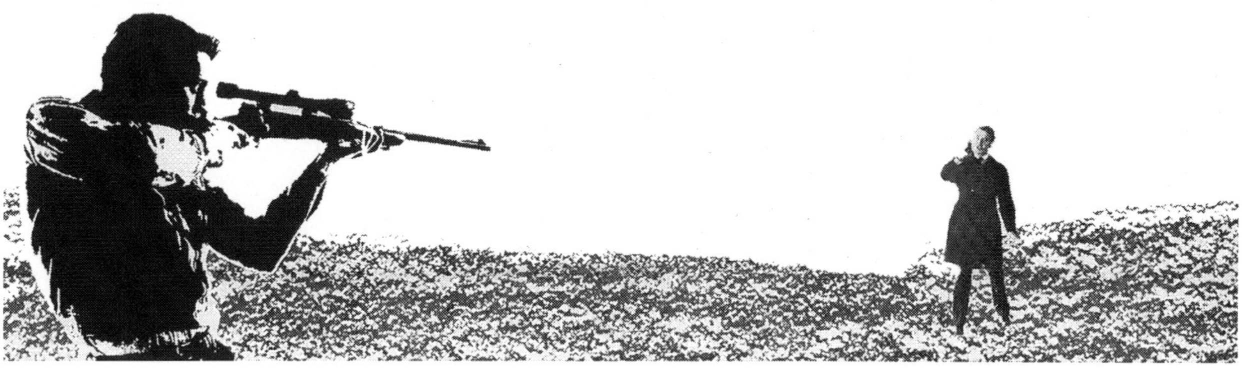

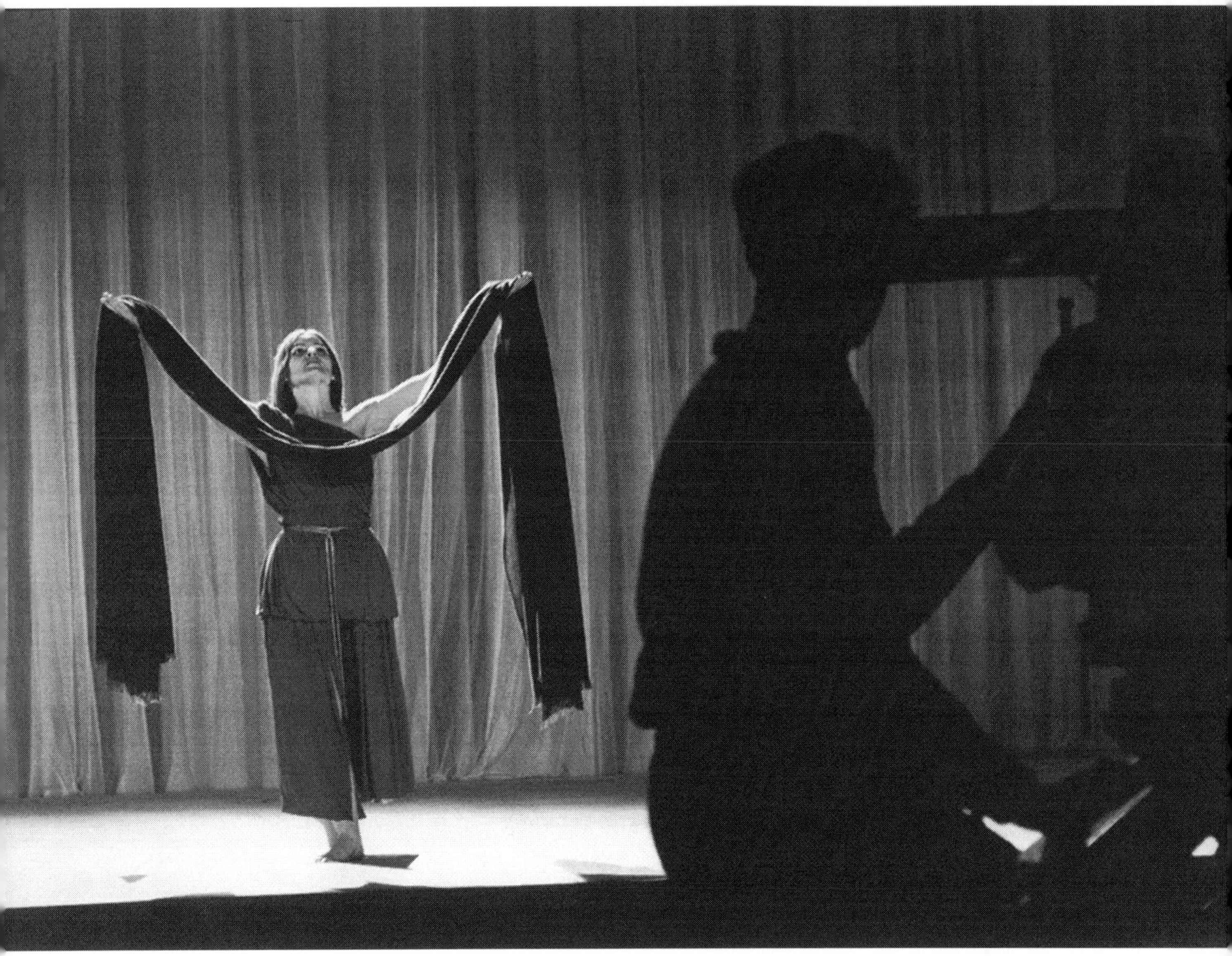

Vivian Pickles in Ken Russell's *Isadora Duncan* (1966)

Six English Filmmakers

by Paul Sutton

Lindsay Anderson
Charlie Chaplin
Clive Donner
Mike Hodges
Ken Russell
Michael Winner

With additional material by

Kevin Brownlow
Brian Cox
Bernard Cribbins
Quentin Falk
Philip Harrison
Jocelyn Herbert
Murray Melvin
Brian Pettifer
Vivian Pickles
Brian Simmons
Rupert Webster

SIX ENGLISH FILMMAKERS

First Edition (April 2014)

Published by Buffalo Books

Cambridge

camerajournal@yahoo.com

ISBN: 978-0-9572462-5-6 - deluxe (colour)
978-0-9572462-7-0 - standard (B&W)

Printed in the USA

Catalogue records for this book are available from the Library of Congress and the British Library.

Also by Paul Sutton:

Lindsay Anderson, The Diaries
if.... A British Film Guide
Becoming Ken Russell

The photographs and posters are from private collections and used in the spirit of education and promotion

Contents

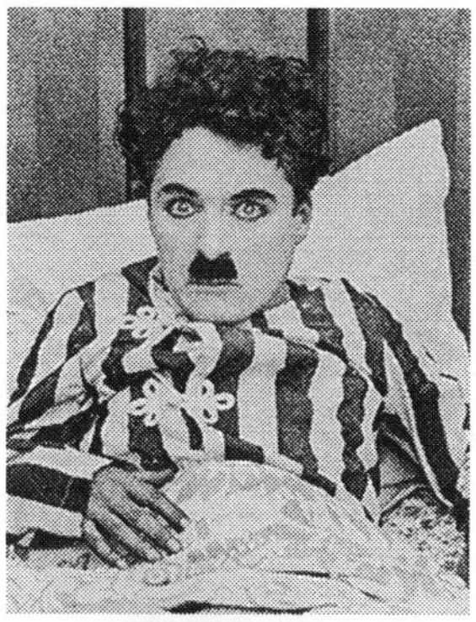
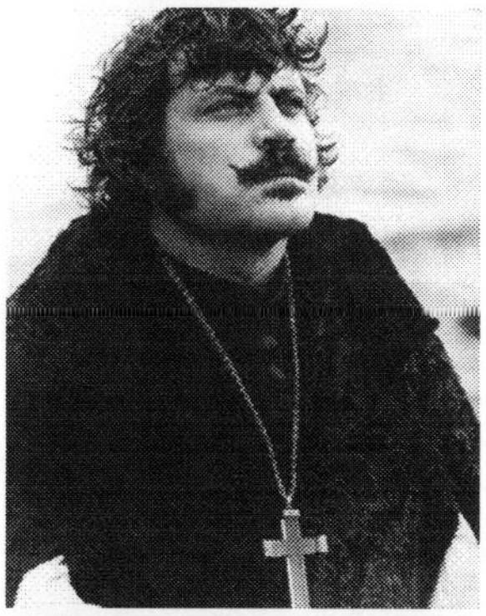
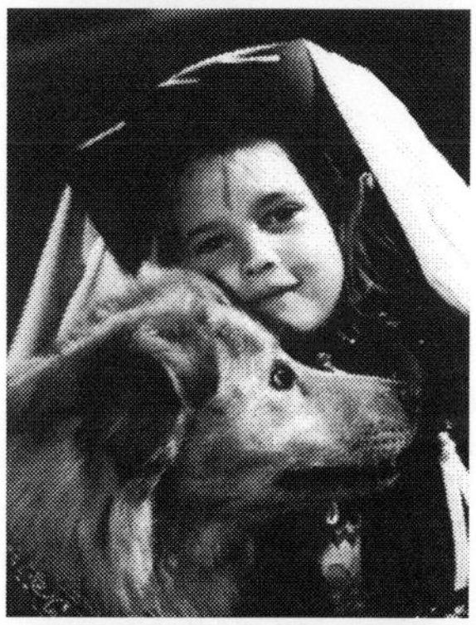
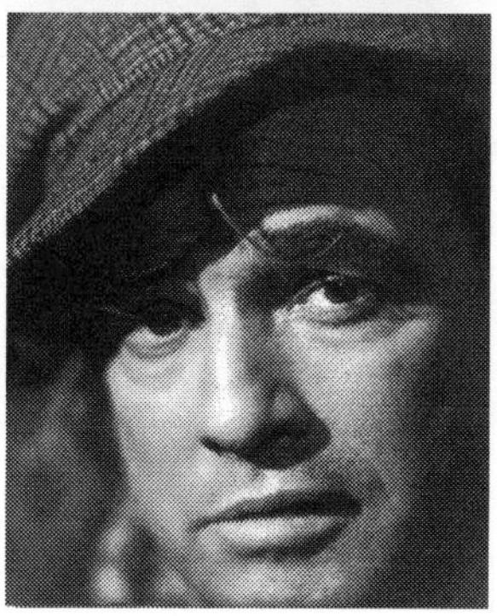

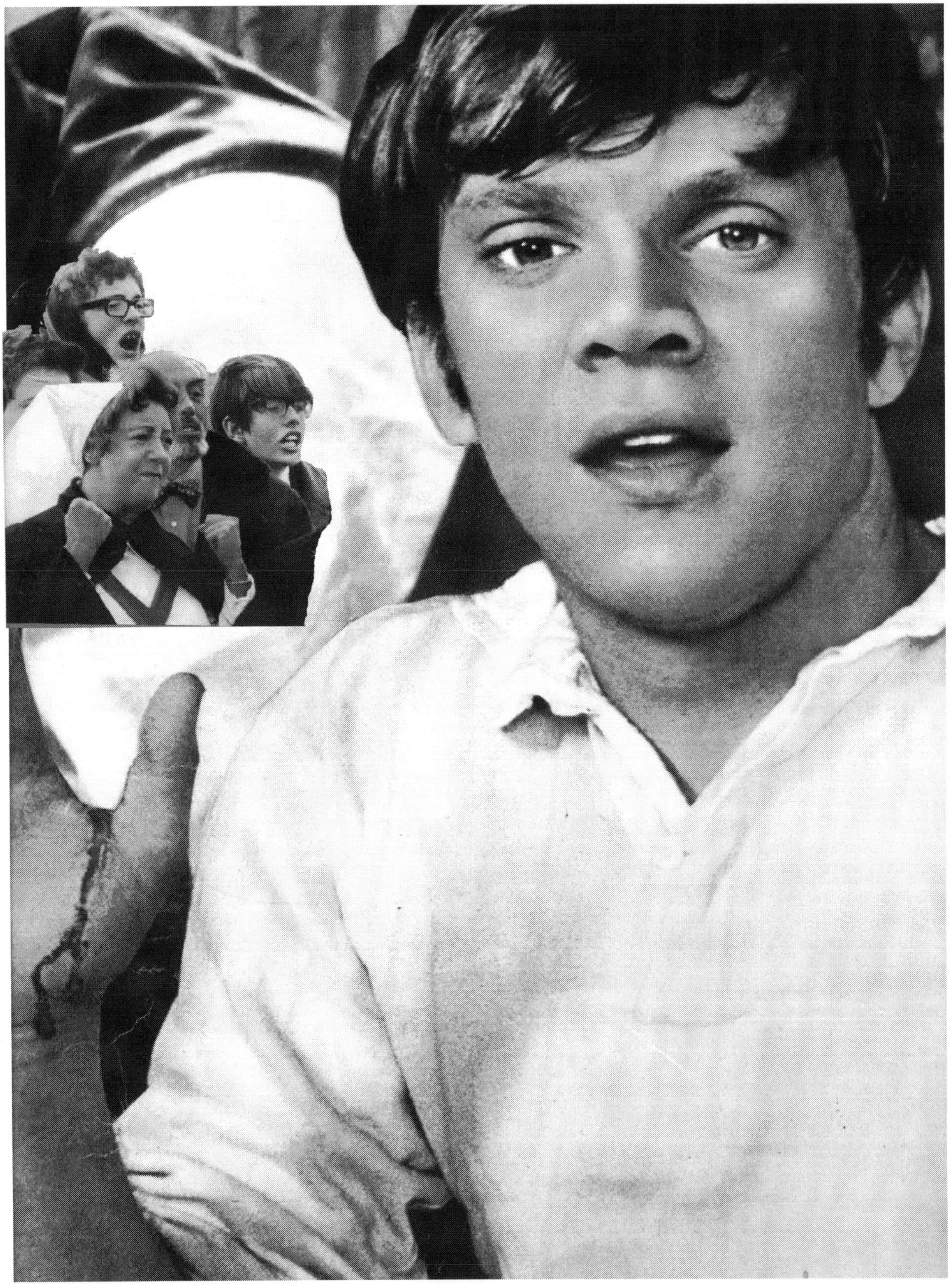

"Real blood!" Artwork from the Italian promotional posters for Lindsay Anderson's *if....*

Lindsay Anderson

"Lindsay Anderson was a brilliant film director -
O Lucky Man was a masterpiece and Britannia Hospital
wonderfully witty and pointed, a feast of telling humour."

J. G. Ballard in a letter to Paul Sutton (13.9.2004)

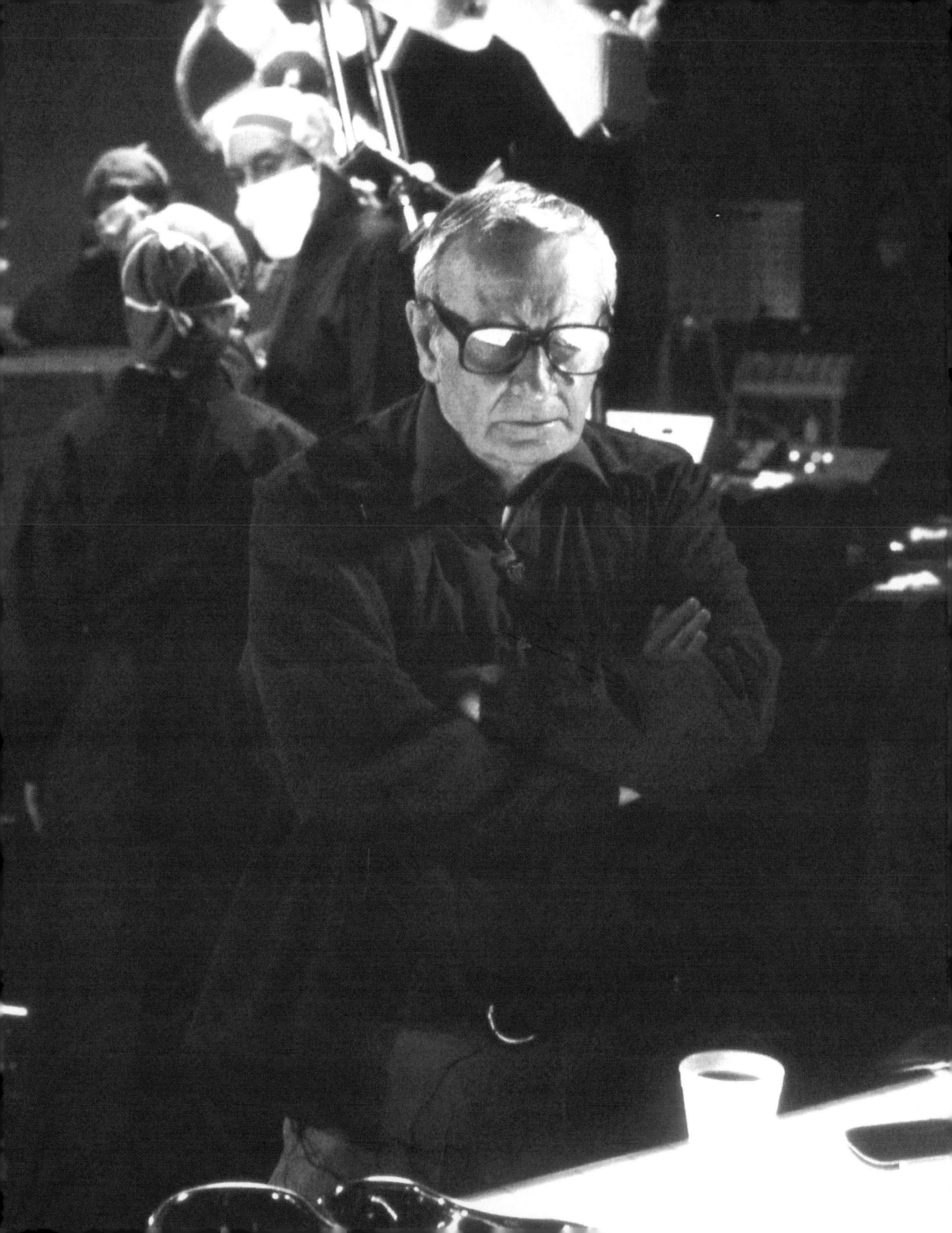

Lindsay Anderson

Born in India to Empire parents (a Scot and a South African), Lindsay Anderson was schooled in England from infancy to Oxford. He lived all his adult life in London and made masterpieces of cinema on the theme of England. The start of my friendship with him began in 1990, four years before he died. Ten years after his death I edited his diaries for publication. The following article is compiled from a strand of our correspondence and conversation on the theme of 'What films and filmmakers are worth studying?' Our correspondence began when I, then a green young man with a particular liking for the films of David Lean and Michael Powell, wrote to chide him for his published dismissal of what I thought was the best of English cinema.

Lindsay, I spent a good week in the Bodleian Library in Oxford reading Sequence, the film journal you edited in the 1940s. I did enjoy them, but you were much too harsh on English filmmakers, particularly Michael Powell and David Lean. In a review of Lean's Madeleine, you describe him as 'the white elephant of British cinema'.

It's pleasant, if also a bit intimidating, to think of you reading *Sequence* nearly fifty years after we produced it. You have to take into account the general atmosphere then, which was very different from today. In those days after the war, the British cinema was, we felt, considerably over-praised, while the American cinema was under-praised. Peter Ericsson and I were tremendously impressed and moved by *My Darling Clementine*, which led us to a proper appreciation of John Ford, while generally Ford's work was neglected. He was only taken seriously, in fact, as the director of *The Informer* (which nobody remembered very well) and *The Grapes of Wrath*. We were greatly impressed, when we caught *They Were Expendable* one Sunday, mysteriously revived at the Granada, Greenwich.

Madeleine is not Lean's best, but he was genuinely world-class. Of Powell's The Red Shoes you wrote: "Never for a moment does the film convince, excite, live. The gaudiness of its trappings only emphasizes the lifelessness and frigidity at the core." Fine words but nonsense in reference to The Red Shoes. You wrote beautifully in admiration of John Ford's work, but you were also full of praise for lesser work by American directors such as George Cukor and William Wyler.

Certainly Cukor and Wyler both produced work at times which was far from their best, but I am surprised to see that you rate David Lean's *Madeleine* with, say, *The Philadelphia Story* and/or *The Best Years of Our Lives*.

You seemed to be attacking Lean because his films were too 'perfect'. In the Free Cinema manifesto you state 'Perfection is not an aim'...

Certainly every artist strives for Perfection, but I still think it's wise for critics to seek not for perfection of style but for depth of content. Both of course. I think you over-estimate the achievements of the British in cinema.

In your introduction to Tony Richardson's Memoir you write 'He failed better', in reference to his own theme that an artist has a right to fail. This suggests an ambivalence towards his work as a whole? The box-office success of Saturday Night and Sunday Morning and Tom Jones brought on a sort of British film renaissance.

Tony Richardson's contributions to theatre and cinema in Britain were remarkable. His strengths were his ambition and his intelligence, rare qualities indeed if we're taking about British film-makers. The 'right to fail' was a policy of the English Stage Company under George Devine and Tony Richardson at the Royal Court Theatre. This meant a pro-humanistic and therefore anti-Conservative approach. Success cannot be measured only in terms of the box-office. I did admire Tony's arrogantly independent stand, his insistence on doing things his own way. Remember, this was the era of Rank and Ealing.

The Long And The Short And The Tall was filmed at Ealing.

I directed the first performance of *The Long and The Short and The Tall* at the Royal Court Theatre (7 January 1959) with Peter O'Toole in the leading role, but I was not allowed to make the film. It was extremely typical of the attitude at the time that when Ealing made the film of *The Long and The Short and The Tall* [in 1961], both O'Toole and I were rejected by [Michael] Balcon. He felt that neither of us were capable of making a film. The film was directed by Leslie Norman, Barry's father.

Didn't you have a contract with Ealing?

I was commissioned by Balcon to do a treatment of *Casualty*, a novel which I thought would make a good film. *[Life on a casualty ward in a London hospital. The book was given to Anderson by Ken Tynan in 1957 when Tynan was a script editor at Ealing].* I got as far with the script as I could but Balcon wouldn't pay for a writer to work with me. When I withdrew from the project, Balcon wanted me to repay all my wages!

Did you?

Of course not.

Well you did go on to make THE hospital drama, Britannia Hospital.

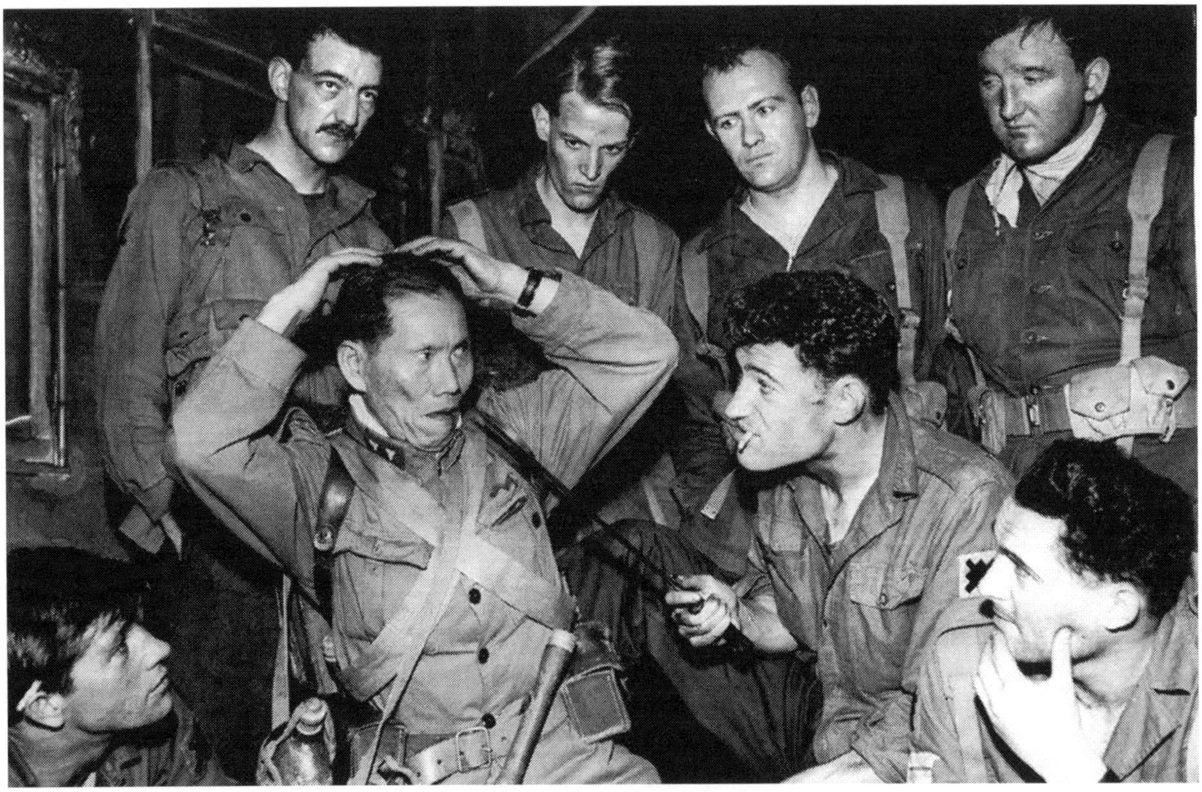

Peter O'Toole and Robert Shaw (lower right) in Anderson's *The Long and The Short and The Tall.*

I did, true.

And you did work for Rank [This Sporting Life was bought by Rank for Stanley Baker, who resented losing the film to Anderson and Harris when Baker's choice of director, Joseph Losey, was rejected]. But you were talking about the strengths of Tony Richardson. Was he one of the greats? Tom Jones and Charge of the Light Brigade are wonderful but on the whole I think his films lack rhythm.

I agree. His films are inorganic, lacking in rhythm and narrative control, spasmodic.

By 'organic' you mean 'natural progression'. Say from the text?

The style or the concept has to be drawn from the material rather than imposing a 'concept' on the material, which seems to be the vogue at the moment. I need to experience the material as closely as I can and let the production evolve from that. With Tony there was never any discussion. He seemed to me to proceed from a cast-iron whim, which is perhaps putting it a bit harshly. He didn't really like actors. He wasn't open to the creative contribution from the actor. He was amazed that the actors in *O Lucky Man!* agreed to come in for that finale sequence for nothing. He wasn't interested in that kind of relationship.

You said you admired Richardson's ambition, but was there ever a more ambitious British film than O Lucky Man!, in terms of scale and scope? The whole of England from the North to the South is opened up. I think it's a masterpiece.

I think the film does carry its message, but it is not rated among the canon of British cinema, probably because it is a dissident picture and Britain is a very conservative country.

What was your aim with the film, apart from holding up a mirror to England?

It was my wish to make a picaresque film in the manner of the 18th century novel, going from incident to incident without a tightness of structure. The film is in two parts. In the first part the hero sets out to be *successful*. Then in the second part he sets out to be *good*.

I understand you shot a now deleted scene in an old folks' home. Was it one 'good' scene too many?

A scene in an old people's home was scripted and prepared but I did not shoot it. I knew at the time it wasn't right. It was too literal. The hero's path to enlightenment comes not by 'action' or from 're-action'. It's a journey [taken] within.

The Zen smile of the finale and the poster? It's a film about a smile; a smile that starts out as a deception, a sale's pitch, and which ends with a smile of revelation, if not happiness.

That's a good way of putting it.

It is a film about understanding the country we live in. A film about 'Getting Wisdom'.

And using that Wisdom to *Transcend*. It's a philosophic sequel to *if....* It shares that Biblical proverb.

['Wisdom is the principal thing; therefore get wisdom: and with all thy getting get understanding'. Anderson put the proverb on a title card in if.... and Arthur Lowe reads it aloud in The White Bus (1967), where it is written in gold on the walls of the library built for the education of the working man]. I'm very impressed by the soundtracks of if.... and O Lucky Man!. You can hear the influence of John Ford at the start of if...., with its sort of overture in the form of a communal song, and the 'real' sounds of shouts of boys in the corridor.

I'm glad you appreciate the care that went into the soundtracks. I think the music and songs by Alan Price in *O Lucky Man!*, and their use, remain some of the most original and effective uses of music in film. The songs helped the anti-naturalistic feeling of the picture. All except one of the songs were discussed, composed and recorded before the film was made.

Robert Altman

Was Alan Price asked to write songs for if....?

No. I did meet Alan before I made *if....*, and we did discuss the possibilities of working together, but *if....* was not a film that needed 'pop' songs. It is not a 'youth picture'.

Wilkinson had previously scored your Julius Caesar.

I chose Marc [Wilkinson] because he was available. I knew I could work with him and I knew he would give me what I wanted, which was what the film *needed*. Film composers have a tendency to give you tunes they've long been holding in their heads which, pretty though they may be, have nothing to do with the film. Then they tantrum when you *cut* or reject music they've laboured over, and which is often very good, but which is not what the film needs. Marc, like Alan, had an instinctive understanding of 'need' and 'style'.

I'm not sure Price's synthesized score was the right approach for Britannia Hospital.

It surprised me.

His O Lucky Man! songs act as a Brechtian chorus.

The influence of Brecht is really in the question of style. *The White Bus*, which I made in 1967, was very important for me. It was the film in which my work developed from a naturalistic or documentary style into something which is much nearer satire. *The White Bus* is a poetic satire, lyrical, humorous. And that really is the style in which I worked in to make *if....* and *O Lucky Man! This Sporting Life* is quite a different kind of film. It's more emotional. Satire would not have made *This Sporting Life* a stronger film. But they are all *realistic* films. Realism is not naturalism. Brecht, in comparing realism with naturalism, made the point that realism is an exposure of the underlying reality of a given situation, whereas naturalism is a reproduction of the *surface* reality. Using that definition *O Lucky Man* and *if....* are realistic films, not naturalistic films. They are films that have strong elements of style and a comment in the style and are realistic in dealing with the basis or the underlying reality. They're not newsreel.

Was O Lucky Man! a commercial success?

It ran at the Warners [Rendezvous] in Leicester Square very successfully. [It was still in the top ten grossing films in London three months after its release]. It made a profit. Then unfortunately we showed it at the Cannes Film Festival which, I am sure you know, is a completely bourgeois event. *O Lucky Man!* is not a bourgeois film so the audience did not like it. Ingrid Bergman, a very good bourgeois actress, was the president of the Jury.

But you've won at Cannes. You're respected abroad?

Abroad one finds oneself respected for being an artist, and that makes a welcome change from being treated as an eccentric uncle, which is usually the case here. The artistic naivety of the English is lamentable. Any departure from naturalism finds one immediately labelled 'obscure' or 'pretentious'.

I suppose the only comparable portrait-of-a-nation film is Altman's Nashville. It was good seeing Malcolm McDowell in The Player.

Bob Altman is a phenomenal chap, full of good ideas. I admire his apparent variety but I'm always disappointed by his *sourness* and by his lack of structure. He seems to have very little sense of rhythm. Malcolm, of course, has a fantastic natural gift as an actor, genuine spark.

He's magnificent in if.... Was an attraction of if.... the opportunity for autobiography?

if... is not an autobiographical film. The script was written by David Sherwin - mostly.

What did you add?

Maturity... The original script was naive and sentimental. The misunderstood hero fell to his death from the roof of the school, rather wastefully I thought.

You kept the roof but gave him a machine-gun.

A backbone.

Your last film with Malcolm is Britannia Hospital. A bitingly true picture of England. An easy shoot?

Well, first of all, it should be noted that *if....* is a Paramount picture and *O Lucky Man!* was produced by Warner Brothers. *Britannia Hospital* was made by E.M.I. a British company. The whole affair was very poorly organised. The production department was never able to get us on to sets that were ready for shooting, and quite unable to provide any alternative weather cover and, I might add, were quite unable to get us any locations either. Every location was found by Richard Tombleson, whom you would have seen as a senior in *if....* [he plays the boy with 'elephantitis'].

I like the film very much, but it lacks the aesthetic qualities of if.... and O Lucky Man! because of the absence of the cameraman, Miroslav Ondricek, and the designer, Jocelyn Herbert? and, I presume, a shorter shooting schedule? Do you like the film?

Very much, but *Britannia Hospital* was a terrific failure critically and at the box-office. It was despised. It's a deeply pessimistic film, a totally satirical view of Britain. It was too fierce and also much too sophisticated to please either the bourgeois film critics or the simple-minded public, who are now incapable of enjoying anything except extravagant escapism.

Like Star Wars. Did you enjoy Star Wars? I did.

I thought it was simple-minded but technically impressive.

But then you wouldn't have cast Mark Hamill in Britannia Hospital?

The casting of Mark Hamill had nothing to do with *Star Wars*. Mark was a replacement for an American actor [Treat Williams] who let me down, and for whom I'd got permission from the British union. Mark was a working actor who wanted the job and who fitted the bill. I was very happy to have him in the film. He did a thoroughly professional job.

[Anderson turned down the role of The Emperor in the third Star Wars film, Return of the Jedi, after turning down an approach to direct the film].

Which British filmmakers do you admire?

Humphrey Jennings, whose output wasn't great, though as substantial as Jean Vigo's, was surely, and still is, one of our finest filmmakers. His films are primarily realist but remember, as a painter, he was influenced by surrealism.

What do you particularly like about his work?

His poetry. His sense of place and community.

I wasn't much impressed by Fires Were Started. Non-actors striking poses à la Eisenstein. Fake fires.

Who do you like?

Ken Russell. Do you like Ken Russell?

I admire his ability to get film's made.

Did you enjoy working for him? [Anderson acted in Russell's wordy, low-powered HBO film, Prisoner of Honor, starring Richard Dreyfuss and Oliver Reed].

It does a director good to find out what it's like in front of the camera. I was impressed by Ken Russell's confidence. He did his own [camera] operating. He's a visual director, not an actor's director as such.

Hit the mark. Say your lines.

A quick run through but no real rehearsal, except for the camera.

Did Oliver Reed behave himself?

His reputation [as a drunk] *has* lessened his standing as an actor. He's a very fine actor.

Quite wonderful in The Devils.

I enjoyed his performance in *Royal Flash*. Properly Teutonic-Aristocratic, brutal, but not unsympathetic.

Will your film about George Michael ever be shown?

I didn't make a film *about* George Michael, I made what I was asked to make: *Wham in China!* A project I undertook in the mistaken belief that the young millionaire genius had interests beyond his own ego. He doesn't.

What films should I see?

It would be important, I think, to see *Spare Time* and *Heart of Britain*, and perhaps also *Words for Battle* by Humphrey Jennings. Marek Piwowski's short films are really outstanding, but have been very little seen, if at all, outside Poland. And sometime I hope you'll be able to see the little film (twenty minutes) I made in Poland called *The Singing Lesson*. I like it a lot.

I will. And Robert Flaherty?

Flaherty is certainly one of the great names.

Was the boy 'wrestling' an alligator in if.... a tribute to Flaherty?

I'm afraid not. I wasn't thinking of *The Louisiana Story*, but it's a nice idea.

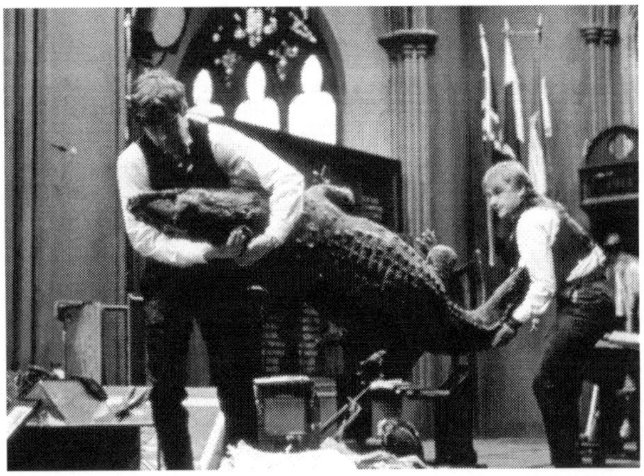

I was impressed with Flaherty's White Shadows in the South Seas which I saw on satellite TV; atmosphere and spectacle but a human centre.

I've never seen *White Shadows*, though I know about it. It hasn't been much revived, but I'd very much like to see it.

I'll try to record it for you. Bunuel?

Bunuel was a great filmmaker, but he did suffer from a falling off of vitality. Inevitable, I suppose. His last films were bourgeois, when you compare them to his earlier films. And he did become a great favourite of the bourgeoisie, like Brecht.

I like Woody Allen, just about everything.

He is very clever, but he was a better comedian than he is a dramatist. I find his dramas sour and lacking in truth. They are all obviously about him, but they are too guarded, too closed, and therefore too false to work as drama. And he's a better director of men than he is of women.

Have you ever met him?

No, but I did have the misfortune to meet Mia Farrow once. A determined woman, with an unhealthy obsession for adopting children.

Do you like Tarkovsky?

I can't stand Tarkovsky, though he's probably a very good director. I just don't like his films.

You must like Orson Welles?

Welles was a terrific talker, highly intelligent and amusing but a great snob.

He did Ionesco's Rhinoceros at The Royal Court when...

Yes, I bumped into him a few times. The first time, in fact, was in the North of England when his stage *Othello* opened and I was filming one of my Conveyor Belt documentaries. I went to a party in his hotel bedroom in Middlesbrough!

I can't imagine Orson Welles in Middlesbrough. Why doesn't Britain produce it's share of great filmmakers? Our two indisputable greats, Hitchcock and Chaplin, both did their best work in America.

The English are innately conservative and innately philistine. British Film production is dominated by self-servers, opportunists and hangers-on who couldn't care less about making 'a great film'. Producers are much more likely to think in terms of the talent associated with the project than with the quality of the script. And the critics are no help. They have become *journalistic*, self-obsessed, so there is now a tremendous gulf between what they write and what anything is *actually* like. I'm totally shocked by the way they hype the mediocre. The defeat of the community-spirited Left of the Fifties by the capitalist-consumer revolution of the Sixties is a factor. But the fundamental problem is The Class System. It stains everything from features to B-films and documentaries. Our documentary cinema was staffed exclusively by graduates from Oxford and Cambridge.

The exception being Ken Russell's work for Monitor.... You worked in America on the TV film Glory! Glory!, Is anything else lined up there?

All the most talented directors are naturally only interested in filming in America, apart from Ken Russell, I suppose. I would rather try to make it happen with fellow-artists here. There is too much "deal making" in Hollywood, everyone obsessed by the day-to-day struggle to get a Deal, regardless of the quality of script.

You have made one American cinema film, The Whales of August, starring two Hollywood greats, Bette Davis and Lillian Gish. That must have been a career high? How did it come about?

To find oneself directing Bette Davis AND Lillian Gish in the same picture surely qualifies as a high point, and I was also very taken with Ann Sothern. It came about because a friend [Mike Kaplan] asked would I direct a film starring Bette Davis and Lillian Gish? I said I would if he could get the money. I didn't think he would get the money. But he did. Incidently, the picture is handled by Nelson Entertainments, a British-run enterprise, though based in Los Angeles. It's not only British filmmakers who have fled the country, it's British money!

Who else would you have wanted to work with?

Of the greats? Jean Arthur, in a remake of *My Two Husbands.*

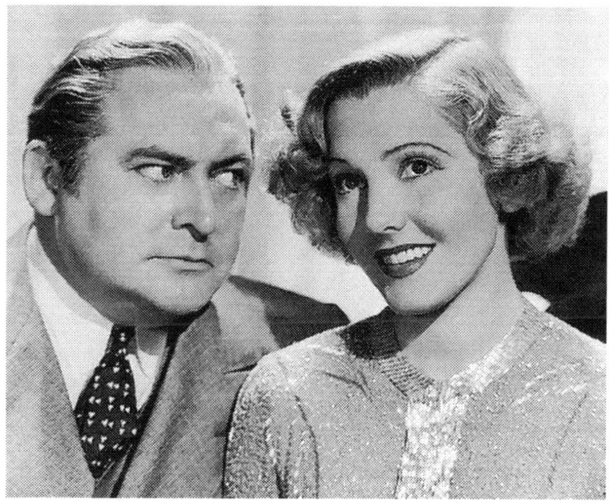

I've only seen her Capra films... and Shane...

Try to see *Easy Living*, a Paramount picture, directed by Mitchell Leisen from a script by Preston Sturges There is a tendency these days to overstress the importance of the director. The writer's contribution is never negligible. *[A banker throws his greedy wife's fur coat from their skyscraper apartment onto Jean Arthur and, in doing so, changes her life. Echoes of the 'golden suit' in O Lucky Man!].* You might also have a look at *The Devil and Miss Jones*, directed this time by Sam Wood, with Robert Cummings, from a script by Norman Krasna *[echoes of Britannia Hospital with its workers' agitation and a senior citizen as the leading protagonist].*

Have any current actors or films impressed you?

I was impressed by *What's Eating Gilbert Grape?* I thought it was original and sensitive.

I preferred My Life as a Dog.

(*Lindsay Anderson sighs*). I thought *Philadelphia* was tremendously well-acted, particularly by Antonio Banderas, who didn't have much to do, and who should have been given more to do, but who really played well. I did enjoy that. I liked Tom Cruise in *The Firm* though I preferred *One False Move* starring Bill Paxton, who gave a very sensitive-dynamic performance. Of course neither film compares with *The Big Heat.*

Any actresses?

Wynona Ryder was remarkably good in *Reality Bites*, very impressively directed by Ben Stiller. Madonna has the right aptitude for work and learning and could be worth watching in the future.

And the British? Emma Thompson? Now almost as prized as Glenda Jackson.

Glenda Jackson was a formidable actress but you could sense in her later performances, particularly on the stage, that she would rather be somewhere else. I remember writing a snide review saying she played *Bernarda Alba* like a Head Girl drafted into a school production and wishing she was outside playing hockey, which was unkind but not untruthful. Emma Thompson was very bad in *In The Name of The Father*, in which she played a 'type' and not a 'person'. But the British public do love bad acting. I wish I could join in with their applause for the populist and the mediocre but I am completely out of sympathy with developments in British and American filmmaking. A new conformism has asserted itself. Cinema is less open to the individual radical voice or talent, with the "Media" more and more supplanting art. The whole spirit is towards "safety", narrow expensive projects ensured by "stars".

Yes, even Coppola has backtracked from Zoetrope to remake Dracula with the current flavours of the month, and your old friend Anthony Hopkins [whose London stage debut was in Lindsay's Julius Caesar, and whose film debut is a cameo in The White Bus].

I thought Coppola's *Dracula* was much too concerned with stylistic *effects* and had no real sense of reality or place or even storytelling. I don't know why Hopkins has become a magnet for prizes. He has always been a good actor but his performances have become all technique and not enough *truth*. *The Remains of the Day* was a traditional English middle-class offering, though a great deal more sophisticated on the surface. One should note it was made by an Indo-American team and financed by the Japanese. All the greatest 'triumphs' of recent years have been completely infantile or appallingly sentimental, tame and respectable.

Schindler's List?

Liam Neeson is an excellent actor but he didn't do a great deal with the part. I thought the film was too "acted" and narratively poor. All my life I've aimed at a style which has been consciously directed away from "effect" and the whole way that movies seem to have gone since the growth of the Film Schools and "Media". I'm more impressed by the technical qualities of the Polish cinema.

Are you surprised by the ascendancy of Sean Connery? Now the world's biggest star.

Not at all. His success is deserved. I've always rated him.

And the finest English actor is?

Gielgud, of course.

Are you not tempted to do more TV in Britain? The Old Crowd was astonishing. [Rachael Roberts and Jill Bennett at a Bunuelian house party. Anderson filmed it on video in three days and a night in March 1978, after two weeks of rehearsals}.

Stephen Frears put that together. He's making his own features now, and rightly so. There's a drive towards standardisation and mediocrity in television. For example, I was invited to make a documentary for Granada Television in Manchester. The subject had to be a Northern one and the

Lindsay Anderson

Walker Art Gallery in Liverpool was suggested. I was tempted until I was told the shooting time was set at one day.

Ridiculous. It sounds more like a film school exercise than a serious attempt to make a film. [Curiously, the last film Ken Russell worked on was a one-day shoot of the Liverpool Philharmonic].

It isn't worth doing anything unless it can be done right. My last effort *Is That All There Is?* was made for BBC Scotland nearly two years ago. An unpretentious work, a fragmented account of my life, English life. It won a couple of prizes in Florence and in Uppsala in Sweden. I'm glad to say that there seems to be a screening date for it on TV this September. Probably that's the end of my career as a filmmaker.

The editorial in the final issue of Sequence, I presume it was written by you, it is in your style, lucid, authoritative, precise, makes reference to The Cherry Orchard. A few months ago, on the Barry Norman show, Maggie Smith said you were trying to raise funds for a film of The Cherry Orchard, and had received a rejection letter addressed to 'Mr. Chekhov'.

True, true. It gave me a good laugh.

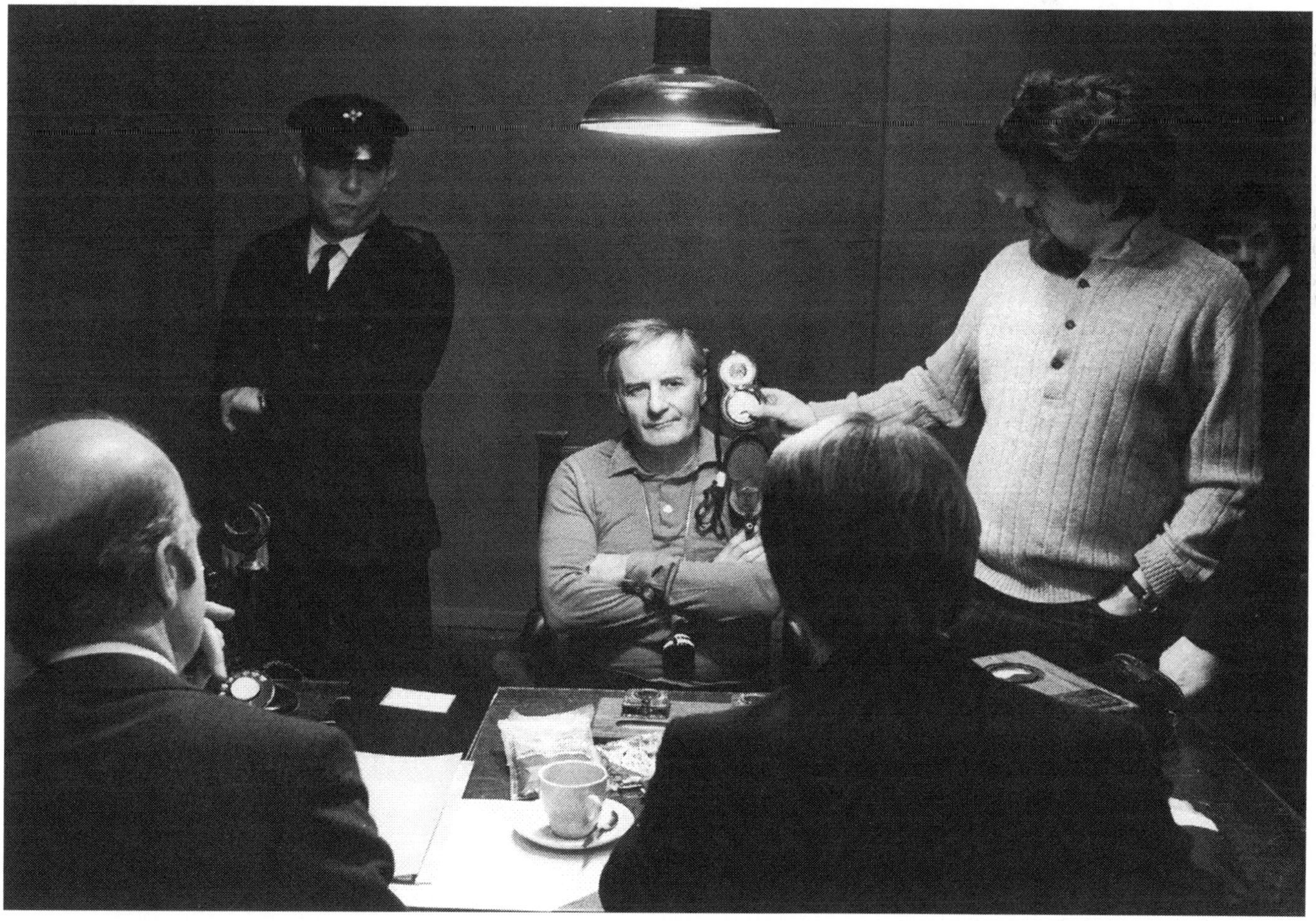

Mirsoslav Ondricek lighting the interrogation scene in *O Lucky Man!*, with Lindsay Anderson himself standing in for Malcolm McDowell who can be seen on the right of the frame.

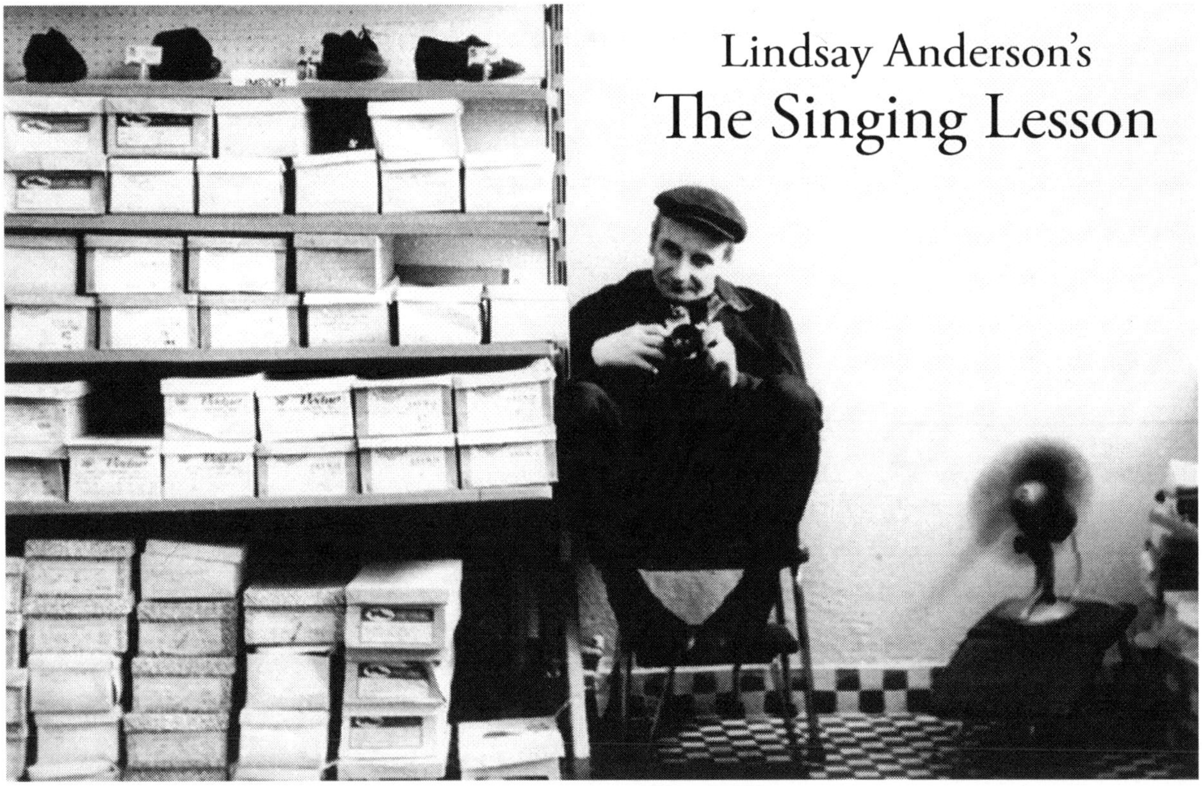

Lindsay Anderson's
The Singing Lesson

Lindsay Anderson in Poland (1967)

As a tribute to Lindsay Anderson, *The Singing Lesson* was screened on the BBC in the week he died. It's a nineteen-minute film of students singing folk songs, intercut with snapshots of Polish life under communism. It was the model for Anderson's rarest film, *Wham in China!* (1985), the George Michael documentary from which Anderson was sacked and not allowed to remove his name. His own cut, deemed to have 'too much China and not enough Wham!', has never been screened publically. He made *The Singing Lesson,* or *RAZ, DWA, TRZY...* (capital letters and dots added by Anderson) in Warsaw between April and July 1967 whilst waiting for the film that became *if....* to fall into place.

Memorial Pictures, owned and run by Albert Finney and Michael Medwin, were trying to secure the financing for *if....* (then called *The Crusaders,* from a script by David Sherwin and John Howlett) whilst easing the rights away from the producer-director, Seth Holt. *The Singing Lesson* enabled Anderson to detach himself from the three-fold work pressures of Memorial Pictures; turmoil at the Royal Court Theatre (where Anderson directed mostly new plays) following the death of the company's co-founder, George Devine; and the signing of a contract to make seventeen television commercials for Kellogg's Cornflakes. Filming *The Singing Lesson* would ease Anderson's conscience and allow him to re-connect with the poetic humanist cinema of his heroes: John Ford and Humphrey Jennings.

In the four years since his debut feature, *This Sporting Life* (1963) won Oscar nominations and Cannes prizes for Richard Harris and Rachel Roberts, Lindsay Anderson had been trying to make another film with Harris, including a version of *Wuthering Heights* scripted by *This Sporting Life* author David Storey. Unable to compete with the superstar salaries offered to Harris in the wake of the Oscar nomination, Anderson had dutifully stepped aside, waiting, as Harris worked in Mexico for Sam Peckinpah; in Italy for Antonioni; in Norway with Kirk Douglas; in Italy again with

John Huston; and onto Hawaii with Julie Andrews. When Richard Harris quibbled about the set designs for an agreed Anderson/Storey/Harris feature film about Dylan Thomas, Anderson drew a line under the years of waste, dropped Harris, and sought inspiration elsewhere.

He sought it first in Paris, where he tried and failed to interest Serge Reggiani in an adaptation of John Osborne's *Inadmissible Evidence* [In 1955, Anderson and Reggiani had worked together on a French production of *Hamlet*]. And he sought it in Poland with Tadeusz Lomnicki, the star of Andrzej Wajda's debut feature, *Pokolenie* (A Generation, 1955). In December 1966, Anderson directed Lomnicki at the Warsaw Theatre Wspolczesnym, in a Polish adaptation of *Inadmissible Evidence.*

Anderson also found inspiration in the humanist cinema of Jan Nemec, Milos Forman and the Czech New Wave. He spent many weeks in 1965 and 1966 criss-crossing between capitalist England and communist Czechoslovakia, studying Czech filmmaking methods and overcoming English and communist bureaucracy to hire Forman's cameraman, Miroslav Ondricek, for the richly poetic 46-minute film, *The White Bus* (1965): the mayor of Salford (Arthur Lowe) leads dignities, and a lost-in-London local, on a tour of the city's industrial, recreational and educational facilities. Complete with explicit nods to Jean Vigo [speech day mannequins], the film turns from black-and-white into colour. It is the only watchable part of a Three Colours *Red, White and Blue* trilogy put together by the Royal Court Theatre's general manager, Oscar Lewenstein, with the lesser chapters directed by Tony Richardson and Peter Brook. Whilst awaiting distribution for *The White Bus,* Anderson rejected an offer of theatre work from Rachel Robert's husband, Rex Harrison (whom he would direct on Broadway in the 1978 hit, *The Kingfisher*); and he rejected film script after film script; whilst taking up the lucrative Kellogg contract, to return to Poland to make *The Singing Lesson.* His diaries record the days of frustration and pleasure:

29 April, 1967

The car came at 6.0 and we went to shoot the wall of the painter's house. God knows if the time of day really made any difference ... but I respect Sigmund [Samosiuk, cinematographer] for demanding it. Then back to the railway station ... and later to the studio. In the streets in the afternoon, with crowds, and Sigmund picking out individuals à la *Words for Battle* [by Jennings] (or *Wakefield Express!*) [Anderson's 1953 film about a newspaper].

1 May

Shoot workers in collar and tie for May Day Kronika ... the weather has turned perfect. Stroll out across the square: then down near Marshalkowska and wander around. 11.00am return to hotel for schedule 'conference'. After 'conference' everyone sits around: I suppose in order not to impolitely dash away ... time? money? I can't help thinking with affectionate nostalgia of May Day last year. Nobody even accepts the offer of a cup of coffee. Finally I say I'm going for a walk, and we troop off ... down to the Palace of Culture for the end of the Parade, now the citizens: schoolboys and girls: scouts ... Atmosphere quite jolly in an undemonstrative sort of way. We were drinking light beers up by the Opera when [Wladyslaw] Gomulka [First Secretary of the Communist Party] started his speech: the usual string of clichés: no one paying any attention. [By thus, The Crusaders script acquired a Speech Day scene, the usual string of clichés, to which no one pays attention when the school hall starts to burn].

2 May

Sudden spasm of self-indulgence as I retired to bed last night prompted me to order two boiled eggs and Café complet ... Do I get any closer to happiness these days? We start shooting at the contemporary Art Exhibition: tracking shot calls for six takes, much to Sigmund's disgust. I don't think Strasek is much of an assistant: which seems born out by delays when we go on to shoot alienation close-ups of shop assistants ... Back to 'O Dreamland' [Anderson's 1956 short about a seaside park].

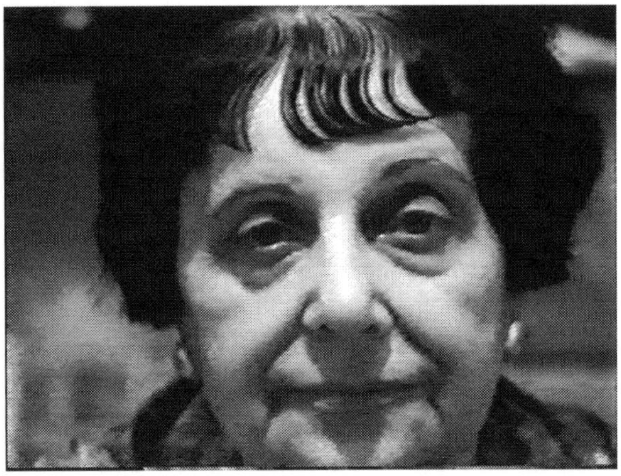

3 May

Last night, David [Sherwin rang] saying that Seth [Holt] was refusing to sign the legalistic document prepared by the lawyers and brilliant [agent] Robin Fox... [father of actors James and Edward]. Shooting at the school: first the love song by - well I don't know her name - sturdy, very charming expression and eyes ... communication with the unit really difficult: I am reminded that Zygmunt is a Pole. His work is really creative: but his mind moves in that mysterious way ... Disaster strikes when I see Andrzej Nardelli [the star of the film] has had his hair cut... We take him to the studio and try a wig on, but he looks like a Beatle. Of course there's nothing to be done. Impossible to get a schedule arranged and working with intelligent anticipation. I get irritated with everyone, including Jeanne with her devoted, stupid eyes, and mind that seems incapable of self-powered dynamic. ['Self-powered dynamic' was the quality which stirred Anderson's muse, and which he associated with Richard Harris, Tadeusz Lomnicki, and Serge Reggiani.]

He continues: "Depressed and empty today...

A letter with Crusaders budget from Michael [Medwin] just makes me feel worse. Keep getting intuitions of that village cottage - far from the Madding Crowd." [He'd inherit from his mother a cottage in Rustington, which he used for work retreats and dreams of retirement]. He stays up "much too late" talking with Tadeusz.

4 May

Shooting: PIERRE sings The Coat, which I find very poetic and suggestive the more I hear it, and the enchanting ANDRZEJ NARDELLI sings Grozski ... unit discipline and communication becomes impossible, climaxing in the disappearance of the entire unit after the first song, which has involved endless delays and unnecessary retakes. I blow my top, and hate doing so, since it has to be at Sigmund. But the working atmosphere gets noticeably better, and Grozski restores our sweet harmony. Rushes at the studio, art gallery and alienation shots excellent. [Andrzej Nardelli drowned in a Polish lake in 1972, when Anderson was in England making *O Lucky Man!*]

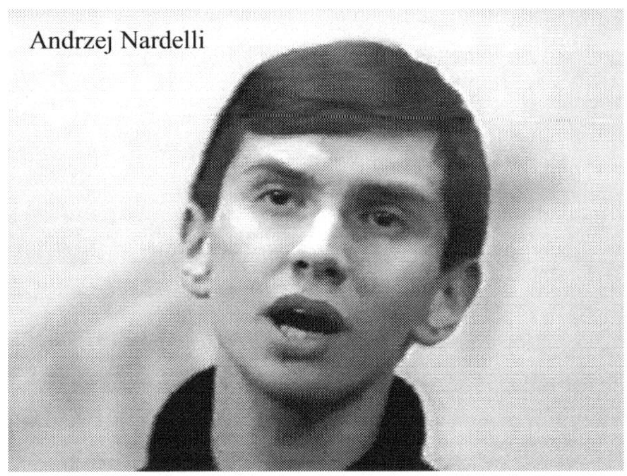
Andrzej Nardelli

5 May

Depressing rushes of two days back - not even synched up yet, which doesn't help. Movement and focus pretty poor. I feel I have been over-ambitious, and they have too politely tried to give me what I wanted. Communications failure again ... Sigmund bought me the POLISH COOK BOOK, just before we shot in Bar Praha. His spirit is beautiful ... But complicated... very difficult to make direct rational communication with Sigmund, he goes off into his own world of thought, sits with that rather oriental, remote delicacy, his light (blue-green?) eyes looking everywhere or nowhere ... He is not lethargic, but he suffers like all the others from that Polish belief in letting things happen. English empiricism but totally without forethought ... schedules can be kept in the head for about five minutes: 'possible contingencies' don't exist, e.g. the chatter about availability of students, cameras, [Professor] Sempolinsky, for shooting this week – with every day a different tale. It's true that in a funny way things do get done, but of course the price is endless waste of time.

7 May
A long, packed day at the school: JEANNE and ANDRZEJ rehearse Panno Sabino ... which we manage to trim to some sort of manageable length, despite everyone's lack of comprehension. God knows how painful Jeanne's hand, in plaster, is: she refuses to admit any handicap. PROFESSOR SEMPOLINSKY arrives, fortunately a bit late... We have a second cameraman, a broad-faced, likeable young Pole. We shoot a lot: a bit grabby: the Professor is impatient. The lights are terribly hot: we waltz and waltz ...
raz, dva, tze ... of course I can't direct it as I'd like. Everything takes too long, and so the shooting has to go quickly. No food, NARDELLI brought a box of cakes: Sigmund, Tony and I repair upstairs for a slug of whiskey. The students are really charming, excellent, good-mannered; hard-working. They are, like the young Czechs, the best possible advertisement for socialism. What will become of them? Nardelli has the most winning charm; PIERRE unobtrusive, but splendid and strong on the screen: MARIAN heroic in his handsome face and powerful build. End the day exhausted but feeling good work has been done ... until rushes.

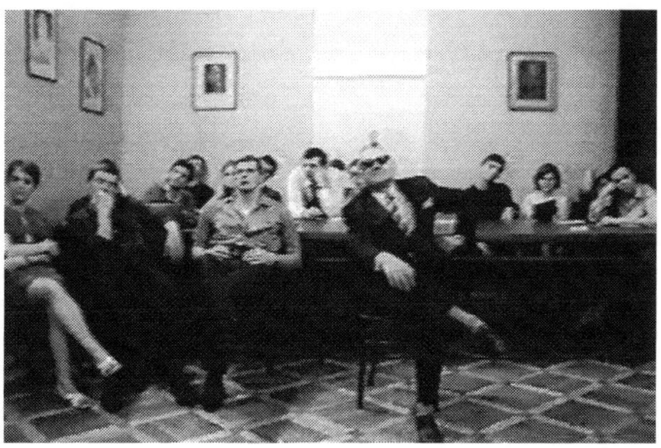

8 May
A reasonable quiet day today - as I remember - I write at the end of the week, having missed days, and they're starting to blur. I think today was MUSEUMS: photos, and a few selective static images. It was also Stasek's name day: which seemed to be a reason why everyone wanted to break early.

13 May
To the Studio early, where Sigmund and I received mysterious packets of zlotys on signature ... payment for 'Documentation', script, scenario etc. Here as everywhere the cinema seems better paid by far than theatre. I have more to come ... Equally have spent quite a lot in the course of shooting. I attempt to instil some idea of professionalism by getting Tony to find out precise details of our takes by phoning PANI JADWIGA at the studio ... imagine the complications ... We shoot GROSZKI with great care and concentration ... Andrzej performs with splendid professionalism and breathtaking charm ... This and Plaszcz alone would make the film remarkable I think. The students overall fantastically correspond, poetically, to my ideal of charm, seriousness, sensitivity, young humanity at its sweet best. I can't see how this film can be other than beautiful, and very poetic: really no boring narrative or informational elements.

May 14th
Was the Tadeusz of *Pokolenie* just my own sentimental illusion: or the Richard [Harris] I first knew? or Serge [Reggiani]? Do they change? or did I lose my illusions? We shoot at the opera: afterwards I and Mirek drink too much cognac and talk balls ... sick in the night!

May 15th
BACK [to London] To no joy: but a world in some ways more alienating in its commercialism and self-imposed corruptions. I get in from the Airport and am plunged into phone calls: Memorial, Leon [Clore, who arranged the Kellogg's contract and who was trying to get Anderson to direct *All Neat*

in Black Stockings], David (Sherwin). Film Contracts, arrangements for setting up KELLOGGS etc. The Price of Freedom. I try to hold the image of Andrzej Nardelli's face — of Sigmund ... Last rushes - The station, the retaken waltz, Warsawa ... on the whole excellent. But in London even the film seems to lose substance. Too thin and 'humane': what would *Sight & Sound* or John Russell Taylor have to say about it? Nothing. It is too simple, too plain.

May 16th
Dramatic sudden immersion in the shit of the KELLOGG'S,UNIVERSAL-SETH-MEMORIAL, GRANADA, ROBIN FOX, ROYAL COURT and all the rest of it ... the feeling growing of my inability to COPE ... to choose ... to conduct a career which in any way satisfies me. Morning inspecting the Kelloggs houses at Hatch End with DEREK BANHAM and LARRY [Pizer, photographer with whom Anderson made 79 commericals between 1963 - 1971]. I ought to write something about Poland: naturally people are just bored by it in conversation ... but what desperate contrasts!

Can we shoot Kelloggs in nine days? Lunch with David Sherwin, then joined by Michael Medwin and Albert Finney, at Escargot [restaurant in Soho] ... Hear more about the SETH [Holt] situation ... He plainly is some very weird kind of neurotic - as I say to David later - like DENIS MITCHELL [documentary filmmaker] - with a sort of obsessive, paranoid quality... all the emphasis on one way 'friendship' etc ... and no capacity to imagine the needs and complexes of others. Another grotesque failure. Meeting with MEMORIAL and CECIL TENNANT - JAY KANTER of Universal: respectful but of course not convinced or optimistic of CRUSADERS' capacity to attract exhibitors. How can I blame them? ALBERT [Finney] really impressive - generous, intelligent, dynamic and confident. Whirl back to interview KELLOGGS artists and FAMILY. WHAT A DAY. No wonder I collapse - David [Sherwin] spending the night - to T.V. and Records.

Throughout the nine days of the Kellogg's shoot, Anderson kept in telephone contact with the Polish editing crew. He edited the commercials with the Czech, Mischa Norland: "I like Misha, he is 'a bit cocky', but with real understanding. Of course he's not English! He catches on very quickly."

Anderson's Kelloggs commercials won the main industry awards that year.

On 7 June, 1967, he took a plane to Warsaw to the *The Singing Lesson* cutting rooms: "Why is there this unforced relaxation, which I cannot find in Britain? Somehow here the emotions flow freely, unaffectedly. We look at the last rushes — Groszki! All [shots of the] last day at school excellent." Later that day he travelled to Kraków ("where the gilt goes off my Polish gingerbread ... met by an uncivil youth who made no attempt to help me") to a screening of a Festival film. In 1965 he had been a juror at the first international film festival in India. In 1966. he was on the jury of the Venice Film Festival. This year, 1967, Anderson was in Kraków to serve on the jury of Poland's oldest film festival. For the next four days, in the sympathetic company of friends, such as Gene Moskowitz and Lino Micciché, he saw twenty or so short films: "Back to the Grand [Hotel] to commence Jury deliberations. The whole experience not bad, and relatively speedy. I kick off by proposing Borowczyk's *Rosalie* for the Grand Prix, and the US *Napalm* as runner-up: this, to be honest, slightly against my better judgement, as I found *Rosalie* in fact rather theoretical, great refinement and sensitivity of style, but somehow unconvincing: anyway *Napalm* took the majority."

Reviewing the full list of prize winners, of which Lerner's anti-establishment film about personal responsibility won the top prize, Anderson notes: "A good list. Where is Britain? Poor and provincial with its sentimental, amateurish Jemima and Jinny, and typical Shell tripe about River Pollution. Squareness of style and imagination sadly apparent." After the festival, Lindsay Anderson went to a screening of student films at the Kraków film school. After watching six ordinary efforts along the lines of *Kirk Douglas visits the Film School*, he was impressed by three films: "A 'black documentary' on boys with nothing to do but stand on street corners and look for girls: an extraordinary recreation (in the studio) of a 'rough cafe', with old drunks, spivs and thieves, and just people getting drunk — funny and intensely heightened reality: and finally *A Provincial Death*, the young student researching in a Monastery who witnesses the death of an old monk. A really impressive selection, bringing gloomy comparative thoughts to a film-maker from Britain."

He is introduced to the director of one of the films, Marek Piwowski. who had asked Sigmund to photograph a film about Youth. Anderson would become Piwowski's friend and champion. He arranged and curated a festival of Piwowski's films at the NFT in 1979. Inspired by the seriousness of approach to filmmaking in East Europe, Anderson revived his enthusiasm for filmmaking in Britain by making an East European film on the universal themes of The Wisdom of Age and the Promise of Youth. The transfer of knowledge and art from one generation to another. *The Singing Lesson* starts with two captions:

'In 1967 Lindsay Anderson was invited
to make a short film in Poland, a
souvenir of his visit to direct a play at
the Contemporary Theatre, Warsaw.
He found a subject at the Warsaw
Dramatic Academy. A group of third
year students present their songs
to their professor and their fellow students.'

'This film is a sketchbook, or a poem.
The words of the songs are not
important, only their themes and
the images and memories they invoke.
The film is dedicated to Professor Ludwik
Sempoliński and the Polish students.'

Captions play an integral part in Anderson's films, from the chapter headings of *if....* , to slogans painted on the sets and landscapes of *O Lucky Man!*, and the news bulletins within *Britannia Hospital.* It was an approach Anderson had used in the theatre: newspaper and stock market headlines formed part of Sean Kenny's set design for *The Lily White Boys* (1960), the musical satire on 'booming Britain' which made Albert Finney a theatrical star.

The opening shot of *The Singing Lesson* has an artfully diagonal composition suggested by the 'mouth' of the clapperboard. On the left of the frame, half in and half out of the shot, a youth holds a clapperboard. Dark-haired and dark-clothed, he stands out against the backdrop of an off-white wall on which are names and dates slope upwards diagonally at the mirror-angle of clapperboard. In the lower-right corner, a dark chair faces the wall to balance the composition: the lower-right with the upper-left. The clapper-youth calls the mark and steps out of shot.

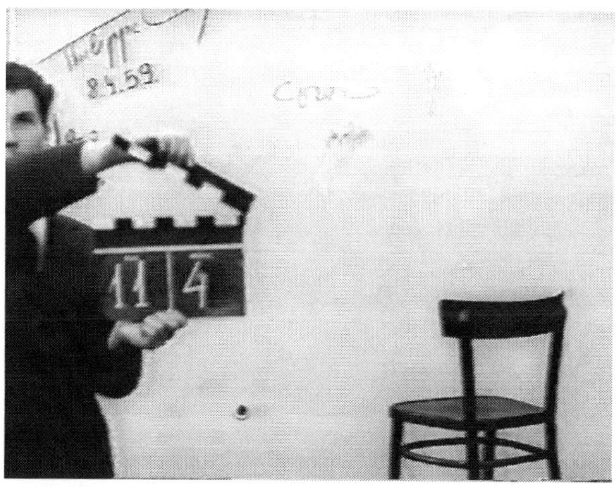

White production credits come and go in a space in the lower-left, their position in the frame set and balanced by the chair and by the writing on the wall. These tableaux of the iconography of learning - the note-covered wall; the forward facing chair, and the youth half in and half out of the frame - set the theme of the film and impart the first lesson: The Importance Of Space in filmmaking and live performance. In filmmaking, the positioning of the camera, and the placing of objects within the frame, is of paramount importance. More than mere pictorial composition it can set the mood and the themes. With *The Singing Lesson*, Anderson wasn't 'recording a performance', he was making a film that could serve as a masterclass for the making of a film.

As the credits play, we hear the natural sound of the classroom, half-hushed, half-expectant chatter easing to silence as the credits end — an introduction Anderson would re-model for *if....* A female youth, dark-haired and in dark clothes, walks into shot and takes away the chair. When she exits the frame, down unseen steps, the scene cuts to a shot of a train passing beneath a railway bridge. A train entering a tunnel is the oldest wink-nudge joke in cinema, but the seriousness of Anderson's tone overrides such crude concerns. Anderson uses it to tie his film of contemporary Poland to the birth of cinema itself, to the train-arriving-at-the-platform films of the Brothers Lumière. When Bertolucci watched Pier Paolo Pasolini make *Accattone* (1960), he observed that when Pasolini did a tracking shot it was like watching the first tracking shot ever attempted, progressing forward by starting at the beginning. Anderson's *The Singing Lesson* starts at the beginning. Inlaid within the shot of the train is the title of the first song: *Plaszcz*, "A song of Poland's inheritance ... the winds of history... I cried Help! Help! No one came".

In the world film canon *The Singing lesson* is a minor work, particularly when viewed alongside equivalent films by Anderson's peers, e.g. the BBC films of Ken Russell (made between 1959-1970) which eclipse it completely (particularly in terms of technique) but one can see the importance of the film to Anderson. He believed not in God but in the community of friends, within whose company he would often break into song. Often the songs were about togetherness. The spur for the film was perhaps the communal singing of hymns in the boarding schools and colleges of his English boyhood, sounds which open the film of *if....*

The Singing Lesson ends with the old professor hurrying forth with great vitality to join two pupils on the stage to show them how it should be done. He dances and sings almost as if he's Chaplin making *Limelight*. The unexpected vitality of the elderly would become a feature of Anderson's films, from the breathtakingly bold entrance of Valentine Dyall in *The Old Crowd* (1978), rushing into a room and staring straight into the camera lens, to the star performances of Lillian Gish (at age ninety three) and Bette Davis in Anderson's swansong feature, *The Whales of August* (1987). Anderson speeds up the action à la Richard Lester. Then the whole class are dancing together and singing *Raz Dwa Trzy* ('one, two, three'); the sequence intercut with matching whip-pan shots of busy people hurrying in busy streets. It's a film about 'desperate contrasts': the happy warmth of a community of artists contrasted with the wet-cold of abstract art, communist concrete and dead-end jobbery.

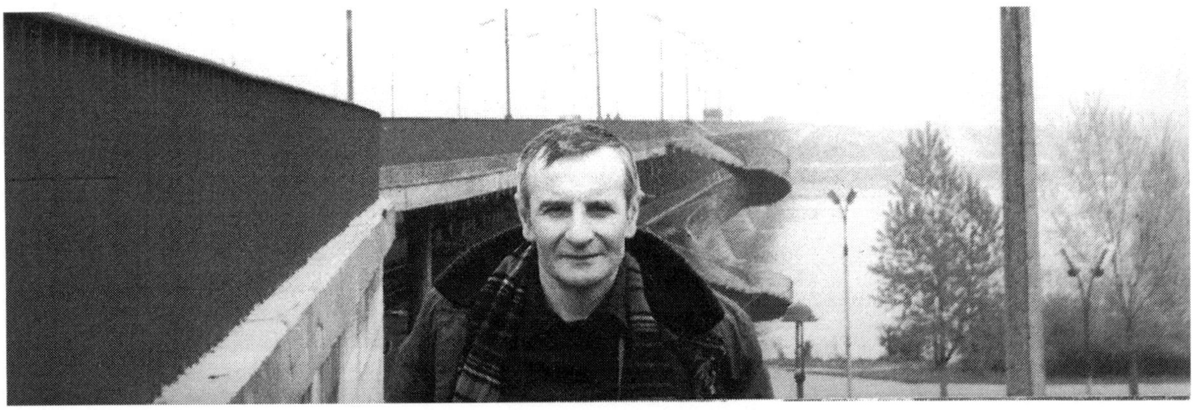

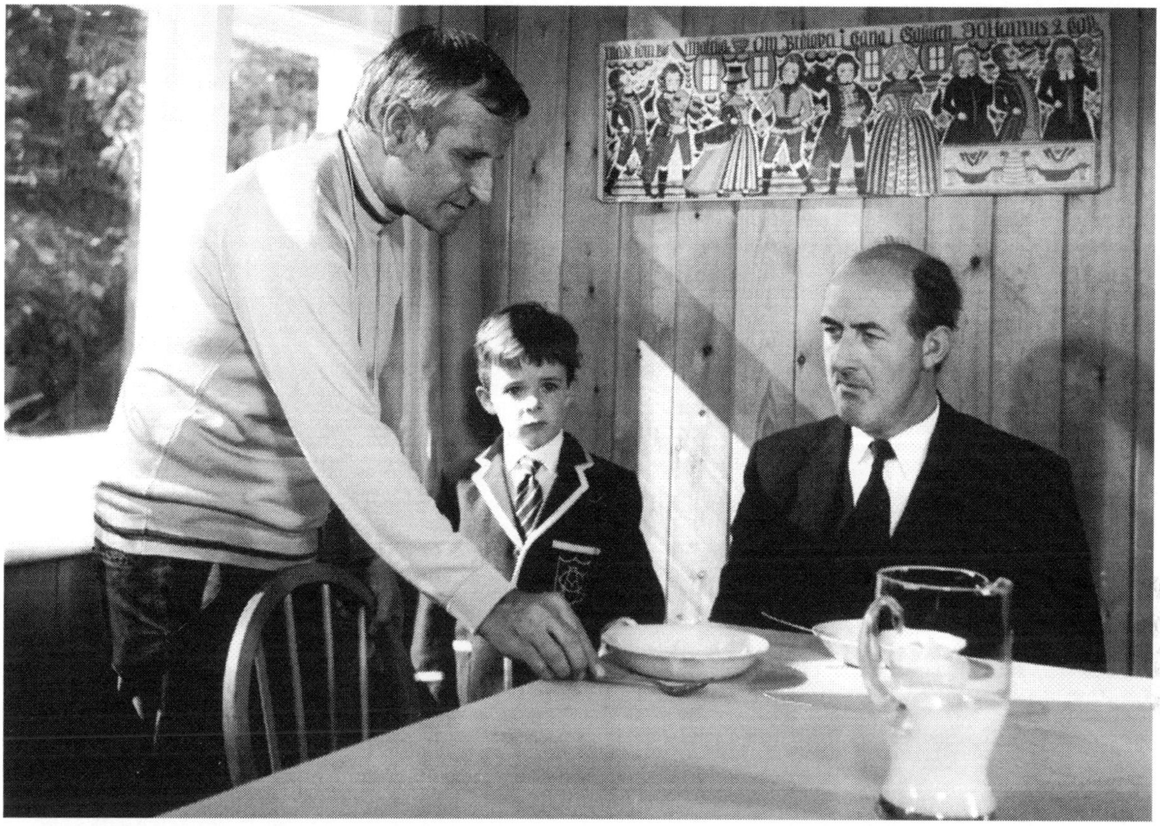

Anderson making '*First Day at School*' for Kelloggs (July 1967)

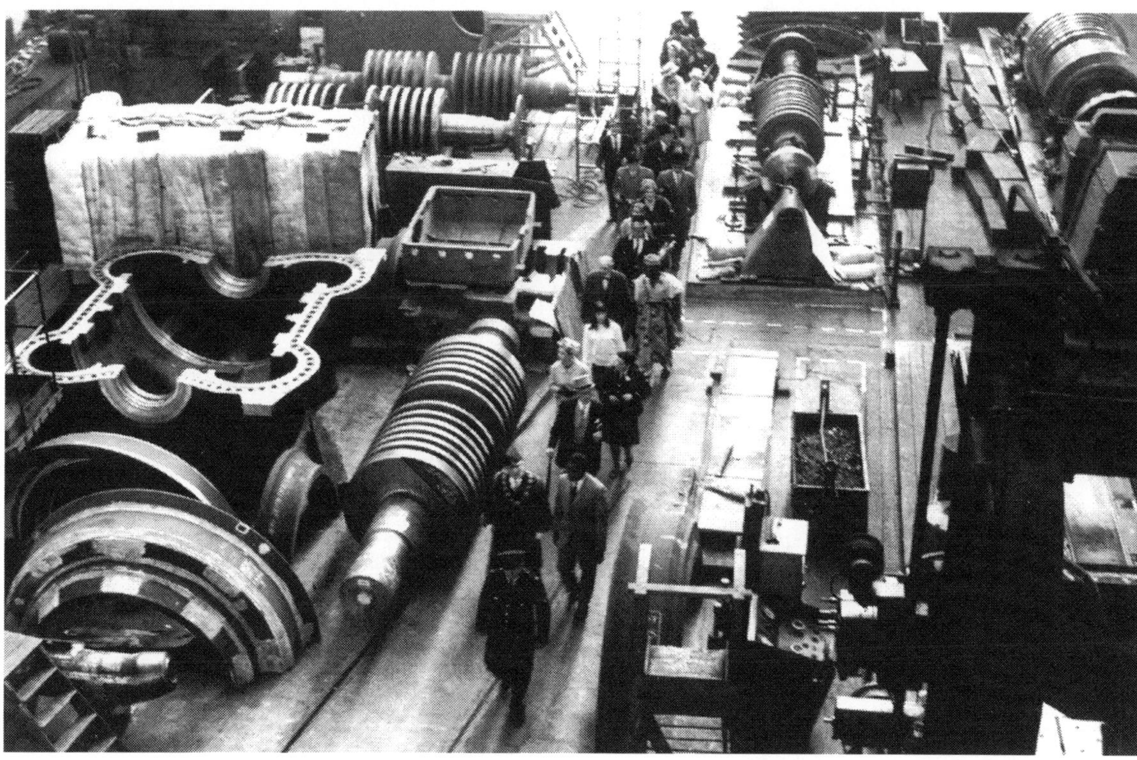

Arthur Lowe leads a tour party through the industrial backbone of England in *The White Bus* (1967)

Philip Harrison Explains How

if....

Got Its Title.

Harrison: I gave Lindsay Anderson the title for *if....*

No you didn't.

I absolutely did. I was asked by Roy Baird [the producer] to go and meet Lindsay, and I met him up in Woodfall's offices, somewhere up in Albermarle Street. I'd been recommended to him by Karel Reisz from my [production design] work on *Morgan!.* .I remember it was a late afternoon, the sun was streaming in, and Lindsay was pacing up and down. He was wreathed in cigarette smoke and firing off questions. I was a bit nervous and stuttered out my answers. I'd read the script and thought it really had something.

The Crusaders script.

Yes, it was called that. He was pacing up and down. He said: "I'm looking for a title." I said: "What about that poem we learned as schoolboys? *If*?
Hewent: "Ah!"
And that was the last I heard of it.

Legend has it that it was suggested to him by his secretary, Daphne Hunter.

Fuck off. Absolutely — fuck off.

I guess Lindsay claimed that because there was a sweepstake of money involved. £100. And he saw it as a way to give his secretary a bonus. Did you turn the job down?

A friend on mine, Brian Eatwell got the job but got fired from it. He's a very good designer but he wasn't the right designer for it actually. He wasn't theatrical enough for it. He was too Brechtian in his approach. Maybe Lindsay was just waiting for Jocelyn [Herbert] to become available. BUT I gave Lindsay that title. Absolutely. And I never heard another word from him. I'm amused because when I gave him the title he stopped in the tracks and went .... That's it. He may have thought he's given me too much already, or am I going to be beholden to this guy?

Rupert Webster

The youngest of The Crusaders, who fought for freedom at the end of *if....*, spent years dodging fan mail from Asia. Now an accomplished guitarist and an exhibited painter, he talks about his brief screen career.

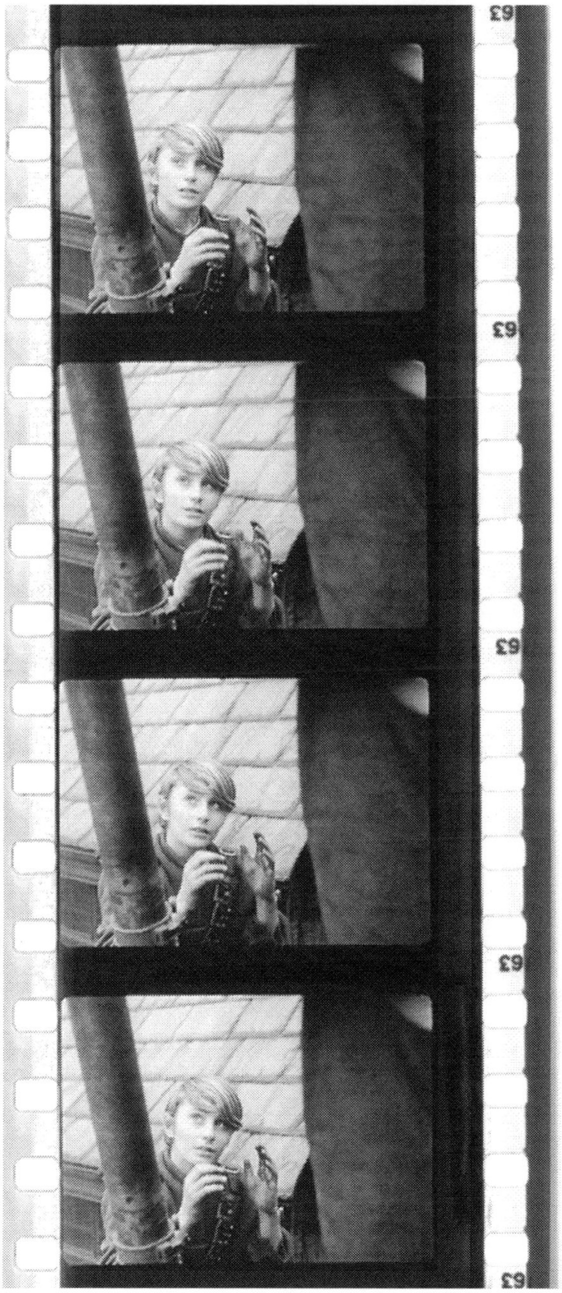

When we were in Cheltenham, I remember watching some of the rushes on a big screen in a tent, and it was so exciting seeing what we had done. That was a huge thrill. I was twelve years old and I wanted to be in the movies. I went to Holland Park Comprehensive, which was fairly free and fast and wild, and I'd appeared in a few school plays, including a big musical production about the Wild West. I got the part in *if....* through a casting agent, Miriam Brickman. I was suggested to her by Roz Chatto, who was also a casting agent. I had auditioned for *Oliver!*, the film starring Oliver Reed and Mark Lester, but I was too tall for that. I had suddenly shot up. They liked me but I was too tall. I was casting about and I remember going in and reading for *if....*, not for Lindsay but for one of the assistant directors. He liked it and, straightaway, he took me somewhere else, and Lindsay was there and I did the reading for him. I don't think the reading was with Richard Warwick, it was with an older chap, but it was the scene where we were in the armoury together. I heard that day, or the next day, that I'd got the part. I was very excited.

With a few of the other kids, I had to go to a fitting at Bermans in the West End to try on the costumes. I really hated the clothes, the school uniforms, the casual clothes and the army clothes. I thought, "God, I'm not going to look good in this lot!" They didn't fit properly. It was one size fits all. You had to request a nip and tuck here and there to improve the fitting. I thought it was a joke. I stayed in digs with the guy who played Machin

[Robin Davies]. There were chaperones and tutors. We had to carry on with our school work which was a giant pain. I thought it was going to be a nice long holiday. I remember going into the town a little bit, and having fun when we had some time off. I can't really remember what we did in the evenings. Some of the shoots started at six or seven in the morning. They liked to get us in early because of the light, so we were probably going to bed as early as they could get us to bed.

One of the first scenes I did was when I'm playing rugger with the new master [Ben Aris]. Unless you know I'm in there you can't really focus on me because I'm at the edges of the shots. I can't actually remember the very first scene I acted in, but I remember having quite a hard time with my entrance scene. I had to do a voice-over on that; my voice wasn't strong enough on the actual soundtrack. A big scene for me was when I'm knocking on Rowntree's door. I had been called back to be Denson's 'scum'. Denson is trying to 'maintain standards' but really he 'wants' this boy. It is actually quite a good scene. There's a lot going on there, although at the start I'm on my own and all I do is knock on the door and move my hair out of my eyes. Lindsay said to me: "This is going to be *your* scene." I was the only person in the shot. I had seen him direct other actors and they had to do it time after time after time and I thought: "Oh, crikey." I did the scene twice and he said: "Perfect!" I was so thrilled. I didn't know about the whole scene, in which one of the prefects says: "Oh, he seems a little lovelier each day" until I watched the movie, and I thought: "That's outrageous!" I wasn't told I was going to be the pretty boy character. I don't think I was ever shown a full script. It was very much under wraps. We were told it was 'adult' but we weren't really told what the story was. I think we were all quite protected. At the time, my sexuality certainly wasn't established. I was aware that Lindsay may possibly be homosexual and I was a bit worried about that. But he was absolutely straight and absolutely professional, always very courteous. He had everybody's confidence. I think the only scene I ever got a little bit concerned with was when I had to get into bed with Richard Warwick. I had no idea that was coming. I thought: "God, what else am I going to be asked to do?" But it was so innocent. And Richard was such a nice chap.

I took my Uncle to a screening in Knightsbridge just before the film opened in the West End. Afterwards he said: "My goodness, that was a hell of a movie!" He was really quite shocked. But he enjoyed it. My mother was very pleased with the way it came out. She thought my performance wasn't polished, that I wasn't 'a proper actor', but she thought I played it right for the character. I thought Lindsay was quite aloof with me. I thought he would work in closer, because he worked very closely with Malcolm [McDowell]. I actually didn't feel that I was being directed as much as some of the other people. A lot of my performance seemed almost accidental really.

I didn't have too much to do with Malcolm, but he was so nice. I remember that I had my thirteenth birthday on the set. There had been a break for something like a month, and when we came back I remember Malcolm saying: "Oh you have grown up and matured, haven't you?" That was the only interaction between us that I can remember. We filmed for about three months in Cheltenham, then we filmed some more scenes at another school, Aldenham School. These were the scenes in the 'sweat room' where Machin gives the speech about "No tinned fruit".

We were all terribly excited when the film opened. We heard about the crowds going round the block, queuing up to see it. When it opened in New York we got an enormous thrill when we heard it had broken box-office records in the first week.

After making the film, I went to King's College, Taunton. It was pretty weird because it was a very similar set-up to the school in *if*.... Suddenly I was back in the setting of the film. I was back to the reality of *if*... but an almost hell-like version of it. A lot of people knew that I'd been in the film and, although I thought I did good work on the film, and I thought it was a good film, I sort of down-played it. I wasn't sure if my screen character was actually a rebel or a 'scum' or something in between and, of course, the Bobbie Phillips character wasn't who I was. It was difficult to ask a friend to 'come and see this movie' in which I was portrayed as a character that I wasn't in real life. It was a little embarrassing. It was one of the first films to deal with that kind of subject matter. It was tough when I was fifteen and trying to get laid.

I did get fan-mail. I was at public school when I got this letter from a girl in Japan. She sent a picture of herself and return postage and a wonderful amorous letter. I was about to write back when, the next day, I got about twenty more letters from Japanese girls. I thought if I wrote to one I would have to write to all of them. The next day I got a hundred letters, then hundreds and hundreds forwarded from the distribution company. I was tempted to write to them but I had homework to do. I feel bad about it now but it was too much. I was swamped and I didn't have a secretary. I was big in Japan, perhaps it was the floppy hair.

I didn't keep in contact with Lindsay after the film. I didn't hear that they were making *O Lucky Man!*. I wasn't in the trade, I was at school, though I did do a few other things, such as a *Play for Today* with Ian Carmichael, who was a bastard but a terrific actor. He wanted to get me fired. It was a BBC film called *Alma Mater* about public schools. I played a school bully, quite the opposite to the part I play in *if*.... . I've often tried to get a copy, and I've met people who work for the BBC but they've all drawn blanks.

I think I auditioned for Ken Russell, I've always enjoyed his films, and I certainly auditioned for *The Triple Echo* which stars Glenda Jackson and Oliver Reed. I was very keen to work with them, and I loved the script, but I went along to the interview wearing seven-inch platform heels, which wasn't a great idea. Those were the days! I would have loved to have met Oliver Reed. He was so great, particularly *Women in Love* and *The Devils*. As an actor he has the full range. He has such a soft side, a vulnerability to him as well as the really strong and powerful persona.

I studied art at the Ruskin College of Fine Art and did my middle year at the Massachusetts College of Art in Boston. That's where I met my wife. I lived in America for thirteen years from 1977 to 1990. I lived round the Fenway, at the back of the Red Sox. I wasn't involved in the film business at all. My mother is an actress. She's a friend of June Wyndom-Davies, a producer at ITV who knew Lindsay quite well. When I came back to Britain, I expressed an interest in meeting up with Lindsay and having a cup of tea. I was aware that he'd made *Britannia Hospital* and *O Lucky Man!* and there was a big rumour that he was going to make *if 2*. I thought it would nice to be around and to be available. I had his phone number and I talked with him on several occasions and we were just about to meet up again, and have tea, and he passed away. I was glad that I'd talked with him. I was sad that I didn't get to see him again and chat. It would have been nice.

I feel very lucky to have been at the reunion of *if*.... at the [2002] re-release of the film. A neighbour, who worked for the BBC, said: "Do you know there is a première for *if*.... tonight?' My mother spent the whole morning trying to get through to the right person but when she did they were very nice and they sent some tickets by courier so we could go. Meeting the cast and crew after 35 years was weird. It was so nice meeting Mary MacLeod. David Sherwin introduced me as "Rupert. He was the beautiful one." and Mary said: "He still is!" She was so nice. On set, she was a real motherly figure. You got that lovely feeling from her, and from Mona Washbourne too. Oh God, she was brilliant. I loved her. They'd bring her in by train, she'd do her shot and she'd be off. She wasn't really a part of the whole experience but what a difference she made! That scene when she is licking her lips when she is pouring out that stew! Robert Swann gave a great performance too. He really was that authoritarian figure, but I thought he was quite likeable. He's a very nice chap. He does car insurance adverts on TV now. I returned from America with thirteen guitars, not counting the five I had to leave behind and, back in London, I picked up my musical career. I've been working with Paul Humphries, one half of OMD. We've put down a few tracks. As a rule I don't like synthesizer pop bands but Paul is a real talent. It impressed me to learn that ZZ Top were fans of OMD. They had huge hits with a synthesized music which became part of their style.

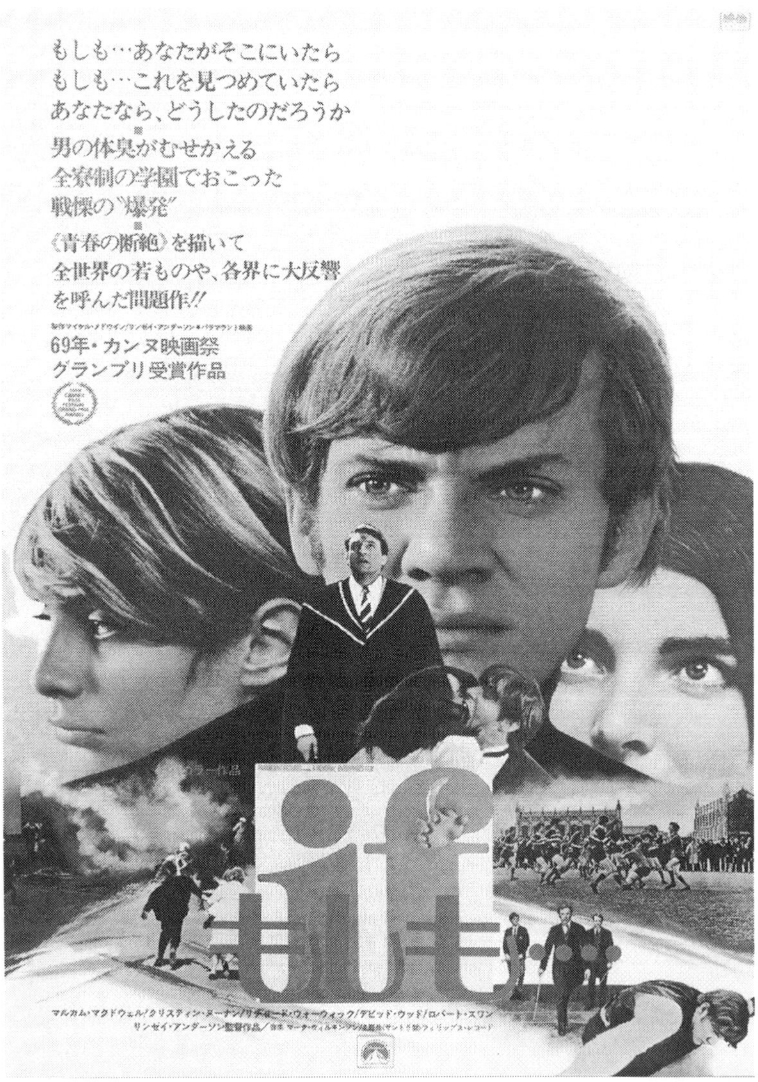

Rupert Webster featured prominently on the Japanese poster for *if....*

His floppy-haired English adolescent look proved to be a particular favourite among Oriental girls; and paved the way there for the frankly astonishing box-office success of the Jack Wild, Mark Lester school film, *Melody* (1971). The 'Webster' look became a staple in Manga comics.

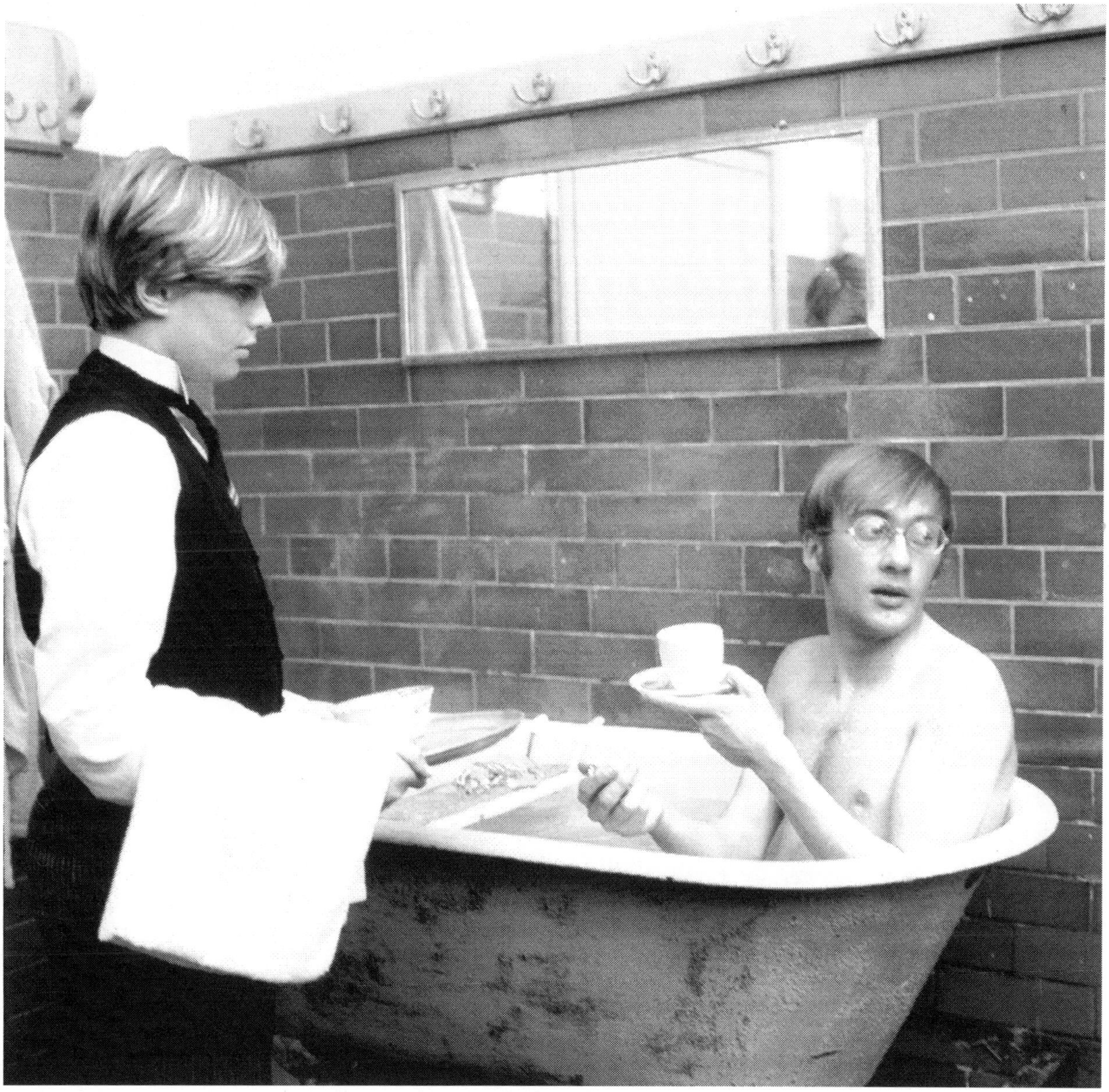

'Scumming for Denson'

Michael Newport

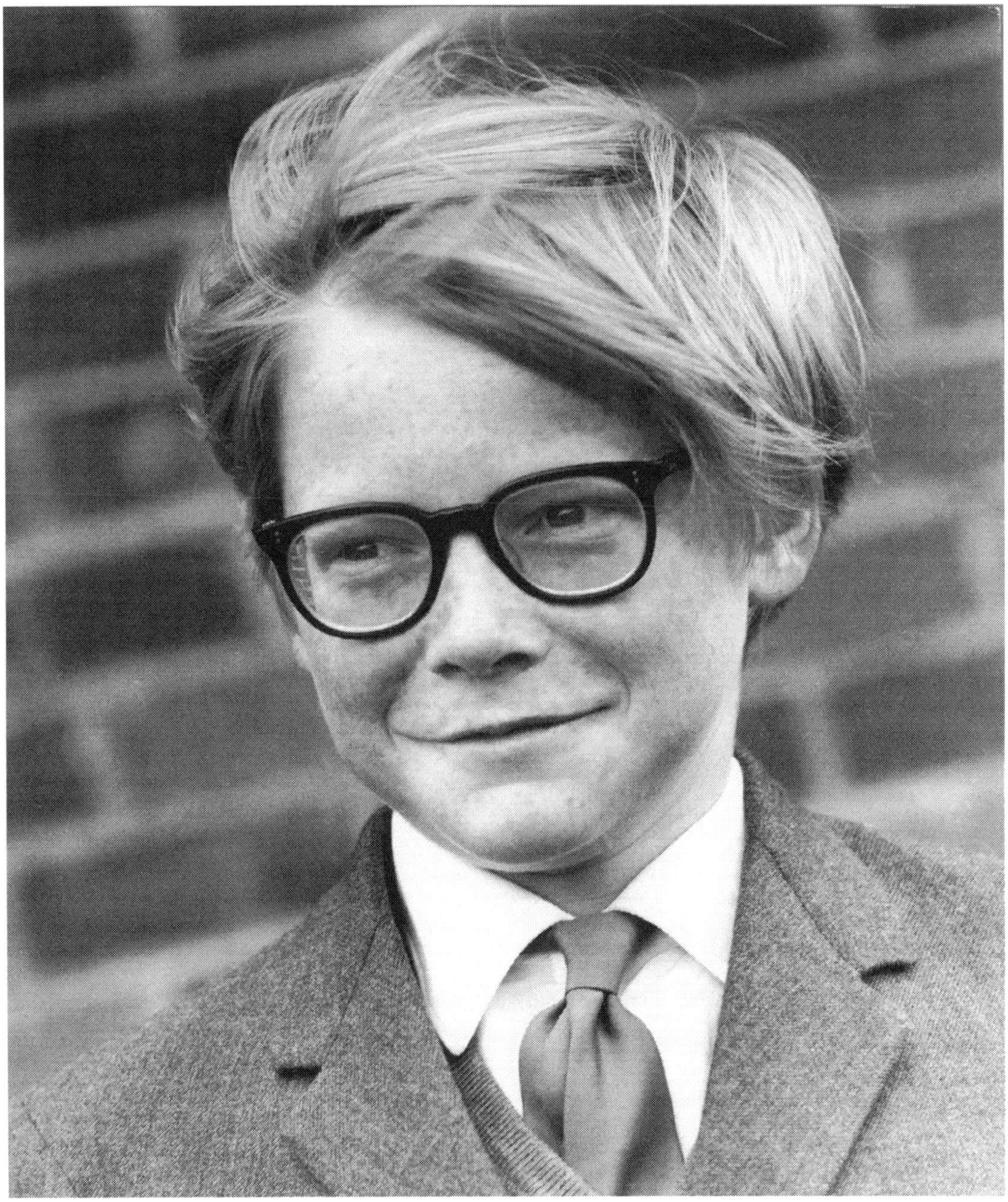

"Masters, THEIR wives, and THEE friends of College!"

John Holmstrom Collection

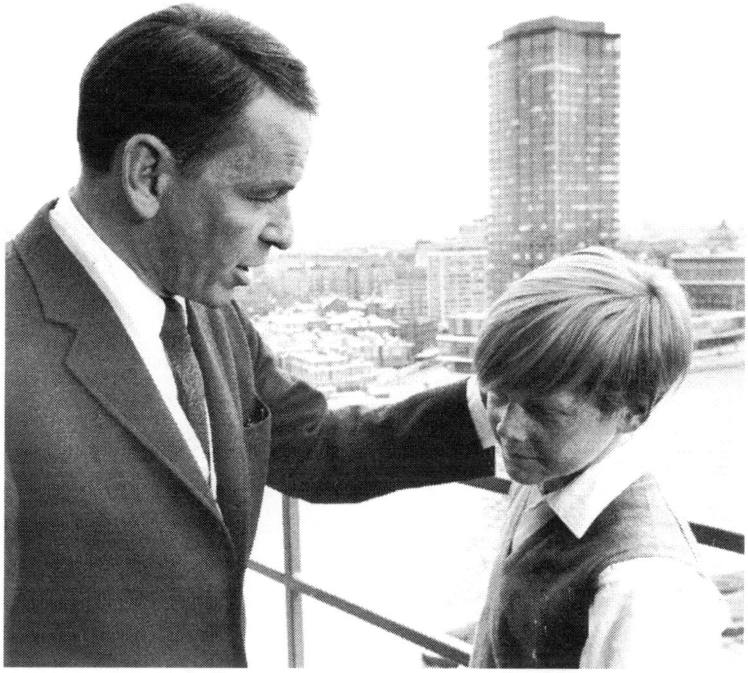

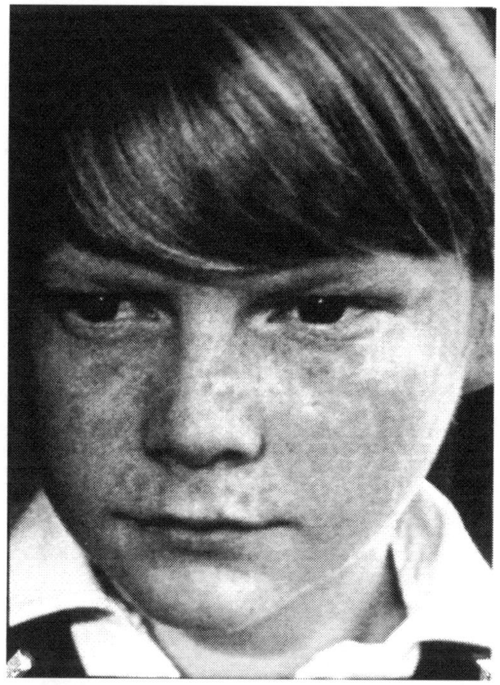

(above) Newport as Frank Sinatra's son in *The Naked Runner* (1967, directed by Sidney J. Furie)

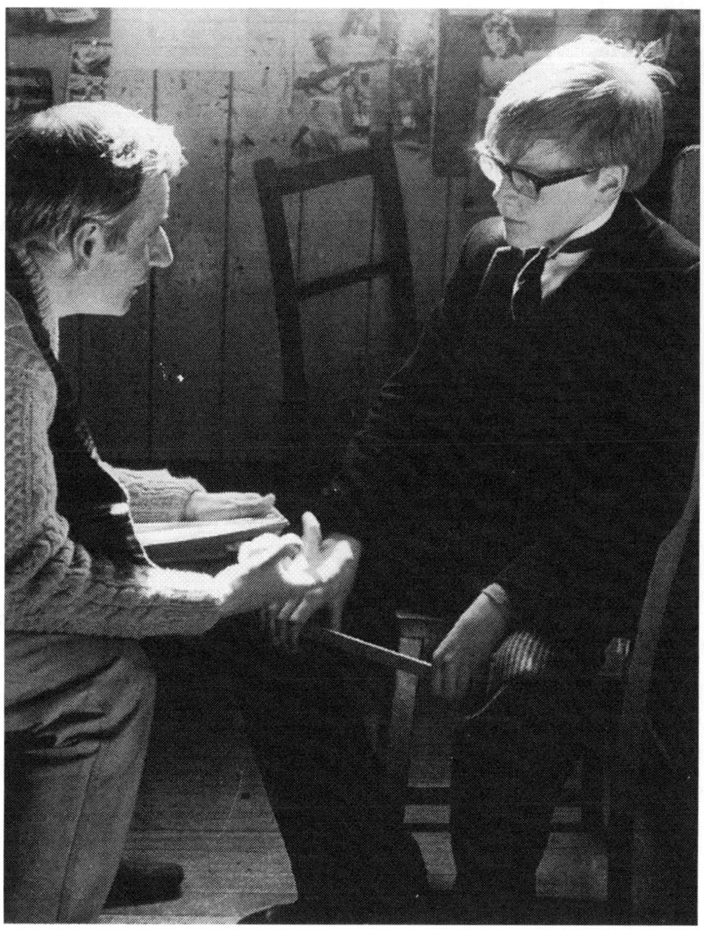

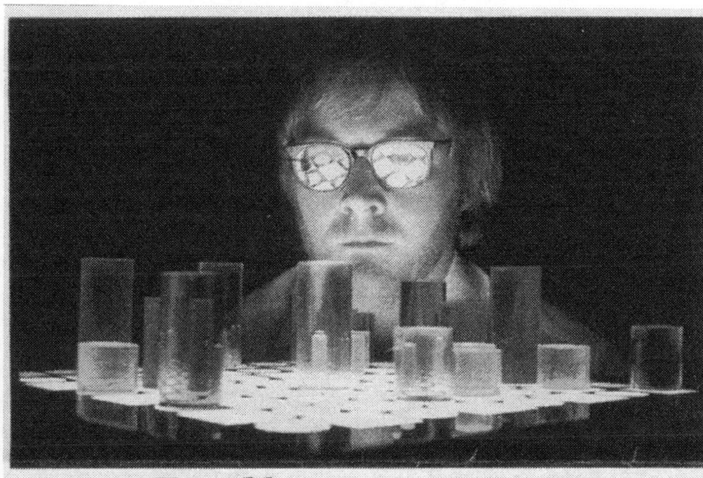

Adrian Murrell

Brilliant move

Michael Newport, dazzled here with his own brilliance, claims to have made the first serious innovation in chess since the castling move. He calls it Spectrum Satellite and, when he starts to talk about it, promptly blinds one with science. The pieces are made of acrylic rods which when lit from below blaze with light at the top. One trouble with chess, Newport says, is that you start by being taught the 'territorial limitations' of the pieces – they can *only* do this or that – rather than their interrelationship on the board. Looking for a way to express the complexities of strategy and so on, he hit on colour. So he has no Black or White; both his queens are red, his kings pale blue, bishops violet, knights amber, rooks green, and all his pawns yellow. The 'Black' pieces are distinguished only by an indentation on top.

Non-players have been sufficiently attracted to learn on his set, and others have remarked on a notable improvement in their concentration. Newport believes that when all the pieces are coloured and lit up you eliminate the danger of 'losing sight' of a piece, which is his explanation for silly mistakes.

Miracles, of 436 King's Road, London SW10, are selling Spectrum Satellite at £275 a time. *Anthony Ellis*

Brian Pettifer

A key member of the Lindsay Anderson Repertory Company, Brian Pettifer made his film debut as the bullied 'Biles' in *if....*; appeared in *O Lucky Man!* and co-starred with Leonard Rossiter in *Britannia Hospital*. He has appeared in hundreds of films and television shows and worked with Clive Donner and Mike Hodges.

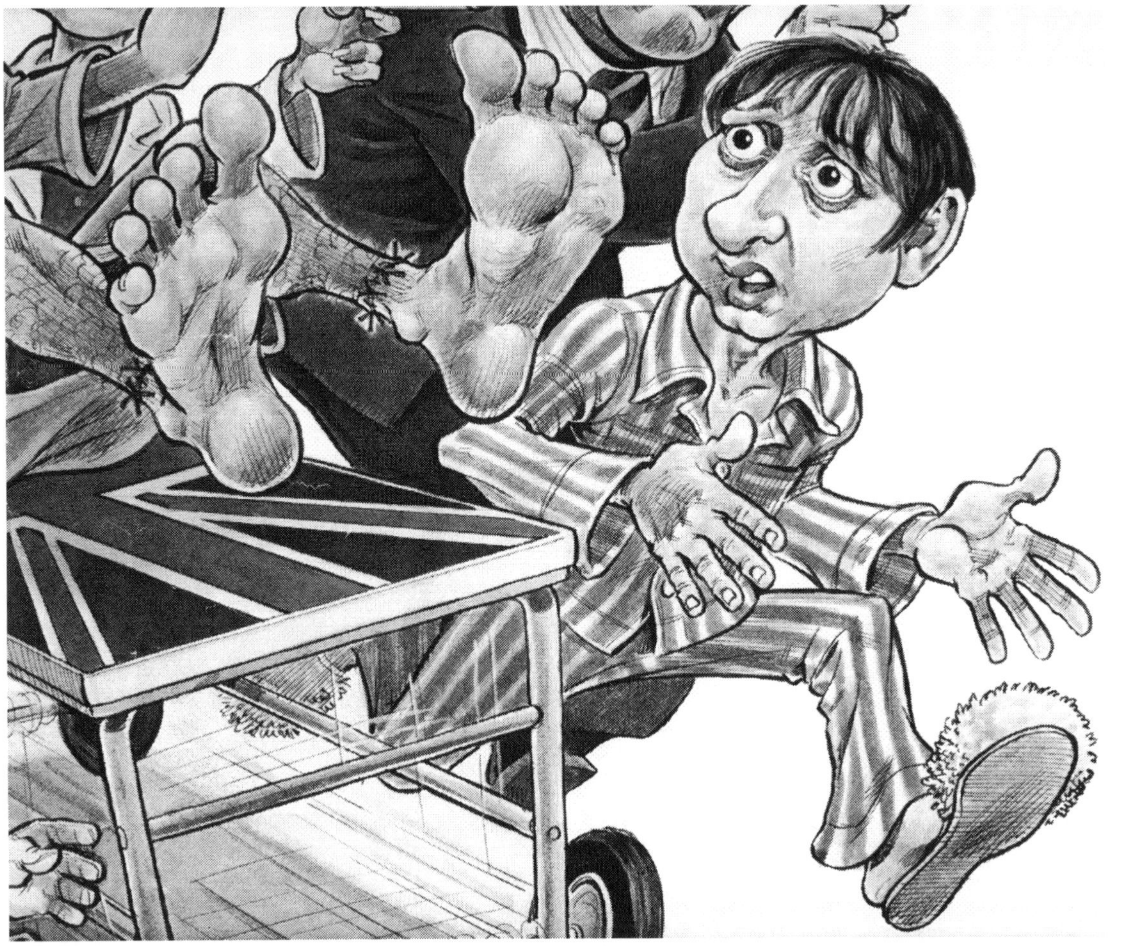
Pettifer on the American poster for *Britannia Hospital*

My parents felt I was very shy. And I was. I was a shy child. There was a junior course at the drama school in Glasgow and my sister had started going. It was twice a week, a Wednesday and a Saturday. They managed to trick me into going along for the interview. Amazingly I got in. I had been there for three days when someone came picking children for a Brecht play and they picked me. It opened up a whole new world for me. I was thirteen. When I left school at sixteen I went straight into a television series which lasted for two years. I was living in London then, and I had an agent, and I'd done some work there. Rudolf Nureyev lived in the flat above. I never paid attention to him, but sometimes I wonder what would have happened if I'd said: "Rudolf, do you want to come in for a cup of tea?" (*laughs*). The agent said to me: "There's an audition for a part in a film set in a school. It's by Lindsay Anderson." I'd never heard of Lindsay Anderson or Miriam Brickman, the casting director. I went along and there were lots of kids there. And I went to another interview at Half Moon Street and every time I went there seemed to be more people. But what did strike me, even then at a young age, though I'd done 60 or 70 television shows and worked with probably 25 directors, was that Lindsay was completely different. He was far nicer. He didn't talk to you as if you were an idiot. He spoke to the boys as if they were equal to him. There was no talking down to them. He was very polite and very nice. He saw so many people, as you know there was a 'casting call' advert in the *Melody Maker*, and he didn't ask me to do much. I think I read one of Malcolm's speeches, everyone read one of Malcolm's speeches, but no one but Malcolm was going to play that part. There wasn't much dialogue and what there was was for Malcolm. And that was my first film with Lindsay. He famously said to Malcolm afterwards: "It's all down hill from here, Malcolm."

Quite a lot of jobs I got afterwards were because the directors were great fans of *if....* I used to say to Lindsay that *if....* has been very good to me because directors like the film. They'd say: "If you are good enough for Lindsay Anderson then you are good enough for me." Virtually straight after *if....* I did *Husbands* with John Cassavetes. My agent, Tom Busby, had been in *The Dirty Dozen* and was a friend of John Cassavetes. So when Cassavetes came over here to shoot the British section, Tom was casting director. It wasn't a big part. It was a bellboy. I had a scene with Peter Falk. It was cut out of the movie because the movie literally lasted ten hours. We filmed at night. We didn't start until midnight and were due to shoot until 8 a.m. but at about 2 a.m. Cassavetes, who was very mood orientated and very indulged, said: "I'm fed up. I want to play cards. It's a wrap." And we went to play cards. He did the most extraordinary things. He'd go: "Action!" and Peter Falk would start to talk, and Cassavetes would run in front of the camera, and shake him and bang his head off the wall. They'd laugh uproariously and Cassavetes would say: "Now do it." And he'd say to me: "Speak when you feel like it." I'd think "What?". It was disconcerting. Falk was very nice.

O Lucky Man! was a delight. I wasn't in it a great deal, unfortunately. I'm in the first scene and I pop up here and there, but not often enough obviously. You see me being released from prison with Malcolm; and I should have been in the pig body but I was too small for the costume. Lindsay looked at me inside the costume and said: "No". Jeremy Bulloch did it.

The scenes with Rachel Roberts were good because she was so nervous. She's giving a lecture in the training room. Arthur Lowe had a line: "Our top salesman at the moment is a wonderful man called John Schlesinger." That's the line he said. You can clearly see that's he's looped the line for the film. Lindsay never mentioned Schlesinger to me, but I suppose losing *Billy Liar* to him must have been a sore point. [Anderson directed the original stage play, and a had a huge success with Albert Finney and then Tom Courtenay in the title role, but the writers, Waterhouse and Hall, sold to film rights to Joe Janni, John Schlesinger's producer, because Anderson was rude to them when the play was in previews in Brighton].

I went to the première of *O Lucky Man!* at the Warner Brothers cinema in Leicester Square and I loved it. I liked it straight away. I liked it more than I like *if....* . There was just so much in it. But at the reception afterwards you could tell that people had liked it but the feeling was that it wasn't loved. People didn't think it was fantastic. The reaction to *if...* at the London Film Festival when I first saw it had been ecstatic.

When Lindsay was putting *Britannia Hospital* together I got a very nice letter from Patsy Pollock, the casting director, saying: 'Dear Brian, Lindsay would love you to play the part of Biles again...' and when I read the script I thought: 'Gosh, Biles has got a lot to do in this one.' Shooting it was a completely different sensation to *if...* and *O Lucky Man!* because there was patently no money. It seemed and felt low-budget. The pressure on everyone, mainly Lindsay, was immense. And it wasn't cast with names. The problem with having Leonard Rossiter in the lead role was that he was too famous from television. He was a terrific actor. He'd worked a couple of times with Kubrick and had a walk-on roll in *This Sporting Life* (1964), but he was known as a 'television actor'. One of the reviews said: "It's a shame it was so resolutely cast from television". Leonard was playing a part that had been written for Arthur Lowe. But by the time they got the money to make the film, Arthur was on the way out. He died soon afterwards. Before filming started, I met Lindsay on The Strand. He looked worried. He said: "I've just been to see Arthur [who was performing in the theatre]. He didn't know who I was." (*laughs*). Arthur did end up in the film and people booed because he dies in the film and he had died by the time the film came out. In the film he makes a valedictory speech about 'This Sceptred Isle. This England' and people booed! Sam Kydd was also in it, but they cut his bit out and he died soon afterwards too. Graham Crowden is fantastic in it, of course. *Britannia Hospital* flopped in Britain, people hated it here, but it was popular in Argentina and France. I was in France when it was on.

I was then hired by Milos Forman to win F. Murray Abraham an Oscar. I was the young man Abraham tells his Mozartian tale to in *Amadeus*. When I first met Forman, at the Savoy, he was charm itself: "It's not a big part but it would be a great honour for me if you would accept it". Then, when we got on the set, he was a complete monster. From morning till night he shouted at everyone and was thoroughly obnoxious. Lindsay came out to Czechoslovakia and spent a couple of days on the set.

I worked with Clive Donner on *A Christmas Carol*. I like Clive a lot. He was very nice, very British, upper class, very pleasant to work with, but the difference between Clive and other major British filmmakers is that Clive's heart was never in the film. It was never a part of 'him'. It was just a job and anyone could have shot the film. I think he was hired because he had worked with George C. Scott before and Scott was difficult. And Clive can do an efficient job. It was a nice job. We shot it in Shrewsbury.

I was reunited with Helen Mirren in *Heavenly Pursuits* (1987) and with Malcolm [McDowell] on *Gulag* (1985). *Gulag* was great fun. We shot it in Norway and Watford, with Watford doubling as the *Gulag* (*laughs*). When you've been to Watford you think: 'That's absolutely right. They've got it spot on.' I had a marvellous death with an axe in the back. I was wearing a padded jacket but I was hit hard. The director, Roger Young, said: "You're anticipating it a bit, Brian." I said: "I fucking am because this guy's hitting me in the back with an axe!" For days after I was bruised. David Keith and Warren Clarke were in it. David said to the pair of them: "*A Clockwork Orange*, I love that film. You both know Kubrick. Why don't we go up there and say hello?". Malcolm said: "Er, no."

I like Mike Hodges. He was very good to work with. His career was in a bit of the doldrums when I worked with him on *Dandelion Dead* (1994), a four-hour mini-series for London Weekend Television. David Thewlis was in it and he was a pain in the arse, and on the cusp of being great in *Naked*.

Throughout my career, Lindsay's work and friendship continue to resonate. For example, I was making *Loch Ness* (1996) with Ted Danson. Mary Steenburgen, whom I didn't know but who was once married to Malcolm, came over to me and, in front of everyone, said: "Gosh, you're in all of Lindsay's films." My stock immediately rose among the company. Ted Danson was very good to me thereafter.

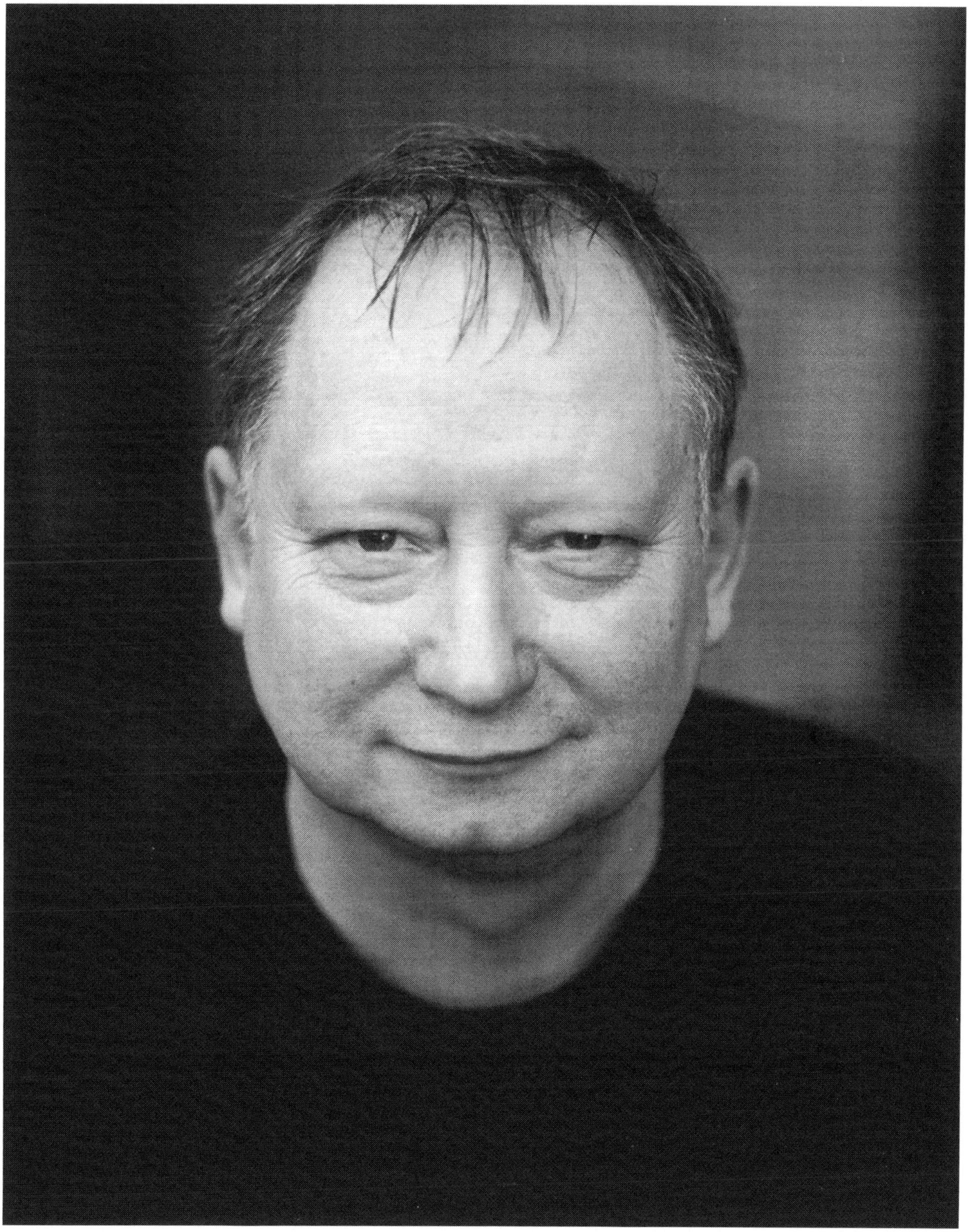

(c) Paul Sutton

Malcolm McDowell

I took this photograph of Malcolm McDowell in New York City in May 2002. I was in New York to introduce screenings of 35mm prints of Lindsay Anderson films showing at the Walter Reade Theatre, as part of an eight-day long celebration of films starring Malcolm McDowell. It was taken in the anteroom of a restaurant off Fifth Avenue where we had just eaten. I'd accidently left my camera on the back of my chair and a waitress had hurried over and handed it to me. McDowell directed the photo shoot. He said: "This is a good place for a photo, with the light coming in from above. Take it here but don't ask me to pose because I won't."

After I'd taken the photograph he said he'd like to introduce me to someone he was sure I'd like: "He lives nearby. Do you want to walk or catch a cab?"

I asked: "If we walk, will you get recognised?"

"Of course! But there's a pattern about the recognition."

"What do you mean?"

"Let's walk. There's something similar about the people who recognise me. See if you can see what it is."

It didn't take long before someone recognised Malcolm. From a truck, the driver shouted: "You're the dude, Man!" and asked him how he was doing.

"Fine," answered Malcolm, "and yourself?"

"Just great, man. Say, it's made my day seeing you. Have a great day."

"I will," replied Malcolm. "Thank you."

The man in the truck waved a farewell and drove away. Then another person recognised Malcolm McDowell. They stopped him and shook his hand. Soon he was recognised by a third. And a fourth.

He said: "Have you recognised the pattern yet?"

I had: "Everyone who has greeted you is black."

"It's crazy isn't it?" said Malcolm grinning. "White folks walk on by but the blacks tell me I'm great and shake my hand. I've got a big black following."

"I wonder why that is?"

"I've no idea. But I did have a black cock in *Britannia Hospital.* That was Lindsay's idea. My cock was painted black. It's the smallest black cock on film."

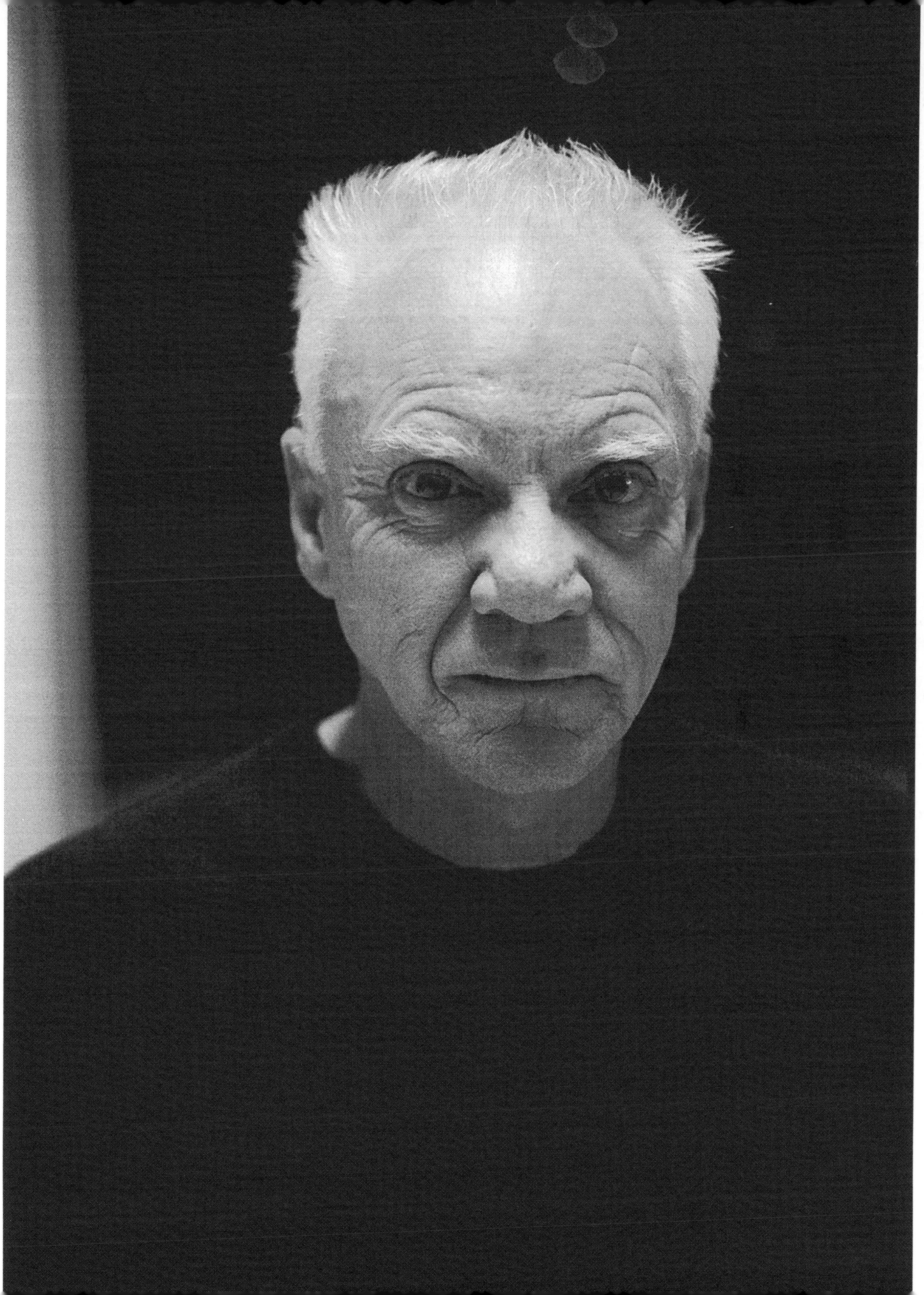

This stunning Warhol-inspired poster was designed by Mike Kaplan, formerly a marketing executive at MGM. Kaplan rescued Kubrick's *2001* from failure after persuading MGM to pull the film from release after a disappointing opening weekend so that he could re-launch it with a new poster campaign. Kaplan's campaign worked. Thereafter, Stanley Kubrick invited Kaplan to oversee the marketing of all his films. Kubrick's *A Clockwork Orange* brought Kaplan into contact with Malcolm McDowell. Kaplan become McDowell's manager and lifelong friend. The lettering on the poster is Anderson's own handwriting to emphasize the 'handmade' quality of the film, and to highlight the integral part played by Alan Price's songs. Kaplan moved into film distribution and production. He produced Lindsay Anderson's *The Whales of August* (1987) and Mike Hodges' *I'll Sleep When When I'm Dead* (2003). Naturally, he has the best poster collection in the United States.

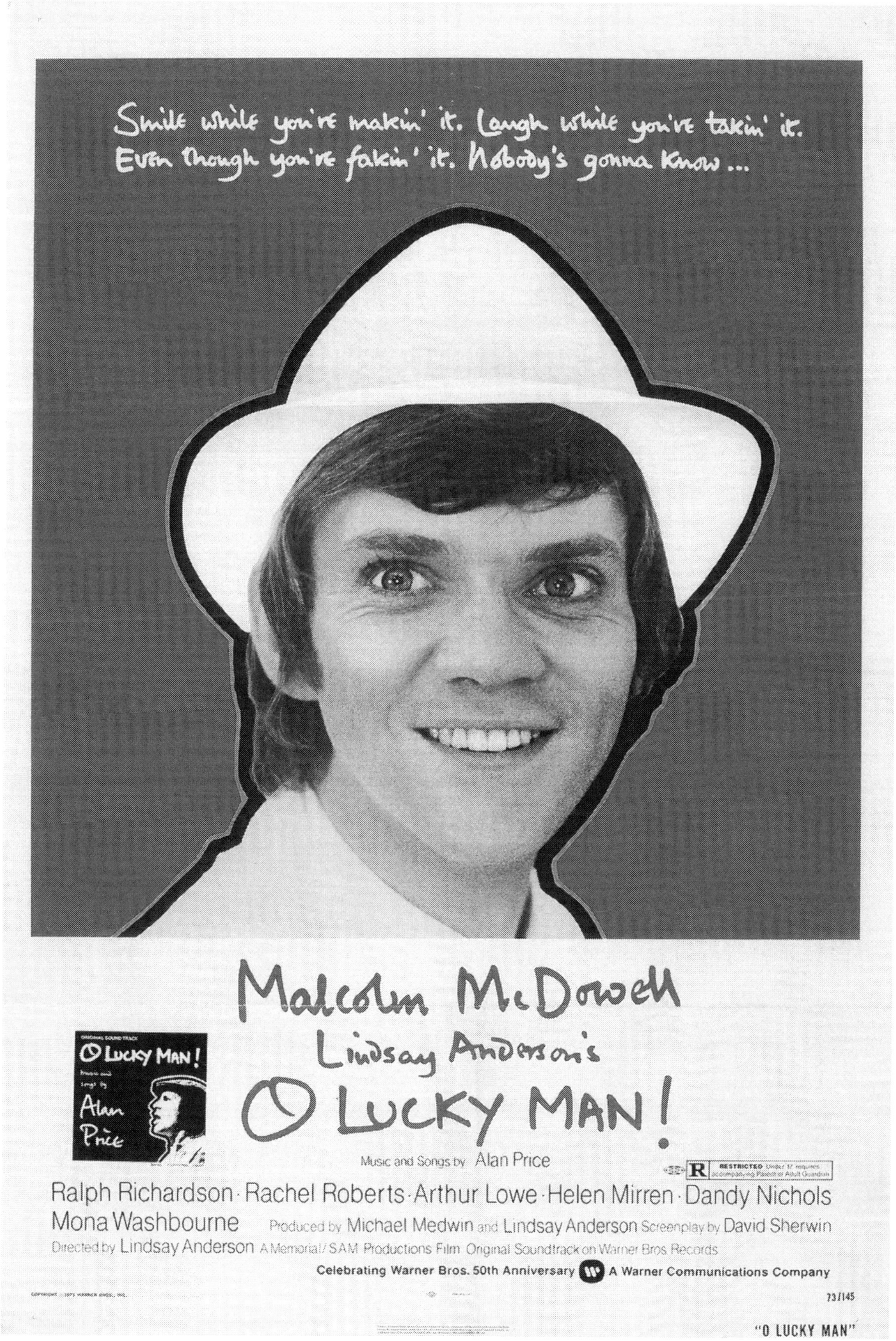
Smile while you're makin' it. Laugh while you're takin' it.
Even though you're fakin' it. Nobody's gonna know ...
Malcolm McDowell
Lindsay Anderson's
O LUCKY MAN!
ORIGINAL SOUND TRACK
O LUCKY MAN!
Music and songs by
Alan Price
Music and Songs by Alan Price
R RESTRICTED Under 17 requires accompanying Parent or Adult Guardian
Ralph Richardson · Rachel Roberts · Arthur Lowe · Helen Mirren · Dandy Nichols
Mona Washbourne
Produced by Michael Medwin and Lindsay Anderson Screenplay by David Sherwin
Directed by Lindsay Anderson A Memorial/SAM Productions Film Original Soundtrack on Warner Bros Records
Celebrating Warner Bros. 50th Anniversary A Warner Communications Company
73/145
"O LUCKY MAN"

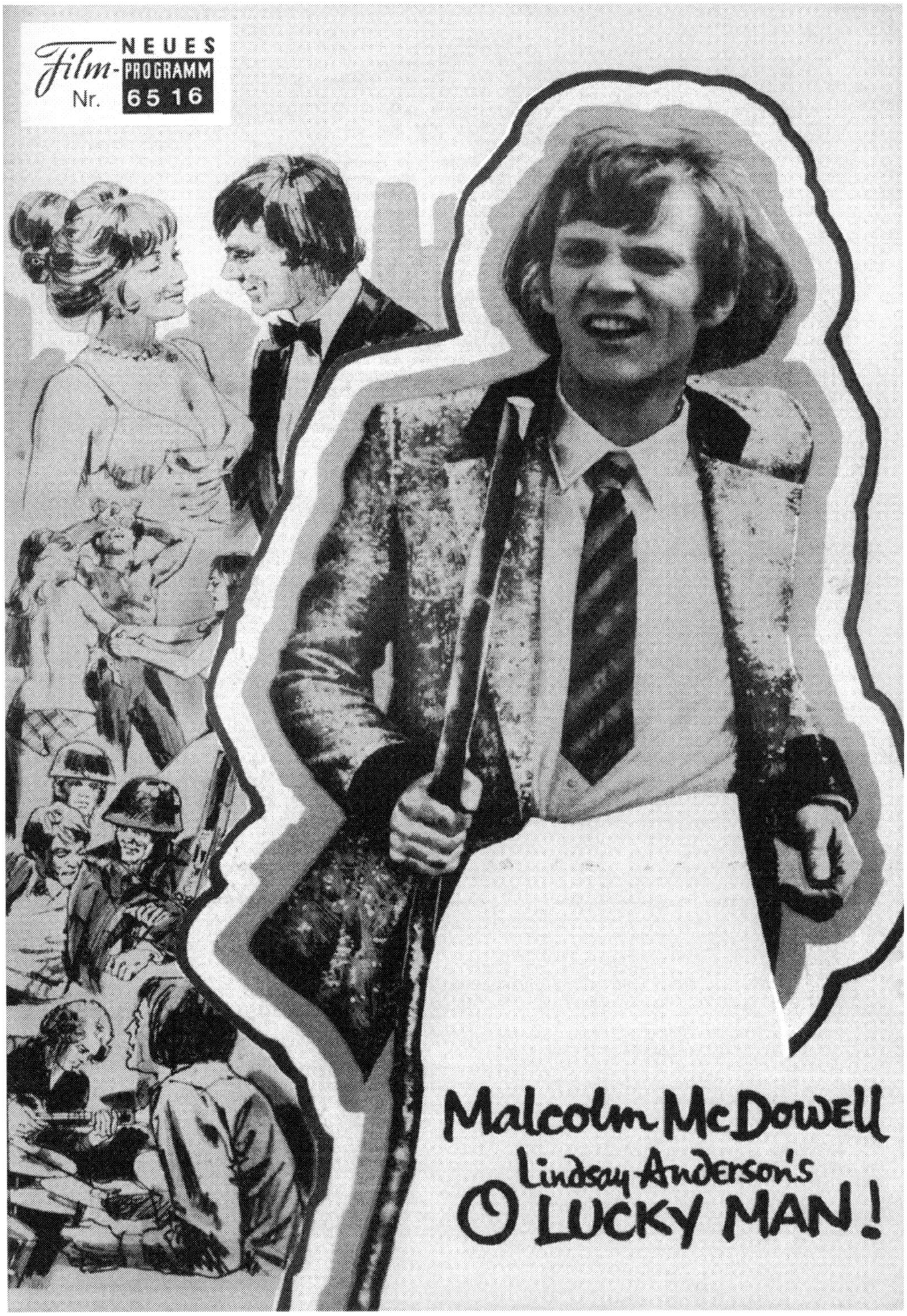

McDowell in his lucky golden suit in *O Lucky Man!*

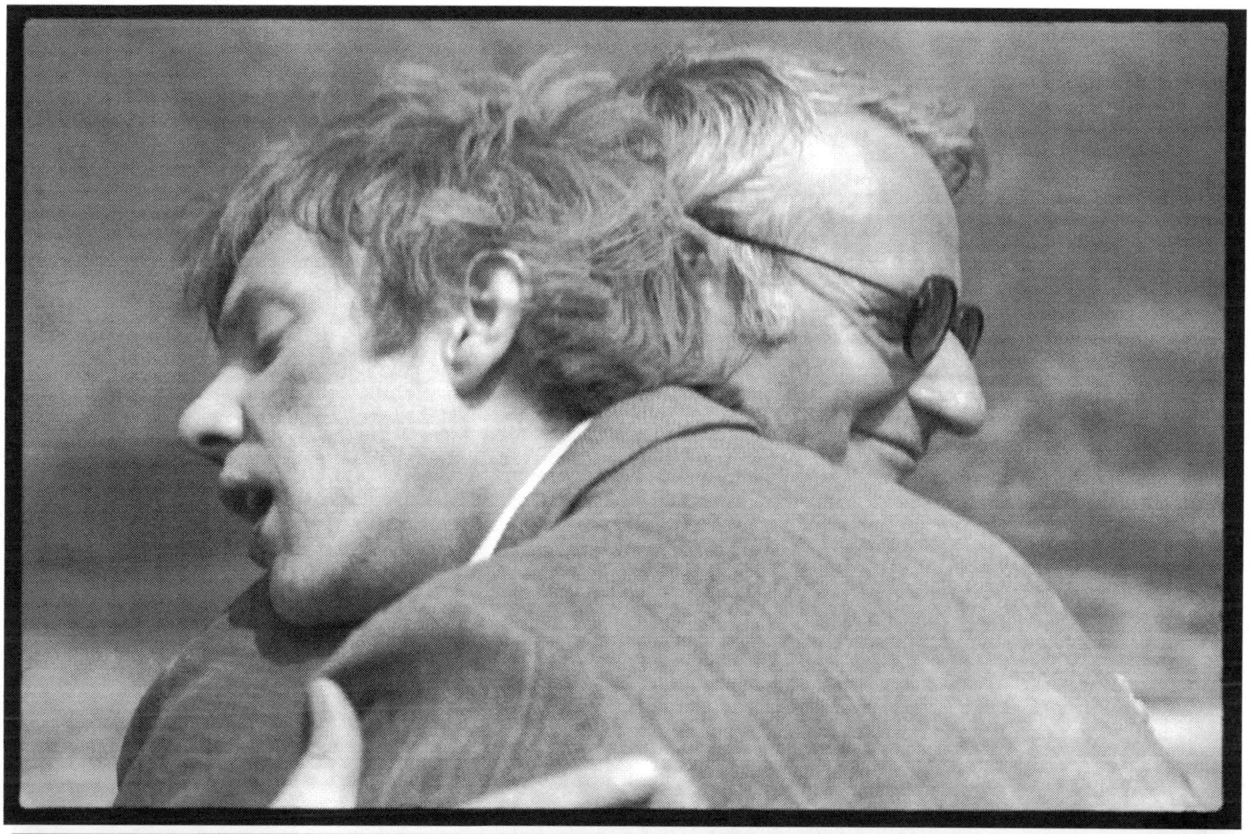

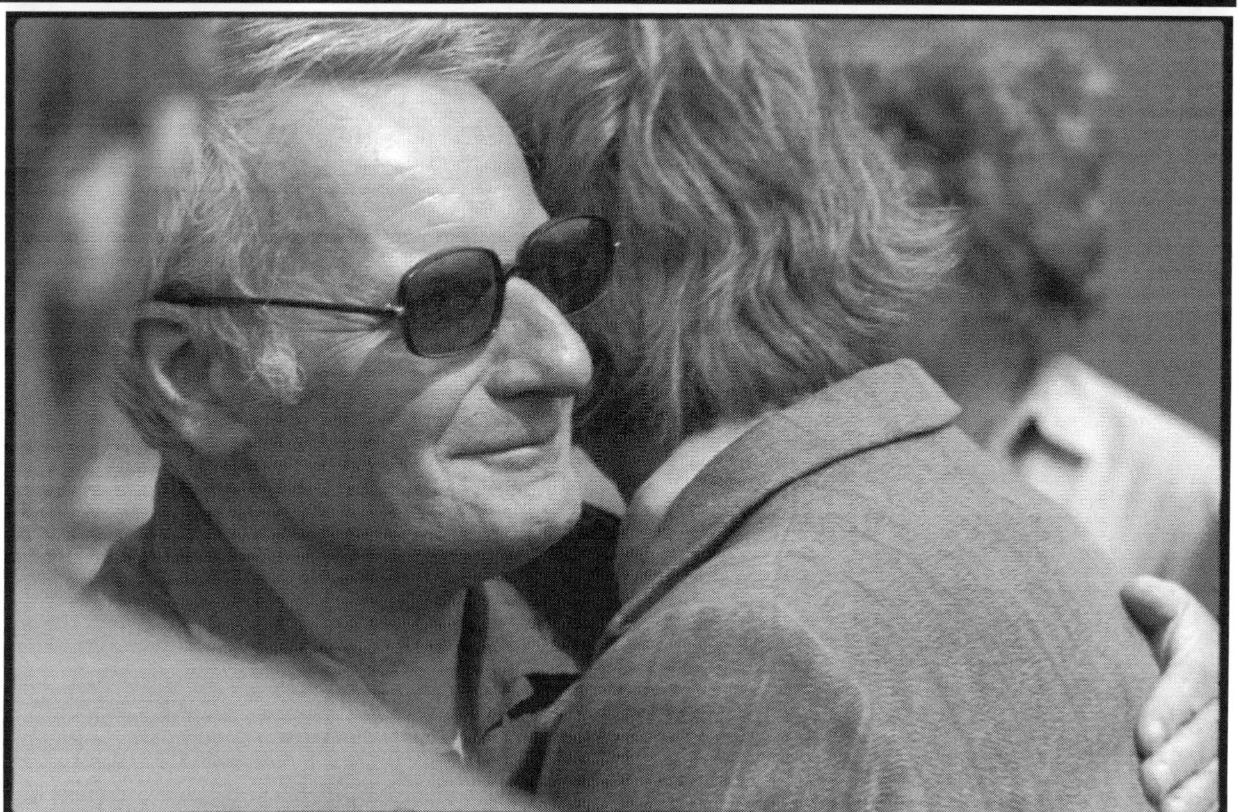

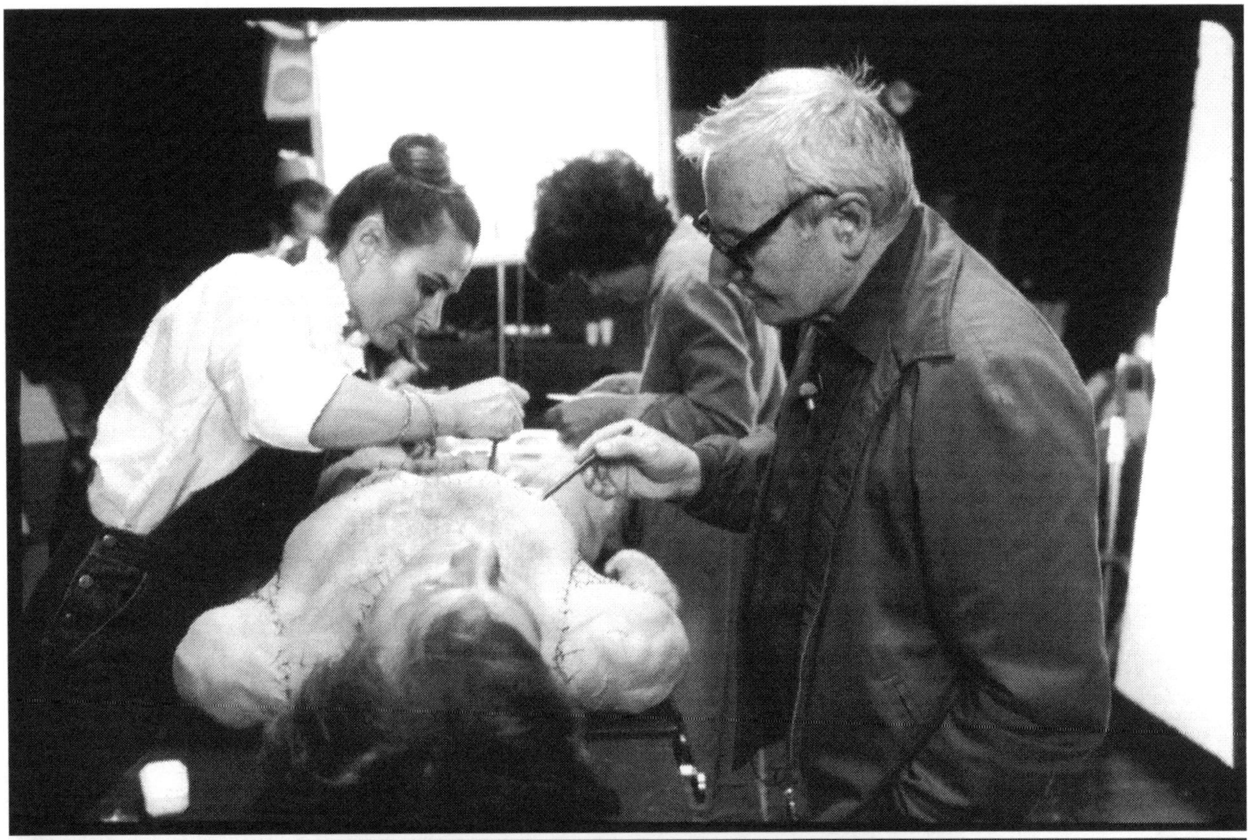

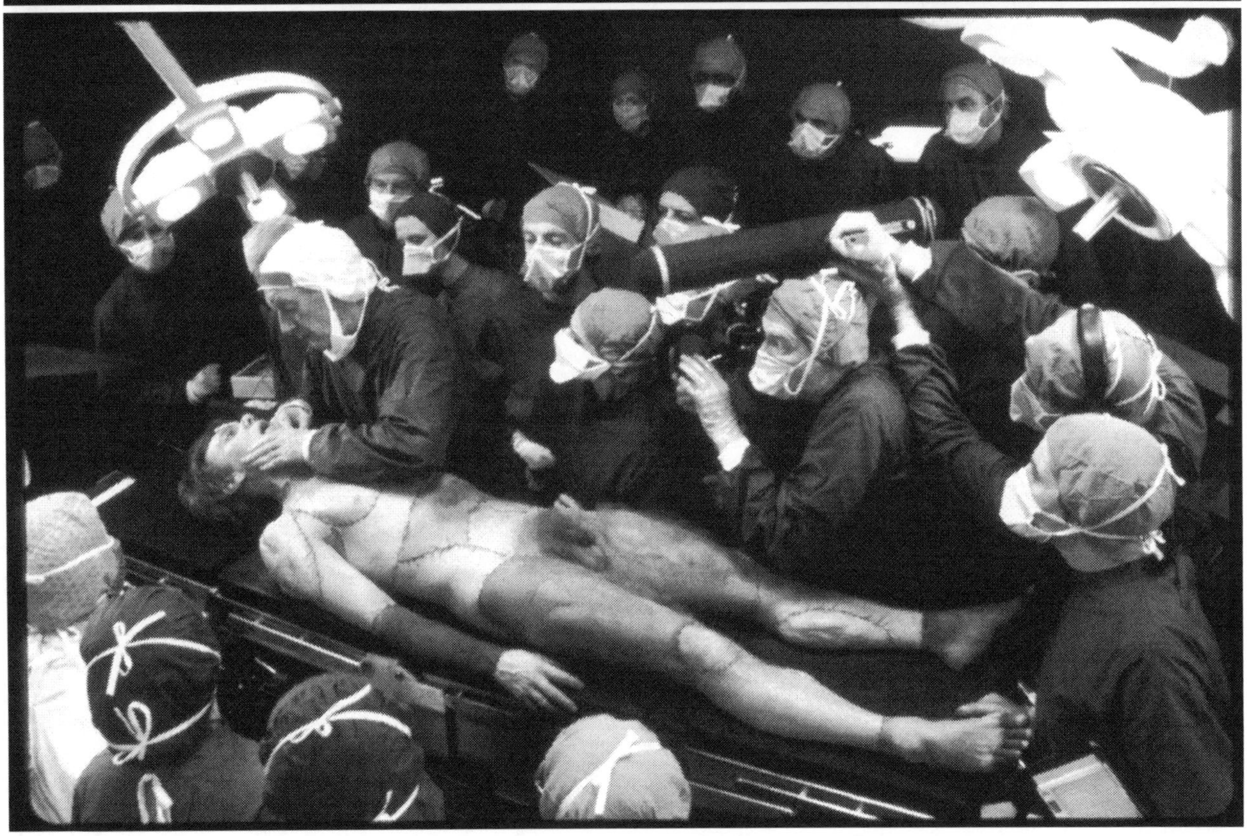

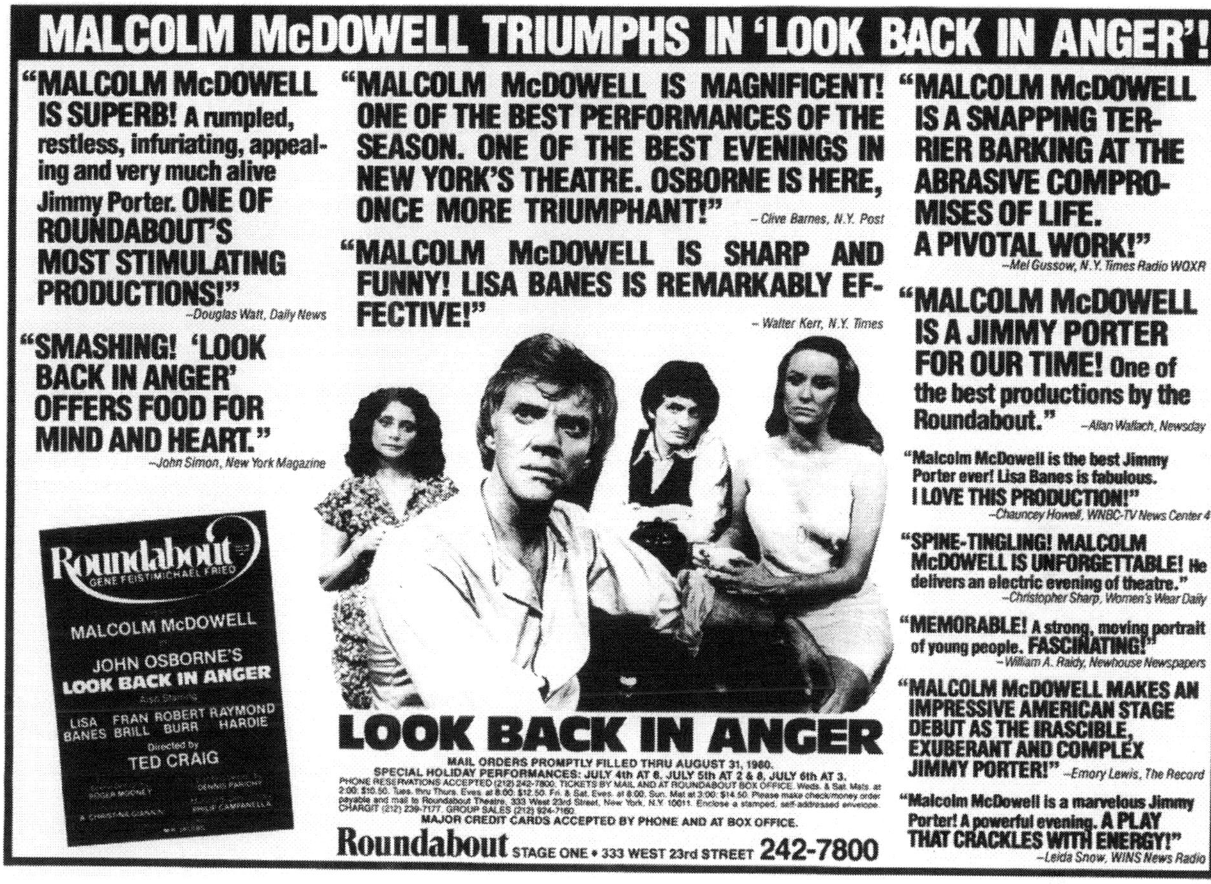

Anderson directed a video recording of McDowell's 1980 New York performance in *Look Back in Anger*. It played on TV in the United States and in Hungary. Warner Brothers released it on VHS.

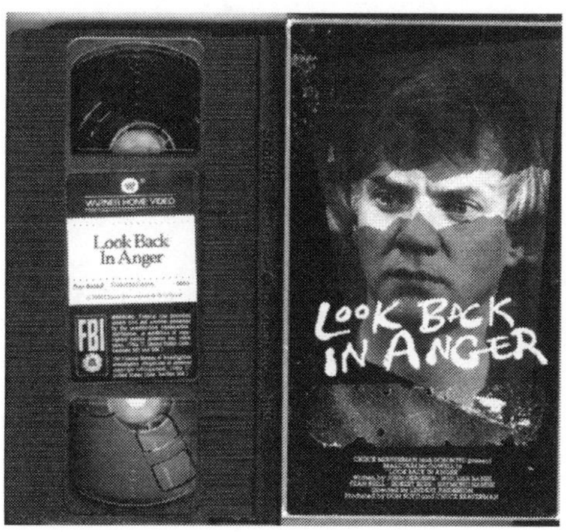

Partly inspired by a letter I found whilst editing Lindsay Anderson's Diaries, in which Lindsay sort of apologises to Alan Bates for misbehaving at a party hosted by Clive Donner, a "malicious-tongued" attack on the "tasteful, passionless respectability" of Alan Bridges, McDowell wrote and performed a one-man show about Anderson and his work (friends and writings). He premiered it at the Edinburgh Festival, performed it in London, and toured it across the United States to deserved acclaim. Mike Kaplan filmed the show, screened it at Cannes, and released it theatrically and on DVD as *Never Apologize.*

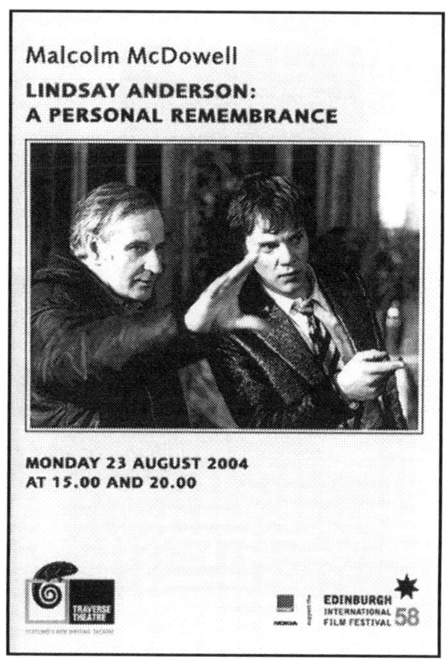

Jocelyn Herbert

In the programme notes for the 1975 Royal Court Theatre production of *What The Butler Saw*, it states that: "Jocelyn Herbert was 'aged by ten years' as a result of working as production designer on Lindsay Anderson's *O Lucky Man!*". In this rare interview, the last she gave before her death in 2003, Herbert talks with me about the director with whom she worked with, and fought with, for almost forty years.

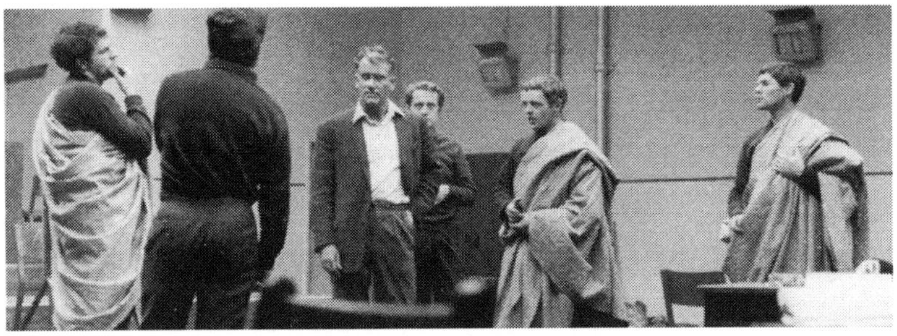

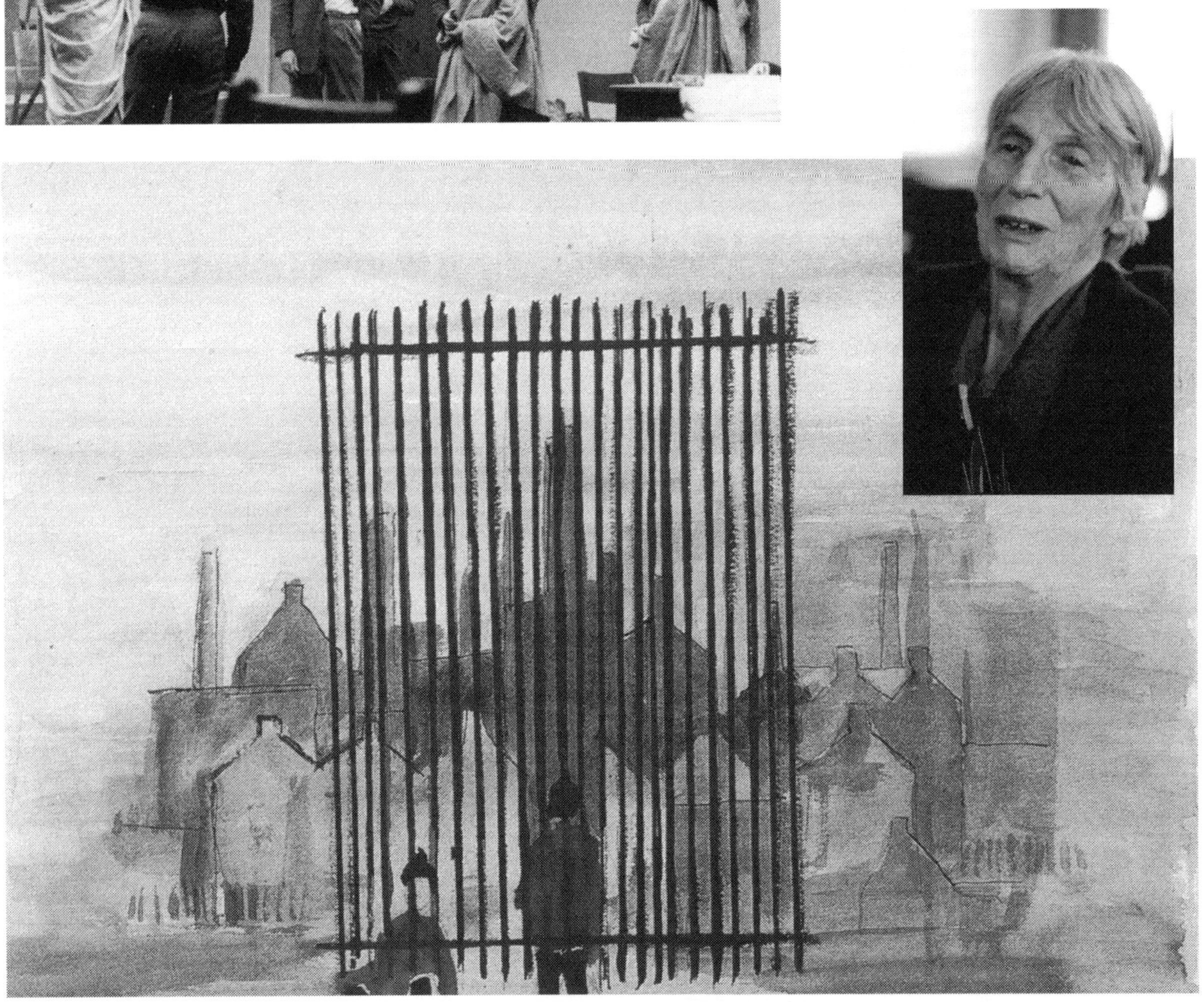

Herbert's design for the prison scene in *Serjeant Musgrave's Dance*.
Her use of suspended symbolic shapes had a profound effect on English stage design.
Ian Bannen and Anthony Hopkins rehearsing Lindsay Anderson's *Julius Caesar* (top).

I first met Lindsay at the Royal Court. He came not having done anything as far as I remember. My first real memory of him is working on *Serjeant Musgrave's Dance* [which opened October 22nd 1959] which was quite an adventure. After I read the play I did some drawings which I showed to John Arden. He seemed to think it was the right idea. Lindsay came along and tended always to say 'No' at first. He'd say: "Well, I don't think that will do!" A good example, which is absolutely typical of him, is that in the play there is a Gatling gun. There were two carpenters in the workshop at the Court who were terribly nice. We had done a lot of plays together. I was talking with one of them about the gun and he said: "Can I have a go at making it?" And he spent *hours* making this Gatling gun. I don't know anything about guns but I thought it was absolutely brilliant. He brought it on stage and we were looking at it when some people came in at the back. I suddenly heard Lindsay's voice saying: "Good Lord! What on earth's that! Terrible!" And this poor man walked off. That was the cause of my first real row with Lindsay. We had a terrible row. I said: "You never think about anybody!" And, of course, he used the gun because it was perfect. That was very typical of Lindsay. Whenever he saw something for the first time he'd be frightened it wasn't right.

It was an important play. It was a British take on what Brecht and Büchner were doing in Germany.

That's right. It's a wonderful play.

The Open University made a documentary about the making of Musgrave. It said that the play had poor reviews and was failing until Lindsay wrote letters to the press telling them how good it was.

Yes. (*Laughs*). He was good at doing that.

Musgrave was played by Ian Bannen, whom Lindsay had used in one of his Sunday plays [Sully's 'Lester Abbs']. But he didn't use him in his films.

Didn't he? No, I don't think he did. He was in [the theatrical production of] *Julius Caesar.*

Yes, he took over from Nicol Williamson, who had taken over from Richard Harris. Julius Caesar was your second production with Lindsay. How did his Caesar differ from what we would have expected from the RSC? In terms of design?

"In theory," he said, "we won't really have costumes." Basically, it was a regular brown suit for everybody. The actors all had a brown suit and they each had a toga which they put on in different ways. The girls had a dress I think. There were awful problems of how to put the togas on. Some had the feel for it and did it perfectly, a lot of them just hadn't a clue and looked terrible. It took George [Devine] to come along and show them. He was a big man and he could put it on and look wonderful. It is quite tricky because it is just a length of material and can look like an old dish-cloth tied round you. I don't think they were made from calico but it was something which draped well. We dyed them and speckled some of them to give them a bit of texture. They were different colours but they were all off-white.

Were the designs well-received?

No. People hardly ever mention the design unless they hate it. The whole overall production was good, I thought. Very very simple. We had very basic, rather abstract, scenery. We did have a tent and we had a huge statue at the back made of metal which stayed until Caesar was killed, and I think there were three pillars.

Can you remember anything about Lindsay's approach to the text? Were you in on the rehearsals?

Yes. We had a long weekend down at our little house in the country. There are some wonderful photos of us wandering around the garden with the book in our hands as we went through the play talking about it. He was very good on text and he

was a wonderful director for actors. I mean they may have hated him at times but they often gave better performances for him than they'd ever give for anyone else. For the David Storey plays he got performances that were amazing. He definitely had a wonderful way of interpreting the text, I suppose. But I remember one play, one of the last ones he did of David's *Stages*, with Alan Bates, which was a love story in a way, and Lindsay just didn't seem to be able to get his way round it. I thought, 'he really doesn't understand this play'. He was always saying to me: "What's it all *about*." The design was very very simple. It only had a chair and a table and practically no other furniture. At the rehearsal I got some things in which I thought were slightly suitable, not necessarily the things we would use, but Alan Bates fell in love with the chair. They were just stand-ins and Lindsay just accepted them as that. Then finally, one day, Lindsay said: "When are you going to get the real stuff?"
Alan said: "What do you mean?"
"Well, these are just stand-ins."
And Alan said: "Oh no, I like this chair I want to keep it." So we kept that particular chair. There was a question of a carpet or not a carpet and always these terrible discussions and rows. Just really to wind me up, I suppose.

Even in the later productions, when you've been working together for years?

Oh yes. It was a tease really most of the time, but it could become quite... Well, I walked out of *O Lucky Man!* at one point. I got in my car and went home. There was a terrible flurry of telephone calls and eventually, to my amazement, Lindsay appeared. And that must have cost him something! Of course I then went back. We got on rather well actually, despite our fights. I mean he really became a great friend and used to ring me up practically every morning: "Well, what are you doing?" "Oh Jocelyn, really!" (*laughs*)

Were any of your squabbles over budgets?

Not much, no. I'm not an expensive designer.

In the Open University documentary on Musgrave you said you encouraged him to have less realistic sets?

Yes. We had practically nothing in the first scene, just a row at the back to give the feeling of a river, with a canal barge and just crates for the soldiers. Then, in the pub scene there was just one flat with a door in it and some furniture. He kept directing people outside the set and I went mad: "Can't you see they're not in the room!"

He worked a lot early on with Alan Tagg.

He did. He liked him very much. What did he do with him?

The Long and The Short and The Tall, and Billy Liar.

Oh yes. *Billy Liar.* He asked me to do that but I was doing something else.

What film work did you do before if....?

I did *Tom Jones* with Tony Richardson in 1962. Tony was at the Court with me at the beginning in 1956. And I remember we all went on holiday to France and we were all reading *Tom Jones.*

And you made a marvellous film.

It was a good film wasn't it? Some of it was wonderful. I was what was called a 'Colour Consultant', which meant that I had to do all the interiors and costumes but I didn't have to do all the building. The whole lot of it was done in the country to start with and then we went to London. I decided to do all the country scenes with greens and browns, Earth colours. When we went to London it became sort of blues and greys, cooler, so to speak. I think that's the only time I have ever attempted that. It was a film very much in two parts. Then I did *Isadora* for Karel Reisz which was really a feast of costumes; very influenced by the Twenties scene of course. David Storey had written a script that wasn't used and somebody else whose name I've forgotten.

Melvyn Bragg. A Ken Russell discovery. He wrote the script for Isadora. Ken Russell also made a film about Isadora Duncan.

Yes, I saw that. I think the Ken Russell one was brilliant. It was actually better.

With if.... did you start working on the production design a long time before filming took place?

No. What happened with *if....* was I was abroad doing *Isadora*. Lindsay kept ringing me up and saying: "Come on. You've got to come back and do *if....*'" I said: "But I can't. I'm in the middle of this film." And this went on and on and I used to say to him: "Supposing I was doing your film and I left in the middle of it to do somebody else's, imagine what you'd say?" Of course he couldn't answer that because he would have had a fit. (*laughs*) But then I finished *Isadora*. I'd hardly got home and he had just got to Cheltenham and had seen what the designer was giving him for the hall, you know the big hall at the end of the film, and he said: "You've simply got to come down."

I said: "Well, what about - "

"He doesn't mind. He would *like* you to."

"Well, you'll have to send a car for me and bring me back." I must say the big hall that had been prepared was hopeless. In these big school halls they have these portraits of old generals and headmasters and things, and he had just blown up portraits of a lot of military people. They didn't look like oil paintings at all. And he'd put them in huge frames. Terrible. And they were supposed to be shooting the day after next. Luckily, I knew the set dresser so we went out, and we sent other people out, to buy things; and we repainted this and that and we did it all in a day, which was pretty good going really. And the designer was helping, you know the one who was there before I came. He kept saying to me: "You must explain to me about Lindsay. Why do I get on with him so badly?" I tried to explain to him. But he hadn't got a clue about design.

Were there any sets built for if....?

The boys' studies. We built all of them and the Sweat Room. We'd build a section then regurgitate it as something else. We built one or two things in Wimbledon I seem to remember. And it was taken down when we had finished and used again for something else the next day. That was always happening. Most of what you see in the film was already there. In the school we used the actual dormitories.

The boy's colourful beakers seem prominent, and the arrangement of the washbowls. Was that how they were set out at the school?

Yes, they were in the middle of the room. I don't think we painted the dormitories but we may have painted the passages. We didn't do much in the school. We certainly built all the studies and made the collages. The studies were all in a group. I made them so that you could pull the walls out not so you could take the camera in but take the camera to the wall. They were much too small to take the camera in. I hate that when you have an enormous space when its meant to be tiny, and it worked perfectly. You could take out whichever wall you wanted.

They're absolutely perfect. I presume the school roof was *the school roof?*

Yes, that's completely as it was.

Everyone I've talked with, who worked on the film, seems to claim credit for the collages. David Sherwin and Malcolm McDowell both added bits.

Yes, and also a young man who has become very famous as a director.

Stephen Frears.

Yes, that's right. He came and asked if he could be an assistant or hang around and Lindsay said: "Well you can do that [the collages]". It was great. We all put things in but, I think, Stephen considers that he did them (*laughs*). They changed all the time too.

One of the last things Lindsay did before he died was present a BAFTA award to Stephen Frears, who said in his acceptance speech: "I've just been given an award by my father."

He was a great help to Stephen. He taught him an awful lot, I think. He was a wonderful friend and influence on so many people. In his flat he housed Patricia Healey, the girl who was in *The White Bus*. And for a long time Frank Grimes lived there with his wife. Frank's baby was born there, or while they were there. Lindsay was incredibly good to them.

He also did a lot of work to get the Czech film makers out of the Communist Czechoslovakia, Milos Forman and Vladimir Pucholt.

I didn't know that.

Yes, he put Pucholt through Medical School {Pucholt became a British citizen in 1975]. A favourite scene in if.... is the one where the new master is shown his room. It's superb.

It is isn't it.

It shows the loneliness and the snobbery and the miserliness. Was that a set?

No, that was a real room. I can't remember now where that room was. I think it was in Cheltenham. It may have been done before I was there. They were already at Cheltenham and I don't remember doing that scene. But, as I say, my memory is pretty bad.

Did you have any say in the costume designs?

I didn't do too much because it started before I was there. They were all typical school things. Some of the film was in colour and some was in black-and-white. I don't really like the colour. I think it looks much better in black-and-white.

The problem with the colour on if.... is that, before the restoration, the prints had faded quite badly. What was your reaction on first seeing the film?

I thought it was a bloody good film! (*laughs*). It really was. The scenes where they are beaten and all the boys sit listening, and when Mick gets up and does that (wipes his eye), ahhh.

Malcolm's performance is terrific.

Oh yes. Brilliant! And the film was so funny wasn't it? The headmaster was so *real*. And the *real* headmaster was always asking us in for sherry. I used to feel terribly guilty that we were betraying him, treating him very badly but Lindsay didn't feel anything like that. I said: "Did you really show the headmaster the script?"
"Oh, yes, but of course I edited it." And there he was at the end taking part in being shot! I'm not sure he didn't lose his job.

There's a legend that he wrote a letter to Lindsay and Lindsay kept it unopened on his mantlepiece for years.

Oh did he? He didn't tell me that. I wonder if he ever opened it? He must have opened it.

It would have been negative.

It would have been pretty rude. I don't think the man was intelligent enough to like the film but it would have been interesting to open it to see. I bet he did open it really. I'd have opened it.

Lindsay was annoyed he was never invited back to Cheltenham College, but I read in The Times that there was a suggestion of getting the school choir to sing at his memorial service?

Yes, I think we did ask them but they refused.

The feeling on set was said to be very good?

That was the sort of thing the actors would say together, probably. I was so busy I never had time to talk to anybody.

Was Lindsay's behaviour better then?

He wasn't too bad. (*Laughs*) He was terrible on *O Lucky Man!*.

What caused the big falling out?

Oh, it was just one of these scenes. I'd been getting a scene ready for the next shot and it was just a very very simple set - it was a hospital bed. And I think he'd forgotten but we had already discussed where we were going to put things and they were all there. He came up and said: "Well that's *all* wrong."
"Well that's what you asked for." He went up the wall (*laughs*). And he said something. I can't remember what, and I said: "All right, Lindsay, that's enough. I'm going." And I just walked out, took my things, and got in my car. It wasn't *just* that. It was an accumulation of endless things 'not right'. My ideas were always used in the end but you'd just have to go through this terrible scene.

How long was that into the shoot? Was it midway?

Yes, perhaps just over midway. We were in the country and Malcolm was all wired up in bed for the scene with the mad doctor. There was still the scenes in the prison to do and all the stuff in the East End.

Malcolm has all these wires coming off him. Burgess offered Lindsay the Clockwork Orange script before Kubrick took it up. Lindsay didn't want to do it; and Stanley used Lindsay's actors! Was the mad doctor scene a conscious reference to A Clockwork Orange?

Not as far as I was concerned. The cameraman was always terribly worried it was going to be like *A Clockwork Orange*. In actual fact, I hadn't seen *A Clockwork Orange* at that time, but Mirek Ondricek was concerned.

Did you discuss things with Mirek?

I did sometimes. It was very difficult because he tended to wait to hear what Lindsay wanted. He'd only not do it if, camera-wise, it didn't work. I remember, after the shoot at Cheltenham, we had breakfast at six o'clock in the morning. It was '68 and all the papers were full with Russians going into Prague. Poor Mirek was devouring them.

Was Lindsay generous with praise whenever he liked something?

Not particularly. He didn't shout it down. "That's okay. That'll do." I don't know how I survived actually. He behaved appallingly badly (*laughs*). I can't remember where we were, Scarborough or somewhere, in a hotel, and everybody was in a rather bad mood, cross about something. We were sitting round having a drink and, for once, everybody was being rather horrid about Lindsay. I can't remember exactly what it was all about but I thought they were being very silly. One of them said: "I don't know why we are all doing this film." I exploded and said: "We are doing this because it's going to be a wonderful film!" Which is what I felt. And they were so amazed that *I* should be saying that that they shut up. It *was* an amazing film. All the different scenes. The one where they decide to send the poison in the aeroplane and Arthur Lowe is blacked up, wonderful! It's astonishing.

I love the scene in the working men's club. David Sherwin told me that the women were meant to be topless and that you and he had to decide who was going to get a shouting at by asking Lindsay why he insisted on covering them up?

I got it, yes. That is true. I did want the women to be topless and it seemed as though Lindsay was going to have them in clothes. I said that the whole point was that it should be a bit unexpected. There was something of a compromise in the end. They had little aprons on. It's a *wonderful* scene.

The announcer is Warren Clarke [McDowell's sidekick in A Clockwork Orange] I'd seen the film three or four times before I noticed that. He fell from Lindsay's favour because he didn't attend the party that was shot for the film's finale.

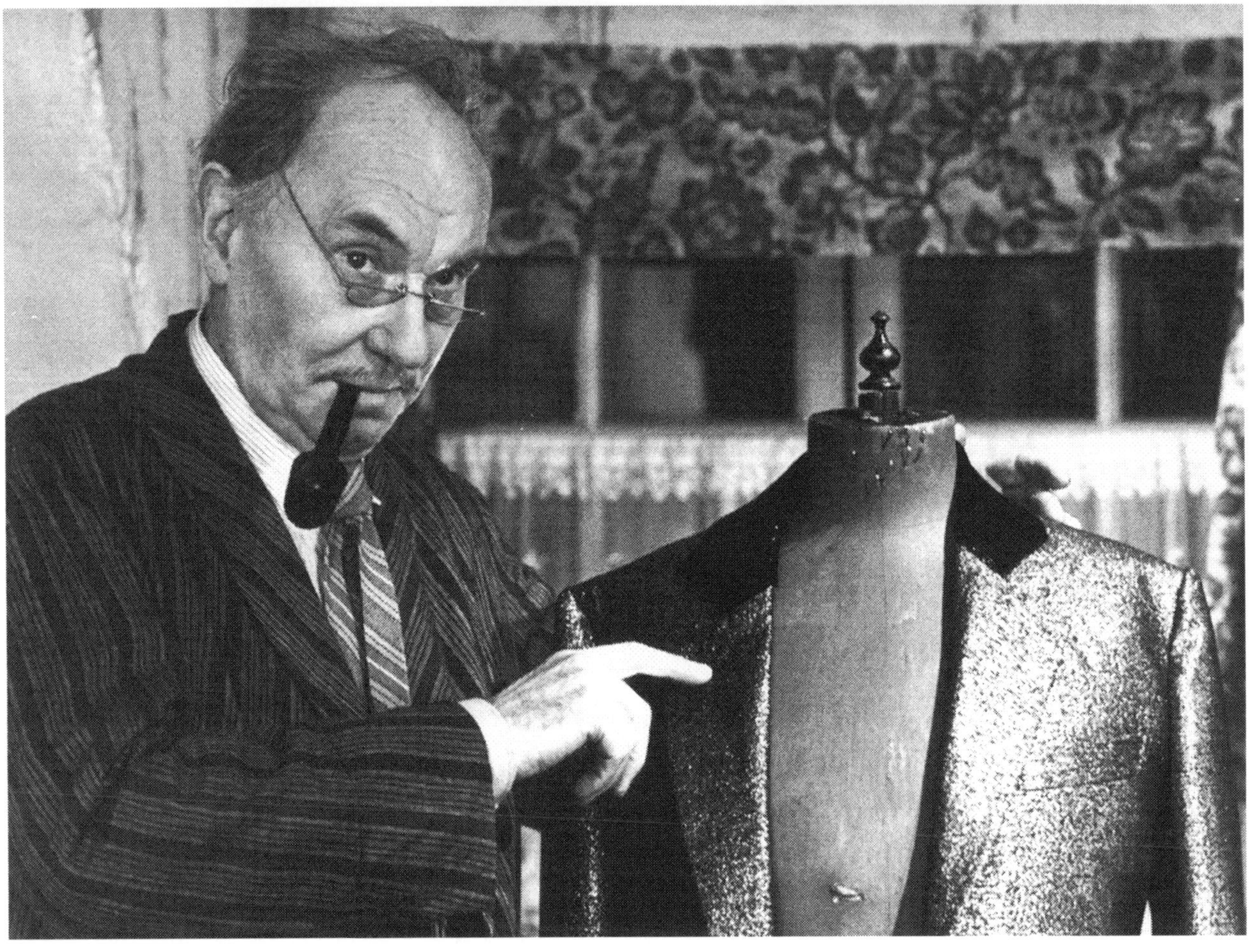

Ralph Richardson with the Golden Suit in *O Lucky Man!*

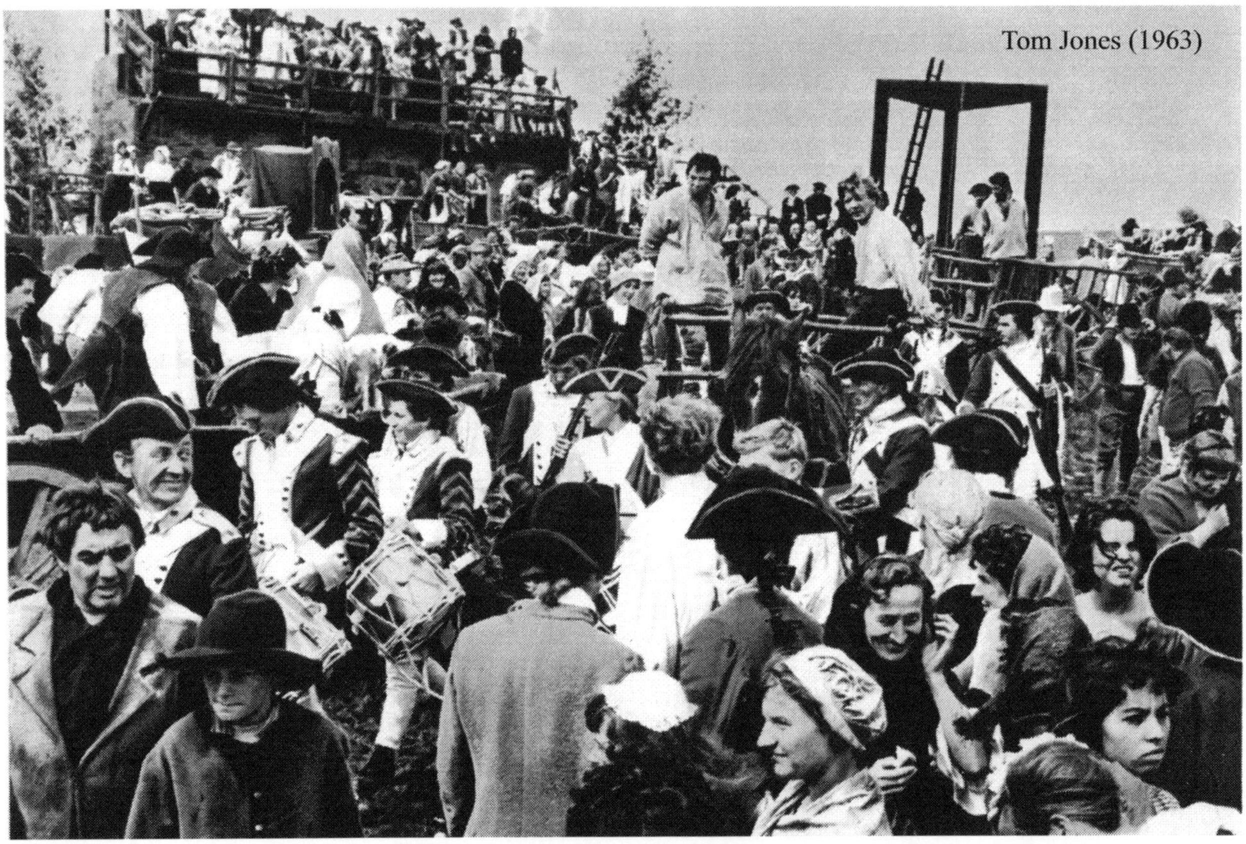

Tom Jones (1963)

I think that was wrong of Warren Clarke. But I think I had fallen out with Lindsay too and I didn't go to the party either! (*laughs*)

O Lucky Man! is an epic in every sense of the word. How much preparation was there?

It was very strange actually, because I'd really enjoyed doing *if....* When making *if....*, Lindsay would rehearse each scene and then do it. He didn't do endless shots and endless shots. One sort of knew what one was doing, and we really had very little money. It is always better to have little money. When I met the first assistant on *O Lucky Man!*, we had a drink and he said: "What's it like working with Lindsay?' and I said: "Oh, it's wonderful. He's a marvellous person to work with." But he didn't turn out like that at all! He was much more nervous on *O Lucky Man!* because *if....* had been such a success, he now had something he had to better. So psychologically he was under pressure, and also the script wasn't quite finished. He was always worrying about the end and trying to write it and finish it. So he wasn't in a good mood like he was when we made *if....* It was very difficult to get much discussion with Lindsay once we were filming because the moment we had finished shooting he'd rush to the hotel because he was still working on the script.

Did you do pre-production sketches?

I did things for the coffee factory and that study where he meets -

Ralph Richardson?

Yes. We found a house and I adapted the rooms.

I suppose the big scene is the nuclear rocket factory.

Oh, yes, gosh! I did a lot of drawings for that and for the countryside and the run up the hill, and when he was inside being questioned. I did a whole lot of those passages and rooms.

Were they built for the film?

I think they probably were there. We just painted them.

Was there a colour scheme for individual sequences or for the film as a whole? I notice that you use a lot of browns and oranges.

Was it because of the coffee? I don't think so, I'm a bit addicted to brown (*laughs*). Did Malcolm have a brown suit?

He had a brown suit and a tan brown jumper and he also wore a golden suit.

Oh yes, that was special. I saw this wonderful material in a shop and I got a suit made from it. There wasn't really any grand overall scheme with the colour. It's not like when I did *Tom Jones*. One of the most involved things were these velvet curtains, huge velvet curtains. The film people, of course, couldn't understand what I was doing. I had to shave them all so they looked as though they had been in the sun. It's terribly difficult. It made them look really old but they looked beautiful still. They thought that mucking up this wonderful velvet was the most terrible thing. And I had to get all these cushions which had to be bleached and ragged and one thing or another. I don't think they had ever seen anybody do all that before. But they always want to take everything home with them, the prop people, not only them, the directors take things home too. If you go into their houses after the film you see all the furniture. Whenever I asked if I could re-use a sofa which I'd bought it had always disappeared.

What happened to the gold suit?

I don't know. It wasn't a very nice suit but it worked when he put it on. It had to be a normal suit and somehow it had to be a sort of surprise. If it had been a funny shape or period it wouldn't have worked.

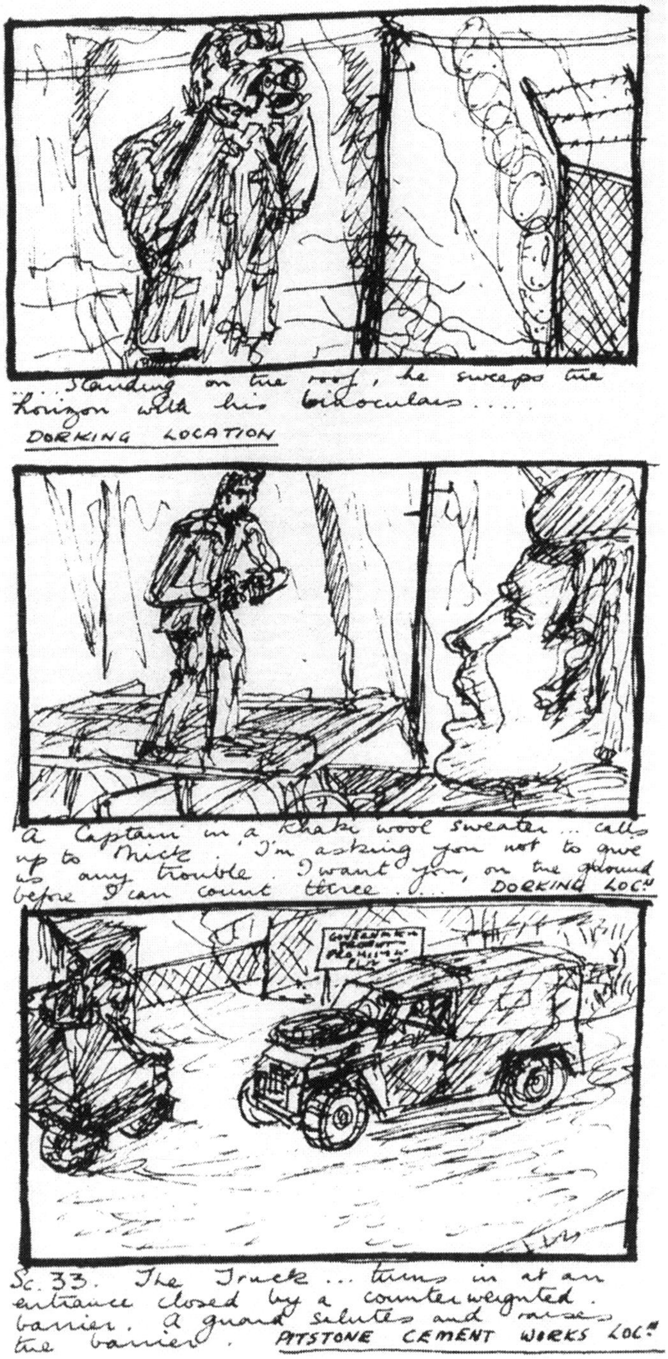

O Lucky Man! storyboard showing Mick's arrival and arrest at the military research station.

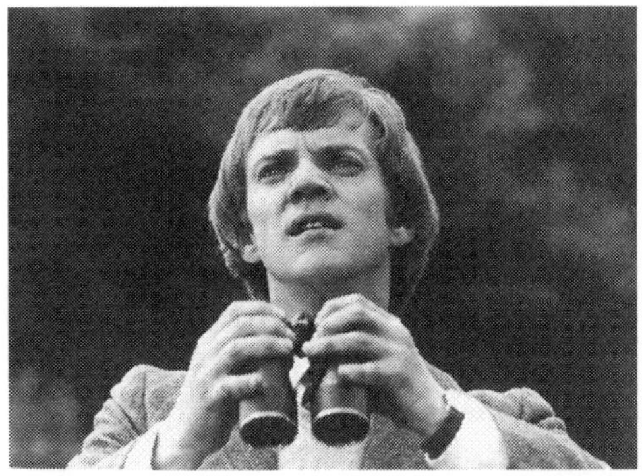

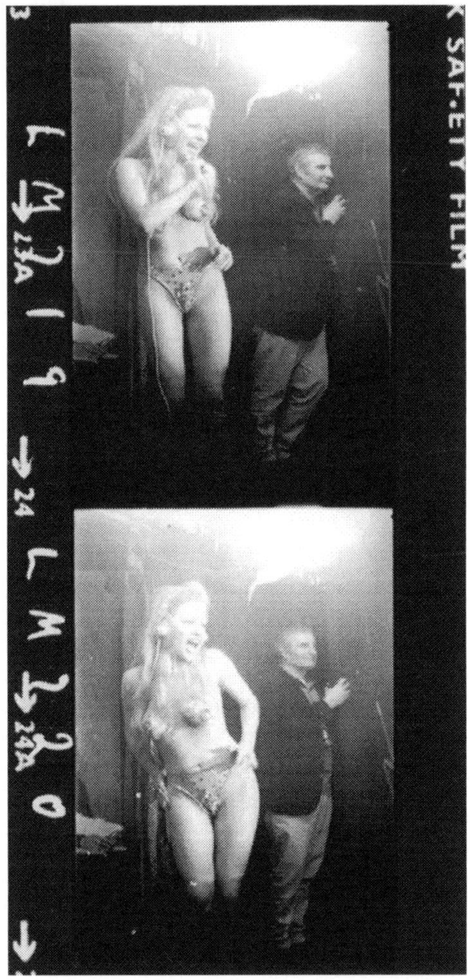

Anderson with a covered-up 'artiste'

And Alan Price's contribution?

They were wonderful those songs weren't they? Absolutely wonderful.

Did Lindsay ask you to design Britannia Hospital?

He did but I turned it down. I think I was doing something else but I didn't want to do it. I wasn't prepared to go through with it all again.

The arguments?

Yes. He had to have someone he could vent his frustrations on and if there wasn't anybody else it was me (*laughs*).

You continued to work with Lindsay in the theatre and you worked with him on his final feature film, The Whales of August. Did you design the film before you went on location in Maine?

The production people came from LA and they had hired two American designers and I don't think they had told them that Lindsay wanted me to be the production designer. Not knowing this, I wrote to them and asked if could they send me photographs of the little house that Lindsay and Mike Kaplan had found for the film, and they weren't at all friendly. Then they wrote to me saying that they would bring all the furniture with them from LA, and I rang up and said: "Don't bring anything!" I'd done *The Hotel New Hampshire* with Tony Richardson and knew I could get it all in Maine and it would fit. And it would look right. When they arrived they had two enormous pantechnicons full of the most unsuitable furniture which I never used. We had to make a new fireplace and it had to be of brick and they said: "We can buy bricks in sheets." I told them: "That won't do at all we must really build it with bricks." It so happened that I had to go to New York about some costumes and, when I came back, they'd built the fire place from this awful stuff, and there was Lindsay fuming up and down. So we called a meeting. In the course of the meeting I had to say: "Why did you not do as I said?" And I added: "In all my life of working I have never before had to work with people who were so unfriendly and unhelpful." There was a terrible silence. They were all very shocked that I said anything. But it made a bit of a difference. They tried a bit after that. But it was not a good atmosphere. And as for Bette Davis, she couldn't bear me. Lindsay and I went to see her in New York. The moment we got to her flat, Lindsay disappeared to the loo and left me holding my portfolio. And she said: "What's that!" I explained: "It just has some drawings in it in case you want to have a look at them."
"No! I've got all my costumes!" she said.
"Oh? Perhaps I could see them?"
We sat down and she gave us a dress parade of all the clothes she had. I knew there was no point in me saying I didn't like them. Actually, they weren't bad, some of them. The way to get her to wear something I'd made for the film was to leave it lying around and she would try it on. If she liked it she wore it.

She was known to be difficult.

Bette had a make-up and hairdresser to herself and she used to send one of these people to me: "Bette Davis (who is blind in the film) thinks it is a rather a shame that Lillian Gish, who can see, is so badly made-up and her hair is always such a mess; and yet she who is blind is properly made-up." I said: "I look at it the other way, I think it is so peculiar that someone who is blind has such exquisite make-up and such a strange hair-do." Funnily enough, the first time I met Lillian she said to me: "You're not going to cover me in that awful yellow make-up are you? You know, that they put on you for television?" I told her "As far as I understand, you can wear no make-up at all and do your own hair." And she did. She did her own hair. It was absolutely lovely.

Vincent Price is known and loved for his horror films, but it was good to see him extend his range.

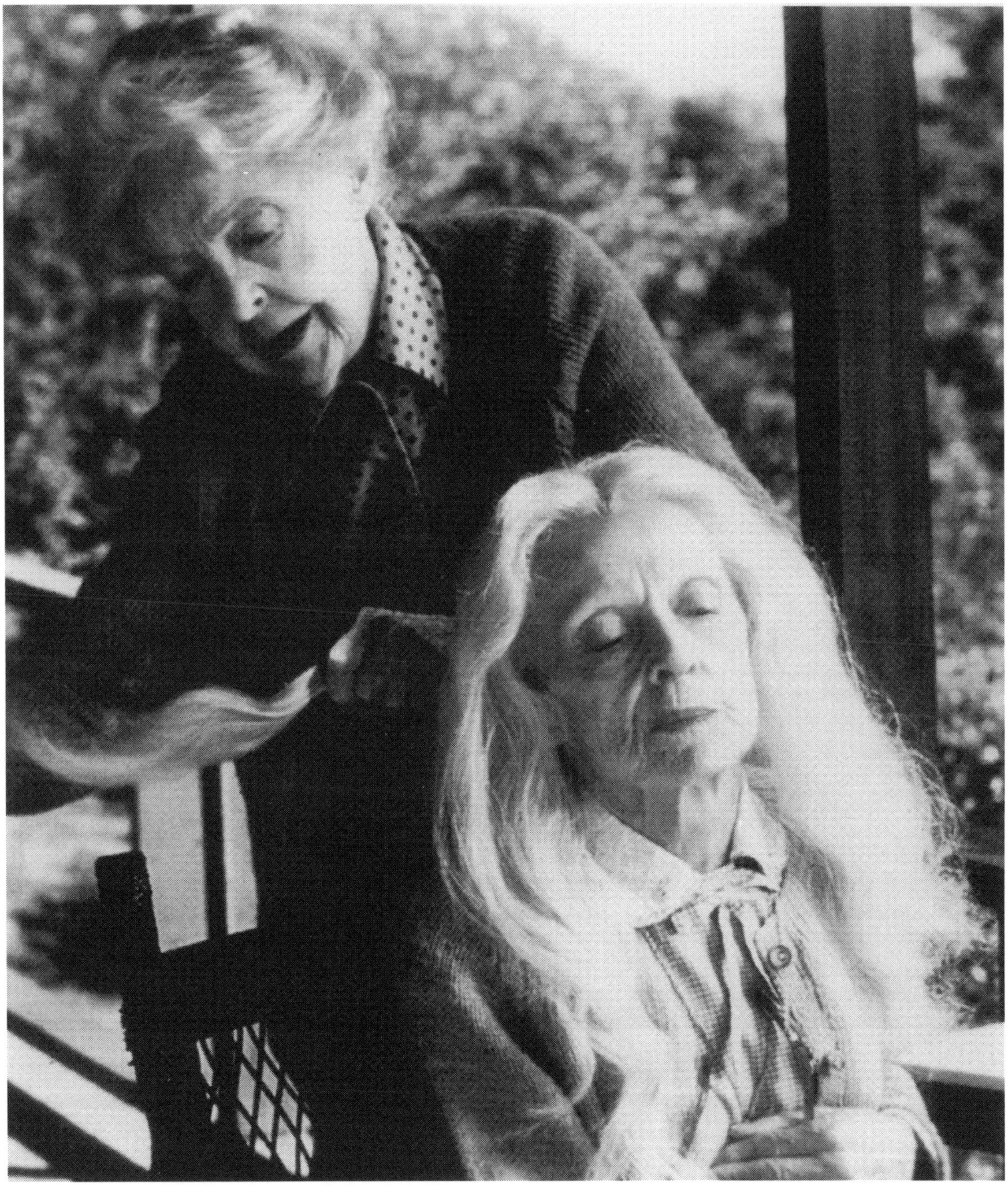

"Lillian Gish and Bette Davis in Lindsay Anderson's Oscar-nominated *The Whales of August* (1987). A major box-office hit in Japan.

Yes. It got him out. He was very nice, a sweet man. Ann Sothern was lovely too.

She won an Academy Award nomination for the film. Malcolm tells a good story about the scoop at casting Lillian Gish but then comes the problem of finding an actress to be her older sister! Bette Davis was younger, but she looked more lived in.

The thing was that Bette Davis wanted it to be her film and she was always inventing extra scenes and things, and I kept saying to Lindsay: "Why do you let her?"
"She's the money," he said (*laughs*). Lillian used to say: "I feel so sorry for Bette. She's so unkind to people." There was this one extra bedroom we used as a bedroom occasionally in the film, but it was really a place where, I thought, the girls could sit when they weren't being used. But Bette just took it over, and Lillian never got near it. She just sat in the corner. But she was wonderful. It was Lillian's birthday and we gave a party for her and she just came in her old anorak. There was a cardigan that I'd found and I'd hung on the door and the moment Bette came into the house she saw it, picked it up, put in on, and never took it off!

What did you think of the film?

Funnily enough, I was amazed by it because Lindsay kept wishing he wasn't doing it, but when he got the actors he was so wonderful with them because it wasn't easy. Lillian was quite deaf and a lot of time he had to speak the words and then she spoke them. And Bette Davis was quite a pain. Of course, Lindsay liked Lillian but he really found Bette Davis much more fun because she was so awful (*laughs*). But eventually she did go too far and he actually said to her: "Look. You're not directing this film. I am." And she walked off the set. Of course she came back. It was very difficult to tell what it was going to be like. Everything was such a battle. For some reason the costume person disappeared and it was impossible to get another at that time and I found myself suddenly making all these white frocks. I remember borrowing machines from the locals. They were so nice the island people. I'll never forget the first time I drove this old bus and had to reverse it. It had a big thing at the back and I drove into a telegraph pole. Luckily I didn't knock it over, and I whizzed away as quickly as I could. It was quite bizarre. I bought a little boat. Before we started filming there was an auction, and Mike [Kaplan] took us to it. There was a little boat going which I bought for five dollars or something. We lived on another island, not on the one we filmed on. There was this big house, and when we finished filming we used to get into a boat. It was a ten-minute ride to a pontoon on the other island, then we'd walk up a track through the woods and go into this marvellous house where there was always a *huge* fire blazing and enormous whiskeys given to you, as soon as you went in, by this very nice man who ran it and who cooked the most wonderful meals. At weekends, when we weren't filming I used to go out in my little boat.

Further Reading:

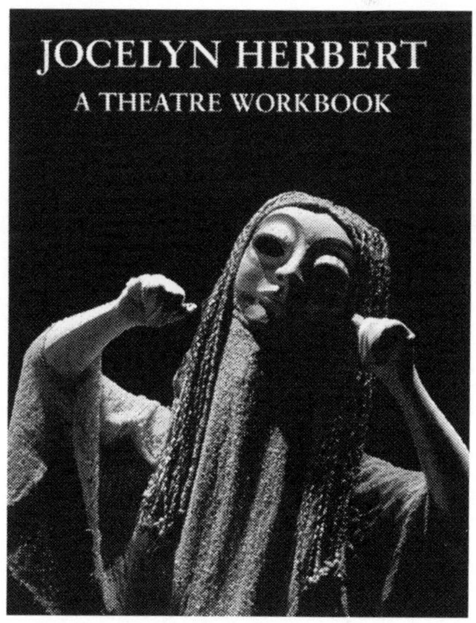

"Lindsay was very cross because I didn't put any films in my book. I hadn't got pictures of most of the films so I thought I couldn't. He was terribly offended."

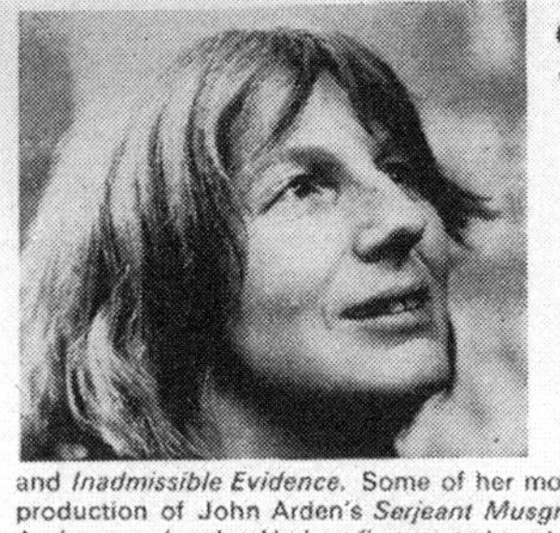

Jocelyn Herbert

began her long association with the Royal Court Theatre in 1955, first as a scene painter in the Workshops and then, after two years, as a designer; her first set was for Ann Jellicoe's *Sport of My Mad Mother*. She worked closely with John Dexter and Arnold Wesker on the first productions of Wesker's *The Kitchen* and the *Trilogy* plays. She designed all George Devine's Ionesco and Beckett productions, and worked with Tony Richardson and Anthony Page on John Osborne's *Luther*, *A Patriot for Me* and *Inadmissible Evidence*. Some of her most memorable designs were for the first production of John Arden's *Serjeant Musgrave's Dance*—also directed by Lindsay Anderson. Jocelyn Herbert first started working in the cinema as 'Consultant' on *Tom Jones*. She followed this as Art Director on *Isadora* and *If....* Her most recent work has been on *Ned Kelly* in Australia and on *Beckett 3* in The Theatre Upstairs.

Alan Price

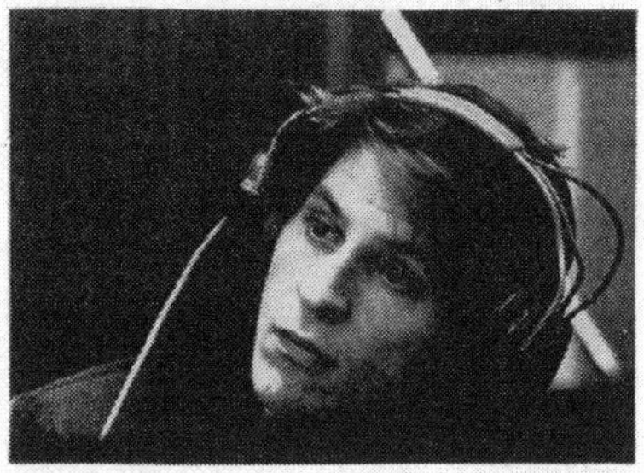

is a Geordie, born 28 years ago in Fatfield, County Durham. He ran his first group, *The Alan Price Combo*, in his spare time after a working day as an income-tax officer. He then became the organist-arranger for *The Animals*, one of the first and most successful of the English rhythm-and-blues groups in the early sixties. In 1965 he founded his own group, *The Alan Price Set*, with which he recorded his first big hits, 'Hi-Lili Hi-Lo', 'Simon Smith and the Amazing Dancing Bear' and his own song 'The House that Jack Built'. In 1968 he disbanded the Set to work on other projects—notably the TV series 'Price to Pay'. Last year he formed *Alan Price and Friends*, did a television series about the development of Pop, *Monster Music Mash*, and a series of concert programmes with Georgie Fame. His current single is his own song, *Sunshine and Rain—The Name of the Game*, and his next L.P. will feature all his own songs. His music for *Home* is Alan Price's first work in the theatre.

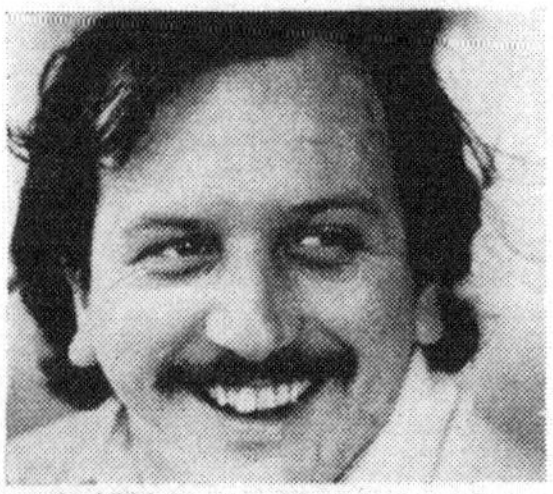

Andy Phillips

Andy Phillips has designed the lighting for all Royal Court productions for the last four years. Born in Staffordshire, where his father was a Baptist parson, he went to drama school in Brighton for two and a half years. He left to form his own company, Group One Productions, in association with Bill Owen and other fellow students. The Company went bankrupt in Edinburgh in 1960, and he went into repertory: he once appeared at the Theatre Royal, Brighton, in *Nude With Violin*.

In 1961 Andy Phillips started as flyman at the Aldwych for the Royal Shakespeare Company, eventually graduating to Assistant Chief Electrician. Five years later he left the Aldwych to take up the post of Chief Electrician at the Royal Court. He has also recently lit William Gaskill's production of *The Beaux' Stratagem* at the National and

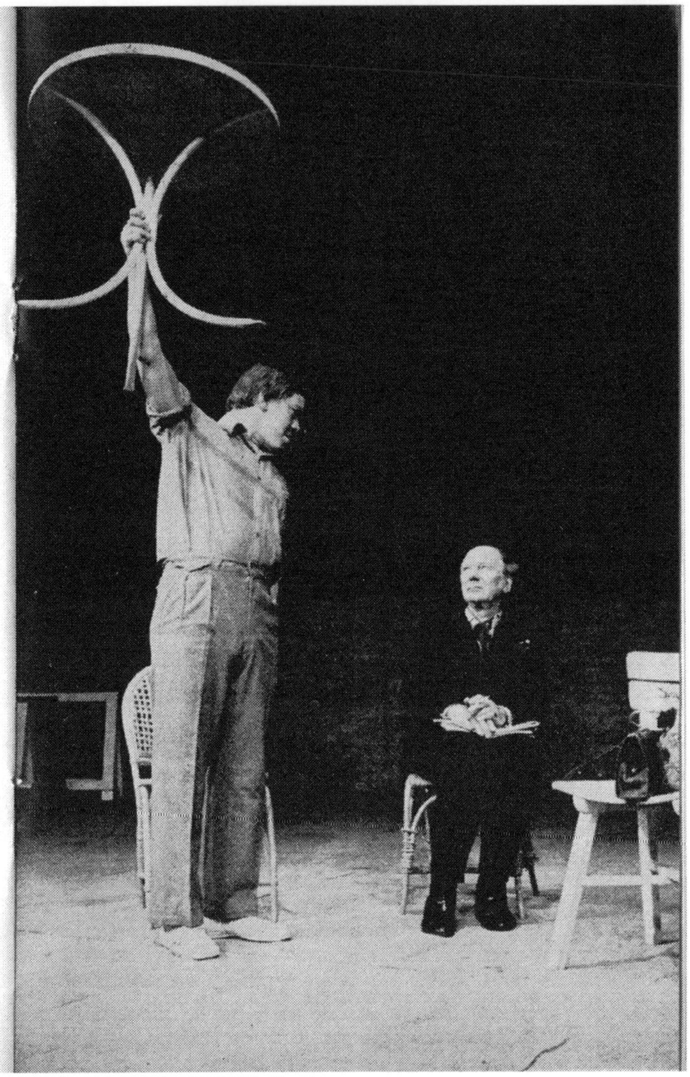

Memorabilia from five of the plays designed by Jocelyn Herbert and directed by Lindsay Anderson, including the programme note for *Home*. Warren Clarke shows his strength to John Gielgud.

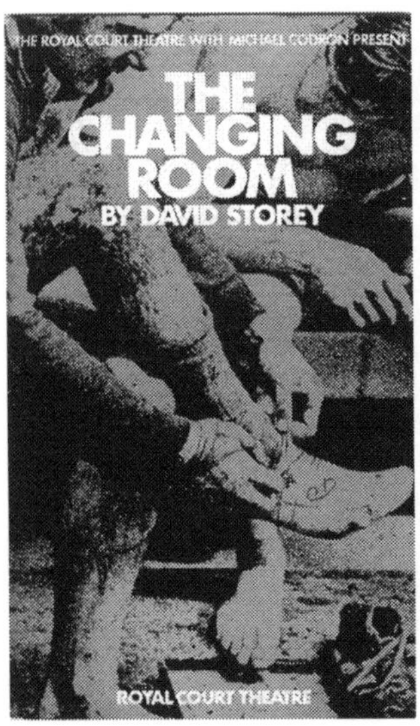

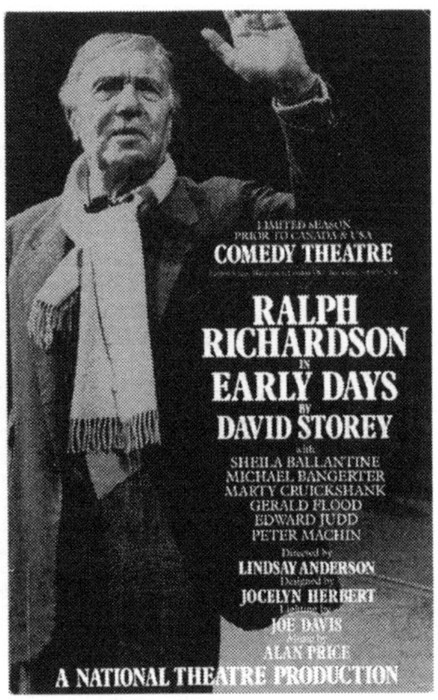

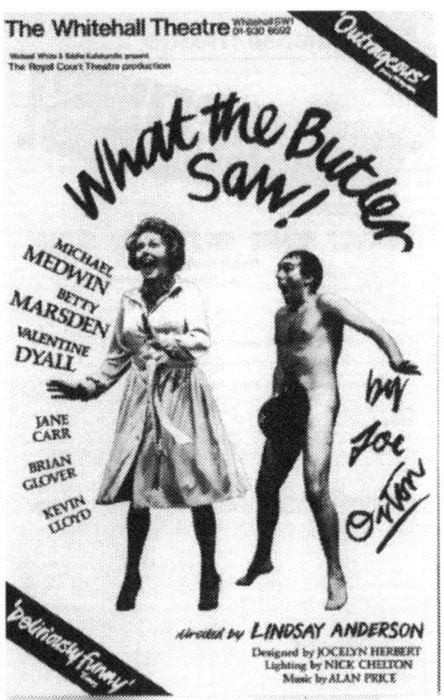

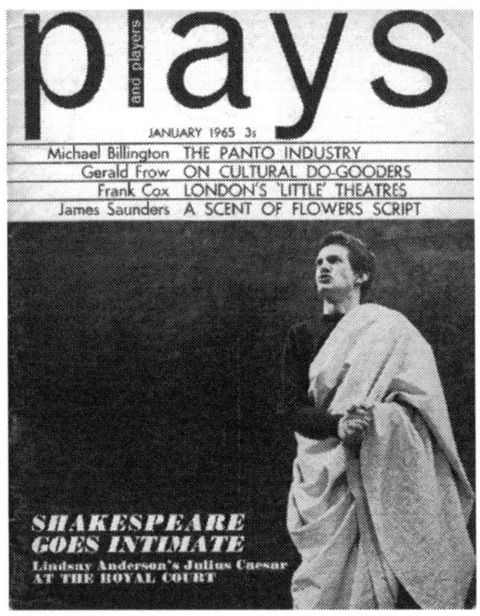

Brian Cox on Lindsay Anderson

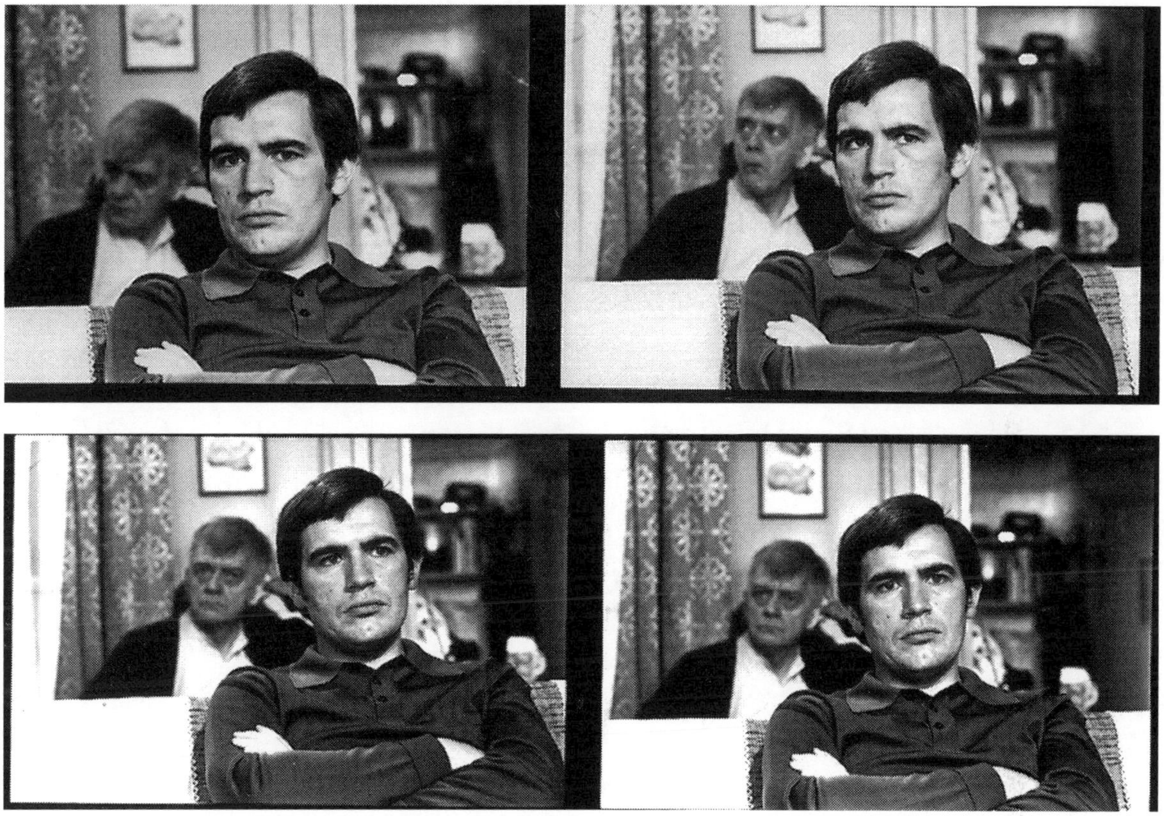

Brian Cox in Lindsay Anderson's film *In Celebration* (1975)

It is important to see Lindsay in the context of post-war Britain. Lindsay was egalitarian, which meant getting at the status quo. He was fed up with the theatrical establishment, and its ineffective training methods, and the limits it placed on what you could produce. To illustrate this point he gave a brilliant lecture at the Edinburgh film festival [in 1993]; basically about the English class system and how, culturally, we were locked by our education. To a certain extent that is still true. He showed two film clips, one of Jack Hulbert, a jolly chap, and he contrasted it with a clip of Fred and Ginger. The limits of one contrasted with the possibilities of the other.

We all have a kind of romantic view of Lindsay, which is a good view. I don't think there is a problem with that, a lot of people really loved him, but he was a very complex man. He had a dark side, which came from his pain, and his background, and his alienation. In the theatre, and in his films, Lindsay's direction was always about 'truth'. Truth is truth no matter what. A lie is a lie. Theatrical lies are sometimes more acceptable because acting is about dissembling, but it is still a lie. Lindsay wouldn't take lying. He was always sneery at the work that was done at Stratford. In many ways he was right because some of the work was quite awful. There was a lot of posturing. Good acting is about 'truth' and being true. Lindsay's great note to me as an actor, and I will always remember it, came when I first walked onto the stage at the Royal Court. I was hired to play a role in *In Celebration*, David Storey's play about a boy who has grown up and who comes back home for his parent's fortieth wedding anniversary. Lindsay said to me: "Don't just do something, stand there!" I'd been too busy acting, trying to indicate what was going on, as opposed to feeling it and getting a sense from within.

Lindsay was one of the great psychological directors. In *In Celebration*, Alan Bates and I played brothers. Under Lindsay's direction, we became very close in a very short period of time. Lindsay's method wasn't that awful Strasbergian emotional memory stuff, it was much more disciplined. He cultivated a more responsible sort of acting. I learned responsibility in acting from Lindsay; responsibility to the text and to the character. I had done it in theory at drama school but 'responsibility' was Lindsay Anderson's *raison d'etre*. He always started with the vein of truth. He used great comic actors, such as Arthur Lowe, who are great because they are truthful. Arthur Lowe was a comic genius. He was rather like a character in *The Lady Vanishes*, a symbol of the English middle-class-men-who-do: bank managers, headmasters, mayors. Peter Jeffrey, the headmaster in *if....*, was another of that type. Lindsay called upon such men because they didn't need to 'act'. They were already 'there'. The audacity of Arthur Lowe playing an educated black African in *O Lucky Man!* was wonderful, and absolutely outrageous.

Lindsay Anderson gave me a base as an actor. He taught me about responsibility. He taught me about attitude. He taught me to never create an attitude because it becomes a series of poses, which isn't 'life'. In *In Celebration*, I was playing a mostly silent character. Lindsay told me I wasn't playing it 'real' I was striking an attitude. That is also the difficulty one needs to overcome when playing material which has a political element. You have to play it for real instead of for attitude. In this he was the opposite of Brecht, though Brecht is sometimes misinterpreted, people forget that Brecht was keen on Stanislavsky.

Lindsay saw himself as a Jonathan Swift, and that is reflected in the films he made. His films were about England. Culturally they were so accurate. He worked brilliantly with the writer, David Sherwin, and that is why it is a tragedy that, in his later years, he was denied access to filmmaking in Britain. He made a few films in America, which were quite good, but they weren't the same. His films and his theatre have these elements of truth and also of theatricality. In theatre, the scenery is theatrical but you must trust the actuality of the specifics and the text. As an actor, he gave you this realm in which you could just 'be'. He allowed the performance to happen. He was always very keen on the specifics. He was very meticulous of the detail in the course of a series of actions and, in this respect, his masterpiece was *The Contractor* [which premiered at the Royal Court Theatre on 20th October 1969]. One of the problems I found with the Royal Court, and with trying to build a career in Britain, is the range of material that you are allowed to do. An actor really wants to be able to take on a lot of different material. One of the reasons I went to America was that, as an actor, I was accepted as a Scot. The country is fundamentally egalitarian. My argument with the Royal Court, and I got shot down for this, is that we were very much cast towards our social type. That was part of the poetics. Sometimes you felt a little bit cramped. I wanted to take everything I learned from Lindsay across the boards into the classical theatre, and into a theatre that was broader than just being 'British'. It was very hard to succeed in the classical theatre and, for a Scot, or a Welshman, it was a doubly difficult job. There were only one or two ever employed. Classical theatre was a tradition of the English, the Oliviers, the Gielguds, the Richardsons. It was not a tradition that Lindsay was really interested in. He was more interested in the actual material of the 'now', and in the political make-up of contemporary England. At the Royal Court, the political background of where you were from was always a difficulty.

Lindsay's great thing was that he was paternal, a mentor and a father-figure. He was very caring in that way. But Lindsay was also quite superior. He was quite patrician. He was a part of the English public school system. The Russians never had that problem. They replaced the Tsar with another totalitarian government but the arts thrived. The culture was rich and you could play anything. From Lindsay I learned to use the tools of who I was. This enabled me to get into the classical theatre and, once I'd done that I wanted to move on. I still love the classical theatre but, like Lindsay, I didn't want to get caught up in that particular tradition.

Saturday 19 October 1974

U.K. industry in midst of a 'nervous breakdown' —Lindsay Anderson

By Quentin Falk

LINDSAY ANDERSON thinks it is "highly significant" that the most-highly-praised British film last year was "Don't Look Now."

Film-makers and critics, he says, just don't want to "look now."

He has now finished filming David Storey's "In Celebration" for Ely Landau's American Film Theatre, with the same cast as his stage production at the Royal Court five years ago.

On the set at Elstree, he told me: "It's a difficult but very valid play to film. I had an offer to make a film of it here when Bryan Forbes took over.

"There didn't seem to be any point in making a film like this in the context of British distribution at that time—or indeed now."

With, of course, the success of the AFT subscription experiment in the States, there is now a ready audience for Anderson's film.

But it is about the current state of the British industry that Anderson feels so gloomy.

"The cinema is and always has been a very strong and significant indication of the imaginative vitality of a nation.

"And I think the British cinema rather correctly mirrors a nation that has ceased to believe in itself, is confused and fatigued, divided and without imagination.

"In fact it mirrors a nation in the middle of a nervous breakdown.

"I think the British industry can now be regarded as a disaster even if from time to time the Americans make a couple of films here.

"First there is the economic factor. We have priced ourselves out of film-making for our own market.

"This has come largely through

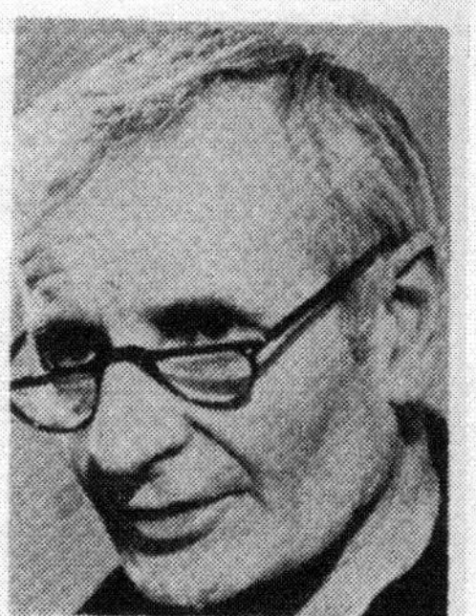

● Anderson—gloomy about the future

letting there grow up a kind of union mentality of legislating for American producers and distributors, of making economic demands on film-makers which assume they have the resources of a major American company, and of not making any kind of adjustment for the home product.

"And, of course, secondly, the British cinema lost its way when it deserted the path of realism.

"It veered into a 'swinging' phase which proved a complete disaster.

Untalented people

"Large numbers of untried and untalented people made pictures, some of which haven't even been shown—and on that score I don't blame the industry."

Anderson believes that British films have currently "regressed to either bourgeois mannerism, nursery infantilism and rather degenerate music-hall tradition.

"To supply fodder for the television industry which needs just fodder from, say, an original film may be good business.

"But to be reduced to making your films, adaptations of something that originally was no more than fodder, is decadence.

"There are themes all round us but Britain doesn't want to face the truth.

"If there was a really vital collection of British film-makers, they would find 15 stories jumping out at them every time they opened a paper."

Caine and Glenda for 'Englishwoman'

JOSEPH LOSEY'S "The Romantic Englishwoman" starts shooting on Monday.

The film, from the book by Tom Wiseman, stars Michael Caine and Glenda Jackson, and is being produced by Danny Angel. Wiseman and Tom Stoppard have written the screenplay. The film is being shot on location in England, France and Germany.

Lindsay Anderson Gallery

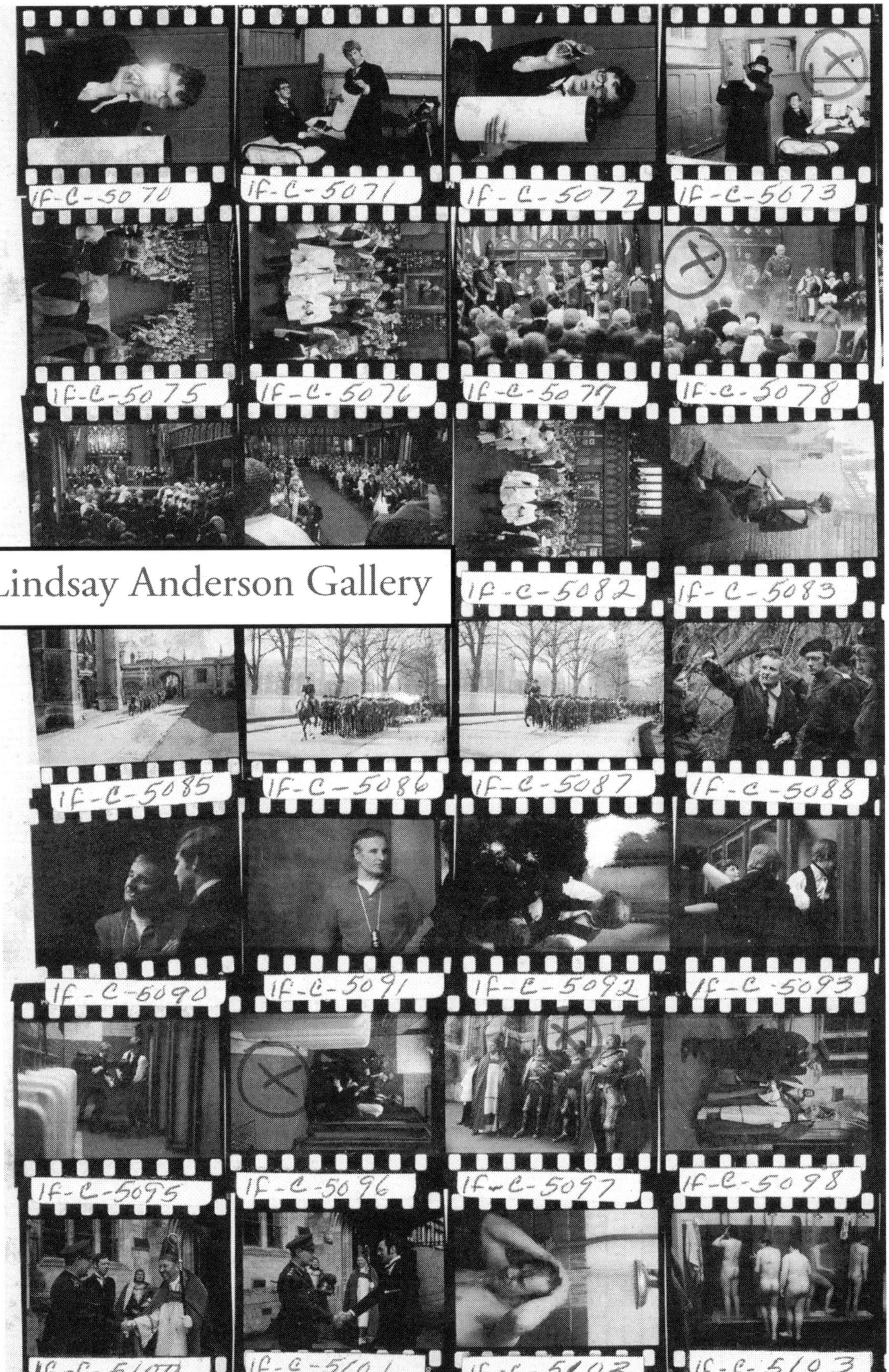

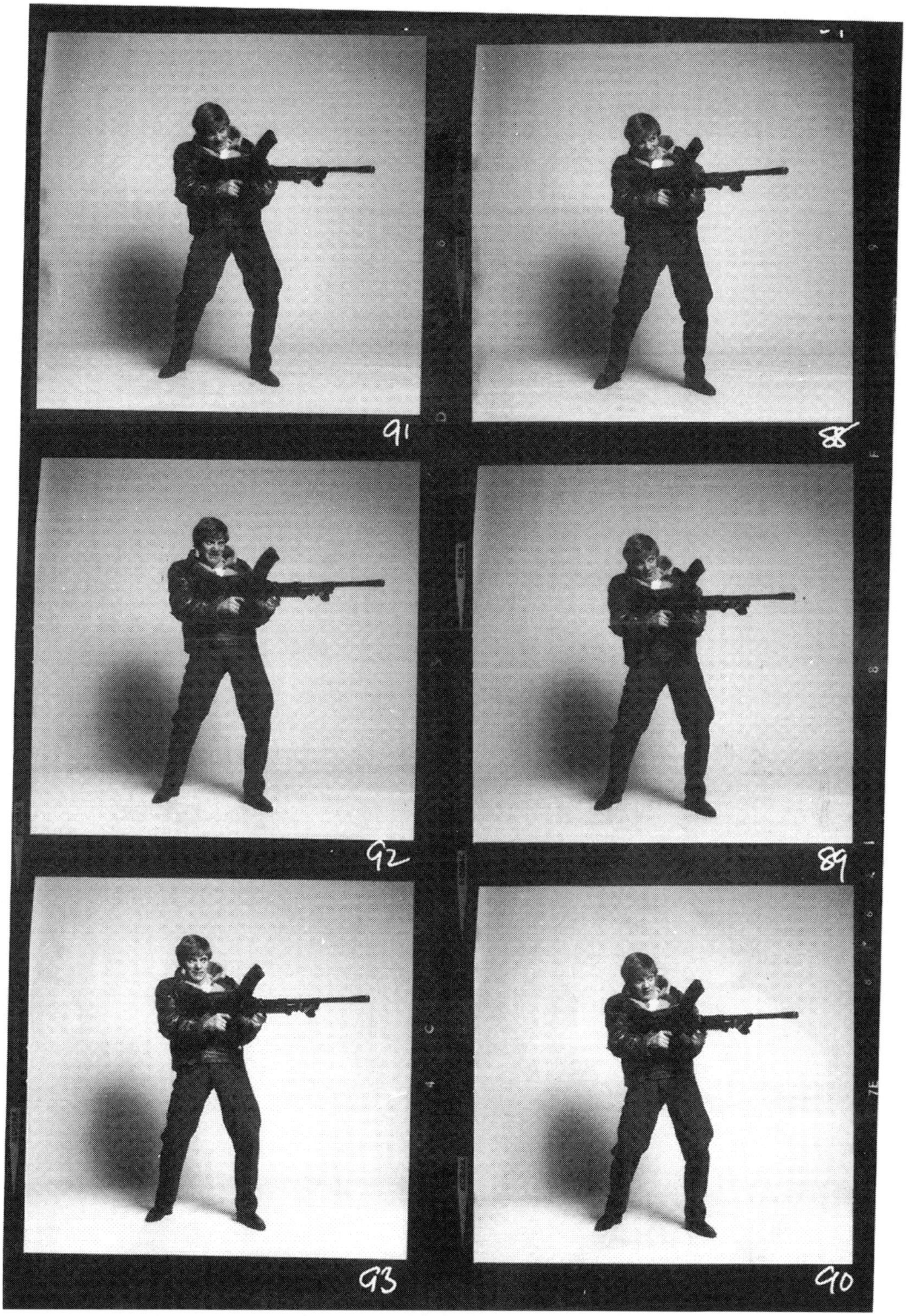

Malcolm McDowell 'Gatlin Gun' publicity shots for Lindsay Anderson's *if....*

"Could you shoot
a Gatling gun?"

"I don't know."

"If you really want a riot
why don't you go at it proper?
Come on, I'll tell you."

*Serjeant Musgrave's
Dance*

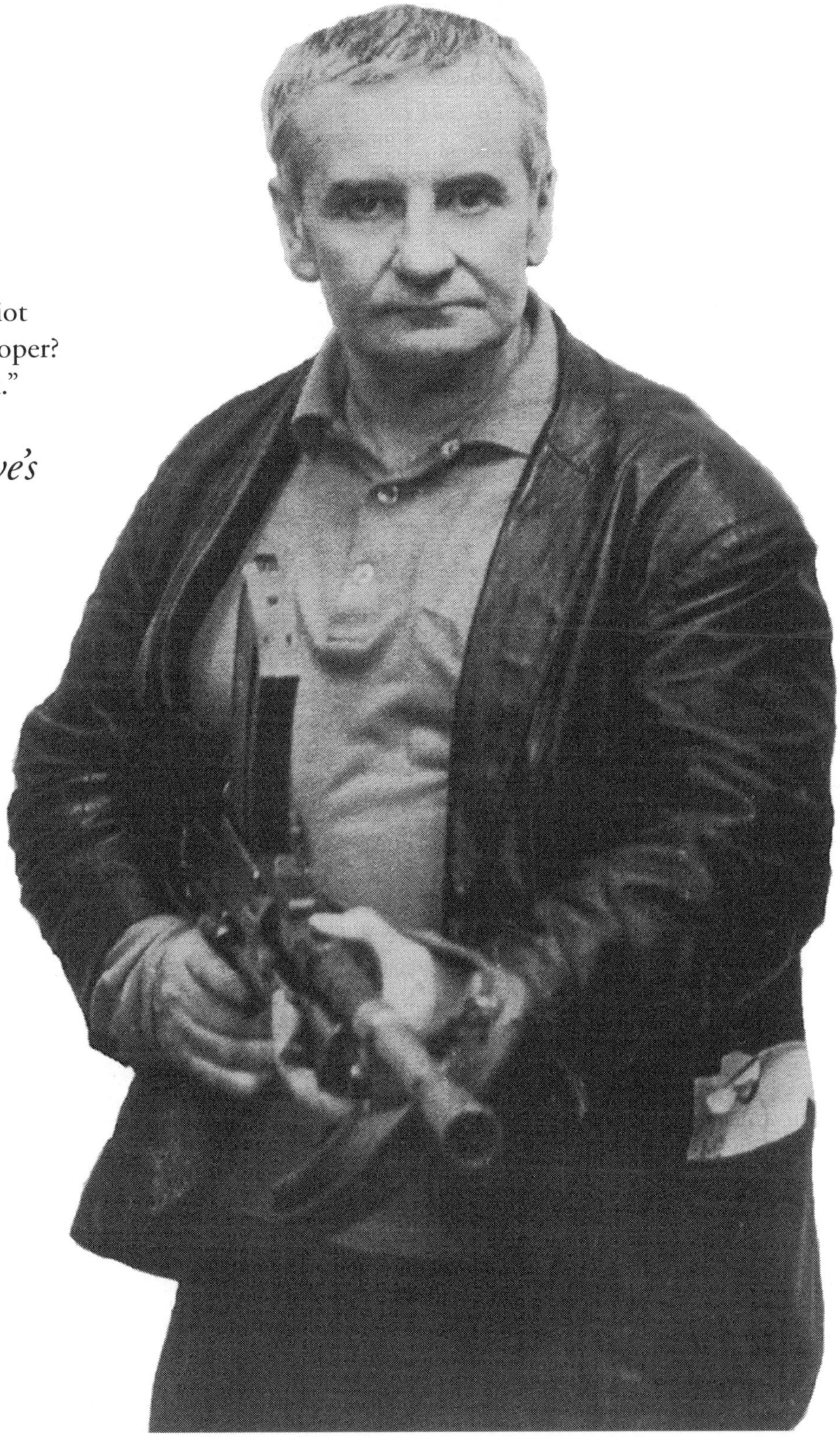

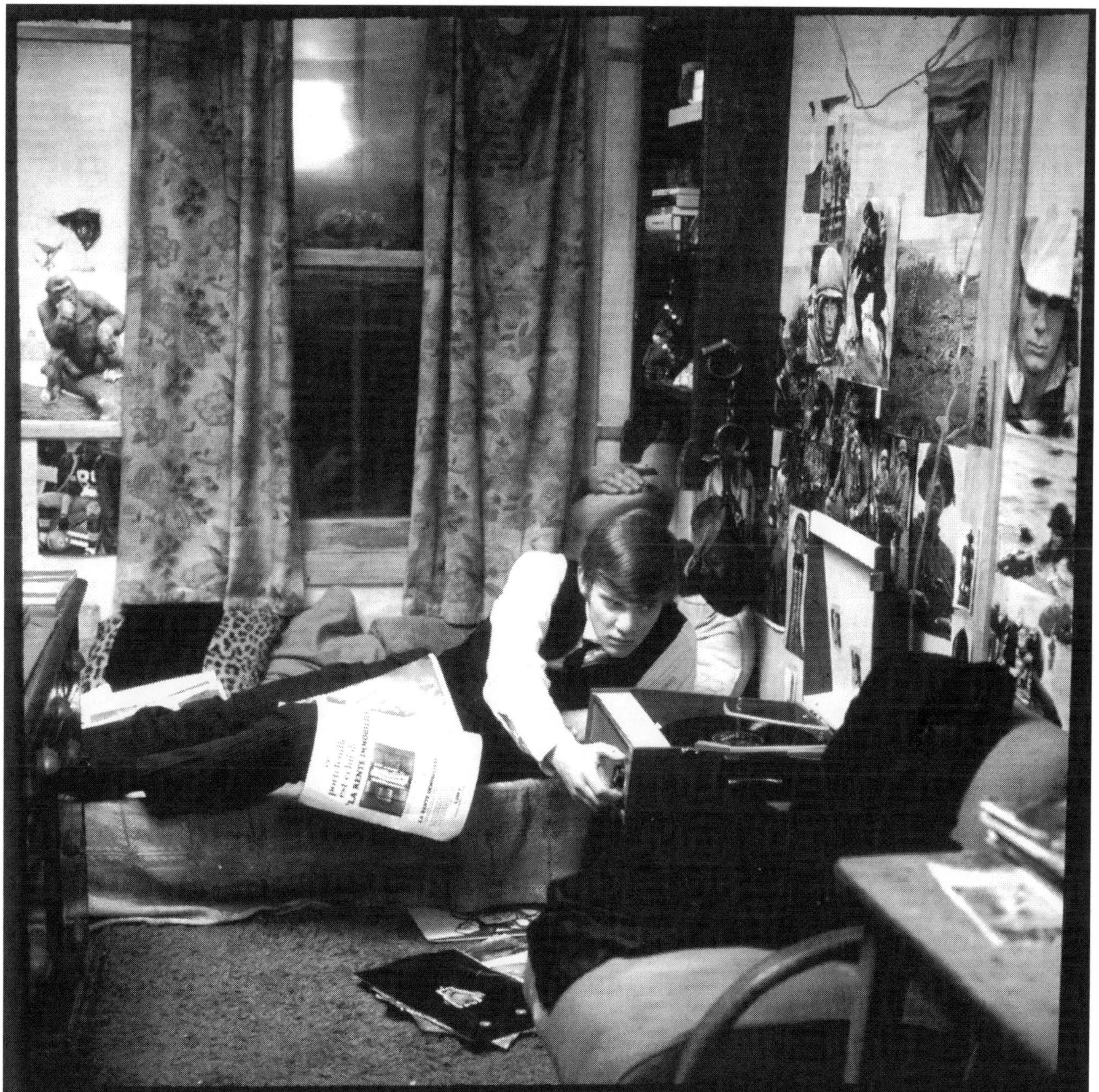

Malcolm McDowell re-plays the Congolese 'Sanctus' in a set built and dressed by Jocelyn Herbert

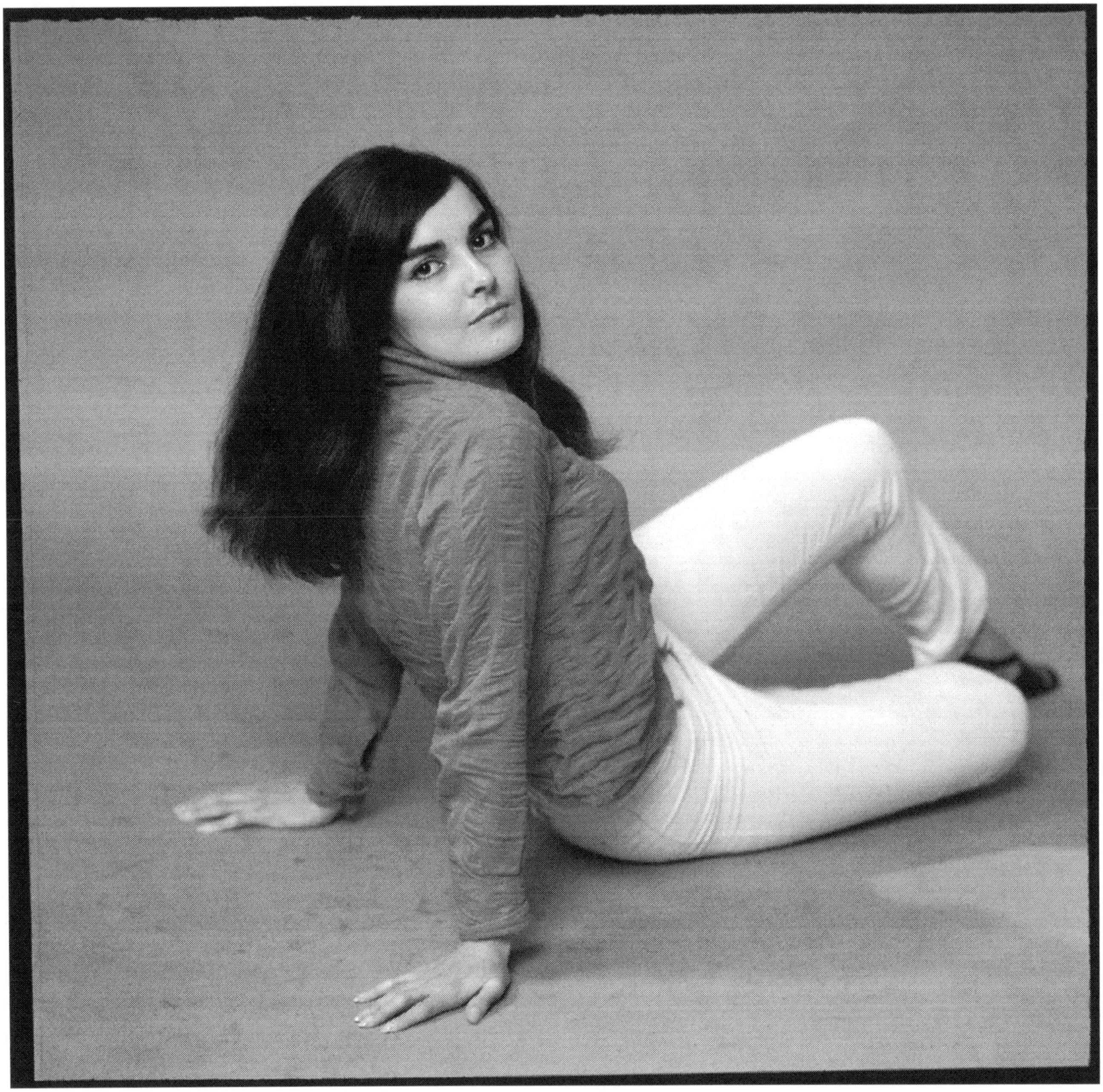

Christine Noonan

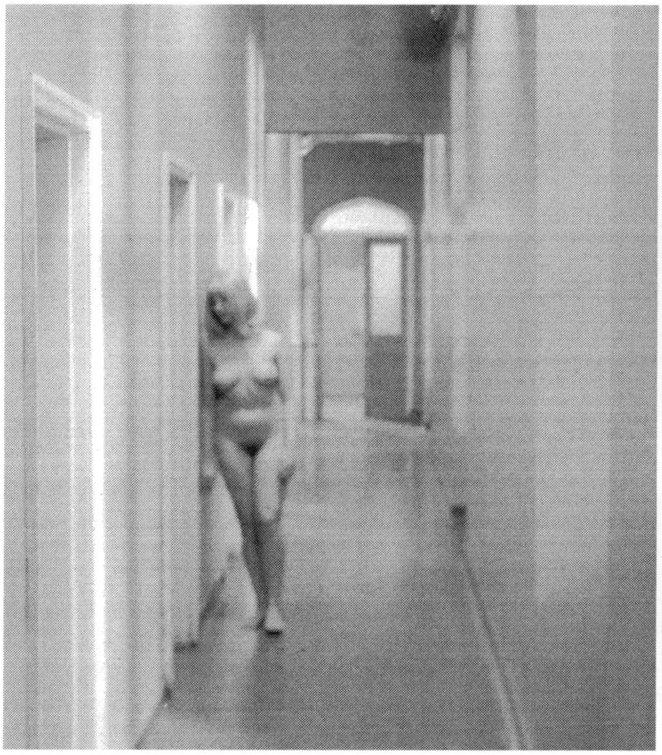

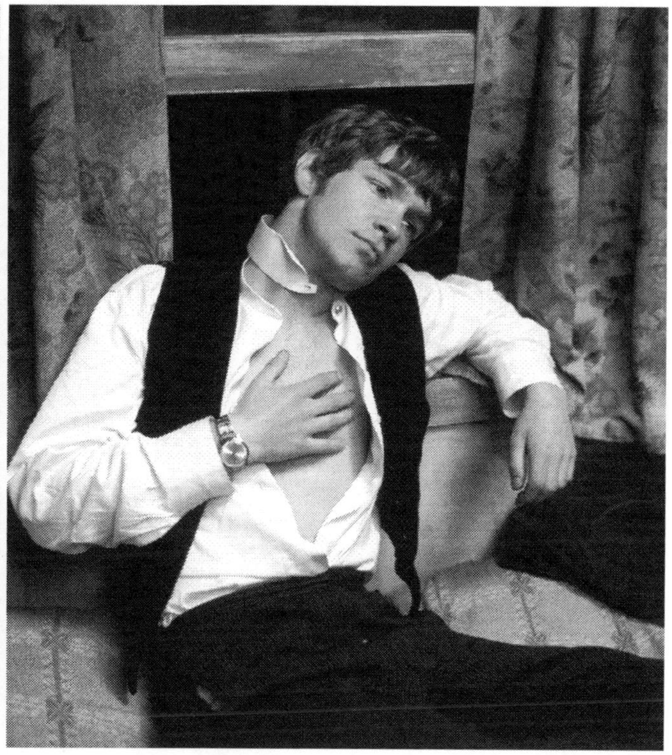

Mary MacLeod, Richard Warwick, Arthur Lowe

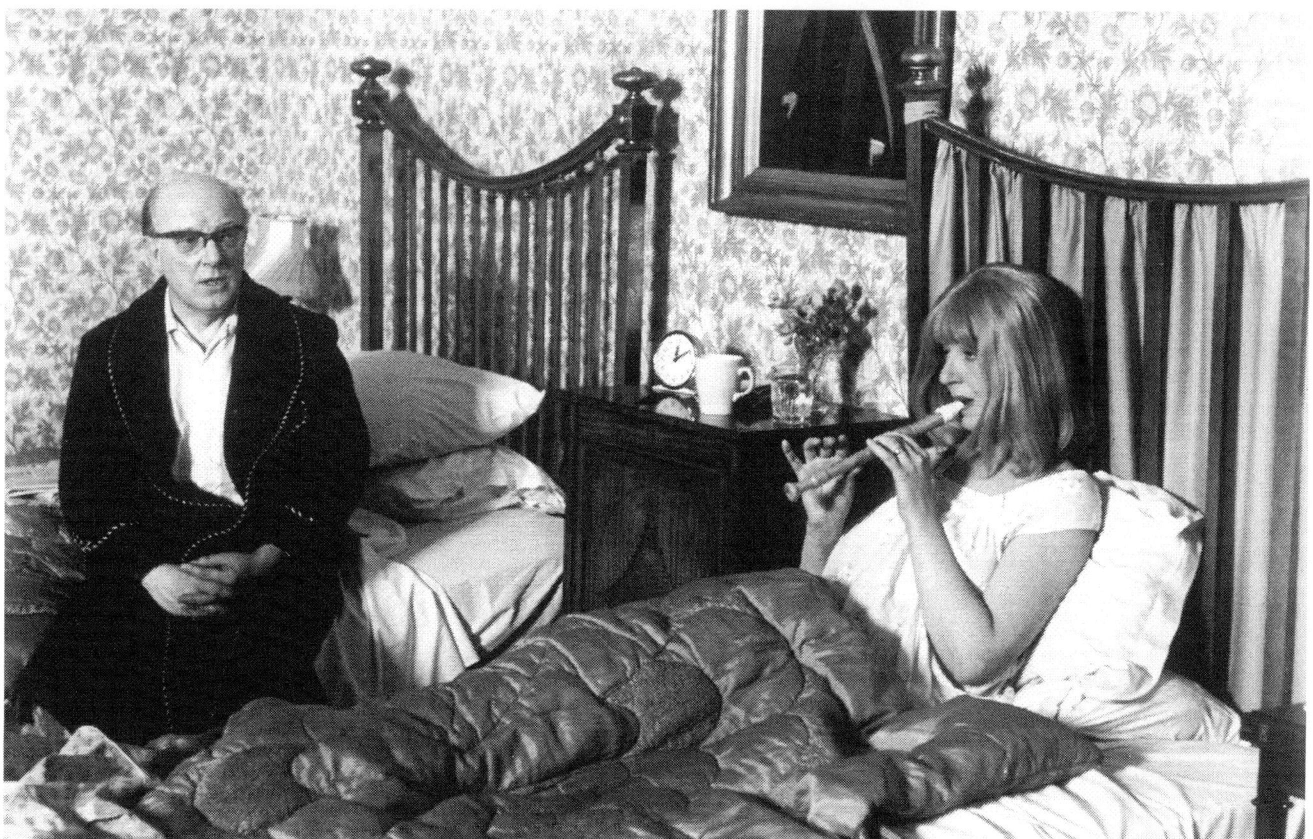

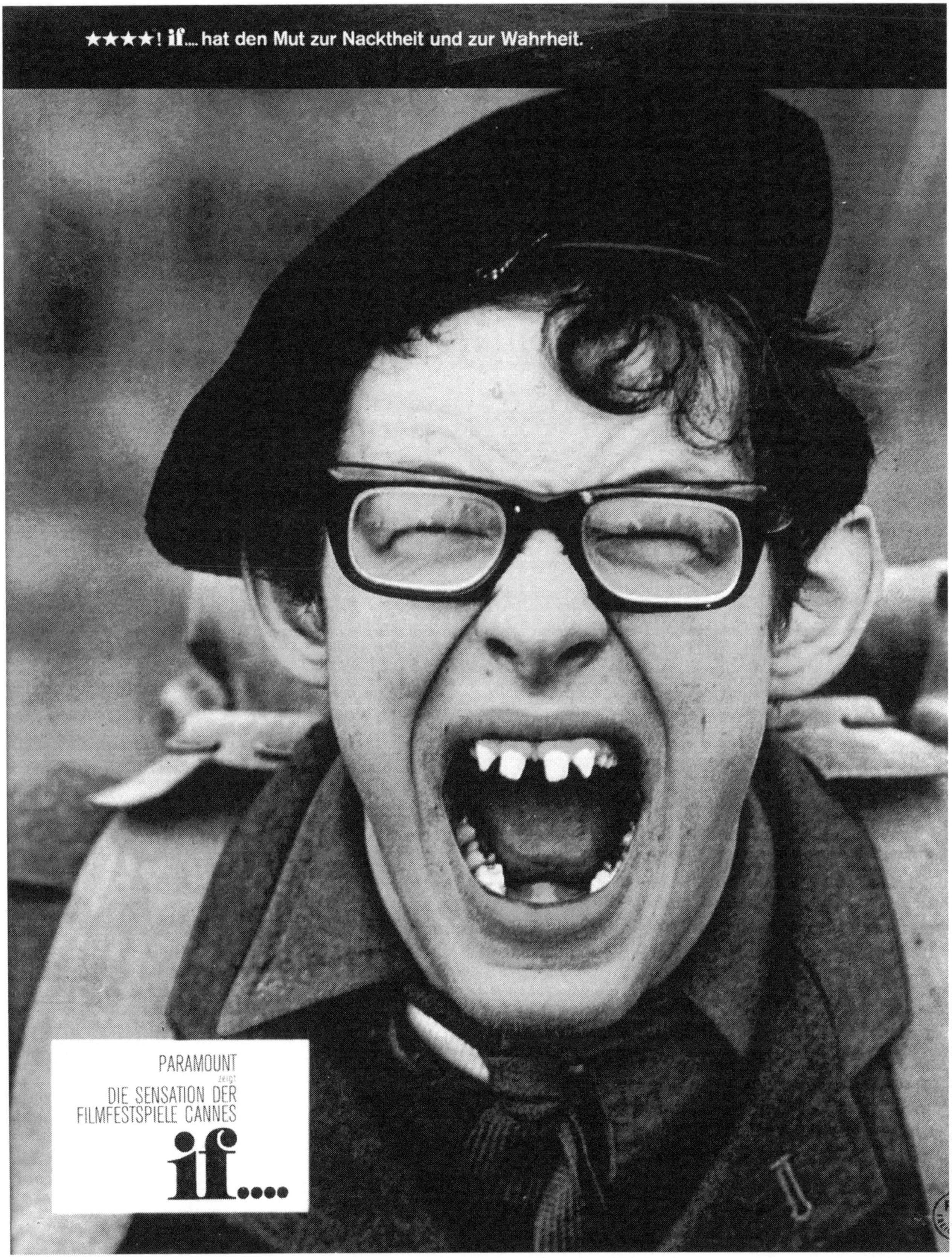

"The Yell of Hate!" Lurid-coloured lobby card of Philip Bagenal, the only boy cast from open audition

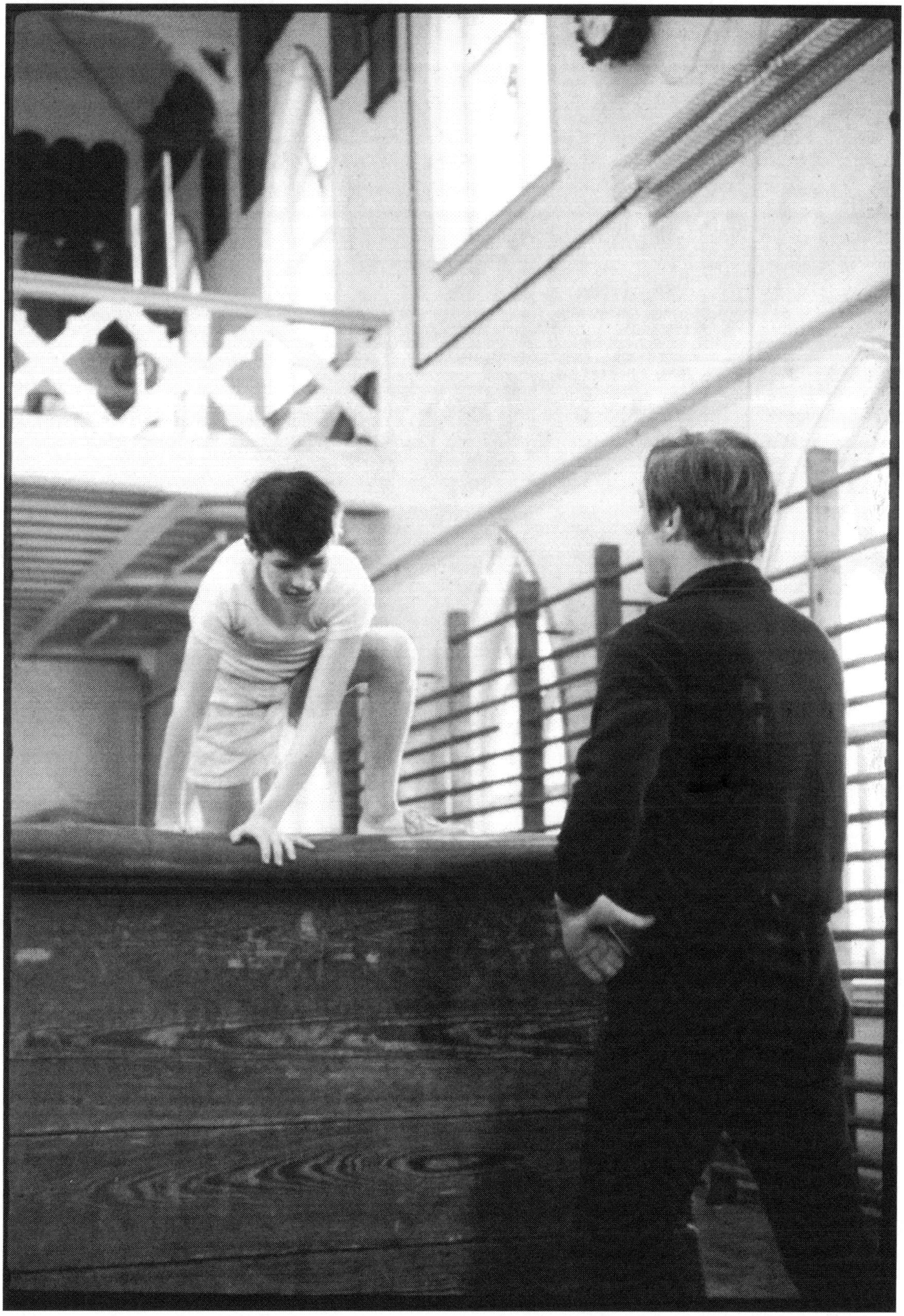

Sean Bury as ‘Jute’, the new boy assimilated into the system

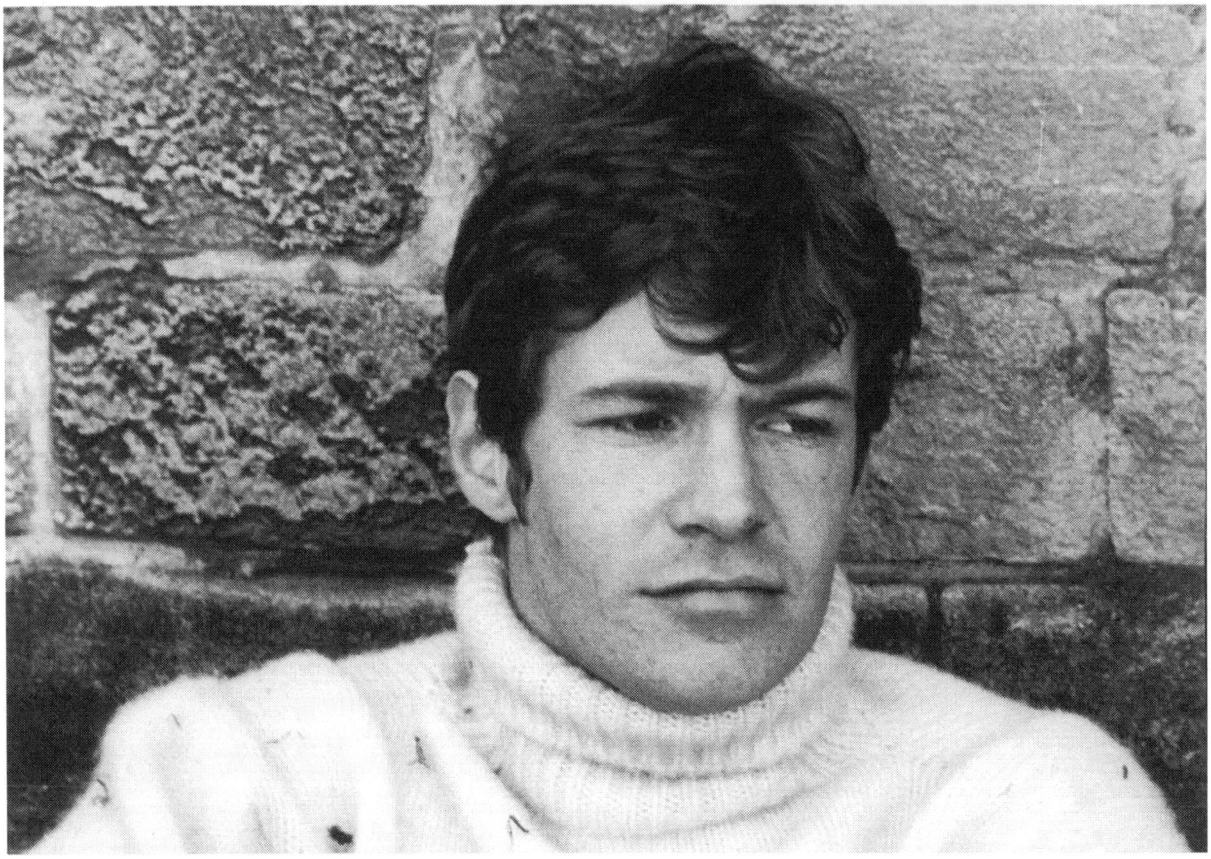

Richard Warwick (above). Lindsay Anderson directs The Juniors

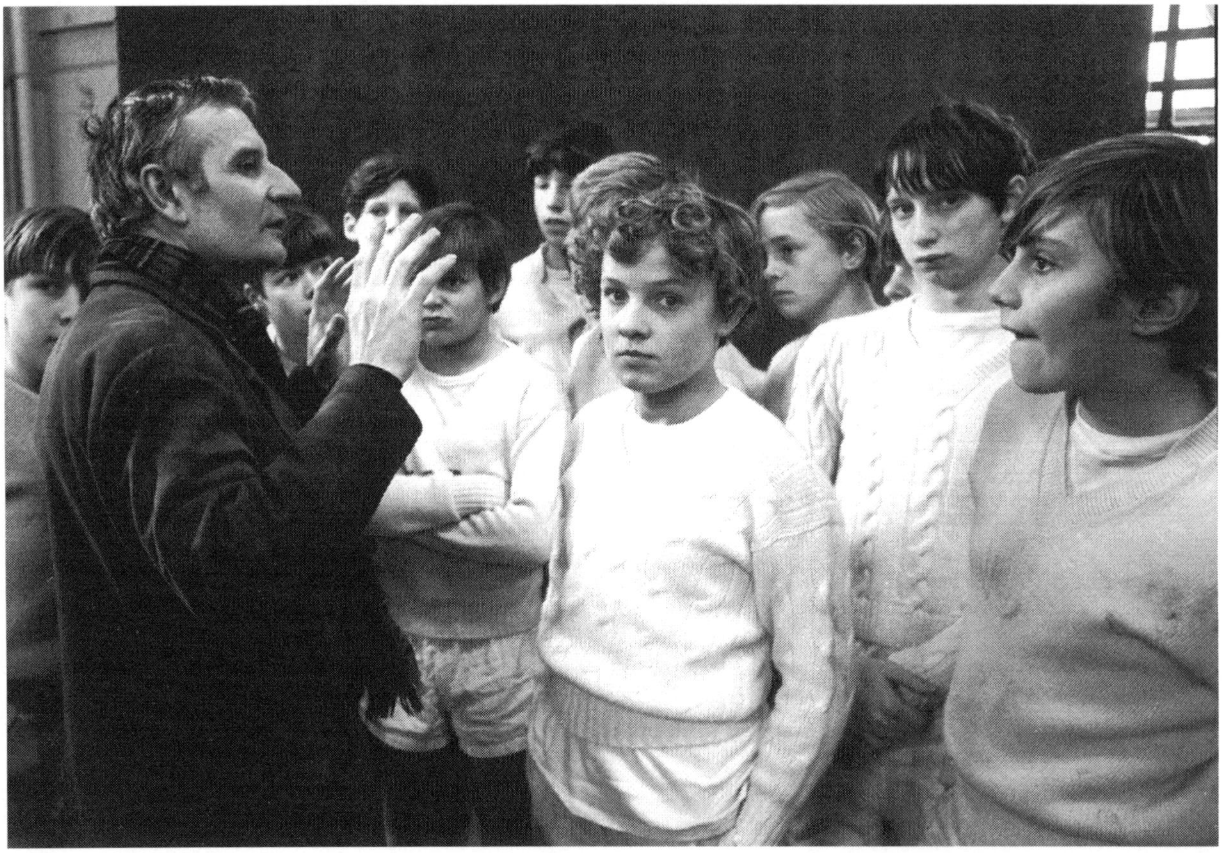

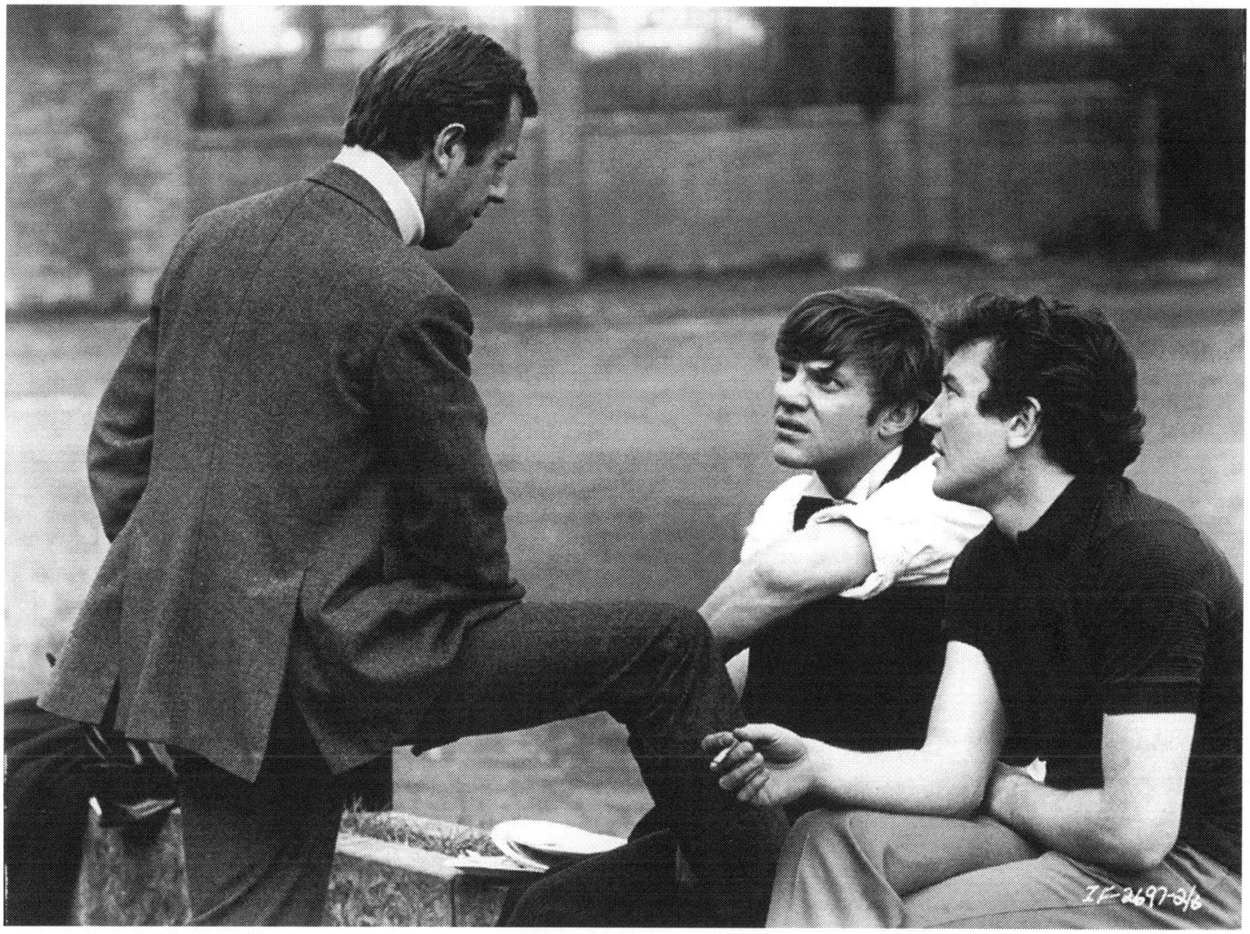

Memorial bosses, Michael Medwin and Albert Finney, with Malcolm McDowell on location for *if....*

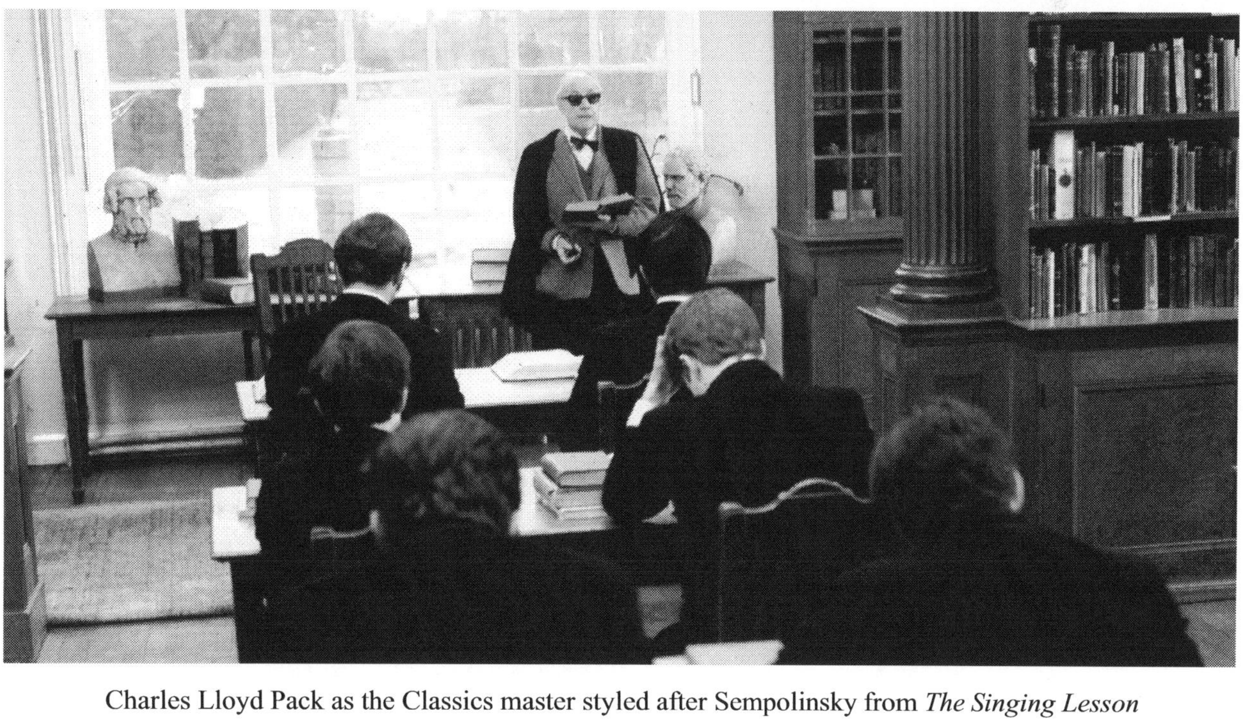

Charles Lloyd Pack as the Classics master styled after Sempolinsky from *The Singing Lesson*

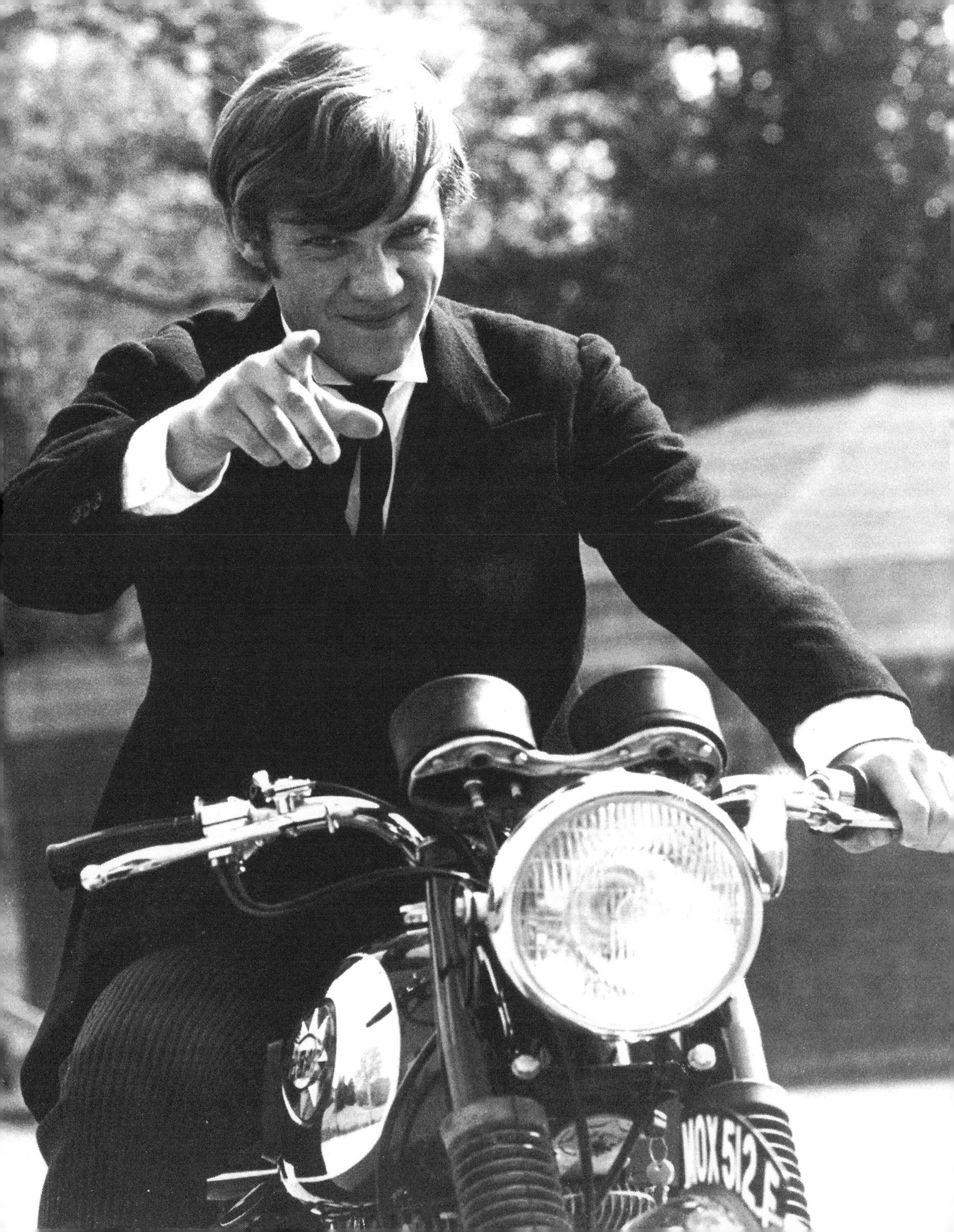

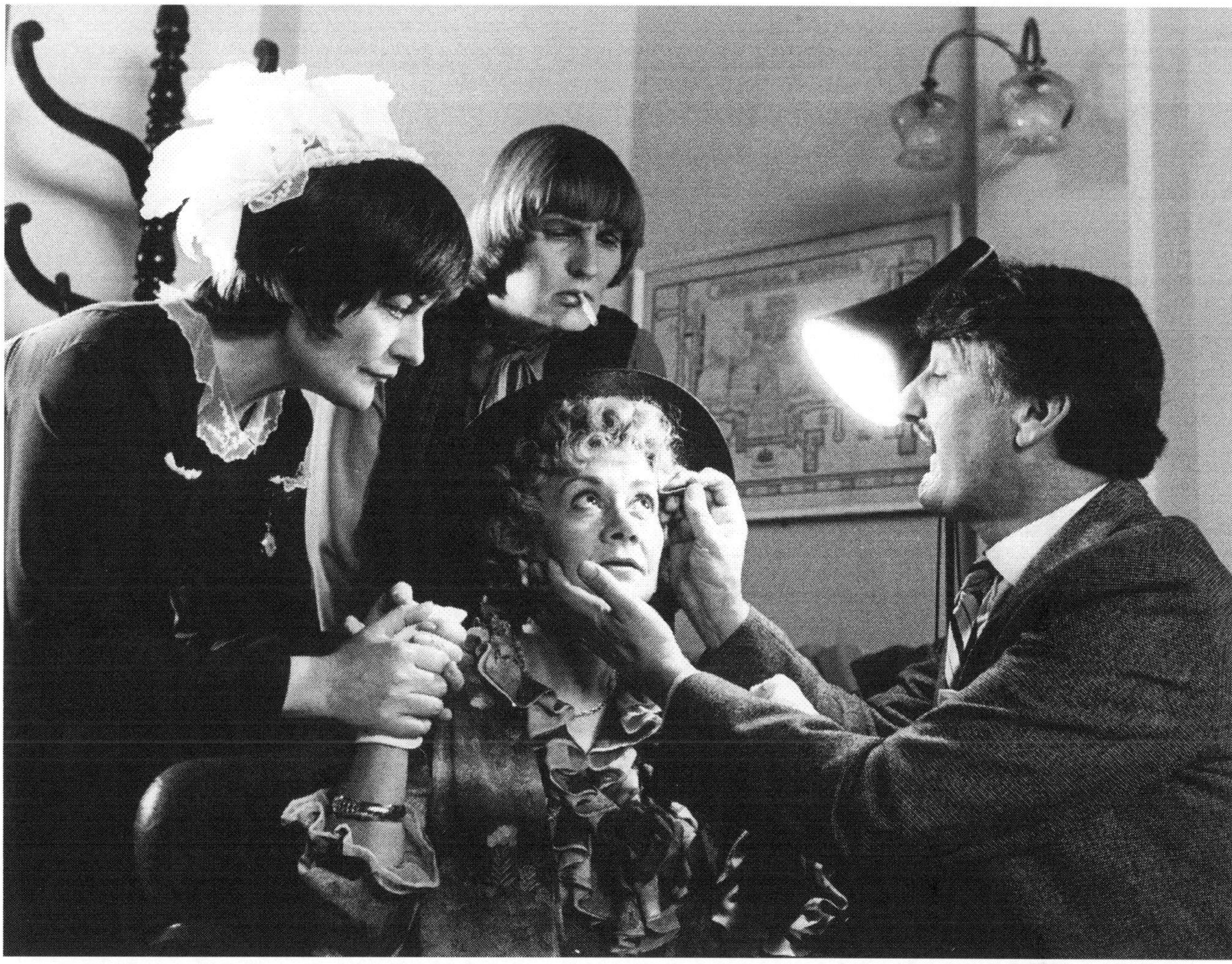

Vivian Pickles as the Matron, Joan Plowright a patient, and Peter Jeffrey as a doctor in *Britannia Hospital*

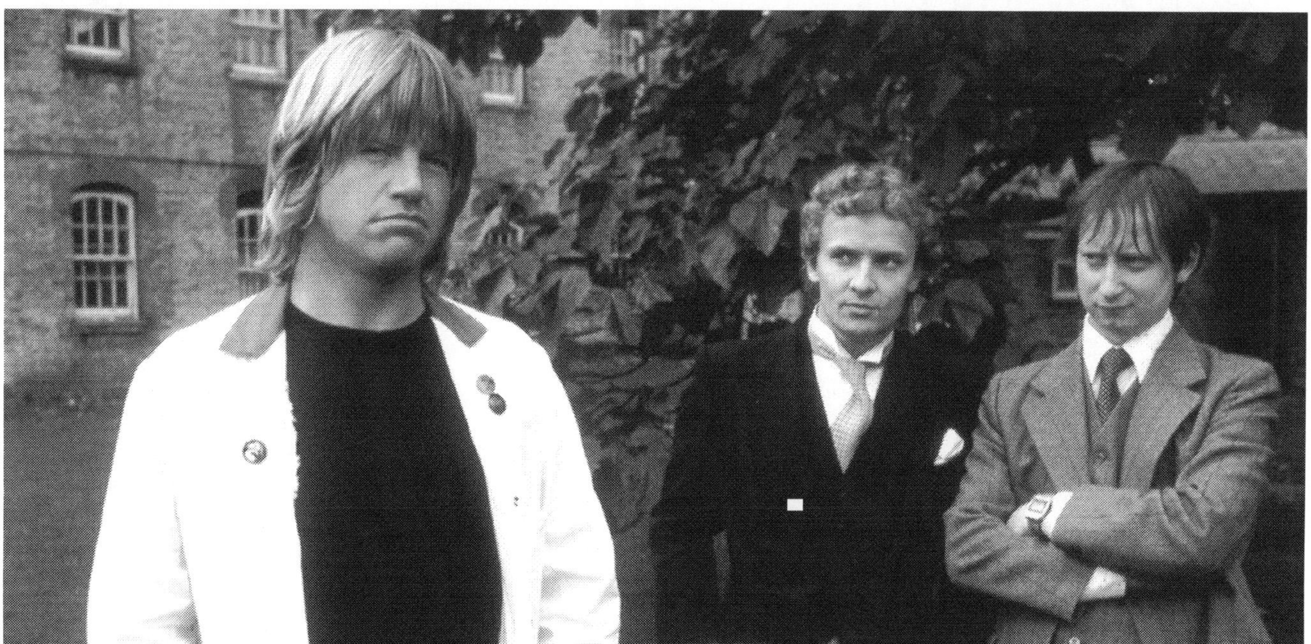

if... boys reunited in *Britannia Hospital.* Robin Askwith, Robin Davies, Brian Pettifer

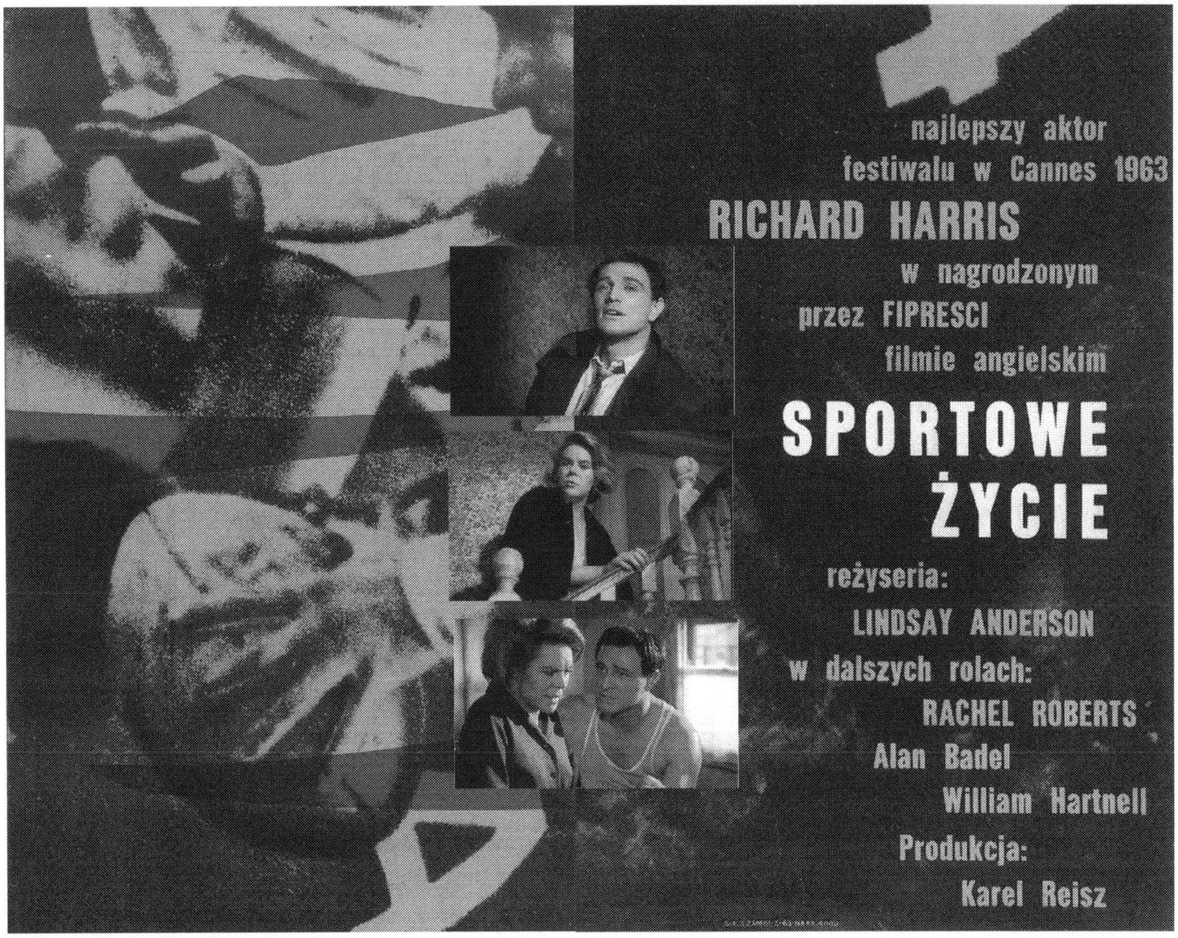

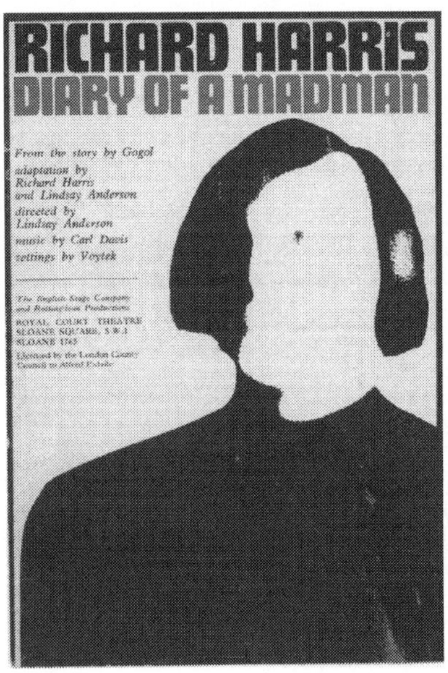

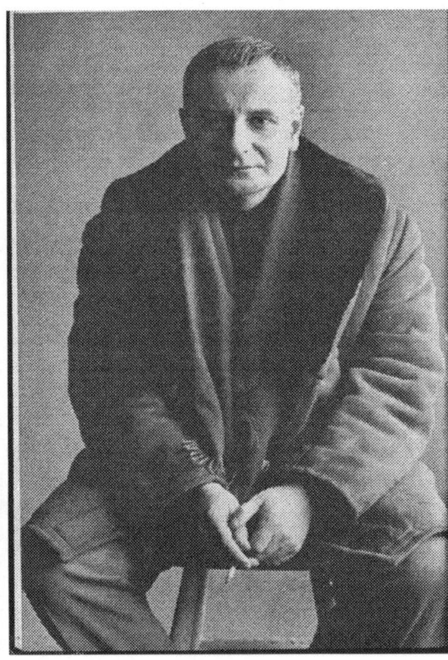

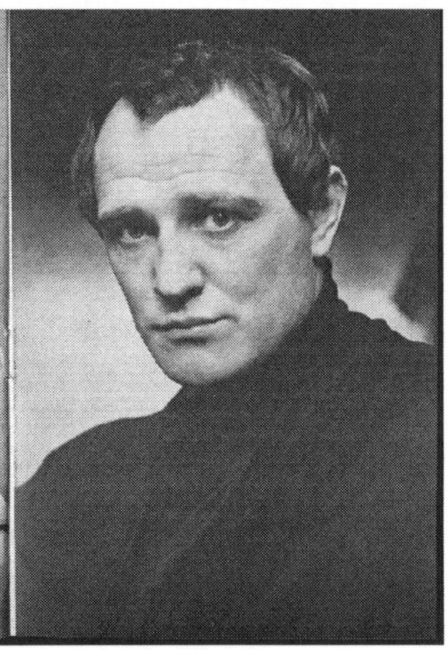

Lindsay Anderson and Richard Harris followed *This Sporting Life*
with a one-man Gogol-inspired play at the Royal Court Theatre, London.

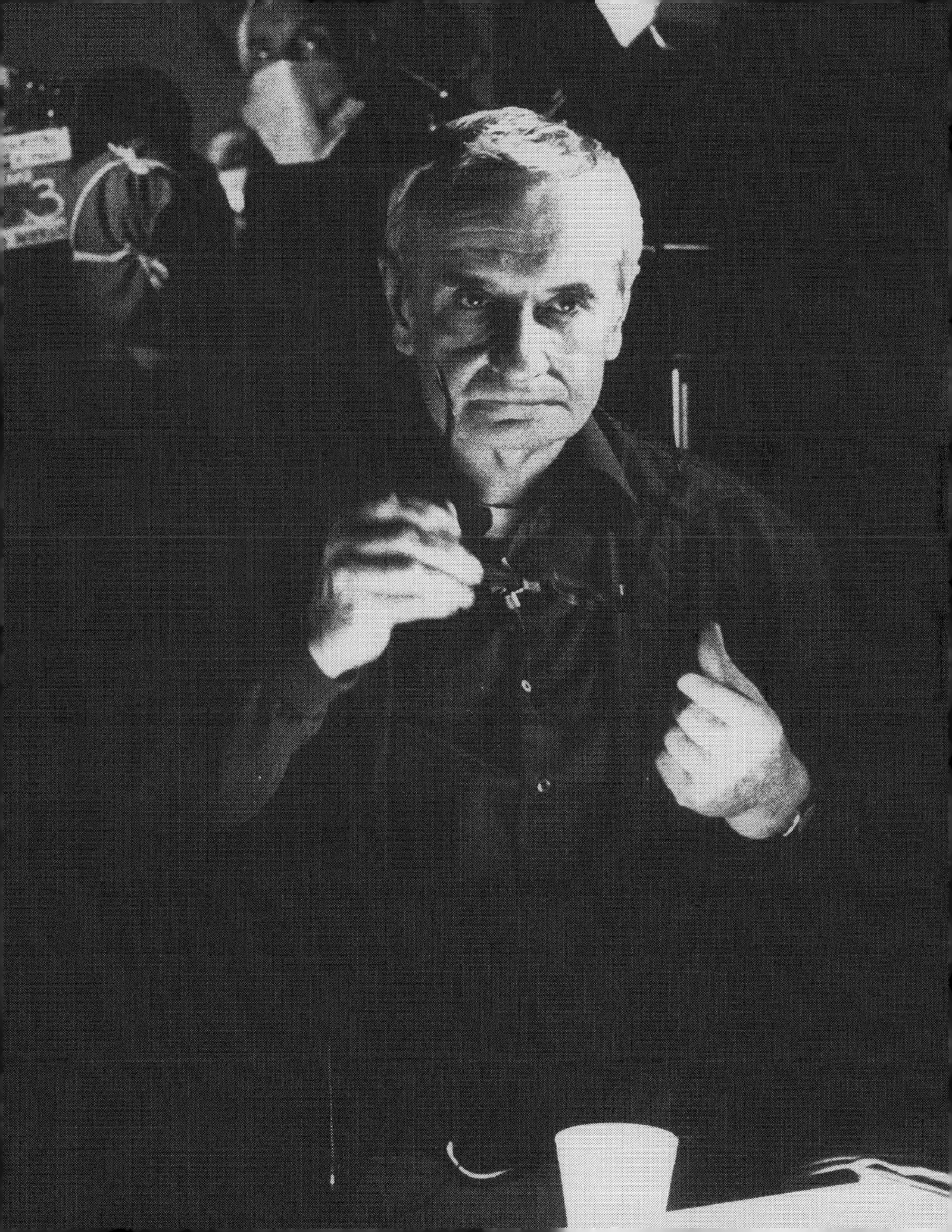

Charlie Chaplin

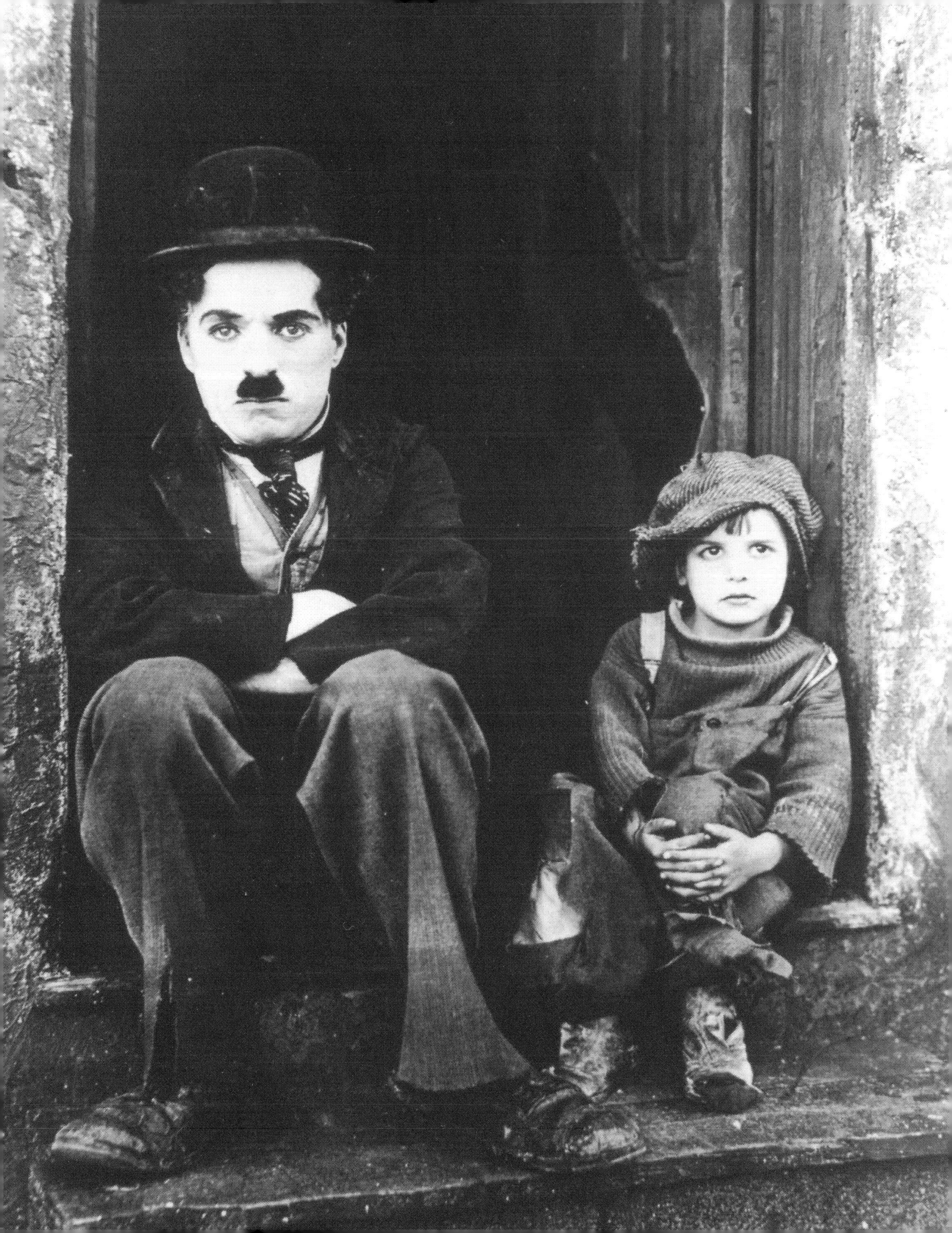

Charlie Chaplin

Kevin Brownlow came to see me in Cambridge on the day he was presenting the première of his film *The Tramp and the Dictator*, famed for the remarkable colour footage of Chaplin at work on the set of *The Great Dictator*. We spent the afternoon talking about the greatest actor-director the world has ever seen. Brownlow sent the transcript of our conversation to the Chaplin family. It helped to persuade them to make the long unavailable silent version of *The Gold Rush* available on DVD.

When did you discover the films of Chaplin?

Kevin Brownlow: I was taken to see *The Gold Rush* and, like many people, I didn't think it was a comedy at all. I thought it was so sad. This was the 1942 re-issue with the narration added. At school, I'd seen Chaplin's short films but I never really grew as fond of him, at that period, as of someone like Harold Lloyd and later Keaton but, eventually, I saw *City Lights* and was converted. Working on *The Unknown Chaplin*, in the 1980s, in which we discovered all his outtakes and miles of rushes, made me realise what an extraordinary artist he was. David Gill and I used to think it odd that people would choose one of those comedians and use them to batter the other two. It wasn't like that in music. People didn't say if you liked Haydn you couldn't possibly like Mozart or Beethoven. It's very very odd. In the film history world, if you are passionate about Keaton you have to denigrate Chaplin and Lloyd. Without Chaplin there wouldn't have been any of the others because he proved that comedy was commercial, almost more commercial than anything else, and he made it possible for all the others to come on after him.

I saw the original release version of The Gold Rush *before I saw the 'official' 1942 narrated version, and I was stunned by it. I didn't like the 1942 version because the narration encouraged the viewer to laugh at and not with the Little Tramp.*

Chaplin and the family regard the sound version as his last word. We've done a restoration of the silent version. It was shown, for example, at the Royal Festival Hall not so long ago, and Carl Davis adapted the Chaplin music for the second one and put it on the first one, and it was a fantastic success.

The scale of the film is extraordinary. When people talk about Chaplin they sometimes mistake him for Mack Sennett, or remember only his earliest shorts shot on tiny sets, but his feature films are massive. On The Gold Rush *we see snowy mountainous landscapes over which 12,000 men are marching.*

The Chilkoot Pass, yes, that's right. It's an epic, but apart from the opening, an intimate epic.

Chaplin began the film on location but withdrew and re-filmed in the studio?

Yes, and it's well done. Even the little house on the side of the cliff, he manages to bring it off.

A Chicken Run sequence was cut from the film, a man in a giant chicken suit, stills of which still exist.

There is still a man-sized chicken in there but there was a lot more to it originally.

In Louis Malle's autobiographical film, Au Revoir Les Enfants, *the boys are shown a Chaplin film, a key point in Malle's development as an artist.*

Yes, and there's a film called *The First Time*, made in Cuba just after the revolution, in which projection trucks go into the hinterland and show films to people who have never seen them. They film the kids reacting to *Modern Times*, and that inspired the recent head of the Cinémathèque, Peter Scarlet, to do the same in Afghanistan. He took Keaton and Chaplin films to orphans who had never seen those comedians at all. The reaction was fabulous.

I think Charlie made comedy 'human'. That's one of his major achievements. He brought pathos into comedy films, pathos isn't sentimentality, sentimentality had always been there in the popular comedy films.

I'd say that's right. That has always been used as a club to hit him with. Pathos in comedy is extremely unpopular now for some reason, but that's perfectly true. It is something the other comedians tried to do as well, not always successfully.

Some of the pathos is exaggerated in Keaton's films.

In Keaton? Exaggerated? Give me an example of exaggerated!

In The Cameraman, the sequence where the woman is drowning, though it is a fantastic film.

The film is brilliant.

I love the superimpositions, the battleship 'sailing' down a New York avenue.

Wonderful. I like The Tong war with the tracking shot when Keaton is on the scaffolding, cranking away and the whole thing moves forward like the tracking shot over Babylon in *Intolerance*.

It's the favourite film of the man who runs the Arts Cinema in Oxford. I think he's got his own print. He shows it every year.

I hope it's the restored print.

I've only seen his print and it seems to be very good. Watching your film, The Unknown Chaplin, in which we see Chaplin at work, he seems to me to have been very much like Stanley Kubrick, in that he'd arrive on set not knowing exactly what he wanted. He'd have enormously long shooting schedules so that he could 'discover' the film whilst working on it, and he'd spend months refining what he discovered. He'd work and improvise until he got what he wanted.

That's right. It amazed me. The evidence came from the material itself, from the miles of rushes, even before we talked to people who confirmed it. He was incredibly insecure, I suppose. When he finished *The Kid* he wanted to put it on the shelf and not release it.

The Kid is simply awesome. And it was one of the three or four biggest money-making films of its time. I love the little behind-the-scenes clip in your documentary where Jackie Coogan dances for the exhibitors!

An Irish shimmy.

It's delightful.

I think that people from my generation were held back from Chaplin because the prints of the early comedies had been duped out of existence. Then they started showing them on widescreen so that you lost the head and you lost the feet and there wasn't very much more to see. *The Kid* was shown in the most excruciating version by DUK Film in the 1950s, whom Chaplin sued, and it wasn't until he started re-releasing them in these beautiful prints did we suddenly see what *The Kid* was all about. In the Chaplin Centenary year of 1989, David Gill and I did a presentation of *City Lights* with a live orchestra, and all the critics helpfully said: "Nobody under forty finds Chaplin funny," so it failed to sell. We were in real trouble because we had a whole week to fill. But when the audience actually saw *City Lights* the word-of-mouth was so good that the bookings went through the roof. By the end of the week it was standing room only! There was so much laughter you couldn't hear the orchestra in certain sequences. We recorded the people under forty not finding Chaplin funny and we sent the tapes to each of the critics, only Barry Norman replied.

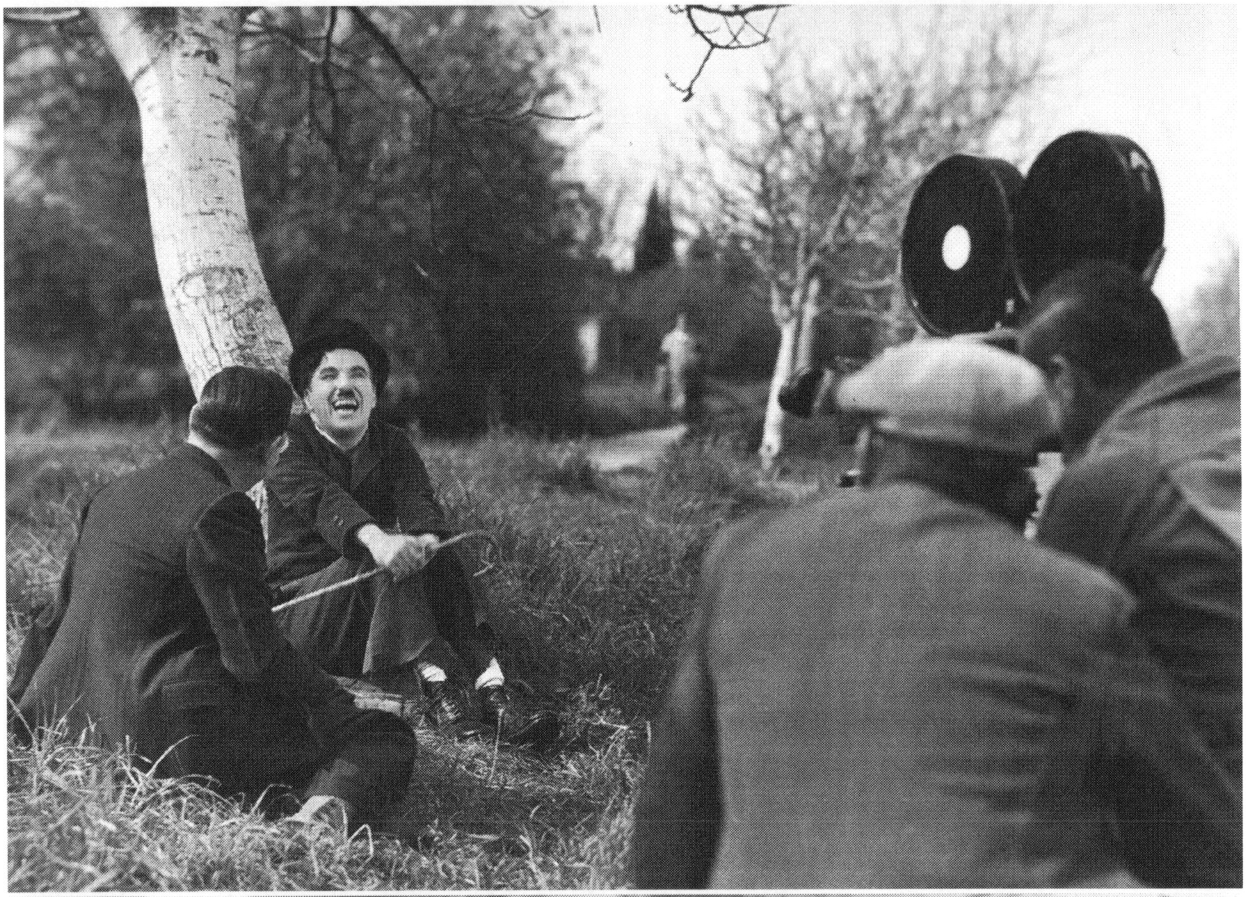

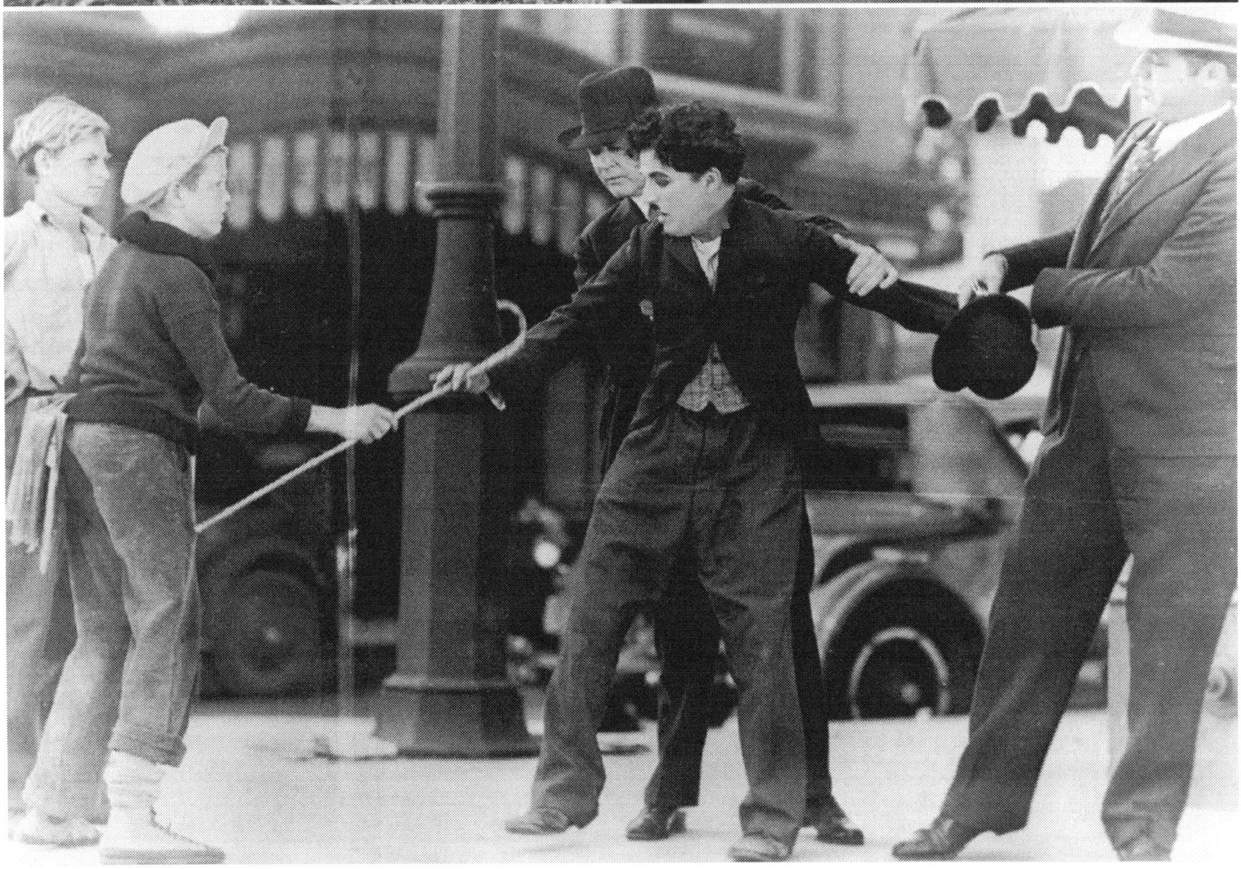

On location filming *Modern Times* (1936); Teased by Robert Parrish in *City Lights* (1931)

Only those who haven't seen a Chaplin film can think he isn't funny. Some of the short films are astonishing, such as The Cure.

Yes. Eight-six years old and it still works.

The timing of the stunts and his stock players, such as Eric Campbell, take the breath away. The scene when Campbell falls out of a wheel chair into a little tiny round pond is incredible. It is impossible not to laugh.

I agree. Although the actual leap was done by a stunt man.

A criticism of Chaplin is that his filmmaking technique is very plain, that the camera hardly moves, but that's simply incorrect. His style is very deceptive.

That's the word. In *Shoulder Arms* when you see him for the first time, the camera tracks with Chaplin down the trench, there's an explosion and smoke fills the screen. He comes out of the smoke and you track all the way back. In 1918 this was advanced and unusual for an American film. But so what if he seldom moved the camera? The direction is absolutely perfect *for him.*

The Fireman is as playfully inventive as a Jean Vigo film, but it was made fifteen years before Vigo picked up a camera. Charlie plays about with the film speed and runs sequences backwards, so that, for example, he slides up the fireman's pole, and 'reverses' a horse-drawn fire engine.

We had no idea how he did the 'axe scene' in *Behind the Screen* [Chaplin strides into the frame and steps over an axe that has ploughed into the floor and missed him by a millimetre]. We could only find out how he did it by looking at the film about forty times. The film as screened is playing backwards.

He's walking backwards but it's almost impossible to tell; the body language is so natural.

Yes, that's absolutely true.

His skill as a performer is undoubtable.

I think television is part of the problem, seeing the films on a 25-inch screen. Chaplin designed everything for a 25-foot screen. When you see him on the big screen, in a print of good quality, you see his expressions, it makes such a difference. When he is reduced to TV you just can't get the same effect.

He's a great comedian, a great filmmaker and a great actor. And, as in the famous quote by W. C. Fields: "He's a goddam ballet dancer."

He was a dancer too. He was an absolutely brilliant mover. David Gill was an ex-ballet dancer and he was always commenting on how silent film stars were invariably dancers as well.

And roller skaters!

In *The Rink* and *Modern Times.*

He's in a department store on an upper floor and there's a big hole in the floor. Charlie is wearing a blindfold and he's on roller skates. You think you know what's going to happen but the genius of the filmmaker is to surprise you. He teases the audience and does a few circular loops that brush the edge of the hole, and he catches you at an unexpected moment.

The Chaplin surprise film that is lost, and I would love to find it, was a gag done for Fairbanks on the set of *Robin Hood*, with the huge castle. You watch the gigantic drawbridge slowly lowering. Charlie comes out with the cat. He puts the cat out and takes the milk in and the drawbridge goes back. Lost! It's such a shame.

A dreadful loss. Let's discuss the sheer inventiveness of Chaplin. When I see a film like The Adventurer I'm stunned by the scale of its invention. From the start. How is he going to enter? He enters from beneath the earth! Which is not what you expect. What is he wearing? Arrow-patterned prison clothes. It's impossible to predict what's coming next. In every sequence in the film he is one or two steps ahead of the audience. And I think that is where his genius lies. He knows what the audience wants and he is going to give it to them but on his own terms, after packing each scene with as many twists and unexpected turns as the narrative can hold.

You're absolutely right, but he went through agony to get it; he had to top himself with every film, particularly when he started making features. The responsibility must have been awful. That's why *City Lights* and the feature films took so long to make. He was dissatisfied most of the time. He couldn't judge his own work. When he had made *City Lights*, which, by any standard is a masterpiece, he wanted to shelve it. Fairbanks persuaded him that commercially it really made sense to screen it to a small group of people and to take their opinion. He said: "You don't even have to be there. I'll tell you how they react." The screening was arranged. Charlie couldn't resist attending. He arrived late and he stood at the back and there wasn't a laugh from start to finish. He was nearly suicidal. When the lights went up. The preview audience were all mannequins!

That's fantastic!

Luckily Fairbanks was his closest friend.

When looking at the character of Chaplin, one must take into account the difficulty of sustaining genius. When people talk about Stanley Kubrick some say he could be a difficult man, but he wasn't world famous like Chaplin, so he didn't have the extra pressures that that brings. When Brando worked for Chaplin on A Countess in Hong Kong he acknowledged Chaplin's genius but said he was a terrible man. He said he found him egotistical and difficult to work with.

But I was on the set of *A Countess From Hong Kong* and I watched Chaplin at work. If you had just filmed Chaplin playing all the parts it would have been perfect. The problem was that he cast actors who couldn't play it as well as he could. Brando is a brilliant actor but it was pointless having him in that role. It was written for an Adolphe Menjou or a Chaplin.

Another great thing about Chaplin is his daringness. Modern Times was a very dangerous film to make in 1935. The Great Dictator was an astonishingly bold film to make in the era of Fascism.

Quite apart from the artistic danger, Trotsky had been killed on the orders of Stalin in the year the film was released. Just before production started, the German-American Bund had kidnapped a publisher in California and were going to kill him. The feeling that these dictators were organising assassinations must have been in his mind. I would not have had the courage to make the film.

And Chaplin was a prime target if a group was looking for publicity. Incredibly, he never lost that sense of danger. The King in New York, completed in 1956, was another daring project. A man who had been thrown out of America made a satire about America.

That was never going to be released in America.

He had been condemned for being political in a country where you are not allowed to be political.

Interestingly, he always said none of my films are political. In *The Immigrant*, when he reaches America, you see the Statue of Liberty in one shot and, in the next, immigration officers rope in the immigrants. He was very worried about that scene. He ran it to his crew and it got by them so he let it go.

The Immigrant shocked me, not for its politics but for its violence. The savage beating in the restaurant of the man who cannot pay his bill stunned me with its violence. It's horrific! And Charlie is sitting there, watching the beating, knowing full well that he cannot pay his own bill. It is a really suspenseful situation. The genius of Chaplin is such that he manages to contrive a stunt in which he is able not only to pay for his meal but to leave a tip!

1
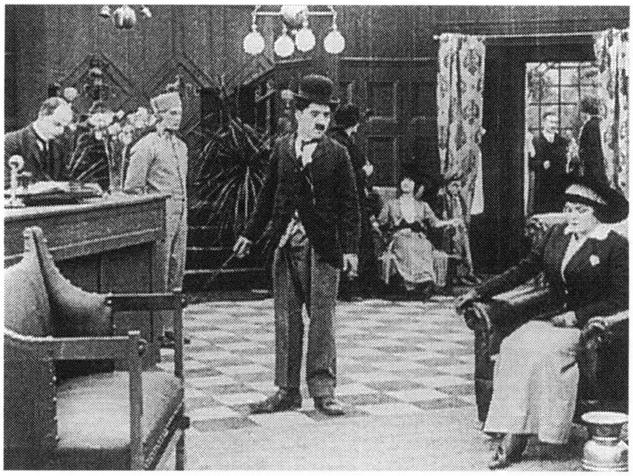

4
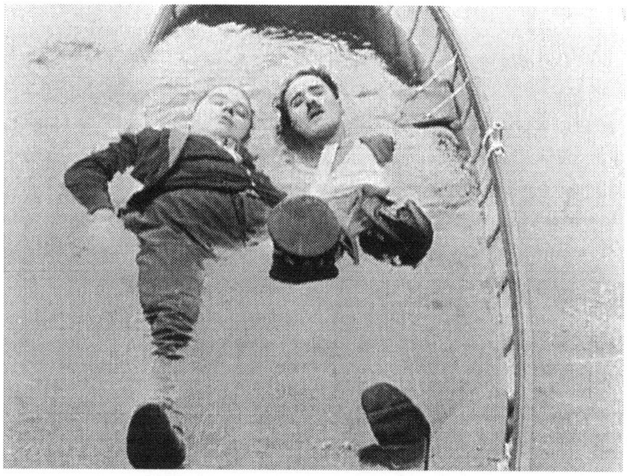

2
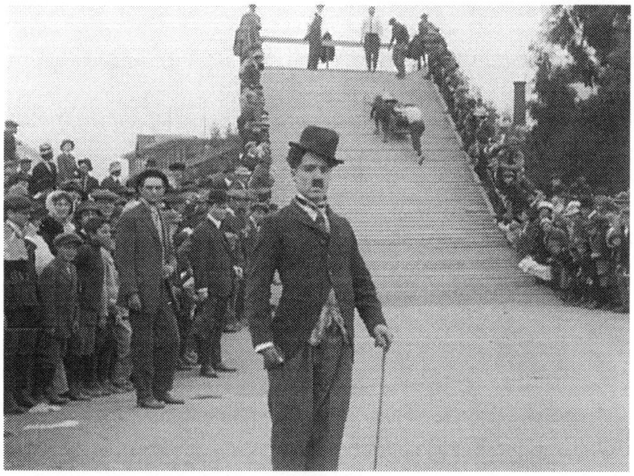

5
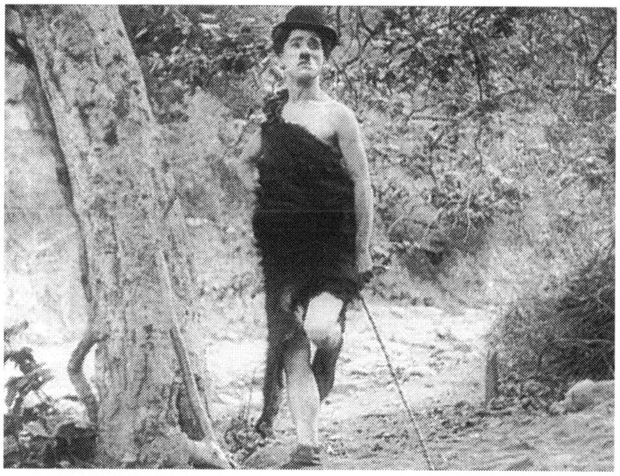

3
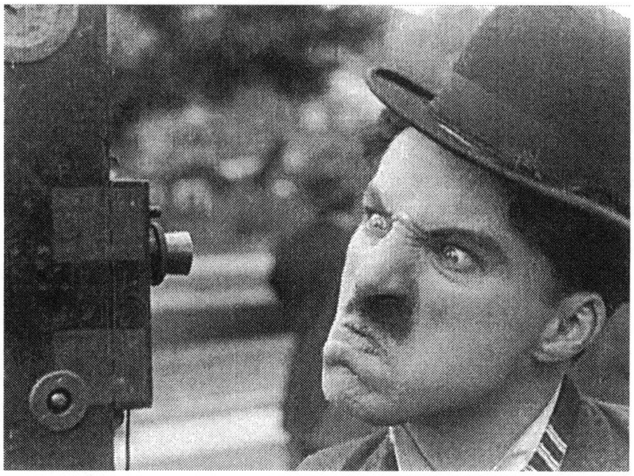

6
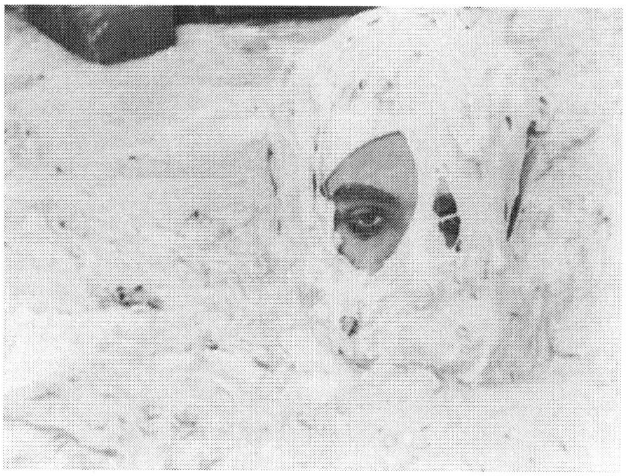

1. Mablel's Strange Predicament
2. Kid Auto Races at Venice, Cal
3. Kid Auto Races at Venice, Cal

4. The Rounders
5. His Prehistoric Past
6. Dough and Dynamite

And when the generous artist finally offers to pay, he refuses! That's so clever. I think he is held at a distance by modern audiences because nobody looks like him anymore, the odd clothes and the ridiculous moustache. They don't understand that that look was quite common at one time for people who were down on their luck and were trying to retain some dignity. That is a drawback, whereas Keaton and Lloyd at least look more or less as one would expect.

No one looks like Keaton!

Dress as one would expect, let's put it that way.

If we are building a portrait of Chaplin we have his boldness and his danger as an artist, which is why he is fundamentally great, to say nothing of his sheer skill as a performer. We haven't really talked about Chaplin as an actor. When sound came in —

He was very brave; the only man who stood out against sound for so long, until he had to talk in *The Great Dictator*.

He did use sound in an earlier film.

Modern Times, but he doesn't talk. He sings.

He sings a nonsense song and it's hilarious and wholly unexpected. Again, he's taking on the new technology and winning on his own terms.

In *City Lights*, when Vitaphone was all the rage, he made the speeches sound as peculiar as Vitaphone often sounded in badly wired cinemas!

Yes, that was terrific. When discussing Chaplin's use of sound we must talk about his speech in The Great Dictator.

Loathed by many people, who say it's a great picture let down by the speech at the end.

I was stunned by it. It was so angry and so forward-looking it was almost H.G. Wellsian. He is putting forth a blueprint for the future. Again one admires his sheer audacity. And to sustain the speech for that length, and at that intensity, from a silent clown, was not what anyone expected.

Yes, that's completely true. And it was 'him'. It was a speech that came not from Hynkel, the character he was playing, not from the barber, it was Chaplin speaking from the heart and saying: "I don't care what you think of it. I have to do it."

The film begins in the trenches.

It picks up where *Shoulder Arms* leaves off.

And Charlie rides an anti-aircraft gun like a bucking bronco.

Yes, it has a sort-of *March of Time* commentary.

And then he takes on The Jewish Question.

Which nobody else was touching in American films. The word 'Jew' was never heard on the American screen.

Was Chaplin Jewish?

No, but the Nazis' thought he was.

In The Tramp and the Dictator you show fascinating colour footage from the set of The Great Dictator. Where did that come from?

Victoria and Christopher Chaplin went to their father's cellar and discovered these suitcases full of yellow boxes of Kodachrome. In one was a larger reel. They took it out, projected it and, would you believe it, put it back again and said nothing. Years later, in France, Christian Delage published a book about the making of *The Great Dictator*. At the launch of that book they revealed that the colour footage existed. Some months after that I was shown the footage and I was too dim to know how to use it. I didn't think it could sustain a complete documentary. The colour footage gave me a dilemma because I'm a passionate advocate for black-and-white, and when you see *The Great Dictator* projected in black-and-white it is so beautifully photographed by Karl Struss that you forget all about the colour. Nonetheless, the colour is fascinating. As is the puzzle of Hitler's moustache and Charlie's moustache. After all these months of research, I still can't work it out. They are incredibly close. Mussolini's chauffeur, who is no longer alive to be interviewed said: "Everyone knew Hitler wore that because it was worn by the best-loved man in the world." But I cannot believe that. If Hitler thought Charlie was Jewish, and he banned his films, what was he doing imitating his moustache?

Did Hitler ban Chaplin's films before The Great Dictator?

Modern Times was banned as Soviet propaganda.

When did Hitler start wearing a moustache?

In the trenches, he had a handle-bar moustache, a droopy walrus moustache and, in 1918, he cut it back to the Chaplin style just as Chaplin was wearing a German uniform in *Shoulder Arms*. It gets very confusing.

In Shoulder Arms he also dresses up as a tree. I laughed from start to finish when I saw it.

Where did you see it?

On video.

Bologna Film Festival just had a showing of it in on the big screen. I didn't think it would work on video.

It did for me. It's an extra on one of those blue-box releases of the feature films. How was The Great Dictator received on its initial release?

Very mixed in The United States, but when it came over here it was manna from heaven. It arrived in the middle of the Blitz and was so successful that if you were in a town with two cinemas both would be running *The Great Dictator*. It was fantastically successful. It made twice as much money as anything he made before.

It made more than The Kid?

Yes, though it was banned from most of Europe.

And how does one follow The Great Dictator?

Exactly. That was the end of The Tramp and the end of that phase of Chaplin. He wanted to make a pacifist comment on World War Two and he chose a very strange way of doing it, one which alienated the Americans completely. Even in the Sixties I was constantly finding veteran Hollywood people who were apoplectic with fury about Chaplin because of *Monsieur Verdoux*.

Astonishing.

Isn't it.

For Verdoux, Chaplin had completely changed his screen persona. He was no longer the Charlie that the world recognised. The grey hair had come in.

Funnily enough the grey hair had come in before *City Lights* and he had to dye it. He went grey very early. He probably went grey because of Lita Grey who gave him a terrible time with the divorce, and then there was Joan Barry.

His taste for very young women contributed to his alienation from the American establishment.

Apparently, in the theatrical circles in which he lived in England, he was taught that if you went for very young girls you were less likely to catch V.D. It's a very real social comment on the era.

I suppose all artists have their quirks and failings. I've only seen Monsieur Verdoux once, or maybe twice, I wasn't terribly impressed with it. I didn't think it was to his normal standard. I was surprised the source was Orson Welles?

Yes, it was. It's a very hard to film to take.

I saw the production sketches at a gallery in Oxford; they were richly full-detailed and atmospheric. They made me think there must be more to the film than I first thought. I need to see it again with my eyes wide open. Evelyn Waugh said something like: "How well we react to 'Monsieur Verdoux' tells us how good we are as human beings."

Did he really?

In a review published in the Evening Standard.

Astonishing.

There's a link with The Great Dictator in that Verdoux is also a murderer.

As an actor in it, Chaplin is brilliant. There's one scene where he plays the piano. There's a knocking which he thinks is from the piano and it's as good a piece of comedy as he has done. It's like the scene at the end of *Limelight* when he loses control of his leg. I watched that a couple of weeks ago with 4,000 people in the great square in Bologna. Hysterical. Yet the great comedy scene with the fleas was greeted with total silence.

Limelight wasn't as much of a risk.

It was an artistic risk.

His music score won him an Oscar twenty-years after its British release. Incredibly, Limelight wasn't screened in an L.A. cinema until 1971! Between the 'double release' of Limelight he made The King in New York, co-starring his little son, Michael. I think the photography is good. It's very sharp and very clear, but I don't think the pacing is quite right. It's too slow.

He rather rejected that picture.

It was the first film he made in England. Was it ever released in America?

I think it was shown eventually, but it was not released in the normal way at all.

You mentioned your visit to the set of his second British film, and his final film, A Countess From Hong Kong. I read your report published in 'Sight and Sound'.

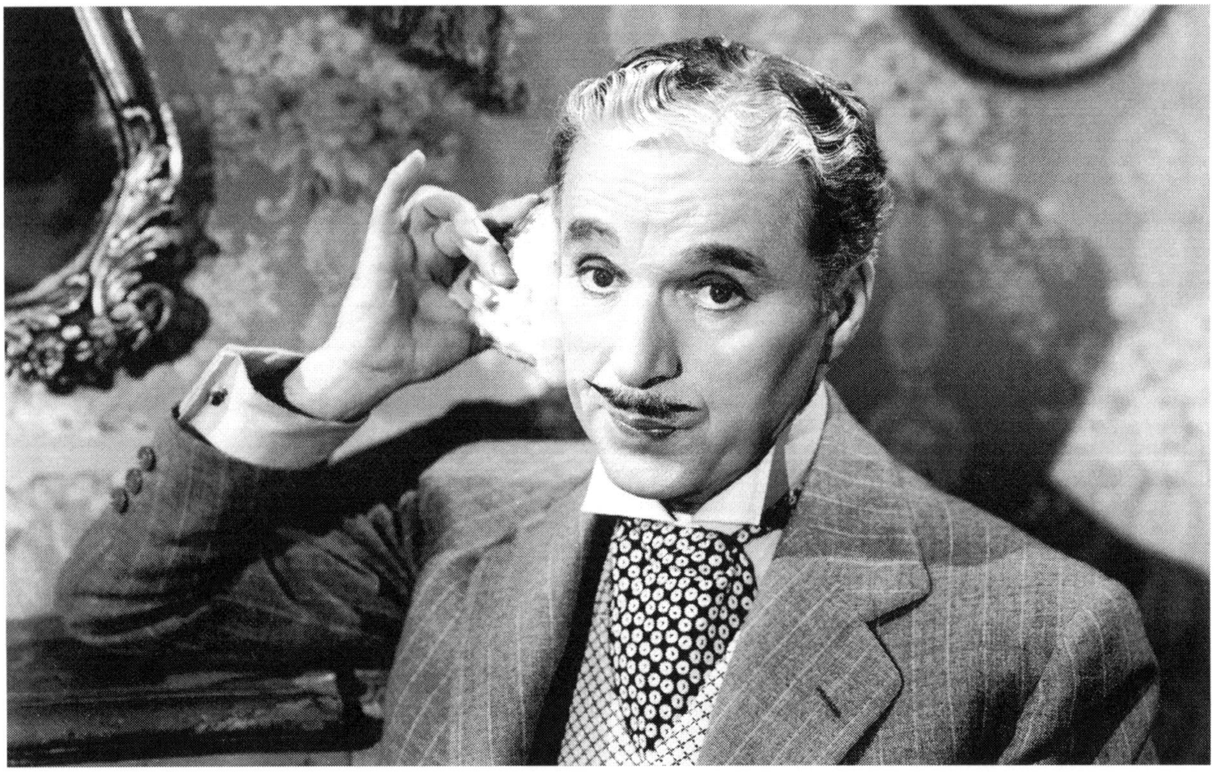

Charlie Chaplin as *Monsieur Verdoux* (1947)

Yes. I went with Gloria Swanson, who had played with him at Essanay in 1915. She thought he was the most creative man you could possibly meet: writer, actor, director, producer, composer.

After which came his Autobiography, which I enjoyed, but it doesn't tell us much about the real Chaplin.

I thought the first third was superb but then there's too much name-dropping. But when you consider he's a boy from the slums meeting royalty and great politicians, it makes sense.

He doesn't talk about his films at all. There are no real insights to his creative processes, which is why your films, The Unknown Chaplin and The Tramp and the Dictator, are so important. They show the process of creation. They let us see how he worked.

He probably wouldn't have wanted that to have been known because his was a pretty wasteful way of working. As a professional that would have worried him a lot.

The endless re-takes; the insecurity.

Yes. Funnily enough, it turns out that when De Mille's first filmed *The Ten Commandments* he was more profligate than Erich Von Stroheim on *Greed!* But no one held it against him because the film made so much money. He said it was not what a film cost that counted but what a film is worth.

Von Stroheim was a genius. I adore all of his film, the nine or ten that I've seen.

He's amazing, and I think he deserves the credit of being the greatest actor of all because he had to act off-screen as well as on. He had to play his role of a European aristocrat. He was a complete phoney, so he had to play that role all the way down the line. And he did it so successfully that Austria and Germany used to send representative to talk to him about military matters. He was never an Austrian officer! He was the son of a Jewish hatter. Fabulous.

He's one of the reasons why Sunset Boulevard is so successful.

I agree. The cameraman, John Seitz told me that Wilder was going to make *The Loved One*, from Waugh's novel, which is why there is all that macabre stuff about the monkey and the funeral, but he couldn't get the rights so he switched the story.

The cinema lost a lot when it lost Billy Wilder.

Cinema lost Billy Wilder long before he died.

Yes, but as long as he was alive there was still a chance of another Billy Wilder film. He had the projects. But he was reduced to spending his last ten years giving interviews.

Or not giving interviews. I tried hard enough.

Did you interview Chaplin? Was he alive when you made your film?

He was alive when we made *Hollywood* [the series for Thames Television in 1980], but not when we made *The Unknown Chaplin*. I laid siege to him once when he was at The Savoy. I was so determined to get through to him that I rang him nineteen times in one day. And I got through! But I was so surprised I didn't know what to say to him! I tried to set up an interview, but he slid out of any commitment. The only man who interviewed him in depth was Richard Meryman, who was given the job of interviewing him for 'Life' magazine at the time *A Countess From Hong Kong* came out. Meryman placed his tape-recorder and microphone over there and Chaplin was way over there sitting by the fire, so the tapes are full of crackling and this distant voice. It's murder to listen to. Chaplin doesn't throw any light on his work in the interview, but there are fantastic things in it, if only one could have gone into them more deeply. For example, Chaplin was fascinated by criminology. He got Winfield Sheehan to take him around the murder sites of the old gangsters in New York.

Now, Winfield Sheehan, an executive producer at Fox, used to be the secretary to Rhinelander Waldo, the police commissioner at the turn of the century and he was a crook. He was getting backhanders from prostitution. Sheehan made it possible for William Fox to make a picture called *Regeneration*, which is one of the early masterpieces by Raoul Walsh, a gangster picture made in 1915 on location in The Bowery. It's the real thing. It is absolutely extraordinary. Anyhow, Chaplin was fascinated by all that and also by The Rosenthal Murder (1912). He describes in the interview how he was taken to meet people who may or may not have been the killers. It was a very famous case in those days. It is fascinating to think that Chaplin was interested in this quintessentially American stuff. I suppose it was because it was happening in the newspapers when he first arrived.

It helps to explain why he made Monsieur Verdoux and, of course, a lot of his films have a cops and crooks theme.

There are many many examples.

One remembers the prison sequence in Modern Times.

Yes! And *The Adventurer*.

I think The Adventurer is the perfect Chaplin film.

How's about *Easy Street*? That's an extraordinary one. He plays a policeman. There are drug addicts. He is very straight about what life was like in the lower depths.

If we were to come up with a scene or scenes that capture the essence of Chaplin, two come quickly to mind: the famous scene in Modern Times where he picks up a red flag that has fallen from a lorry and tries to give it back at the moment a protest march enters the street - the innocent trapped - the political message and the sheer funniness of it are pure Chaplin genius. Also, in City Lights, the scene where he stands in front of a shop window and is looking at a nude.

Yes. I show some of the rehearsal footage for that in *The Unknown Chaplin*.

And he pretends not to be looking at the nude. He films it from an unexpected angle - from inside the shop looking out - so we can see Charlie, and it is framed so that we can see what he is looking at, and, importantly you can see the whole street behind him from which the gag comes forth. He looks at the nude and is a bit embarrassed to be seen looking at it, then he thinks to himself, 'Why should I be embarrassed? I'm an adult man and it's a work of art' and, as he steps back boldly to get a better look, you see the sidewalk elevator opening up behind him! And he sustains the gag. You know what is going to happen but Charlie keeps throwing in the twists and keeps coming up with better gags and stunts. It is perfect. It's inventive throughout. The camera is in exactly the right place (which is the essence of cinema) and there is also the rudeness of it. Chaplin's comedy was often rude.

He was constantly being attacked for vulgarity. In *The Kid* when his hand is wet after holding the baby, he does it again in *The Great Dictator*, that was regarded as absolutely shocking in those days. It's extraordinary how things have changed. That level of puritanism was a drawback if you were seeking middle-class acceptance.

He was rude but he wasn't sexy. Comedians and sex didn't come in until Marilyn Monroe?

No, Clara Bow.

Of course. I haven't seen many Clara Bow films; only a couple of 'It' girl films, which screened at the Broadway in Nottingham last year. She's more 'cutie' than 'sexy' to me though. I guess it's a question of taste.

Constance Talmadge, whom you would have seen in *Intolerance*, in which she is a bit OTT, was, in her normal films, very sexy and very funny. They go back to 1916. And some of the earlier French comedies were very risqué.

Which Chaplin scenes you would show to demonstrate his greatness?

I would run *The Kid*, the whole film, though I showed it to my daughter when she was very small and she was in floods in tears at the plight of poor Jackie Coogan. At the end, I said: "But didn't you find the funny bits amusing?" She said: "What funny bits?"

I love the scene of Jackie Coogan cooking the food like a fast-food pro. It's a beautiful performance, a great piece of direction. I love too the scenes set in a dream-land of heaven where everyone is flying around on angel wings. It's not what you expect.

The heaven scene was much criticised at the time.

It takes the film into a whole new area. I love it.

Of great Chaplin moments, I would certainly include the clock scene from *The Pawnshop* which, ever since I was a kid, has impressed me enormously. An alarm clock is brought in to be repaired. Charlie looks at it and does a complete surgical operation on it using an old-fashioned telephone as a stethoscope. He puts it into his hat and squirts oil on it. He gives it back completely wrecked. But the boxing match in *City Lights* is the finest scene in any Chaplin film from the point of view of getting an audience hysterical.

For an illustration of the Chaplinesque pathos in comedy, the start of City Lights is the perfect example. A blind girl thinks he is a rich man because she has heard him step from a limousine. It's also naughty because he watches her, admiring her beauty, and pretending not to be there. Unwittingly, she throws the flower-water over him, and he tiptoes away. You can almost see the 'thought' process. It's a scene beautifully illustrated in The Unknown Chaplin where we see him refining it and making it better.

The clincher. The other scene which always jumps into my head is the very small moment in the chase in *The Adventurer* where he puts a lampshade on his head and becomes a standard lamp!

Richard Attenborough picked out that one for use in 'Chaplin' (1992). Attenborough's bio-pic wholly fails to convey the genius of Chaplin and the scale of his popularity but, to Attenborough's credit, he ends his film with an extended clip from The Kid that really says 'This Is Charlie Chaplin'. Will Chaplin's pre-eminent reputation last forever? I think it will.

Whenever we do a presentation of a Chaplin film with live music it's always a tremendous success. It sells out and people *love* it.

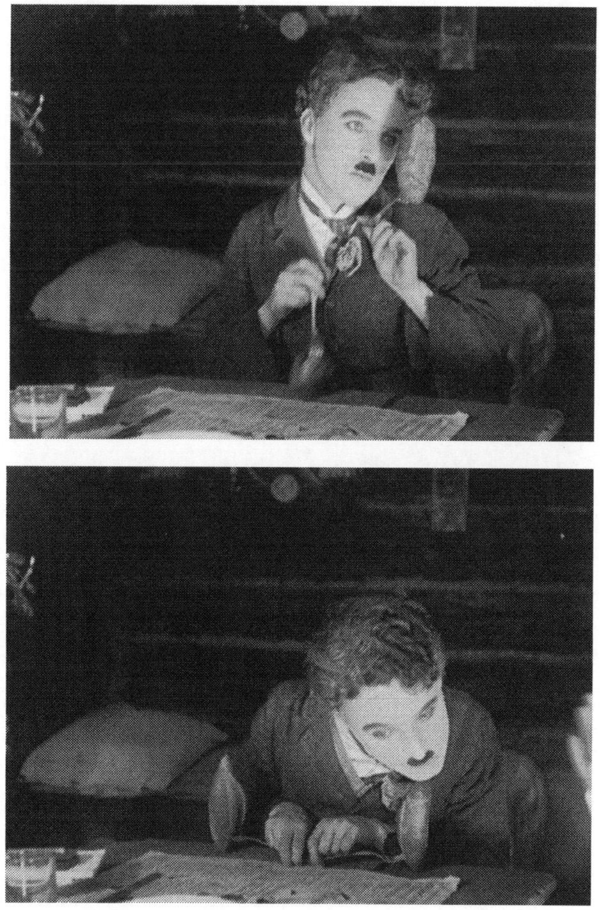

The Dance of the Rolls (*The Gold Rush*)

A Charlie Chaplin film is currently screening somewhere in the world with a live orchestral accompaniment.

For details visit: www.charliechaplin.com

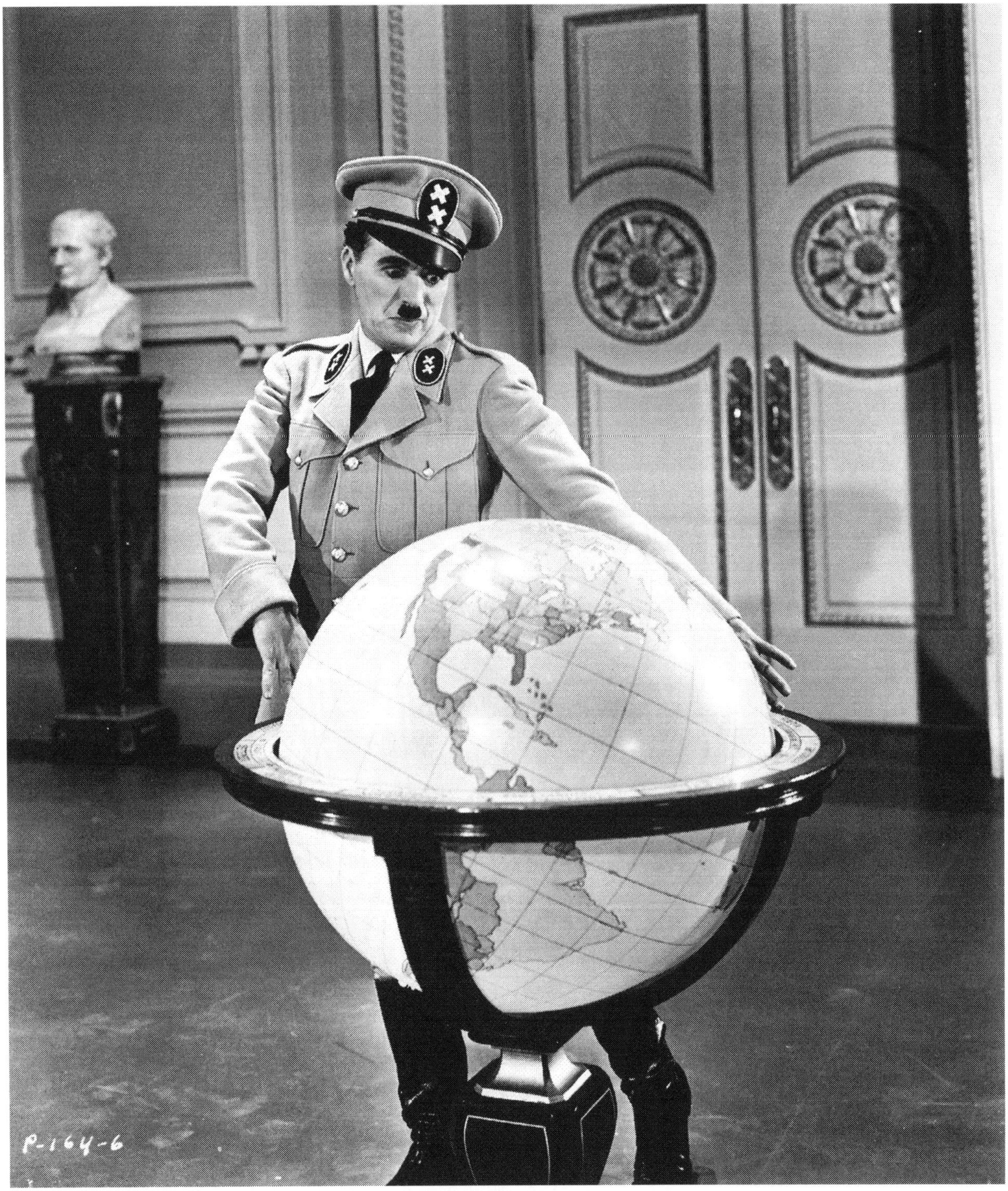

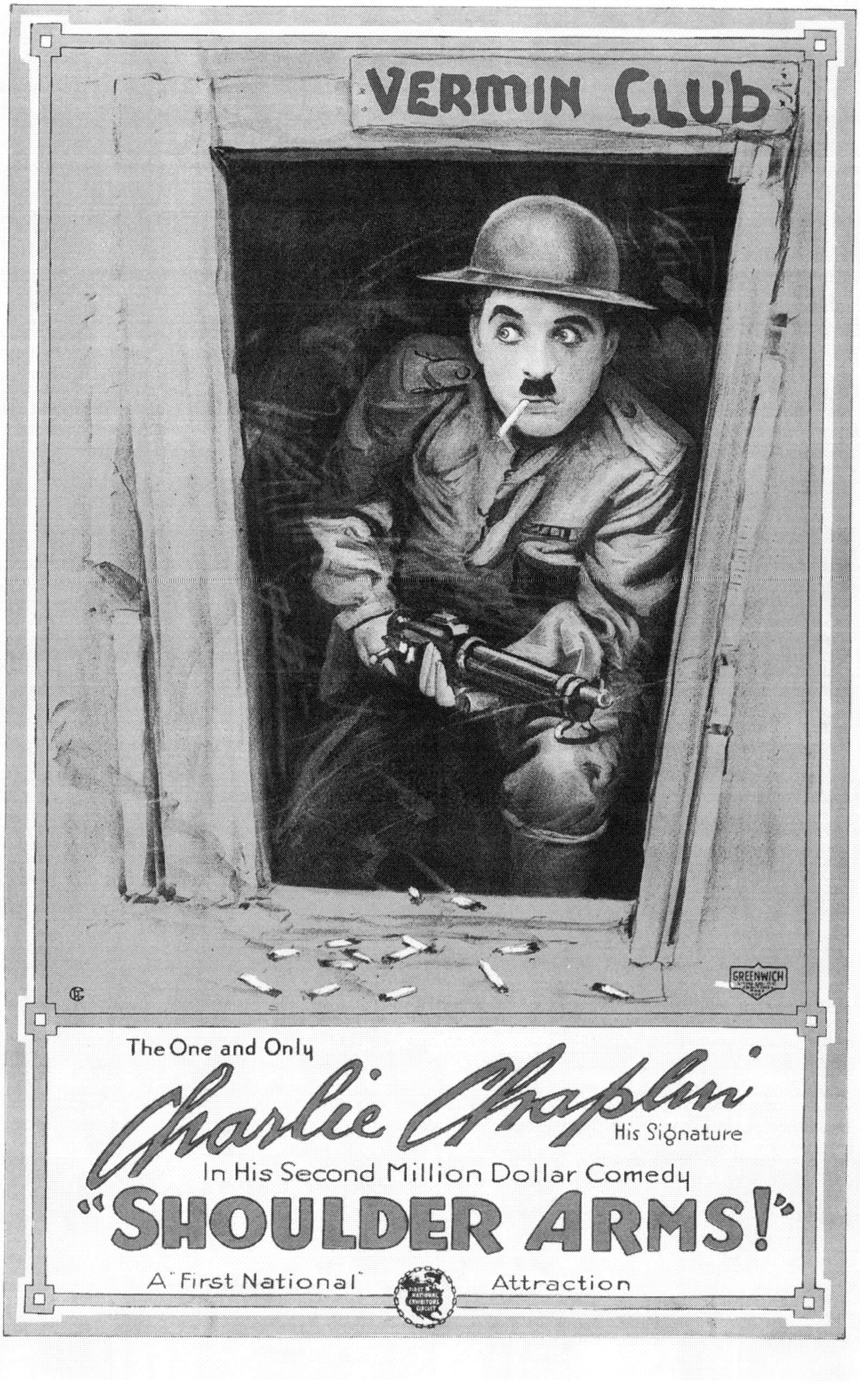
VERMIN CLUB
The One and Only
Charlie Chaplin
His Signature
In His Second Million Dollar Comedy
"SHOULDER ARMS!"
A "First National" Attraction

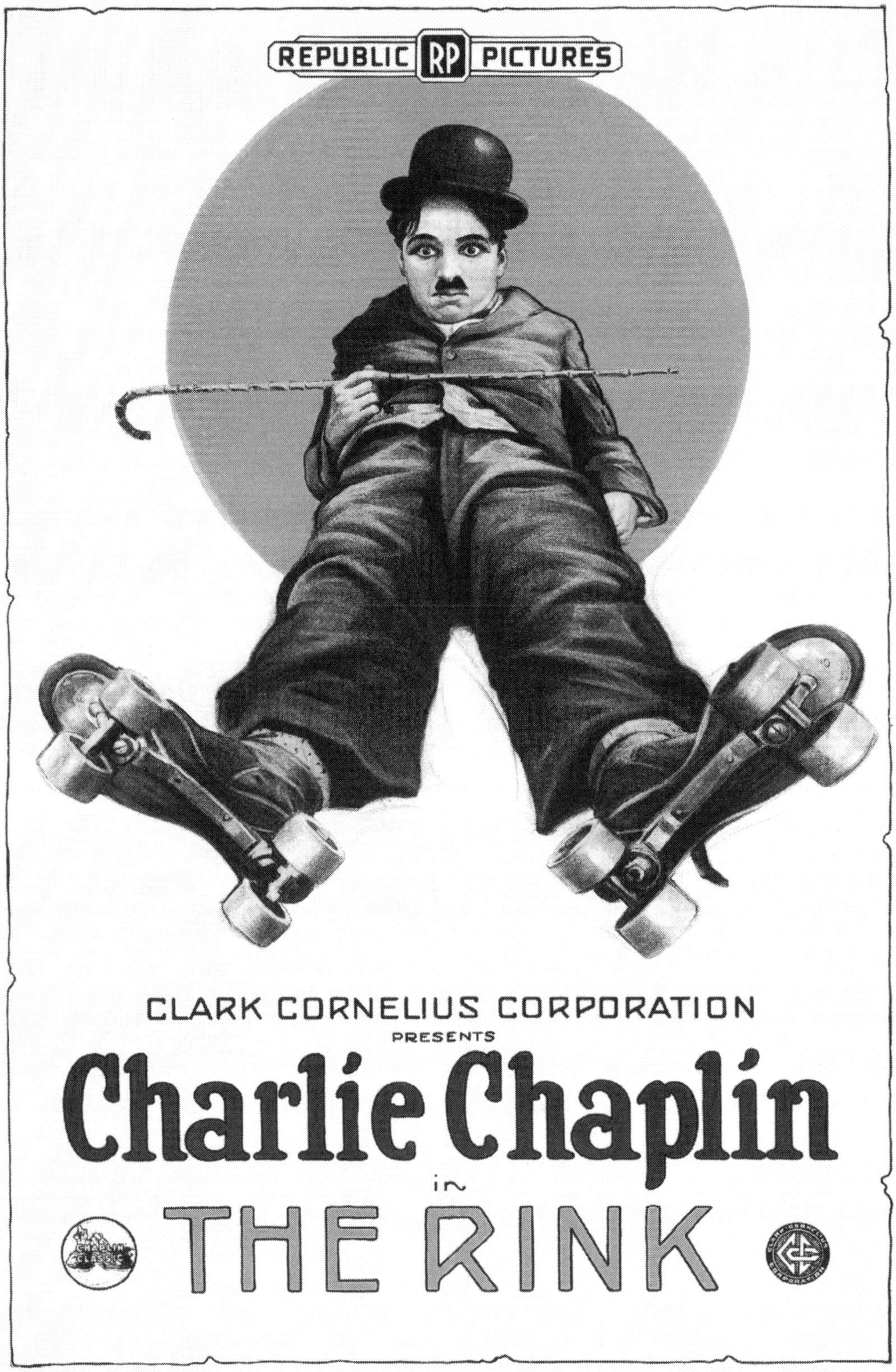
REPUBLIC RP PICTURES
CLARK CORNELIUS CORPORATION
PRESENTS
Charlie Chaplin
in
THE RINK

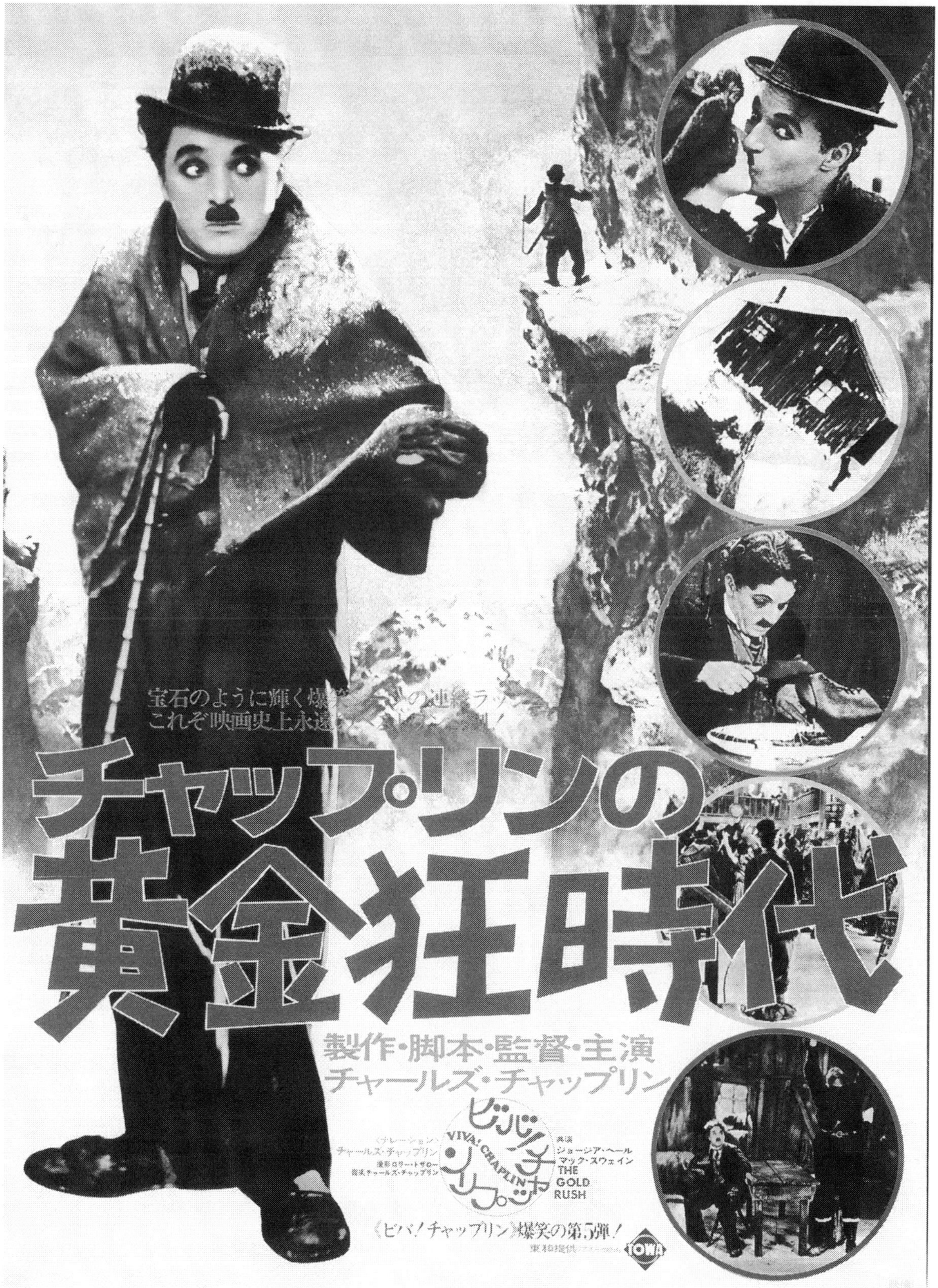

The Gold Rush (Towa, 1974)

Clive Donner

I took this portrait of Clive Donner is his airy and art-filled apartment on the Thames in London. His tastes were sincere and his collection impressive, including Rickard's costume designs for *Alfred The Great* (1969): "She hated signing them. She was so cavalier about her work that her original drawings kept turning up in the Portobello Road". I framed Clive beneath the confident nude which recalled the playful tone of his brightest and most popular films.

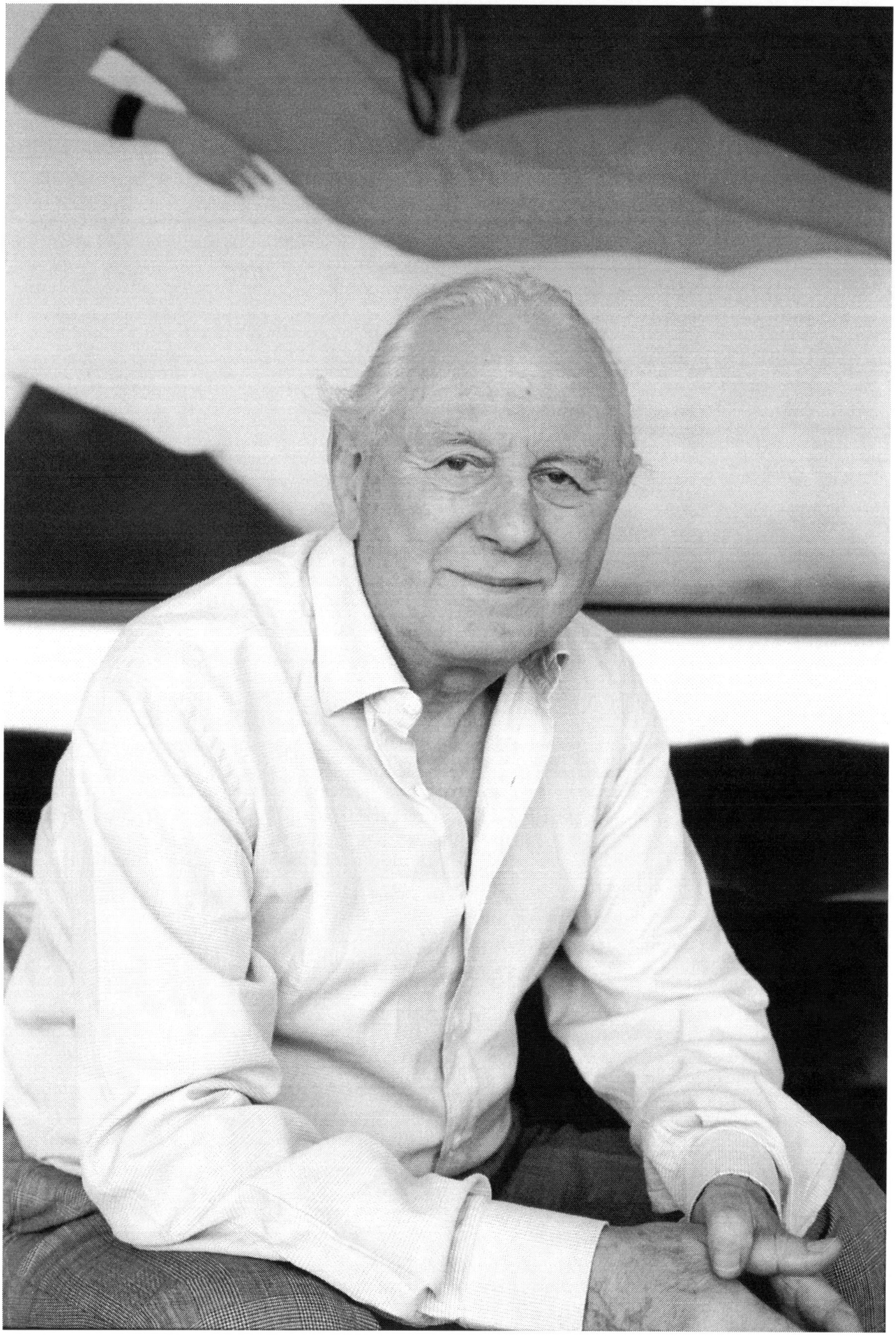

Working from Woody Allen's first screenplay, Clive Donner made the biggest grossing comedy film of the 1960s. He directed the first and best adaptation of a Harold Pinter play, but he never made a masterpiece. He was a craftsman not an artist. He rose from the cutting rooms of Denham and Pinewood, where he worked with David Lean, to direct Woody Allen, Peter O' Toole, Peter Sellers, Jack Lemmon, Michelle Pfeiffer, David Hemmings, Ian McKellen, Terence Stamp, Roddy McDowall, George C. Scott. He married Jocelyn Rickards, the costume designer of Antonioni's *Blow-Up* (1966). I met Clive towards the end of his life. Jocelyn was blind. He was absolutely devoted to her.

I left school at fifteen and was working at Denham studios at sixteen.

Where David Lean made his first masterpieces, Brief Encounter and The Dickens films. Did you work in the cutting rooms with Lean at Denham?

Yes, and also at Pinewood when Denham merged with the Rank studios at Pinewood.

In many ways it was a golden era for British films, but this was the time when Lindsay Anderson was really slagging off British cinema.

Lindsay was full of disdain for The Rank Organisation when I was working there, and he would still be saying the same things. He wouldn't have changed his mind; and indeed he was *right* because the essence of British films at that time, particularly at Pinewood, was to make middle-class films for middle-class audiences. And that was it! Lindsay and I were very good friends. For all those years, when I was working in films and making films, Lindsay was fascinated because he wasn't. It was a long time before he did make a film and it was inevitable that he would get there. I used to talk with him a lot. David Lean was my hero at the time and Lindsay thought he was the absolute pits.

I know he hated Madeleine (1950). You were in the editing room on that? I thought it was pretty good. The sound of distant pipes.

There's a wonderful shot of David's in *Madeleine* where she comes downstairs because her lover is in the sitting room and it's a long shot of her coming down. David did it with such a lens in such a way that the whole of her dress swings up, and it's very erotic. It was very cleverly done. I described the shooting of it to Lindsay. He sighed. He wasn't impressed. When the film came out, he wrote in his review something like: "fancy-playing with lenses isn't filmmaking."

I think what Lindsay objected to, in regard to David Lean, was that Lean was a master filmmaker, with a peerless command of all aspects of filmmaking, but chose, in Lindsay's opinion, to waste his talent making middlebrow party-pieces showcasing his wife. Like yourself, David Lean's first strength was as an editor. Lean's editing certainly made Pygmalion (1938).

It was a good mix of talents. Anthony Asquith was a remarkable man, a drunk filled with self-loathing but a sweet adorable guy and a very good filmmaker. He just had this awful thing of being the son of the Prime Minister (*laughs*). Lean and Asquith *did* work closely together. I was working in one of the projection rooms at Pinewood, waiting for David to come in, and Puffin (Asquith) was there just finishing off what he was doing. And David came in just as he was going out, and David, who was not very sweet, said sweetly: "Hello, *Puff*." (*laughs*)

I like Robert Morley's performance in that. Actually I like Robert Morley in anything.

Curiously, Robert he wasn't really an actor. He was a performer. Even when he was young, because of his shape and his size, he played pompous characters and very successfully. It almost looked as though he wasn't acting. The man and the part seemed to be the same, but it was much more subtle than that.

I suppose, apart from the product, one of Lindsay Anderson's reasons for hating Pinewood was that it operated a 'closed shop'.

Pinewood at that time was ... if you were 'in', and you had to 'in' in various ways, certainly the Freemasons was one way, the art department, there were a whole lot of stuff that I thought was despicable and I had nothing to do with. And I was much disliked for having nothing to do with it. But I was protected by the fact that I knew David Lean and Ronnie Neame and Anthony Havelock-Allan. I worked for them on very successful pictures and so became part of the Pinewood establishment without joining up with all of those gangs.

Your first solo credit was the editor of a non-David Lean Dickens, Scrooge (1951), directed by Brian Desmond Hurst, starring the great Alastair Sim, and acknowledged to be one of the finest films of the 1950s.

Oh, really?

In many countries it's a staple of Christmas broadcasting. Unfortunately, last Christmas, it played here on Channel 5 in a copy of a colorized NTSC tape that ghosted and all the blacks looked grey.

Oh dear. Maddening. Maddening.

Did you know you were making a classic?

Of course not. I had been working as a first assistant in the cutting rooms for a picture by Brian Desmond Hurst. The man who was meant to be editing the film had been a sound editor and wasn't really interested in editing *Scrooge* so off he went and I had the opportunity to take over. That was marvellous. It was made quite quickly by a distributor, George

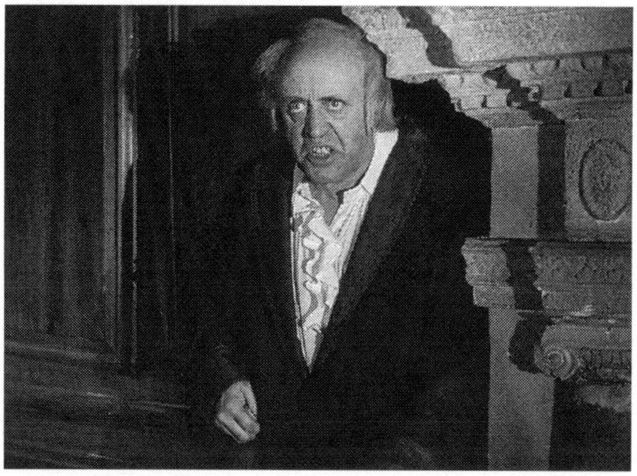

Minter, who usually made pictures like *Old Mother Riley*, but he had also made *Tom Brown Schooldays*.

A terrific film.

Yes. The company didn't cut corners but the corners were tight. We had a very good cast, an unusual cast actually, Mervyn Johns, Kathleen Harrison, Michael Hordern.

Your next major triumph was Genevieve (1953), the biggest box-office hit of its year.

Indeed. There were a lot of films in between.

Fill in the gaps.

There was *The Card*, the Alec Guinness picture.

Directed by Ronald Neame.

That's right. Then I did *Meet Me Tonight* (1952), a weird little film. When Rank made *Brief Encounter*, they got the rights to the nine plays by Noel Coward published as *Tonight at 8.30*, which he wrote for himself and Gertrude Lawrence, and they started making them into films. One of the ideas was to take three plays and turn that into a three-hander.

The portmanteau film, Dead of Night (1945) had been a big hit.

Yes, that's right. That was the thinking behind it.

Was Meet Me Tonight successful?

I don't think so. I don't think it was very good, though I have a great admiration for Anthony Pelissier, the man who directed it. A *curious* chap. He was a protégé of Noel Coward's. His mother was Fay Compton, so he was deep in the whole Coward world and he really knew the material. The best play of the group is *The Red Peppers,* in which Kay Walsh and Ted Ray play a pair of second-rate musical comedians who are squabbling all the time. I like it. It's got something interesting things in it, in terms of the performances, the attitude to film, in the way Anthony handled it. One of the other ones was *The Perfumed Oak,* which every amateur dramatic society in the world has done. We did that with Stanley Holloway, who was very good.

You said Rank films were strictly for the middle-class market. Didn't they have an eye on the export market?

They tried to make a go in America but it didn't work.

How did Genevieve do internationally?

Huge!

It has a German director/producer and an American writer, William Rose, but it's so wonderfully British. How did the job come about?

Where someone comes from has never been a factor for me. I don't go in for any of that. Henry Cornelius had been very successful as a director at Ealing and decided he didn't really want to be under the yoke of Mick Balcon, which was a benevolent yoke but a yoke nonetheless. So he went solo and made *The Galloping Major.* Then he did *Genevieve* at Pinewood. He was both the director and the producer. I went to see him. He said: "This script. Go through it and tell me how much you think we *don't* need to shoot." I did. Then he said: "I'd like to see something you have edited." I showed him some of *Meet Me Tonight.* He said: "I like the way you edit it." And that was it. We started shooting a few weeks later. Cornie was a very very gifted man. He was born in Berlin and brought up in South Africa. He studied with Max Reinhardt in the theatre and, in the thirties, went to work in the movies in France with René Clair. When he saw what was happening in Europe he came to London and worked for Korda as an editor. He edited a lot of Korda's top productions, including *The Four Feathers* (1939). He was a very independent-minded man.

Was Genevieve shot in such a way as to make it easy to assemble?

I had lots of arguments editing the film. Cornie had absolutely no interest in the technology of filmmaking. He felt he didn't understand it, or that he wasn't very good at it, neither of which is true. He'd say: "Let's do this and let's do that."
And I'd say: "You can't do that." "Why not?"
"Because it just won't work."
"What I *want* to do *does* work."
And he was nearly always right.
Rank wanted us to make the film using back-projection. I told Cornie: "Don't! Have nothing to do with it. This is *not* a film for back-projection!"
He said: "Fine, let's shoot it on location."
Michael Stringer, the production designer, came up with the idea of putting a car on a low-loader so we could then track everywhere. And so we'd go bowling off down the lanes with the car on the back of a lorry. The cameraman was Chris Challis, very distinguished. Cornie was forever doing things that you shouldn't do. Chris would look at his light metre and say: "We can't! Here's the metre. The needles at zero!" Cornie would say: "Shoot it. It doesn't matter." When we turned over [started the camera], Chris turned his back. He couldn't bare to watch what was going on. When I put the picture together, Cornie came to see it and he said: "I think I must be getting old." (He was only forty). I couldn't have got it together as quickly as that." And we virtually didn't touch it. Inevitably one does make changes but, basically, the first cut was it. When we showed it to the Rank Organisation they loathed it. Earl St John, the head of the studio, wanted to cut it down and release it as second feature! Earl was an

American, a great big man. His claim to fame was that he had organised the first Wild West Show down Regent's Street.

That's quite a claim to fame!

It is indeed! But it doesn't help you to be the head of a studio! He didn't at first like *Genevieve* but, because Henry Cornelius was also the producer, the studio could do nothing but to go with it. We had a sneak preview at a big cinema in Camden Town. From the moment it started, the audience loved it. Earl, sitting next to me, grabbed my arm and said: "Listen to them, kid. They're laughing! They're laughing!" And it was a huge success worldwide, and remains so. It came out in 1953, the year of the Queen's Coronation. On the 50th anniversary, a huge London-to-Brighton vintage car rally was organised and I was asked to go along and say a few words but I couldn't go. I wrote something which Cornie's widow read out. The film's popularity goes on and on.

I think a part of its appeal are the locations. You were right in refusing to use back-projection.

You couldn't have done it any other way. In a way the film *was* breaking new ground. It was showing middle-class people behaving as they really do and not the way, generally speaking, actors had portrayed them in the movies.

What always makes me laugh is the way the men scream with laughter at each other's misfortune.

That's right. Cornie and I became close friends. I edited his next picture, *I Am a Camera*, starring Julie Harris and Laurence Harvey, which was...

Awful. Too much of the film was in the studio; massive sets, full-size streets and full-size cars.

I know. Fake cars and fake trains. Cornie wasn't comfortable with it, I think, because the story was set in Berlin. Cornie was uneasy about Berlin. I bought the record of Kurt Weill's *The Threepenny Opera*. I said: "Hey, Cornie, let me play you this!" And I put it on and he told me to take it off: "I don't want to hear it."

The first film you directed, The Secret Place (1956), had East End teenagers and diamond thieves. How did the opportunity to direct come about?

An organisation called Group Three was set up, I think by the government, with the aim encouraging young filmmakers. They worked at Beaconsfield and they made some quite interesting pictures. Because I'd edited quite a few films at Pinewood, and they were successful, I was very much in demand. Group Three got in touch and said: "We think some day you'll be a producer." And I said: "Yes, I think so too." We talked and agreed to stay in touch. I'd just finished editing a film for John Bryan called *The Purple Plain* (1954), starring Gregory Peck. I'd edited three films for John and he wanted me do his next picture, a Dirk Bogarde film about a small boy.

The Spanish Gardener, a lovely film.

Yes, it's a charming film. It has great charm and a lot of subtlety, but I said to John: "Thanks very much but Group Three want me to direct." John said: "Don't do anything. Let's see what I can organise here." At that time, John Davies, of the Rank Organization, was trying to expand into America, and he wanted to increase production at Pinewood. Four of us were elevated from the ranks: David Deutsch, a great friend, became a producer; John Hawksworth, an art director, was also made a producer, he later made *Upstairs Downstairs*; Anthony Perry, from the story department, was made an associate producer; and I became a director. They put Anthony and me in an office together and told us to 'find a movie to make'. It took me a long time because the kind of films I wanted to make were not the kind of films that Rank wanted to make. After a lot of unsuccessful attempts to find the right project, Anthony told me his wife had written something I might like. I read it and said: "This is what I want to do." It was *The Secret Place*.

Basically it is a story of youth finding its ideals shattered. The war had ended years ago but the war was really still with us. In London it existed very strongly. The bomb sites still existed. First and foremost I wanted to make a film that was entertaining, one that held the audience's attention, but I wanted also to make a film that didn't play down to the audience.

The Monthly Film Bulletin wrote: "Gains strongly over the average British crime thriller in its concern to establish a realistic background and setting."

Absolutely, but quite a lot of it was shot in the studio. The locations were in Bethnal Green. The studio went crazy. John Davies said: "*Why* do you want to shoot it in Bethnal Green? It's a terrible part of the world. Why can't you do it somewhere more agreeable, like Streatham?" Unbelievable! But John Bryan, the producer, was supportive and we did it our own way.

Ealing gave themselves a big boost by filming Hue and Cry on location on East End bomb sites. Was that an inspiration to you?

It was an inspiration in the sense that the 'sets' were there. One didn't have to go out and build a bomb site. They existed. All I was saying was let's use it. People live there.

Among the rubble. Rather like a Rossellini film?

There was certainly something of that in it. The principal character was a girl. I tested endless girls and I found one who was absolutely marvellous, an East End girl who had just come out of RADA. She was sexy and she was beautiful and she could act. John Davies saw the tests and said: "Yes, she's very good but I can't take her." I asked: "Why?" He said: "I've got nothing else to put her in. Your film is a one off. I don't have any more films for a cockney girl." I told him: "She doesn't have to play cockney, she can play with a standard English accent." We did more tests but he wasn't having it and I lost out. Of course, all the way along the line, waiting for me in the wings, was a girl called Belinda Lee, one of the kids from the Rank Charm School, sexy, from a well-to-do middle-upper class family in Budleigh Salterton, way down there in the West Country, and very innocent in a way. I more or less had to accept her. I looked upon it as a challenge. It was *tough* to begin with but it worked. She had marvellous on-screen presence and she learnt as we went along and she really did very well. Have you seen the film?

I haven't seen The Secret Place but I have seen Belinda Lee on the screen. She's a real beauty.

She was married to Cornel Lucas, the in-house photographer at Rank. She married him just before we started shooting. Belinda hadn't played any major roles, but she was playing Shakespeare's Rosalind in Regent's Park and I went along to see what she could do. I was really rather impressed. She had tremendous stage presence. She was such a beauty. It was packed with school kids and somehow or other she brought them in, she held their attention, which I thought was 'helpful'. She said the thing she enjoyed most was that the kids would come along with their books to follow the play: "I kept making jumps and cuts and they'd all be changing places trying to find out where they should be." She had a kind of, she wasn't a Rachel Roberts by any means, but she had a gentleness in her quirkiness. She had absolutely no idea about her beauty. None. One day, we were talking and I put my hand on her back. I said: "Belinda, what's this?"
"It's my waspie."
"What's your waspie?"
Apparently, at that time, all the girls were wearing these very tight bras, not really bras but corsets, that they were tied up in.
I said: "Belinda, you're a young healthy girl with a great body, you don't need that."
"I couldn't possibly appear without my waspie on."
I said: "I think you should think about it."
A little while later, we were doing the scene where her boyfriend takes her to a swanky apartment. If the heist that they are planning comes off she's going to be transported away from Bethnal Green to live

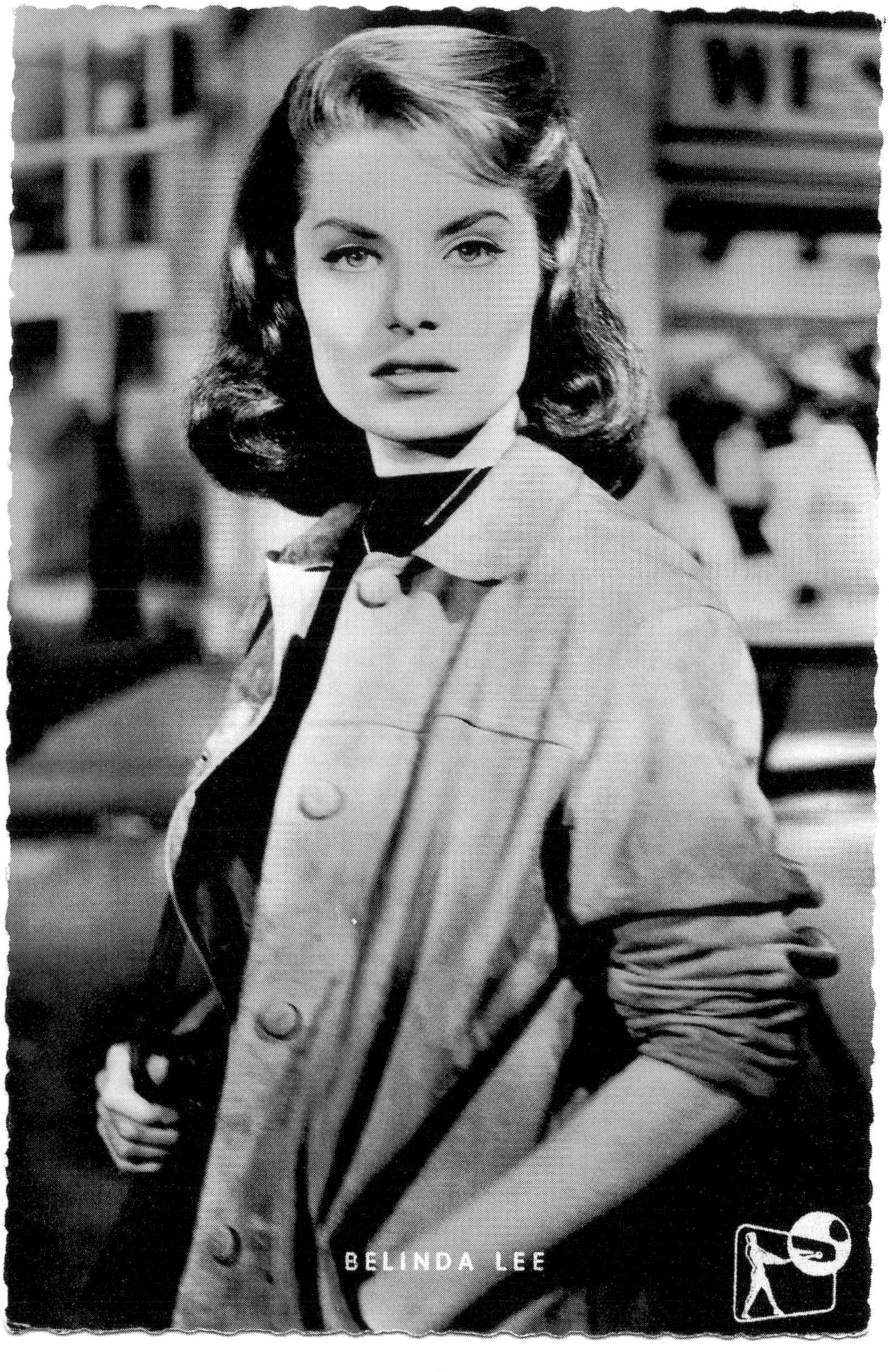
BELINDA LEE

in what to her would be paradise. Beautifully shot. Just before we started shooting, she said to me: "Do you notice anything different? I'm not wearing my waspie." For her that was a huge jump from the stifling rich background towards something she hadn't even thought about when she went to RADA.

She had a continental film career. She worked with Francesco Rosi, Marcello Mastroianni...

She had terrible bad luck. After making *Secret Place* she did quite a few films for Rank, such as *Miracle in Soho*, God, a terrible film, and then she was doing a film, I think, in South Africa, [*Nor the Moon by Night*] with Michael Craig, when she fell in love with a Vatican prince. He wasn't a prince but he was aristocracy. They had a rip-roaring affair that was all over the papers. John Davies and The Rank Organisation were furious. She was convinced he would leave his wife and children and go off with her. Well, of course he wasn't. And didn't. And her heart was broken. I'm not sure if she was fired from Rank or if she quit. She started getting parts in Europe and was doing well. The films weren't always very good but because she was so marvellous to look at, and people on the continent recognised it and didn't have the uptight neurotic British thing at all regarding sex, she was being talked about and noticed. She went to Hollywood, where she was seeing all the right people, and they were interested in her. It looked as though something was about to happen and, one night, she went out and was in a car crash and was killed.

An Italian professor got in touch and is writing a book about Belinda Lee. He's absolutely passionate about her. And because of him, the National Film Theatre did a season of Belinda Lee films.

I've got a postcard of her, a promo piece from your film [hands the postcard to Mr. Donner].

Beautiful. Use that as an illustration. The stills you've used in the one book of your that I've seen [Camera Journal 2] are *wonderful*. That stuff with Malcolm [McDowell] is *sensational*.

I shop for them. All handpicked. I've managed to buy some colour slides from MGM for What's New Pussycat? Your second film was Heart of a Child, a boy and his dog story set in the Austrian Tyrol. The boy runs away with the dog because his brutal father is going to sell it to a butcher. The boy is beaten to within an inch of his life for selling it to a vet, and has to get the dog back because he thinks the vet will pass it onto the English who eat dogs!

That's right.

What inspired that? A desire for a holiday in the Alps?

No, not at all! *The Secret Place* was very successful but it wasn't what John Davies wanted to do. The story department kept sending me things. I kept reading them but I didn't like anything. One day they sent a script and they said: "We don't like this but you might." I read it and said: "I'll do it!" But Joyce Grenfell, who was head of the story department, said: "I'm terribly sorry, Clive, but John Davies has now read it and he says that under no circumstances will the Rank Organisation do this film, nor will they show it on the Rank circuits. It was *Room at the Top* (*laughs*) I was getting really very cheesed off. I went away on holiday. They rang up and said: "You're good with kids. [Child actor, Michael Brooke had got good notices for *The Secret Place*] We've got a film for you." I was under contract. I was in the Bette Davis situation.

Were you as monstrous as Bette Davis?

I would like to think so (*laughs*). I would like to think that she and I have something in common. And that's how *Heart of a Child* came about. The Head of Production at that time was Sydney Box, an old rogue, but I rather like old rogues. I like people who are prepared to do things other ways. Sydney played absolutely by the rules but he bent them all over the place. He and Betty Box were making the films that John Davies wanted middle-brow films, easy listening, easy looking. We made the film. It wasn't a very happy experience.

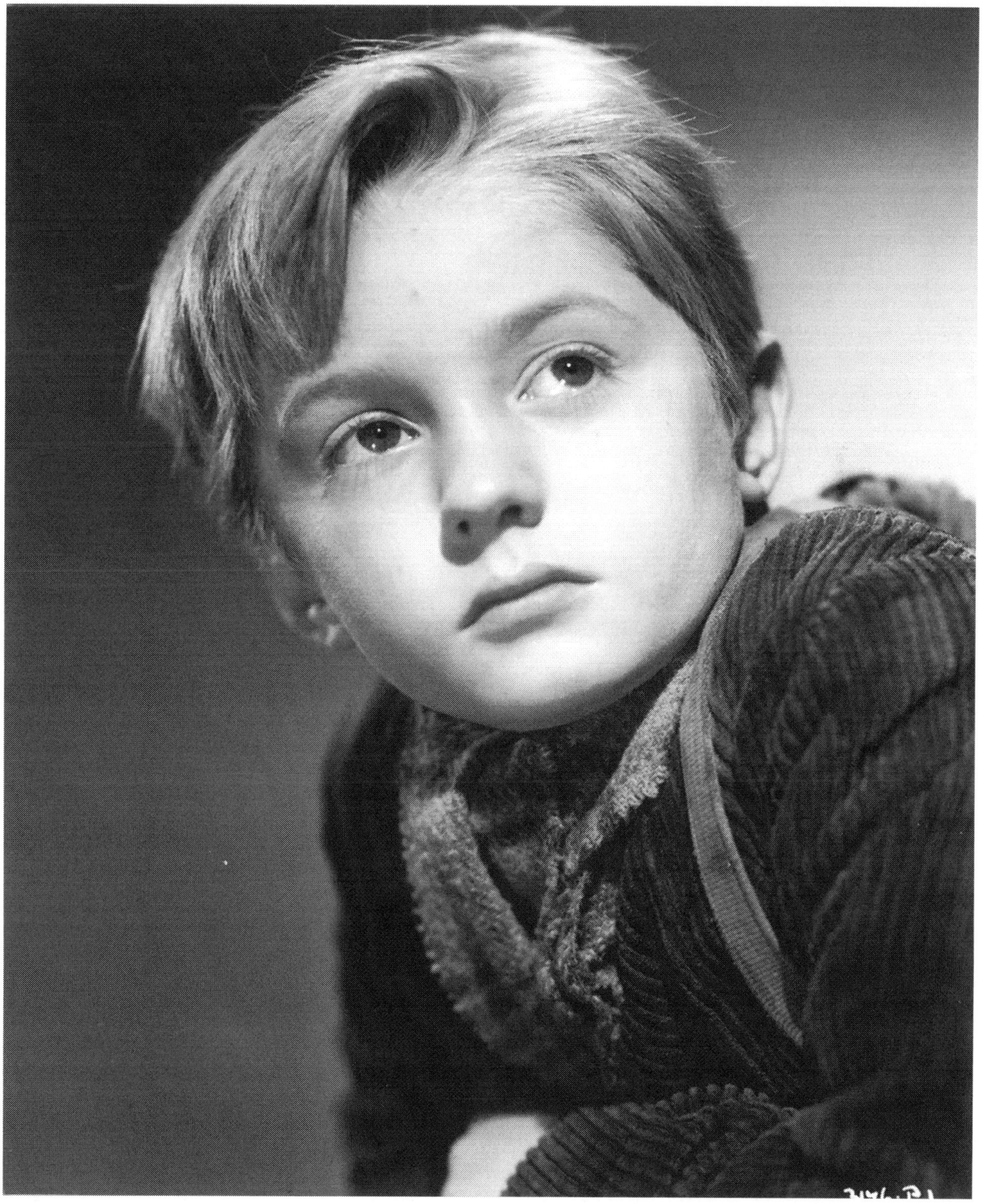

Richard Williams in *Heart of a Child* © Rank/ John Holmstrom Collection

The film wasn't widely admired. Part of that must be critics' aversion to boys and dogs. The boy is called Richard Williams. No relation to the famous animator who worked for you on What's New Pussycat?

Dick Williams? No, no, no.

Was the boy part of the package or did he come up through an audition?

God. I saw *endless* boys, *endless* little beasts. He was good actually. He was a good kid.

Next up were several Edgar Wallace second features, hour-long dramas [now available on DVD]. Every bookshop in Germany has an Edgar Wallace section.

After *Heart of a Child*, John Davies' plans for the studio fell down and everybody was given the sack, including my good friend, David Deutsch. David's father was Oscar Deutsch, who built the Odeon cinema chain. The Odeon Leicester Square, it is Oscar Deutsch. Therefore, in a funny kind of way, David was a Prince of Wardour Street but he was a regular guy, a very good chap. We were all out of work. A lot of us got jobs making commercials so we were able to survive. David got a job working for Nat Cohen and Stuart Levy at Anglo-Amalgamated. They made very successful low-budget films, including the *Carry On* series made by Gerald Thomas, a very good friend. We both came out the army at the same time, and we had cutting rooms next door to each other. We were both mad about car racing when it first started here at Silverstone. Gerry was a very good driver and I was very good at navigating. We used to do a lot of rallies. We used to have great fun. His elder brother was Ralph Thomas, who was unspeakably boring! (*laughs*). Ralph *desperately* wanted to be an important director but never made it. And Gerry, the younger brother, a great big fat man, came into my cutting room one day and said: "I'm having a terrible time with this sequence. I need a close-up of Kay Kendall looking right. Have you got one?" I was doing *Genevieve*. "I'll have a look for you."

We tried it out but it didn't work. We thought it would be fun to swap shots. Gerry then made *Carry On Sergeant* (1958). He said: "I think you'll like it." He went on to be *the* comedy filmmaker of this country.

I'm not a big fan of the The Carry Ons but they did provide a financial backbone for the industry.

Yes, absolutely. It is very easy to sneer, but there *are* some funny jokes in them.

And they are well-photographed.

Yes, it was the best that Pinewood could offer, technically *always* impeccable. Gerry loved doing them, slogging away in the cutting rooms next to me. I was right in the midst of doing what was actually fairly important work for me and he was slogging away at one of his *Carry Ons*. I never thought he had a funny bone in his body. And I'll deny saying this if ever questioned, but it was 'The Gang' that made them work. I said: "Don't worry, Gerry. I promise you, you'll get a season at the National Film Theatre before I do, and he did! (*laughs*).

We wouldn't have had the Carry Ons, and that financial backbone, without Nat Cohen and Stuart Levy.

Nat and Stuart were extraordinary. Absolutely archetypal West End Jewish businessmen. I don't know how they started but they did very very well, and they were honourable men. They wanted to make more interesting, more important films, and because they were gamblers they were prepared to gamble, to back some hunches. David said to me: "Do a few of these Edgar Wallace's because if Nat sees that you can handle it, then we can get onto something else." I did three I think. Nat's horse won the Derby when we filming. I had to stop filming because the crew had all had a flutter and couldn't concentrate on anything but the race. They helped a lot of us indeed. Subsequently, they gave John Boorman his first chance with *Catch Us If You Can*. John's a great guy, a very good director, a very talented filmmaker.

John Schlesinger made *Far From The Madding Crowd* for them. A wonderful film.

Photographed by Nic Roeg.

Yes. I taught him all he knew (*laughs*).

Nic would hate me for saying this because he has made five truly outstanding films, but I'm not sure that his greatest contribution to the cinema isn't the work he did as cinematographer. Much of his cinematography was sublime.

Absolutely. And he *would* hate you for saying that!

David Lean spotted his talent and hired him to do the second-unit for Lawrence and the principal photography for Zhivago but the two men didn't get on.

Nic and David weren't made for each other at all. The first time Nic and I worked together was on a commercial. He was the camera operator.

In 1962, you made a television film about Sir Francis Drake, which featured Jean Kent as Elizabeth I, and which starred Michael Crawford.

It was a Lew Grade production. I did two for him. I did that and *Danger Man*. The thing about Lew is the orders come down from on high but the work is good. Then I made a film called *Some People*, produced by Michael Birkett, whom I'd also met when I was making commercials. He was a first assistant. We'd done a lot of commercials together and we became close friends. *Some People* came about through Gerald Thompson, the advertising agency, who had been approached by The Duke of Edinburgh Award scheme to make a documentary. They said to me: "You've done a lot of work with kids." I was asked to meet a man called Bill Heels, Colonel Heels, the guy in charge. He was enchanting, an old army man who had been a monk. I told him I was a bit wary of all that Kurt Hahn stuff.

Muscular Christianity in the great outdoors.

He said: "Let's go round the country. We'll see what the audience we are looking for are like." We spent two or three weeks going all round the country. It was a wonderful time. I saw kids on all levels, from public schools right down to sink schools. We went to police colleges and clubs for un-clubables, amazing stuff. At the end of it, Bill and I talked and I said: "The kids who go to see documentaries in schools or at the YMCA or at the Church Hall are not the kids we are hoping to attract. To catch the kids who have fallen through the net, we should make a feature." They accepted the proposal and we made the picture and it was a big smash.

With Kenneth More and David Hemmings.

Hemmings was one of the kids, yes. I'm not sure when he started acting, he'd been a famous child singer, of course, but he'd been doing it for ages. He was very proficient, very good. I remember he did this children's thing for the BBC at the end of which the credits were wound up by somebody. David was standing by the guy doing the winding and, as it came to his name, he put his finger on it and was fired on the spot! He was fired from doing anything again for the BBC! He's a rum lad. He had every kind of gift, a singer, painter, poet. He started the production company, Hemdale. David was extraordinary. He had extraordinary energy as well. His trouble was he got bored very quickly.

Did the finance come from the D of E scheme?

No, it came from Nat Cohen. Nat was clearly looking for a gong (*laughs*).

You worked with Michael Birkett again on the film of Pinter's The Caretaker, financed by the great and the good, including Noel Coward.

Robert Shaw was a great friend of Noel's ... I think it was something to do with Jamaica and an ex-wife of Robert's. The film came about because Donald Pleasence was in *Heart of a Child*. That's where we met and became friends. We wanted to work together again. I saw *The Caretaker* on the first night. He asked: "Do you think *The Caretaker* would make a film?" I told him I thought it would. He said: "I'm off to America to play it there. Come on over and we'll see what we can do." We knew that the first thing we had to do was to talk to Harold [Pinter]. I told him I wanted Michael to produce it. Harold and Michael and I met and agreed to work together. It was the beginning of an absolutely impeccable friendship and work situation. None of us took any money except that we all owned a bit of the film. There was absolutely no problems at all. When we couldn't get the finance, Michael said: "We've all got friends who have got a lot of money. And some of them have said to us, if you need any help we would be happy to. If none of us takes any money upfront I think I can knock the budget down to £30,000. We can do it for that and still be able to pay the crew properly." And that is what we did. Michael went round and we were oversubscribed like that (*clicks fingers*). It was amazing. Of course, the circumstances under which we made it were impeccable. The people who we had working on it were first rate: Nic (Roeg) -

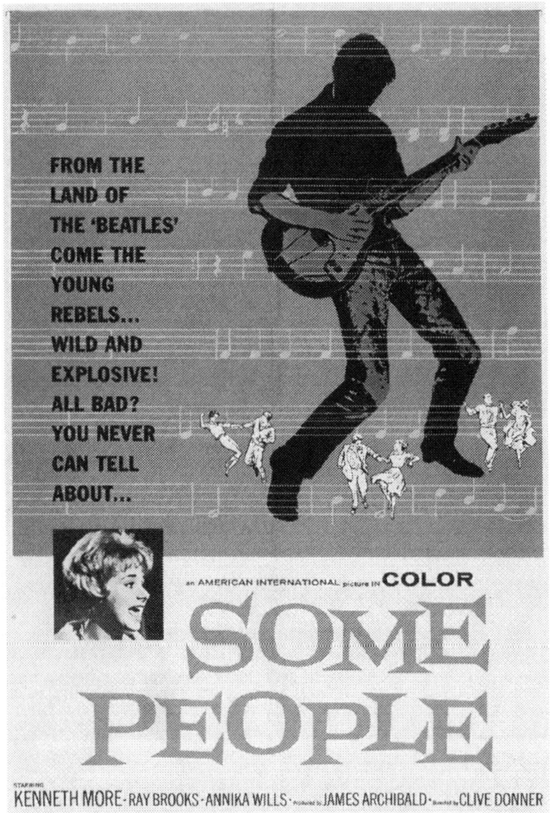

Painting with light and shadows. The opening shot is terrific, the glow of a cigarette from the driver in the dark of a car and a hand that comes out. It really sets the tone; and it sets the character played by Alan Bates.

Secretive.

Secretive but with a smile. The film is on the edge between laughter and tears, which I suppose is one definition of drama, and the film gets there right from the off. Annoyingly the print on the BFI DVD jumps at the beginning.

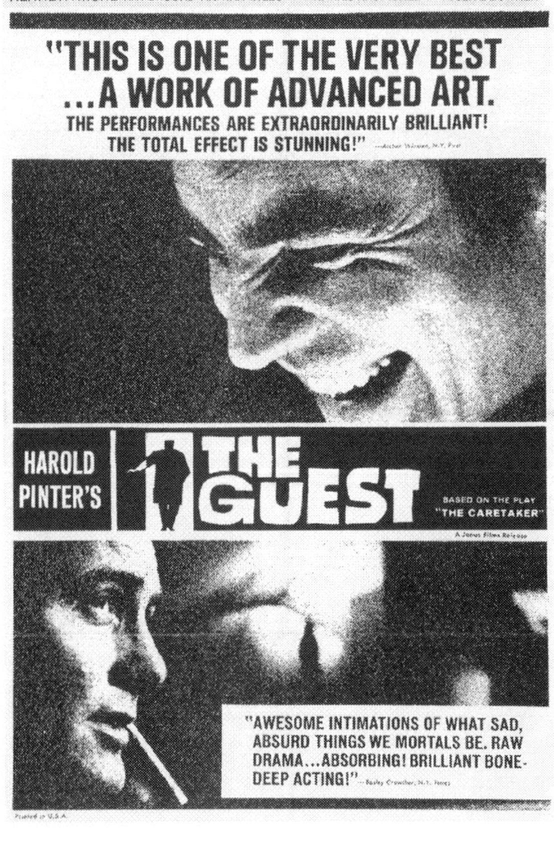

Does it? We'll have a look. Mind you, I didn't have any DVDs until I got that. I had to get on to my chums at the BFI and ask how do I make it work? (*laughs*)

What also impressed me about The Caretaker was Pinter's discipline for writing for the cinema, which really came to the fore in his great films with Losey. He wrote a new introductory scene for The Caretaker, but had the discipline and the commonsense to ditch it. The additional scenes that are in fit perfectly and all are cinematic.

We sat down and we went right the way through the text together, looking at where we should make cuts and additions. Harold said: "What are we going to do about things which would happen in reality?" I said: "We'll do them. We are not on the stage. We can go anywhere we want to." Harold said: "There were places in the play where, when I was writing it, if I had been able to do those things I would have done them." Donald out in the street; Alan in the garden looking at the pond; the couple next door who go by; Alan giving Donald a lift in the car. That's all he wanted to do and, clearly, that was all that was necessary. One didn't need to over egg the pudding. Harold's instinct for it *was* there right from the beginning. The making of *The Caretaker* coincided with Joe (Losey) shooting *The Servant*. They were happening at the same time.

I like the soundtrack. The sound of distant trains, a barking dog...

Because of the setting the soundtrack had to be of an entity. It couldn't be something outside it, such as a Mendelssohn string quartet. What I really wanted was not music but sounds that had a musical quotient, 'reality' sounds, such as a bus going by or the sound of the water dripping into the bucket. I said: "That is where we will find our score." My girlfriend at the time worked at the BBC. She told me about their electronic workshop, a weird room with lots of wires and these somewhat obsessed people who created wonderful noises. Ron Grainer, our composer, who had done *Some People* and who would also do *Nothing But The Best*, created a score out of the reality sounds and handed it over to the boys in the electronic workshop. With Ron, they put the soundtrack together. It is reality chosen and tweaked to create sounds that would enhance aspects of the film.

Then you made what many look upon as your best film, Nothing But The Best.

I'm glad people think that because it is an important film to me. It came about because of David Deutsch. That happens so much in the profession, in other professions too, things come out of the friendships you make. The filmmaking world is full of these talented and gifted people. You find them or they find you and, if you're lucky, you find the right ones. My work with David Deutsch led to me making *Nothing But The Best*. Again, Nat Cohen was the producer and financier.

So if you would have said 'No' to those Edgar Wallace films you would not have had the opportunity to make Nothing But The Best?

Exactly! Exactly that!

On Nothing But The Best you have a perfect cast, including Denholm Elliott, who gives his signature role. And he has the perfect death...

That's right. Denholm was quite a bit older than the rest of us. He had been the golden boy of the theatre and, somehow or other, he dropped out. He had gone to America and floated around Hollywood and was out of it. Then he was back in England and David Deutsch said to me: "Denholm Elliott's back. His agent says we should see him." We saw him and we spoke and I said: "You've got it." And it made his career again.

He plays a character called 'Charlie Prince'. Not a rude reference to Prince Charles?

No! That never occurred to me! Was he even born? I've no idea (*laughs*).

The film is full of surprises, not least Willie Rushton without a beard at the Hunt Ball. Miriam Brickman was the casting director. Everyone I talk with mentions Miriam. Malcolm McDowell told me he owed her everything [she was the casting director on if....]

Nothing But The Best was the first film of mine for which she did the casting, although we had known each other for a long time. She was the great casting director. She was extraordinarily perceptive and intelligent. Very loving. She had a much deeper vision of whatever it was she was looking at or looking for.

For example, when we started casting, she said: "When an actor comes in I don't want you to be surprised or worried that I won't be looking at the actor. I'll be looking at you." She wasn't looking to see if the actor did the right thing. She was looking to see if they were what Clive wanted. And if its is not what Clive wants, why doesn't he want it? She read my reactions. Casting wasn't a one-man decision. It was an interchange between the two of us.

I like the little things, such as when a character enters a bank, a church organ plays on the soundtrack. It's not subtle - money is the new God - but it is funny.

Yes, that's right.

It's a rich film that keeps you laughing and the finale doesn't disappoint.

We had faith in the material. We believed that if we did it this way we would be rewarded.

It was written by Frederic Raphael.

Yes. It was a good script.

Was Room at the Top in your mind?

Not at all, I thought the book was good but I didn't like the film.

I thought Laurence Harvey did a good job, but he didn't quite get the accent right... 'Room' was hailed as The New Realism but all the key scenes were shot in the studio. Bad back-projection.

The reason for that was the past generation of producers. In that case they were good producers, John and Jimmy Woolf, but they were under the influence of the old.

Which company owns Nothing But The Best?

There's a problem. The ownership of films goes round in circles. It has ended up at Warners. There's a guy at Warners who is on the board at the BFI. Rick somebody. We are hoping that maybe he can get the BFI to release it.

Raphael won the Writers' Guild Award and Nic Roeg won a BAFTA nomination for it, but your next comedy, What's New Pussycat? really opened the doors.

After *Nothing But The Best*, my agent rang and said a man called Charlie Feldman is coming to town and he wants to see you.

Did you ask: "What has he produced?" (The Seven Year Itch, A Streetcar Named Desire...).

I did, yes. Charlie is a curious character.

He lost his reputation at a stroke with the film he made after yours.

Yes, he did. He came to London and said: "I've got four films and you can do any one that you want." One was *The Group*, which Sidney Lumet eventually did. I didn't know enough about middle-class American College girls so that was out. One was called *Eternal Fire*, a crash-bang-wallop thing, so I said: "Not for me." Then Charlie said: "I've got a crazy comedy called *What's New Pussycat?* and... there's *CASINO ROYALE*." Nudge-nudge wink wink. (*laughs*) I agreed to read the script of *Casino Royale*. It was Ben Hecht's script at that time and it was terrible. Unusable. Hecht *was* a great writer but the awful thing, as happens all the time, is that the spark goes. What was once hot and fresh passes on and new things come up to replace them. It's the nature of things. I went to Charlie and told him: "I don't want to do *Casino Royale*: I enjoyed the book very much, but I don't honestly see a way it can work, certainly not the way the book is structured". About three or four Bond films had been made and Charlie was trying to cash-in on it. Quite apart from the difficulties of competing with Sean Connery and all of that, I didn't think a film about a casino would work. It *is* the story of a casino. There's some exciting stuff before you get to the casino, but once it's there that's it. That's why I didn't want to do it. But I said I'll do the other one. He said: "Okay. It's written by a crazy young guy called Woody Allen, but you don't have to have him, don't worry about it,

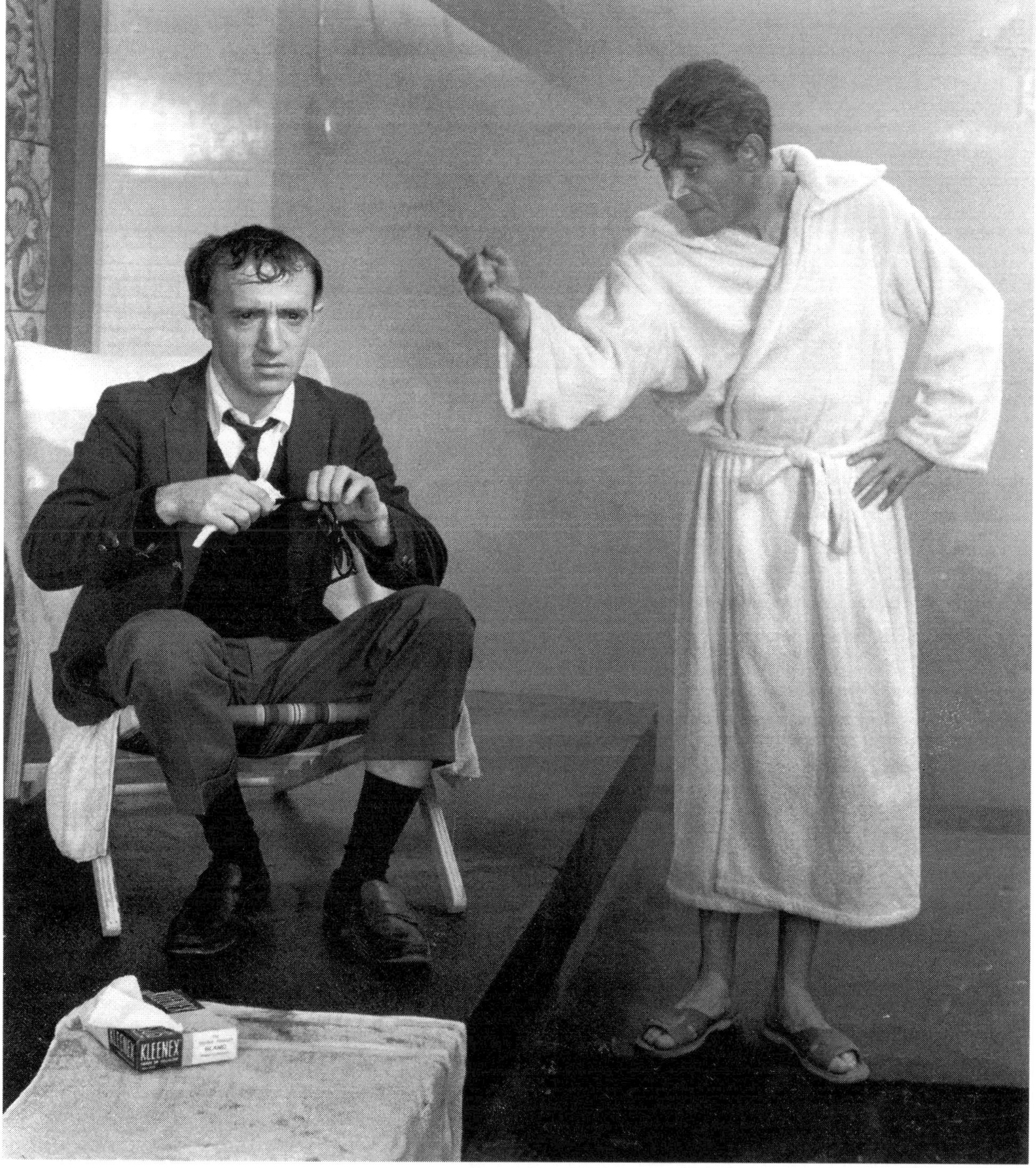

Woody Allen and Peter O'Toole in Clive Donner's *What's New Pussycat?*
The biggest money-making comedy film of its time.

he's not necessary." (*loud laughter all round*) Really! But he said: "You'd better come over and meet him." I went to New York and was met by two of Charlie's henchmen and off we went to the Vanguard Theatre. Woody was playing. It was his last night. He was there with one of his agents, a close friend who would be with him throughout the making of the film. After the show, Woody came and sat with us and I told him: "I liked your show very much."

Was he playing clarinet?

No, no, he was doing his routine, his stand-up. I said it would be great if we could get together and talk. And Woody said: "Yes". I stayed in New York for about five weeks and worked with Woody on the script. We would meet almost every day to talk and to discuss it. In the end what I said is: "What we are talking about here is the most expensive art-house film ever made." It was always going to be an expensive picture, but it was never going to be quite on the scale that it became.

Woody has said he wasn't happy with Pussycat and that, in future, he would only write screenplays he could direct.

That's right.

When asked why he didn't like it he gave as an example that he'd written a scene set where a couple make love in an elevator, which would be funny if filmed in New York City, but the lavish production in your film made the elevator look like a Parisian brothel, so the joke had gone."

Why? (*dismissive snort*). Why had the joke gone? I don't agree with him.

Of course not. It's your film. To Woody it looked like the most natural thing in the world to make love in the 'brothel' elevator.

I know what he felt, but you see, one of the things about Woody, for whom I have nothing but absolute admiration, I think he's absolutely okay. And when he says if he had directed it, it would have been twice as funny and half as expensive, or whatever, *of course it would* because that was the film *he* was making! Not the game that we were into. Anyway, listen. That's really old stuff. Woody and I were *fine*. Though he would occasionally, at some of my jokes, give me a look.

You worked with Woody on the main body of the script, but you re-wrote the ending with the two Peters, the two stars. Is that true?

It's a bit complicated. I've never really spoken before about *Pussycat*, and there's a lot to tell, and one of the reasons I haven't is because I'm totally on Woody's side in every way. The film he wrote was a vehicle for Warren Beatty but Warren Beatty dropped out, and that was all because of Charlie Feldman. Charlie adored Warren. They were very close, but Warren didn't want to play in the film with Capucine, not because he didn't like Capucine, but because he didn't want to work with Charlie's ex-girlfriend. And he knew that because she was an ex-lover of Charlie's she would be in the picture. And she was. And she was very good. So that's why Warren dropped out. The next thing I heard was that we, Woody, Woody's manager, and me were summoned to the South of France. When Woody arrived in London from the States, expecting to make the film in London, I met him at The Dorchester and I said: "Woody, don't unpack."
"Why?"
"Because we are going to meet Charlie in the South of France."
"What about my laundry?" said Woody. I said: "You cannot have flown the Atlantic just to have your laundry done at the Dorchester! I met Charlie this afternoon and he thinks it would be a good idea to film it in the South of France." "Why?"
Anyway, we went down to the South of France, the Hotel du Cap. It was extraordinary. the girls, the big pool, Charlie with his Majordomo who looked after everything for him, John Shepbridge, and Woody hated it. He hates the sun. Charlie loved to take people to one side and say: "Come and talk to me."

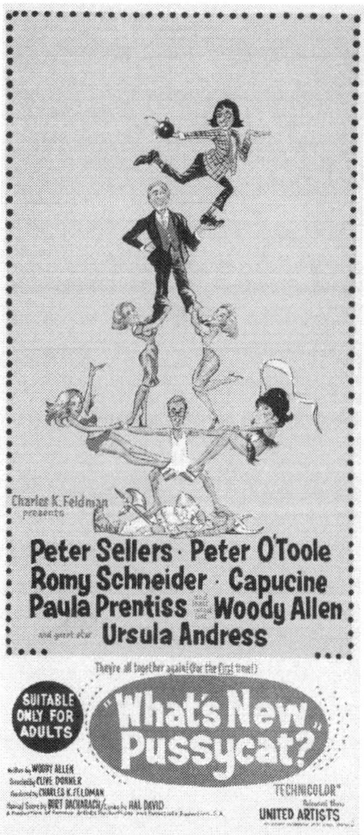
Charles K. Feldman presents
Peter Sellers · Peter O'Toole
Romy Schneider · Capucine
Paula Prentiss
Woody Allen
Ursula Andress
They're all together again! (for the first time!)
SUITABLE ONLY FOR ADULTS
"What's New Pussycat?"
CLIVE DONNER
CHARLES K. FELDMAN
BURT BACHARACH
HAL DAVID
TECHNICOLOR
UNITED ARTISTS

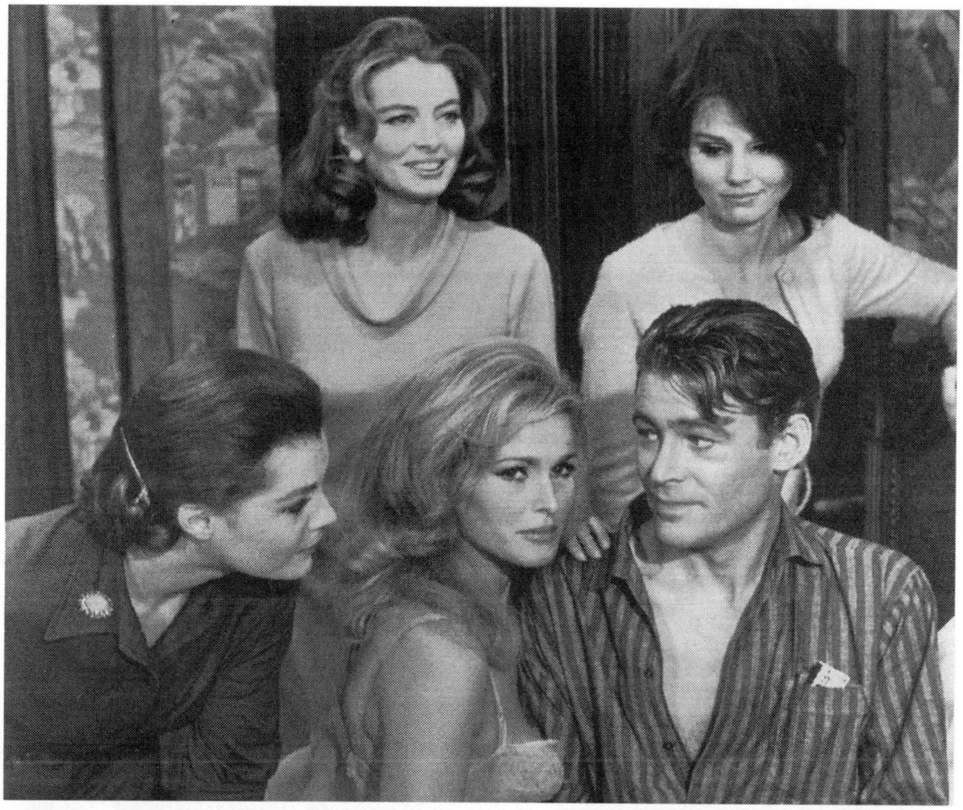

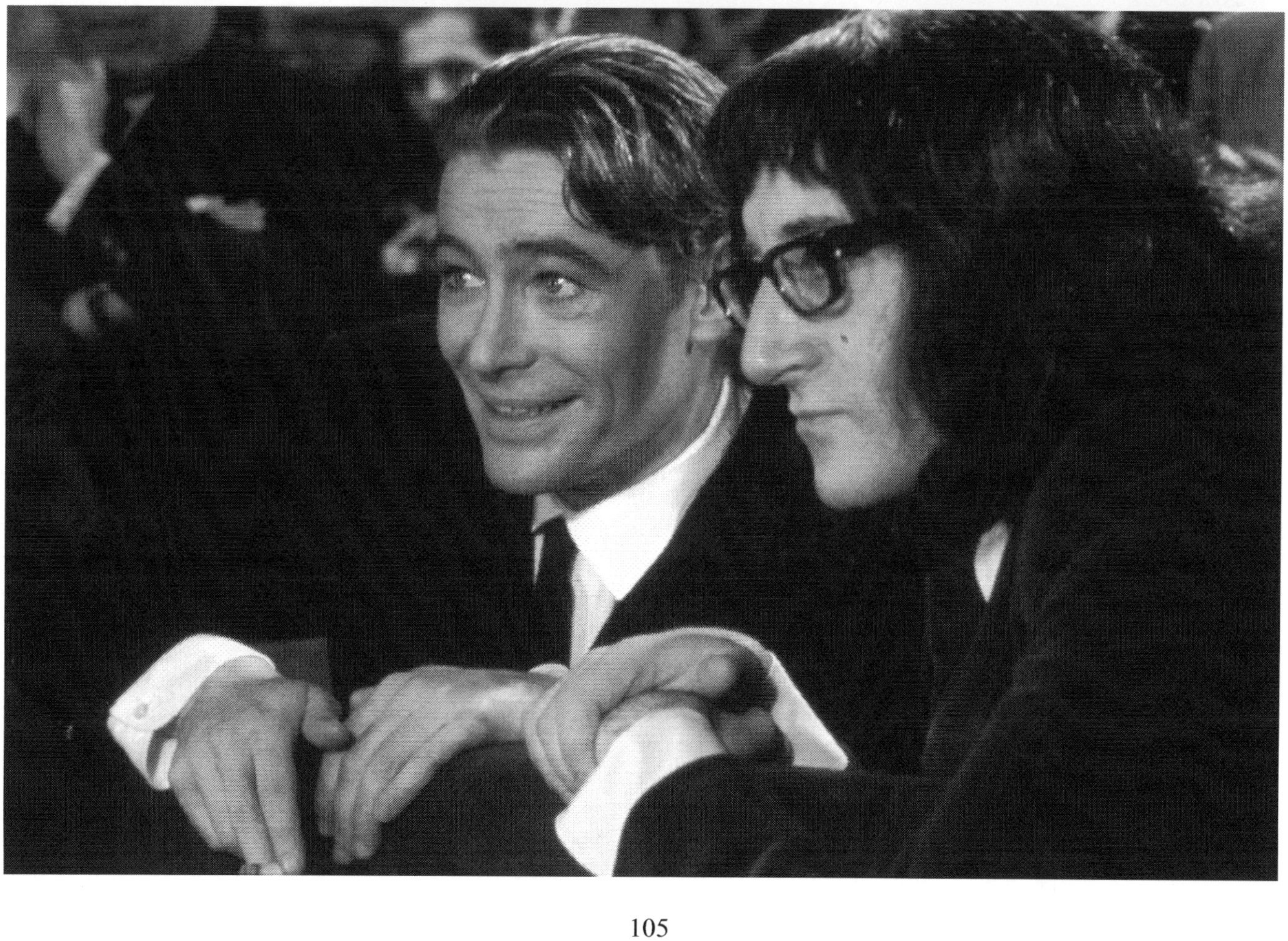

When we arrived, he took me to one side and asked: "What would you say to O'Toole?"
I said: "He'd be very good. I've worked with him and I know his work in the theatre, and he's a very good comedian". And so it happened. Woody and I were despatched to go and have a swim. Woody said: "I hate swimming!" It was *torture* for Woody. He absolutely hated it.

You and Feldman were making a big star vehicle and not 'a Woody Allen film'. Woody Allen films didn't exist then. When was Peter Sellers hired?

Once O'Toole was on board. The film kept growing and growing. The film went 'BIG' because Charlie now had a *real* star. We had everybody we wanted. There were many things wrong with Charlie, but one thing he knew was how to put on a big show. In came all the girls, from all over Europe: Ursula Andress, Romy Schneider, Capucine, of course. I was very fussy, very picky in regard to the shooting and casting. Charlie would say: "I hate her she's got a big ass." And I would say: "But she acts well, Charlie."

It was quite a coup and quite a risk to cast Peter Sellers because he'd had a few heart attacks?

He'd had the first big bad heart attack in Hollywood when working on a Billy Wilder picture called *Kiss Me, Stupid*. He was in intensive care but he came out of it. He was replaced on that picture by Ray Walston. When we were talking about who to cast as 'Fassbender', Charlie had some extraordinary ideas: "How about Charles Boyer?"
I said: "Don't see it, Charlie." (*laughs*)
"But if you want him I can get him," and he picked up the phone, called New York, and asked him: "Oh, you're not free, Charles? Never mind." (*laughs*). Peter's name came up and Charlie asked would I be prepared to talk to Peter? I said "Sure". I went to London and we met. We knew each other. He had just got over the heart attacks and he wasn't insurable, but Charlie wanted him. Peter and I talked and at the end of it, Peter said: "Yes. I'd like to do it." He did it because he trusted me.

And his ill-health didn't hinder his performance.

Not at all. Not a bit. He really went for it. There was one moment though that I'll never forget. We were in Paris, getting ready to shoot the Viking Funeral on the banks of the Seine, and all the celebrities in Paris had come along to watch. I got a call that Peter was is in his caravan and wanted to talk with me. I went along and he said: "Feel my heart." "Are you all right?" "I'm feeling all right but I've called for a doctor." The doctor came and inspected him and said he could go ahead with the scene but he must be returned to his caravan between takes. It was freezing cold outside. We brought him out, filmed a take, and took him back to his caravan. There I was, freezing on the banks of the River Seine, with all of Paris watching on, and my leading man about to die!

Peter Sellers wears a crazy long Beatles wig. I'm not sure that that works. Whose ideas was it?

It was his. It was a choice between a long one and a short one and I said: "We are in so deep (*laughs*), don't let us start getting cold feet now. Just go for it!"

It became the biggest grossing comedy of all-time.

Of it's time. I believe so, yes.

Despite of it going out X-rated in this uptight country of ours. There's an audacious bit in the film that made me scream with laughter, when Peter O'Toole sees Richard Burton in a bar and asks: "Are you Richard Burton?" Burton replies: "No, I'm Peter O'Toole." Then O'Toole says something like: "God bless you, you must be the greatest man who ever lived." You do something similar in Charlie Chan with Richard Hatch, who isn't in the same league as O'Toole. He goes into a bar and asks for a 'Captain Apollo', his character name in Battlestar Galactica.

I like slipping little things like that in, little jokes to cheer me up. I used to do it quite often.

Was it your idea to get Richard Williams to animate the credit sequence?

Yes. We were friends. I thought he was brilliant and I told Charlie this is who we should have.

Then he did the credit sequence for Richardson's Charge of the Light Brigade. A fine film.

Yes, though *Light Brigade* came out first.

When were Tom Jones and Burt Bacharach hired?

We were making the picture when we started talking about finding a composer. Charlie said: "Sinatra says we should have a guy called John Williams. He says he's a bright young guy." I asked: "What's he done?" And he said: "Well, Frank says he's great."
"I'm sure Mr. Sinatra's right but..." I really wanted Dudley Moore, but Dud really didn't want to go for it. He had too many other things going round his head. Poor darling. So Charlie was in the foyer of the Dorchester and in walks Angie Dickinson. He said to her: "Hello, my darling. What are you doing here?" She said: "I'm with my boyfriend."
"Oh, really, who is that?"
"Burt Bacharach."
"Who's he?"
"He's a musician."
"Is he any good?"
"He's wonderful."
So Charlie rings me up and says: "Have you ever heard of a composer called 'Burt Bacharach'?"
And I said: "Yes!"
"Do you think he'll be any good?"
And I said: "Yes!"
He was in London with Angie because he was conducting for Marlene Dietrich, who was playing at the Savoy. It was arranged that we would all go the Savoy that night to see Marlene. Afterwards we talked to Burt and to Hal David, his writing partner. Heady stuff! Wonderful. That's how it came about. The next day, Burt and Hal came to see the movie and they loved it, but Burt said: "I have a commitment in Hollywood." "Don't worry about Hollywood," said Charlie. "I can get you out of that!" And he did. (*laughs*)

Raymond Durgnat described the film as "Lubitsch on roller skates."

Wonderful! When you see him, thank him for me.

I will. You then made my favourite Clive Donner film: Here We Go Round The Mulberry Bush.

It's your period isn't it?

I wasn't even born then (cough). I think it is one of the ten best British films of the Sixties.

Thank you. It was one of the pictures I made for United Artists. At that time, United Artists' policy was 'Trust the filmmaker'. They trusted me. Use your instinct to get the right people and once you've got them you *trust them*. That's the way to get it right. That's *not* what happens today. A sad, sad thing to have happened

It will get better.

Of course it will. Things'll change.

I notice the film has additional dialogue by Larry Kramer. How was he? He co-wrote Ken Russell's Women in Love, which was a massive hit and a great film, but Ken was furious Larry took the credit for the screenplay.

If you can think of the two worst people to put together it is Ken and Larry. Larry Kramer was hysterical. A bright guy. Yale. Smart as can be. Neurotic as can be. Gay but not officially out in those days. He was in England working as a story editor for Columbia, choosing stuff for them to make films of. This was at time in the Sixties when -

Wardour Street was full and alive.

Yes, it isn't anymore. You know the old joke about Wardour Street? The only street in London that's shady on both sides! (*laughs*) And alas it *isn't* any more. Anyway, Larry Kramer was very, very good at his job. Sharp. He had very good taste. e.g. he was the one who pushed them into making *The Spy Who Came In From The Cold.* Without him Columbia would never have made it. But he really wanted to be a writer and a producer. He liked a couple of my films and we knew each other around. We would meet socially. He was tremendously supportive. At that time, the guy who made everything work at United Artists was David Picker. There's such a good story about Picker. His father and his uncle were both executives at United Artists. David was the kid who came in with all the ideas. He was a bright man, a big man with a lot of dignity. Mad about movies and mad about British movies. Back in England we are struggling along trying to get movies made. The National Film Finance Corp. would say: "£4,000 for the rights to *Tom Jones*? We can't afford it." United Artists would say: "£4,000? Sure." They spent that much on an evening's meal. What nobody knew at the time was that the father and the uncle and all the elders of the tribe were saying to the young David Picker: "You're crazy. What are we going to do with that Limey film?" When *Tom Jones* was screened for the executives, the father and the uncle all came in to look at it. And when it was over they said: "Well, there you are, that'll teach you." (*laughs*).

Oh dear me. Tom Jones is a masterpiece.

Yes. However, I am not here to praise other people (*laughs*). I said to Picker, and to the head of U.A. in London, that I wanted to do this film and that there couldn't be any stars in it because there weren't any teenage stars and they said: "Okay, if you can bring it in at a price, you can do it." I had the idea that if I went to the United Artists music department I'd find a great score, and that's what I did. I found a group called The Spencer Davis Group, one of whom, Steve Winwood had left to form Traffic. With them on board it meant that, whilst making that movie, I didn't have any executives breathing down my neck *ever*, .

Because the music guaranteed an audience?

Yes. I knew exactly what I wanted to do. People would say to me: "Why do you want to do this movie with *kids*? You're always doing pictures with *kids*." And I said: "They happen to be an audience and I happen to be interested in them."

How did you end up filming in Stevenage? A concrete utopia with a style and symmetry that Antonioni would die for.

The New Towns were being built and the idea formed in the back of my mind. I remember talking to Michael Birkett about it years before I made the film.

Where did you find Barry Evans?

He'd just come out of drama school. He was a strange and interesting and difficult young man. He was an orphan who had been brought up in children's homes, not Bernardo's, the other one. He didn't know who his parents were. He wanted to be an actor, so the charity helped to get him a place at a drama school in Swiss Cottage. It's still there. He was a difficult little bugger, clever, smart, charming. And he got himself expelled. The guy in the film who plays 'Spike' was also at the school and can vouch for this story - when Barry was expelled, the Head of the School called the class together and said: "I may have fired Barry, but he's got more talent than the whole of you lot put together." He got a place at the National Theatre and he *loved* being there. It was like a home for him. He had small parts in the plays and he really used to make something of them. He did a play for Zeffirelli in which he had one moment and it was magic. He did a little film for John Schlesinger about students at drama school [*The Class*, first broadcast on the BBC's *Monitor* show, April 1961]. Larry Kramer and I were seeing people for the part and this guy walked in. I looked across at Larry and Larry looked across at me and I wrote on a piece of paper, 'He's it.'

He's terrific in the film. Have you seen Ferris Bueller's Day Off? Matthew Broderick addresses the camera and brings you in on his life in the way that Barry does in your film, and has a Union Jack on his door.

That's right.

It seems to be a kind of -

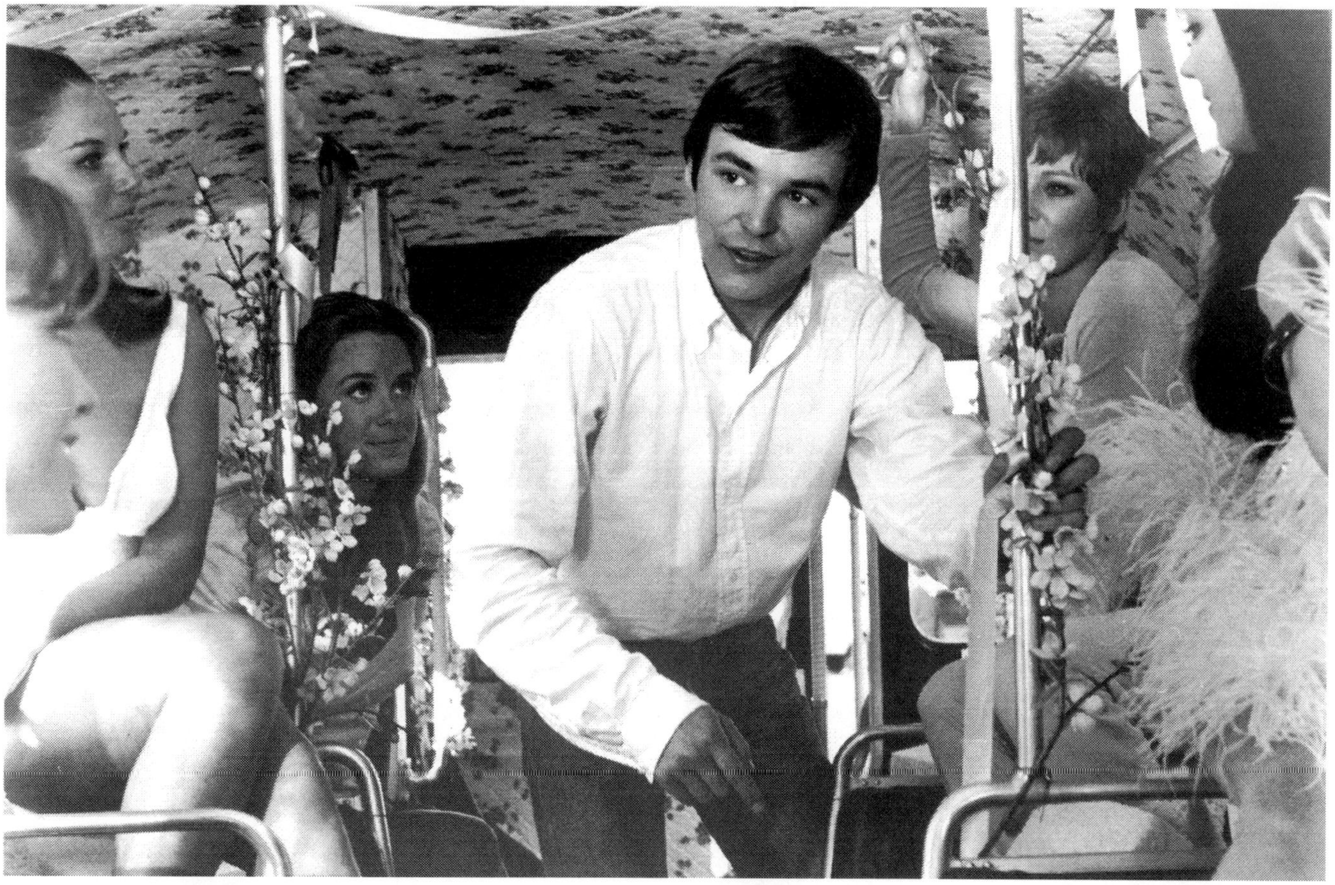

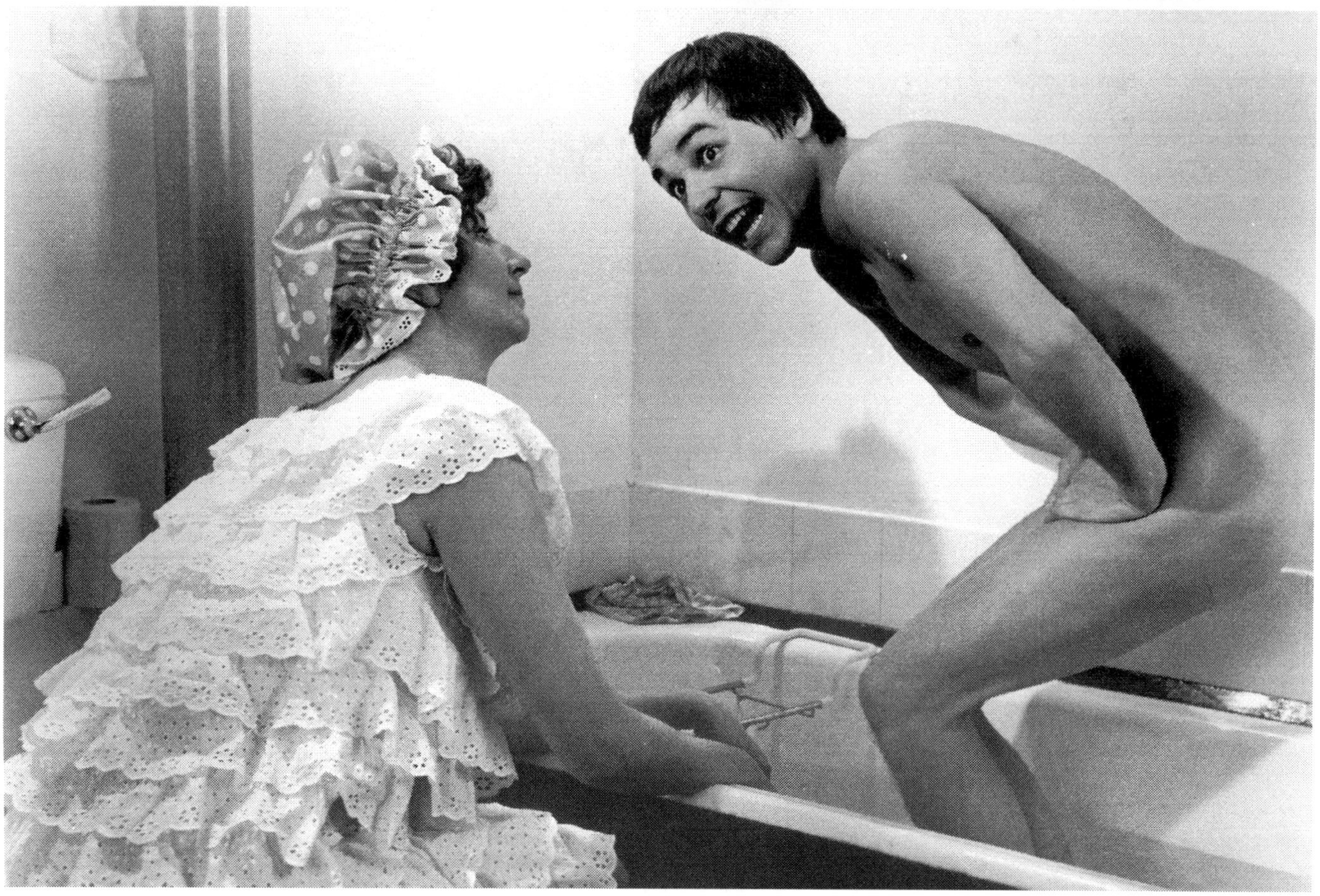

Homage.

Yes. It's sad how Barry ended [dead at fifty three from drink and possibly murder].

Awful. The film was a big success and after the film he was very successful. He was furious with me. He said: "I never wanted to be a star! I just wanted to have my nice job at the National, where I just do my job and I enjoy it and I love the people." He was in several hugely popular TV series and he just walked away from them, time after time after time. When *Mulberry Bush* opened in America we did a lot of big publicity, television shows, but Barry had a cold and arrived in a bad mood. We got a doctor in for him. On one breakfast show he was asked: "Gee, Barry Evans, what's this film about?" And when he replied: "It's about this guy who wants to get laid?", you could see them panic. One day, the people from *The Johnny Carson Show* came to talk to the publicist who was there with Barry to talk about him coming on the Carson Show. And Barry talked himself out of it. The guy from Carson said: "Listen, Barry. If you don't want to be on our show, that's fine. There's lots of other people who do." The publicist went white. I said: "Why did you do it, Barry? It can't go on." We were going over to the coast and they rang me and asked: "What's going to happen when we bring him to Hollywood? Is he going to behave like this? Forget it. We'll do without him." It broke my heart. It hurt us for publicity. And that was Barry. That's not a story I've ever told. There's no reason not to, I just don't feel good about it. It still upsets me.

I was a fan of the film before I saw it. I was about fifteen when I found a very sexy centrespread from it in a magazine.

We were breaking a few barriers. The scene where they go swimming.

The breasts.

Exactly. The censor, John Trevelyan (*groan*), said: "No, no, no, we can't have that!" I said: "All the girl was doing was taking her top off. Kids do it!" He brought in his boss, Lord Harlech, a nice man, to adjudicate and Harlech said: "It's a very nice film but, no, I don't think so." I was *furious*. It went out cut. Over the years I had done a lot of work in prisons, giving talks and making presentations, and I was asked to bring in my new film. I showed the 16mm copy and it had the tits in! The men were in uproar and the place fell apart.

Using your movie to incite riots in prisons.

(*Laughs*) Yes. That's right. I'm all for it.

There were censorship problems again later on with Stealing Heaven. Seven-minutes cut.

The director's cut did get released on video.

Some of your early films were American financed but was 'Luv' your first 'American' film?

Yes it was. It was the first time I'd made a film in Hollywood. It was the wrong film done in the wrong way. We should have done it as a smaller film, very much more intimate and made it much more snappy. Instead of which it was blown up out of any connection with the humour and the wit that originally was there.

But you don't turn down an opportunity to work with Jack Lemmon, a Hollywood legend.

That's right. Jack Lemmon was the most remarkable and the most rewarding person to work with. As Billy Wilder said to me: "Happiness is working with Jack Lemmon." It's true. The film had a curious history. It was a play by Murray Schisgal, first performed at The Arts Theatre in London, with Fenella Fielding playing the lead. Mike Nichols picked it up and directed it on Broadway with Eli Wallach, Annie his wife, and Alan Arkin. My agent asked me to see the play on Broadway because they thought there was a movie in it. I thought Mike had done it very well, he's a very skilful comedy director, but it didn't connect with me. It may have connected with New York audiences but its 'reality' didn't connect with me. Anyway, they said they wanted me to do the picture. And I had the opportunity to direct Jack Lemmon, Peter Falk, Elaine May; and I thought I could see a way of doing it. What really and truly happened was that I bumped into The Hollywood System. What The Hollywood System wanted, and all that it knew, was making films that they could control, and which were done at a certain price. The first thing we shot were the outdoor scenes on the bridge, which was great and fine and funny. But just before we started shooting I found out that it was going to be in widescreen. *Luv* is not a movie that should be in widescreen.

You think 'bridges' and you think 'widescreen'.

They probably did. I think they thought: "Hey! It's our big picture with Jack so let's give him the big screen!" That meant I was knackered.

No, one of the glories of Mulberry Bush is the visuals. Thomson's cinematography. The horizontal townscapes, the beautiful parallel lines. Are they not in widescreen?

No, it's certainly not. It's standard. Then I discovered that not only were we going to shoot it in widescreen but certain scenes that *had* to be shot on location were going to be done in the studio! such as the end of the film where they all fall into the water. The whole thing was built on two huge stages in Columbia Studios. My heart was sinking all the time. The film was falling through my fingers. I hope I never have another experience like that.

It was a stage play and it was being stretched out?

That's right. And there was no *feeling* in it. The only feeling I got into it was when we were out on location, when we were up on the bridge where Jack was doing his stuff. There were some ladies sitting way down there. We started shooting and Jack did a very funny thing where he hangs onto a piece a rope and he comes up and does this funny bit of business. When it happened, this woman, from way down there, started laughing: "Ha! Ha! Ha!" And I said: "Cut! Who was that! Who the fuck was that!" And Jack said: "It's my mother." (*Laughs*). An example of how the film went wrong is the scene in the Chinese restaurant. I set it up the way I wanted to film it and when I came back, the cameraman, Ernie Laszlo, and his operator, had decided that I wasn't taking advantage of the widescreen so they spread everything out. It had taken hours to set up in the first place. I said: "What are you doing?" And there was a row, but I'd lost heart by then.

But you've mostly fortunate with your cameramen. You've used a lot of world-class people.

That's because the photography is the most important thing. Everything else doesn't matter. It is what goes into the lens that counts.

How did Luv do at the box-office?

It had very bad pre-run reactions, which is nothing new, but it was really doing badly right up until the night before its release and studio thought they had an absolute dud on their hands. But the first night, the press and the paying public were there and it was a smash! And it went on to be a big hit.

Apart from the problems on *Luv*, which wasn't easy, I love *working* in Hollywood. I did not enjoy *living* in Hollywood. When I was making *Luv*, David Hemmings came over to do the film of *Camelot*, in which he played Mordred. I rang him up and he said: "I hate Los Angeles. There's no centre to this town." I agreed with him, and said: "But don't worry, we'll sort you out." And we did and he had a good time and he ended up spending his life there.

You worked with him again on Alfred the Great.

Yes. It was produced by Bernard Smith. MGM. pursued me with the project. I read the script and it was not my cup of tea. It was miles away from anything I had done or wanted to do. I was interested in making films that had a mixture of reality and non-reality. *Alfred* was 'historically real'. It dealt with something that actually once happened.

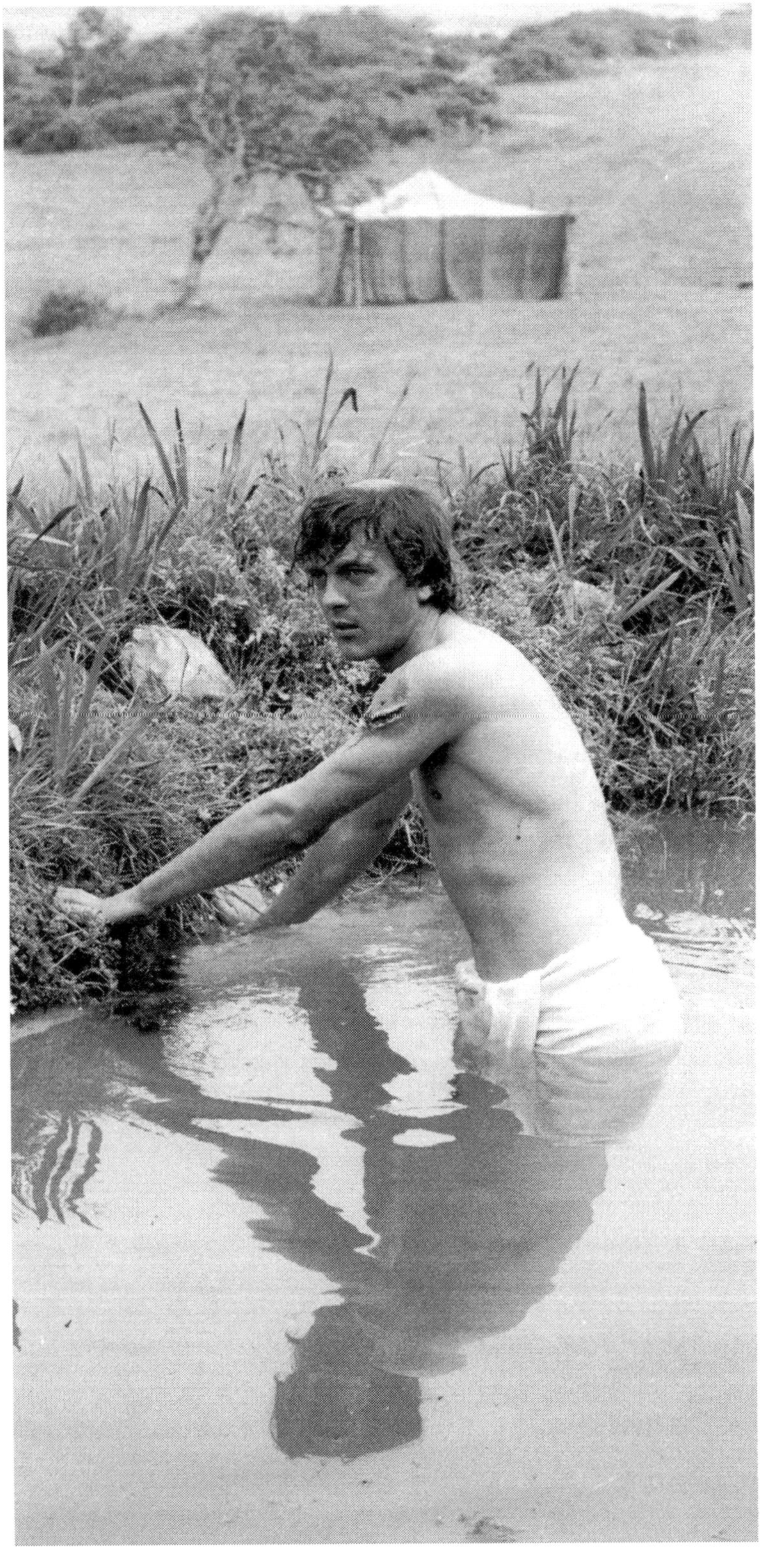

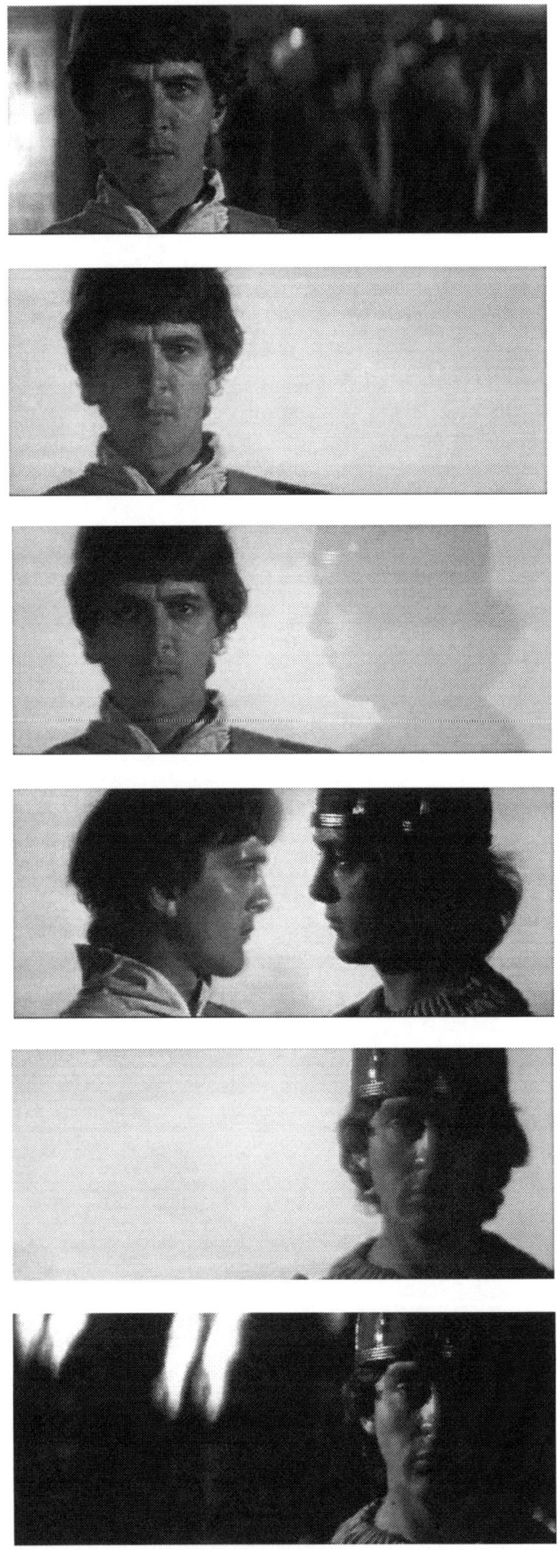

David Hemmings as *Alfred The Great* (1969). A trainee priest becomes a warrior King.
The pre-credit sequence foreshadows Ken Russell's *Tommy* in the Pop Art colours and the location-change dissolves.

And you'd have lots of people telling you if you got things wrong. The History Societies.

Tell me about it. "He wouldn't have been writing in Latin at *that* time it was three years later..." But MGM kept coming. I was making *Mulberry Bush* at the time, and Bernard Smith flew over and pestered me. I listened because it wasn't rubbish they were talking about. It could be quite an important project.

It was given a royal première.

Two royal premières. The first with Prince Phillip. The second with, I think, Princess Anne, which was fun. But the reason I didn't want to do it was that I didn't like what was on the page. I couldn't work from the script they had. It was written by James R. Webb, a real old-timer, very clever, very good, but of another era. Bernie said: "I'll make a deal with you," (somebody in Hollywood always says: 'I'll make a deal with you') He said: "I'd promised Jim that he would have a chance to talk with whomever directed it and that he could go through the script with them. Will you do that with Jim?"
I said: "Okay, fine." But at the end of it I told him: "It isn't going to work, Bernie." He said: "Okay. Now it's your shot." I went to the writer, Ken Taylor, and during our talks the thing began to turn over. I began to find a reality in it for me.

A modern resonance?

That's right. I began to find a pattern of behaviour that I could understand, so I said: "Yes". It's an experience I would never have missed. From my point of view it's a very important film. It's a film that I put more into than I had ever had to put into a film before or since. Not only the whole business of getting the history right but getting the script and the design right. I had Alex [Thomson] photographing it. And I had Michael Stringer, the art-director from *Genevieve*, and the studio gave me every bit of support they could, including the costume designer, who was a girl called Sally Jacobs. But her husband had just got a job in Hollywood and they had a new baby and so she couldn't do it, so they suggested I see a lady called Jocelyn Rickards. And that was it. We fell in love and we have lived together ever since. It was wonderful working together. It totally changed my life.

Jocelyn had worked with David on Blow-Up (1966).

For Antonioni, yes. Jocelyn got on very very well indeed with Antonioni, apart from the fact they were able to speak French together. He could speak English perfectly well but pretended he couldn't. Bernard [Smith] went to the Hollywood première of *Blow-Up* and, like everyone in Hollywood, immediately wanted to make a film with David Hemmings.

I heard you used a trick learned from Antonioni in the making of Alfred The Great. You painted the grass the right colour green?

True. True. We filmed in Galway where the grass is always green except when we wanted to film it! It was the hottest summer on record and the green, green grass was brown (*laughs*).

Apart from entertaining the audience what were you trying to achieve with Alfred the Great?

The film shows that in any circumstances, if you believe strongly enough, there is always the possibility of finding a solution to any problem. In the film, Alfred's victory comes at a terrible cost. At the end, many men die for what, in reality, was a straightforward little skirmish. We made it into a big battle but it wasn't really. Nevertheless, the feelings that the film expresses are true.

The battle scenes are impressive particularly since you always know who is fighting who, a common failing of epic cinema, and the viewer gets some understanding of the tactics. A couple of times you use an overhead camera looking down on the battlefield, not simply to provide some very cinematic and aesthetically pleasing shots, but to clarify the tactics and strategy of Alfred's army at war.

It varied, e.g. the first Danish assault coming down from the hill had an entirely different structure to it from a filmmaking point of view. *That* was to just show a terrible mechanised force, implacably coming down a hill, believing they are walking into an easy win. And then, of course, from the sides you get Alfred's pincer movement, a brilliant strategy on Alfred's part. The second battle I did do from a helicopter shot. It starts on the white horse. We start close on Alfred and we pull right the way back so that you see the whole of the battle going on. The point was not just to do a clever shot but to show that the whole of that battle was terrible: people slugging away at each other and really hurting each other; and nothing really happening. It was just stand there and kill. There was no real strategy to it at all. I find that the most moving part of that is the end when the women are looking for their dead husbands. For the last battle, Alfred did choose to manoeuvre his troops into an arrow shape. Having found that out I worked from that image. Once I find a way into planning a scene everything becomes, not easy, but everything starts to connect: the structure and the emotion and the styling of the film as a whole, and that's what happened there. I had five or seven cameras shooting the battle, which took two or three weeks to stage and film. One of the cameras was on a rostrum because that was the only way to see over the tops of the shields, which were made from staves of wood and which were just above the height of the fighters. I built the battle on the basis of that necessity. It wasn't a question of going high to look down on it as it were from God's view, but so you would actually be *in* it rather than remotely serving it.

Did you have a problem getting the rushes?

No. I've never been itchy about rushes. The editor was Fergus MacDonald, a brilliant editor whom I'd worked with often. He had been away, directing and working in Canada. I met him walking through Wardour Street and I said: "Fergus! What are you doing?" He said: "I'm back. I need a job."

"Do you want to work for me?"

"You bet."

And he became my editor, a wonderful editor, silent, never spoke unless he absolutely *had* to speak. Fergus saw the dailies and that was it as far as I was concerned. I'd trust his judgement. I have always felt too, and I know this is heresy today, that the whole business of watching a scene through the video monitor is wrong. Firstly, I don't want everybody looking at it and, secondly, I'd rather watch the actors. I am the only person on the set whom the actors have to log onto. And if I am sniffing over there looking into a video screen it is not the same as if I am standing here (*close*) and watching you and giving close personal direction.

And that sort of attention is absolutely necessary when the actors can get lost in the production. I've got a press clipping which trumpets the film's epic credentials: "3,000 meals and 200 gallons of tea were served every day ... Local craftsmen made 4,000 arrows, 1,600 swords, 1,800 spears, 1,500 shields..." It demands to be seen on the biggest of screens. Mike Kaplan told me I haven't seen it until I've seen it on the big screen.

We made special 70mm prints and they do look wonderful. I'd love to be able to see it again in 70mm projected on the widescreen. Tony Sloman [world-renowned lens maker and colleague of Kubrick] is very interested in seeing if we can get a 70mm print. Do you know where there is one?

I'm sorry I don't. Maybe Bradford has one? They do a widescreen festival every year. I'll ask them. In the last phase of the last battle, Ian McKellen orders the men, women and children to fight to the death. He is rapidly heading to immortality as a great man of theatre and cinema, but Alfred The Great was his very first film.

Yes, it was. He'd done quite a bit of theatre at Oxford but he certainly had no real experience of filmmaking. He was very reluctant. He wanted to do it but he wasn't sure. I adore him but he was being a bit of an old fuss pot. He finally agreed to do it. He brought an intellect and a kind of curious honour to the role; his character, Roger, lends his wife to Alfred because clearly Alfred is in a terrible state and needs a fuck. "Here you are." That's not what is said in that scene but that's what's actually going on. It was why you never hear Vivian Merchant speak. I didn't want her to get in the way of what was going on with the men. It wasn't a question of her fancying Alfred. It was an act of love from Roger to Alfred. Ian was marvellous. The long speech when he meets Alfred, when Alfred gets there and he comes and talks to him, he did the speech in one take. We'd talked about it and done the usual preparation and he delivered. I said: "It's *marvellous*. Would you like to do an other?" He said: "Well, I wouldn't do it any differently." So we didn't do a second take. We moved on.

What had you seen him in that made you so keen to use him? Had he auditioned for you?

He didn't audition. I'd seen him in the two Bernard Shaw plays that really made his name, *A Man of Destiny*. He was very well-known at Oxford, was in plays in the West End, and he was making a name for himself. I thought 'this is the guy to go for'. When the film was finished and I was editing, the phone rang and it was David Lean, who was preparing to make *Ryan's Daughter*. David said: "This fellow, McKellen, what's he *like*? What do you *think* of him?" I said: "He's the most exciting actor of his generation, David. Grab him."
"Do you *really* think so?" "I really do."
"Thank you very much."
And that was almost all the conversation. I knew that he'd been having some terrible ideas for the part of the shell-shocked boy. He'd wanted John Gielgud, Marlon Brando. Then he took this rather curious actor -

Christopher Jones.

Who I thought gave a rather good performance.

I agree, but imagine what McKellen could have done with that role?

Exactly!

Lean had to dub Christopher Jones, though he looked fine on-screen.

He is more than that. There is a sense of the innocent who has been wrecked by war. He was able to do that very well. Jocelyn (Rickards who designed the costumes) wore all of his clothes, particularly his boots, to wear them in. They are about the same size. Christopher is tiny.

Aesthetically they are at opposite poles, but there's a little of Lawrence of Arabia in your film of Alfred the Great. In both films, both men become horrified by the fact that they begin to take pleasure from killing. There's the clash between the Pagan man and the Civilised man.

Indeed. And also the sexuality.

Was Lawrence a conscious influence?

Not at all. I loved it but it wasn't an influence. When I was making *Alfred*, David Lean came to Galway and we met and we talked a lot. He wanted to know what I was doing: (*whispers*) "What are you doing? What are you doing?". He was looking for locations for *Ryan's Daughter*, an absolutely great film, but *Lawrence of Arabia* stands as his masterwork.

Didn't you help to provide the editor for Lawrence?

Annie Coates. She was Rank's niece. A good girl. She'd worked in the laboratories at Rank. I got a phone call from the studio head telling me they were sending me a new assistant: "She's Arthur Rank's niece. You'd better look after her." She was game and great fun, a lovely big girl, a very good assistant, *absolutely* straight, no nonsense. We became, and still are, very good friends. She was my assistant for a few films. After I had done *Scrooge*, I went back to Pinewood where I was working for Ronnie Neame on *The Card*; then Noel Langley, who had written the screenplay for *The Pickwick Papers*, wanted me to edit it. The last thing I wanted to do was to go back to George Minter. I told him I was working on something else but that I had a marvellous assistant. "I can lend her to you, and when I've finished I'll come over and take over," knowing full well that, when the time came, Annie would win them over. And she did. I couldn't do Ronnie's next picture, so I said: "Take Annie." And from that moment she went up and up and up. These were David Lean's men. It was quite natural that she would eventually do *Lawrence*.

Looking through the cast list of Alfred, I notice a Michael Billlington playing the part of 'Offa'. Is that Michael Billington, the theatre critic, who introduces the DVD of The Caretaker?

No! No, no, no, no, no, no, no.

Damn, I thought I'd made a clever connection.

The Michael Billington in the film was a good actor who thought rather highly of himself. He was always going round saying: "Harry Saltzman wants me for the next Bond film". Things like that.

Before we leave the Viking era, have you seen The 13th Warrior?

No, is it good?

It's the best American film for some time, if you ignore the budget, and the fact it lacks a bit of bang in the final act. There's a long gap between Alfred and your next film. What were you up to?

I was exhausted and needed a break. I retreated to directing theatre at the Nottingham Playhouse. That was a very good experience.

Anything new or was it all rep?

Nothing new, no. I did Pinter. Shakespeare, mostly. I loved it. It's so much easier than filmmaking. With filmmaking you're faced with a problem and you think, "fuck" I've got to do something. And you do something there and then. With theatre, you watch from the stalls and you think: "That's not right" so, that evening, you go to the bar and have a chat with your friends and sort the problem out that way, dealing with things privately, quietly. It's easy. With filmmaking you have to be fully prepared and absolutely at the top of your game, in terms of your imagination and deftness and resourcefulness, for you have to deal with the situation there and then. Maybe an actress can't get the right performance? You've only got one chance to get it right. And you must never bully them. Never.

Your next film was Vampira with David Niven [Dracula revives his wife with blood from Playboy models. She turns from white to black, and loves being black]. Had you seen the American blaxploitation horror films, such as Blacula?

I hadn't seen *Blacula*. There was another one that I had seen.

Blackenstein?

(*Laughs*) I think those sort of pictures are very tricky. Polanski came adrift on *Fearless Vampire Killers*.

He did. I don't like that film at all. The tone is wrong. The actors hit all the wrong notes.

In a funny kind of way you need to have *more* time, *more* money, *more* attention to detail all the way through to pull those kind of films off. You can say, 'Corman does it', or people working for Corman, but there's a kind of camp quality in all of that as well.

Yes. Coppola worked for Corman, and he did go on to make an interesting version of Dracula. He'd had the training I suppose. Three things worth mentioning about Vampira are David Niven, of course. He's a character one could talk about for the rest of one's life?

David could talk about David for the rest of one's life! With David Niven what you saw is what you got. He was very very funny, urbane, very professional.

The film has a song by Anthony Newley, whom I've liked ever since I saw him as the Artful Dodger in David Lean's film of Oliver Twist, a powerfully sad and intelligent performance that inspired me to go out and buy his greatest hits recording.

Some of his songs are marvellous.

The third is the production design by Ken Russell's friend, Philip Harrison, whose next films were Russell's Lisztomania and Valentino. I loved the coffins, the sliding glass one, and the fold-away double coffin.

Philip's a wonderful designer. Very creative. Vangie [Harrison, his wife] did the costumes.

In America, Vampira went out as 'Old Dracula' with the tag-line: 'If you liked Young Frankenstein, You'll love Old Dracula!'

Yes, but I think Mel's picture was better.

It is, but that is as good as he got.

I caught *Silent Movie* recently, by chance, and it is a fascinating film.

I haven't seen Silent Movie, or Robin Hood, Men In Tights! (Clive Donner laughs). Even his titles are funny. There's a Mel Brooks link to The Nude Bomb which you made in 1980. Didn't it originate from his Get Smart TV series?

Mel did have something to do with it. That was quite an interesting experience. After making *Alfred The Great*, a producer called Jennings Lang got in touch with me and said he'd very much like me to do some movies with him. I liked him very much but nothing came of it. Years later, I was in London, and I got a phone call saying Jennings Lang wants me to go to America to do *The Nude Bomb*. I knew the show, some of it was very funny. The film rights were owned by Universal and they were hoping that a film version would inspire business abroad for the TV show, which was unknown everywhere except America and France. I was intrigued by the offer. And it was a good experience, except that it trailed with it five other producers who had been involved with the show. The real key to the film was Don Adams who played 'Maxwell Smart'. Don's a very interesting, very clever man and it became apparent when making the movie that if Don had an idea it was the right one. We'd change whatever we were doing to go with it. He was an experienced man of comedy who knew the show and knew what the audiences wanted.

Back in 1974 you made Rogue Male with Peter O' Toole. Alastair Sim and Harold Pinter. I've been re-reading the first volume of Peter's autobiography and he talks a lot about his obsession of wanting to kill Hitler.

It is very much a key film for him. When we contacted Peter, and asked him did he want to do it, he said: "Of course." Freddie Raphael had written an excellent script. Have you met Peter?

Not yet.

I've known him for a long time. He's odd. He's a very odd man. You never quite know what he's thinking.

I know he's very bright.

He's very bright and he's very funny and he has a very clear view of what it is that he wants to do. And he'll go on and on and on until he gets it done his way. It doesn't always work. When we started shooting *Pussycat*, I think it was the second day, and there was a scene on the stairs with Romy Schneider and him. I took one shot from this way, and I was filming the reverse shot from the other way, and Peter said: "She's looking at the wrong side of the camera."
I said: "She's not. Don't worry about it."
"Look. I've just done a picture with David Lean, I know about these things."
"I don't care what you've done." But he had to go on and on. He wouldn't give up. He may have changed now. He's gone through so many curious phases in his life. But he's a true eccentric.

And a genuine talent.

Ahhh, absolutely. And when he gets the bit between his teeth he really gets it going and, like every good actor, he knows he's got it going. On *Rogue Male* we were working on quite a tight budget, which was fine, we had enough time to do what we needed to do, and Peter was always prepared. He had done his homework. I found that the first take I did with Peter was okay, but I'd see things in it that could be better. Now, traditionally, you go on either until you think you've got it or, if you are in a lunatic mood, and you don't know what you're looking for, you go on for hundreds of takes. It happens, but never with Peter. He would turn up and he would do it, and it was apparent to me that some changes could be made, not that his performance was bad, because Peter didn't do *bad*, but I'd say: "What about this, this and this." He'd say: "All right." We'd do it for a second time and he would put the changes in. Then I'd say: "Okay, let's try one more." And it would go right. Time after time after time. It is important to have good relationships with actors because we, the director, are their only lifeline to what is going on in the scene. One shouldn't indulge them, and you need to smack their wrists now and again.

You tell a good story on the commentary on the DVD of The Caretaker. Robert Shaw, who has been much noted for his 'competiveness', is shouting and ranting and you go up to him, hold his arm gently and say: "It's okay, Robert." And he calmed down.

Yes, I'm glad you got that. It is something that nobody ever talks about. All these drama schools don't know what they are talking about. There are elements about directing that you only really learn about when you get out there. You either make it work or you don't work again.

Rogue Male was made for the BBC?

Mark Shivas, the producer at the BBC, rang and said we are going to make three films about English espionage agents prior to the Second World War and would I do them for television? I said: "Of course but, Mark, I don't make a difference between filming television and filming cinema films. They are *all* films. It is *all* filming. They may be shown under different circumstances but that doesn't mean I'll approach them in a different way." The media is irrelevant. And consequently, *Rogue Male* was my first film for the BBC but it looks like a cinema film.

Films and Filming carried a photo-feature. What struck me though, when watching your tape of it, was how good the script is.

Ah, yes. It is.

It's thrillingly tight and packed full of unexpected twists and turns. O'Toole's character takes a pot shot at Hitler and yet becomes a parasite in his own country. He digs himself into a hole, literally.

Raphael's screenplay gave a very solid base for the actors to work on, in terms of creating something that was a *visual* experience, within a strong dramatic structure. The film was very skillfully put together. It was adapted from a very good book by Geoffrey Household, written largely about his own experiences. Freddie extricated from it the parts that would tell the tale well. Hollywood bought the novel and made it into a movie called *Man Hunt*, directed by Fritz Lang.

It isn't as good as Rogue Male.

I'll tell you why it isn't. In Lang's film, the hiding hole is like this (*huge*). In the book, and indeed in my film, the O'Toole character escapes from Germany on a boat and it is the mate who agrees to hide him. When Fritz Lang made the film, Fritz chose my very best friend, Roddy McDowall, to play the part. Roddy was a little boy, a little bit of schmaltz coming in. Also, Fritz knew nothing about England. He had no experience of the Blitz or anything like that, and Roddy would always be correcting him! Lang's film had absolutely nothing to do with the book, but it's worth watching.

It is studio bound and it lacks authenticity.

The *huge* room! I did like the pin in the girl's head though.

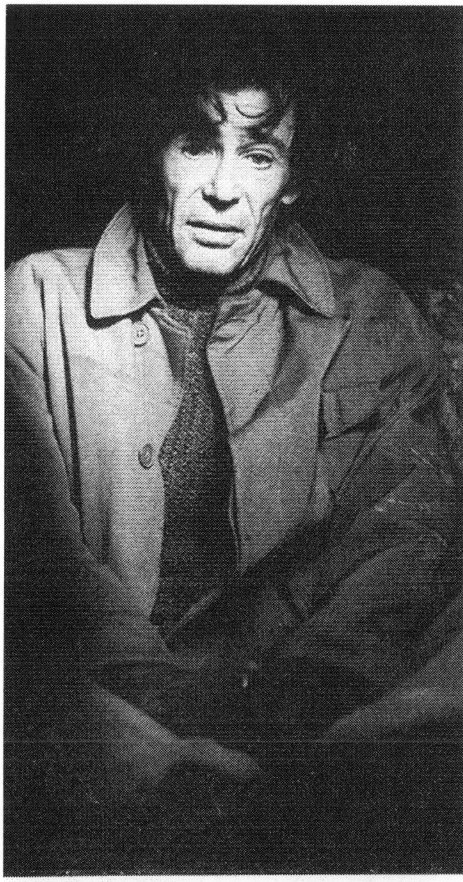

Peter O'Toole as Sir Robert Hunter—the would-be assassin of Adolf Hitler

ROGUE MALE

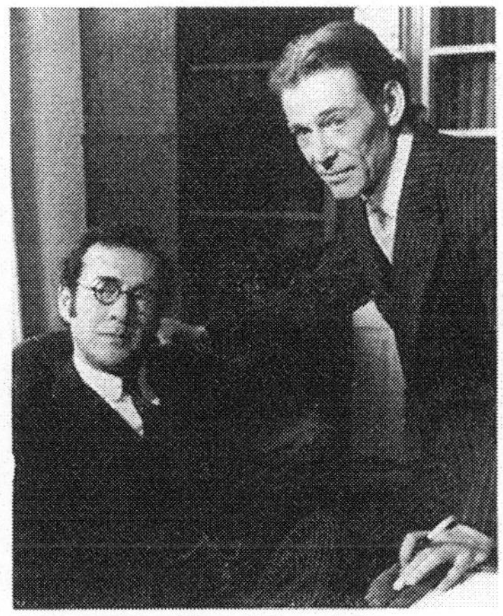

Hunter visits his solicitor Saul Abrahams (Harold Pinter) for advice and financial assistance

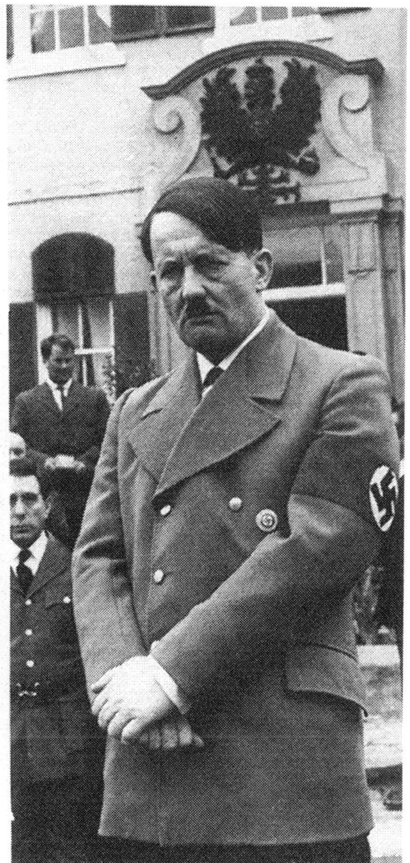

Michael Sheard as Adolf Hitler

Directed by Clive Donner from a screenplay by Frederic Raphael. With Peter O'Toole as an English aristocrat who attempts to assassinate Adolf Hitler just prior to the outbreak of World War II; after he fails he is tracked by not only the Nazis but by the English police as well. Co-starring Alastair Sim, Cyd Hayman, Harold Pinter, John Standing and Michael Sheard. A co-production by the BBC and Fox, it was produced by Mark Shivas

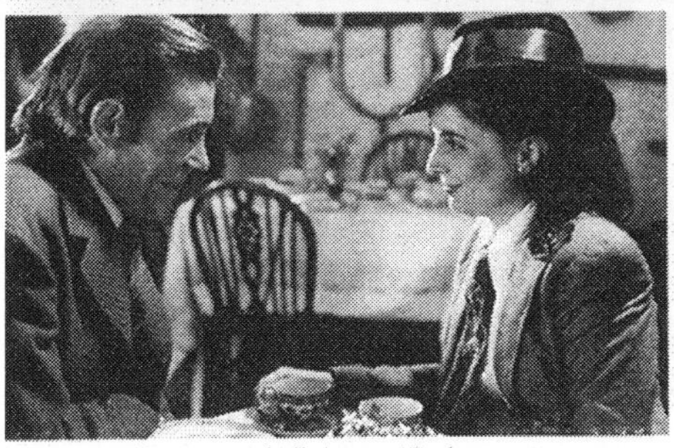

Hunter with Rebecca (Cyd Hayman), the girl whose death he sets out to avenge

Attempting to evade his Nazi pursuers, Hunter takes up residence in a hole in the ground

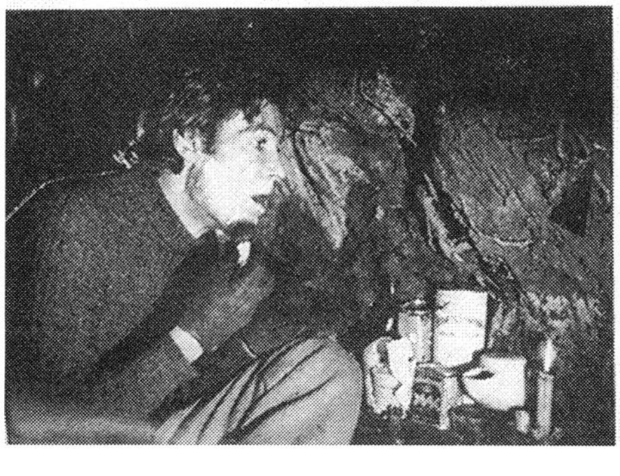

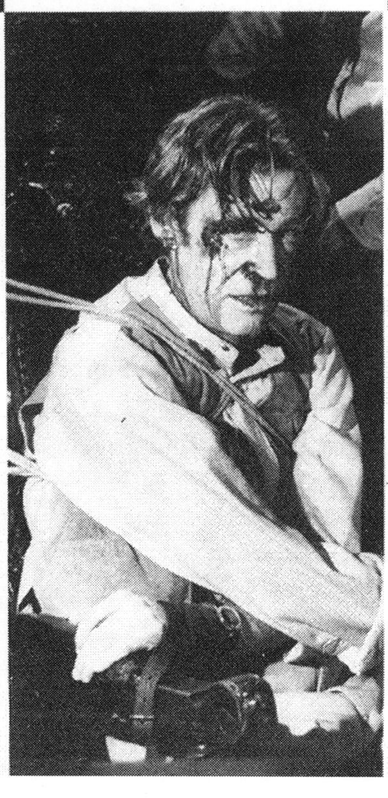

Tortured by the Germans, who find it hard to believe that Hunter acted alone

After escaping from the Germans, Hunter seeks the help of his uncle (Alastair Sim)

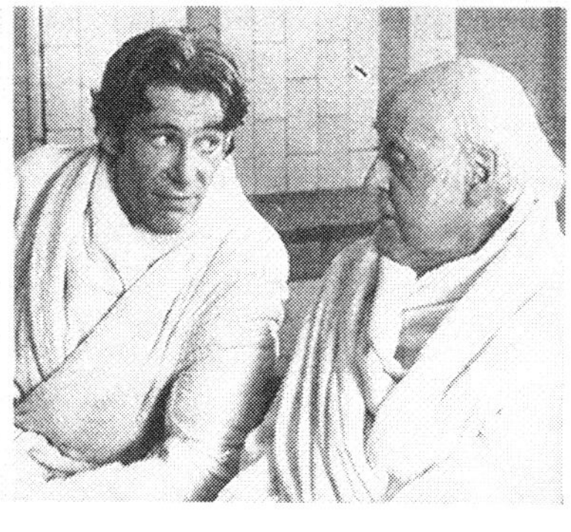

Films and Filming, October 1976, p48

I was impressed by the physicality of O'Toole's performance, crawling across wet mud, digging into the earth with conviction and vigour.

Oh, absolutely! He was committed to it very deeply. And I took the precaution of running the cast list past him. He had no problems at all but Peter was perfectly capable of saying: "I don't think we'll have her," and I wanted to be sure we didn't end up with a situation. It was a wonderfully free and easy film to do. Mark Shivas is a *marvellous* producer. He gives you absolutely everything you need and let's *you* take advantage of it. He's a magical guy.

It's surprising Rogue Male is rarely revived.

We had screenings recently in Paris and in Telluride. Three screenings in fact because there was such a demand for tickets. O'Toole is trying to get it back out. It was owned by Fox, and they sold it on to someone else who sold it on to someone else. The BFI are getting in on the act and Peter's agent is getting in on it. [Poorly-mastered copies from a bad tele-cine are now available on DVD].

Spectre, the pilot you made for a Gene Roddenberry series sounds intriguing. There's a good cast: Robert Culp, John Hurt, Gordon Jackson. I haven't seen it. It sounds like a cross between Sherlock Holmes and Quatermass?

Yes, very near. Gene Roddenberry was a fascinating man. He was trying to launch another television series using the idea of Sherlock Holmes as an occult sleuth. He'd been trying to get the project going for some time and eventually they said: "Go over to England and see what you can make of it."

Where did you make it?

Out at EMI. At that time, if you had an American actor you could cast it. And the money was okay, so you could get John Hurt. Gene's idea for this particular story was a wealthy man using occult means to make money. In all of Gene's stuff there is a strong moral point of view. But *Spectre* didn't really have an ending that was satisfactory. It's quite exciting in a cheesy sort of way but it didn't really have the quality that makes you *think*, which, at the root of it, was what Gene was very much about.

The greatest guest star in the Star Trek films, the man who kills Captain Kirk, is Malcolm McDowell. You first worked with Malcolm on She Fell Among Thieves (1978). Tom Sharpe wrote the script. It is a murder mystery set in a French chateau in the 1920s.

That's right. This was the second of the three films I did for Mark Shivas, *Rogue Male* being the first and *The Three Hostages* by John Buchan, being the third. They were stories by pre-war writers writing about the British secret service in one form or another. *She Fell Among Thieves* was written by Dornford Yates, who wrote in the twenties. He was a fascist, but he did write a lot of very popular stories. He's worth checking out. However, when we came to do the script, I mentioned I'd worked with Tom Sharpe and I knew that Tom was an enthusiast of Dornford Yates' work. Tom took bits of *She Fell Among Thieves* and added bits of his own to make a very ingenious, witty little film. It's one I like very much indeed, and Malcolm is marvellous in it. It's lovely to look at. It's an adorable film.

Malcolm had done an earlier telefilm with Olivier, and Alan Bates. The Collection (1976).

Pinter, of course.

A fascinating film. Larry camping it up and chewing the scenery. Malcolm loves it. She Fell Among Thieves sold well and launched the Mystery! series on PBS. Was it filmed in France?

No, if you go down the motorway into Wales, just before you get into Cardiff there's a castle, modern, built in the 1870s, called Castle Coch. We filmed most of it there and some in Twickenham. I had Brian Tufano, *the* BBC cameraman. More recently he did *Billy Elliot* (2000).

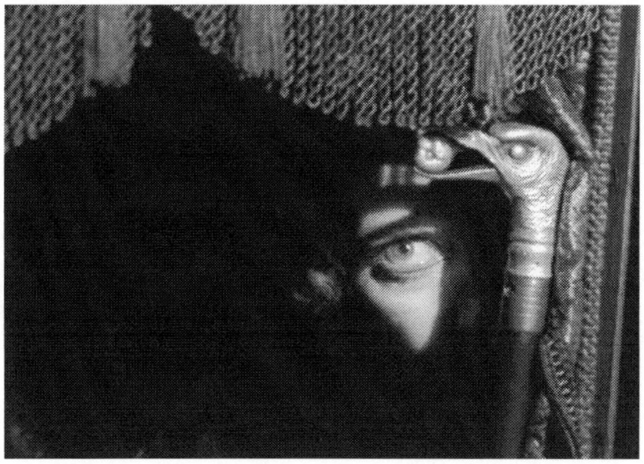 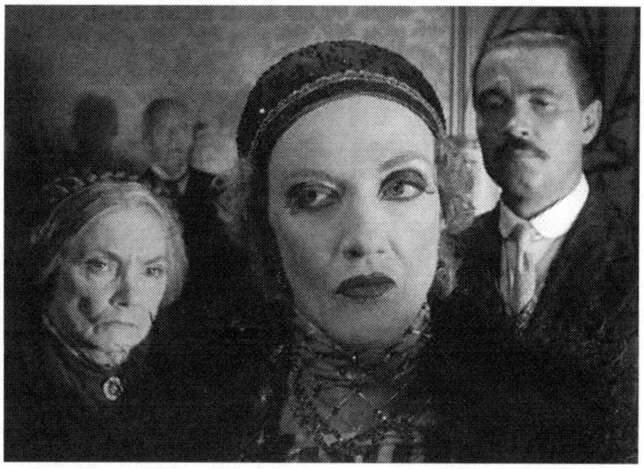

Eileen Atkins in *She Fell Among Thieves* (1978)

I've chatted with him. A good bloke, documentary background so he always makes good use of natural light whenever possible, but there's some good Gothic compositions in the film.

Yes, I was pleased with them.

Eileen Atkins has the Bette Davis role, and Bernard Hill pops up briefly.

And there was Michael Jayston, a fascinating actor. He did a marvellous *King Lear* at the Royal Court.

I'd love to have seen that. I did see his other regal role though, Nicholas and Alexandra, *in which he signs away the throne of Russia to Vivian Pickles's husband. You concluded the Espionage Trilogy with* The Three Hostages, *with Barry Foster and Diana Quick.*

Everybody thought that that was going to be the real big one. Barry plays it absolutely dead right, he's a very good actor, but it needed something more than 'right'.

It needed a McDowell or an O'Toole?

Exactly. However, it is impeccably made with some fascinating stuff in it. It also has a certain political relevance with today. It is about a man who is out to conquer the world. In this case he's an Englishman trying to turn the English establishment upside down, and turn it into a fascist state or some other kind of state. There is a link with the internal problems going on in England, the kind of things that are happening within ethnic communities. It is there, but not explicit.

Malcolm McDowell worked with you again in the 1980s on Arthur the King, *also known as* Merlin and the Sword. *It is available on DVD but I haven't seen it. The reviews haven't been good.*

It's a joke. It was a good script but a terrible production. We had to create Camelot. We set out looking for locations and, on the advice of one of the assistant directors, we found 'Camelot' in Dubrovnik. We flew in, over this incredible castle, and I said: "That's it! We'll do the show right here." It's very long and there is some truly terrible acting in it. Edward Woodward and Malcolm were wonderful though. They were absolutely superb, very funny together, they often had me under the table, but there were a couple of people who shouldn't have been in the film.

Rupert Everett?

I didn't say that. He's a very talented boy.

I like him. He acts in good films all over the world, with great directors, such as Francesco Rosi, but no one sees them. He's a male Belinda Lee, though I hope he has a happier ending. Any final thoughts on Arthur?

Arthur is not uninteresting but it's pretty boring. It had a terrible producer-problem.

You've already mentioned Roddy McDowall. You made

a couple of films with him: Thief of Baghdad and Charlie Chan & The Dragon Queen.

Roddy McDowall was an extraordinarily fortunate young man. He started acting when he was seven or eight. He had an older sister and his mother was very keen on them being in films. When the war came, his father was in the Merchant Navy. He sent the two children to Hollywood; and Mrs. McDowall, with her two chicks, got them into the movies straight away. And it happened to be a very good time. The first thing Roddy did, of course, was *How Green Was My Valley*. It won the Best Picture! All his life he was an avid enthusiast about films and photography. And he's a very very good photographer. I never saw him without a camera. For a long time he did 'kids' stuff, in competition with Freddie Bartholomew. He wasn't just an actor who stood there, he became very adept at communicating what he felt. He was a bit pushy, he had other ideas, but he wasn't a show-off, and his films all went very well. His best friend at that time was Elizabeth Taylor. I got to meet him when I first went to Hollywood just after *Nothing But The Best*. We shared the same interests and we became friends and remained very close friends thereafter. He had a very rough time after he got past adolescence. That's the difficult time for child actors. Can they make the leap up into becoming a professional adult actor? Rod handled it very well. He did a lot of Rep. He really worked it the hard way and, although he was out of it in Hollywood, he got to Broadway. The big hit, the thing which turned him back into a movie star, was a play called *Compulsion*, about Leopold and Lowe, two wealthy young boys who kill another boy. Roddy was in it on Broadway with Dean Stockwell. From there he did an Ariel for John Gielgud. He was in *Camelot* with Richard Burton [and Julie Andrews; in *The Fighting Cock* with Rex Harrison]. He created the air of being an unusual talent. First of all he was an Englishman, even though he became more and more accepted as an American. Suddenly he was back in favour again, not so much in Hollywood though he did a bit of work there, but in television. He did an enormous amount of television. He directed a film, *Tam-Lin [The Devil's Widow]*, starring Ava Gardner, a curious film, very interesting, worth a look. Then he settled down to being an elder statesman in Hollywood and he worked all his life. And all of his life he took photographs, everywhere.

He's best known for The Planet of the Apes films.

That's right! It was ironic that the film he is best known for is the film he is least recognisable in.

Except for his voice.

I know. Nevertheless, it was extraordinary that when he was in Hollywood or in London, the mob of autograph hunters and paparazzi knew he was in town and they'd all come round. His car was had the registration number 'Moppet', the Variety term for a child actor. I said: "You're a fool, Roddy. They know it's your car and they'll come at you with a knife one night." And it could have easily happened. But he would go anywhere and be a normal person, and everywhere he went it was: "My God, it's Roddy McDowall!" Absolutely incredible. Everybody in Hollywood knew him, and everywhere he went he was welcome. When he started to get old, and just before he got ill, he went on the board of the Academy and looked after the finance! He was a warm and loving friend. When we gave up our Hollywood home we always stayed at Roddy's. He was the most hospitable guy. Very often he would have people to dinner. He always had about eight people to dinner. To be invited to Roddy's was regarded as being very special. Nobody *ever* told tales out of school. People trusted him and looked after him in that way. I was there one night and I *knew* that he had had Greta Garbo and Mae West over to dinner, and I said: "How did it go?"
"Oh, a lot of talk as usual."
I asked: "Who won in the talking stakes?"
He said: "Mae, of course."

Roddy plays a good part in The Thief of Baghdad.

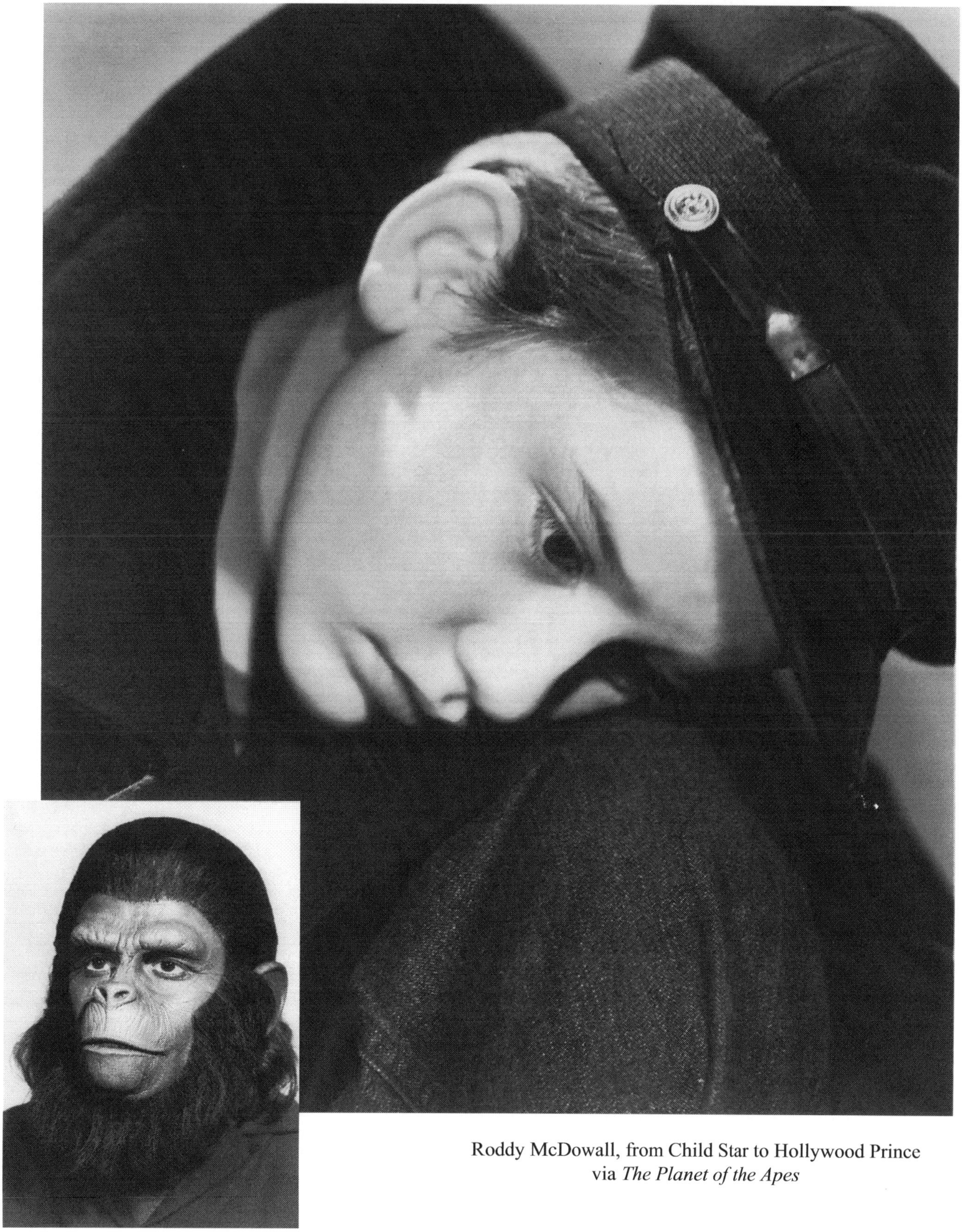

Roddy McDowall, from Child Star to Hollywood Prince via *The Planet of the Apes*

He wasn't bad was he? The thing that was wrong with that picture was that it didn't go far enough. It's nice to look at but it didn't have quite enough juice in it. It needed more vigour!

It is written by Andrew Birkin, who wrote a beautiful book about J. M. Barrie. And the film has a good cast, Peter Ustinov, Terence Stamp...

It's an American television film and they tend to be overlong. We were making films that were too long. They needed them to be three hours long but what we really wanted was a two-hour film that was compressed and had it all in. It was too slack. And, in the end, in the back of everyone's mind, and quite rightly so, there's the Korda version, not to mention the one by Douglas Fairbanks. So you are on a hiding to nothing.

Michael Powell directed the Korda film.

Michael Powell was one of them! He *wasn't* the only director at all, *four* worked on that film.

He took the credit.

He certainly did! As the years have gone by he managed to push himself up and everyone else out! In my film everyone does their work well but you come out thinking: 'Why don't I feel something more about it?' because there are some good things in it, but it wasn't fresh. Terry Stamp wobbling in on a... (*laughs*)

He's watchable, as always, but a little below par.

I love Terry and he is a little below par in it. I sometimes see him around and he hasn't changed at all. A gentle man. And what an amazing career!

Pasolini, Fellini, William Wyler...

And he disappeared off to India, and all that, and burned a lot of money and came back. Did you see his first film, *Billy Budd*? Wonderful! A wonderful, wonderful film.

Directed by Peter Ustinov who plays a good part in Baghdad. You've worked with him often, including a Poirot, Dead Man's Folly (1986).

He is a great unique English European. He has an extraordinary mind. His lineage in terms of culture is incredible. His knowledge of life today is immense, not just in terms of politics, and the enormous amount of work he does for Unicef. He has friends and connections around the world and, on top of all of that, he is the funniest man in the world. He is just hilarious. And what's more, he can't stop. That's the sad thing. If you spend working time with Peter, you'll get the repertoire. The curious thing is that he is because he is so well-known for his one-man shows, he isn't well-known in the way that say, an actor like Alec Guinness, who's from the same generation. Alec is lauded and Peter, although much loved and deservedly so, is seen as someone who is enormously talented and entertaining but who doesn't go much further. Some of his work is absolutely first-rate, *Billy Budd* (1962) is a dynamic piece of film-making. Brilliant and moving. It stands *way* above a lot of the auteur stuff that gets shunted around.

He did a superb film with Anthony Newley when Newley was a little boy.

Yes. *Vice Versa* (1947).

In Charlie Chan and the Dragon Queen, Chan is played by the great Peter Ustinov and you've got a cast that features three of my favourite actresses: Rachel Roberts, Angie Dickinson and Lee Grant and also Michelle Pfeiffer! Several internet fan sites talk about the famous Pfeiffer kissing scene.

I'm glad to hear it. They were a wonderful cast. It was made for an odd production company, we didn't quite know where they came from. It wasn't a major studio and although nobody short-changed us there was always a feeling that something might happen. The only thing I'll say about the picture is that, great though all the cast were, the sheer joy of that picture

was finding Michelle Pfeiffer. I said to Jocelyn: "Okay we've found a girl."
"What's she like?"
"Fine." Jocelyn went off with Michelle to get her some clothes and when Jocelyn came back she said: "That girl's not *fine*. That girl's a *star*." At that time, Michelle was a kid running around on the surf in Orange County. She had never had silk close to her body. Jocelyn took her into very expensive shops. And she was not exactly innocent but rather like of a tabula rasa, a plate you could put what you wanted onto. And, thanks be to God, she went on to do some very good and very important films. She's spectacular in *White Oleanda*.

To Kill a King was a Jack Higgins thriller about a Gestapo plot to kidnap the Duke of Windsor.

That nutty picture. It was a Bill Storke picture so we had an absolutely smooth production, Bill's a terrific producer, wonderful. We made it in Portugal and Paris. He invited Roddy over to Lisbon to take photographs. There are two very interesting performances in the film that make it worth seeing. One by John Standing playing the Duke, a man who suddenly realises he has got himself into an inescapable trap. John's a very interesting actor. He brought great depth to his role. He is also in *Rogue Male*. And the other performance is by Teri Garr, playing a nightclub singer. Teri's a marvellous girl, marvellous actress. She had started as a hoofer, as a chorus girl on Broadway. If you asked: "Did you ever meet Shirley MacLaine?' "Sure I knew Shirley." She knew absolutely everybody. She'd danced with them all! I'm not mad keen about Jack Higgins but *To Catch a King* is a good thriller. The story was pretty close to happening in real life. We know that the Duke and the Duchess met Hitler at Berchtesgaden, so his position was untenable. When the Duke was in Portugal he was trying to get home but neither the King nor Churchill wanted him back. They bunged him off to the Bahamas, where he became governor. The hero (Robert Wagner) is an American in Lisbon running a bar, kind of a crib from *Casablanca*. A nightclub singer gets involved in the plot to kidnap the Duke, and she has to get out of Lisbon with the information that they are trying to kidnap the Duke. There's a sequence I shot in Lisbon of Teri running away and boy could she run! She was fantastic!

Oliver Twist and A Christmas Carol were two very successful American television films you made with George C. Scott. I suppose the money to make them came with Scott?

Yes, absolutely. Bill Storke had been an important executive at C.B.S. and had moved onto making films that were better than the average television films. When it came to *Oliver Twist*, Bill arranged for me to meet George C. Scott and the writer, James Goldman. I was living in Hollywood at the time and I flew to New York to a lunch meeting with George in James's apartment overlooking the Metropolitan Museum. George is a *presence*. Big. You can't take your eyes off him. It was an average conversation. Chatty. We talked about wigs and this and that and it was easy and jovial. Then I decided that I had to deal with the 'problem' and I had to deal with it now. I said: "Mister Scott. It will not surprise you, that it is well-known, and it has come to my attention, that there are times when you do like to have a little drop to drink." Bill went green. George sat there and he did a George face. And he said: "I'll be on time. I'll know my lines. And I won't take a drink when I'm working." But I don't think he ever forgave me.

He did work with you again.

Oh, yes. But he still... sometimes he would give me a look. I loved him actually. A great man who ruined his life with booze, women and with attempting to *fight* the establishment, self-distributed his films. He fought and he lost, as you do.

Oliver Twist got a theatrical release in England.

A royal première! for The Queen! at the Odeon Leicester Square. One of The Ladies came up to me afterwards and said: "The Queen had a little cry." (*laughs*).

The film starts with a nice montage of kid's faces as the soup's being served up but thereafter there aren't many kids in it. They've disappeared when you get to Fagin's den.

They're there, there are about eight boys, but you never get them all together singing and dancing because it's not a film by Carol Reed. There was no attempt to fill it up with boys because what was important was to tell the overall story, not cloud it with stuff that really has no place.

The boy [Richard Charles] playing Oliver is from the Mark Lester school of outrageously innocent and pretty infants.

Yes. He was not from an acting school at all. He was a kid I found. He loved playing football.

You used him again in A Christmas Carol (1984).

Yes, he played the Dauphin. He doesn't do anything in the film. He's just a great face. A sweet kid.

You cast Tim Curry as Bill Sikes; a rather different version of the role than the Sikes we are used to.

George said to me: "I want a Bill Sikes who will threaten me". There was some talk about casting a big huge Jewish guy, who makes very interesting films but I can't remember his name, but I didn't want that, that would too obvious. If you had George and you had an equally powerful man there's nothing in it. But Tim was threatening in an entirely different way, sheer malevolence, which gave George something extra to work with. George told me: "I was not expecting that. If Sikes would have been just another big guy, I would have known what to do, punch him, but with Tim I had to think again. I had to find a way to be frightened of him."

Tim does come across as very dangerous. I think he's a very underused actor. Scott picked up an Emmy nomination for his second film with you, A Christmas Carol, which brought your career if not full circle, back onto the Scrooge story, but told now for an American audience?

No. I was making it for myself. I *always* do. Sometimes, but not often, I've fallen into a trap and failed to be able to do what I've wanted to do, but all the films that are important to me were made the way I wanted to make them.

The film has a real Victorian feel with lots of carols sung in the streets. It's a very moving film.

Thank you. That's what I was after. It's a film I'm proud of.

Where was it filmed? The locations were atmospheric and in period. London?

Shrewsbury.

It worked perfectly. Was the terrible model of a church tower a throwback to the Alastair Sim?

No. It was what I was given. On a television schedule you sometimes have to work with what you're given.

With respect though, the film of the year was A Passage to India, by your old friend, David Lean.

David was editing *A Passage To India* and I was walking up the corridor past his room and he came out: "Have you got a moment?". I told him I had. He said: "Have a look at this." He was working on the scene where Peggy Ashcroft is running down from the Marabar Caves. I sat at the Movieola and David said: "Do you notice anything?"
I said: "No, it's wonderful how you've done it."
David said: "You're absolutely sure?"
I said: "Yes. Why?" When I was looking it, like all editors I put my hand there so I could feel the film going through, it's something you automatically do, and he said: "No, take your hand away." If there was

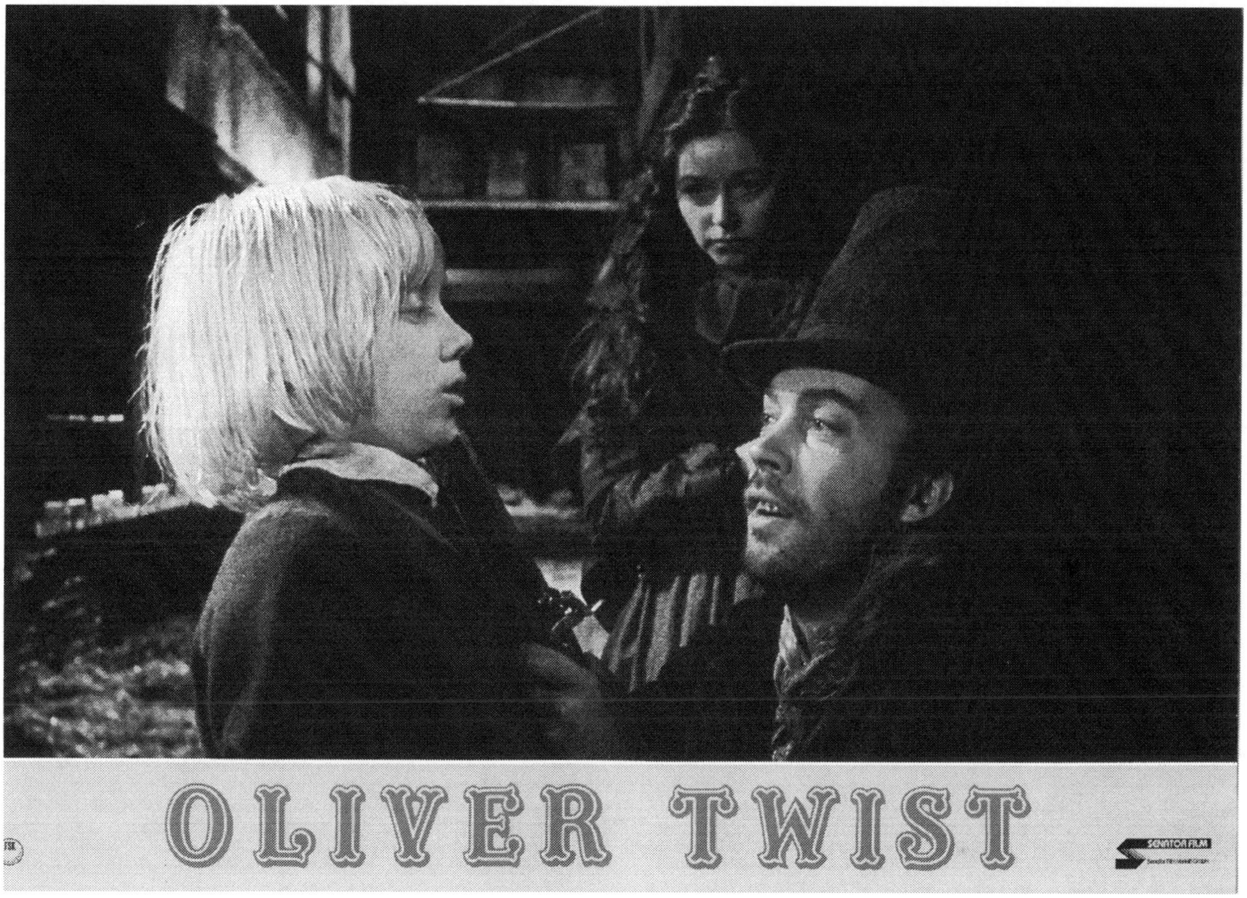

Two good Dickens by Donner. Tim Curry as a quietly dangerous Bill Sikes.
George C. Scott, a quietly moving Ebenezer Scrooge.

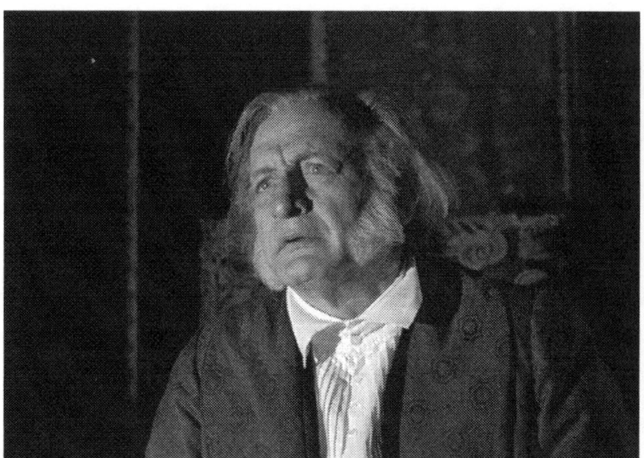

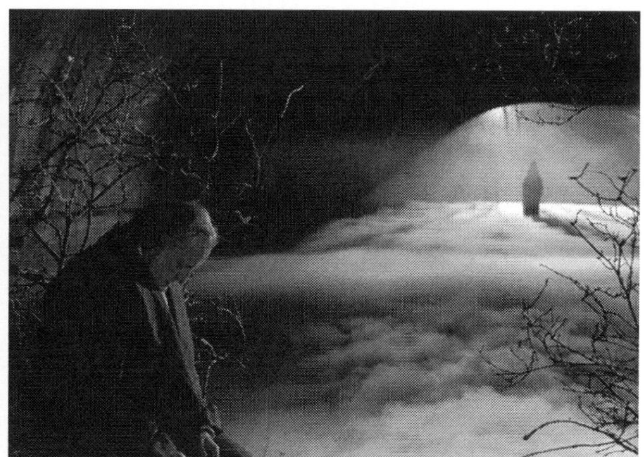

a cut in it and he knew I would feel the cut. He wanted to know whether or not it worked without me *seeing* the join. And it did work.

You are well-known as a good director of children, and also for having this mix of fantasy and reality in your features, so it was quite natural for you to make Babes in Toyland with a pre-teen Drew Barrymore.

Well, round about that time I was a having trouble finding material that I wanted to do, and the material I wanted to do I was finding very hard to get accepted, but I was getting a lot of work, and a lot of offers, particularly from C.B.S. for American television for transmission worldwide. I think I made six or seven pictures for them. Some of them worked extremely well, such as the George C. Scott ones, but *Babes in Toyland* was just something I was offered to do and something I thought would be quite fun to do. It was. There were some interesting things to be got out of it but, from a production point of view, it was torture. We shot it in Germany, in Munich, which was fine, very well organised, but the American 'producers', they call themselves producers but they don't 'produce', they just look after the finances and were only interested in getting it done as quickly as possible. I had some terrible things happen. When Drew arrives in Toyland and there's a bit of fun, and she saves the day and she's on a cart and they are all going round in circles. For the dance, I was using Eleanor Fazan, 'Fizz', who worked for Lindsay Anderson, of course, and who was full of enthusiasm and ideas. We rehearsed it in the morning and we had to shoot the whole sequence in the afternoon! And Fizz was in tears because she had worked out a whole lot of exciting fun things to do and the 'producers' had it all cut. They wouldn't let us have the time. And this went on all the way through the film. It was a battle.

To put anything creative onto the screen?

Yes.

Some of the songs are fun, but the 'Cincinatti Song' sounds just like 'Supercalifragilisticexpialidocious'.

Yes, well it's Leslie Bricusse isn't it? (*laughs*)

And you have a Hollywood golden boy acting his heart out - Keanu Reeves.

Nobody had heard of him. He was just a great lolloping kid who came in and he was great, wonderful, worked very hard, did very well. He was a very hip, quiet kind of guy. I liked him very much indeed, generous, a nice boy. And, for that kind of boy, from where he was coming from, at his age, it is not easy to start playing that kind of role, which can be a bit cheesy if you are not careful. In the context of a fairy story he made it real. Keanu brought a believability to it. You may not have believed the whole film but, within that, Keanu and Drew were perfectly believeable. There was no messing around, no campness, no silliness at all. They played it *very* well.

Bertolucci said something similar about why he picked him out to play Buddha in Little Buddha. There's an openness or an honesty about the way he performs, almost a blank canvas.

Absolutely. From that point of he's a very consistent actor. I've seen the new *Matrix* film and, I must say, I think he looks marvellous. All of the kids and all the little children just loved it and they adored doing it. The problem as so often happens was that I wasn't my own man on it at all. It was a fight every hour of the day to get the thing that I wanted to do *right*, and to get it done *properly* and to get it so that it *worked*. It was terrible.

It is difficult getting hold of the full version. It's available at ninety minutes, but originally it was about two hours?

It was more like three, four hours with commercials. Having a 90-minute version is very sensible. You can sell it easier and more kids will see it. There were things in it which were too long, for example, the march of the toy soldiers goes on and on and on and on. We were short! We needed more footage.

Because you have to fill the allotted time?

Yes. That old adage about 'Never work with kids or animals' is still true about animals but it doesn't apply nowadays to children, it's applies to the parents of the children. I've worked with a lot of good children. Children come to auditions with their parents. I was in Hollywood casting *Babes in Toyland* and a woman came in with her little boy and he did his stuff and read a little bit, and all of that was fine, and I said: "Thank you very much indeed. That was very, very nice." And his mother stood up and she gave him a nudge, and he looked at her, and she gave him another nudge. So he came up to me and he said: "Mr. Donner. I *love* you." (*laughs*) Jesus!

Were you sick on him?

Not on him. He was okay. I should have been sick on his mother.

Of your later films, the most highly regarded is The Scarlet Pimpernel (1982) written by James Dean's friend, William Bast. It stars Anthony Andrews, fresh from his triumph in Brideshead Revisited, and Jane Seymour and Ian McKellen. Bast had just won an Emmy for The Man in the Iron Mask.

He's a good writer. Anthony can drive you mad. He can be very fussy. But on this picture he didn't fuss. He and Ian and Jane Seymour, who is very good at being Jane Seymour, all worked very well. Sometimes you come away from making a film feeling good that you made it. Most of them I do, not all, but certainly that one. The *Pimpernel* films Leslie Howard made in the forties were wonderful but they were of the period. I was trying to bring some whiff of the reality of history, a sense of what it would have been like to actually be there.

It's a richly dressed film.

Jocelyn is one of the best costume designers in the world but she can't do it anymore. The costumes were by Phyllis Dalton, who did *Lawrence of Arabia*. The producer was David Conroy, whom I've worked with often and always happily. A good producer is *essential*. Most of the time you don't have good producers, you may have nice people, but David Conroy was a good guy and a good producer. I despise people who are known as 'producers' who have nothing to do with the real concept of being a producer. A producer is somebody who takes responsibility for the material right the way through and deals with all the problems; who makes sure the director has everything he needs to get his job done properly. Curiously, on *Luv*, the back-up producers were very good to me. They did not hustle me at all. The real problems with *Luv* were that we were doing the wrong film in the wrong way. We should have done it as a small film, much more intimate and snappy. *The Scarlet Pimpernel*, as I've said, was produced by David Conroy, a very bright man who went to the BBC and made some important pictures, including *War and Peace* which was wonderfully spectacular. He's worked with independent companies. He asked me to do *The Scarlet Pimpernel*. From the moment we started work I knew we talking about the same thing. He was the *producer*. He was there with me, to help me, wanting to know what I was looking for, whether the production departments were providing me with the things that I needed to make decisions. When it came to casting he didn't intrude. He never sat in on the casting but he knew every actor I was seeing. I'd tell him my decisions afterwards and there was only one instance where he didn't agree. He didn't let me have somebody whom I wanted to cast. In *The Scarlet Pimpernel*, for the part of Marguerite's brother, a handsome looking fellow who just jumps around a bit, Miriam Brickman arranged for this young man to come in to audition and I saw him and said: "Yes!" David said: "Let's have another look." Then said: "I think he's marvellous but I'm worried. He hasn't done enough. I don't think he's ready." I said: "He *is*, David. He is." But I lost.
And that was Daniel Day-Lewis.

(loud laughter): Dear me! I hope you still hold that against him?

(*laughing*): I do. I do. I'm seeing him for lunch next week. But he's a good pal. Making a movie is such a complex thing you need people like that who you can bounce ideas off. A person like David in the background doesn't half make life easier. Did you ever come across a character called Noel Davies? My closest friend. Adorable guy. An actor who became a very successful casting director. I miss him. Queer as a two-bob bit. He was one of those people who was *bright* and intelligent and *honest*. He would not and could not let you down on *anything*. Consequently, the actual making of *The Scarlet Pimpernel* was a joy. Apart from anything else we had wonderful locations. Conroy gave me every conceivable opportunity to go round the country looking at stately homes to find the ones that were the very best.

And Jane Seymour has rarely been better.

Yes, she wasn't bad. Very attractive. Not a lot of range but within that range she delivers. She played on Broadway with Ian McKellen and Tim Curry in *Amadeus*. Anthony Andrews' wife had been at RADA with Jane and so they were chums. They were at ease together. Anthony, Jane and Ian working together in harmony. Ian would sometimes have some weird ideas of how to act or stage things. "I don't think so, dear. Not this time. Do it in somebody else's production."

His Richard III is very striking.

I loved it. I really liked it.

He filmed London as you've never seen it before.

Yes, the director, Richard Loncraine is somebody else who has got his own view of things. One final thing to note on *The Scarlet Pimpernel* was that the costumes again were by Phyllis Dalton. She was a remarkable woman. She had an eye for what was right without it being fussy. When the actors were on the set everything about their costume not only looked right and were right but you knew they felt right. People like Phyllis and like Eleanor Fazan who work

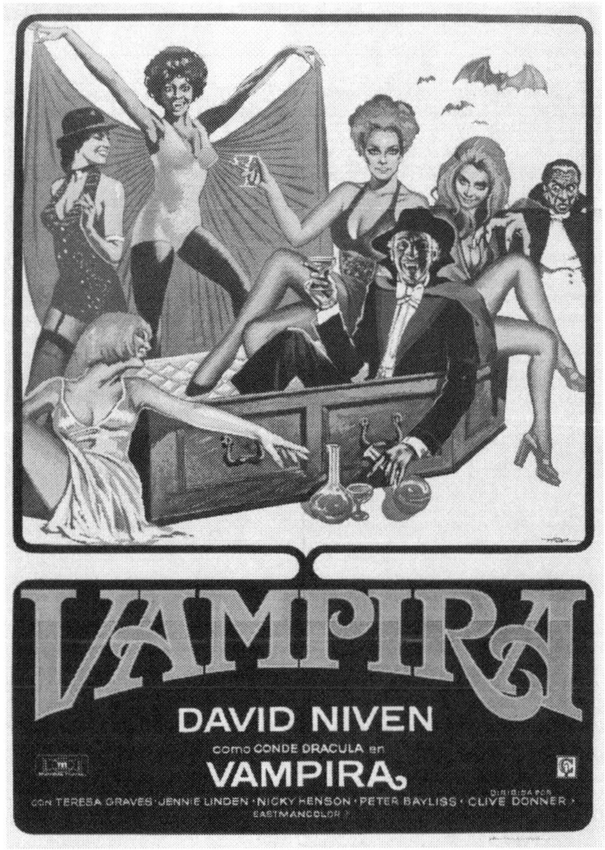

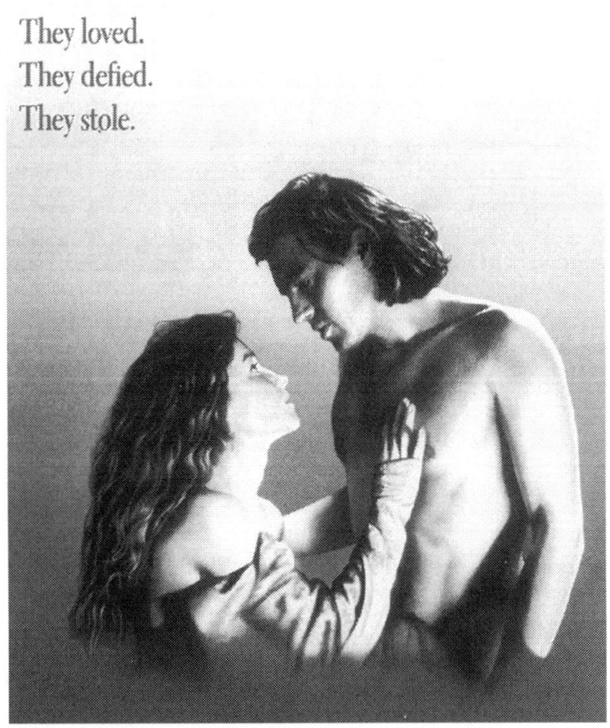

with you are gold. They are always on your side. They will always try to understand what you are trying to do and they will help you to do it. If you can you work with people like them as often as you can.

Stealing Heaven reunited you with Denholm Elliott and tells of the doomed 12th century love between Abelard, the great teacher, and Heloise.

It's very hard to talk about it. The producers were Susan George and Simon MacCorkindale. Susan's smart and Simon is a good-looking handsome clunk but perfectly okay; as an actor, a bit stiff but he can do it. As I understand it, Simon's brother is a lawyer in Los Angeles and was able to set them up with a pool of money. They chose the book, it's a really difficult story to do, and they asked me to direct it and I was very happy to. They didn't interfere that much, but neither did they contribute that much, actually that's a bit unfair, but the two people who really made the film work were my first assistant director, Bert Batt, in British movies Bert Batt is a name to conjure with, a man to go into the jungle with, a wonderful guy. The other was an extraordinary Greek Cypriot called Andros Epaminondas. Andros is really smart. He was born and brought up in England, of Anglo-Greek parentage. His father had sweatshops in Soho. Andros was mad about movies and he got himself a job with one of the big companies and then, somehow or other, luck shone on him and he fell into the lap of Stanley Kubrick. Andros worked for Stanley for eleven years, in which he did everything for Stanley. He would go to Montevideo to make sure that the print was properly aligned, and that the screen was right. He dealt with absolutely everything for eleven years, after which Stanley said: "It's time you went out on your own. I'll give you this lighting company." And he gave him a whole lighting company in London, which did very well, until he got bored with it. He married, has two lovely children and he no longer works. He looks after the children. He's a *fascinating* guy. He's filled with energy. On *Stealing Heaven* nothing got by Andros. As a film director, whether you are making a huge MGM epic like *Alfred the Great*, or you're doing a TV film for the BBC, you do need people like Andros around you. People whom you can trust. Even if you don't like them, if they are the right person for the job you *have* to like them and you *must* give them the job. Otherwise you are not being true to yourself. And that's what it all comes down to: being true to yourself.

I like the way you link the film of the past with the present in the title card at the end telling us where Abelard and Heloise are buried and that lovers still leave flowers on their grave.

When I showed the film to my agent he said: "You've saved the best scene until last." The young man who played Heloise's son was fantastically good-looking. He was found by Simon. We were filming in Yugoslavia and I sent Simon down in Zagreb to scour the bars for a suitable face.

I notice that the lead actors have beautifully shining eyes, spotlights reflected in their eyes, and that makes them very appealing. Was that a conscious effect you strove for?

No. The photographer was Mikael Saloman who, after this picture was immediately snapped up for two films by Spielberg {*Always* and *Arachnaphobia*]

There are some dynamic 'Spielbergian' lighting effects, such as the beams of lights on the students' faces when they are looking through slits in the rafters at Abelard (Derek De Lint) being tempted by the naked woman.

Yes. Mikael was very good but only within a narrow range. For example, Jocelyn (Rickard, who worked as the visual consultant) and I would show him the paintings of Giotto, which formed the basis of our concepts for the visual design, but he didn't really understand what we were getting at. What did you think of the music? We got hammered for the music.

It's interestingly eclectic. The mix of synthesizers with

plainsong, and with all-female plainsong, is very bold. But it creates the right mood. There were synthesizers in Chariots of Fire.

Exactly. It helped to make the film more resonant and more modern.

I saw Boheme, the modern English updating of Puccini's opera that you did with Tony Britten.

That was really Tony's film. Tony is the original and only begetter of Music Theatre London and he asked me to be a board member. He started off, about twelve years ago, doing a *Figaro*. Then, later, at the Drill Hall, he said he wanted to make a film. I said: "'If you want to make a film, and you are serious about it, then we have to sit down and talk." And we did. In the main I didn't do much. All the casting and directing was left to him. I worked as the executive producer: I checked on the script, very intensely. I checked on the lighting cameraman; I found and chose a location, once, when they were stuck and, of course, I helped a lot with the editing. And that was it. It's a production of *La Boheme* unlike any other, and it's Tony's picture. It's not my picture. I wouldn't want it attributed to me.

I think it's main asset as a film is that the singers act naturally. Berlioz was always complaining about the inability of opera singers to act.

Yes. That took a lot of work to get right.

Was casting a problem on Charlegmagne. A Franco-Italian-German co-production?

Not at all. The French wanted so and so and the Germans wanted so and so and I said: "No, no, no. It's very simple. What I'll do is have Italians playing Italians, French playing Frenchmen, Spaniards playing Spaniards."

And Frank Finlay as an Englishman.

He plays a character called 'Alcuin', an English priest who became a friend of Charlemagne's. He met Alcuin in the aftermath of defeat at the Battle of Roncesvalles (778 AD). Up until that point Charlemagne had been a Jack the Lad, always victorious, and suddenly he was smashed to the ground. His way of dealing with it was to berate God: "Why did you desert me?" He met Alcuin who becomes his close advisor. Frank is marvellous in the role. The story of Charlemagne is a great one, a brilliant man, great lover, endless wives, the maker of the first Holy Roman Emperor. I'd loved to have made it my way as a great feature on a bigger scale. I could have done with having many more extras, but we got by. There's tons of stuff in it. It's grand to some extent. It's not all to do with ritual, though ritual is there, it is also to do with 'men', there were few if any woman of influence at the time. It's human and personal.

Where did the crew come from?

The production crew were Italian and they were wonderful. They really came up trumps with everything as far as they could. It was a very exhausting shoot. On the last day of shooting we started shooting in the afternoon because we were going to shoot the last scenes at night, and I was having a late lunch on the location with the French executive and I said to her: "Oh, Thank God, this is the last chicken meal I'm having in Hungary." She said: "Don't be so sure..." We edited the film in eight or nine months in Paris. I worked with Tom Schwalm, who is German but he lives with his family in England. We had worked together on a little thriller I'd made in Germany called *Terror Stalks the Class Reunion*. Not that exciting but not bad. It didn't quite come off as well as it should. It was very helpful having a German-speaking editor on my side in the editing room because when arguments came up with the French and the Italians, and there were quite a few squabbles, he was able to calm things down.

Charlemagne was something of a return to the spectacle and main themes of Alfred. A medieval epic where the central figure is a young king torn between the need for war and the horror of war.

Yes. It was a three-part film, three one-hour films, put together to celebrate the creation of the European Union; Charlemagne had created the concept of Europe. The money came from France, Italy and Germany. Each one had their own particular view of what they wanted to see. The Vatican was terribly important to the Italians. The French had a very strong feeling about 'Europe' because of where they lay geographically. I worked on the script for nearly a year with de Gaulle's historian, Marcel Jullian, a very prestigious writer, and, every month I would have meetings with representatives of the three countries and we would argue about the script. It was absolutely fascinating. A wonderful learning experience. The film was sold and was acclaimed in every country in the world except England, where it was never shown. The BBC turned it down! The word they used to turn it down was 'accessible'.

Terrible. They should have been sacked. The same clots also rejected Gérard Depardieu's Napoleon.. It's ironic that the great flagship of the BBC for many years was Kenneth Clark's Civilisation, which, of course begins with Charlemagne. Then the BBC was held in high esteem; domestically it is now regarded as something of a joke. You said you made the film in Hungary?

Yes. That worked very well. For the famous battle from the Chanson de Roland, I found this extraordinary extinct volcano that looked like the ragged Spanish mountains. It worked perfectly.

Did it come in on time and on budget?

Yes! Of course! At the end of two years work, after finishing the editing and the dubbing, and after I had checked the print and handed it over, it opened the Monte Carlo Film Festival. We had a massive screening with a lot of the cast and it was great to see them again, and it was the end of a marvellous period of work. There are things in it that I wish more could have been done, more soldiers, more extras, but nevertheless some of it is very good. It ends on a tremendous upbeat. It's a film I'm proud of.

Are you optimistic about the future of film?

We are still making films that are about dialogue, not about emotions. Cinema is getting a bit stale. It's all 'What's the story? Who's the heroine?' The commercial structures of filmmaking, certainly as far as America and Europe go, are what they have been ever since film was invented. It is time for some changes. And I think they will come. The younger filmmakers are not as addicted to -

The classical narrative?

Exactly. One of the reasons it is hard to find *good* new subjects is not that they don't exist but our *attitude* to film is trapped in amber.

We spent a couple of afternoons watching films and looking at paintings. Clive Donner showed me the books in his library. He was particularly proud of a complete set of Lindsay Anderson's journal, *Sequence,* which he'd had bound and which he was leaving to Mike Kaplan, but his most treasured tomes were perhaps the four inscribed volumes of *Double Exposure*, photographic portraits taken by Roddy McDowall.

Donner: "I wish I could remember her name."

Sutton: "Don't you have a Halliwell?"

Donner: "I don't have a Halliwell. I dislike him so intensely I won't have him in the house."

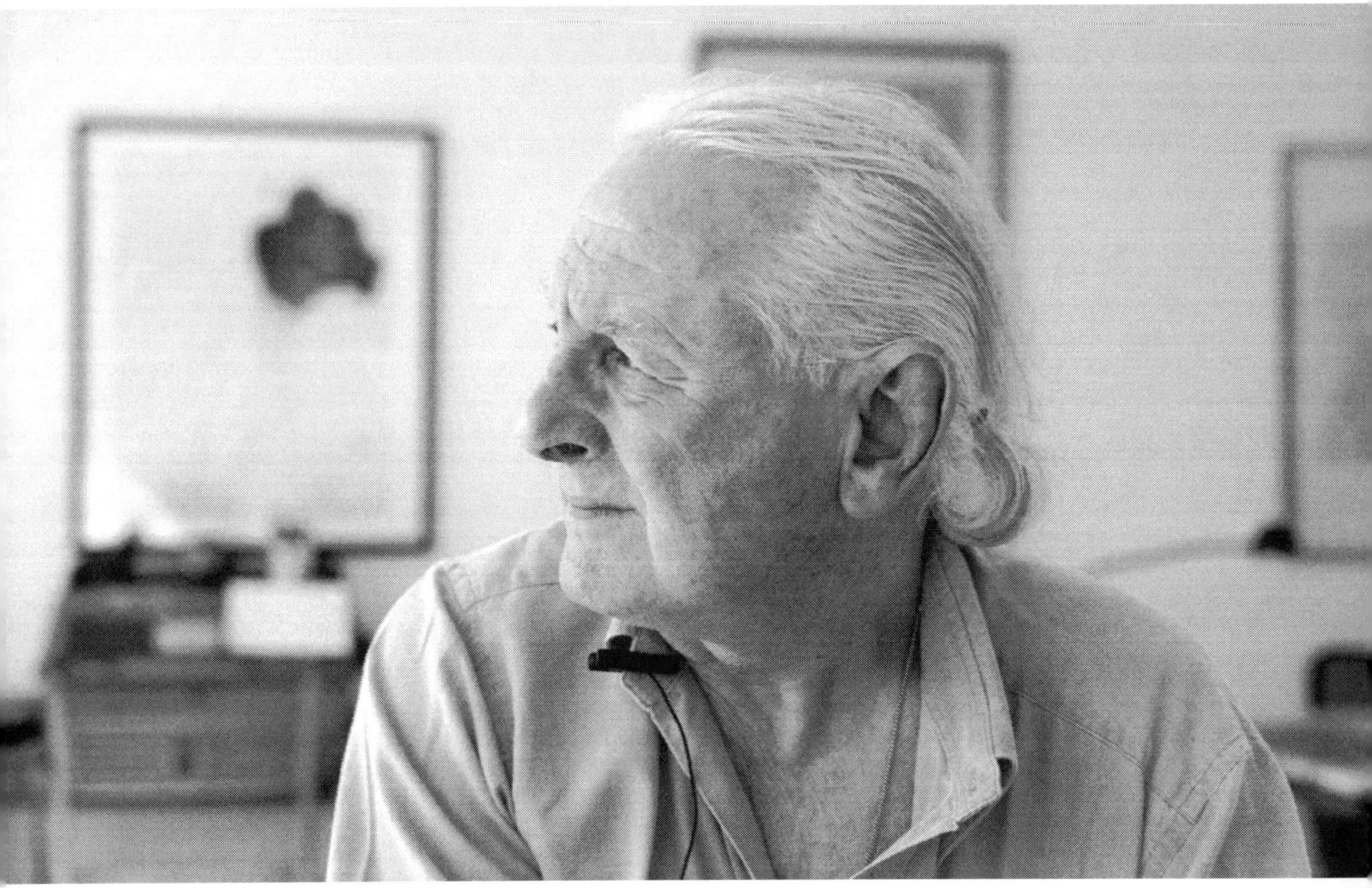

© Paul Sutton

Mike Hodges

I spent a few days on the set of Hodges' *I'll Sleep When I'm Dead* (2002), and had a private dinner in a fine restaurant with Charlotte Rampling, where I disgraced myself by eating all her chocolates, but no matter. It was a most relaxed film set. Clive Owen got a little annoyed once when the producer gave his mobile number to a French journalist, but that was nothing a pint in the nearest pub couldn't fix. But relaxed film sets don't necessarily lead to the making of fine films. *I'll Sleep* suffers from a lack of on-screen energy, the inglorious theme of male rape, and a star too hidden beneath unsympathetic make-up. That said, it's a film that should be better known. "It's a step in the right direction for me," said Clive Owen at the cast and crew screening at BAFTA, where he stood proud against a mild ribbing over what seemed certain to be a Hollywood turkey, Bruckheimer's *King Arthur,* which Owen had just finished working on. "Oh, come on. What does anyone really know about King Arthur?" Owen's star first shone in Hodges' exquisite chamber piece, *Croupier* (1998). Mike Hodges directed Michael Caine in *Pulp* (1972) and *Get Carter* (1971), still the finest English thriller in colour. He directed Mickey Rourke in a *Prayer For The Dying* (1984) and Rosanna Arquette in *Black Rainbow* (1989). He made the one true Felliniesque Science Fiction Film, *Flash Gordon* (1980), Fellini's own having been left on the launch pad at the end of *8 1/2* (1963). He also made the splendidly dark *The Terminal Man* (1974), adapted from the novel by Michael Crichton. It earned Hodges a rare fan letter from Terrence Malick.

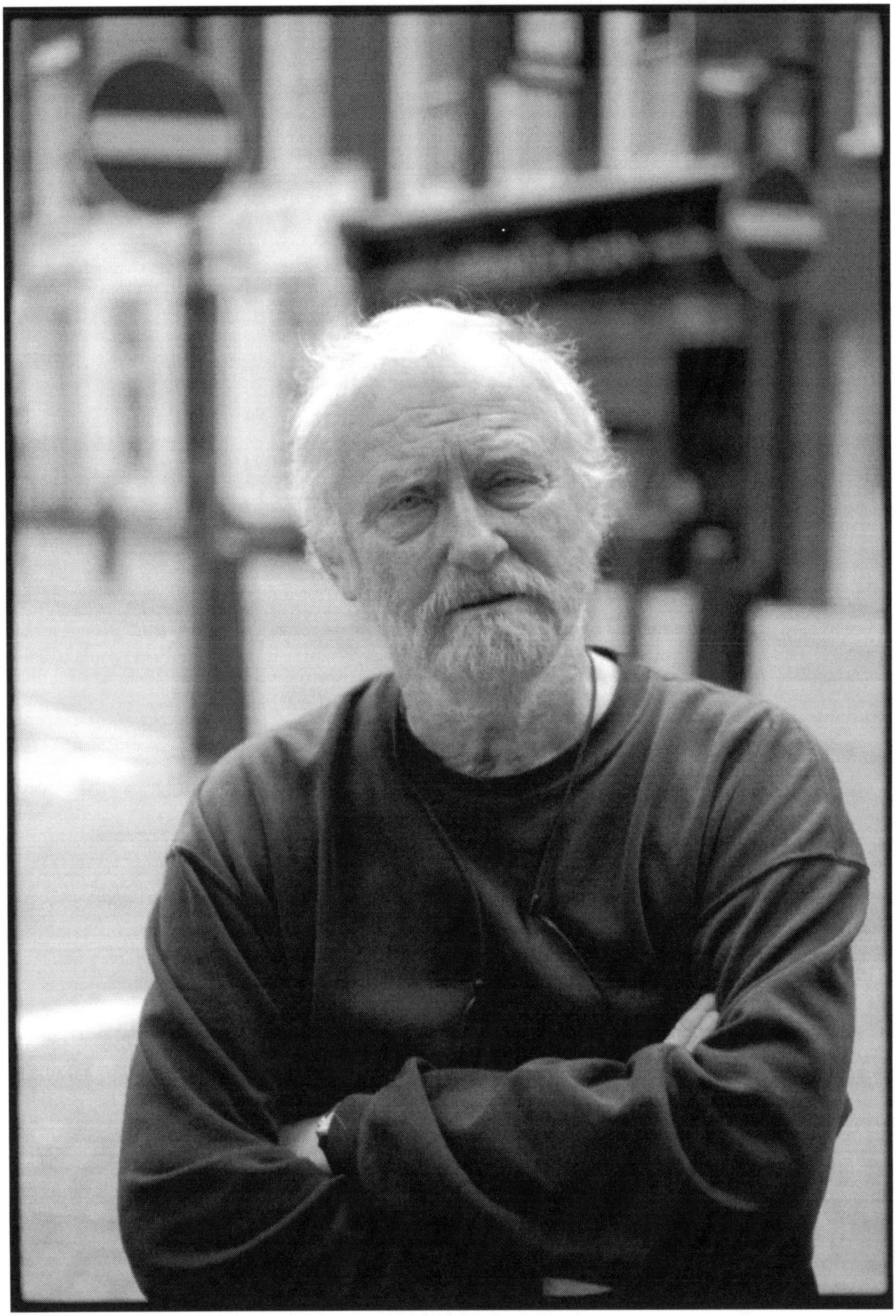

"I felt real, rather sudden sympathy, comradeship for Malcolm;
and we greeted each other with a rush of affection.
Mike Hodges came with him: a pleasant, small man with a beard."

Lindsay Anderson, The Diaries (1 January 1974)

When I saw Croupier the thing that first struck me was the credit 'A Mike Hodges & Paul Mayersberg Film'. The writer given equal weight.

That's right. If I had written it myself, and I have written a lot of my films, it would be okay to call it 'A Mike Hodges Film'. But I must say I don't like the possessory credit and I don't think it means very much. It means something if you are a Spielberg or a Hitchcock but there are so many no-nos who make films.

Boys whose life experience consists of being raised by mummy, sent to film school, then making a film.

Yes, complete unknowns, and they get this possessory credit. I don't know why that situation has come about. Credits have to be earned. If you worked with the writer, solidly, as I did with Paul Mayersberg on *Croupier*, with Trevor Preston on *I'll Sleep When I'm Dead*, and with Tom Stoppard on *Squaring the Circle*, it's incomprehensible to call it 'A Mike Hodges Film' without including the writer. I consulted the writers all the way down the line. If I was going to change something in the script, or I was thinking about changing something, I would consult them.

Croupier is a film about a writer, and about writing. He works in a casino but he isn't a gambler. He repeats the point that he doesn't gamble. He's a writer, Jack Manfred, who takes risks. He becomes the character he is writing about.

Sure.

He's played by Clive Owen, who has a great stillness, or sureness about him, a magnetic star quality. It's a real movie star performance but he wasn't a star until he made this film. I know you don't do readings when you're casting. How did you come to cast Clive?

Patently it was incredibly important to get the casting of Jack Manfred right. I worked with a very good casting person called Leo Davies. I saw a lot of actors. We narrowed it down to four, all suggested by Leo, and I did actually on this instance do a camera test with the four actors. It was a very simple thing. I wanted to see them in a tuxedo. More importantly I wanted to match the voice with an image. One of the four actors was Clive. I had really already made my mind up with Clive but, because the role was so important, I just needed confirmation. He had those saturnine good looks which casino owners love to have. There's a lot of sexual undercurrents in gambling and in casinos. I don't mean there's much flirting that goes on, it's very much ...

I know what you mean. It's a common phenomenon. In Cambridge, the young people employed to wear waistcoat and boaters and to entice people to go punting are all fantastically good-looking. It's as if it said on the job description 'previous modelling experience essential'.

Exactly.

The character Clive plays is fascinating. He immediately brings the audience in on his side by taking us into his confidence (in voice-over) and talking to us as his equal. He takes us into the world of gambling, where he seems very secure of himself. He sees and understands everything, every little trick, and he explains it all to us. But there are signs that this impressive confidence is a facade: his beating of a man who cheated is prolonged beyond the bounds of what we would expect from a reasonable man. It's interesting too that he makes a great fuss about being so methodical and so ordered and yet he breaks all the house rules about fraternising with staff and customers.

Yes. He is a fascinating character. You're right that it is as much about writing as it as about gambling. Part of the character's complexity comes when he gets absorbed by the book he is writing, and by the character he is creating. He becomes almost like an actor. He has to go into situations to find out what he's going to write about. When I write my scripts I like to go into the situations I am writing about. I don't want to be killed or shot if I'm writing a thriller, but the involvement of the locations is of incredible importance. I will go to the locations and try to find characters or read up about characters. You become a sponge and absorb everything that happens to you. The other wonderful thing about researching on location are the little accidents that happen. In *Croupier* all sorts of accidents happen to Jack, for example, he meets Matt and realises that he is writing about the wrong person. Paul's first drafts of the script were actually about gambling, and about the croupier from the outside, until he realised that the croupier, in a way, is right at the centre of the roulette wheel. That enabled him to draw this extraordinary character who I think is very representative of the times that we live in.

Everything's on the surface.

That's right and, in addition to which, the life that is described is the life that we are all sharing, and it's the life that aristocrats used to lead. Aristocrats had time on their hands and they had money. The same sort of corruption and the same necessity to alleviate boredom has now reached millions of people. Millions! Court life then was like 'Hello' magazine now, but now we are all a part of that nonsense. Previously we were peasants and we were outside of that 'lucky circle'. If it was a lucky circle.

Like Barry Lyndon in a sense.

Exactly. And it has extended to such a degree that an enormous amount of people gamble.

From a nation of shopkeepers to a nation of gamblers.

Absolutely, but even further than that. The obsession with money is paramount now. Money is the paramount driving force. When Paul came to me with the script, originally it seemed to me to have that texture to it, that feel, without being heavy-handed. I realised that the sounds of the casino itself should go outside the casino because that was what the film was about to me.

There's a lot of subtle visual detail, particularly early in the film when we are being encouraged to look and listen. The casino tables and chairs are blue with a red trim, which is repeated on some of the chips; the red of the chips is the same striking shade as the publisher's window frames, Jack's telephone and the strawberries on his father's bar.

I must confess that it wasn't my request and it wasn't something I was aware of. I'm slightly against colour-coordinated films now. I was much more interested in the fact that there is no natural light in the film.

There are several scenes in which we see the main character walk down a staircase, he visits his girlfriend at work and stands on a down escalator with her and, of course, he lives in a basement flat. Was that all part of the 'underground' or 'underworld' theme?

That was definitely intended and that was all me. In the original script, Jack's flat is on the first floor which, for me, was completely wrong. It had to be a basement. Many casinos are in basements. It was a conscious effort to suggest an Orpheus in the Underworld, a journey into Hades. Everything feels that is underground, subterranean. Casinos generally don't have windows.

So the gambler loses all sense of time. The finale is very satisfying. One expects thrillers to have a twist, but Croupier provides four or five unexpected twists and turns. Each of which comes off.

I'm glad. It is a gamble. The twists at the end of *Croupier* were a gamble and, obviously, one hopes they're successful. But the biggest gamble in *Croupier*, and in *I'll Sleep When I'm Dead,* is that audiences are very conditioned. It's a very Pavlovian job being a director in some ways, and one that I don't relish. I try not to push buttons

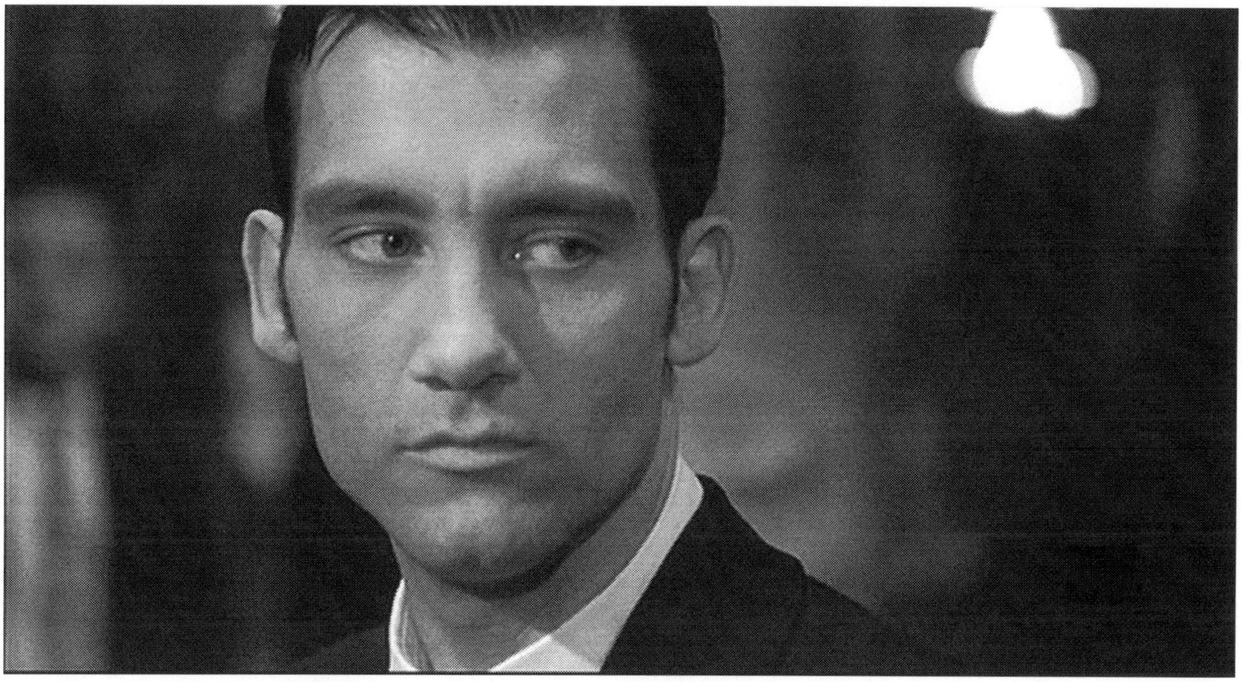

Clive Owen in his star-making turn in *Croupier* (1998).
Distant echoes of *Vertigo* as he is transformed from dark to blond.

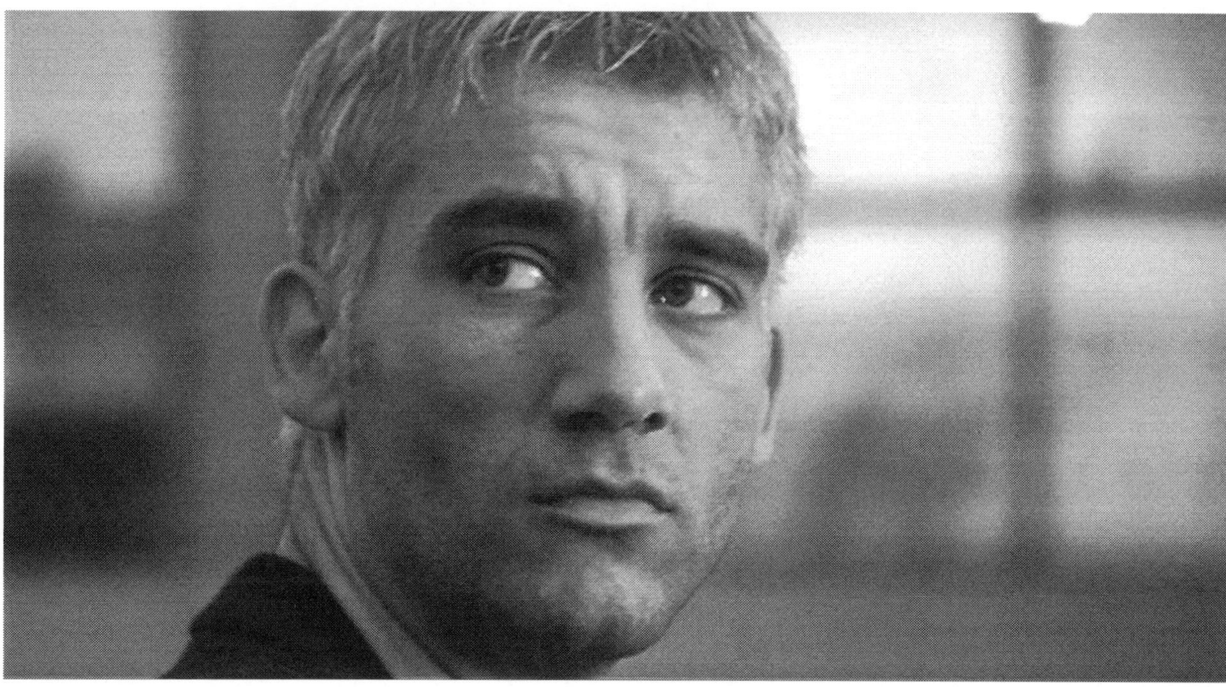

to make audiences react. I don't use music in that way. I don't make films like that, though *Flash Gordon* is an exception.

Dale recoils in horror and the music crashes.

Exactly. It had to be like that in that film, you couldn't dodge the issue in *Flash Gordon*. But in my more adult films. Actually Flash is quite adult in many ways -

Zarkoff's political agenda; the very amusing rudeness, such as the panting that precedes a forest boy's initiation -

And if you look closely you can see John Osborne masturbating furiously with a big staff (*laughs*).

It's a film I've seen often and I enjoy very much. How did you get the job?

Because Dino De Laurentiis like-a-my-face. Really. That's what he told me.

Didn't Nic Roeg have something to do with it?

Nic Roeg put me up for it. He was originally asked to direct it back-to-back with a sequel but he suggested me for the sequel. I met Dino at the Connaught [Hotel in London] and we talked and I thought about it and I turned him down. A little while later, Dino and Nic had had a falling out. Nic left the film and Dino asked me to direct the first one. I wasn't confident about directing a special effects picture but I accepted the job to please my children and I'm glad that I did.

Which suggests it was fun to make?

It was. It was completely improvised. I had no idea what I was going to do from day to day.

Because the script kept being changed?

No, though much of the dialogue was improvised and added to. By fun I mean the daily work of overcoming crazy problems. Such as how do we get them in and out of flying worlds, coloured clouds.

How far you put your tongue into your cheek?

Oh, there was no problem there (*laughs*). It was just a matter of respecting the source, a prime-coloured strip cartoon. Dino thought it was a serious film! (*laughs*)

It was a huge hit in England. It outgrossed everything that year, including Raiders of the Lost Ark.

I'm surprised it hasn't been re-released in the wake of *We Will Rock You* [the Queen musical]. There's a lot of money to be made there. But as I was saying, in my more adult films, I certainly try not to be manipulative. I want to allow the audience their own thinking time.

An element I like a lot in Flash Gordon is that Flash is easily the dullest character. Everyone seems to be having fun at his expense, they tease him and sport with him, then they let him win at the end.

Yes. He's an innocent. He's the only innocent in the film.

It's a good performance by Sam Jones. I heard you'd screen-tested Kurt Russell?

I did. I tested a lot of people, but Kurt was completely wrong. I wasn't looking for a movie star I was looking for a quarterback. Thick as a plank.

The character, not the actor?

Sam was all right, but seventeen weeks of working on a big film went to his head. He didn't come back after the Christmas break after surrounding himself with managers, and the managers took on Dino and lost. I had to finish the film with a stunt double.

Much of it?

Not that much, but a lot of Sam's voice is dubbed by another actor.

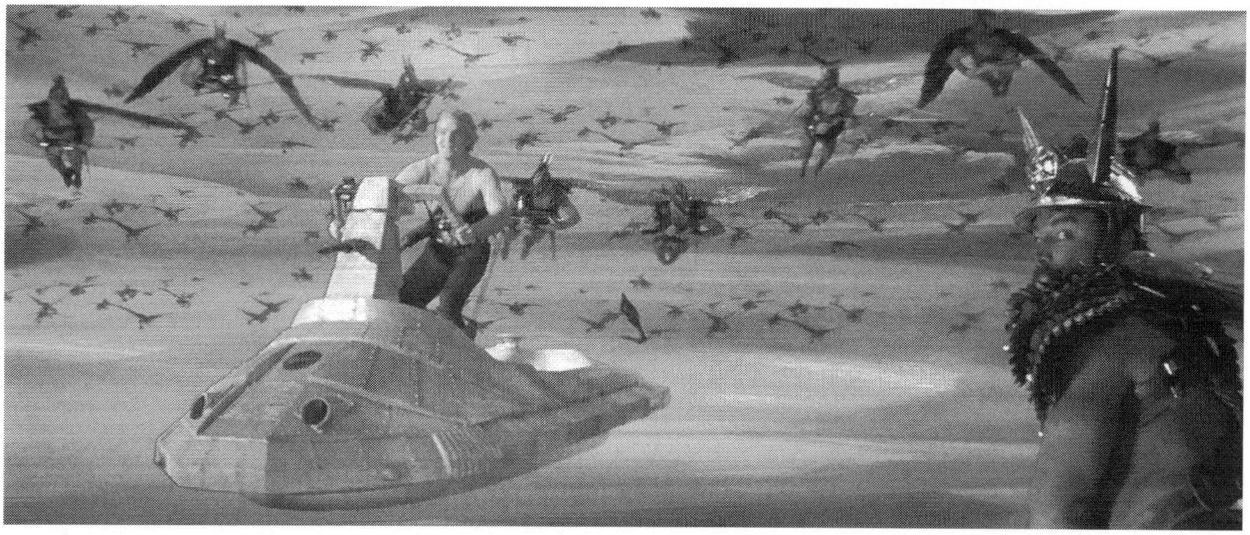
Respecting the comic-strip aesthetic. Cheerfully bad special effects. Just look at those matte lines!

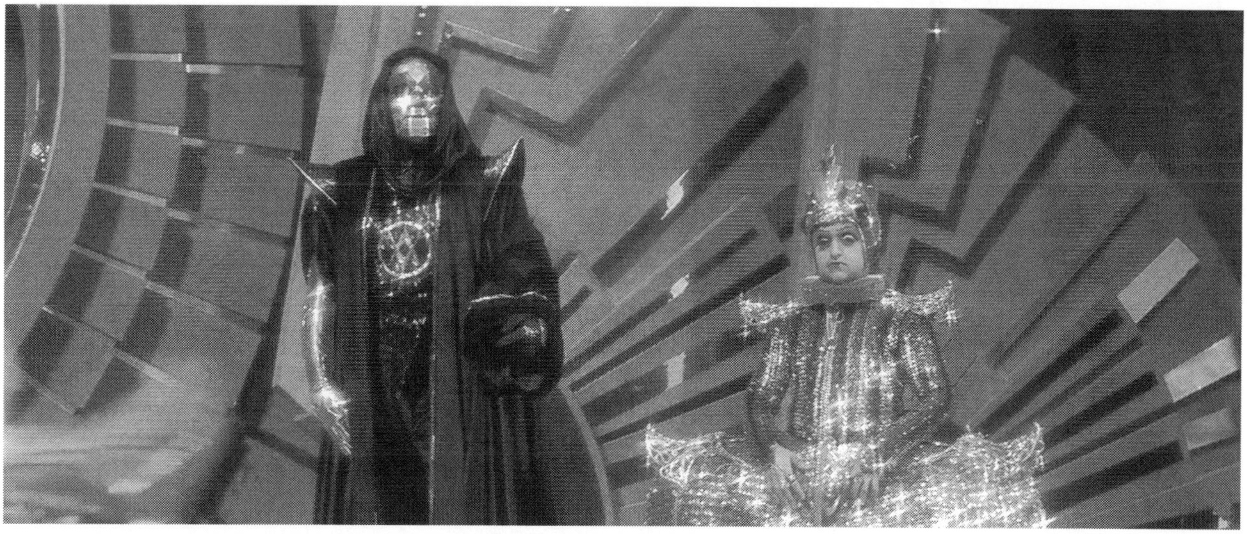
On the right, and on a leash, a dwarf called 'Fellini'. "I rather regret that now," says Hodges.

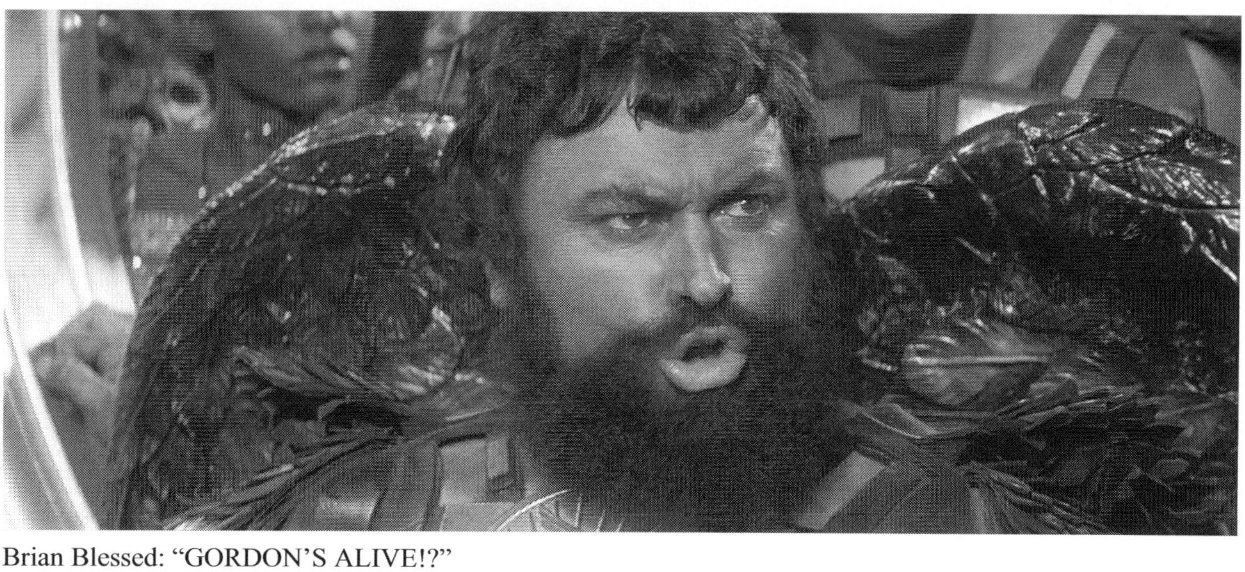
Brian Blessed: "GORDON'S ALIVE!?"

I didn't notice. I guess my ears were too tuned to the music. In Flash Gordon you use music as a driving force to power the action, but Croupier and I'll Sleep When I'm Dead both have sequences when you use music to create silence. In Croupier, there are two in-a-car scenes in which the driver turns off the music off to heighten the tension.

Yes. I've noticed that young people get into a car and loud music will start with the engine. All you hear is a drum machine going away. I incorporated it into the film because it seemed to fit the character. It was my own observation. It was never in the script. It was source music as opposed to music written by the composer. I used it more effectively when she gets in the car and the music is blaring yet again. She is screaming. There's a fight going on, and it heightens the drama of the piece. I've always liked using source music. It can be used very effectively. In a film I did called *Black Rainbow* there's a medium, and towards the end of the film there's this discussion about showbiz. And if you listen to the music in the background there's a corny singer giving it his all. It's sentimental and it's everything I hate about show business and it underscores the scene.

Fellini is the master of using source music. He'll use circus music in a street scene and have a parade of clowns playing the instruments.

Yes, exactly.

You supervised the English version of Fellini's And The Ship Sailed On (1983), but before that you'd worked with Fellini's designer on Flash Gordon. Danilo Donati. Was that difficult?

It wasn't easy. Dino was awe of him because of the work he'd done with Fellini, so Danilo had a lot of power, and he didn't speak English at all, neither did his crew, and I spoke no Italian. His designs looked good but they were sometimes impractical. For example, the big forest set was so full of trees there was nowhere to put a camera. There was no room for one! I had to chop down a few trees.

Metaphorically or actually?

(*laughs*) Both!

I'll Sleep When I'm Dead is a more complex film than Croupier, but it seems a very simple film. The main theme seems to be Death. Everyone in the film, with the exception of Sylvia Syms as the landlady, has the Sword of Damocles hanging over their head. And it's the most unsentimental film about Death that I know.

Yes. Well I am getting on now and I was brought up a Catholic and Death has always been part of my films. It's interesting that my first *World in Action*, which I did in 1964, was called 'The English Way of Death'. It was an examination of the undertakers world. Jessica Mitford had brought out *The American Way of Death*, a very amusing book.

Forest Lawns?

The whole caboodle actually. As well as being brought up a Catholic I was brought up during the war. In 1945/46, when Belsen and the horrors of the death camps were revealed, I was fourteen. And it wasn't hidden from us. Catholicism, with its iconography of death and the contemplation of death, and the fear of dying in sin, was deeply imbedded in me. As a child I was a believer. Capped off with the revelations of how horrendous human beings could be with each other, death became a part of my life. And I don't think it is an unhealthy part. It seems to me you act differently if, every day, you are conscious that you are going to die and that the people whom you are with are also one day going to die. You may act with more generosity, perhaps, and more love and more affection. And that is a serious thing to contemplate. Pretty much everything I've ever done has been imbued with an element of death, and with a consciousness of it: *Get Carter*, *Pulp*, *Terminal Man*, *Prayer for the Dying*, *Damien*, *Croupier* and so on [such as *Suspect* (1969) and *Rumour* (1970) made for Euston films' Armchair Cinema wing and now available on DVD. They are essential Mike Hodges]. The other thing that's interesting about *Croupier* is that the ball stops on -

Zero.

And Margaret is dead. When your number comes up that it is literally it. You think everything is under control then something happens and it all unravels and you are dead. *I'll Sleep When I'm Dead* isn't just about death though, it's also about male eroticism.

It takes the basic premise of Get Carter*, in which a man returns to his home town to investigate a death in his family, uncovers a sexual crime, and sets about avenging the crime. But 'I'll Sleep' takes this a stage further, Will Graham seeks not merely to avenge the crime but to destroy everyone's memory of it and to stop news of it spreading, because to him, buggery is worse than death.*

Sure. And it gets worse and worse for him. He is told that Davey (who kills himself after being raped) ejaculated, in other words, implying that he'd enjoyed it. It is all to do with the culture. For men like Will Graham, male rape undermines the whole structure of their society where the male is the matriarch.

I like the rich layering of detail in 'I'll Sleep'. One example is the boxing motif. When you first see the hoodlums in the back of Malcolm's car, one is looking through a boxing programme. A little later you catch, in the corner of the screen, a young boxer out running, accompanied by his trainer on a bicycle, and when Will sees a vision of his dead brother, the brother is shadow-boxing. It is placing the brother in the gangland milieu; and it is helping to build up a portrait of an area of London ruled by the underworld.

Yes it is. Boxing was always the working class way out. It was also a comment on the fact that male tactile sports hide a lot of homo-eroticism. To me, American Football is game that seems to be designed by and for homosexuals. All those beefy men with silk-clad bottoms sticking up in the air. It's a most bizarre game. I gather quite a few of the players are homosexual, and I've no objection to that, but I do object to the fact that it's obligatory to present this macho image. Many of the stars of Westerns were homosexual and I find it terribly funny that they presented this macho male front. The macho posturing, and this preoccupation with masculinity, particularly in America, has been a disaster for the world at large. The film looks into that area in a rather unusual way, I think.

A unique way. I can't think of similar example.

The rape itself is frugally handled. I used to wake up wondering how I was going to film it. The script is fairly blunt, which it had to be. Trevor writes what happened, and it's my job to stage and film it in a way that is watchable. And the rape has no significance other than the effect it has upon the young man concerned.

And the knock-on effect.

That's right the knock-on effect. If he hadn't committed suicide no one would have found out. He probably would have never told anybody that it had happened. That's the ramification of the suicide. The suicide leads to the whole unfolding of the story. And Boad, the character played by Malcolm McDowell, would have got away with it, as most people who do it do get away with it. Rape is a crime about power, the perpetrators know that it's the way to demean or to destroy somebody, particularly if the victim is a macho male. If you notice that when Turner's assistant is stitched up by Will Graham's old gang, they defile him by turning him into a woman, by putting him into a woman's dress and make-up. In the script they just shave his hair, but that wouldn't do because whole theme is this strange area which all men are conscious of, and which most men want to sublimate. It is an uncomfortable area that I was anxious to explore, without being obvious. Including the boxing, I might add. I don't know where it came from. I just said to Jonathan, why don't you do a bit of shadow-boxing before the rape? And I built on it. In the park I was going to have people doing tai-chi, I love parks early in the morning, but I thought it would be better to just have a boxer going round.

A lot of the henchmen have bleached blond hair. At one time that was taken by the macho society to be a sign of femininity.

Exactly, as in *Get Carter* of course. I had two characters in *I'll Sleep* bleached: Miles, the guy who makes the phone call at the party at the beginning. You had to remember him. Bleaching his hair showed off his face. I thought he looked terrific. And Turner's henchman.

I like the little scene with the guy who first spots Will on his return to London.

He is a very good boxer that guy. He's really up there in his weight division. And that was his first role.

He looks so right. And his whole attitude is so wrong. He judges Will Graham solely by his looks and declares that this former king of the underworld is now 'nothing.' And it also helps to imply that the tentacles of this crime empire are everywhere.

Sure. You're right.

Talking of boxers, you directed Mickey Rourke in A Prayer For The Dying. I think he brought a lot to the film. There's always something going on in a Mickey Rourke performance, and I don't mean showy. There's quite a lot of James Dean in him.

Yes, he's a very instinctive actor. He does a lot of improvising and a lot of thinking. You couldn't rehearse with him. You just point the camera and he does his stuff.

And he does go deeply into his characters. I'm talking about the IRA tattoo.

Yes, that was for the character. I told him to get a temporary one but he got a real one, and it went septic.

Much like the English press reaction when they heard about it.

Yes.

More apoplectic though than septic. 'How dare an Irish-American actor say that English Imperialism is wrong'. Both Croupier and 'I'll Sleep' have a Clive Owen transformation scene, in 'I'll Sleep', he turns from looking like a tramp into a sharp-suited gangster, almost as if to say that you can't do the job unless you're wearing the right clothes.

Sure. It's a ritual as much as anything. If you are going to revert to being a gangster you have to look like one. At the beginning when we find him, apart from the very first scene, he looks like an animal, and people say he looks like one, but he is trying not to act like one. Animals kill.

But he turns his back on the man in the woods who has been beaten up.

The man being beaten up is incidental, except that it is reminding him of the world which he has rejected. He turns his back on it, as he does again at the end of the film. The transformation comes when he decides to stop *looking* like an animal and instead *act* like one. And of course he looks like a business man. The jungle nowadays is in business. I'm reading a book called *The Iron Triangle*, which is about the Carlyle Group which controls the American financing of defence. These men are animals but they wear wonderful clothes. They are in their own little jungle, and

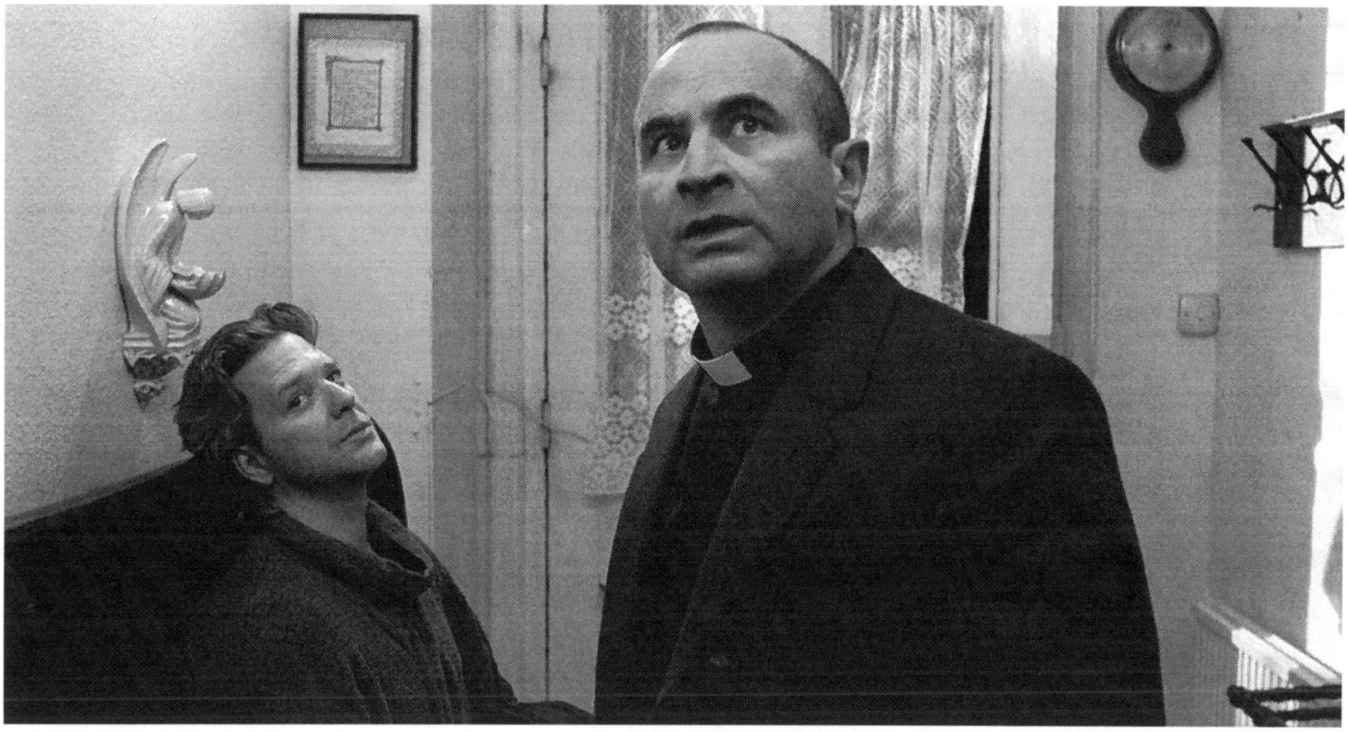

Uncharacteristically blunt symbolism as an angel prays over Mickey Rourke in *A Prayer for the Dying* (1987)

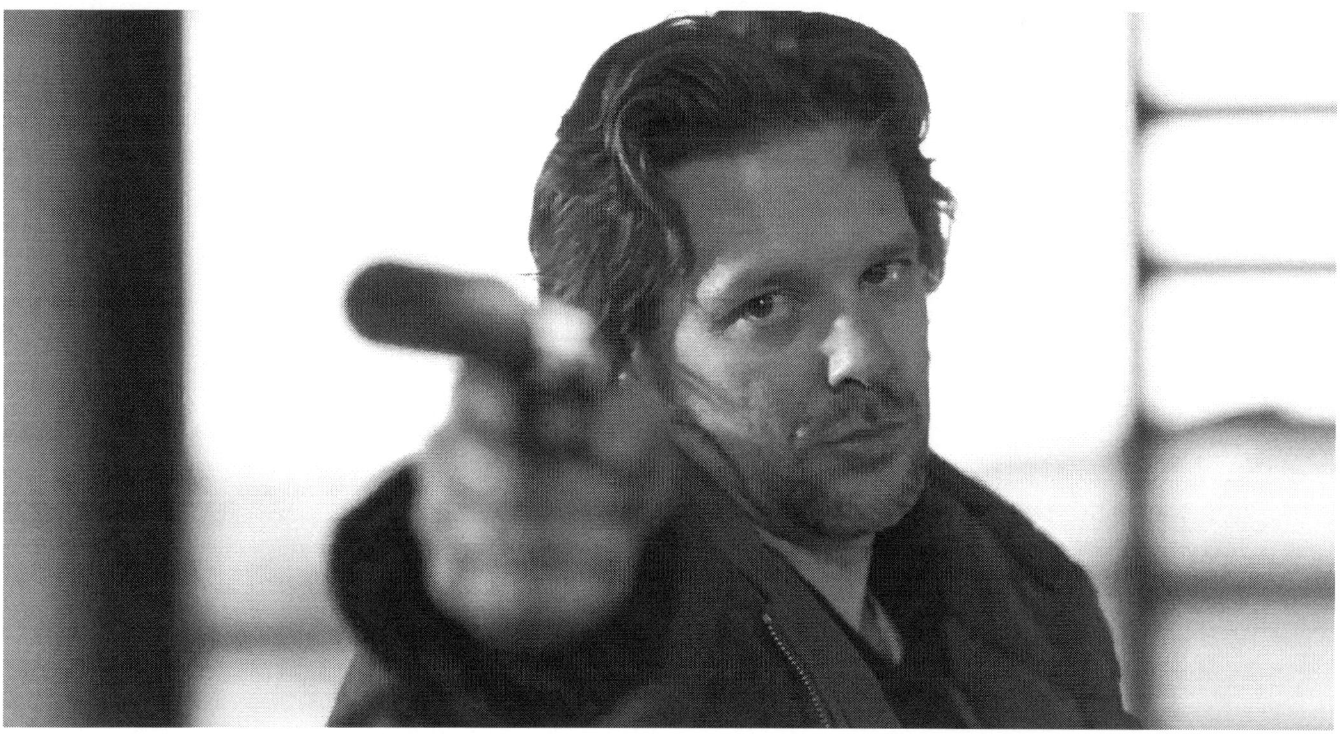

unfortunately one has to be a part of that jungle, and that's how the Iraqi War begins. The first time Will turns his back, the man calls to him, and he changes his mind and goes back to help him. The second time is the repeat at the finale, when he tells Boad that he is not going to kill him now, and I do the same thing there. I track with Will, the camera on his back, and he stops and, like he does the first time, he turns round only this time to kill. It is strange that I've made two films where the focal point is the metamorphosis of the main character, both played by Clive Owen. In Paul's script for *Croupier,* Clive had long hair which is then cut, because you can't be a croupier with long hair, but that wasn't enough, and, because it was a very short shoot, and we were shooting all the casino scenes in Germany in which he had short hair, and then the scenes where he had long hair in London. I hate wigs. I decided to keep the hair the same length and change its colour from blond to black. There is one scene, where he's selling his car, and there is a little bit of wig on the underground.

And the hat?

Paul had written one scene with a hat in it, and I built it up to make it his 'thinking cap'. I thought it would be good to have him wearing the hat the very first time we see him writing. Marion (Gena McGee) 'wants to live with a writer'. She's romantic. There's one moment when he's writing and he hasn't got the hat on and she puts the hat on him. The hat is a part of her image of him as a writer. Writers wear hats.

Both films start and finish at the same point. Apart from being aesthetically pleasing it does create a sense that you've created a world, that the story you have told will continue long after the credits are over. Was that a part of your plan? To make a world?

Absolutely. Good films always do that. They take you into a world that the filmmakers have made. I think that's the key to a good film. If you don't enter that world, the film, for you, is a failure. Every time I start a film I try to go somewhere different, to somewhere I have not been before. And you, the audience, hopefully will find it different as well.

I know you have wanted to work with Malcolm McDowell for a long time, there was talk of you working with him in the early Seventies, and I know he was uneasy about doing the male rape.

He's wonderful, Malcolm. I was nervous in some ways. Malcolm is an extremely brave actor. He does wonderful things, always, I think. And I didn't really want 'brave' acting in that scene I wanted it to be quite subdued. I was curious to see what he brought to me. He was wonderful. I think his speech at the end was absolutely fantastic. What he has to say is so pathetic and so stupid and so sad. And for two lives to go for this ridiculous *male* jealousy is very sad. The thrust of it, to use rather a crude word in the context, is jealousy and the fear of growing old. In the original script 'Boad' (McDowell) was about the same age as Davy. It was interesting making him older, and I also made 'Helen' (Charlotte Rampling) older. It's very understated. Can audiences understand why Davy committed suicide and why Will shot Boad?

I'm sure they can. And it is more powerful the second time you see it. And it really did need the shooting of Boad.

Audience satisfaction is always interesting, and how to achieve it. The gamble is that you never know. I think the cut from Will throwing the door open and putting the gun up, to the gunman sitting on stairs above Charlotte, she looks almost dead, it's a very odd and wonderful cut. I'm very proud of that cut.

That scene is something that haunts you after you've seen the film. Did she die? Did Will come to the rescue?

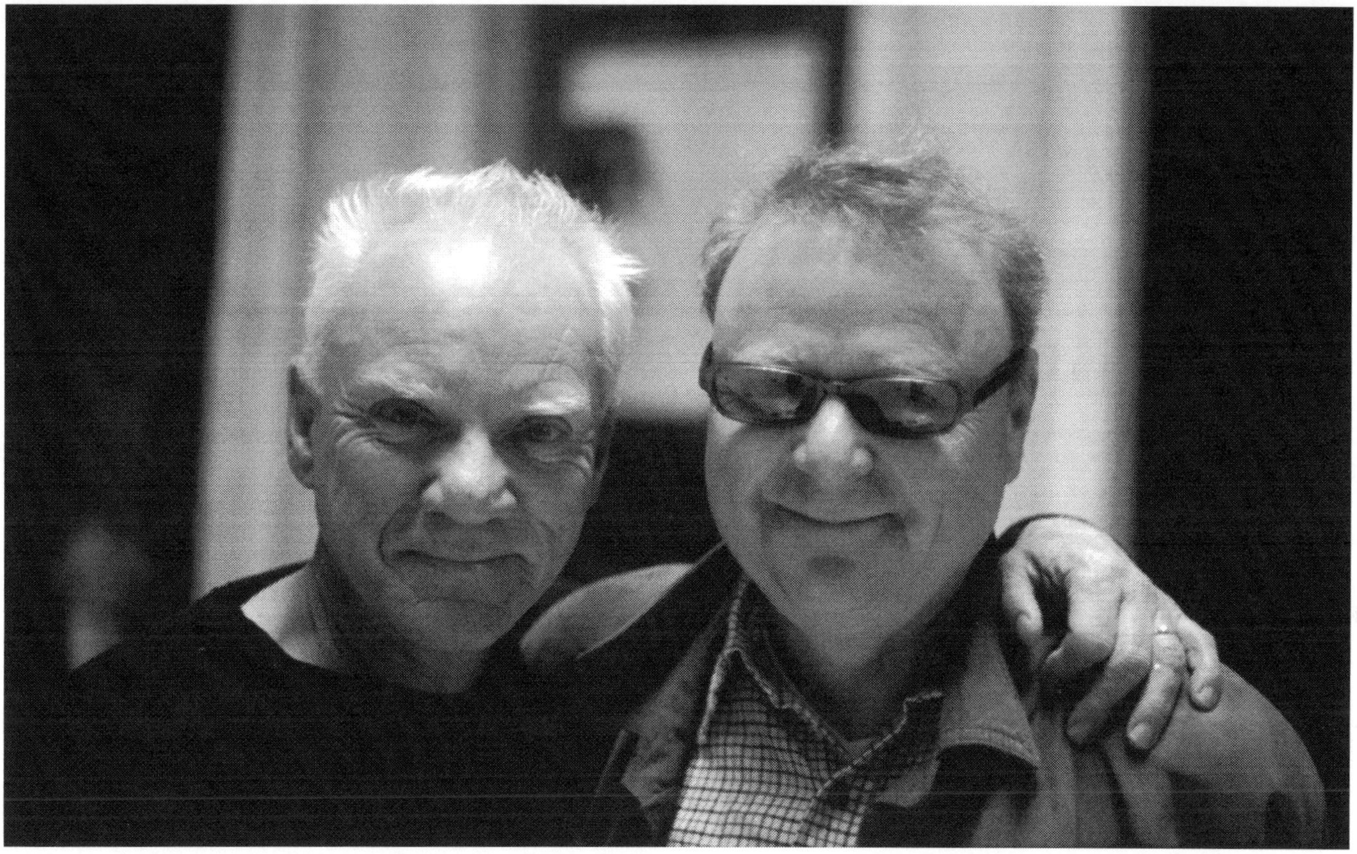

Malcolm McDowell, Mike Kaplan and Clive Owen on the set of *I'll Sleep When I'm Dead* (2003)

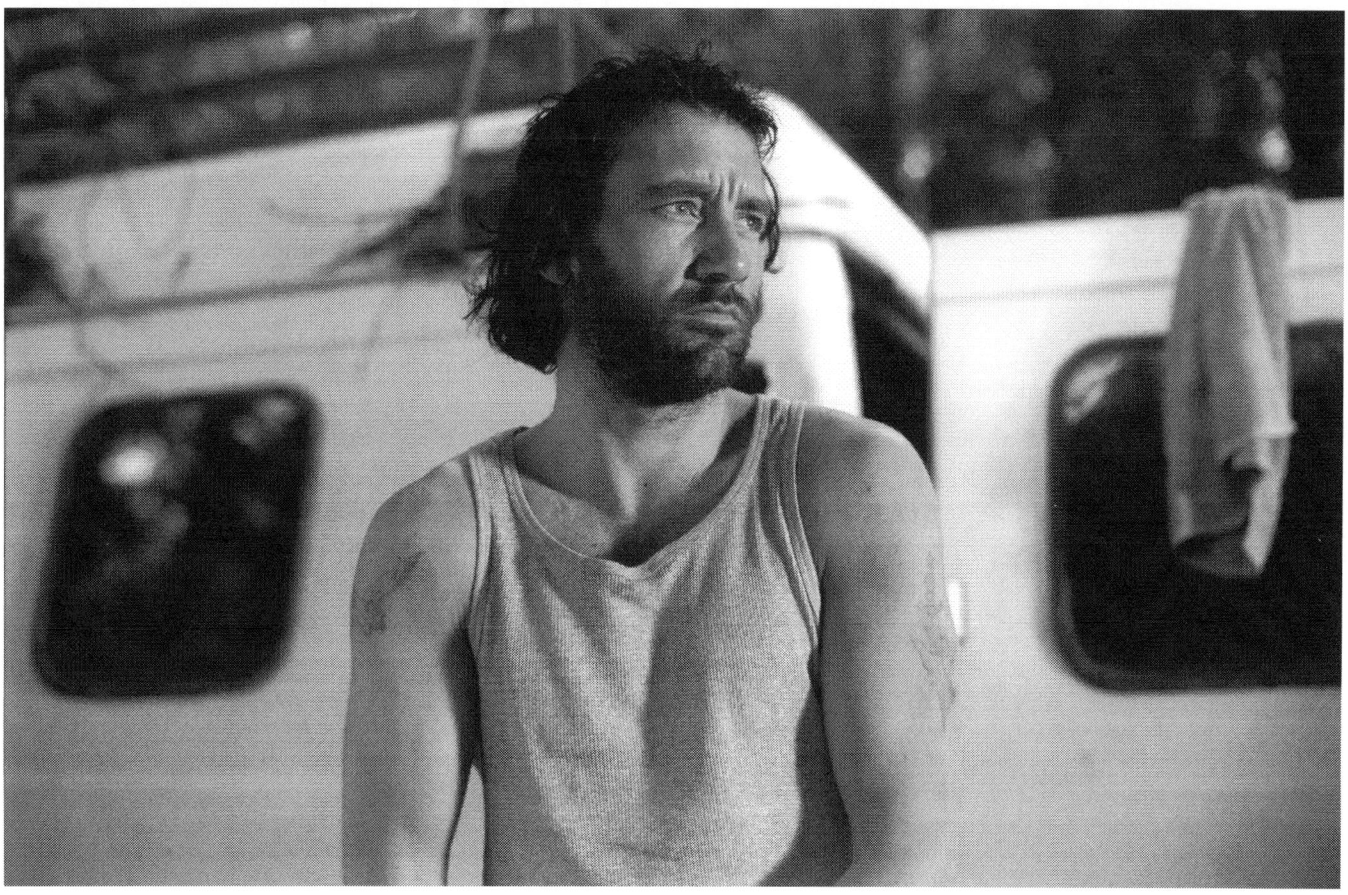

Exactly. I love that. And what else *could* you do? Have a shoot-out? It wouldn't happen anyway. And Will knows that when he kills again he has blown it. The police would be involved and they'd track him down, etc. His whole life has just unfolded. Gary Indiana, an American writer I like very much, noted that words said by Will at the beginning of the film, and at the end, echo the words said by Boad. They are almost the same, 'about the way he smoked a cigarette, the way he walked', but one set is loving and the other is hateful. One is a declaration of love, the other a declaration of hate.

A happy accident?

It was, I admit it. I didn't pick up on it until we were editing.

The first thirty-minutes or so reminded me of Carol Reed's Odd Man Out, in which James Mason goes on a journey through city streets, meeting a whole parade of unusual characters, who have only one moment or one little scene. The final character is a man so eccentric he can only be played by Robert Newton.

Oh, Robert Newton is great in the film!

He is. There's something about that journey and that parade in I'll Sleep. You've mentioned the man at the party, there's the taxi driver, the man riding a bike in the alleyway, the landlady ...

You're quite right. I love Carol Reed. As a director he is terribly underrated. And of course, I was alive when his films were coming out. He was the equivalent, say, of Spielberg. They were the kind of films we used to go to see every week. Imagine that? It was a wonderful time to be watching films.

British films.

Exactly.

Terminal Man left me with a similar feeling. It played on my mind. The theme of a man who loses control to such a degree that he loses his identity is very powerful, but I also believed in the man as played by George Segal. It was a wonderfully human performance.

Yes. The film was not successful when it came out. It was made long before Michael Crichton was the major novelist he became, and they sold it as a sci-fi film. It was too strong to be released in Britain. It has had an extraordinary life though in America on television. And it's been very successful. I know because I get the residuals. Part of the problem with the initial release was that Segal was known as a wonderful 'light comedian', a bit like Jack Lemmon. I'm not decrying light comedians in any sense, but Lemmon had always had these serious roles as well. Maybe they didn't take to George as an ordinary man?

Didn't Terrence Malick have something to do with getting the film released in the States?

He did. He wrote me a fan letter and Mike [Kaplan] used the letter in the trade ads. ["I have just come from seeing *The Terminal Man* and want you to know what a magnificent, overwhelming picture it is. You achieve moods that I've never experienced in the movies before, though it's only in hope of finding them that I keep going. Your images make me understand what an image *is*. Not a pretty picture but something that should pierce through one like an arrow and speak in a language all its own..."]

The production design of The Terminal Man is striking. Very cold.

That was me. And that was a conscious case of colour coding. I wanted to shoot it in black-and-white but Warner Brothers said 'no', so I decided to shoot it in black, white, gray and skin tones.

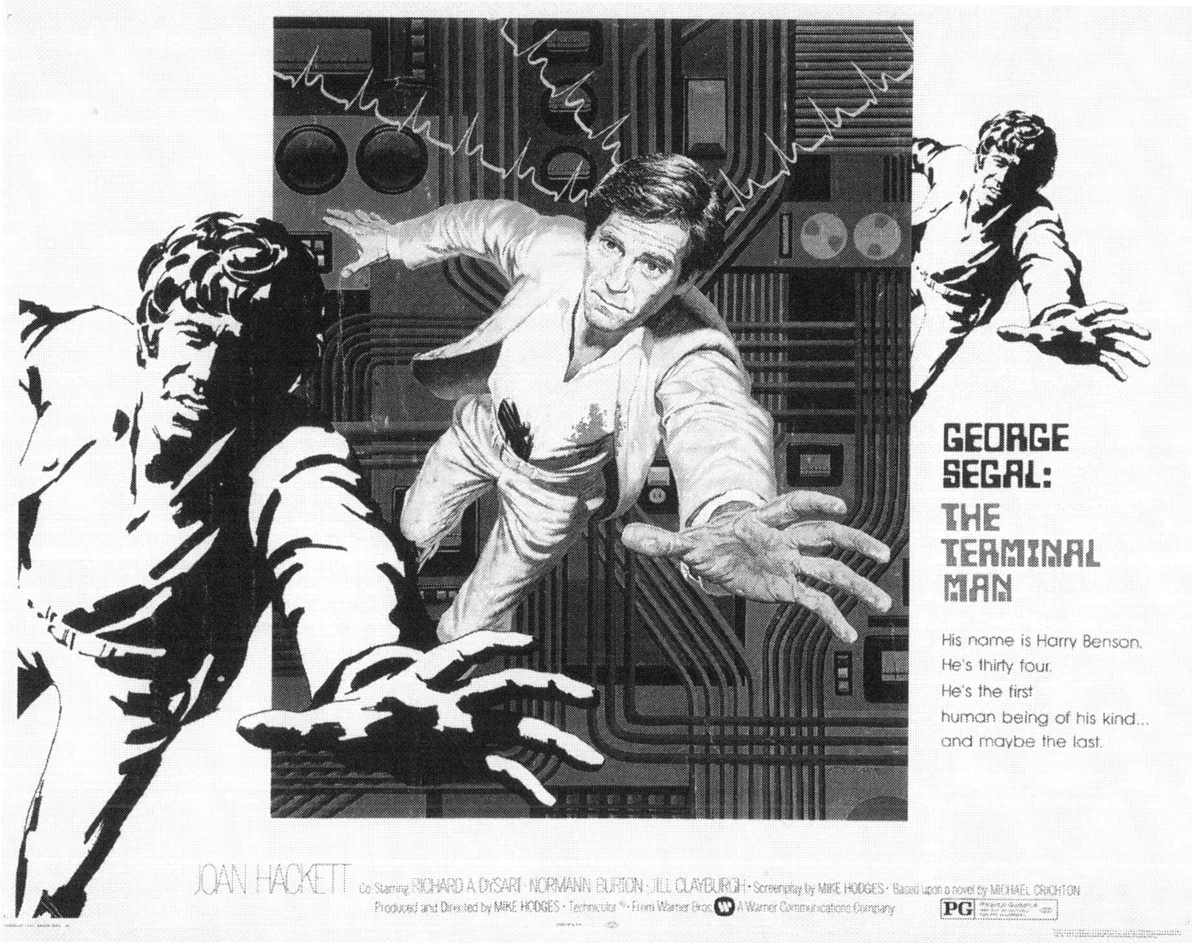
GEORGE SEGAL:
THE TERMINAL MAN
His name is Harry Benson.
He's thirty four.
He's the first
human being of his kind...
and maybe the last.
JOAN HACKETT Co-Starring RICHARD A. DYSART · NORMANN BURTON · JILL CLAYBURGH · Screenplay by MIKE HODGES · Based upon a novel by MICHAEL CRICHTON
Produced and Directed by MIKE HODGES · Technicolor ® · From Warner Bros. A Warner Communications Company
PG

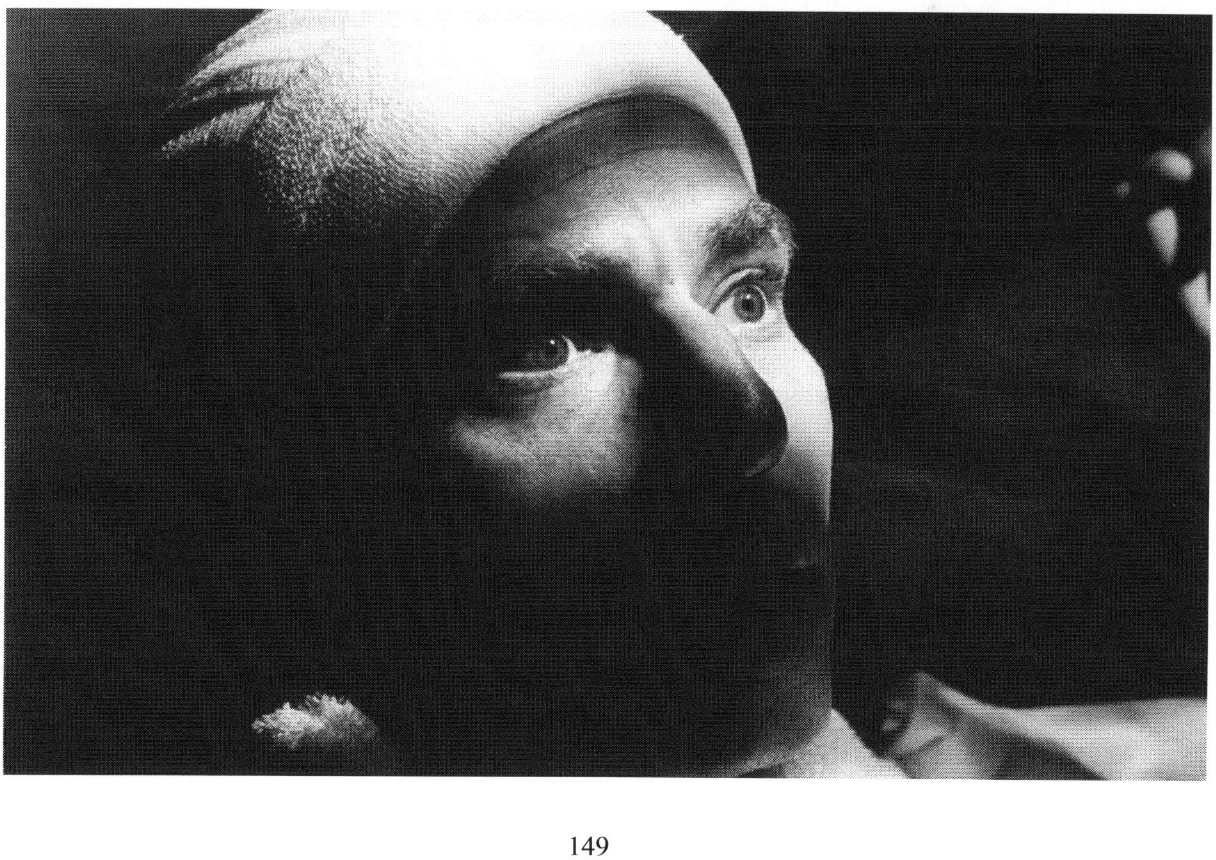

Then I decided I would use colour just at specific moments, such as when he gets stabbed, the red rose, and the blood. I don't think I would make a film like that again. If it has a failing it is that it is almost too self-conscious, though that approach suits the film. I made some changes to Crichton's novel, which is a good novel but, because it was about a man who is scared of becoming a machine, and the machines are taking over, Crichton set the finale in the basement of the hospital.

You chose a cemetery.

Being an ex-Catholic, I wanted something deeper than just a shoot-out in the hospital. I thought I was pushing my luck to say he should escape into Forest Lawn cemetery.

Evelyn Waugh country.

I had always loved that novel, *The Loved One*. George Segal found the grave and then did that wonderful thing, bowing to everyone before jumping into it. It was so curious and, in my opinion, appropriate. But bizarre.

Did you make many changes for the director's cut of The Terminal Man'?

It's only one cut, but it's three-and-a-half minutes out of the film.

I presume all that sentimental stuff at the start?

That's right. That was put in because Warners said there was no one to root for, and I agreed to it so I'm not complaining. I was grappling with American audiences weaned on sentimentality so I tried to help by putting that scene at the beginning. I had shot it but I changed its position and put the photographs in. And I hated it every time I saw the film. It was very 'television' and it was the wrong way to start. I did the cut yesterday and it is fucking wonderful! The most satisfying cut I have ever made in my life. And it works! The helicopter is lifting off, and you hear the sound of the helicopter. You go the black and you hear just this piano, the Goldberg Variations. It is just terrific! People must think I'm mad but it has bugged me for thirty years and I wanted, at least once before I popped my clogs, to see it with the scene removed.

The use of the music in the film reminds me a little of the way Kubrick uses music in Barry Lyndon, which I think is a masterpiece. The film is paced to the music and the music is paced at the beating of the human heart. One can't listen to music 'at pace'. The music creates a mood of thoughtful contemplation.

He made a big mistake with *Barry Lyndon* by having an interval.

Not at the screening I saw.

When the film came out it had an interval which was a terrible mistake, because he perfectly built up this world, and you were in it, you felt you were obliged to straighten your collar and pull your stockings straight, and then came the interval! And you went out and bought a hot dog, and then he had to build it all up again. But you are right it is a great film. I think there is an audience out there, and a considerable audience, for films that have a different pace from most of the shit that's put out. You should see the trailer that Paramount did for *I'll Sleep When I'm Dead.*

Wham-Bam-Thank You-Mam!

Yes, including the metamorphosis. Have they no trust at all in audiences?

I don't think they have.

And this is Paramount Classics. I kept saying: 'We agreed that this is a film for adults, for sophisticated people. At the moment they've done the whole campaign with the aim of attracting morons.

So they'll get the wrong people to see the wrong film.

Yes. I wouldn't want people going to see this film thinking they are getting *Get Carter*, because they are not. *Carter* was thirty years ago. I've made lots of different films since.

Get Carter was your first film and is perhaps more popular now that it has ever been. I think a good place to start when talking about it is the soundtrack, not just the music score, but the fact that, from the very start, you use natural sounds almost as rhythm. I'm, of course, thinking about the noise of the bridges as the train passes under them.

Correct.

And it is a film where the soundtrack and the visual are elaborate and yet simple, and working in perfect unison.

I am *obsessed* by sound. Again I suppose because I was brought up in that era where sound *was* really used well by the great British filmmakers, Powell and Pressburger, David Lean. Lean was incredible with sound. I was brought up in an era where the use of sound was important. Something happened, I think in the late sixties, when pop became the vogue and music just washed away everything. It was crudely used. Music in films now is used to mask the insecurity of the filmmaker. Music has become meaningless, except to *tell* you how to feel. Often you can see a reasonably good film ruined by intrusive music. You can always tell a British Miramax film by the music.

The English Patient was over-scored. The film rendered wholly unmemorable as a result because, as you say, the music is doing the thinking for you.

True. The same happened in *The Madness of King George*. The music got between you and the King. It's such a wonderful performance by Nigel Hawthorne but the music comes in and is used in such an appalling way. Now, and this says a lot about the society we live in, most people can only watch a film when they can eat at the same time. And if the film is quiet they feel embarrassed about eating. It's all about money. The majors want the public to pay to see the film and pay to be fed at the same time.

I'm forever telling people off for eating loudly in cinemas. I'm the horror of the Cambridge Arts. Back to 'Carter' there's a mournful music motif that, to me, wouldn't sound out of place in a Spaghetti Western. It adds a melancholy grandeur.

Yes. I love music, and I listen to it avidly all the time, so I'm won't use it unless it has a purpose. I met this wonderful composer, Simon Fisher Turner, who is fantastic to work with. We never go into a studio with musicians. What used to happen was that you had the score written and you would screen the film and record the music. It was a stultifying experience. It was too late to do anything. It was, of course, different with *The Terminal Man*, I just sent the film to Glenn Gould and that was that. *Carter* was a very small recording session. And because it was so small I was able to control it. The theme you mention was embedded in the opening music and luckily I recognised that the motif could be used as the theme for the whole film. I wanted something simple. I always want something simple. I said to Roy [Budd]: "Pull it out". I would then sit there, as we went through the film, and I would tap him on the shoulder and say where I wanted it to go, for example, when Carter sees his brother, and, of course, at the end of the film. Film scores at that time were a 'big deal', 'big' scores. Roy was a young man but he was a part of that 'big' tradition, of which *Goldfinger* is a good example.

Big, orchestral and brassy.

Yes. And once the 'big score' gets going it is like a tank in way. There's nothing you can do to stop it. Scores like that are fine for those types of film, but *Carter* was a small film.

There's a little moment in Get Carter which nobody talks about, probably because it is a pure accident, but it's no accident that you kept it in the film, that encapsulates what is best about your films. There's an overhead shot of a car pulling up at a jetty and a pigeon runs away from it. It doesn't fly as one would expect. It runs. Brilliant!

I put that pigeon there. I went down personally and put that pigeon there. Everyone seems to storyboard these days, but they don't seem sensible to me. I have used them. I used them for the operation in *The Terminal Man*, because it was so complicated and because I could use them as a way of recording what had been done in the operation. And for *Flash* [*Gordon*] I had them for the special effects sequences but I never paid any attention to them.

And the pigeon sequence in Get Carter?

I did indeed. For me the real joy of filmmaking is making discoveries on the set, improvising, allowing for the unexpected. When I first started making films I would lie awake at night going through the next day's work, thinking about this tracking shot here, then this cut there, then you'd go in in the morning and discover that the set wasn't quite as you'd expected and you have to scramble your ideas and start again. Now I get a good nights sleep, and I go onto the set, see what's there and what that allows, and I build the scene then. That allows in all the little accidents and it also allows the scene to build organically. It's the best thing I learned. There is one scene in *Carter* which I have always been pleased with, the scene when Carter catches the little guy and brings him up to his hotel. To do that scene in the conventional way, frankly would have taken two days, and the cutting, from him to him and so on, would have made it look like Wimbledon and I hate that. It was my first feature film and the schedule was tight. And I worked out a better way to do it. Luckily I had a star, Michael Caine, who was fantastic to work with. He was quite prepared not to have a close-up and to play a lot of it off his back! I was able to work in this little thing, almost like a dance, with a whisky bottle that is thrown and caught, and because it's all done in one shot you see *everything*, and because you see everything you have to choreograph the actors' every movement. Or preferably not to have any moment. Scenes usually dissolve when there is a lot of close-cutting. *I'll Sleep When I'm Dead* was a 29-day shoot and there is hardly any close-cutting at all. I hold on Malcolm at the end when he makes his speech. The Americans would have been cutting all over the place.

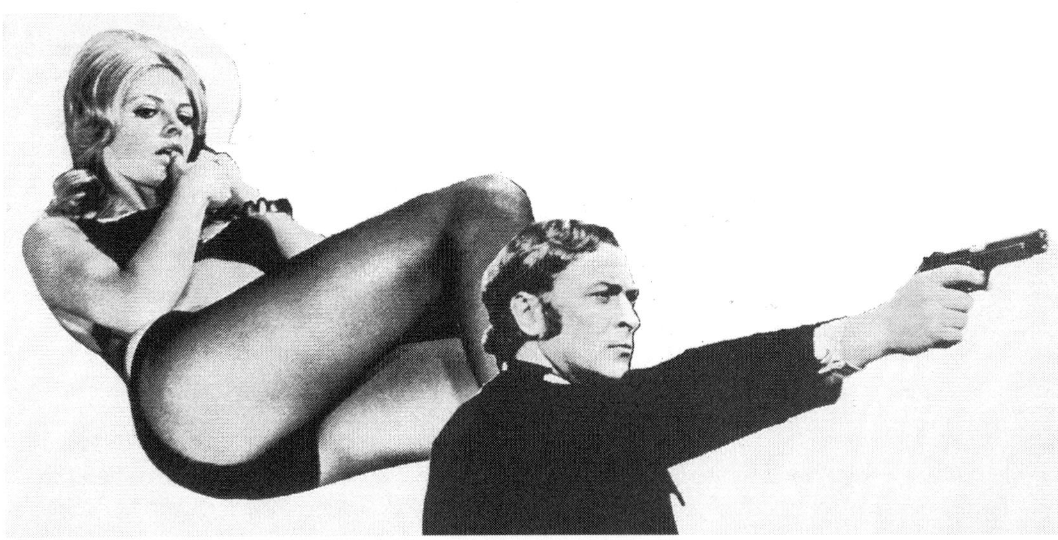

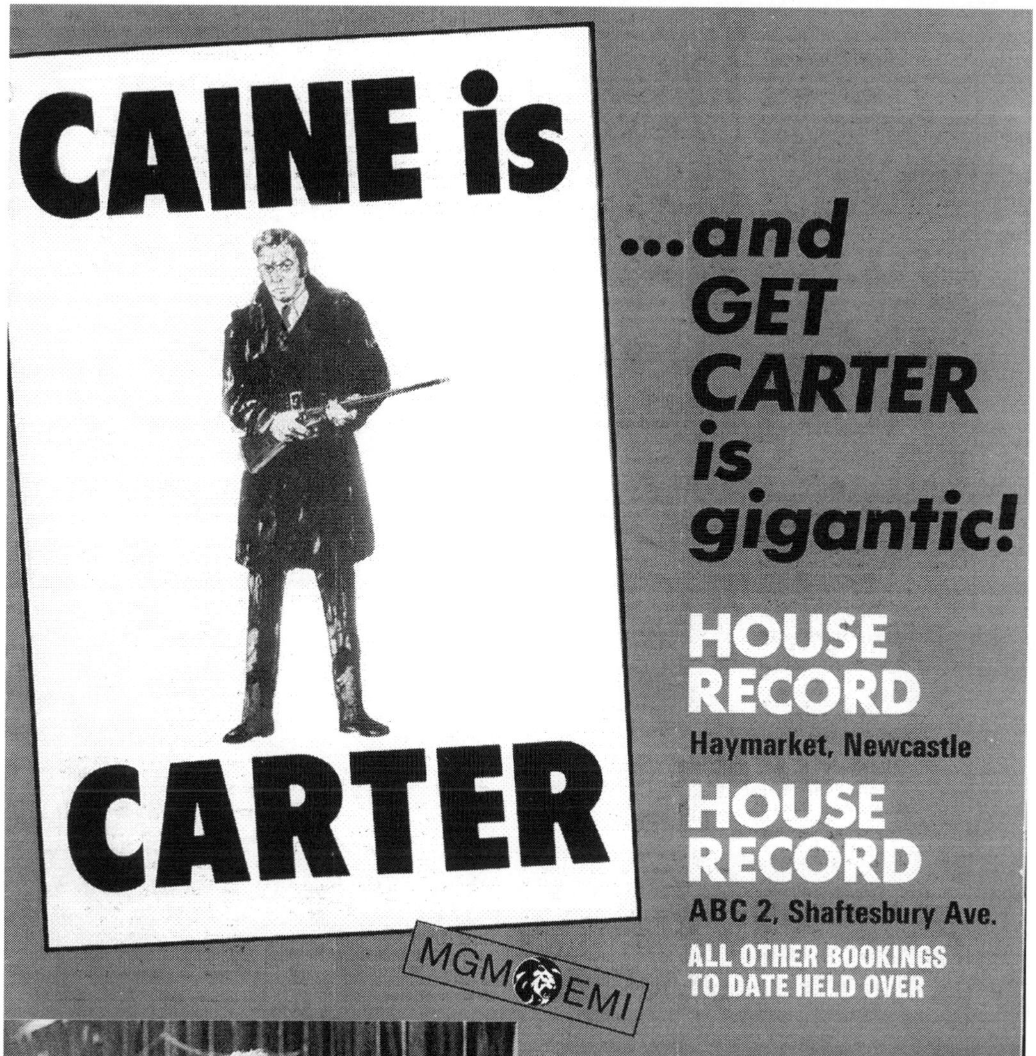

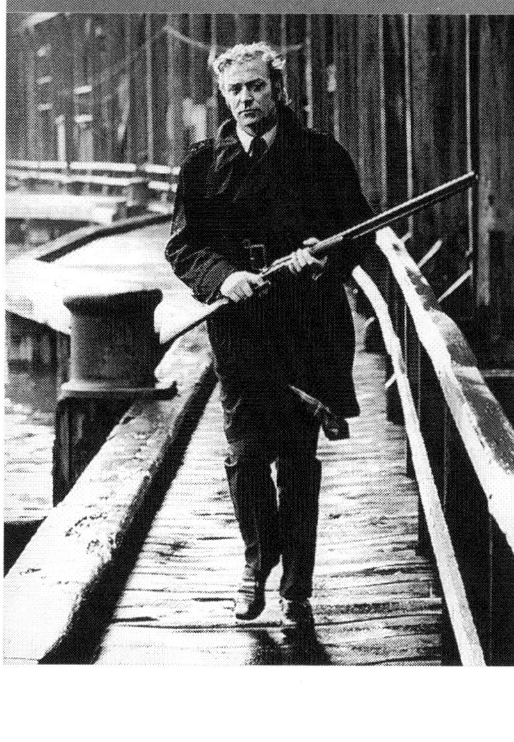

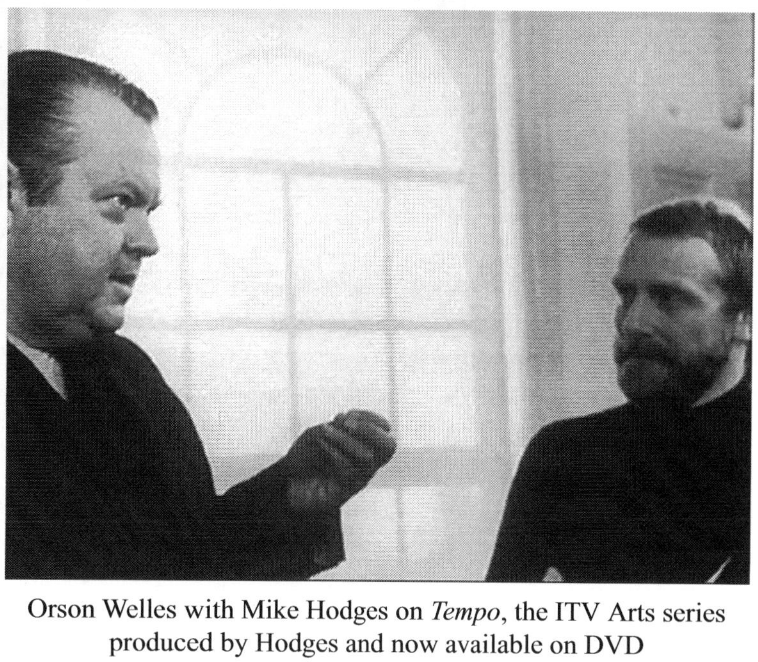

Orson Welles with Mike Hodges on *Tempo*, the ITV Arts series produced by Hodges and now available on DVD

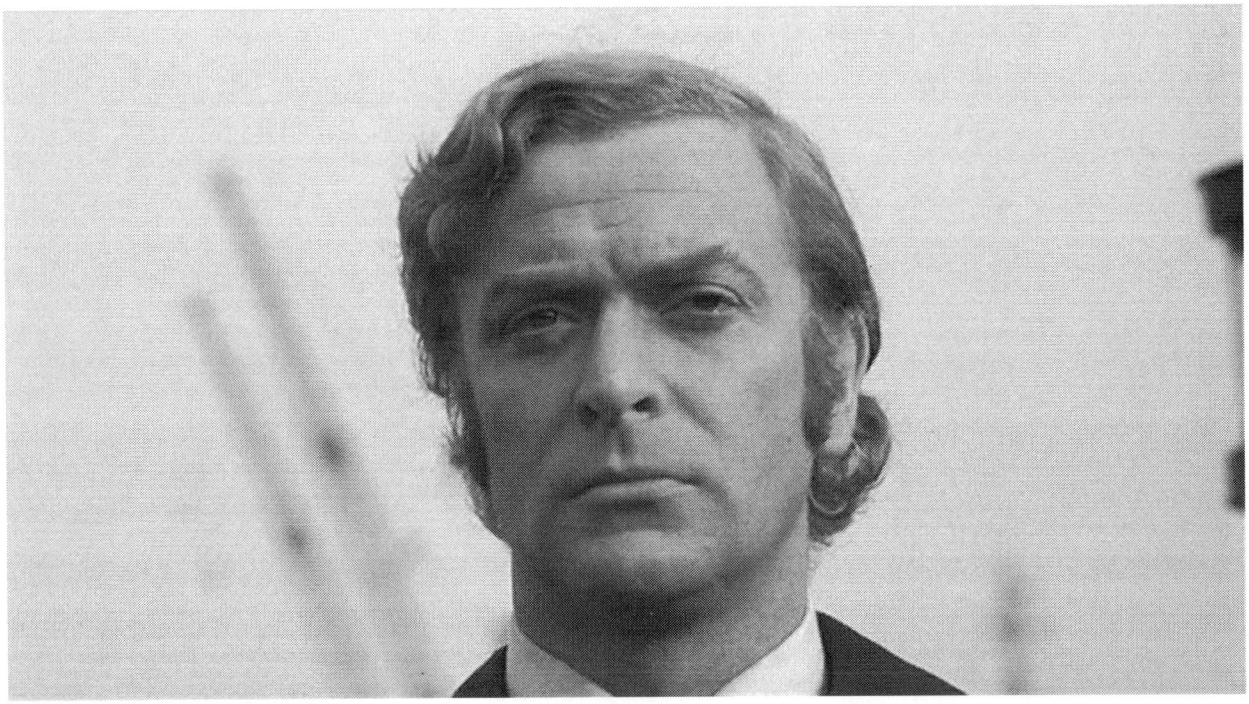

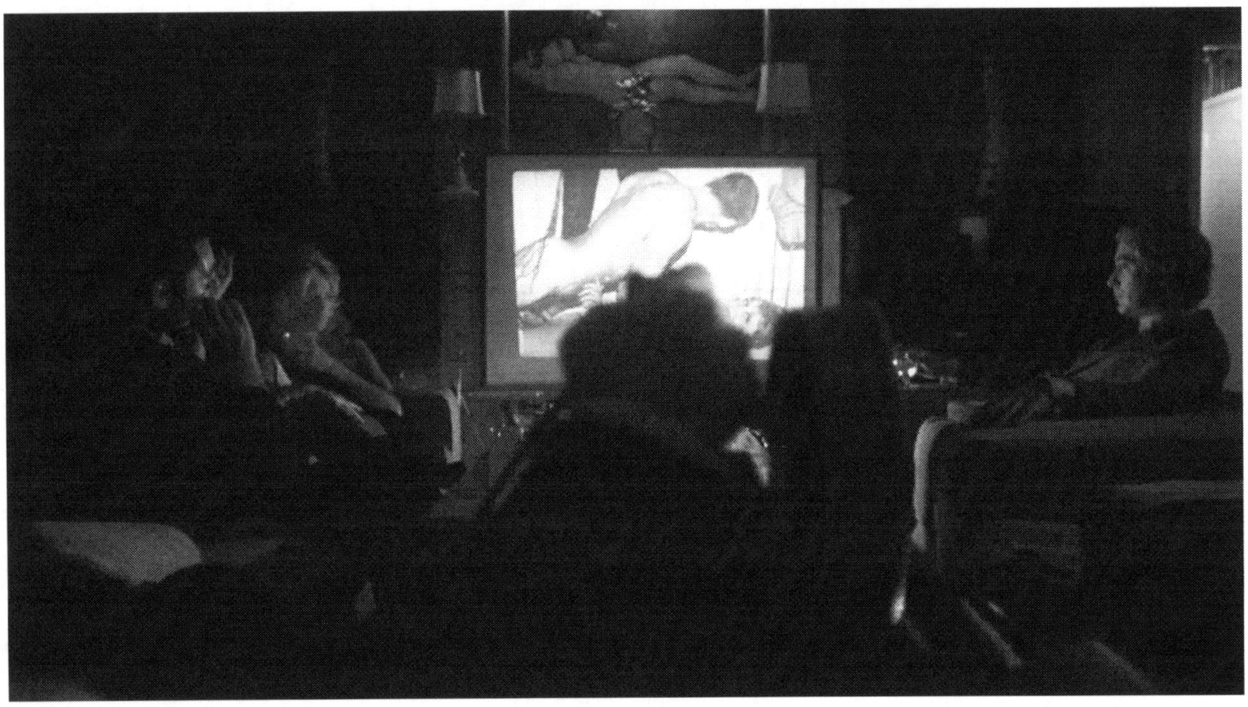

If Hodges had managed to get this pre-credit shot past the infamous censors, *Get Carter* would have been the first English film with an on-screen erection. The film wasn't released uncut until 1993.

Ken Russell

"A nice enough chap, breezy and unpretentious."

Lindsay Anderson, The Diaries (22 May 1991)

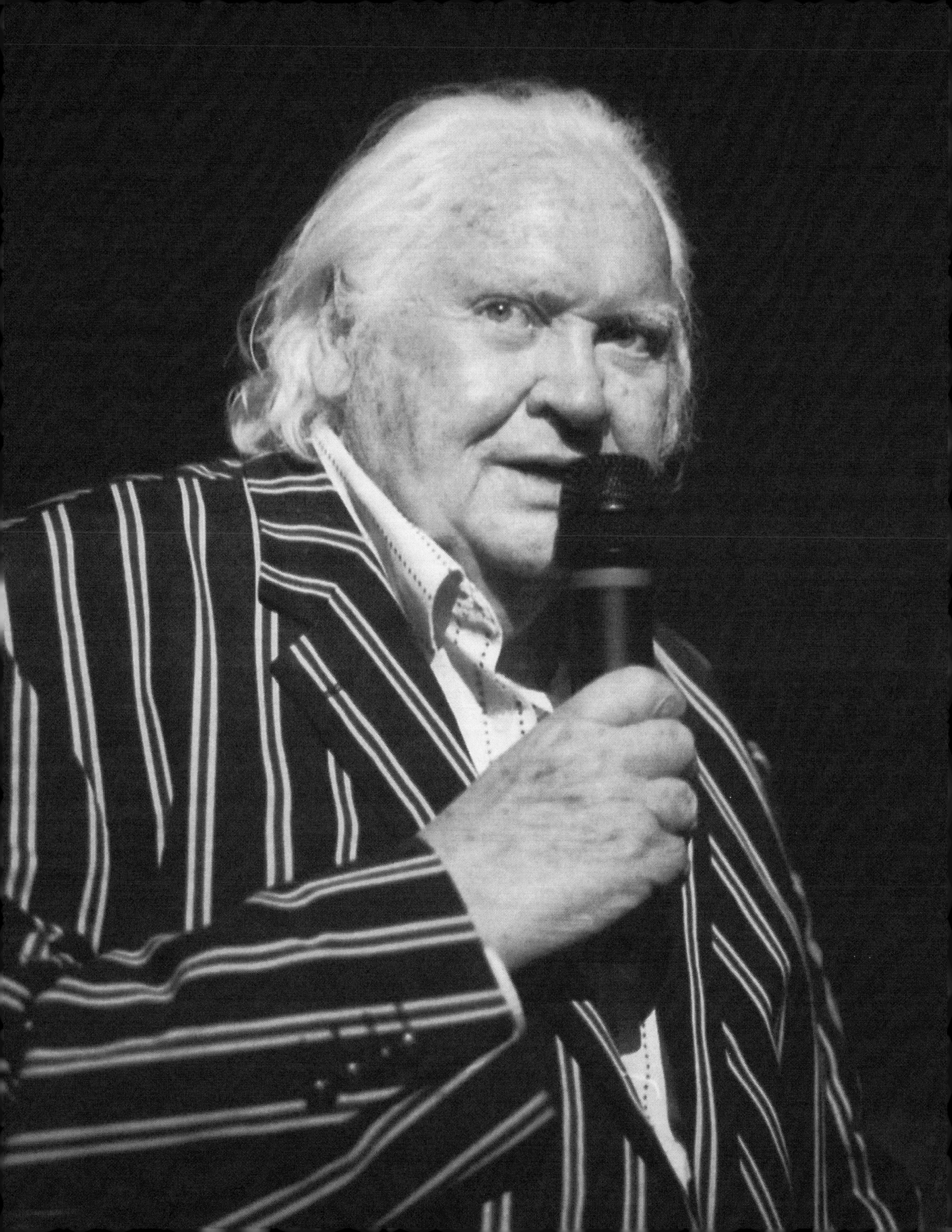

When I showed this photograph to my mother, she was taken aback by the strength of Ken Russell's poise and expression. She said: "He looks so strong. He'll live forever." I took it in the stalls of the King's Theatre in Southsea, Portsmouth. A very special venue on a very special night. It was the 25th September 2010. Ken Russell is talking about making *Tommy*. He filmed the famous Pinball Wizard sequence with The Who and Elton John in this very theatre. Possibly a tenth of the entire population of the city of Portsmouth is in the film, an aural and visual spectacle on a scale unmatched in the history of English cinema. A few months previously, with Ken and his wife, Lisi, I'd attended an Academy Award's tribute screening of the film in a packed Los Angeles theatre. More or less the first question asked by the bedazzled audience was: "How *much* did the film cost?" It's huge. The answer is "Not much, really". It was an aspect of Russell's genius that he could get so much on to the screen for so little money. Ken Russell's entire output of more than eighty 35mm films, which included building and blowing up the walls of Loudun (twice), and taking William Hurt on a transformative hallucination to the very atoms of Creation, was made for less than a third of the budget, say of the remake of *Fun With Dick and Jane* (2005). A few hundred of the many thousands of Portsmouth locals who appear in *Tommy* (holiday camp patron; followers of the messianic deaf, dumb and blind kid who sure plays a mean pinball; costumed partygoers who flee from Southsea's coastal pier as it burns down on camera for real) were at the screening, which was preceded by a new film made by locals about their time on the set. A good tribute band played songs from The Who, live from the stage, and one of the pinball machines had been restored and was available to play on. I notched up a score so low that a deaf, dumb and blind man wouldn't struggle to beat it.

Disability is a theme of the film, and was one that got Ken Russell into trouble, pilloried by the press of the day for using real disabled people in the 'healing', 'celebration', and 'protest' scenes. The papers, the unions, and the older members of the Great British public were horrified that Russell was doing able-bodied actors out of a job. Didn't he know that imitating paraplegics was a way to win awards? And didn't he know that disabled people should not be seen and not be heard. That was what it was like in 1970s England. Naturally, the disabled themselves were thrilled to be asked, and they delighted in taking part, in *belonging*. Ken Russell Hitchcocked his way into a wheelchair and can be seen twisted and waving with joy (or is it anger?) at the New Messiah, a Lourdes-like contingent craving to be blessed. He counted himself as one of the afflicted for he had always known that he was 'different' and, for all his public bravura, he was cripplingly shy. The cameo was also perhaps a way for Russell to confront his own fears of illness and disability. He was dying when I took the photograph. He had almost died ten years before when he caught the MRSA superbug in a filthy English hospital, but had been caught and saved by the love of a new wife, Lisi. She had nursed him back to something like health and she added ten years to his life.

By the time he reached Southsea to revisit a scene of former glory, Ken Russell had all but lost the ability to walk, and was suffering from almost regular strokes and memory loss. He looked old, so very old. And unwell. But although this evening was a celebration of work he had done more than thirty years ago, he and his wife had brought along young friends from the New Forest avant-garde groups for whom he was writing a film.

Soon after he started speaking, Ken Russell was distracted first by me crawling on the floor between the seats to get into the right position to take the photograph (I was using a fast new film by Kodak, and had a good lens, so didn't need to use a flash) and he gave me the briefest of looks that said: "Paul, what are you doing?". Then he was distracted by a shout from a paraplegic young man in a wheelchair away to his right. The young man, over-excited, was making more noise than he realised. He was laughing and shouting, shouts not of words but of twisted noise. Ken Russell cast a look at the young man, and then kept him in the corner of his eye as he carried on talking about *Tommy*. And as he talked, and the young man railed, Ken Russell seemed to grow taller. The pained and excited boy, a boy who was damaged yet full of spirited life, seemed to awaken something in Ken Russell. The illnesses that were killing him seemed to be falling away and he started to look strong again. Was it fear? Or was it courage? I think he was setting an example.

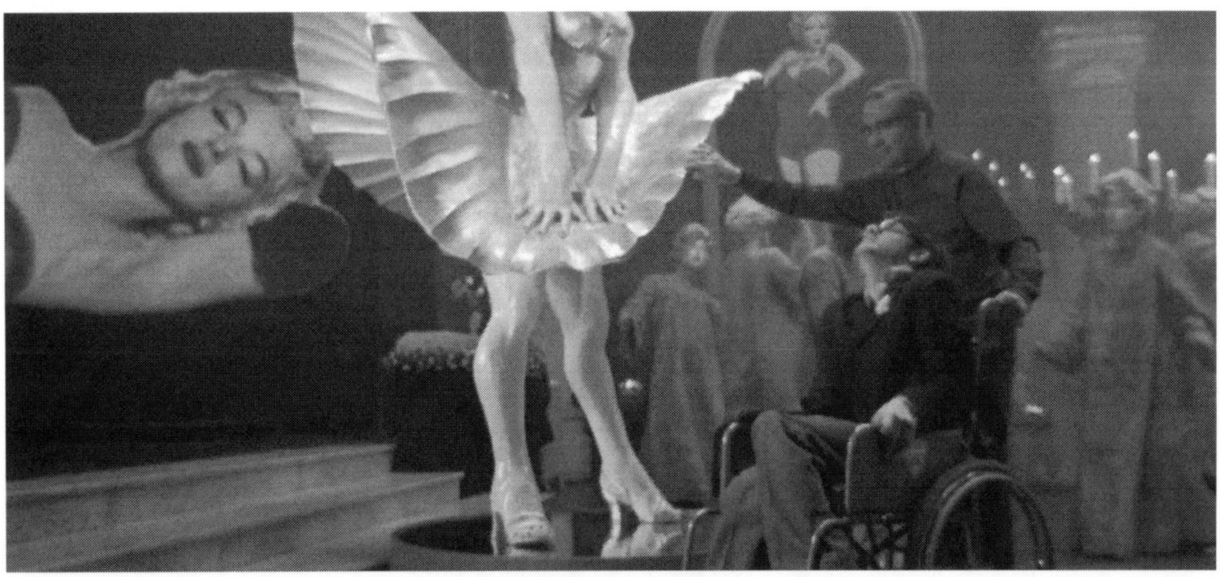

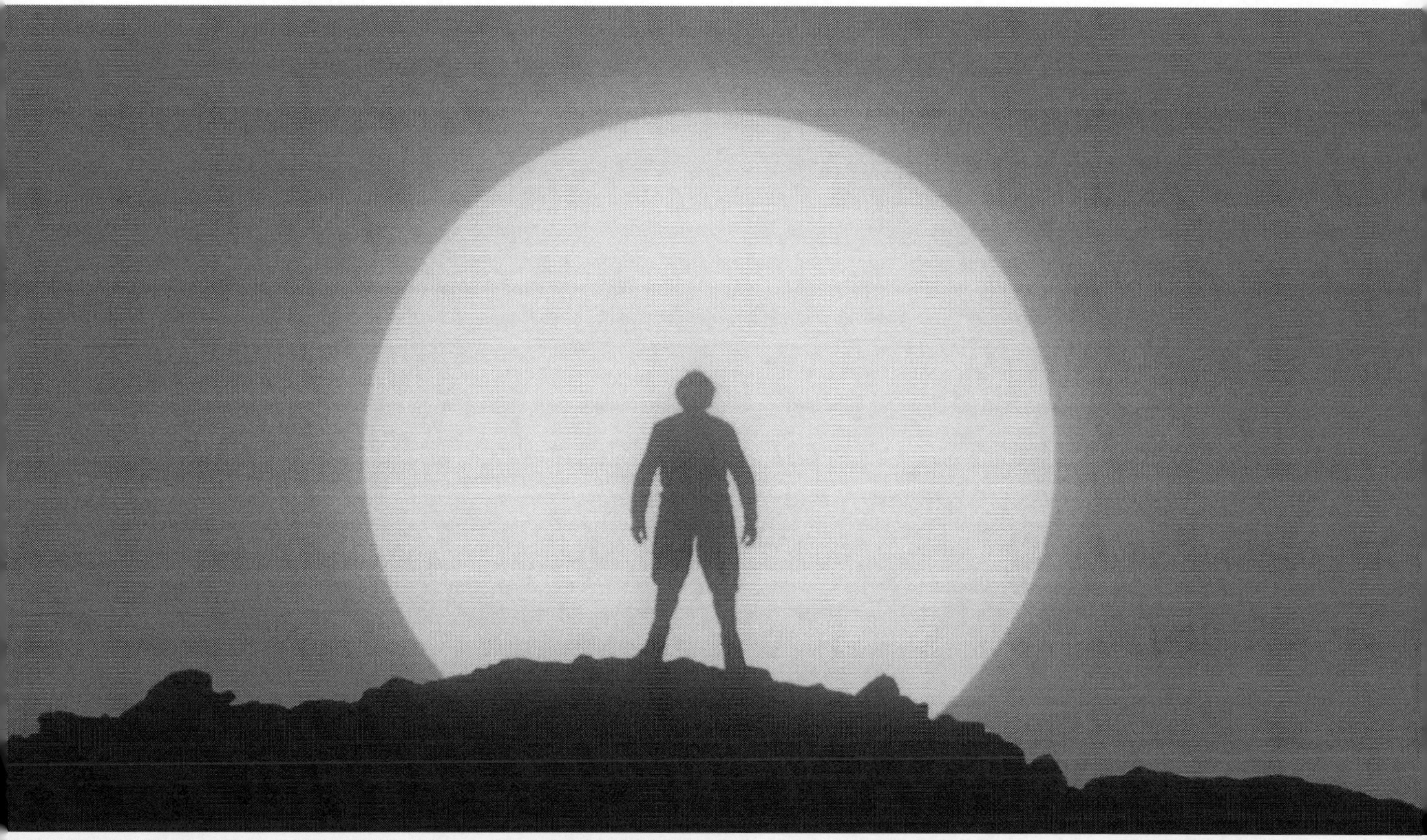

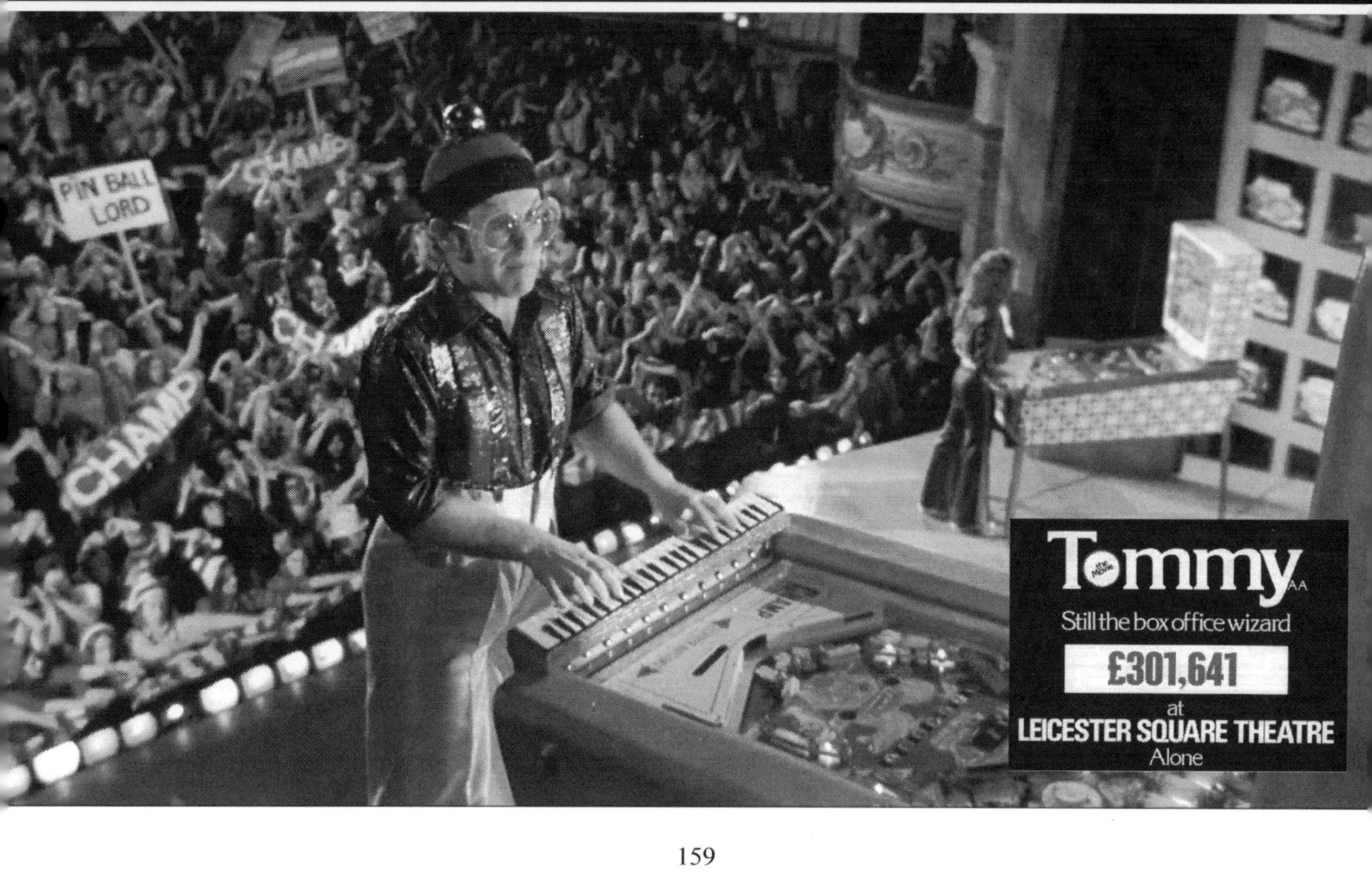
PIN BALL LORD
CHAMP
CHAMP
CHAMP
Tommy the Movie AA
Still the box office wizard
£301,641
at
LEICESTER SQUARE THEATRE
Alone

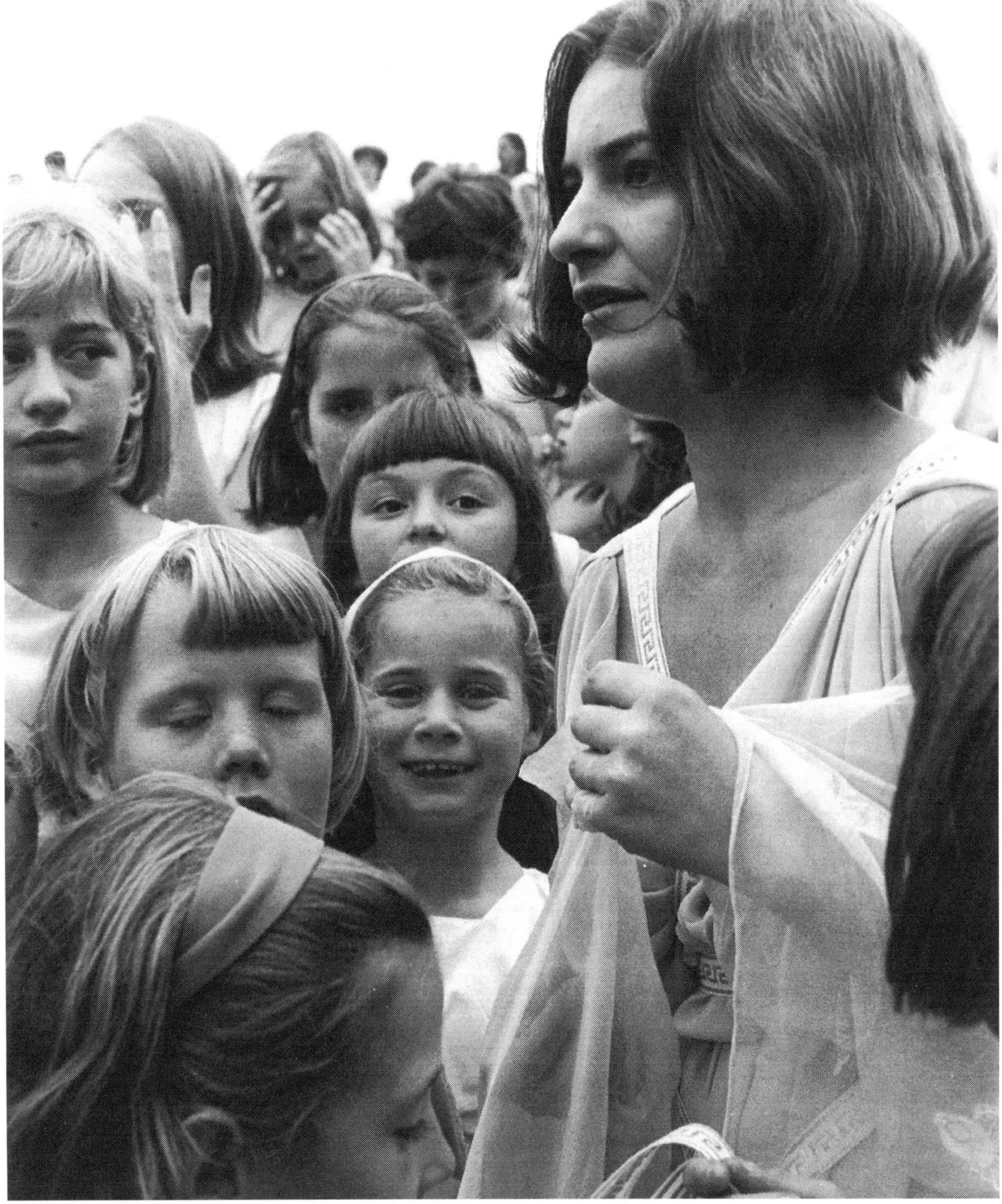

Vivian Pickles on the set of Ken Russell's Isadora Duncan (1966)

Vivian Pickles, Brian Simmons and Paul Sutton

Talking about Ken Russell

In the first five years researching the full biography of Ken Russell, I had hundreds of conversations with Russell and with people who worked with him. This is a transcript of one of the conversations. I'm with Vivian Pickles and Brian Simmons. Vivian gives what I sincerely think is the finest performance by an English actress on 35mm film. The film being Ken Russell's *Isadora Duncan* (1966). It was seen by 12.4 percent of the entire population of Great Britain on 22nd September 1966. Brian Simmons was a BBC soundman who worked on *Isadora Duncan* and who was working as a freelancer when Russell hired him for *Women In Love* (1968), *The Devils* (1971) and *The Boy Friend* (1971). He won an Oscar nomination for *Braveheart* (1995) and he worked on the last ever scene of the last George Lucas *Star Wars* film, *The Revenge of the Sith* (2005), which, coincidentally, was filmed on the same stage at Elstree as the very first scene of *Star Wars* (1977). This conversation took place at BAFTA in Piccadilly, London on 30th March 2010.

Vivian Pickles: Brian, I've got to ask you about that swimming pool scene in *Isadora*. The sound is bouncing off the walls. Why didn't you fix it in post-production?

Brian Simmons: It was the BBC's policy to try to record the sound 'live' and 'original'. If it was barely acceptable it was fine. If it was totally unusable they might re-do it in the studio, but very reluctantly. One of the most poignant scenes I remember was when the children have died and you dance to the *Gymnopédies*

VP: Ken was the first to use that piece of music. Everyone copied him and they still do! It's marvellous how he gets the music so absolutely right.

BS: I was a little in awe because I had never worked on anything quite so grand. It was one of the BBC's big prestige productions. 35mm. Shot by one of their best cameramen, Dick Bush. Do you remember the medal the crew gave you? For Valour.

VP: Yes! It was a Victoria Cross. I've still got it. Dawn Alcock [make-up] gave it to me, bless her. That was brilliant. It meant more to me than *anything*, just *anything*.

BS: It came from the crew because we felt that you had taken more than anyone should take. It was a tough old shoot. It was very demanding.

VP: It was. Absolutely. But it had to be got right. It had to be right.

BS: Ken had a huge reputation because of his *Monitor* films. He could be difficult. He could be temperamental. He could be extraordinarily demanding but you felt that there was a talent and there was a vision that he was trying to achieve, and you got swept along with that. It wasn't 'Him' and 'Us'. We were all in the barrel together. And we were all in his sights at one time or another. The crew had a camaraderie. And we knew we were working on A Ken Russell Film and we felt driven by that. It's remarkable. And he never changed.

He was like that thereafter. On every production I did with him after he was always that way. I threatened to walk off every job I did with him.

Paul Sutton: I am recording.

BS: I have to tell you that when we go twenty years later, twenty years after doing *The Boy Friend,* I got a call to do *Lady Chatterley* for Ken. It was meant to be a feature film with the BBC putting money into it. I went to the production meeting at Pinewood. I hadn't seen Ken for years. We are sitting in the boardroom and at the end of the table is this wonderful white-haired, rosy-cheeked, jovial old man, almost like Father Christmas, a lovely man, and people were coming in shaking his hand. I thought this is going to be all right. I am twenty more years experienced. I'm not as green as I was way back then. I'm going to be able to handle this. And he has obviously mellowed. Wrong! How wrong could I be. He hadn't changed one single bit. He was just as demanding on *Chatterley.* But the good thing about it was we were more experienced and we found a way of handling the situation. Not long before that I'd done a documentary on wine for television in Spain, all the Sherry business. I became a bit of a fino snob. I introduced the idea of a fino break at 11 o'clock. Not overtly, but covertly. Just to help us get through the day. We'd go to the electrician's truck which had a refrigerator and out would come the fino for the DP, myself and selected crew members. Ken got to hear of it. So Ken joined us for fino. Then Ken probably felt guilty because he was consuming but not contributing, so he took to delivering half a dozen bottles of Chablis. And so we had rather a jolly shoot, although as always with Ken it was stressful. But there was that kind of recognition that we all needed something. It was a signal that we're all in this together and we've all got to come through it.

VP: I've been watching Paul Merton's television programmes about early cinema. He reminds me of Ken in the early days. The cockiness. The throwing off terrible jokes, boy jokes, and getting away with it. There's a likeness there. And there's a sense of a one-track mind that they aren't 'in' with everyone else. They are individual. And they have no fear at all.

BS: That's how it appears, but we don't know what doubts or fears Ken had.

VP: He *had* a very clear idea of what he wanted.

BS: Absolutely.

VP: At my interview he told me what he was going to film and that's exactly what he did.

BS: He had his visualisation and he would go for it absolutely.

VP: He would see it in his mind. And if it wasn't there on the set, or he wasn't getting what he wanted from the actors, he'd be absolutely furious. He'd rage until he got what he wanted.

BS: That is the mark of an auteur.

PS: But he *was* very nice to you, Vivian, when the BBC came to film *him* filming *Isadora.*

VP: Oh! Do you remember when they came to film him filming? And we are out in an awful woodland doing some dance barefoot. And suddenly it's 'Vivian darling, do you mind...' and I thought, 'What's this?' It was Ken acting the nice director, going on with this nice dialogue. Later on, he tried to have a conversation with me on camera for their camera. 'Oh God!' I thought, 'I'm not playing that game'. He must have known that was how he was expected to behave as a director.

BS: You really did work hard on *Isadora* and it was such a physically demanding role.

VP: It certainly was.

PS: And your performance was adored. You won award after award for it, in an era when they meant something, including the international one at Monte Carlo.

VP: Oh, that was fantastic. I'd never been aware of a standing ovation before. I was standing at the back of the cinema and saw the whole audience stand up and applaud the film. The awards were presented later, not in the cinema but at a grand regal ceremony with the Prince of Monaco. When I went up to collect my award I was wearing a striped-coloured Kaftan with gold-braid edging, which was very new fashion. I knew the French would adore it and they did. When entering Monte Carlo you have to show your passport. When the guard opened my passport and saw my name, he looked up and said: "Congratulations!" I'll never forget that.

PS. You wouldn't get that in England! (*laughs*).

VP: Brian, how did you get into the BBC?

BS: I came out of National Service and I wanted to be an aeronautical engineer, but because I didn't get a good enough grade in Maths I couldn't go to university. It was tough in those days, not like now. I came out of the air force and really had no direction. In the air force I shared a room with a third assistant director, who had worked with people such as John Paddy Carstairs and on those English comedies. His stories were about the closest I got to the film business.

PS: Carstairs worked with Norman Wisdom. [A young Vivian Pickles has a blonde-beauty cameo in *Trouble in Store* in which Wisdom sings to her].

BS: I think he did, yes. I got a job as a lab technician which was boring and unfulfilling. Somebody said 'The BBC are advertising for sound people in radio'. I applied and got a job in radio. I went to the BBC and thank God for the BBC. It was my university. Residential courses out at Evesham. It was fantastic. I went from radio to television. I did *Z-Cars* live.

VP: Did you? I did a *Z-Cars!*

BS: Wasn't it an adrenalin rush?

VP: Yes! Oh my God.

BS: Phenomenal. And all the things that used to go wrong with the back-projection. It was twice a week.

VP: I did an *Emergency Ward Ten* too.

BS: Ah, but that was the opposition. Commercial television.

PS: Do you remember John McGrath? In addition to *Z-Cars*, he wrote *Billion Dollar Brain* and *Diary of a Nobody* for Ken Russell. Ken speaks very highly of him.

BS: John? Yes. He was quite tall and had a shock of hair.

VP: A lovely man.

BS: Very nice, yes.

PS: He introduced Ken to Michael Caine.

VP: He had a huge influence on Ken. They were very close actually. They often had spaghetti evenings together, with Shirley cooking.

PS: Ken's a good cook now. He likes being in the kitchen.

BS: Spaghetti was the lingua franca in those days. I remember making spaghetti for Vanessa Redgrave.

VP: John McGrath suggested me for *Diary of a Nobody*. I wouldn't have met Ken if it hadn't been for John McGrath. I'd played a barmaid in *Z-Cars* and got a laugh on one line and a close-up! (*laughs*)

BS: What year, 1961? 1963? That would have been with the original team, with BRIAN BLESSED! Mr. Blessed.

VP: Did you do the episode with Gordon [Gostelow, my husband]. He played a tramp in a prison cell. The episode called *Canada*?

BS: I did the whole series. I was doing two episodes of *Z-Cars* back to back with *Compact*. The senior

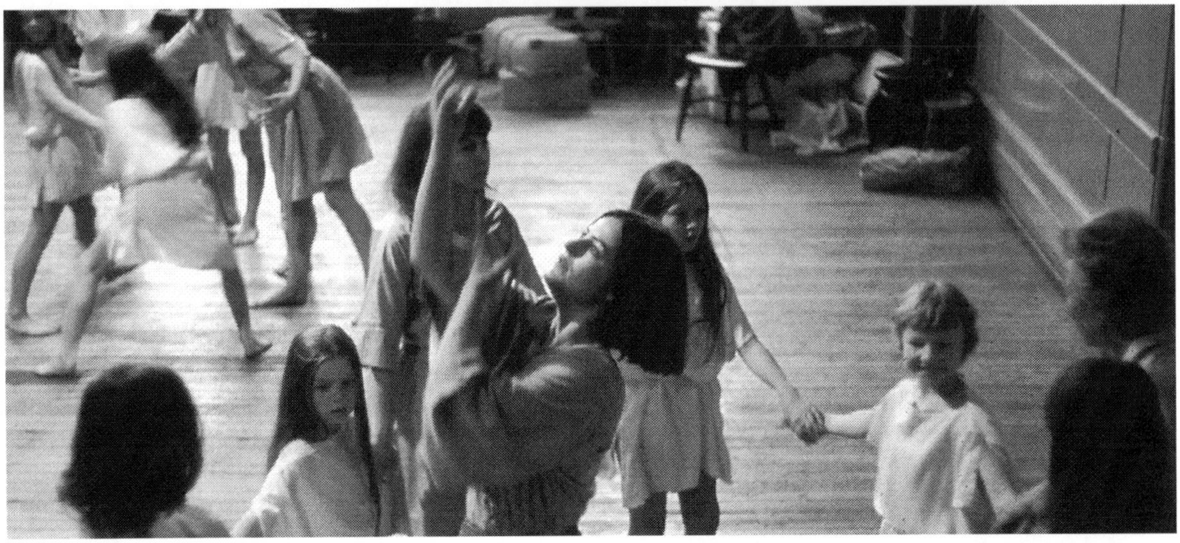

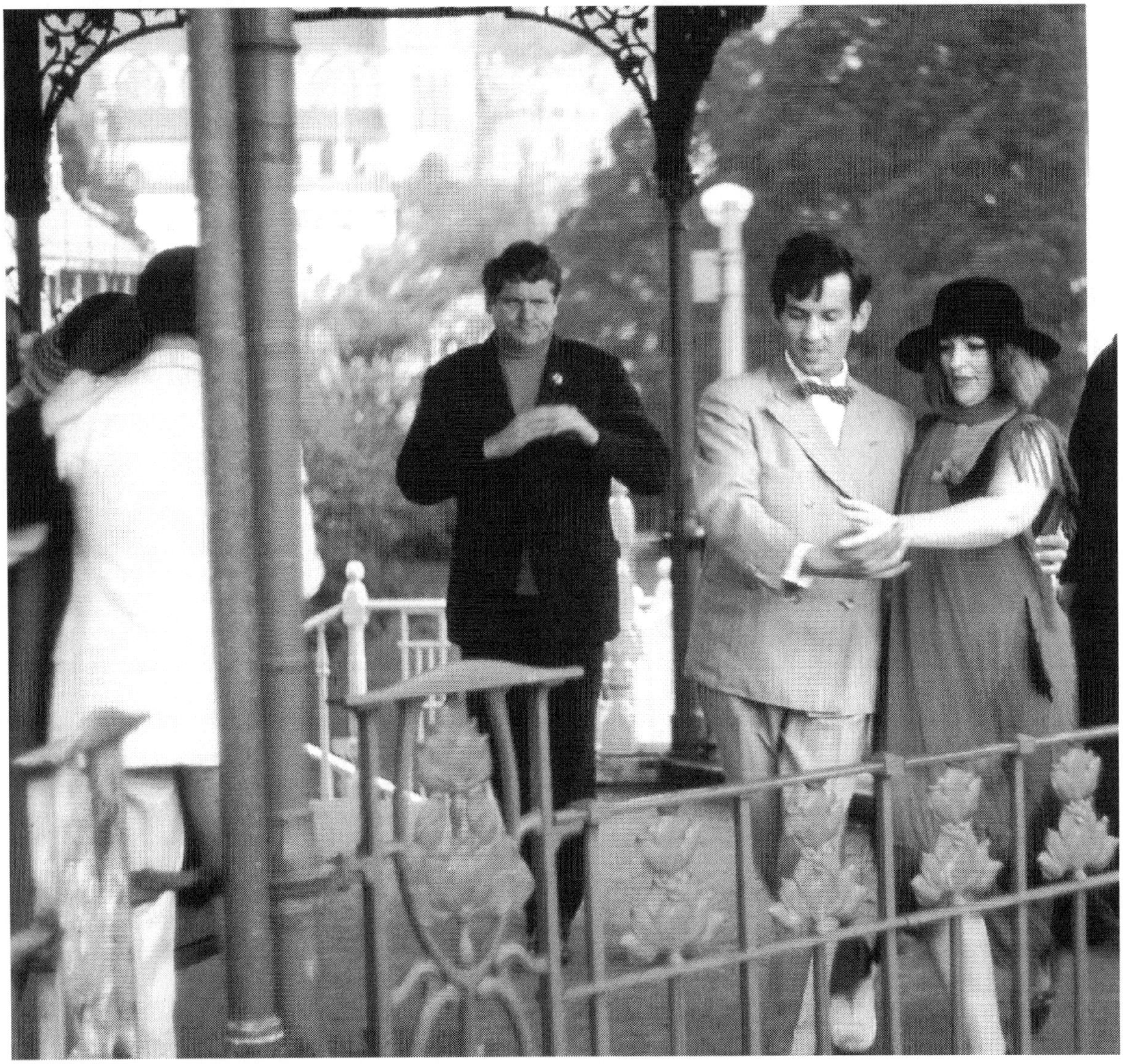

Ken Russell directing Vivian Pickles in *Isadora Duncan* © David Hurn / The Vivian Pickles Collection cameraman on our shift was Michael Bond, who wrote *Paddington the Bear*. He wrote the recommendation for my move to the BBC film unit.

PS: Ken is very generous like that. He'll always write recommendations. It sounds a fascinating time to have been in *Z-Cars*. It was a real training ground for some real talents, including Mike Hodges, Ken Loach, Colin Welland...

BS: Yes, Colin was one of the four principal cops, with BRIAN BLESSED!

PS: Brian's best loved of course for playing the Big Bird Man in Hodges's *Flash Gordon*. Have you often worked with Brian?

BS: Not for a while after *Z-Cars*. I met him briefly at Kenneth Branagh's house when I did a little film for Ken. He's a good friend of Kenneth Branagh. And, of course, he visited his wife on the set of *The Legacy* (1978). Dick Bush was the DoP and the director was Richard Marquand, a lovely man. Do you remember Richard Marquand?

PS: He directed *Return of the Jedi*.

BS: That's right.

PS: And *Eye of the Needle*.

BS: Very good. You should be in a pub quiz.

PS: I'm pretty good in pub quizzes.

BS: The connections, the spider web of associations.

PS: English cinema has such a rich history. It's why I'm determined to talk with everyone who participated, so I can keep that history alive. It's why it's such a shame that Harry Benn has died. All that knowledge and experience and it has gone - and gone unrecorded. [Harry Benn was Ken Russell's money man/producer].

BS: In my Guild I've initiated an audio archive of our people, technicians who worked on iconic British pictures. And they're going so fast.

PS: Yes, it's why I was so keen to speak to continuity women such as Angela Allen because they have a different set of eyes on set to the actors and directors we always hear from. They have a different perspective.

BS: Everybody looks at it from their own perspective, obviously. Though we're a big family while we're working, we are still compartmentalised. You have your own perspective. I'm sure another department will have quite different memories of the same film. Like I said earlier, on my first film I was an oily rag on the floor and knew nothing of the politics, nothing of what goes on behind the scenes.

PS: Ken was always hiring outside equipment on his films for the BBC, always starting with £5 for a rented zoom lens from Samuelsons. And that didn't endear him to the hierarchy at the BBC who kept trying to cut corners and costs. They were always trying to get him to film on 16mm instead of 35mm and, because of his great reputation and because he was an independent, they always failed, until colour came in.

BS: The BBC up until probably mid-sixties were shooting on 35mm black-and-white. The reason they went to 16mm was because they couldn't afford colour 35mm.

PS: Ken only agreed to do the Strauss film [*Dance of The Seven Veils*] in 16mm colour because they wanted him to make it in 16mm black-and-white, as a pat on the back for his Oscar nomination for *Women in Love*!

BS: When we did *Alice in Wonderland* in 1966, we had quite a cast...

PS: Including Vivian's husband.

BS: Gordon was the gardener.

VP: Yes.

BS: That cast was spectacular. We got one week into shooting and Jonathan Miller said: "Everyone back to BH." {Broadcasting House]. We stopped filming. There were all kinds of gossip and rumours about why we had stopped shooting, because this was a big 35mm production with a wonderful cast. The next day, Jonathan called us all together and said: "You wonder why we've stopped shooting? The BBC was approached by Seven-Arts, the American production company, because of the calibre of the cast. Peter Sellers and co. They want to take it on, and release it internationally as a feature film, but only if we shoot it in colour." But the BBC said 'No'. So we carried on where we left off. This was before the BBC Enterprises recognised that there was a world market out there.

PS: Their short sightedness is incredible. I've seen colour photographs from the set of *Alice in Wonderland.*

BS: I've got loads of rather bad colour filmstrip from the film. From the lab we got short ends of colour negative, scrounged it from them. We loaded up 35mm spools and used it on our stills cameras. Then we gave it back to our lab contact to get processed. It came back as a strip. I've got them at home all cut up but they are faded now. They need serious retouching.

PS: You can do it with a scanner and photoshop.

BS: It's so time-consuming.

VP: Is there a museum for things like that?

PS: Yes, but they tend to be run by management cows with degrees in management and no interest in film. For example, listed in the catalogue of the special collections of the British Film Institute is a letter Ken Russell wrote to Michael Balcon in the 1950s, saying I'm a young man and I want to be a film director. I asked could I read it, and use it in the biography. They can't find it. Not only can't they find it, but they don't seem to give a damn that they can't find it.

VP: They can't be bothered.

PS: Ken gave them his own 35mm and 16mm copies of his films in return for them making copies for him onto VHS. They did two or three then couldn't be bothered with the rest. So he doesn't have copies of his own films anymore. One they did put on tape for him was *Preservation Man* (1962), his film about Bruce Lacey. So I've got a copy of that tape made from Ken's print. When they screened Ken's 35mm print at the retrospective in 2007, the sound from the last two or three minutes of the film was missing. They'd lost it. It now only exists on the VHS tape, which I've had converted to DVD.

BS: There's no excuse today for films not to be archived properly. It's so easy with digital media.

PS: Only one of Ken Russell's films seems to be completely lost. A film about the choreographer John Cranko, which he made in 1960.

BS: Was that before *Monitor*?

PS: It was for *Monitor*. It's called *Cranks at Work*, about a revue Cranko was casting, rehearsing, performing. Bernard Cribbins is in it. I've managed to find a transcript and the day-to-day shooting schedule.

VP: Brian, did you ever work with John Mack? A sound recordist who worked on *Cleopatra*?

BS: No.

VP: Ahh. I was going to ask what happened to him.

BS: He worked in the recording room in dubbing theatres in America. I don't know where he is now. I always say we're just miners at the coal face down my end of the game. We're struggling to keep up with the circus.

PS: That reminds me of Ken's wonderful film *The Miner's Picnic* (1960). I wish I had a copy.

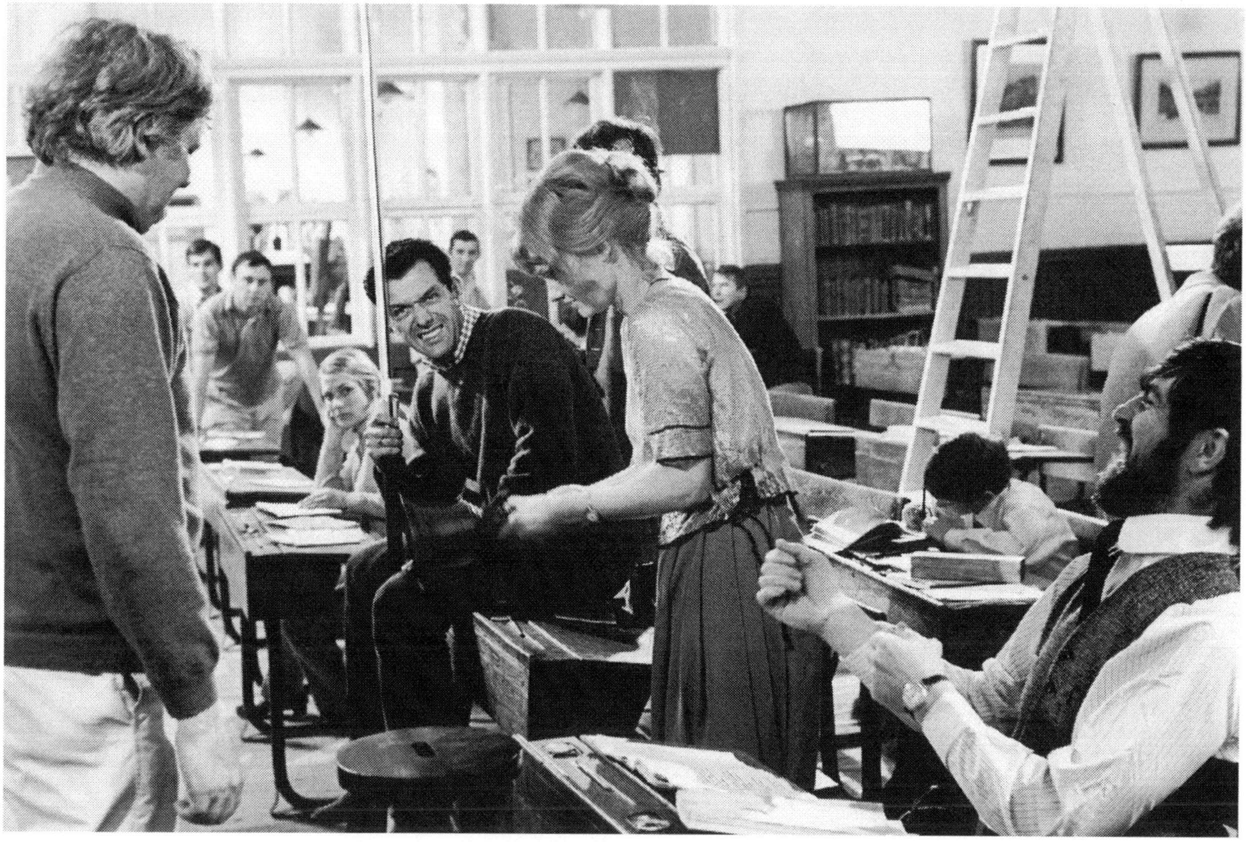

Ken Russell, Brian Simmons, Jennie Linden & Alan Bates making *Women in Love* (1969)

On the massive set of *The Devils* (1971)

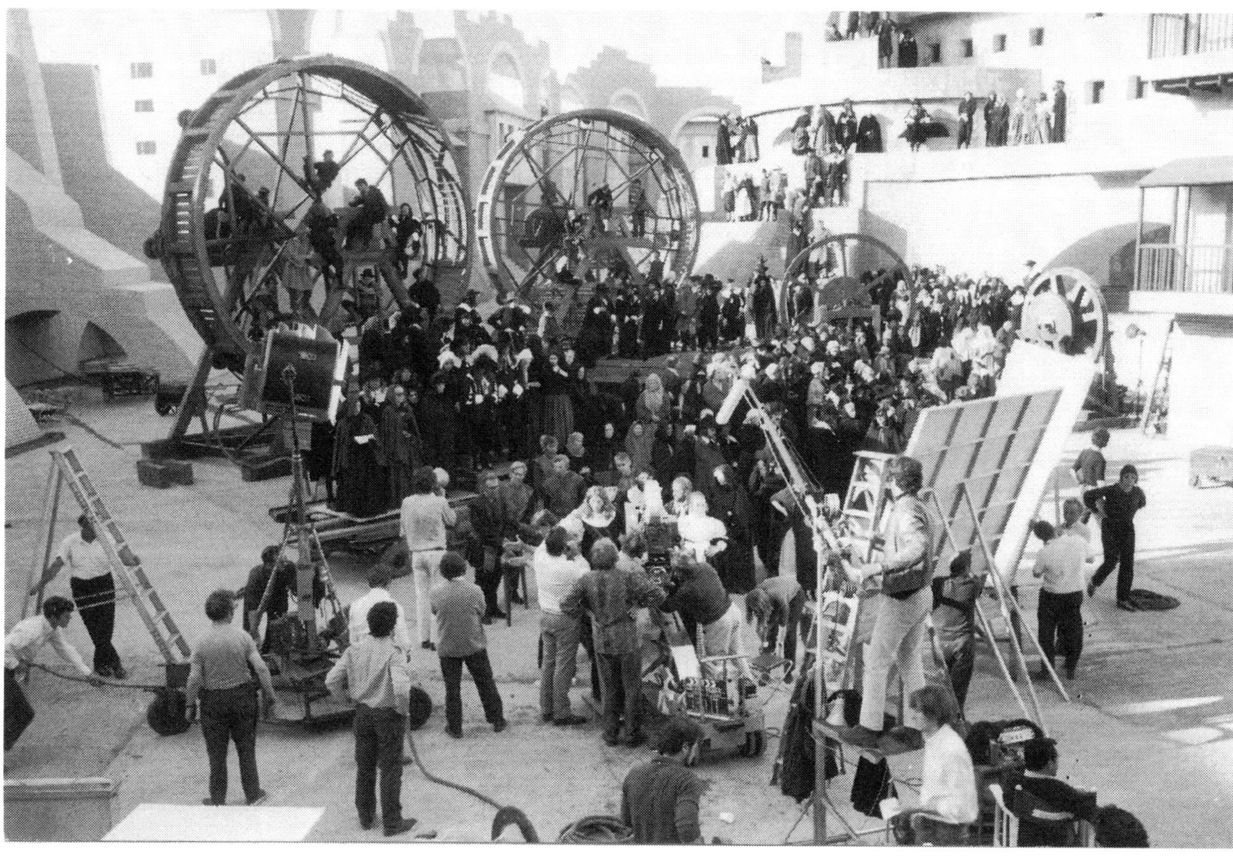

BS: Yes. I think I've got a copy of *The Miners' Picnic Revisted* where he revisits the town forty years later. It's quite a moving film. It's a comment on what happened to communities in the mining areas. I remember *Women in Love*, of course. We were in North Shields filming the mines there.

PS: It was the same mine he used in *The Miners' Picnic*.

BS: It was. And it was probably unchanged from when it opened. When we shot *Women in Love*, the mine hadn't changed from how it was in the Twenties, the same period in the book. It was amazing. Absolutely amazing. Victorian.

PS: With Oliver Reed heaving those huge great lumps of coal. One of the extraordinary things about *Women in Love* is that it is a visual film about dialogue; a film about conversation, and conversation which is full of ideas, intellectual concepts. We never get anything like that now.

BS: We rarely get 'talkies'. It's actually quite refreshing to get a movie which is an ensemble dialogue piece, where the story is important and told through the inter-relationship of people talking, communicating.

PS: With Oliver Reed giving you problems with his whisper-shout delivery?

BS: Ollie could out drink everybody and still come in in the morning and hit his marks and know his lines. He could go from a whisper to a very forceful projection. We had one camera. We had rehearsals. We had cover. We knew there would be an establishing shot and there would also be an opportunity to get in closer. Nowadays you have two maybe three cameras, you can't get a microphone in a good position, you have to use radio microphones. You are constantly compromised. We were able to get much better quality sound on *Women in Love*. The whole thing was more disciplined. Ken was not predictable. That was one of his fortes. He was totally unpredictable but, because of his discipline, you knew instinctively what the sequence of shots might be and where the cutting point might be. He knew how films were constructed and we, the sound crew, could anticipate the problems and address them before they actually occurred. Now whether he wanted you to do that or not is another matter. But you could say, "on the next shot can the actor play the preceding line? because it will cut better". Nowadays it's totally different. Directors don't seem to have an idea in their head of how they are going to construct a scene or how to cut a scene. It makes everybody's job more difficult. There is no working piece by piece and crafting each shot and scene for the best. What I like about *The Boy Friend* was not the Busby Berkeley, but the actuality, the material shot in the theatre, both on stage and backstage. I have a little bit of pride in the thought that I captured the 'live' theatre, the sense of being in a theatre, whereas today they wouldn't accept that kind of openness, that theatrical projection from the stage. It would be closer dialogue and ADR. In Ken Russell's *The Boy Friend* you can hear the actual footsteps on the stage. And you think you are there. You are really there watching it happening in that lovely old almost empty theatre. My job was to try to make it sound real. These day, the job of the sound recordist is to make it sound artificial. The post-production people have taken over and made it heavy with music and sound effects. Dialogue seems not to matter much now. What you do on location in film today is unrelated to the environment. We've been conditioned by American television and American movies into thinking that we have to be right in there, so intimate.

VP: I can never hear what they're saying on American television. It's maddening.

BS: I get frustrated of course because the music and effects are so dominant, it is kind of saying that the dialogue is unimportant. They've lost touch with the audience. Do you know where you are? Do you know where you're going? Do you know where you're coming from? I fear for the future with 3-D. The visuals are going to be so dominant there is going to be no room for the story.

PS: I was disappointed with *Avatar*. The 3D, when seen in a standard theatre, isn't as good as in the 3D films I saw in the 1980s. Maybe because my eyes were better in the 1980s.

VP: Television is going to have a go with it, aren't they?

PS: Yes, they're trying it with football games. It won't last. It's a long way off the quality of 35mm.

BS: I can see the value of 3D for football or that kind of thing where you are re-creating a spatial reality. Quite recently Channel 4 did a 3D evening where they put out old footage from the Queen's Coronation. At around that time a friend of mine gave me a 3D DVD, a horror movie.

PS: *My Bloody Valentine? Final Destination?*

BS: *Final Destination 3D*. (*Vivian Pickles laughs*)

BS: I've got a big screen TV and the glasses. I put it on. It's not my kind of movie. You have a scene where there are three characters and some dialogue but the vase in the foreground is in 3D and it's very distracting. The foreground is more important than the dialogue even in a dramatic scene! How's that going to work in a truly dramatic situation? You want to be aware of the foreground but your focus has to be through to the characters. In 3D films, the lamp becomes the dominant character. 3D is going to be visually distracting to the point where you lose track of the story and the emotion and the interaction. And I wasn't listening to what was going on. It's just as well. I purposely didn't go to any of the 3D screenings of *Avatar*. They sent us a 2D screener. I watched it as a conventional film. The visuals were stunning. The CGI work was stunning in 2D. And you could focus on the story and on the narrative. How banal it was! It was absolutely derivative crap. The whole point of *Avatar* was the 3D experience.

PS: The only time the 3D worked for me was the little jelly fish floating in the air. A throwaway effect and completely pointless. *Avatar* is *My Left Foot* for the Gameboy Generation.

Vivian Pickles laughs.

PS: A crippled Oirishman plugged into a video game. One of Ken Russell's big strengths as a filmmaker was that he is one of very few English filmmakers who can use three-dimensional space properly. Placing figures in the landscape, where the landscape is used to reflect or comment on the character's psychological state. And the way the actors move in that three-dimensional space. And those incredible three-dimensional sets on *The Devils!*

BS: The walled city of Loudun, on the backlot at Pinewood, was the biggest set built since the volcano in Bond. I think the shooting of *The Devils* took twelve to fourteen, fifteen weeks. Movies in those days did take that long. These are my photographs from the set of *The Devils*. That's Judith Paris. She refused to have her head shaved.

VP: How did she get away with it, I wonder?

BS: They were given extra money if they had their head shaved. She just refused. That's Murray. There was one scene with Murray Melvin up in the rafters, overlooking the orgy, and he's masturbating. And, of course, he's got the camera on him. "Action, Murray!" And one of the crew yells out: "What's it feel like doing it in front of a bunch of professionals?" That's a photograph of my boom operator, and that's David Watkin.

PS: Doing the crossword?

BS: Yes, I took a picture of David asleep on the grave of Shelley. Sadly most of the crew on *The*

Devils are gone, including David Watkin. I wish I had more photographs from *The Devils*.

PS: I've got quite a few. In my researches, I've managed to track down the large format contact sheets. Including the scene with Spike Milligan.

BS: That's a lost scene. I remember that scene quite clearly because it *was* adventurous bringing in Spike Milligan, who was known for not being a serious straight actor. It was a one-day shoot. This scene was in the condemned cell. And it was wonderful watching two actors at work, and seeing how well the scene worked. It was a shame it didn't appear in the film, and it's a tragedy that it's lost because it's probably the only truly dramatic role that Spike ever did.

PS: Ken's 1959 film with Spike Milligan is very creative.

BS: It's so difficult getting hold of copies of Ken Russell films, even copies of the big movies.

PS: I can help you out with most of them. Though some which are available, such as *The Music Lovers* and *Lisztomania,* are shockingly bad British transfers. Was making *The Boy Friend* noticeably more stressful than *The Devils*? Ken says it was, Brian Murphy says it was - on the grounds that you couldn't escape back home at night.

BS: It's true we were trapped in the theatre or the hotel, and all sorts of things were going on.

PS: Having talked with David Watkin I've heard all the gossip, so there's no need to mention any of that. But why was Terry Gilbert sacked? He and Ken had been best friends for years. They went back to Ken's ballet days. The choreography was taken over by Christopher Gable and Tommy Tune.

BS: Terry left. I do remember that he was no longer there and Tommy took over.

PS: I know Terry was annoyed he didn't get a credit on *Dance of the Seven Veils* and he wrote to the BBC saying a credit was in his contract. Murray Melvin told me that the official reason was that Terry couldn't teach 'tap'; but that the real reason will have to wait until we meet up for dinner next month.

BS: I did work with Terry on another film.

VP: Terry and Selena [his wife] did a lot of work with the ballet in Cardiff. I worked with Selena on the stage when I was a child. We were both about twelve or thirteen. Our lives paralleled very closely. She told me how liberating *The Devils* had been for her - being naked. She'd never felt so free. And Dorothy Tutin, a neighbour of mine, was always raving about how free she felt when working with Ken because there was no ceiling. She gave more for him than she ever gave for another director. Actors like that. I think the well-known Italian directors are a bit like Ken in the way they treat the artist. People slave for them. It's a similar thing that happens there.

BS: The only one I worked with was Zeffirelli [on *Tea with Mussolini*] and he is a bit like that.

VP (to PS): And so's the one you like.

PS: Bertolucci?

VP: Bertolucci, yes. And the people working for him love him.

PS: Italians do understand the privilege of working for someone who is genuinely talented. But you do have to produce the goods.

VP: Yes.

BS: They give you the freedom to create the roles?

VP: Yes.

BS: Can't that be a bit intimidating? Don't you need at least a bit of directorial control to say 'Slow down, you're going too fast'?

VP: Yes, but then if you work with someone like [John] Schlesinger or [Lindsay] Anderson they are tuned in to the very music of your sentence and they want it *specifically* on a note. And they'll give it to you. Lindsay will ape it and you've got to copy him, sometimes, because he knows what he wants. He can't tell you how to do it but he'll show you what he wants, and that's *maddening* to an actor. *Maddening*. But Ken is absolutely free and it's all from you. He couldn't *direct* actors but he *could* make a picture. If somebody moved and spoilt the frame of it that would annoy him. When an actor did that it was agony for him. If they were doing what he wanted it was perfect for him. Absolutely perfect.

BS: As the years have gone by I've spent more and more time in the presence of actors acting and I've gained a huge respect for what you have to do, and what it requires.

VP: Yes, Brian, we were lucky because we came into the profession with directors who had worked in radio before they came into films, so they were literate, and some of them came from theatre, so they had an essence of the acting quality. Now, people come straight in on the visual, and they don't have any idea of theatre, or even of language. It's very different.

BS: It's astonishing how many film directors you see whose previous work was in pop videos. They come from a very visual background, which is fine, but film isn't all about 'flash', and storytelling isn't all about 'flash'. I did a film with Pacino, who is a fascinating actor to watch and to work with. Totally focused. You can't talk with him when he comes on set. You don't have that 'Good morning'. He's in character and doesn't want to be distracted. As soon as you learn that, it's fine. It's not 'he's ignoring you'. You respect his inner space. He will do a take, and then he'll do another one. By three the director will be happy and say: "Fine, thank you"' and Pacino will say: "No, I'll give you one more, a little different. You'll like this one". He does another one, a different performance. Something else has come out of it. The director is happy. "Just one more, Mikey. I've got one more." And he will give you seven. Some will be OTT, but in there you have a variety of interpretations which must be a gift to a director. That to me is the most astonishing. To see that diversity.

PS: That's the kind of actor Kubrick liked. It's why he hired people like Peter Sellers, who could give him variation after variation from which he could pick and choose.

VP: I felt sorry for those who didn't know how, when Ken couldn't direct them. I started to help them. I would say to them quietly: 'If you do this and you do that'. Ken couldn't do that for them.

BS: Now that you say that, I don't remember Ken directing the actors much. He would set the scene. Because I worked with Ken on three projects in quick succession, I had no yardsticks. It's only now looking back I realise how little input he did give in 'acting directing'.

VP: He was happy when directing one person. He could focus on one person. As soon as another one came into shot then he had quite a problem.

PS: Did you have a problem with the sound from Ken playing loud music on the set?

BS: On *The Devils* we used to play music there because it would heighten the mood when the nuns go into hysterics. That would drive the visuals. There wasn't anything there particularly for sound. We weren't shooting dialogue. It was nuns going berserk. (*Vivian Pickles laughs)*

BS: Anything that added to the atmosphere was quite right. I'm all in favour of that. Some directors like to keep a little bit of music being played just to keep an atmosphere on set, but usually when you try that, in very short order, the director of photography will say: "Cut that bloody noise off! I

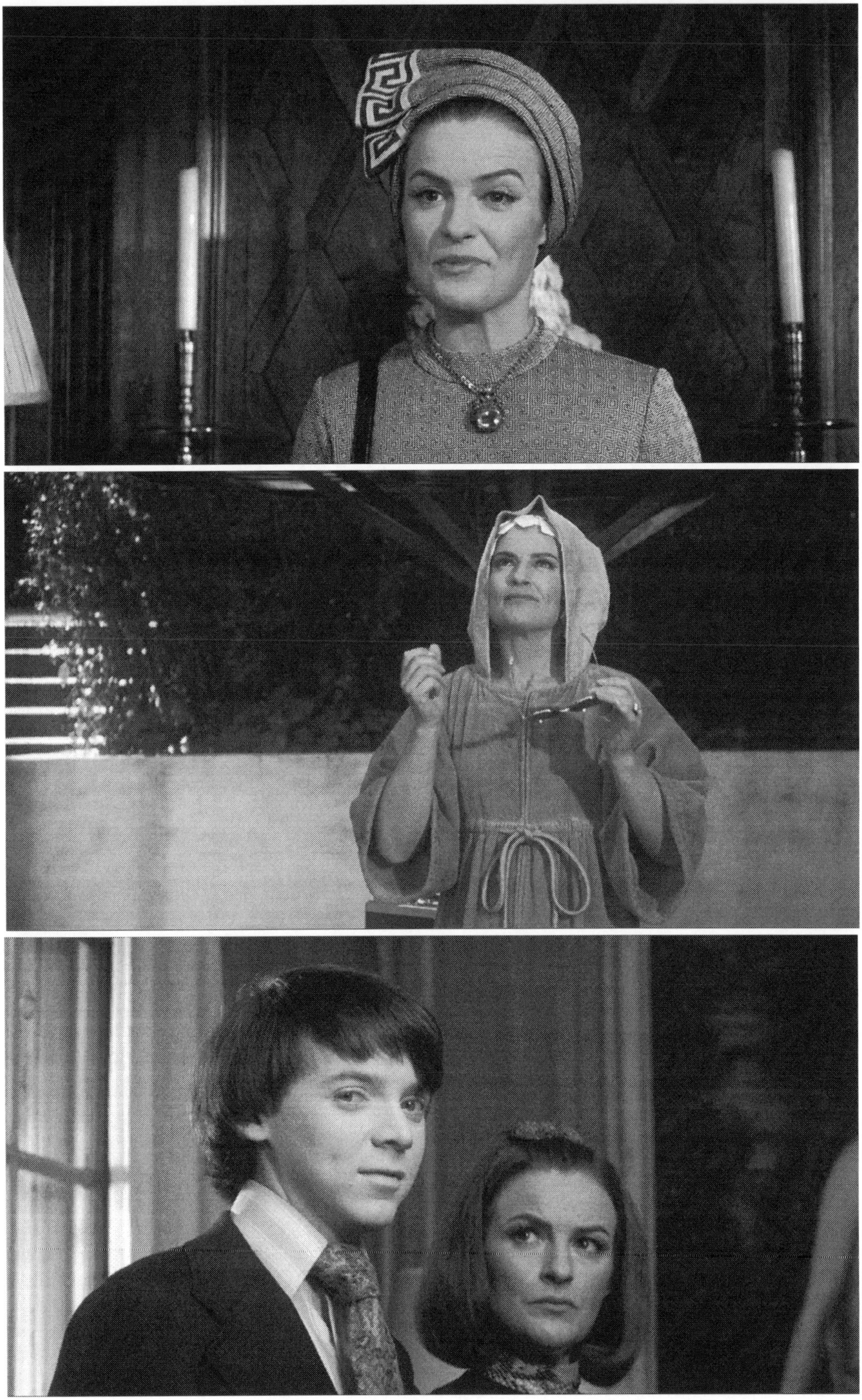

Vivian Pickles with Bud Cort in Hal Ashby's *Harold and Maude* (1971)

can't talk to my gaffer. We're trying to light." But Ken did like it during the shot to boost the energy. On *The Boy Friend*, there was an awful lot of playback because of the musical numbers. Of course, playback at that time was fairly unsophisticated. When we were shooting the film, the musical numbers were played by a man at the piano in the pit, Peter Greenwell. We had problems with cueing the playback. Ken used to get *furious* with Maurice, the playback operator. Whatever Maurice did was wrong and Ken would tell him off. We devised a flag system. We gave Ken a red flag and a green flag. When Ken waved the green flag it was to start the playback. When he waved the red flag it was to stop it. Ken would frequently get it wrong, but nevertheless poor Maurice still got told off!

PS: Did any of the directors you worked with later on ask about Ken and his methods? The reason I ask is Peter Suschitzky didn't have good memories of working with Ken, but George Lucas ran *Valentino* before hiring him for *The Empire Strikes Back*. But then, few Americans are cine-literate when it comes to English cinema.

BS: Occasionally directors are interested that I worked with Ken, but I can't remember any discussing him. Not the Americans. Maybe Atom Egoyan. The European directors would be more aware of Ken.

PS: Egoyan is an interesting filmmaker but I haven't liked any of his films.

BS: I think part of the problem is that a lot of the American directors I've worked with are too young to have remembered Ken's films.

PS: Which is why we need to get the films back out, properly. I was with Ken Russell and Derek Malcolm [of *The Evening Standard*] a month or two back, and Derek said to Ken he'd seen *Crimes of Passion* again in preparation for meeting him and that: "It's a much better film now than it was when it came out." Ken said: "No, it's always been a good film. It's you critics who got it wrong." Many of Ken's films are still great.

BS: I think *The Boy Friend* is high camp. It is what it is. It stands on its own. *The Devils* stands up. It's very powerful. It's church. It's politics. It's all in there.

VP: Did you like working with Americans? Did you find it different?

BS: There are individual Americans I've enjoyed working with.

PS: Who has impressed you?

BS: Mel Gibson on *Braveheart*. I was very impressed by Mel. To direct and act is an awfully difficult thing to do. And yet he always had time for you.

VP (to PS): You've been working in America a lot recently, for months on end.

PS: When they want you, they bombard you and expect you to drop everything and come 'Now!'. But when you ask them for something they don't return your call. If you are not there you don't exist.

VP: I've only been to America once for a film [*Harold and Maude*] but I found it so different. Because they were so proud they would never ask for a rehearsal. They always had to be full of confidence - 'No, we can go for it' - and of course they couldn't (*laughs*).

PS. In addition to Hal Ashby, you've worked with other American directors, such as Franklin J. Schaffner on *Nicholas and Alexandra*. His *Planet of the Apes* made him my first 'favourite' director. And you did *Candleshoe* with David Niven and Jodie Foster for Disney.

VP: Oh, that was wonderful working with David Niven and Leo McKern (with whom I had worked before) and Helen Hayes whose voice I adore, and darling Jodie Foster aged twelve or thirteen. Jodie was such a trouper, bless her. She was fascinated

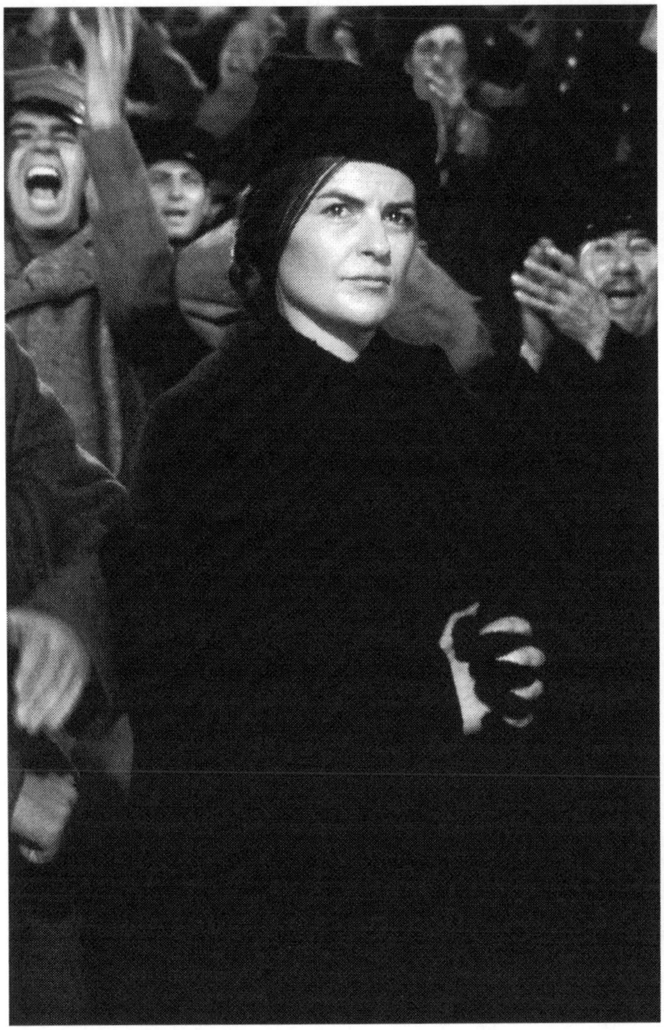

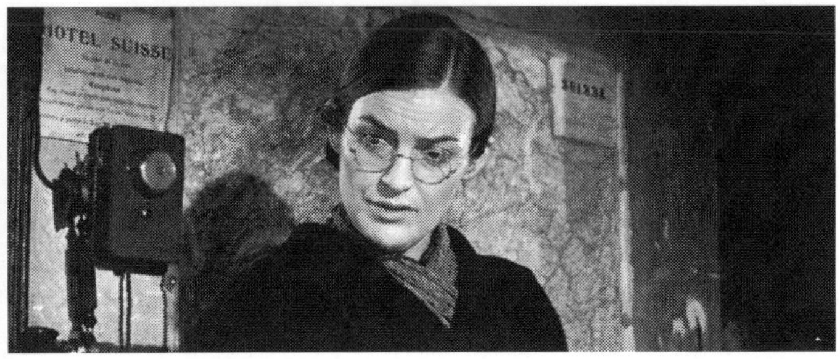

Vivian Pickles as Mme. Krupskaya (Mrs. Lenin), and her husband, Gordon Gostelow, in *Nicholas and Alexandra*

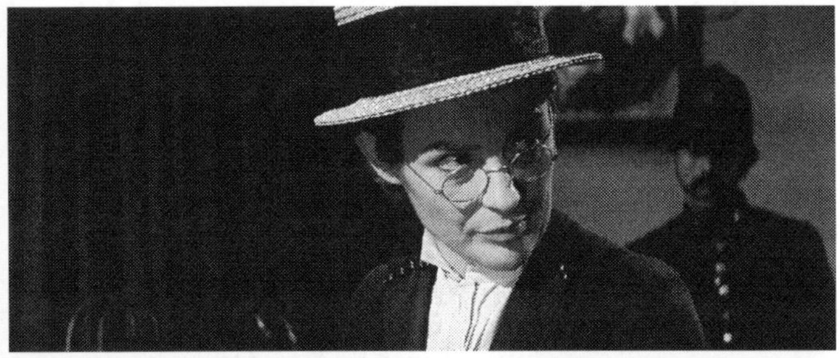

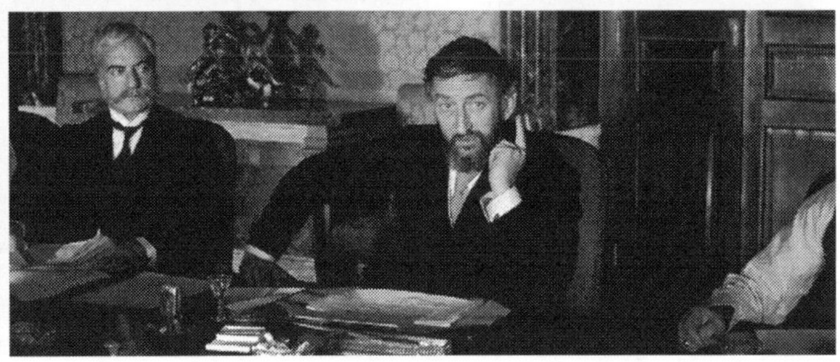

by my doing a cockney accent, and wanted to sit next to me to discuss it between takes. The crew were British and solid. It was made at Pinewood Studios, whereas on *Nicholas and Alexandra* we filmed from Madrid Studios in Spain. Franklin had a dialogue director, David Giles, who rehearsed us beforehand. It was very clever of Franklin to hire David because most of us knew him well from our London work and were very comfortable with him. Franklin would be up a crane checking the sight. I was so impressed with the Spanish extras. They were so disciplined, so professional, listened to whatever was being directed, and their acting was for real, always. Marvellous to work with.

PS: Brian, was *The Great Gatsby* (1974) a British crew? I know Jack Clayton directed it; and Robin [Vidgeon] was on the camera crew.

BS: It was predominantly American. We did it out on the East Coast and the East Coast crew resented us because *Gatsby* is intrinsically American and they felt it was their property. And they had a British director; a British DoP; British designer.

PS: Shirley Russell was asked to do the costumes but Ken wouldn't let her.

VP: Really?

PS: Yes. It's a Twenties setting. She was the world's expert on clothes of the period. She'd have been marvellous, and the film won the Academy Award for costumes. But Ken needed her for his own films.

VP: Brian, do they ask you to teach? Film schools?

BS: A colleague who teaches at the National Film School has asked me several times but I'm very reluctant. I would not be very positive. I don't mind mentoring them but I do think they need a huge injection of reality. The business today is not like it was when we started. Young people are being misled about 'media'. They are hoping for a future which doesn't exist for ninety-nine percent of them.

PS: I was with Ken Russell a few weeks ago when they screened *The Devils* for a group of 'media' students. The level of the questions Ken got asked was idiotic. The first one was: "I read on IMDB that the film won lots of awards. Did that please you?" The students had no interest at all in the art or the craft of cinema. And it meant nothing to them that this Giant of the cinema was in the same room as them, *for them*, and they had been given the privilege to speak to him. And, of course, they had to watch the film projected from a bootleg DVD because Warner Brothers won't release it.

BS: I have a problem with the younger generation who want to come into movies who have no knowledge of the history of movies. They don't know anything before *Star Wars*. They have no film cultural history. They have no interest.

VP: That's right.

PS: It's like training to be an artist and your knowledge only goes back as far as Damien Hirst.

BS: I'm sorry, but 'artist' and 'Damien Hirst' do not belong in the same sentence.

PS: Exactly. And that's the students' reference point.

BS: One of the regulars in my local pub is a joiner who sometimes puts desks into recording studios, so he has a kind of connection with the business. We were talking about movies. He said: "The problem is there is nothing I want to go and see. It's all CGI movies and vampire films. Have they never heard of *Nosferatu*?" You don't get that from film students.

VP: It's broader than that. I was in the hairdressers and some music was playing. I said: "That sounds like Carmen Miranda." He leant forward and said: "Vivian. Only you and I in the whole salon would know who Carmen Miranda was. He told me of the problems he had talking with these young girls in his salon. He said the gaps are getting shorter and faster.

BS: You are on set and you're chatting away with film crew members, and you're not name-dropping but you say, "I was on a film with Gregory Peck," and they go: "Oh".

VP (*recoiling in horror*): Oh, don't. Don't.

BS: And you say: "Do you know who Gregory Peck is?" "Er, no." The films he did are iconic.

PS: It's not that they don't know. It's that they don't care that they don't know. But having said that, I'm always pleasantly surprised when I make one of my rare visits to the National Film Theatre, usually to see a 70mm presentation, because the magnetic sound system there is superb, and there are more people there now under the age of twenty-five than there were when I used to go often when I was under twenty-five. There was a time when all their patrons had grey hair.

VP: What you say about the future is the same with young actors today; when you talk to them you know there's no future for them.

PS: There is still a future for genuine talent and the star performer. I was knocked out by Mickey Rourke's performance —

BS: *The Wrestler*. Absolutely! Absolutely!

PS: And they went and gave the Oscar to a TV Movie of the week performance! And they wonder why the standards keep falling. They prize the mediocre and run from the great.

BS: Mickey Rourke was wonderful. But could he give another performance like that? It was his whole body. He was so battered. He'd been a boxer. And his performance was magical.

PS: Acting is all about movement. Stillness and movement. With Ken Russell, for example, how an actor moves is usually more important than what they say. In *The Wrestler*, the performance was there in the body language.

BS: But Mickey Rourke is that man because of his own life experience. But I suppose acting is, in part, drawing from your own experience?

VP: I had trained as a dancer and I had used it in musicals, but nothing like *Isadora Duncan*. Before I signed the contract I said: "I want a month's rehearsal and I want to rehearse with the children myself." I wanted to take their classes so they were used to me as a teacher. I don't know if they paid me for that.

PS: I'm sure they didn't pay you. Murray and Brian [Murphy] and the dancers on *The Boy Friend* didn't get paid for the dance training they had to do. Seven weeks!

BS: They did have Harry Benn. Harry wouldn't pay for anything if he could avoid it.

PS: I would love to have talked with Harry Benn, and to get the production files for the films he made with Ken.

BS: I'm surprised he lasted so long. He was seriously asthmatic.

PS: Was he married?

BS: I presume so. He has a son.

VP: That dates you, Brian (*laughs*).

BS: I hold my hand up and say I'm of the older generation.

VP: Will they look back on today's generation with the same awe?

BS: One of the problems is overkill. There's too much stuff out there. You can get totally swamped and you have to be very discerning. But going back twenty years or more there was less. It wasn't as difficult to make good choices. Are you a Londoner?

VP: Yes.

BS: Do you remember the Everyman cinema in Hampstead. That was my education. That's where I saw the films of Jean Cocteau; the Gorky trilogy; *Rashomon*. Also I saw Hollywood films there, but they were bloody good Hollywood films, film noir. Hollywood was producing good films.

VP: Mind you, only the Everyman was showing them.

BS: There were certain cinemas in the West End where I got an eyeful of Brigitte Bardot.

(Vivian Pickles laughs).

PS: Returning to the subject of Ken Russell. I've read the production records and know that this lady turned him down *twice*. For *Rousseau* and *Dance of the Seven Veils*.

VP: It was just after my boy was born. And the *Rousseau* was only a one day job.

PS: A *two* day job.

VP: When you are raising a child you can only afford, emotionally, to do one film a year, and the thought of that has to give you enough adrenalin to organise the child and house-care arrangements, and it has to fit in around my husband's work. Both parents can't be away working, especially when you believe in getting the first five years right for your one and only gorgeous son, Harry Gostelow.

PS: It was lovely seeing Harry in the stage version of *Diary of a Nobody* [in 2009], but I kept hoping to see you arrive carrying a giant tree of a gift.

VP: (*laughs*) That was a super scene [in Ken's film]. and Murray and I couldn't stop laughing at each other. We shot the film outdoors under a specially made up Twenties backlot that Ken built behind the studio to get the correct period light. The whole cast were comics and everybody was terribly funny. We laughed at each other a lot. It was delightful. But *Isadora* was far more serious.

BS: Ken launched my career. I'm proud and privileged that my career started with Ken. Ken Russell IS a part of film history, and it's nice to be a part of that, although he drove me mad.

VP: Yes.

BS: There are times when I could have throttled him, and times when I'd almost want to put my arms around him.

VP: Yes, because the work one did with him one couldn't have done with anyone else.

BS: Absolutely. Yes. I owe a lot to him. He has a justifiably high place in the British canon.

PS: He is a giant of British cinema. And he did get definitive performances, from you Vivian; from Glenda [Jackson]; Alan Bates; from Oliver Reed in *The Devils*. Reed would not have given that performance for Michael Winner. No disrespect to Michael Winner.

BS: All disrespect to Michael Winner. Michael Winner was a great supporter of Cannon Films which decimated the British Film Industry.

PS: Cannon certainly did destroy it. But why was the British Film Industry allowed to be sold, hook, line and sinker, including the studios where they made *Star Wars*, to two Israelis [Golan & Globus] who had done nothing but *Lemon Popsicle*?

BS: Has Michael Winner ever made a decent film?

PS: He made *Lawman*, which is terrific.

BS: Oh, yes, with Burt Lancaster. You're right. If Winner didn't exist we'd need to invent him because we'd be short of an awful lot of stories.

(*Vivian Pickles laughs*).

PS: Vivian turned him down of course.

VP: The part he offered wasn't my cup of tea. It was early Michael Winner and I wasn't interested in being in the kind of films he was making then.

PS: We need more Michael Winners really. We need an English producer who can raise the budgets to pay the casts that Winner did. He was the only man in London doing that so he gets all the flak.

BS: He made some commercial successes, but he didn't make a film which stands high in the canon of British cinema. *The Death Wishes* made money but they're distasteful.

PS: *The Mechanic* is pretty good. There's a good story when Ken Russell and Michael Winner gate-crashed a union meeting. They travelled there in Winner's Rolls Royce. The unions in control of the studios were trying to stop film directors from shooting on location; trying to force them to pay a studio fee *if* they filmed on location. Ken marched in, wearing his polar bear fur coat. Stomped to the front and said: "I made a film in your studio and the sets fell down!" Then he started shouting 'Off! Off! Off! Off!' and caused such a ruckus that the meeting had to be abandoned. The unions got their own back years later when they chased Ken out of town when his producers insisted he use a non-union actress for *Fanny Hill*.

BS: Was that not made in the States?

PS: Not by Ken. I meant *Moll Flanders*. The unions put a worldwide embargo on it. The producer, Guccione, sued Ken and lost. But that took a year of Ken's life.

BS: I've got very mixed feelings about the decline of the unions. I come from a union background. One of the sad things about the industry is that we no longer have rules. The free market principle has opened the doors to non-talent and non-experience

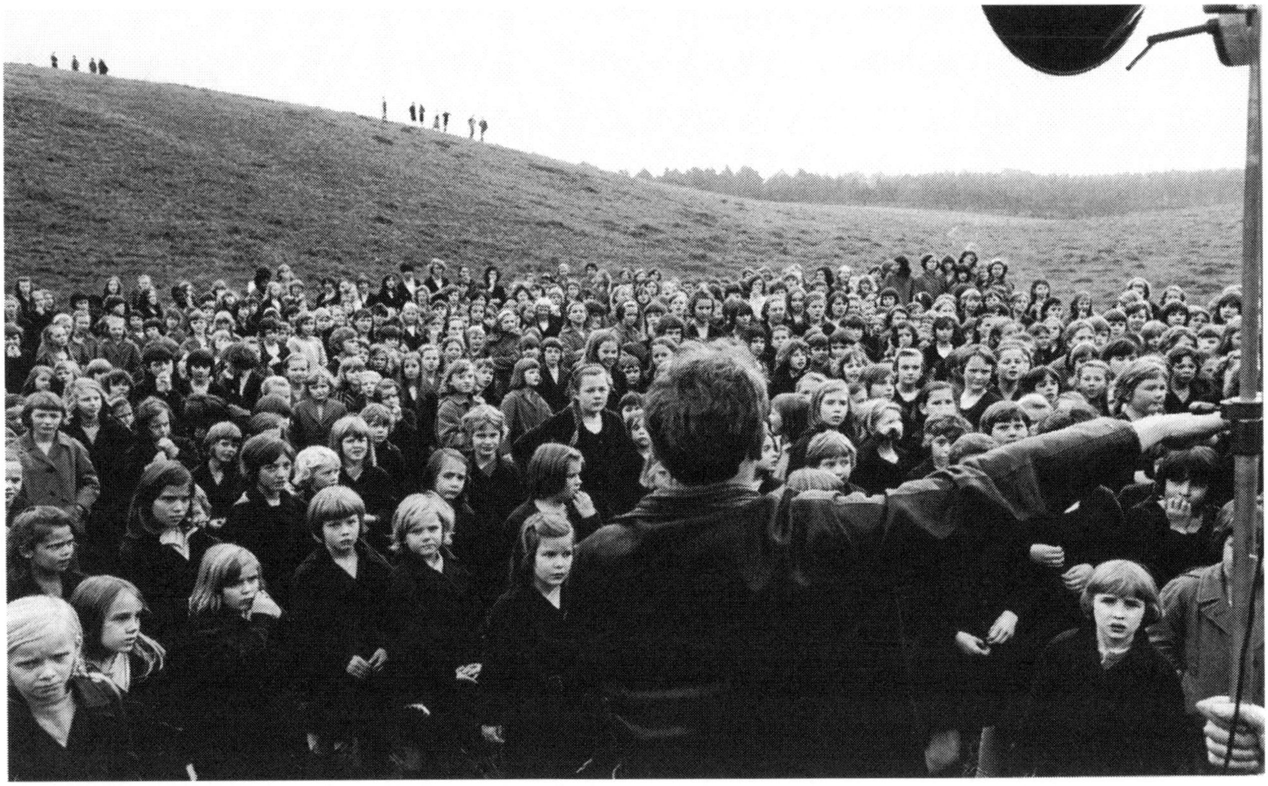

Ken Russell readies 500 girls to dance in the astonishing finale to *Isadora Duncan*

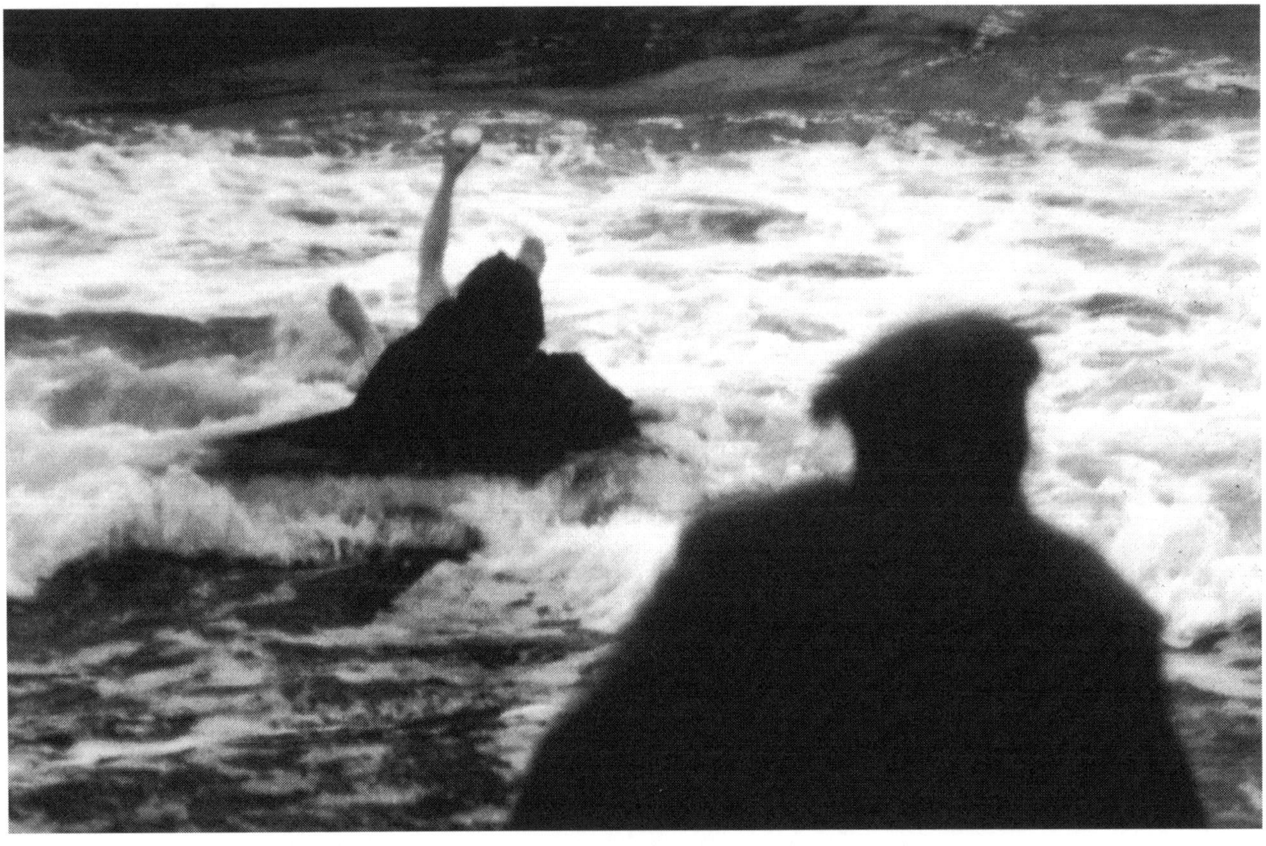

When Isadora tries to kill herself, Ken Russell himself pulls her from the sea and it has degraded the business. It's now a race to the bottom. In the film business, the closed shop worked because it regulated the intake of people. It made sure that there weren't more people than there was production. Now we have open doors. Hundreds of thousands of young people wanting to come into the business but there is no business. And they are diluting what work there is and degrading it.

PS: It's like what you said, Vivian, about *Isadora*. You could get the rehearsal time and whatever you needed to be able to do the job properly.

VP: It's structured. Both sides need to know the rules of the game, otherwise it is freefall and anarchy. Unfortunately, anarchy is to the benefit of a few. In America the unions seem to be strong.

BS: In America the unions are much stronger but they still have their problems. They're being nibbled away at. The members aren't happy with the bosses.

PS: That's always been the case with unions.

BS: In the Seventies, there were stories of leaders of the unions being taken to lunch by producers and giving away concessions that were outside the agreement. But there was a little bit of flexibility. You could always say to the crew: "We'd like to work on." There was an understanding. Now it feels like it is driven by accountants. It feels totally impersonal. And the workers feel that they don't matter. If you don't matter how can you contribute your best?

VP: I loved the American system of overtime. They have three bands, bronze, silver and gold and they were all greedy to have that extra overtime. Three times a day, at set times, your pay went up and up. In England overtime had one set rate.

BS: Golden hours they called it. I think it still happens. There's an American DoP called Haskell Wexler, made his own documentaries, including one called *Who Needs Sleep?*. In 1996, I think it was, because the crews were beginning to work excessive hours, although admittedly they were paid, but the production would drive them to work seventeen hour days. On one particular production, I think it was *Storyville*, one of the camera assistants was driving home on the freeway and fell asleep. He was killed and left a wife and two young children. People are too driven and too tired. Wexler, who did *Medium Cool*, and the famous cop film with Sidney Poitier and Rod Steiger, *In The Heat of the Night*, took up the cause and, over four years, made a documentary about sleep deprivation, with directors, actors, commentating. At the end of the day it all came to nothing because he couldn't change a culture which was commercially driven. Wexler was sent threatening letters from film crews who said 'If you don't like it, get out of the kitchen. We don't want our hours regulated, we want the money'. They were prepared to work themselves and their colleagues into the ground because the overtime was more important to them than their family. In England we do have Health and Safety laws.

PS: I think, in England, in the Seventies they were both wrong. The unions were wrong because they actively did shut down production.

BS: Once Thatcher came in and the anti-union legislation came in it became a slippery slope.

VP: I liked it when we didn't work with non-Equity members.

BS: Now you don't have to be in Equity to act?

VP: No, and that's just awful.

BS: Why do you say that? Because it has lowered the skills?

VP: It has. I think it has.

BS: To be in Equity you had to earn your stripes before you got your ticket.

VP: You had to have training.

BS: That's a similar situation to what we have. A producer can pick anybody off the street and put them into your job. They seem to accept that they know nothing.

VP: When you are working in comedy and you're acting with someone who hasn't played in theatre it's very very hard work, particularly if you are working with young girls, for example who are playing my daughter. Their timing isn't there. It's there for them but it's not there for the scene.

PS: Malcolm McDowell said the one thing he learned from Guccione's *Caligula* was that it was better to work with monsters who were professionals than amateurs who were nice. With amateurs it was always a disaster and it made it harder work for everyone else.

BS: This is not to say you don't occasionally get the genuine talent.

VP: Yes, absolutely. But the decline in standards is across the board. It's wherever you go.

BS: When the CBI turns round and says we are being presented with university graduates who are no good to us, and they are talking about going back to apprenticeships, they have recognised that you cannot carry on without proper training. And by training I don't necessarily mean technical training. The technology of filmmaking has changed. The styles, and disciplines, of the filming process are constantly evolving. Using photographic film imposed a discipline that was lost with the introduction of cheap digital media and the move to multi-cameras. A director had an idea of the construction of his film and needed to be clear on his set-ups, and his cutting points, because he wouldn't have the luxury of selecting, in the editing process, from multiple takes on multiple cameras. The discipline extended to all the crew. Today, with the facility to shoot many takes and from a variety of angles on a single set-up, the technical crew is often 'out of the loop' as to the directors intentions and it is frequently sound that has to make the most compromises in order to attempt to accommodate all of the possible variables. It's not 'wrong' per se. It's different. It's our job to evolve with the times. There *are* good films being made. *Das weiße Band* [*The White Ribbon*] is a remarkable film.

PS: It is, but it is very much of the 'old school', shot on 35mm, and built around the traditional discipline in performance and construction. The thing which disappoints me about current cinema in English is its instant forgettability. Nothing sticks. The reason for that is that filmmakers are no longer thinking in terms of the 'image'. The art of composition, of which Ken Russell was King, has been lost. The camera wobbles because they think that adds realism but it doesn't. When I walk down a street, and am looking around, my head isn't wobbling all over the place, it's balanced. The rapid-fire cutting, from the multi-camera source, as you say Brian, means that the geography of the scene is broken, and the value of each image is less. Less, less and then lost. When I close my eyes I can still see the films of the greats, every frame of say, a Fellini, or a Kubrick or a Ken Russell. But as Ken himself once said: "My films won't last forever. People will only be watching them, oh, for about three or four thousand years.

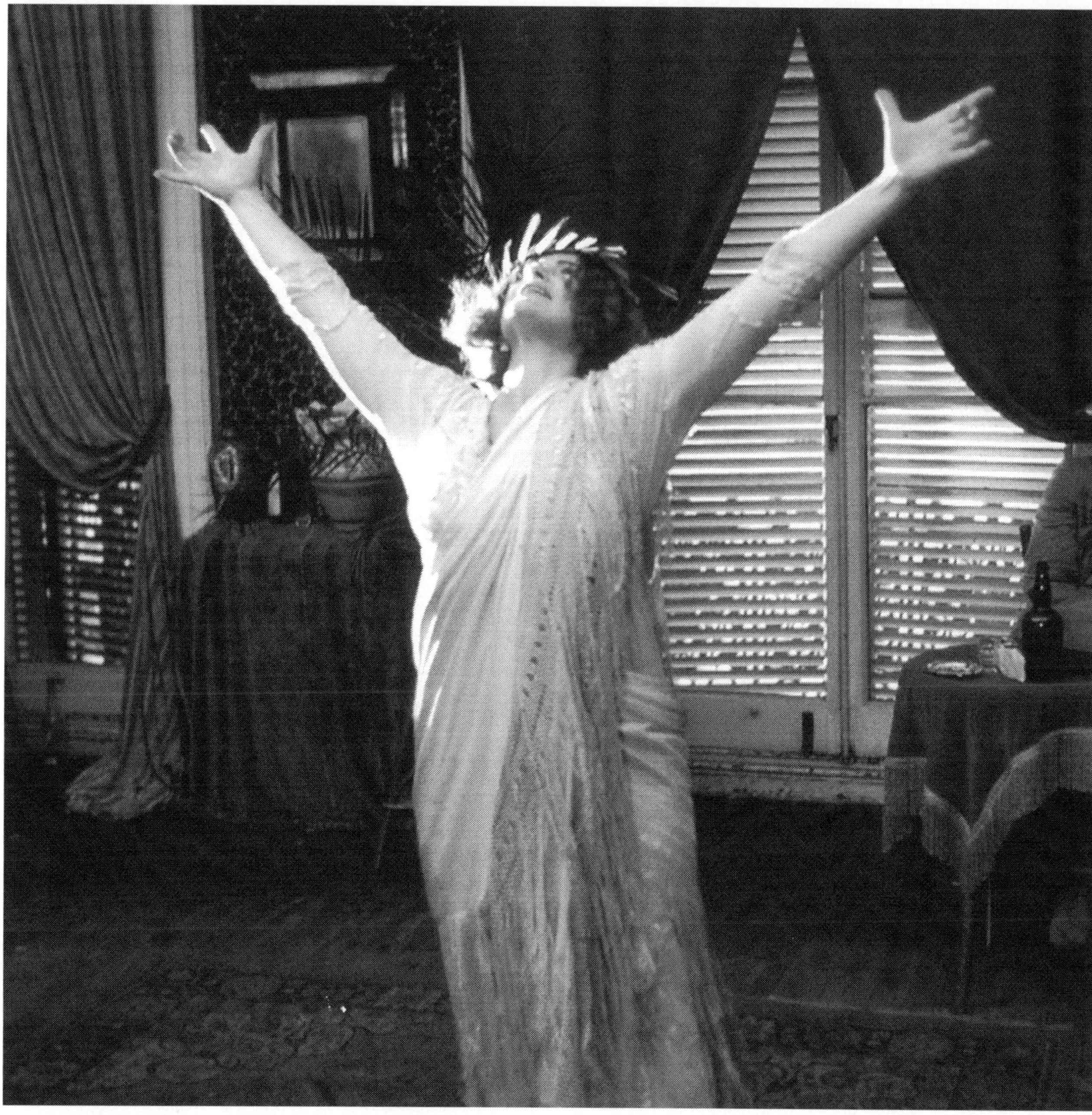

Crowned with thorns, Vivian Pickles dances in *Isadora Duncan.* Flowers for Murray Melvin in *Diary of a Nobody*

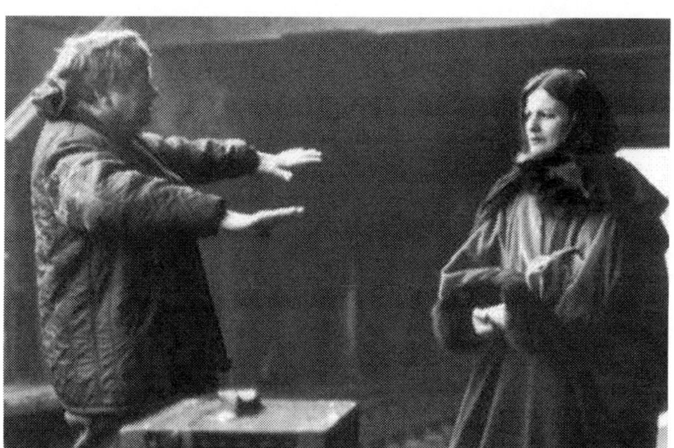

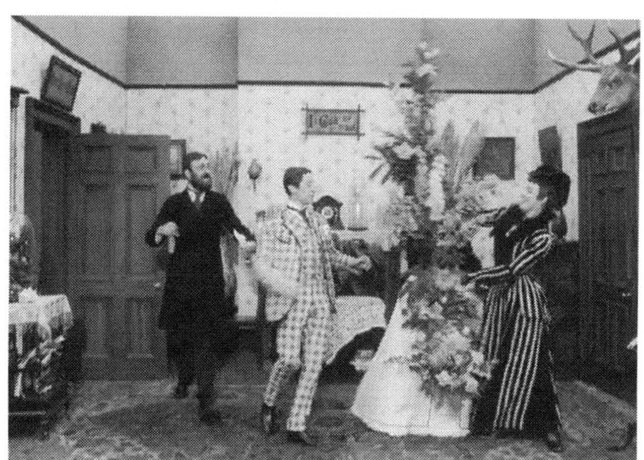

Spike Milligan in Ken Russell's *The Devils*

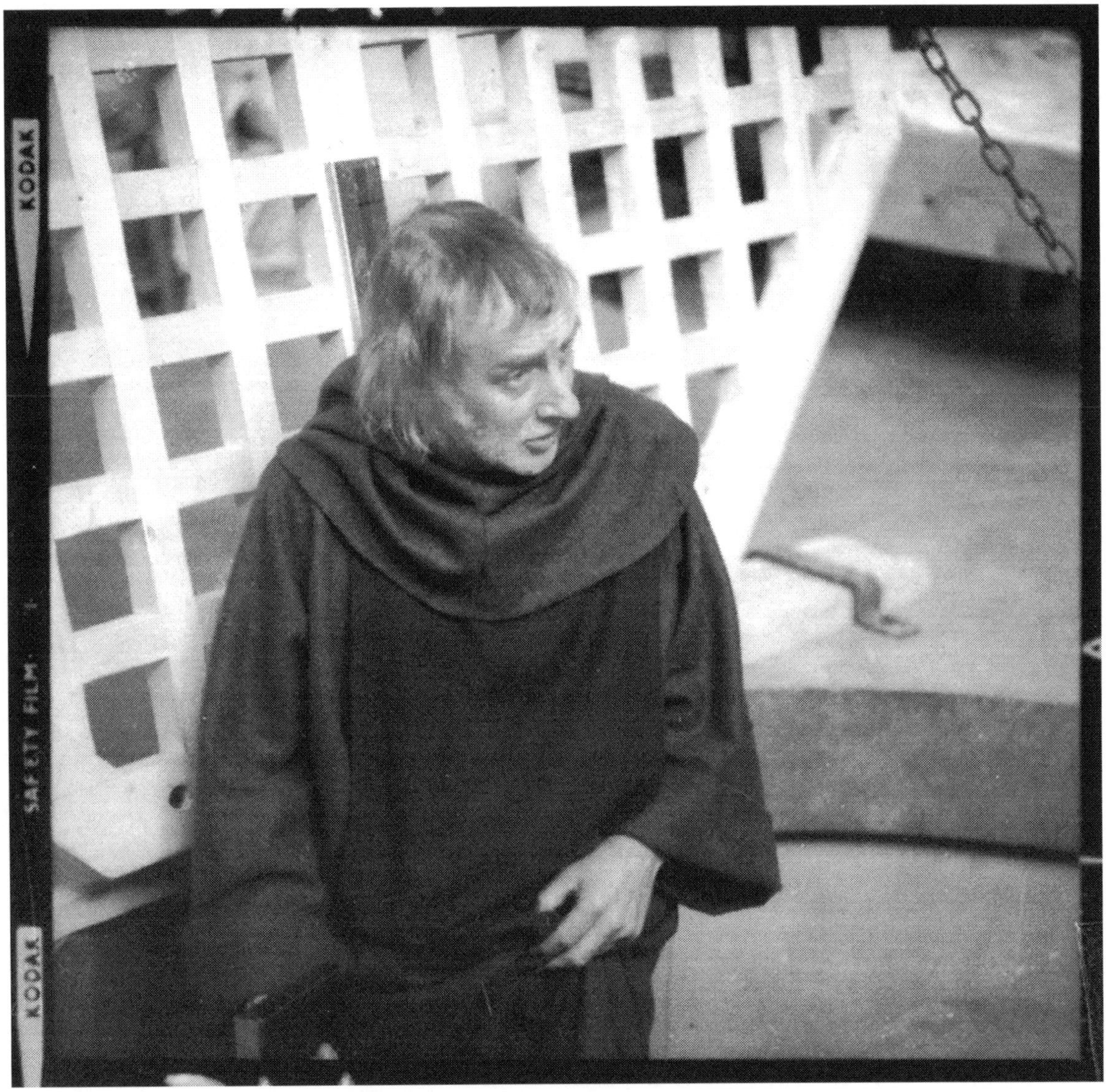

In 1959, in his first year as a professional filmmaker, Ken Russell made seven short 35mm films on subjects as wide-ranging as the poems of John Betjeman, the music of Gordon Jacob, the new national obsession with the guitar, the joys of Mechanical Instruments, the paintings of Roberts Colquhoun and MacBride, and the nonsense poetry of Spike Milligan. The Milligan film, called *Portrait of a Goon,* was a successful attempt by Russell to find a visual style to represent Milligan's newly published verse. Images, such as Milligan silhouetted against the sun atop an English Monument to God, and backscreen projection used as 'mind transport', would be perfected in *Tommy* (1975) and *Altered States* (1980). The Milligan film, financed in full by the British public, can be seen, free of charge, in British Film Institute mediatheques. Milligan himself adored the film and owned a 16mm print. Thereafter he kept up a correspondence with Russell, offering him work and asking for work. At a semi-secret screening of *The Devils,* in Bath in 2002, a few days before the restored film's screening at the National Film Theatre, Mike Bradsell, Russell's editor, broke the news that Russell had cast Milligan in a now lost scene in *The Devils*.

Bradsell had put back into the film almost all the many shots removed by directives from Warner Brothers and the British censors. In answer to an audience question about 'what was still missing', he said: "A scene with Spike Milligan as a humble priest. When Grandier [Oliver Reed] is awaiting the trial, the scene which now has Dudley Sutton coming in with his troops and breaking up the place, taunting him about why don't you offer up your pain to God, Ken wrote a scene about a simple country priest who had heard about the predicament. He visits Grandier to give him comfort and he is the one who says: "Why don't you offer up your praise to God?" It is a two-minute scene. It cut together perfectly. Ken actually said it was a bit out of kilter with the rest of the film and, in a way, Spike Milligan upstaged Oliver Reed. He decided not to use it. He did his best to try to explain to Spike Milligan that there was nothing wrong in what he did. It was Ken's error, and that the scene needed to be done differently to maintain instead the rather cynical attitude of Baron De Laubardemont, the character played by Dudley Sutton. I hung onto [the print of] this scene for a couple of years. Then one day, the phone rang and it was Ken. He said: "Have you still got that Spike Milligan scene? Can I borrow it back because somebody wants to interview me for a magazine and I want to be able to show them it."

I said: "I know it's not my property but I'd love to remain the curator of it."

"Yes, yes, of course," said Ken.

"But if I lend it to you, you'll lose it, Ken."

"I won't. I promise I won't."

But he managed to lose it. It really was a good scene."

Did Ken Russell lose it? Or did he destroy it? Deliberately? Murray Melvin explains:

"It was such a wonderful scene, the Father Ambrose scene. In a conversation with Ken, I had said: "Do you know, if you hadn't given me this part [Father Mignon], which is lovely, I would have liked to have done that. It's such a beautiful speech and it's such a beautiful scene."

And he said: "Yes. I'm getting Spike Milligan."

There was a pause and I blurted: "*Spike Milligan*?"

I was on a film earlier on with Peter Sellers, that Peter Medak started to direct, called *Ghost in the Noonday Sun*. However, Peter Medak was sidetracked, and Sellers brought in Spike to finish directing it. I thought Spike was such a self-publicist. However, here we were doing *The Devils*, and that's what made me say: "*Spike Milligan*?"

And Ken looked at me and he said: "Well, he thinks he's Jesus Christ, doesn't he?"

I said: "He might think it, but..."

Come the shoot, the rest of the company were called at lunchtime. I remember bumping into Ken and asking: "Oh, how's it going with Jesus Christ?"

Ken told me: "He can't do it."

And I said: "Oh? Surprise me."

"He just can't be *true*. Come and watch."

I said: "Oh, no Ken. I couldn't possibly."

"Why not? Don't be silly. Come on."

"No, no, no. It would be too embarassing."

And he went back and they carried on filming after lunch for a couple of hours. Spike couldn't do the 'humble simplicity' that the part demanded. Ken wasn't a director who could tell you *how* to play a scene, he just knew by instinct when it was wrong. So you had to pull something out of the bag. Ken didn't recast it. He realised he could do the film without the scene. One doesn't feel there's a scene missing. At this juncture the lawyers were summoned.

I remember Harry Benn saying "best if we don't mention it". It's possible there was an agreement twixt Ken and Spike, at the parting of the ways, that Spike's involvement with the project would not be talked about. That it why there was no mention of it in the press. Amazing when you think of the PR that would have been generated at the news of the then much talked about Spike Milligan working with the great Ken Russell! It was all quietly hushed up. Which is why there was no expectation of a Spike appearance before the film was released. Crafty Spike. Bet you that is why Ken wanted to borrow the film from Mike. Ken knew he would 'lose it' to save Spike's blushes and prevent any legal trouble."

Ken Russell was making *The Devils* when a hell of censors and lawyers broke lose to attack his most recent film, *The Dance of The Seven Veils* (1970), a mostly dance and mime film on the theme of the Life of Richard Strauss. In conspiracy with the cowed production company (The BBC), the film was banned worldwide after a single screening. The ban is still in force today, not because the film is obscene or libellous, but because of the pressure of lawyers and the lack of backbone by the production company. Similarly, in 1965, Ken Russell's *The Debussy Film*, whose final scenes of haunting were a clear influence on Kubrick's *The Shining* (1980), was withdrawn for decades because the ears of a distant relative of the composer were bent by the whispers of Edward Lockspeiser, a journalist who had lost his own part in the film. *The Diary of a Nobody* (1964), the first Ken Russell film to star his Famous Company of Players (Murray Melvin, Brian Murphy, Vivian Pickles), an exquisite Chaplin-esque comedy, was banned and withdrawn for generations (and is still unavailable) because of the inanities of distant relatives of the 'rights' holders. The best of Ken Russell was being buried from view. The art and the artist were under attack. And he was losing.

In the early 1980s, Ken Russell would lose a year of his life, and almost his home, fighting a lawsuit brought against him by the pornographer Bob Guccione, when the acting union in England prevented Russell from making *Moll Flanders* for Guccione, who wanted Russell to cast a non-union actress as Moll. Russell would win that lawsuit, but was always fearful of the threat of litigation for the damage it did to his art and his muse.

He put a call through to Mike Bradsell and asked could he "borrow back" the Milligan scene.

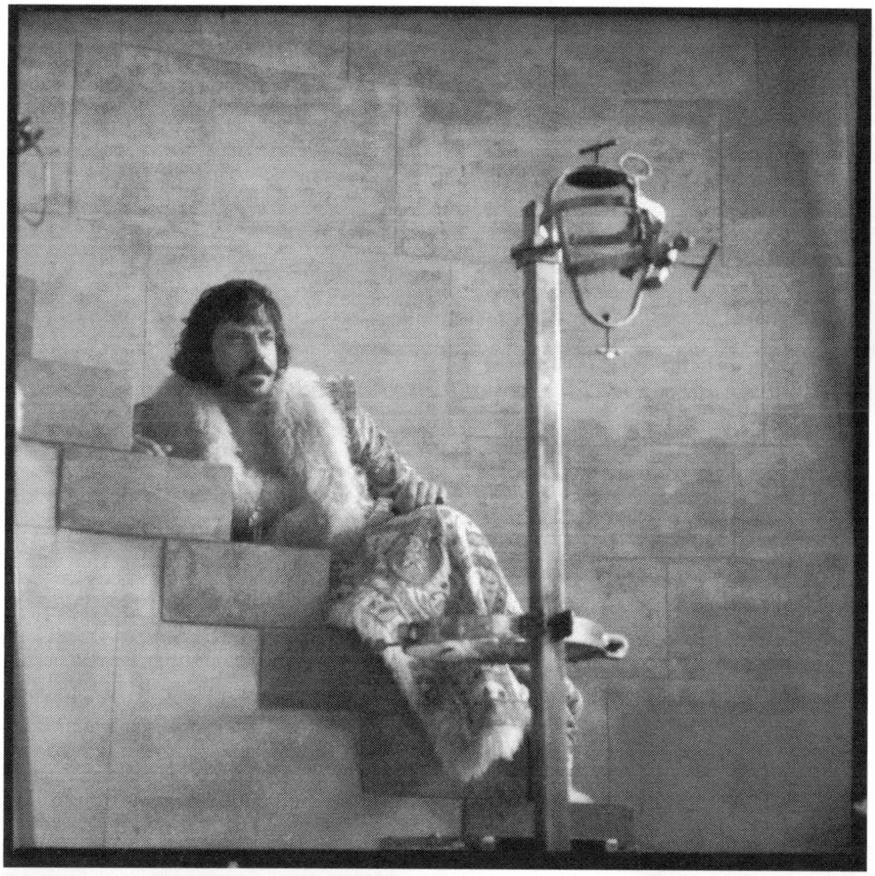

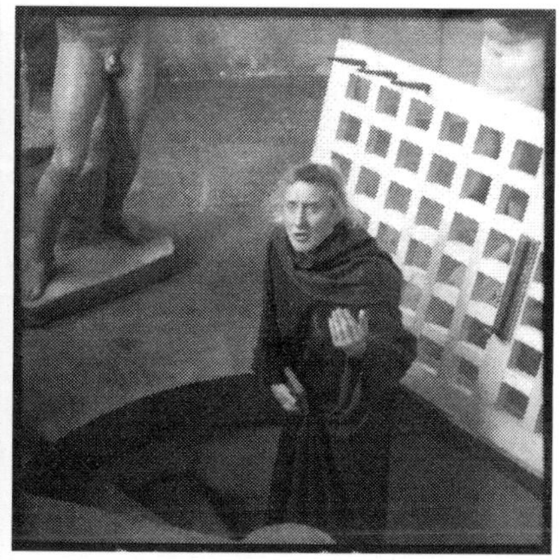

In a room dressed with broken bodies, statues foreshadowing the tortures to come, a village priest prepares Father Grandier for death by telling him that God wants him to die as he lived, with all the flaws of being human.

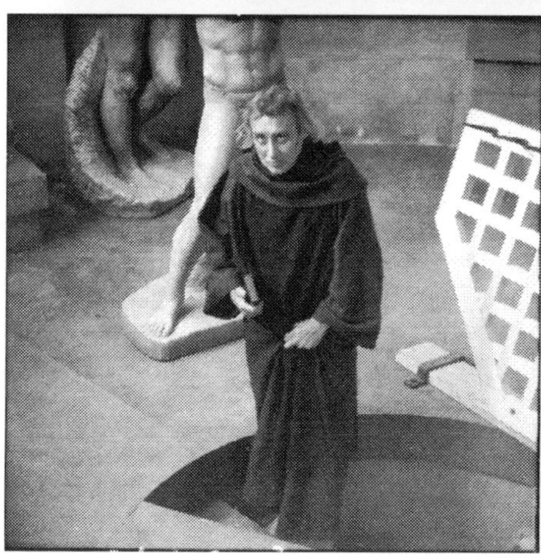

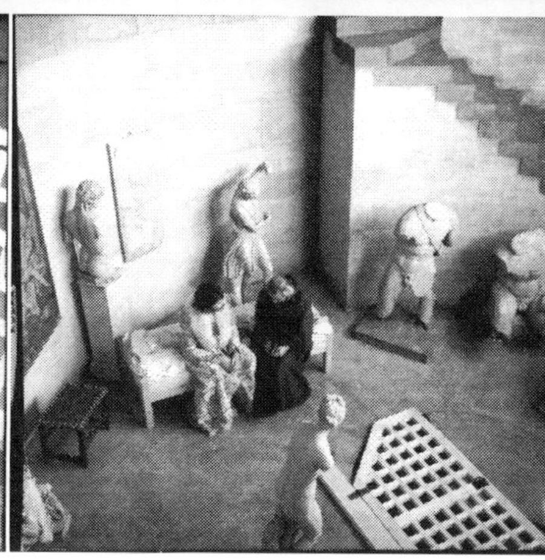

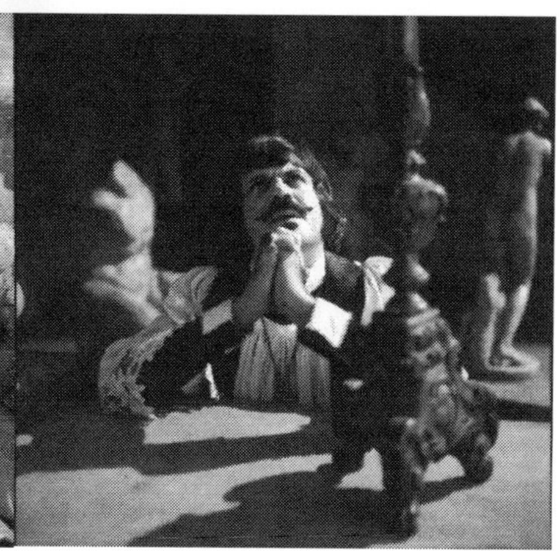

The Lost Spike Milligan Scene from Ken Russell's *The Devils*

59. <u>EXT. CONVENT YARD. DAY</u>

JEANNE has hanged herself from the tree. LAUBARDEMONT rushes through the teaming rain, hauls himself up on the branch and cuts her down.

JEANNE
I wanted to make amends - I have wronged an innocent man.

LAUBARDEMONT
My poor deluded child. It is not you speaking, but the devils within you trying to protect Grandier. The exorcists have failed - we must resort to sterner measures.

60. <u>INT. GRANDIER'S CELL. NIGHT</u>

GRANDIER lies on his bed - he cannot sleep. Outside the cell he hears drunken Breton sightseers - singing.

GRANDIER
God I want... Christ! I need Thy... Christ, Christ ...
(he cries: he cannot pray he is afraid)
God I thought I had found you and now you have forsaken me. What is there in myself which makes for a purpose? Nothing. Nothing.

The cell door opens - a figure enters.

GRANDIER
(leaping up)
Madeleine, what have you done to her?

FATHER AMBROSE
My name is Father Ambrose, I know nothing of your Madeleine. I was told of your trouble, my son. The night can be very long.

GRANDIER
Yes.

FATHER AMBROSE
I thought I might read to you. Or if you'd like it better, we can pray together.

GRANDIER
No.

FATHER AMBROSE turns to go.

GRANDIER
Stay with me.

AMBROSE stops and turns. The JAILER closes the gate, locks it and goes away.

GRANDIER
Help me.

AMBROSE
I will try.

GRANDIER
They are destroying my faith.
By fear and loneliness, now.
Later by pain.

AMBROSE
Go to God, my son.

GRANDIER
Nothing going to nothing.

AMBROSE
God is here, and Christ is now.

GRANDIER
Yes. That is my faith. But how can I defend it?

AMBROSE
By remembering the will of God.

GRANDIER
Yes. Yes.

AMBROSE
By remembering that nothing must be asked of Him, and nothing refused.

GRANDIER
(rising)
Yes. But this is all in the books. I've read it and understood it, preached about it a thousand times. And it is not enough. Not enough. Not now.

AMBROSE
God is here, and Christ is here.

GRANDIER
You're an old man. Have you gathered no more than these sanctimonious platitudes in all your years? Wait, I'm sorry. You came in pure charity. The only one who has done so. I'm sorry.

AMBROSE
Suffering must be willed, affliction must be willed, humiliation must be willed, and in the act of willing ...

GRANDIER
They'll be understood. I know, I know.

AMBROSE
Then you know everything.

GRANDIER
I know nothing. Speak to me as a man, Father. Talk about simple things. What does God want of us?

AMBROSE
Ourselves.

GRANDIER
But I am unworthy.

AMBROSE
Have you greatly sinned?

GRANDIER
Greatly.

AMBROSE
Even young girls come to me nowadays and confess things I don't know about. So it's hardly likely that I'll understand the sins of a young man of the world such as yourself. But let me try.

GRANDIER
There have been women and lust; power and ambition, worldliness and mockery.

AMBROSE
Remember. God is here. You speak before Him. Christ is now. You suffer with Him.

GRANDIER
I dread the pain to come. The humiliation.

AMBROSE
Did you dread the ecstasy of love?

GRANDIER
No.

AMBROSE
Or its humiliation?

GRANDIER
I gloried in it. I have lived by the senses.

AMBROSE
Then die by them.

GRANDIER
What did you say?

AMBROSE
Offer God pain, convulsion and disgust.

GRANDIER
Yes, yes.

AMBROSE
Let Him reveal Himself in the only way you can understand.

GRANDIER
Yes. Give Him myself.

AMBROSE
It is all any of us can do. We live a little while, and in that little while we sin. We go to Him as we can... All is forgiven.

GRANDIER
Yes, I am His child. It is true. Let Him take me as I am. So there is meaning, after all. It is not nothing going to nothing. It is sin going to forgiveness. It is human creature going to love.

Ken Russell directs Spike Milligan as Father Ambrose in *The Devils.* © Ken Russell

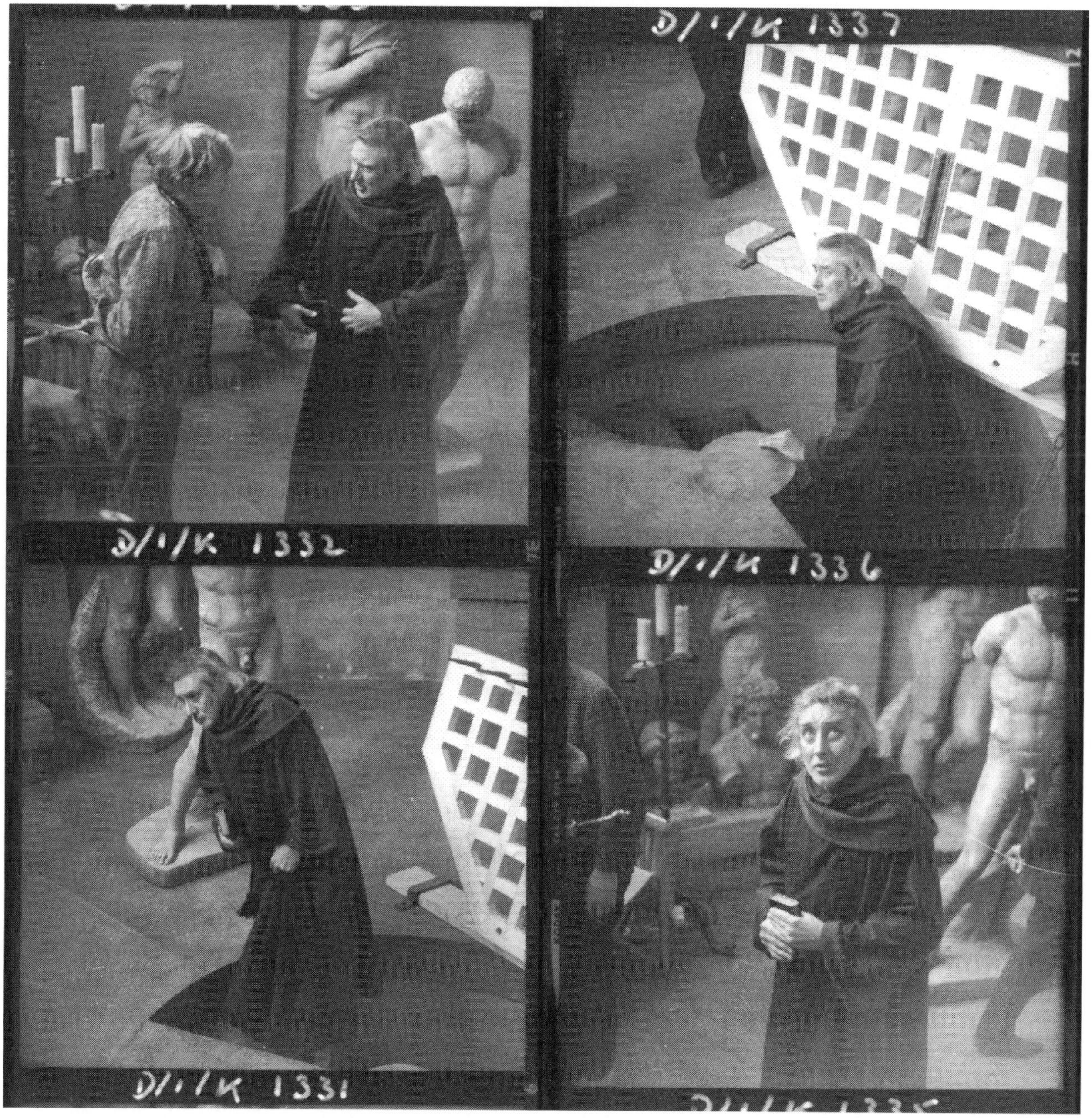

Philip Harrison
From *Vampira* to *Lisztomania*

I saw Vampira last night and particularly liked the coffins, with the sliding glass tops and the fold-out double one that Niven takes to London with him. You could certainly see the step from there to the glory that is Lisztomania. I don't suppose Ken looked at Clive Donner's film did he? Soon afterwards he wrote his script of Dracula, set in the 20s.

I haven't seen or even thought about *Vampira* for ages except once or twice to boast that I had worked with David Niven to people who had probably never heard of him anyway. It was around the time Bryan Forbes took over ABPC/EMI Borehamwood studios and 'revitalised' it with a few old friends including Clive. There was immense confusion with the script during shooting, it being a confusing story to begin with, and Niven blacked-up after having bitten a black lady; the continuity became very muddled after this point and I think there was a lot of panicked re-scheduling and re-editing. I don't suppose Ken would have seen the film by choice. My designs were very much Ken's sort of thing though. *Vampira* was an uphill job but with Ken it was encouragement. That's not to say Clive wasn't supportive but I was apt to go out on a limb and not let on the extent of my notions until they were a *fait accompli.*

Thinking about it Ken may well have seen it... Clive I knew quite well as he was attached to Jocelyn Rickards, costume designer on *Morgan!,* with whom I had made friends. She had possibly championed me to Clive.

On Lisztomania, did Ken keep adding things?

There was an element of 'a work in progress'. Ken's a polymath. He knows a lot. I would never have interfered with anything editorial in the slightest, or queried anything. All I'd ever ask him, if I didn't understand something, was 'What was the reason why it had to be...". I shouldn't even have asked that. It's got me into trouble. "I want it. Just do it." I'd say 'Why?' only because I might then be able to get it even better.

A set I did enjoy was Liszt's bedroom with the bedpiano and the piano-fireplace.

Everything was pianos. Ken kept saying we want Expressionist sets. I thought that was what Expressionism was. Now I know a bit more I know they're not really expressionist sets. They're pretty broad. I remember doing all the musical scores stacked up. Hundreds and hundreds of scores.

Wagner sits on them.

And the steps, were they all musical clefs? There were musical icons everywhere. We went mad buying all the old pianos we could possibly get, and we got a lot of them! Wooden-framed pianos that were worthless because they couldn't stay in tune. You could get them for a fiver each. All the piano people in London couldn't believe their luck because we were buying them by the dozens! We made that beautiful glass piano too. Very early twenties in style. There was an amazing deco one on the revolve.

The one that fired flames?

(Laughs) We had everything. Colin Chilvers, the effects guy, had a wonderful time. He was very very good indeed. You do the design and you present it to Colin and you say: "Can you make this work?" And he'd say: "You have to make this bigger here, and you'll need to put a cable there'. If possible, you work as early as possible with the effects guy so you don't have to keep modifying the thing when it's built. Les Bowie did a model shot for us and I learned a chunk of stuff from that from him. A pan down from the big round window at the top of the tower with his arms out. You pan down to the

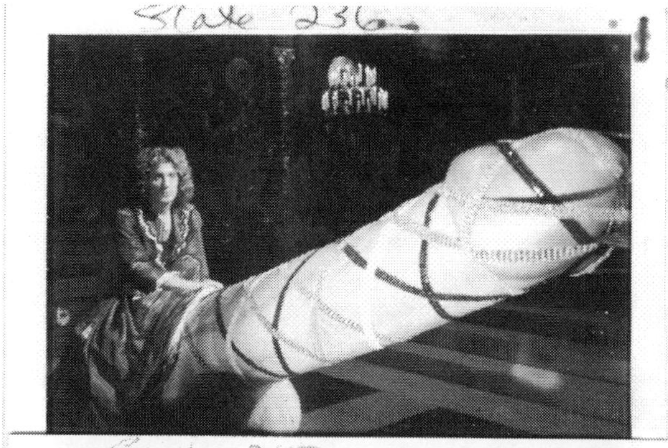

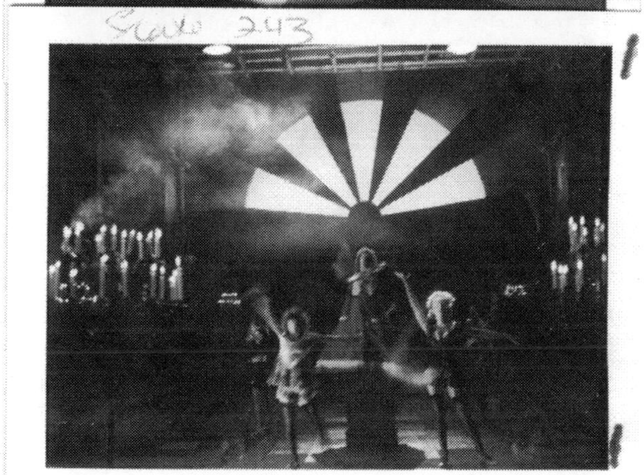

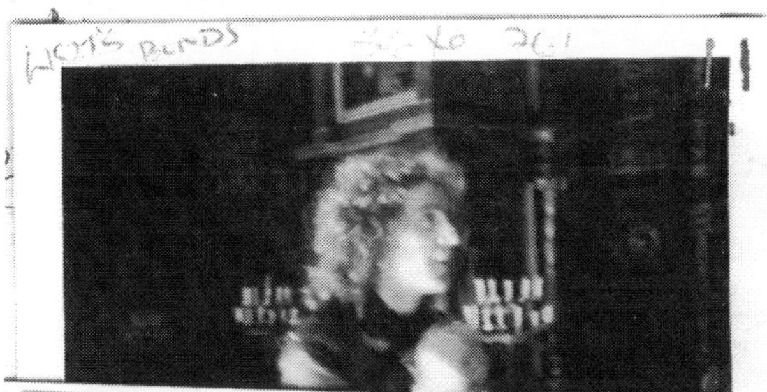

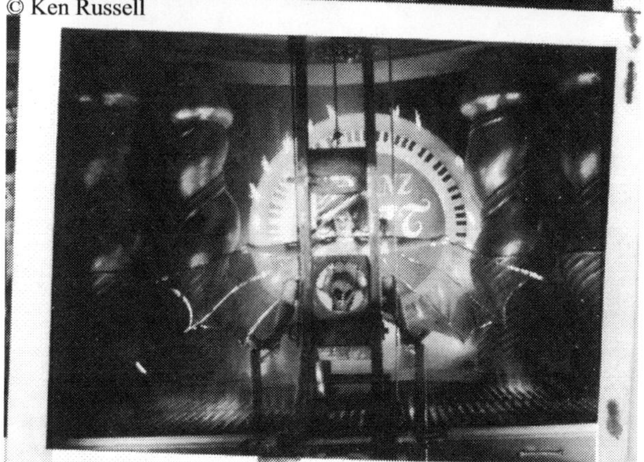

© Ken Russell

street. An explosion happens. It's the 1870 war. The family are running towards you. It was a very good learning process for me. I loved doing it.

The arrival of Rick Wakeman as Thor was a last minute addition.

With his long blond hair. He had a bit of a Danish warrior face. That set was another masterpiece, I think. I had three or four typewriters on each side, and they were alternating, making clattery clattery music. Two at the foot and two at the head were quadrophonic disc gramophones, which had four discs on a stack. Each with a horn. It's a gramophone casebook. It actually existed. We just copied it. I got four of them made. It was terrific to get that work done. Colin Chilvers got some beautiful wooden plate press cameras made. I made a round dressing room mirror with oil lamps around it because it was pre-electricity! I think we had something outside through the window. You could see the front of the marquee or the front of the theatre and I had a big revolving sign made, all lit by oil lamps or candles!
It was pretty elaborate considering we really didn't have a lot of money. Lovely things. I loved the guitar that was a machine gun. It was absolutely fabulous. It had to have a gun effect so it was all elaborately rigged up to make bursts of flames, muzzle flash like a machine-gun.

The Ringo Starr set was all black but it was all mirrors as well. We found a mirror place in the city. For some reason we'd gone for some ordinary rectanglular mirror shapes. But they also made mirrors of all different shapes, and all their offcuts were marvellous shapes, squares that had had circles cut out. We said: "We'll have the lot". We took a skip load! (*laughs*). We stuck them up on the flats. I kept one of the pieces for years. We also went to a Rockwell glass factory, which makes the kind of drinking glasses you get in schools. There's a huge machine, as big as a house, that makes them. White hot glass pellets of glass are shot around, with these wonderful bits of metal. And out comes glasses at the other hand. But it leaves a residue of these wonderful molten shapes of glass, which look like molted wax but it's clear. I put one on the bedpost in *Lisztomania*. About five years later it just exploded!

Ken sent me to see Oliver Reed to keep him happy. They had a jingoistic script about a Colonel. Oliver's house was a huge place. I got there early, about half-past nine. By eleven o'clock we were paralytic drunk.

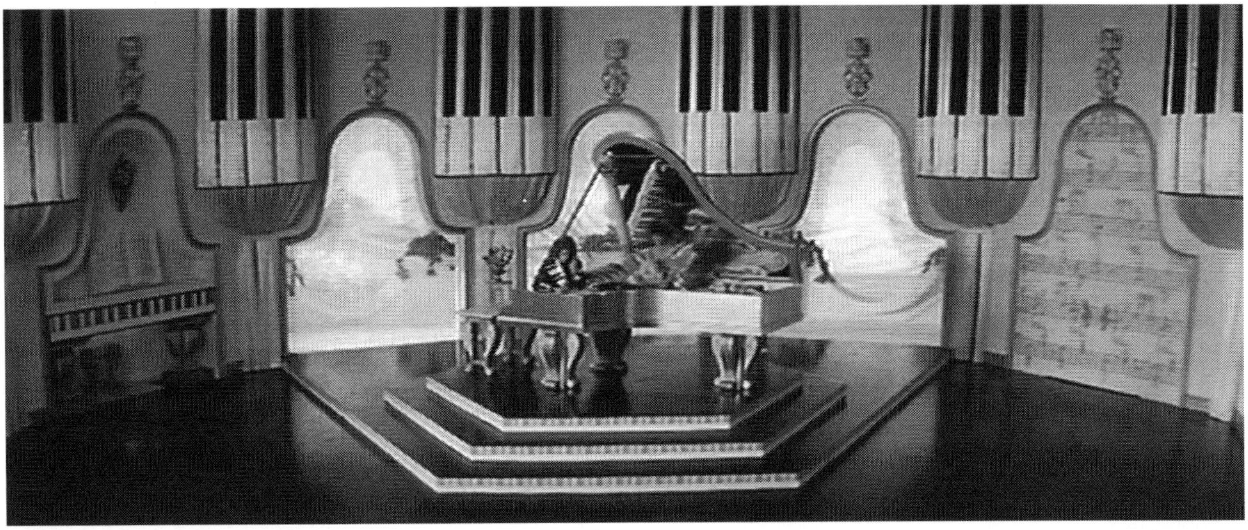

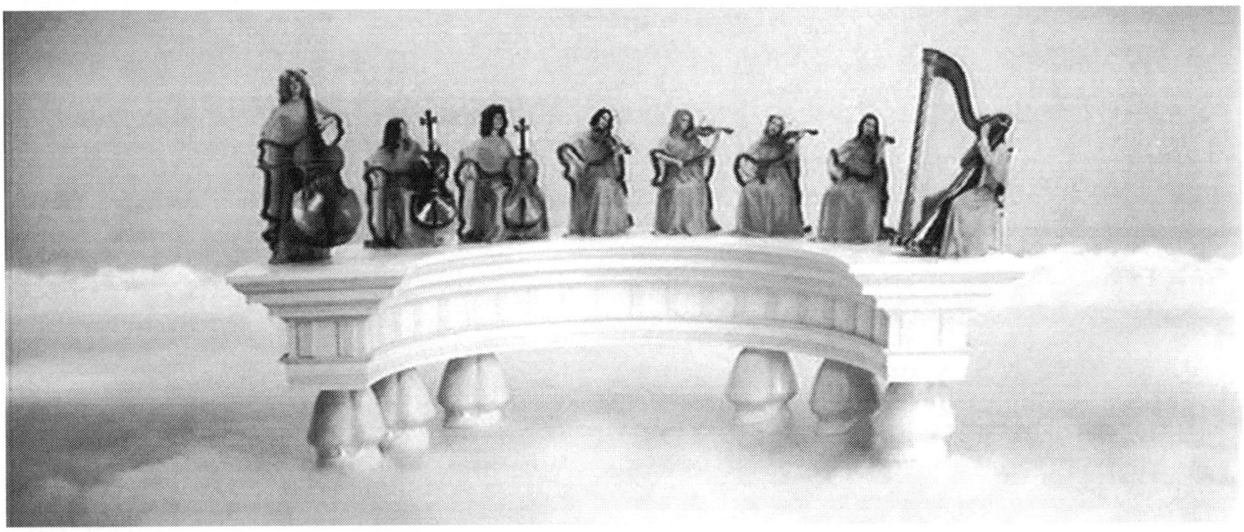

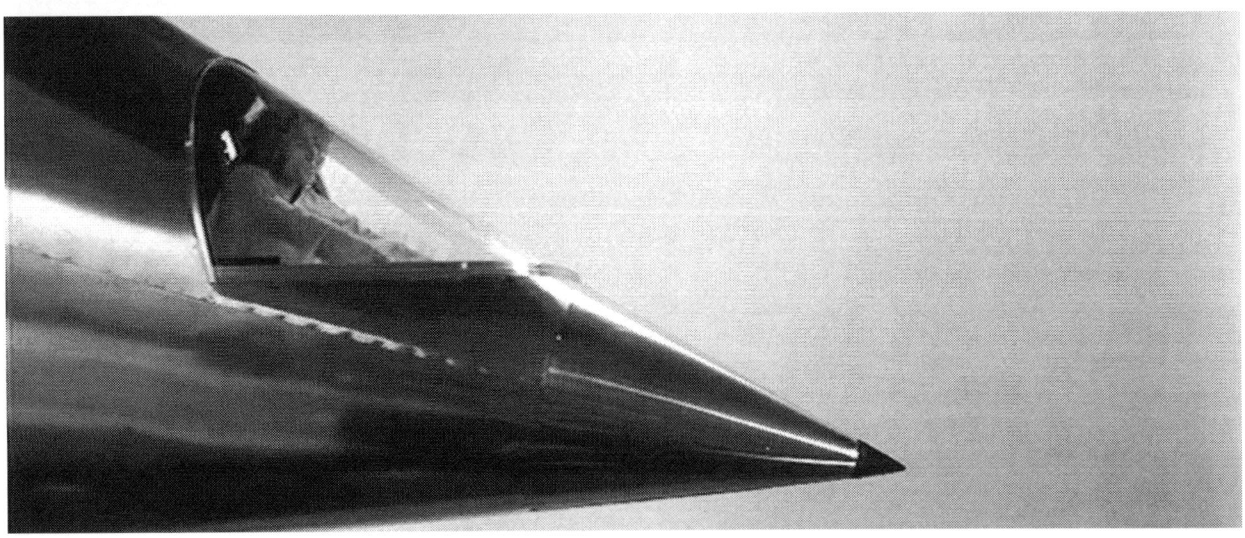

Bernard Cribbins: "I was NEVER a ballet dancer."

Ken Russell's film *Cranks at Work* (1960) is lost. The only print screened on the BBC on the 24th April 1960 as part of the 49th edition of *Monitor*. The show also featured an interview with W. H. Auden at home in New York City and a film about *The Strange World of Hieronymus Bosch*. Shot on 35mm in London and Brighton, Ken Russell's film included a startling sequence shot by Russell of John Cranko's ballet, *Antigone*, then in repertory at the Covent Garden Opera House, and the film showed Cranko preparing, rehearsing and performing his revue, *New Cranks*. The *New Cranks* show was designed by Tony Walton, who would design Russell's own putting-on-a-show spectacular, *The Boy Friend* (1972). Cranko's revue was performed by Billy Wilson, Yolanda Bavan, Gillian Lynne, Carol Shelley, Johnny Wade and Bernard Cribbins who, in Russell's film, sings *Other People, Ugh!* (inspired by Jean-Paul Sartre). Cribbins' performance in the Peter Sellers film, *Two-Way Stretch* (1960) had recently been lauded. He was England's newest film star. Ken Russell met up with Cribbins in November 2009, and interviewed him as part of an irregular column Russell published in *The Times* newspaper. In the article, Russell declared to the world that Mr. Cribbins used to be a professional ballet dancer. When I was researching the making of *Cranks at Work,* for the second volume of the Ken Russell Biography, I chatted with Cribbins:

"Not long before he passed away. Mr. Russell, bless his soul, did an interview with me for *The Times*. The article he wrote was absolute total nonsense. I was never a ballet dancer. He wrote about me being with The Ballets Russes. I was furious and at the same time amused. My friends would have loved that. I was NEVER a ballet dancer. Total bollocks. Absolutely nonsense. I'd been in musicals where you all caper about. But certainly not a ballet dancer."

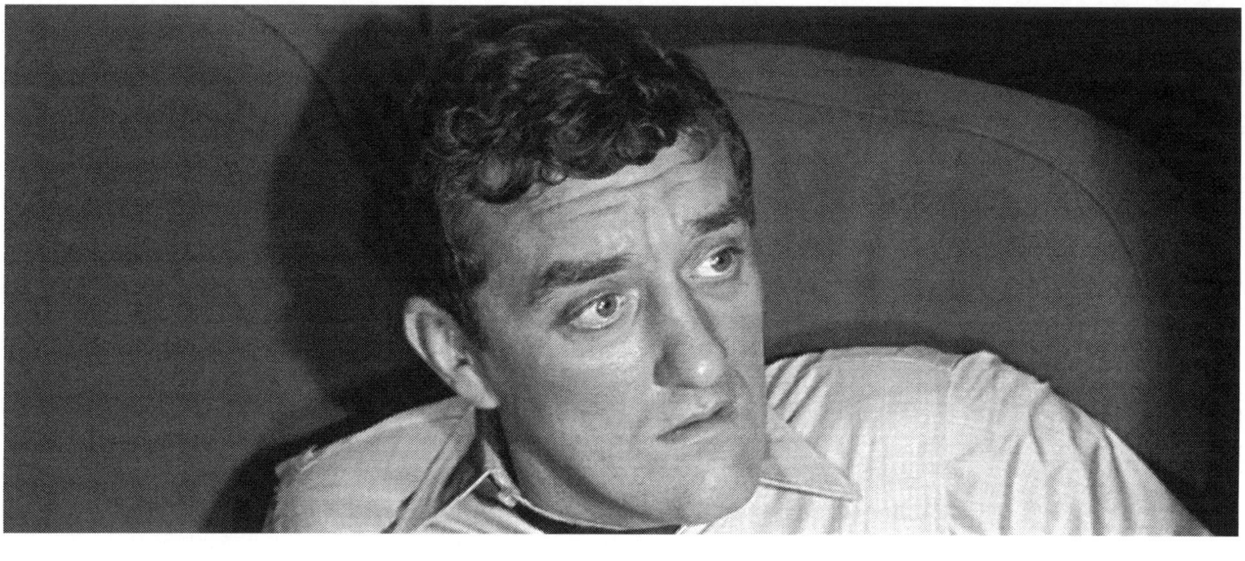

Ken Russell Gallery

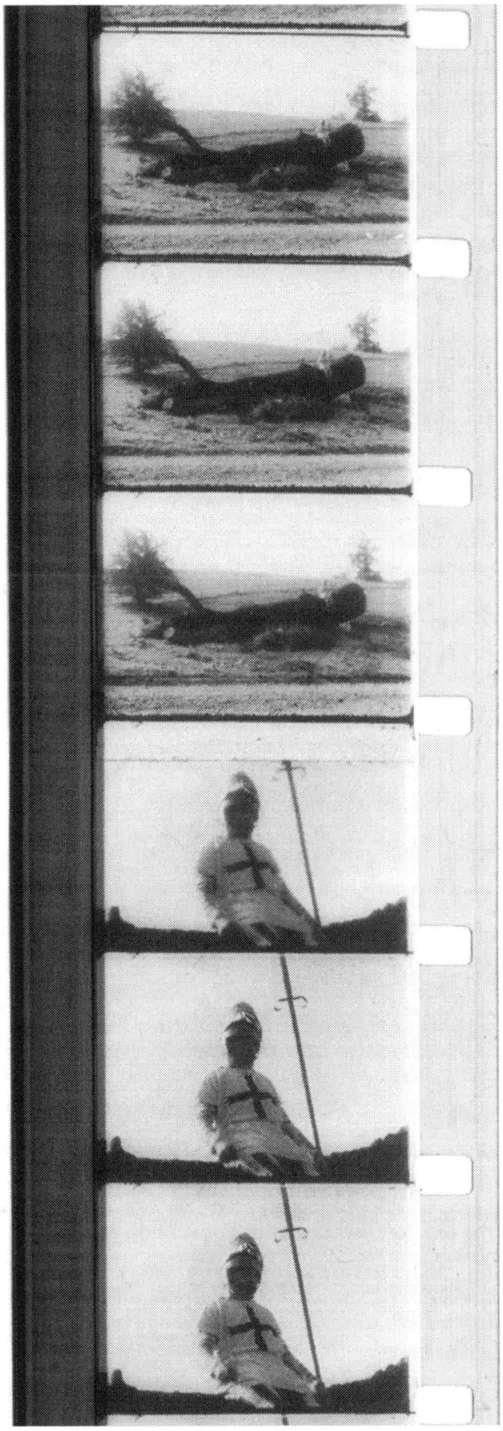

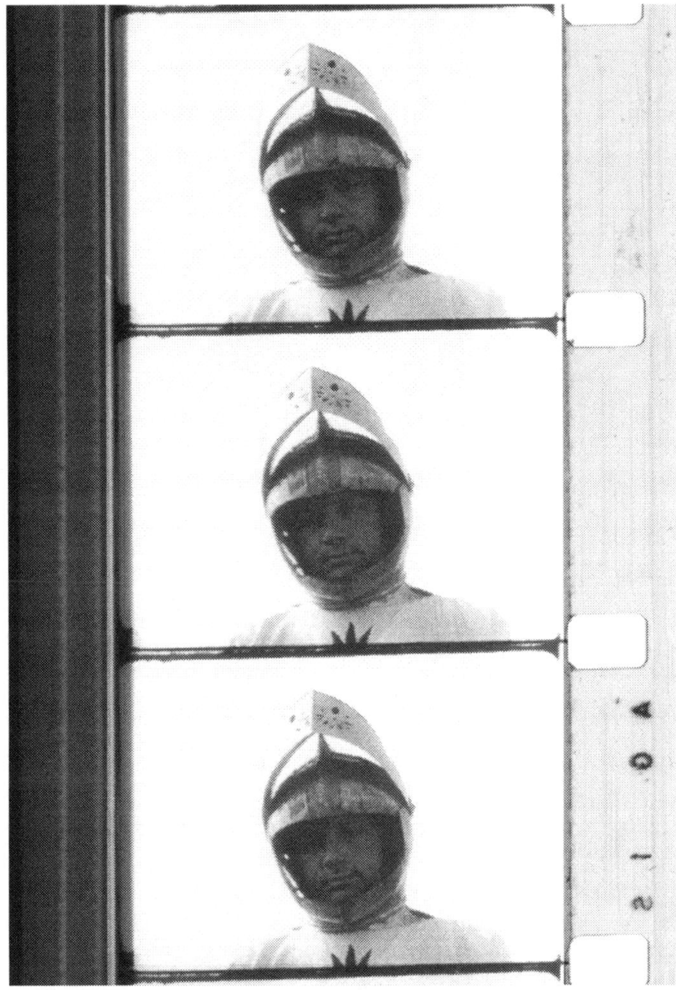

Ken Russell himself in *Knights on Bikes* (1957)
His oldest surviving film

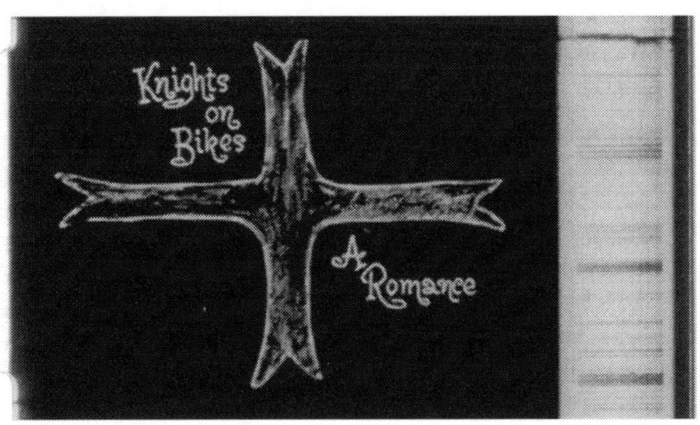

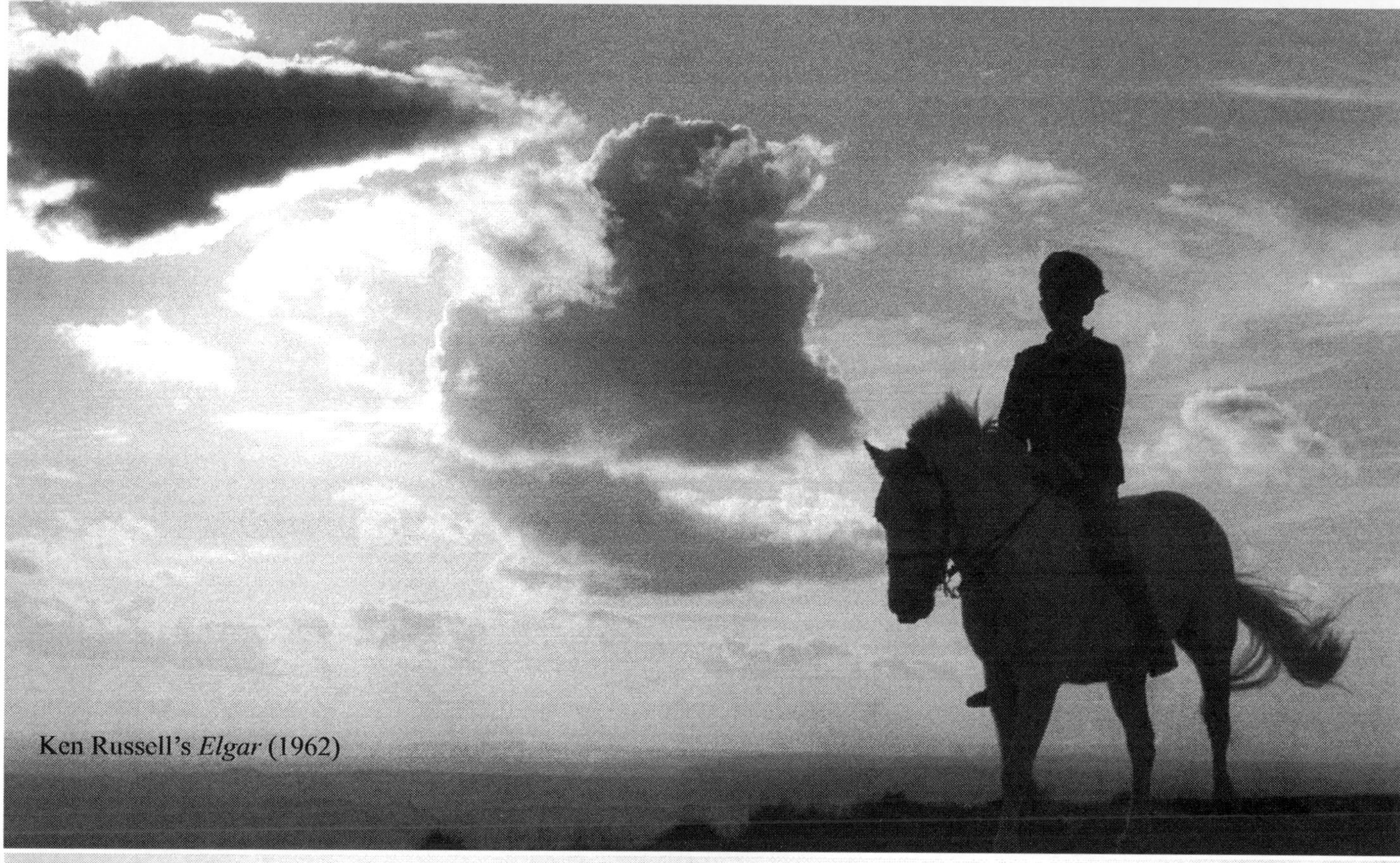

Ken Russell's *Elgar* (1962)

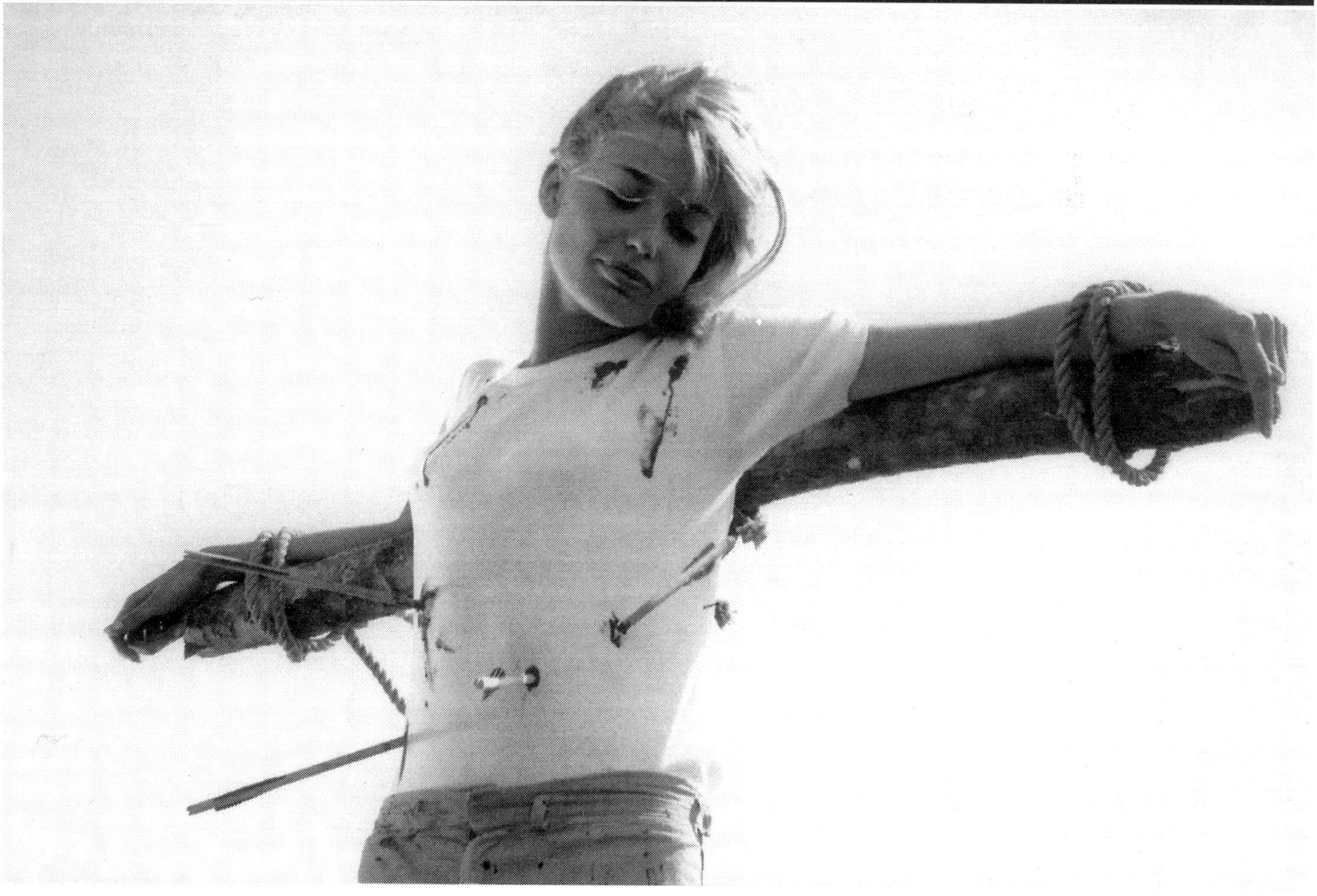

The opening scene from Ken Russell's *The Debussy Film* (1965) © Anne James

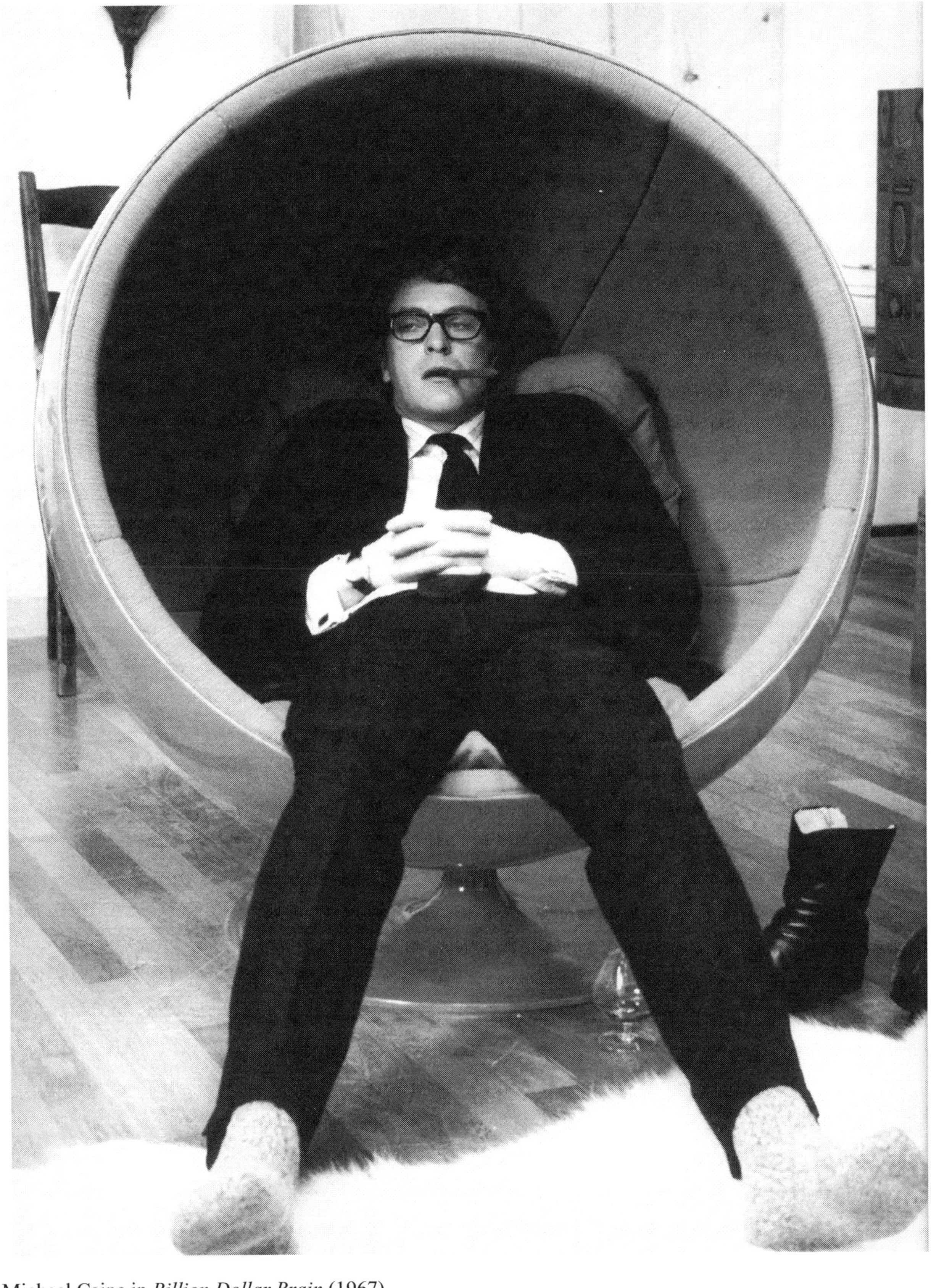

Michael Caine in *Billion Dollar Brain* (1967)

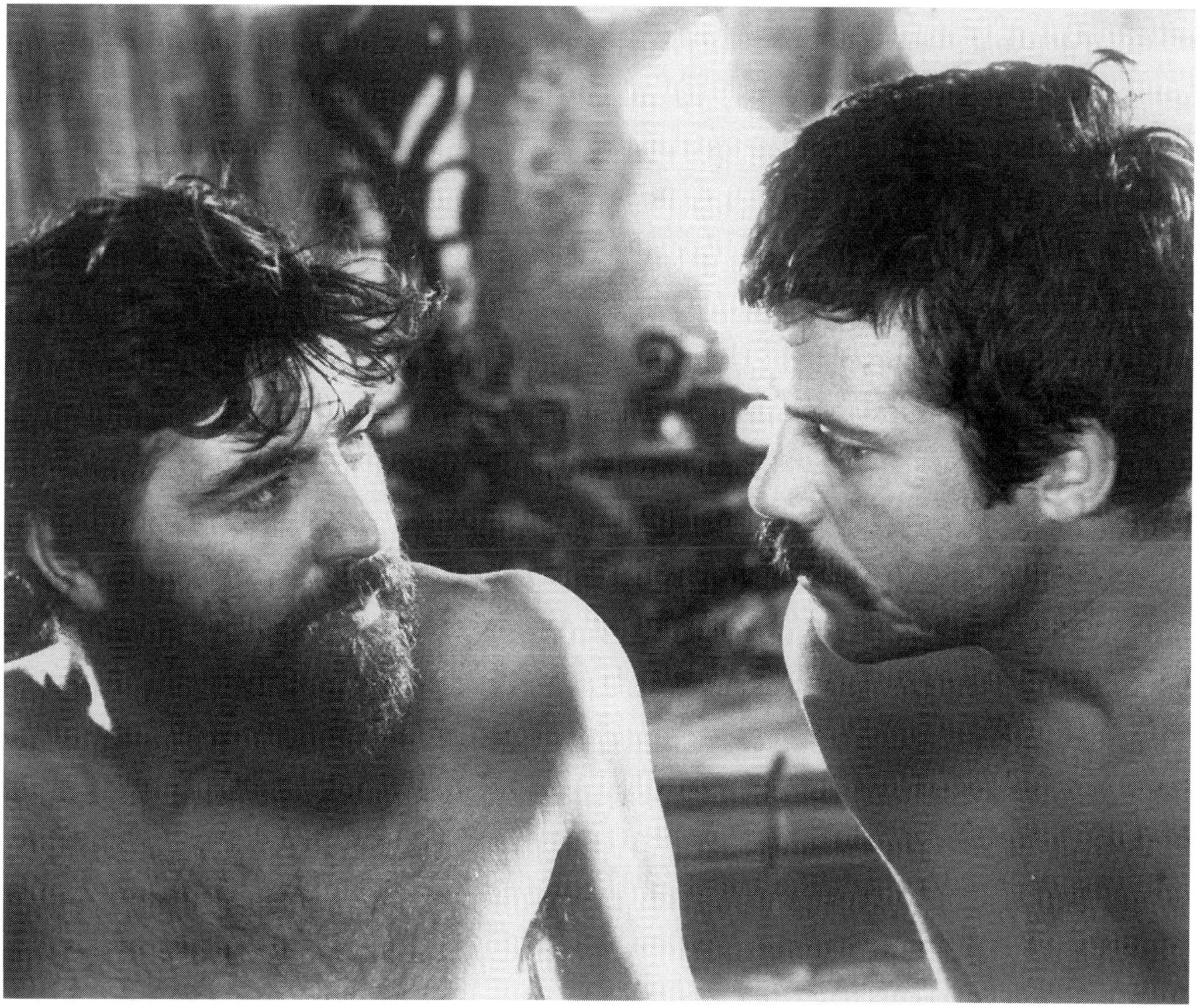

Alan Bates and Oliver Reed in *Women in Love* (1969)

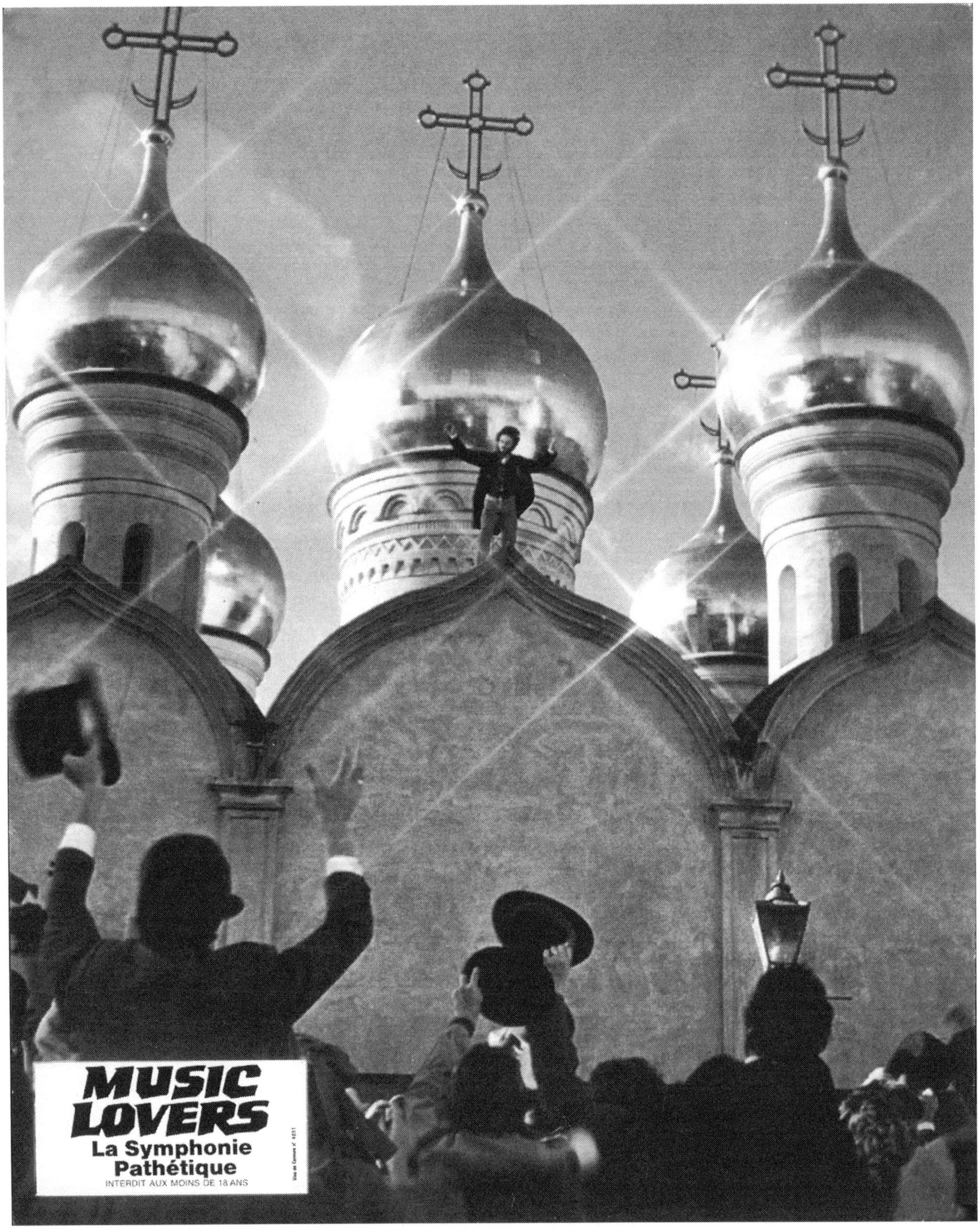

Richard Chamberlain as Tchaikovsky on a set which drew in Muslim visitors wanting to worship. More than half a million tickets were sold for the film at the Odeon Haymarket, London. Breaking all box-office records.

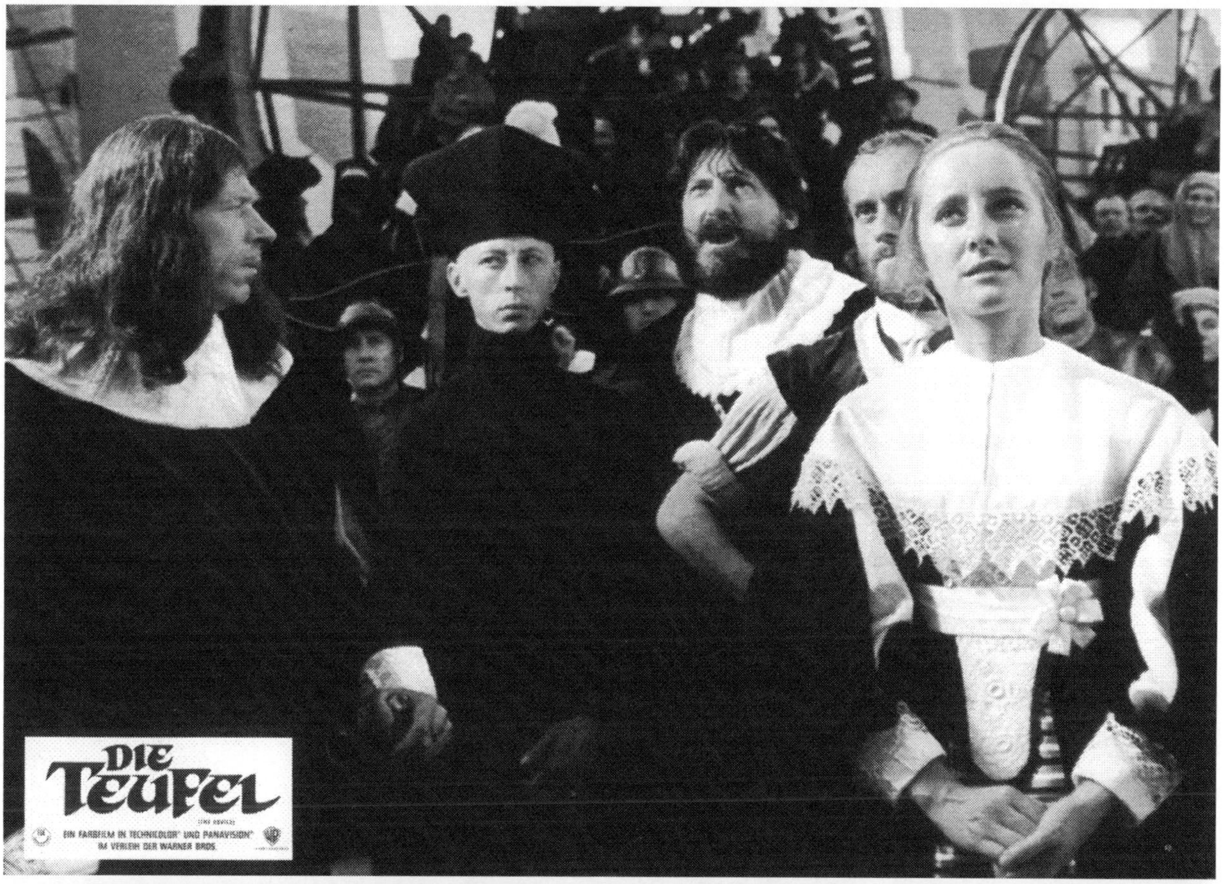
DIE TEUFEL
EIN FARBFILM IN TECHNICOLOR® UND PANAVISION®
IM VERLEIH DER WARNER BROS.

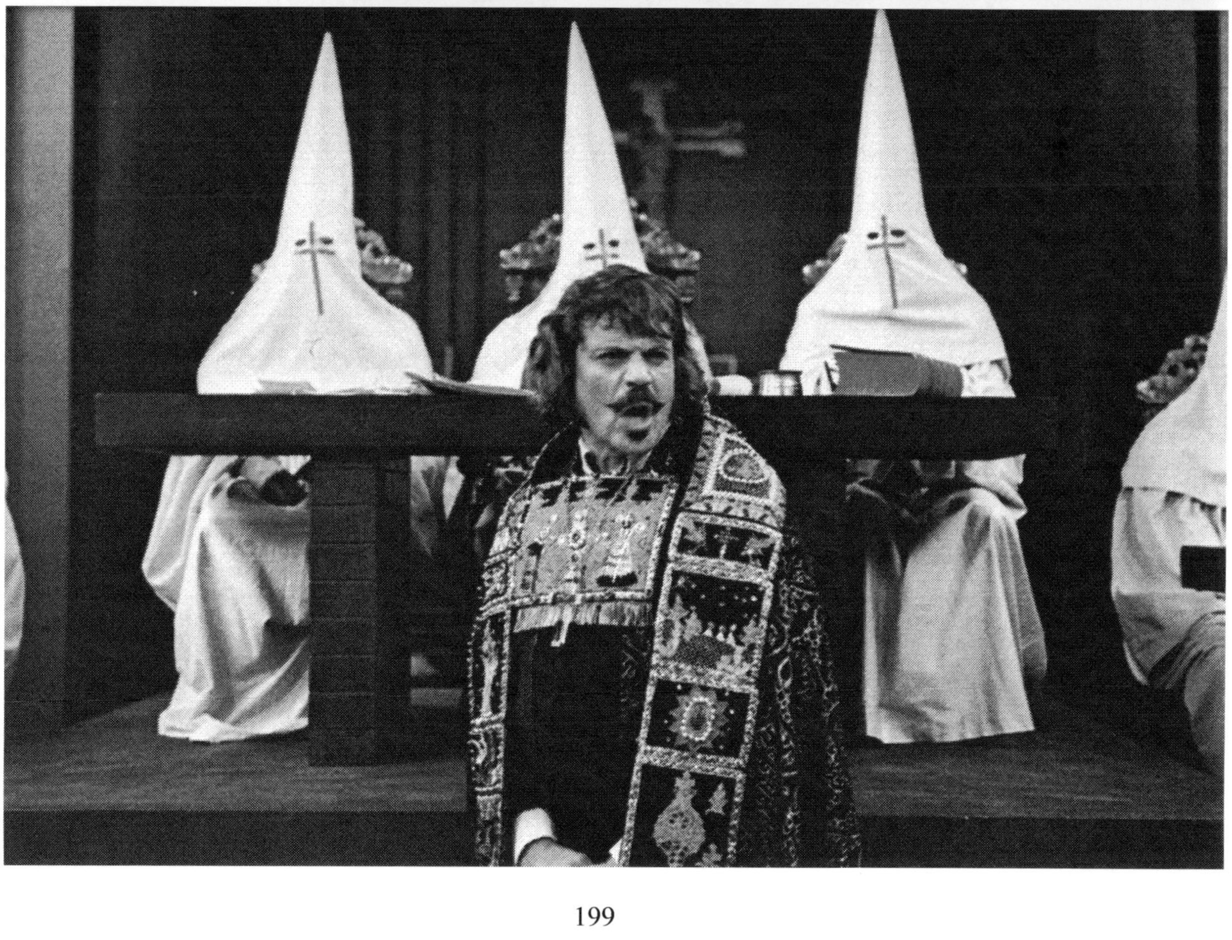

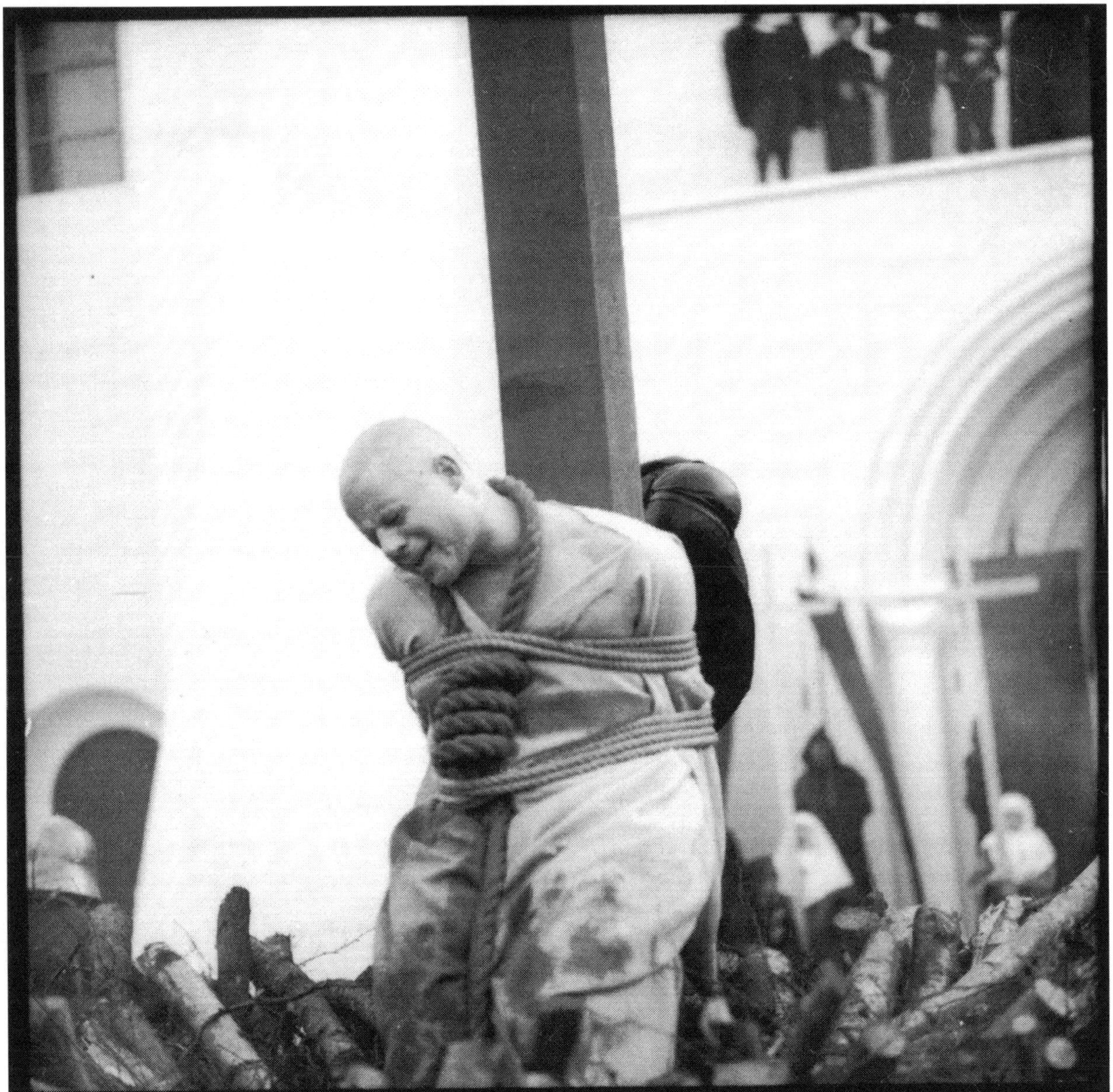

Oliver Reed as Father Grandier sacrificed by the Church and the State in *The Devils*

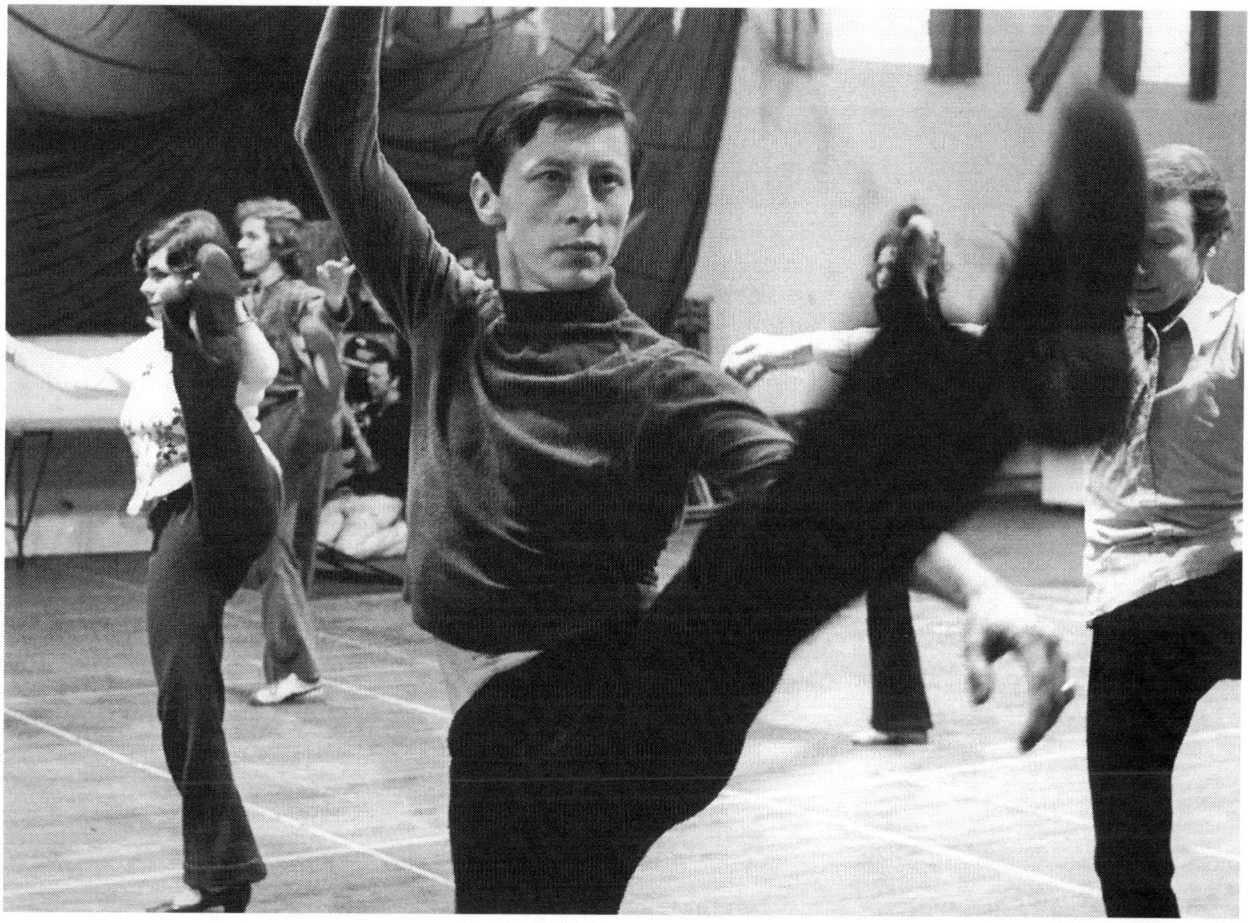

Murray Melvin in rehearsals for Ken Russell's *The Boy Friend* and filming *The Devils*.

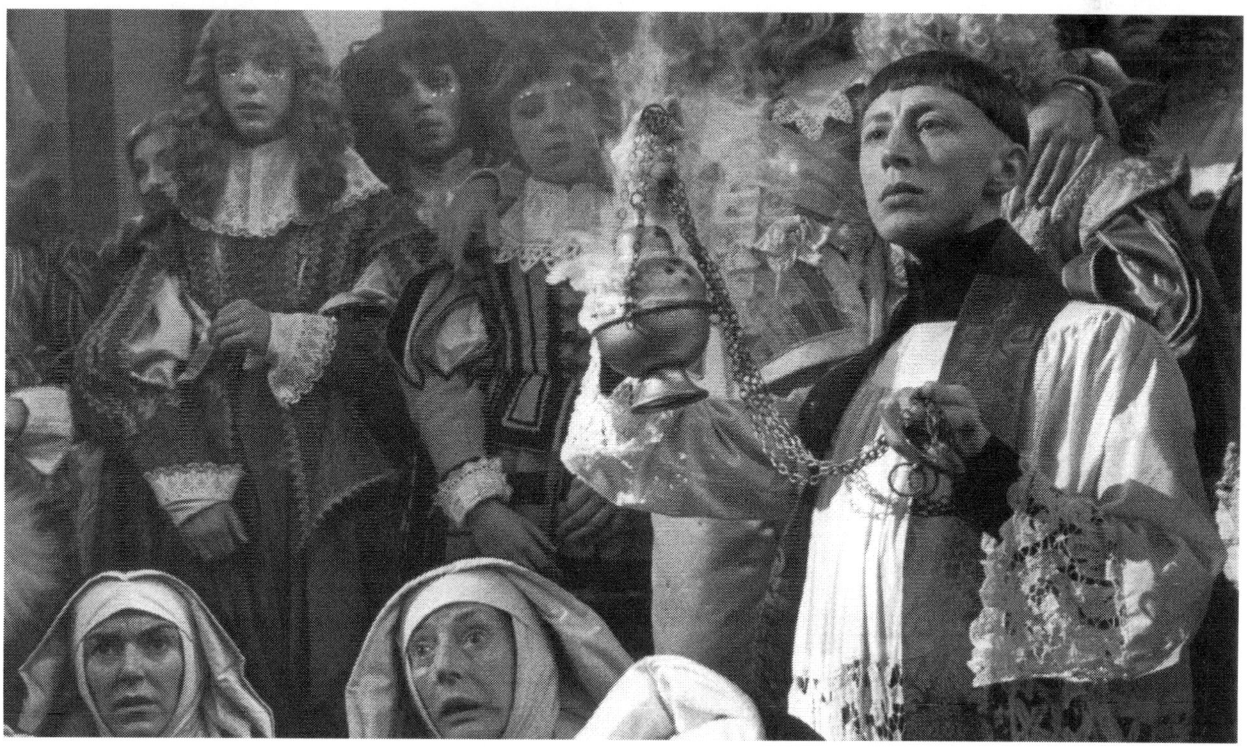

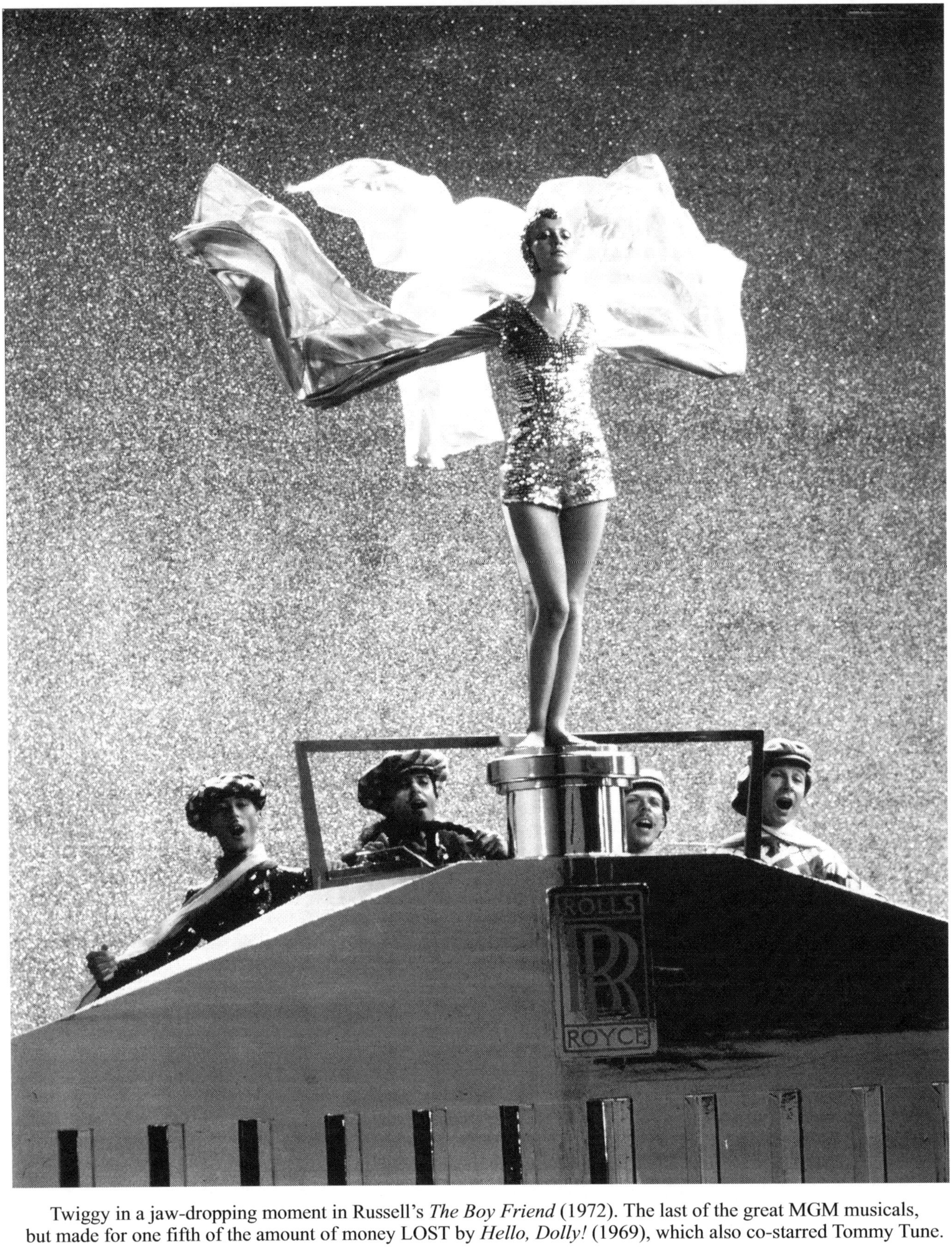

Twiggy in a jaw-dropping moment in Russell's *The Boy Friend* (1972). The last of the great MGM musicals, but made for one fifth of the amount of money LOST by *Hello, Dolly!* (1969), which also co-starred Tommy Tune.

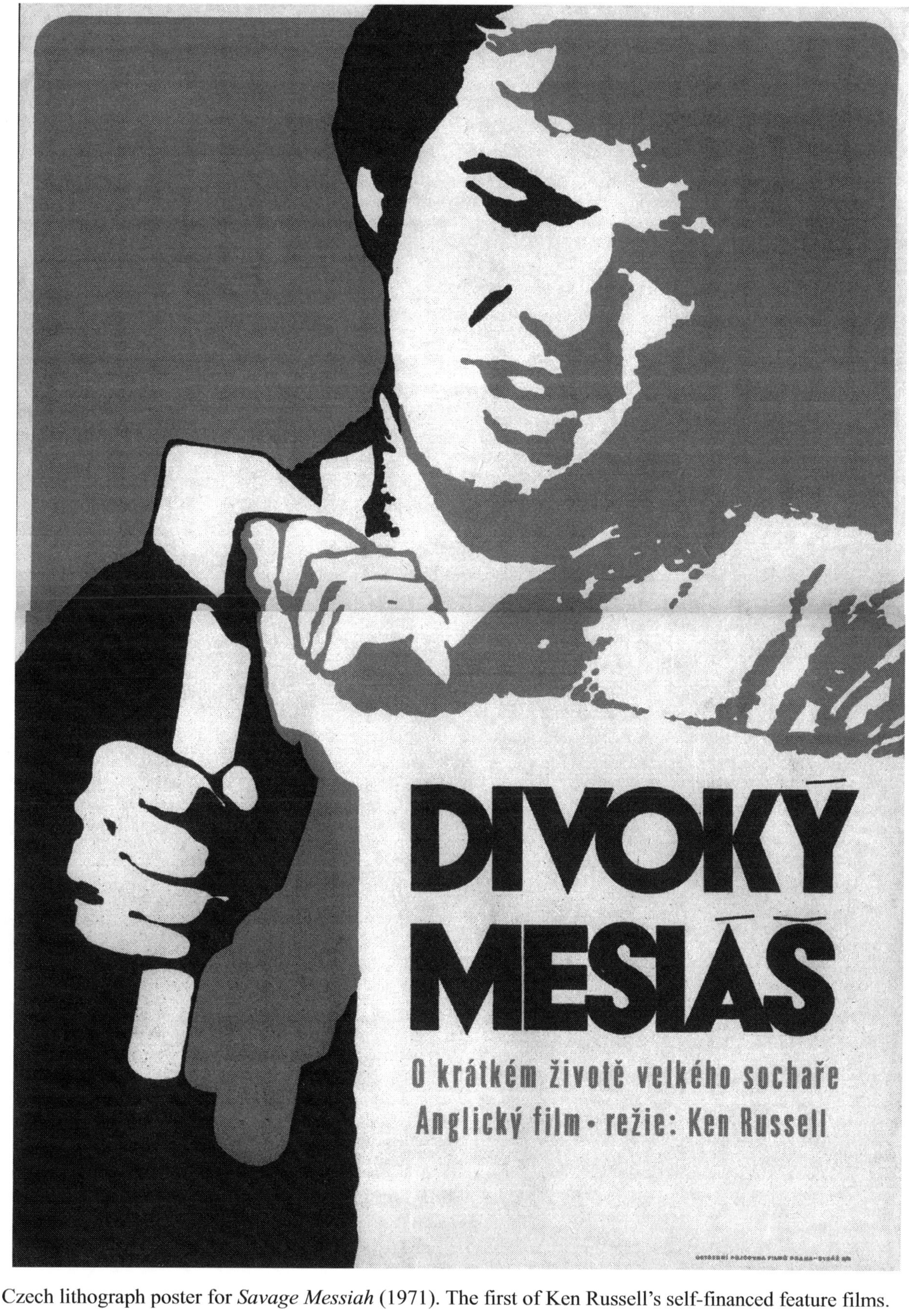

Czech lithograph poster for *Savage Messiah* (1971). The first of Ken Russell's self-financed feature films.

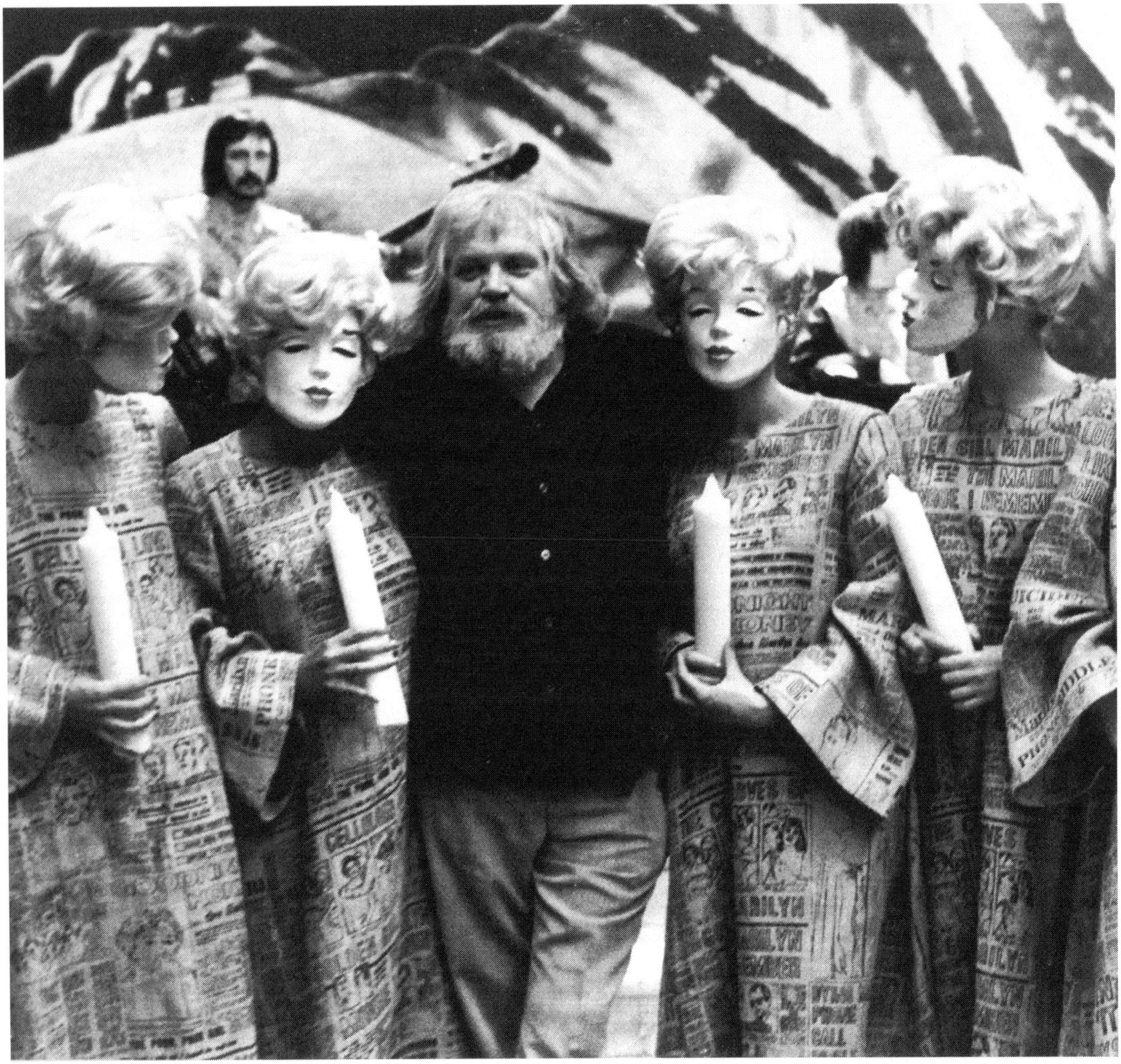

Ken Russell with Marilyn Monroe-masked idols in *Tommy*. Pop-Art images of Monroe appeared in many of Russell's films, starting with a billboard appearance in *Guitar Craze* (1959)

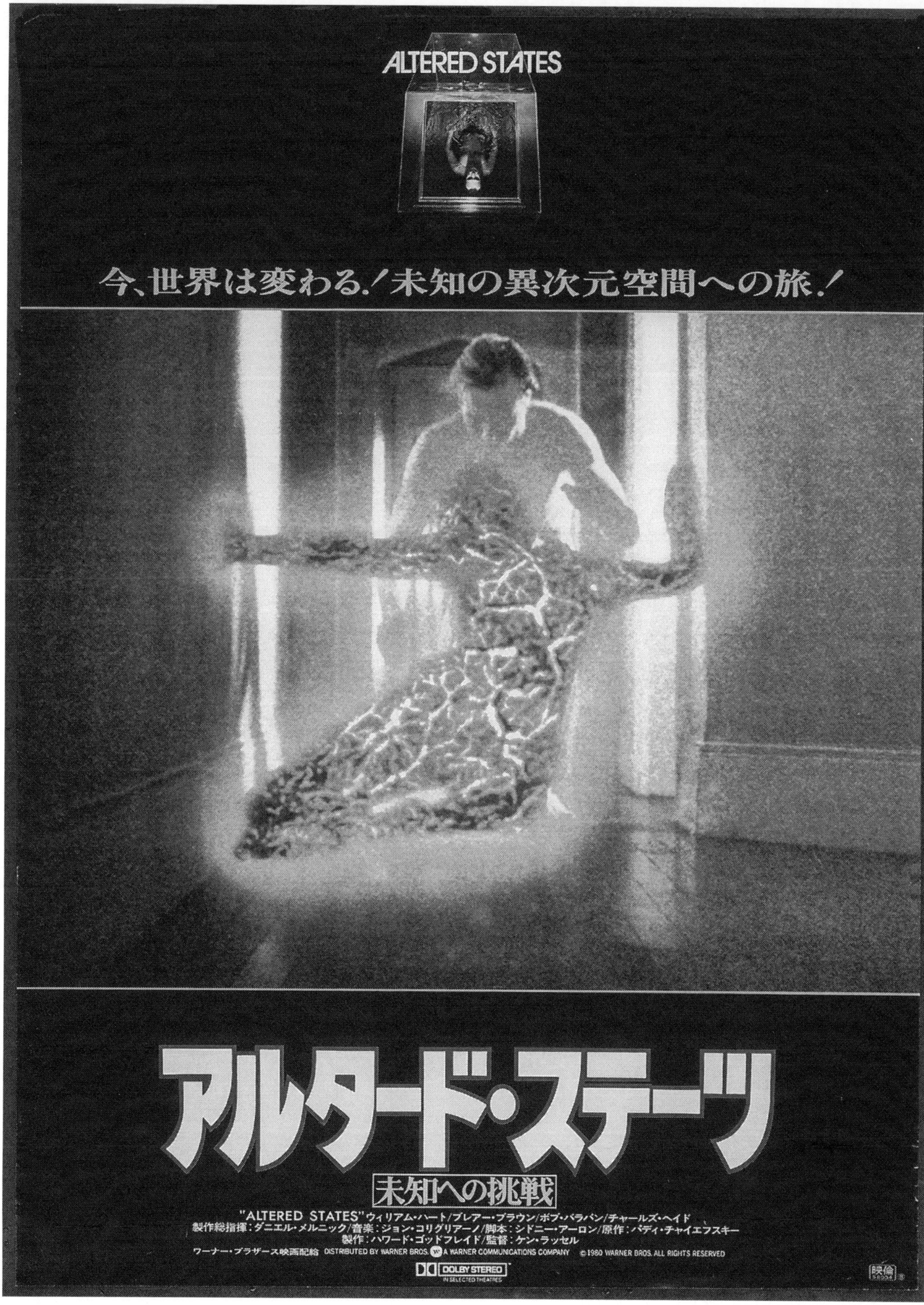

ALTERED STATES
今、世界は変わる。!未知の異次元空間への旅。!
アルタード・ステーツ
未知への挑戦
"ALTERED STATES"ウィリアム・ハート/ブレアー・ブラウン/ボブ・バラバン/チャールズ・ヘイド
製作総指揮：ダニエル・メルニック/音楽：ジョン・コリグリアーノ/脚本：シドニー・アーロン/原作：パディ・チャイエフスキー
製作：ハワード・ゴッドフレイド/監督：ケン・ラッセル
ワーナー・ブラザース映画配給 DISTRIBUTED BY WARNER BROS. A WARNER COMMUNICATIONS COMPANY © 1980 WARNER BROS. ALL RIGHTS RESERVED
DOLBY STEREO
IN SELECTED THEATRES
映倫

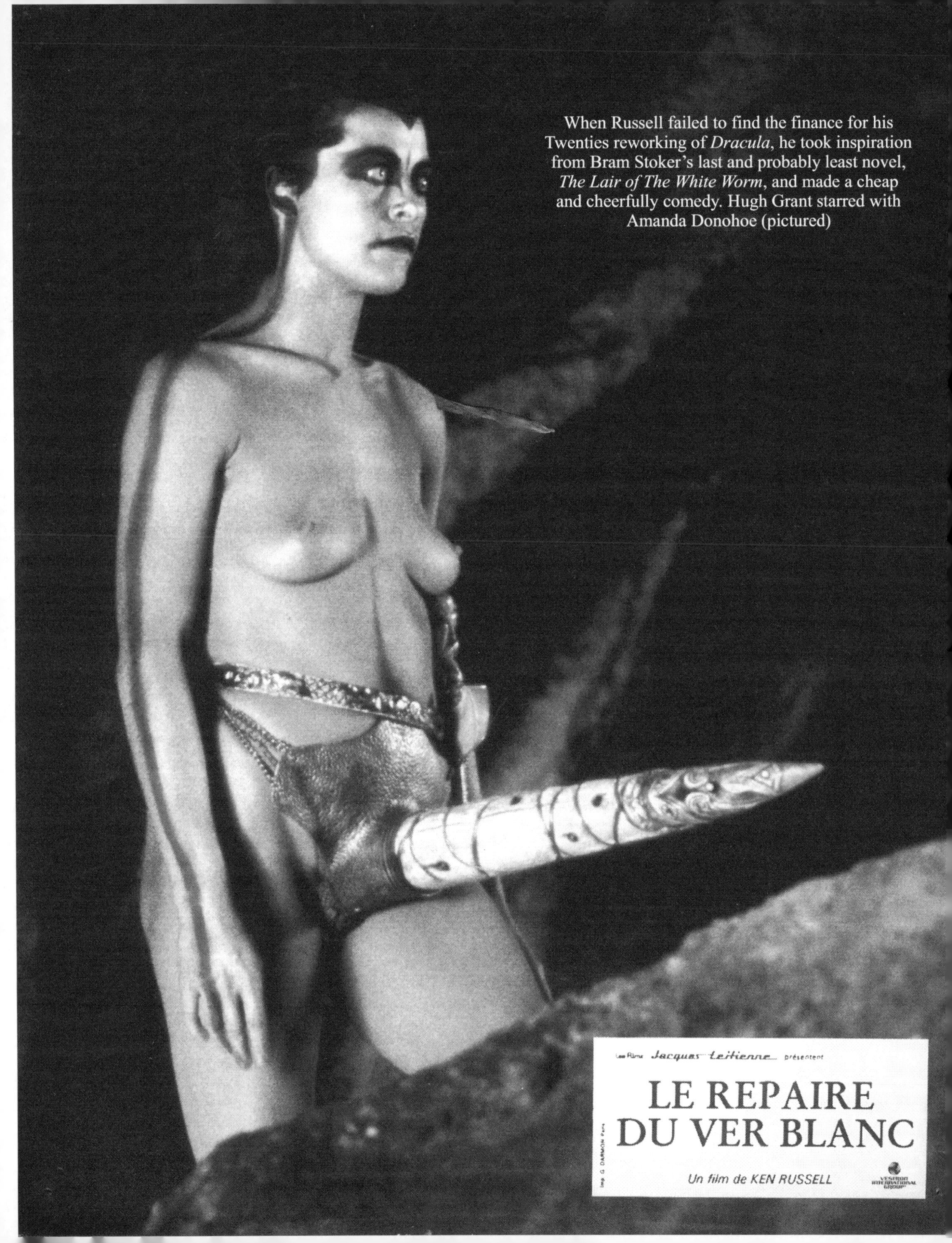

When Russell failed to find the finance for his Twenties reworking of *Dracula*, he took inspiration from Bram Stoker's last and probably least novel, *The Lair of The White Worm*, and made a cheap and cheerfully comedy. Hugh Grant starred with Amanda Donohoe (pictured)

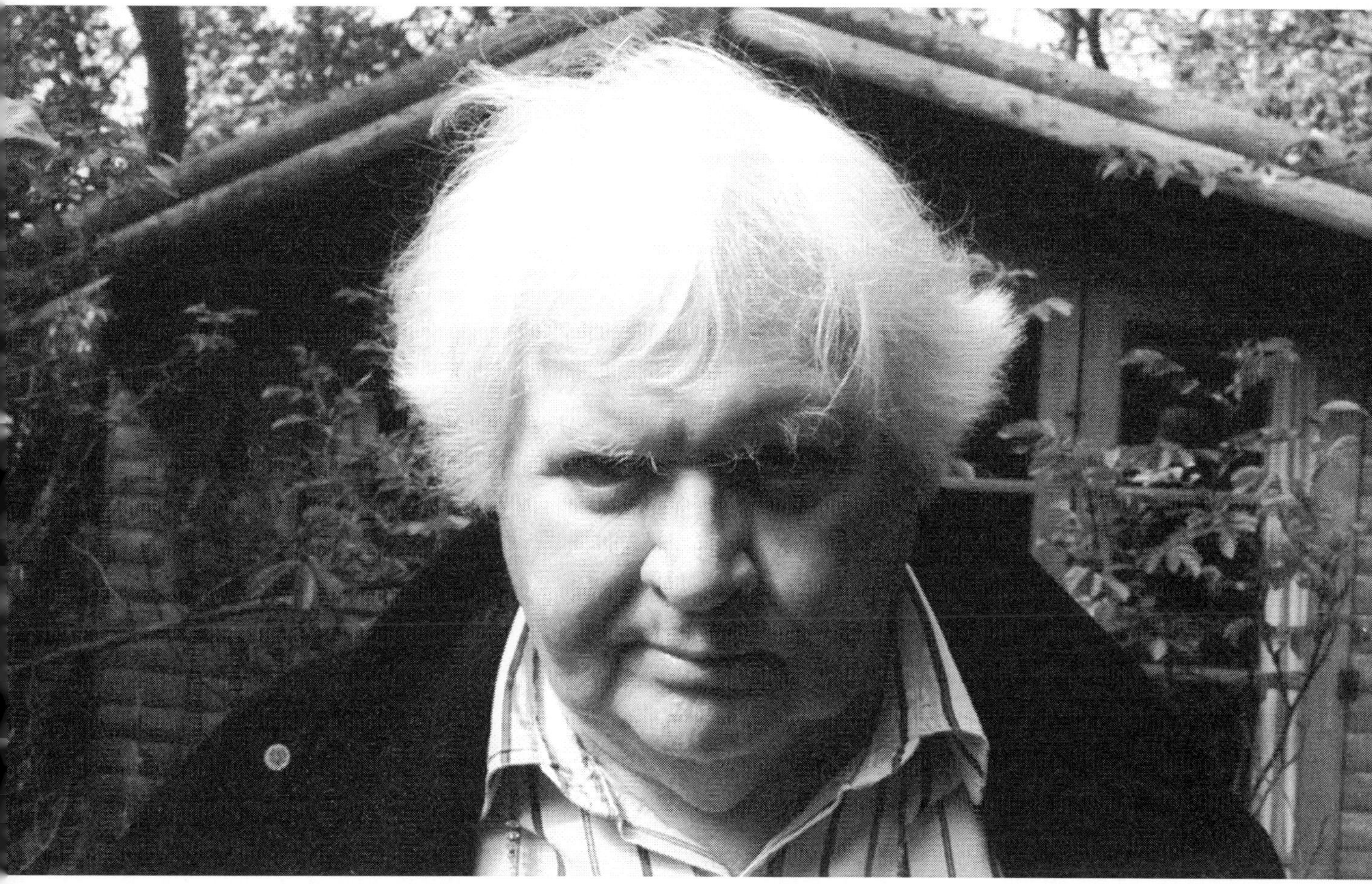

Ken Russell died peacefully at home on 27th November 2011. He was given a Viking Funeral. An effigy of his wife was thrown onto a burning ship at sea that carried his ashes. New Forest archers fired arrows (health-and-safety despots refused permission for flaming arrows). A fleet of mourners, including Judith Paris (overleaf), threw petals and sang:

'How Do You Say Goodbye To a King',

written for him by Lisi Russell and David Massengill.

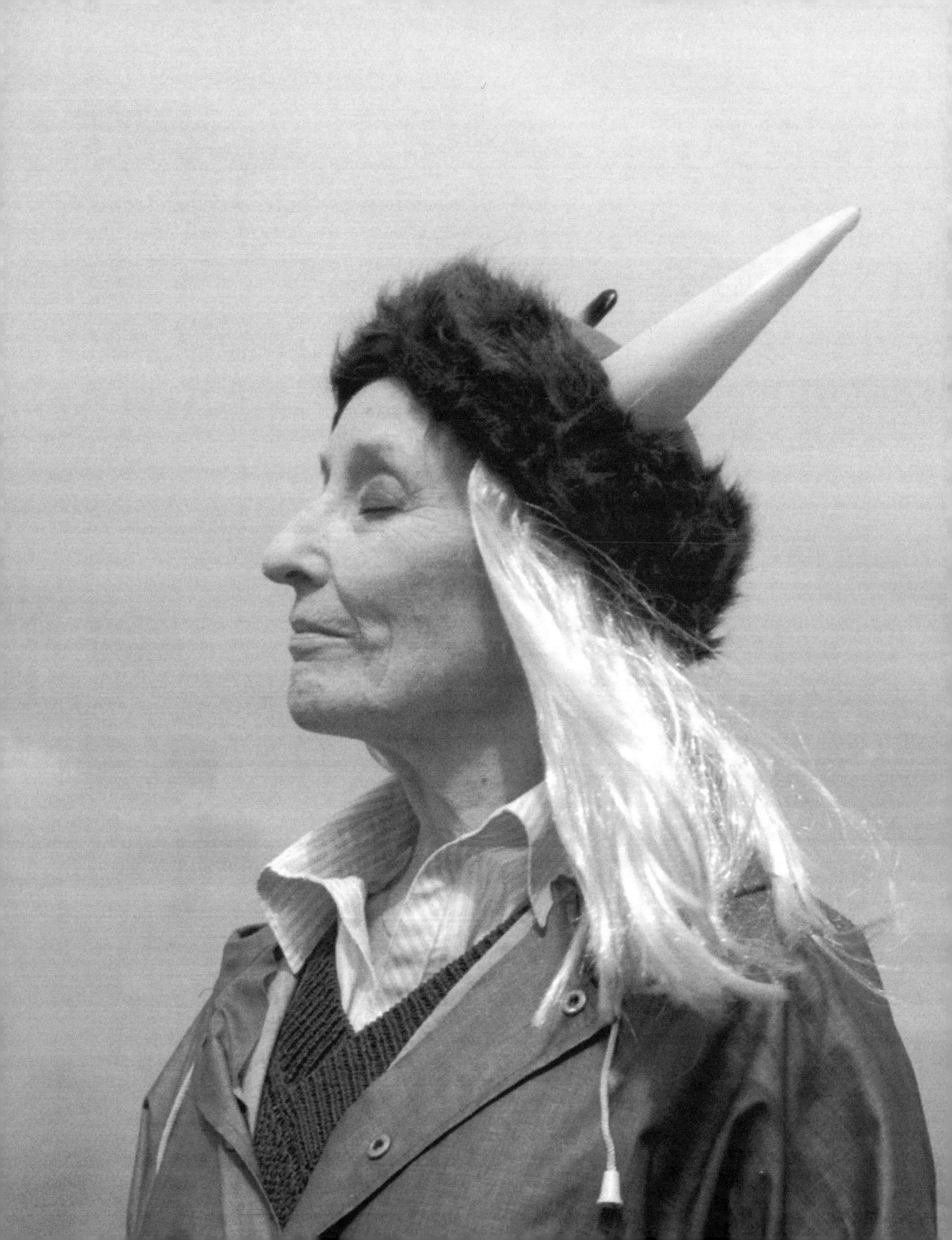

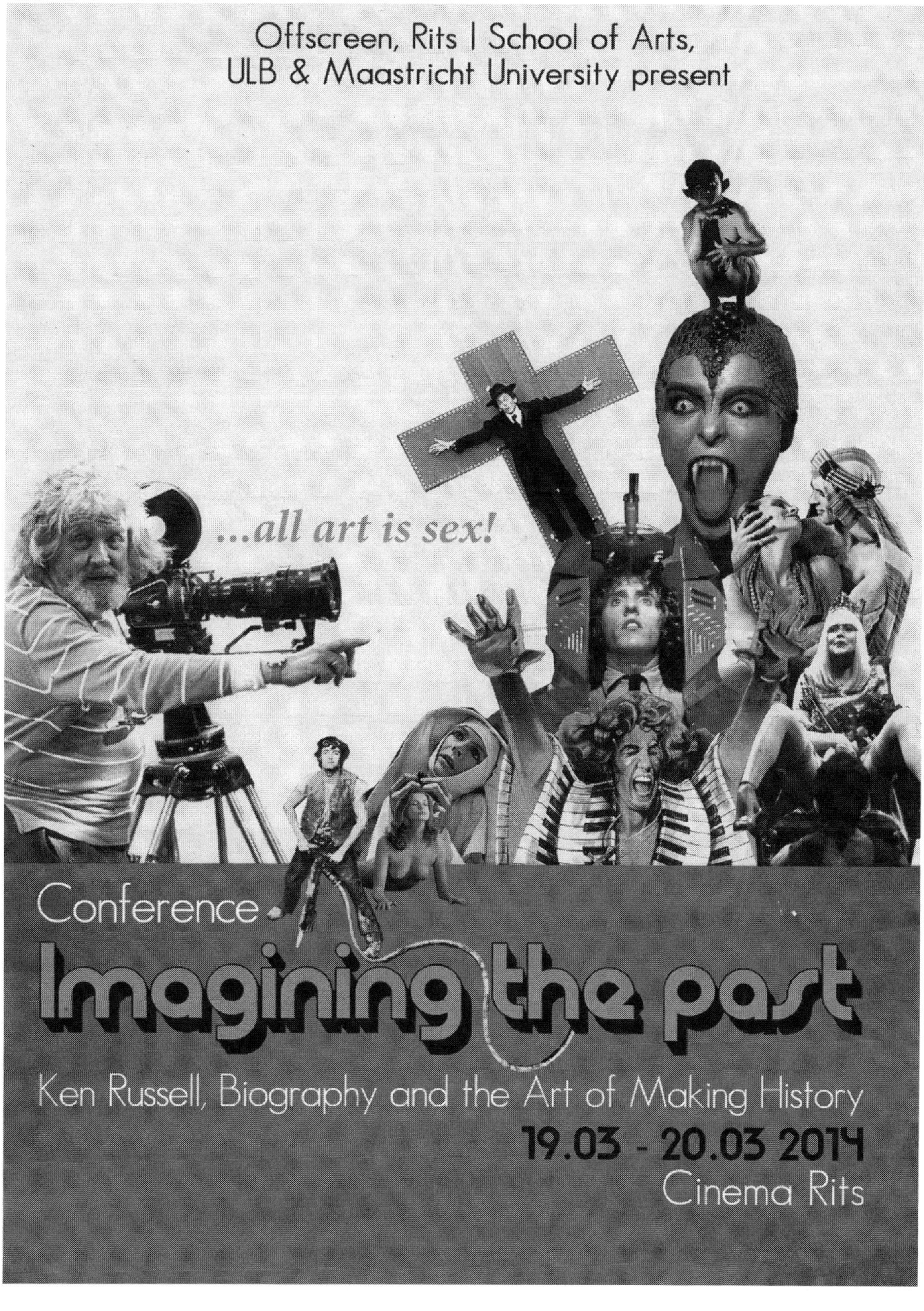

Academics from Belgium, Britain and America gathered in Brussels in March 2014 to present papers on aspects of Russell's art. Concurrently, twenty-seven of his films were screened at The Cinematek, Cinema Rits and Cinema Nova, where a lifesize re-creation of the *Altered States* isolation tank was installed.

Michael Winner

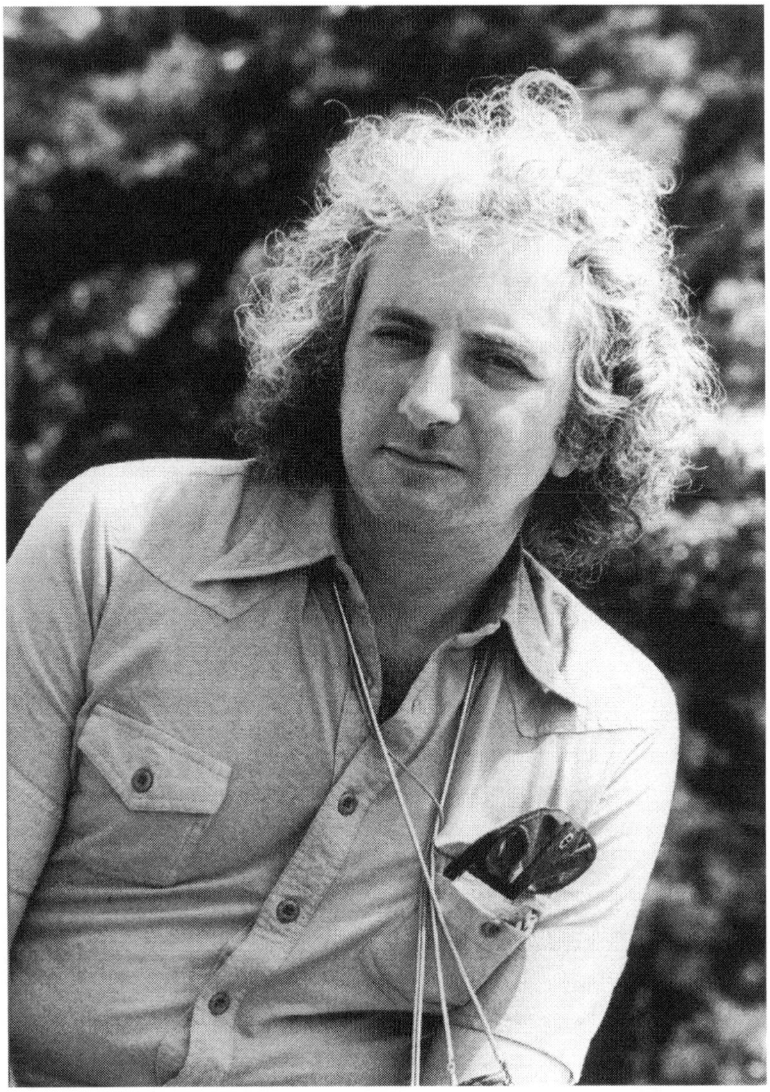

Michael Winner (1977)

In April 2002, Michael Winner invited me to his famous forty-seven room mansion in Kensington, possibly the most impressive private house in London. I was invited to talk about films. His films. Through the front door he led me up a wide curling stone staircase to his office. On the way up the stairs he shuffled through a handful of letters that had come through the letterbox that morning. Now sitting behind his desk, he opened one of the letters and said: "You've come on a good day." It was a royalty cheque for television screenings of one of his six Charles Bronson films. "A cheque for £35,000 for *The Mechanic*, a film I made thirty years ago but which still plays on peak-time television all over the world. Not bad."

Then he pressed 'record' on his own tape-recorder and said: "I'm recording this conversation to make sure I'm not misquoted." He felt he had not been treated fairly by the press. The English press always had difficulty coping with Winner's virtues: hard work, self-promotion and a strong Jewish sense of humour. The English, a nation characterised internationally as lager louts, censorious prudes, officious health-and-safety dwarfs, and as having more than a fair share of genius, have always been a humourlous lot. When the tape reached the end of side one and clicked off, Winner, the son of a Russian father and a Polish mother, made a small show of not flipping it over for he had given up his belligerence. He was impressed I had come prepared. He told me I was the first person in "many years" who had done him the courtesy of seeing most of his films. This was in an era before downloading, when film historians had to track down viewing copies through correspondence with private collectors. During the conversation, Winner glowed with pride and pleasure. And that was good to see.

When the interview was over, he thanked me and said: "I'd like to give you something." He went over to the bookcase, to the left of the desk, and pulled out a box-file from which he took out a booklet originally published to accompany a lecture he gave at the National Film Theatre in 1970, and into which he'd pasted updates. He inscribed it and said: "There aren't many of these left. I'm glad I've got one to give to you."

He asked would I like to borrow photographs to publish with the article, which I was writing for *Camera,* the Cambridge University Film Journal. I told him I would, but added that I didn't need any of Oliver Reed because I'd just bought a big job lot of Reed photographs off ebay. He said he'd tell his office to send me a selection of stills. I promised to scan and return them the day I got them.

The photographs duly arrived, and were scanned and returned the same day. When the journal was published, Michael Winner sent me a thank you note and asked did I return the Oliver Reed photographs?

I wrote back saying I didn't borrow any Oliver Reed photographs. The ones I'd used were from my own collection.

Thereafter he blanked me whenever he could. Indeed the only time we talked again properly was when I writing the biography of Ken Russell. He telephoned me to confirm a couple of stories that Ken Russell had told me, in which Michael appeared. An edited transcript of my conversation with Michael Winner was published in *Camera 2*. The unexpurgated transcript is published here for the first time.

On his death, Michael Winner's valuable and sincere work in organising public memorials for police officers killed on duty was mostly neglected as the newspapers filled with kiss-and-tell stories by attention-seeking actresses who, from a 2013 perspective, condemned Winner's behaviour and attitudes of forty years ago, whilst ignoring the fact that their own behaviour then and now was appalling. Michael Winner's achievements as a film producer, particularly in regard to the efficiency and the effectiveness of his budgets, in star-casting, and in international ticket sales, are unmatched in the history of British cinema.

Are you ready?

I'm absolutely ready, Paul.

In 1962, the producer, Daniel Angel, fired Joseph Losey from West 11, a film written by Willis Hall and Keith Waterhouse. He hired you, and taught you a life's lesson in filmmaking: 'Be your own producer'. Is it true he wouldn't let you cast Julie Christie in her Oscar-winning year?

He said she was 'a B-movie actress'! In 1962, I'd made my first feature film for him, *Play It Cool,* at Pinewood Studios with Billy Fury, Bobby Vee and Helen Shapiro. Billy was a lovely boy and a wonderful singer. In the film he sang *Once Upon a Dream.* It's still one of my favourite records. The film made a fortune but not for me. I was a hired hand. I wasn't allowed a percentage. Then, also for Danny, I did a very strange film at Shepperton called *The Cool Mikado* with Frankie Howerd and Tommy Cooper, Stubby Kaye. I was under contract to Danny Angel during that whole time.

I haven't been able to see The Cool Mikado.

It's never revived.

Is it any good?

It's not much really. One or two scenes.

Then you made West 11? [a poor young man in Notting Hill agrees to carry out a murder].

West 11 was kind of a copy of a book called *The L-Shaped Room,* which Jimmy Woolf made into a film, directed by Bryan Forbes. Angel fired Losey, who had Warren Beatty and Claudia Cardinale! (*loud laugh*), and he offered it to me. It was a very good job; a classy script. I tested Julie Christie and Danny Angel said she was a B-Movie actress. It was at a time in her career when she had been rejected by Clive Donner for *Nothing But The Best*; her Rank contract had just been cancelled because they thought she was no good; and she had been rejected by John Schlesinger for *Billy Liar*; to which you will say, 'She was in *Billy Liar*!' and you'd be right. She's in *Billy Liar* but the film started with Topsy Jane. I met John in London, when he should have been [filming] in the North and he said: "Topsy Jane's ill. I'm having to take Julie Christie". So when we tested her she did have this aura of defeat. Her test came back. We screened it. I thought she was marvellous. Danny Angel didn't agree and, in front of a crowd of people at Associated British Studios, added: "Who would want to fuck Julie Christie?"

I said: "Well, I would for a start."

He said: "That's because you're a homosexual!" I'm not a homosexual. He was just being offensive. That's the sort of person who ran the British film industry at that time! That sums up the British Film Industry. They all wore suits. They all drank gin and tonic. And that was their attitude. Nasty old men. So we didn't get Julie. When she won the Oscar for *Darling*, produced by Nat Cohen, the greatest movie executive in Britain, I rang Danny Angel and I said: "There's been a terrible mistake, Danny. A B-movie actress just won the Oscar! You'd better get on the phone quick and ask for a re-count."

Sean Connery was dying to play the lead in *West 11.* He was shooting *Dr. No*, which everyone in the industry thought was going to be the fiasco of all time, and I was making *Play it Cool* at Pinewood at the same time. They were all laughing: '£1.2 million spent on a film starring a Scots fellow who had only done B-pictures!' Sean came on to the set to meet me. Danny turned him down. I'd interviewed Oliver Reed and wanted him for *West 11*, but if the producer thought Sean Connery was a B-picture actor you can imagine what he thought of Oliver Reed, who was known only as a Werewolf! James Mason wanted to play the villain. Danny Angel rejected him as 'a has been'! (*loud laughter*).

So instead of Sean Connery, Julie Christie, Oliver Reed and James Mason you had to use?

Alfred Lynch, Kathleen Breck, Eric Portman. We made a second picture that year. In America it was called *The Girl-Getters*, and it was called *The System* here. It was crucial in launching my career in America. And I thought, now I'm producing the film I can get Julie Christie, because she would have been perfect for the film. We were good pals. She said to me: "They think I'm so terrible in *Billy Liar.*" They insisted she went to Birmingham Rep to learn how to act! I wish I had kept the postcard she sent me from the Birmingham Rep saying how bloody tedious it was. So I didn't get Julie Christie then either! I did get Oliver Reed though.

West 11 got good notices for its location photography, and location shooting became a big part of the Michael Winner style. Was it always there? I know The Cool Mikado had [the title] scenes photographed in Tokyo; one of your very early films, Out of the Shadow, had been praised for the location photography of Cambridge. Some Like it Cool was famously filmed in the grounds of Longleat House and a nudist camp.

I started out making twenty-minute shorts that played the cinema circuits. I'd make them with a unit of two people, the cameraman and me. We shot them silent. Any equipment we had we had to carry on the bus. When we enlarged the unit to four people, to accommodate sound, we still couldn't afford to shoot in the studio so, when we made our little comedy shorts, we filmed in people's houses. I was steeped in that kind of shooting. When I was preparing to make my first *real* movie, *Play it Cool* at Pinewood, a film set in the clubs of London, I asked could I shoot it all on location in real places. I was told to make it in the studio because: "That is how we do it here. We don't want French New Wave wobbly cameras here in England!" I *knew* it was better to shoot on location because you get more value for your money. If you film in someone's house you can see out of the window. You can't see out of the window in the studio. Behind the window there is an electrician reading a newspaper.

You mentioned The System. It's a notable film for three reasons: 1. Oliver Reed. 2. The mood. It has a remarkable sadness. And 3. Nic Roeg's photography. A year or so earlier, Reed had shown a lot of promise in Losey's The Damned, in which he plays a gang member, a role and a performance that, in the early scenes, has striking similarities with Malcolm McDowell's role in A Clockwork Orange; but The System is the first film in which Reed's charisma, and sexual magnetism, come across, right from the very first time you see him, watching as the train comes in.

Oh yes. He's a movie star.

Did you know the film was going to make him a star?

You can never know. I can't say that I'd seen all of his films but when I met him, when I was casting *West 11* in 1962, I felt a very strong affinity with him. I felt that what I'd seen in the room I could use on the screen. We didn't test him [for *The System*]. We didn't make him read. We just gave him the chance. On *The System* I had total control. It was the first film I produced and directed myself so I was able to get good people in it, such as Harry Andrews, a wonderful actor, and David Hemmings. It was one of Hemmings's first films. He had had a walk-on in *West 11*. He got paid £35 a week [for *The System*]. I remember there was a lot of discussion over whether we should pay Hemmings the extra £5 up from our offer.

Was he still a singer at that point?

No, he wasn't singing. He was doing conjuring tricks all over the place. A likeable chap.

There's a Mexican film called Y Tu Mama Tambien, which is a sort-of Mexican version of The System. It is Mexican where yours is British. Two seaside tales of sexual joy that conclude with a strain of melancholy as a 'liberated' older woman goes her own way.

A lot of my films have been copied massively. Do you want a coffee?

Yes, please.

[To Geraldine: "make us two coffees"] Peter Draper, who wrote *The System*, lived by the sea in Torquay, a brilliant writer. He wrote two of my films, *The System* and *I'll Never Forget What's 'Is Name?*, both fantastic scripts. I'd put a call out to agents for original material. I've always tried to make films from original material, written for the screen, not adapted for the screen. And a fourteen-page outline came through my door from Peter Draper about a group of boys at the seaside trying to sleep with all the girls that they could. It had been rejected by everyone. Peter had published a book, a very good book, called *A Season in Love*. I liked the book so I paid him to write me a proper screenplay. It took me two years to get someone to back it. Funnily enough, I read in the paper this week that Julian Fellowes, who got the Academy Award for *Gosford Park*, said he decided to enter the film industry, and become an actor, when he saw *I'll Never Forget What's 'Is Name?* It's always interesting when you read about something that was going on parallel to your own life and people who have been influenced by the work you were doing.

What did you think of Gosford Park?

Pleasant. It was pleasant.

I love Nic Roeg's cinematography in The System. All the night shots by firelight.

Remarkable. Nic was the second-unit camera operator on a very tacky TV series called *Mark Saber* [*Saber of London*] in the fifties, where I was first assistant director with him on the second unit. Nic was always moaning that time had passed him by and he'd never get anywhere!

He's an amazing talent. Before What's 'Is Name, there was Oliver Reed and Michael Crawford in The Jokers.

That was a big hit. After *The System* I did a film called *You Must Be Joking*. A funny film. Did you ever see it?

Yes. Terry-Thomas with a hunting horn, and an animated credit sequence by Bob Godfrey. [A group of handpicked soldiers are given 48-hours to collect Terry-Thomas' five symbols of the British way of life, including 'a lock of hair from a French pop singer. London being the capital of world pop]

That's right. A funny film, a great collection of English comics [Bernard Cribbins, Arthur Lowe, Denholm Elliott, Lionel Jeffries, James Robertson Justice...]

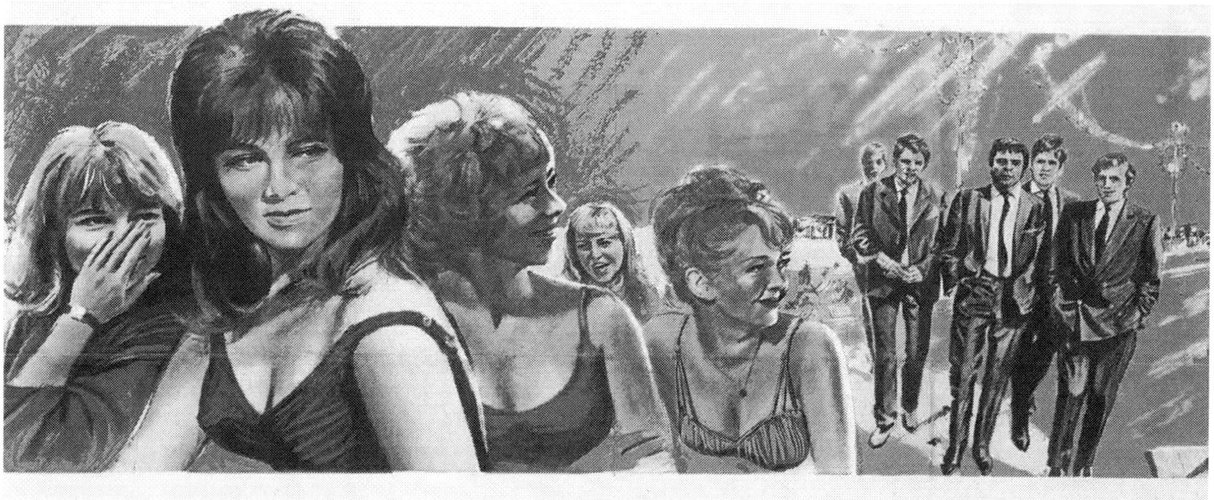

Poster art for *The System* (1963)

And an unknown American in the lead [Michael Callan, he had been a hit in Cat Ballou]. Presumably to get an American sale?

It was an American production by an American producer, Charles H. Schneer, for the British arm [Ameran Pictures] of an American company, Columbia. It wasn't a hit. And I was in trouble. I was out of work. I had the script of *The Jokers* and everyone had turned it down, except Universal who hadn't answered. One Saturday, I was in my office in Piccadilly and I got a letter from a man called John Gardner, who later wrote the book of my film, *The Stone Killer* [*A Complete State of Death*]. He now writes the James Bond books. It said: "Congratulations on your reviews in *Time* and *Newsweek*." I thought, 'This man is mad'. I'm out of work. I haven't made a film for nine months, and he's congratulating me on my reviews in *Time* and *Newsweek*, which come out on Wednesday and this is Saturday! If there had been a review on the Wednesday I would have known about it before now. Since I had nothing else to do, I went and bought the magazines. They were *raving* about *The System*, released in America as *The Girl-Getters*. *The New York Times* had printed the quotes in a big display ad. I was the hottest director in America and I didn't know it! I took the ad and had it photocopied at Victoria Station where they had a machine. Photocopying was in its infancy in those days. You put it in the machine, and black came out white and white came out black. On that Saturday afternoon, I took the ad to the home of Jay Kanter, the newly-appointed head of Universal. He had been Marlon Brando's agent. I put it through his letterbox. In my desperation to find work I'd brought on board a couple of producers, both useless, one of them was called Maurice Foster. I phoned Maurice and told him that I'd had these rave reviews and I've put them through Jay Kanter's door. "That won't make a difference," said Maurice. "Who cares about the director?" That's what he said. On Monday morning, at ten o'clock, Jay Kanter rang Maurice and said: "If Universal can have a six-picture deal with Michael Winner, he can start the movie tomorrow." So, the funny thing is, I was made by the press.

I like Reed and Crawford but I can't believe they are brothers. One, brooding and masculine. The other, fey and sprightly.

Crawford didn't want Reed to be in the picture. He wanted Stanley Baker. I said: "No, Michael. I'm going to pick Oliver Reed." *The Jokers* made them both bankable.

Did they get on during the shoot?

Of course. They're professional actors, but Oliver did get annoyed by Michael's meanness. Oliver was always very generous with his money.

What do you mean by meanness?

Well, he wouldn't buy a round or pay for a meal. He stood Oliver up for dinner once so Oliver hunted him down and held him upside down over the fountain in Trafalgar Square until Michael coughed up the cash (*laughs*). He was screaming! But it was my cash! I'd paid for the meal! (*laughs*)

I like the film for the sheer audacity of the plot, a scheme to 'borrow' the Crown Jewels, and the fact you shot on location inside The Tower of London!

They threw us out of The Tower! They got fed up with us, so we sent people in disguised as tourists, with a camera called the Eimo, which almost looks like a tourist camera. We couldn't shoot in the Jewel Room because it was being re-built, they were moving the jewels, so we used the main courtyard at Eton College. And we built the Jewel Room. When the film was about to come out, I read of two boys at Cambridge University who put a Morris Minor car on the top of King's College Chapel! You're at Cambridge so you know -

How on earth?!

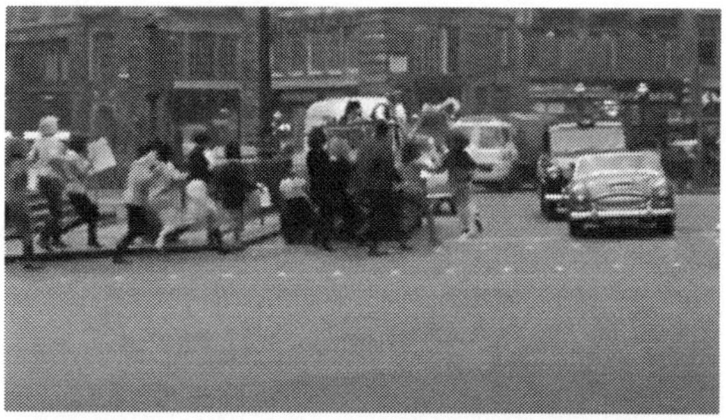

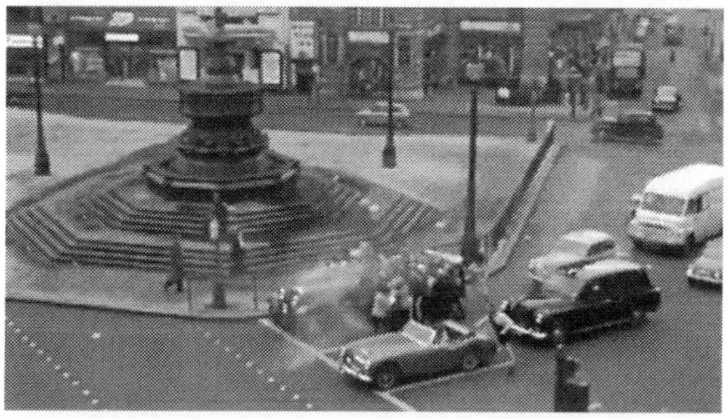

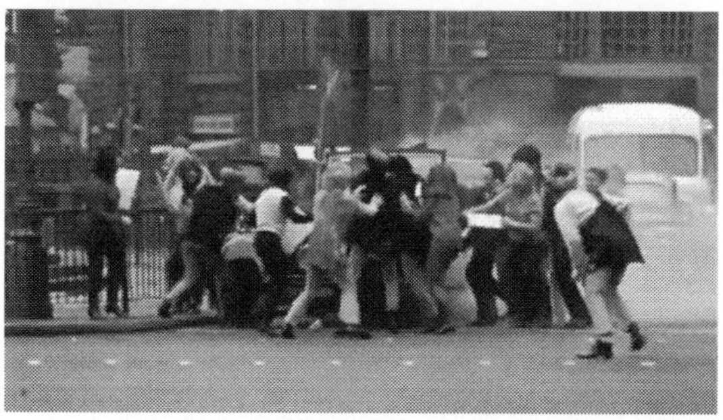

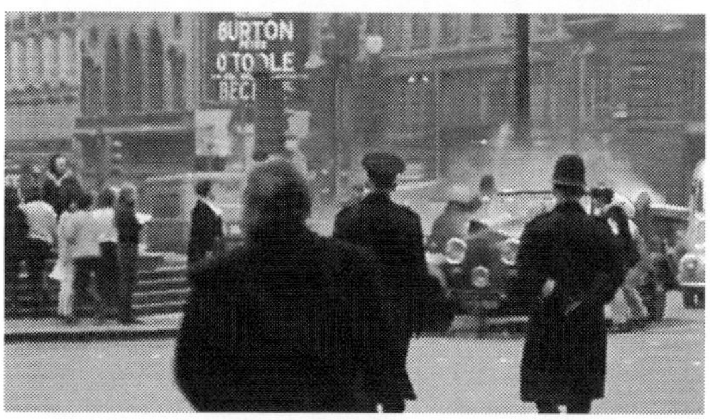

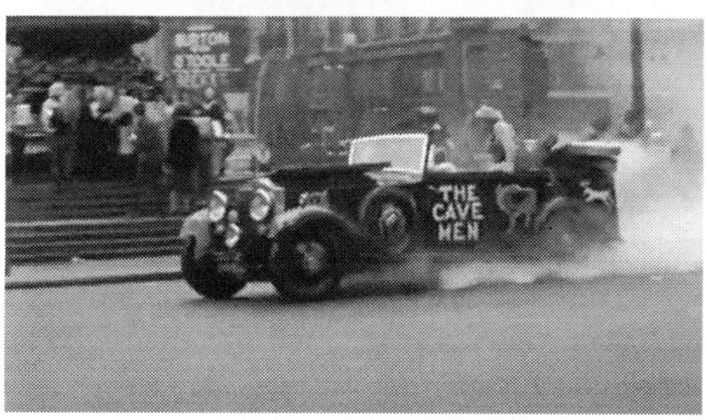

You Must Be Joking!

Not a good film, but its importance in English film history stems from an over-heating car stunt Michael Winner staged in Piccadilly Circus, which briefly obstructed a single lane of traffic. For decades afterwards, the police used it as an excuse to prevent films from being made on the streets of London, at a cost to the country estimated in hundreds of millions of pounds.

Notice the theatre advertising Richard Burton and Peter O'Toole in *Becket* (also photographed by Geoffrey Unsworth). Later that year, Burton and O'Toole would share the screen again, briefly, in Clive Donner's *What's New Pussycat!*

I know! How? The car was put on top of the chapel and photographed sitting there! [*Winner's recall is a little inaccurate. In 1958, Peter Davey put an Austin Seven, all but identical to the Morris Minor, on top of the Senate House*]. So I said to Jay Kanter, on the Saturday after the film opened, I wanted these boys to climb inside the Tower of London and put up a sign that said: "We saw *The Jokers*." They would be arrested, they'd have to be arrested, and in court on Monday morning they would say the film inspired them to put the sign up. I got a couple of hundred quid from Jay Kanter to pay a detective to go to Cambridge to get the boys and take them to The Tower. They had grappling irons, ropes, everything. And no knives. The officer told them they'd be held inside if they were arrested whilst carrying knives. It was the night the jewels were being moved from the old Jewel Room to the new one! There were seven hundred policemen on duty! The army was there! The beefeaters! At four in the morning, my man on the scene rang me and said: "The boys have been in and they've come out."

"Have they been arrested?"

He said: "No". They'd climbed all over the tower. They put up a notice saying 'This is a joke', which was not what we asked them to put up, and were now standing outside the Tower at four o'clock in the morning! What do we do?"

I told him: "You've got to phone the national press. Otherwise they'll take the sign down and there's no evidence except our word." So he phoned all the press. It was a Sunday morning, when no one is there anyway, and all but two of the press put the phone down and said 'pull the other leg'. Two turned up to photograph the boys. The stunt didn't get the coverage I expected it to. But the film was a box-office smash [and nominated for a Golden Globe for Best Foreign Film].

Did Universal give you a free hand to make it or were they on your back?

I was completely left alone. There was one day when they called me up and said: "There's a scene in the rushes that isn't in the script." I said: "I know. And tomorrow you might get another scene that isn't in the script. You're getting more than you paid for." And they were. That couldn't happen nowadays, of course.

A lot of your early films, and many of your later ones, are about a man who is not happy about his situation.

Nearly all my films are about that: a man trying to make a gesture to prove he is a person. In *I'll Never Forget What's 'Is Name* Oliver Reed breaks up his desk; in *The Jokers* they steal the Crown Jewels to give themselves personae. They weren't going to sell the jewels. *Death Wish* is the same. To some degree this happened by accident because I didn't originate many of the scripts, but I picked them from what was available.

Another starting point for many of your films is 'an investigation'. This is true of your earliest films, Shoot To Kill (1960) and Out of the Shadow (1961), and it is true of your star-studded films later, such as The Big Sleep (1978) and Appointment With Death (1988). Were Chandler and Christie influences?

No, until I made *The Big Sleep* I hadn't read a word of Chandler. I never read books. I still don't read books. I was influenced by Carol Reed's *The Third Man*. At the start of my career a number of the second features I wrote were basically poor copies of Carol Reed. I can't remember them very well. I wish I could get them on video. The one feature of mine which I can't get on video is *Won Ton Ton [The Dog That Saved Hollywood]*. It flopped. A lot of top directors made flops at the same time about Old Hollywood: Schlesinger, Bogdanovich, Ken Russell. Dozens. The studios were throwing money at films set in Old Hollywood but nobody wanted to see them. *Won Ton Ton* is a funny film. I don't care what the press thought of it.

Films and Filming raved about it.

They gave it the award for The Comedy of the Year. *That* film is a funny film. Peter Falk rang me a couple of years ago. He said: "Michael, I've just seen *Won Ton Ton*. I can't understand why it got bad reviews. This is a very funny film."

I'm looking forward to seeing it.

I don't know how you'll get it.

One of your films which is available in America on DVD is I'll Never Forget What's 'Is Name.

That has my voice-over on it, You have to get your DVD player adapted. The fellow who sold it to you will adapt the machine so it can take American and British and everybody's. It's very easy to do.

Again, the premise is a man challenging the system, but the twist is that he challenges it 'through integrity'.

He wanted to go back to his roots. He wanted to get out of the rat race. There is a wonderful speech in that film, by Orson Welles, about waste: "The whole world will be under three hundred thousand tons of waste..." Wonderful speech, very ahead of its time in that respect. Orson said to me: "I hope you don't mind if I rewrite my lines in the script?" He told me personally he'd rewritten the Ferris Wheel scene in *The Third Man*, so how could I object? "Orson, please, do what you like." He became a very close friend. Everyday, his secretary, Miss Rogers, would be on the set typing. I'd wait breathlessly for what he'd rewritten. She'd hand him the pages she'd typed and not a word had been changed. Nothing! Not a word. But his secretary was typing all the time. I said: "Orson, forgive me, I'm waiting for a rewrite. I haven't had one yet. If Miss Rogers isn't typing rewrites what is she typing?" He said: "Oh, she just takes out the stage directions for me. I can't rewrite the script, it's so good."

Yes, the dialogue is brilliantly concise. It is a masterful film that was ahead of its time. And it was ahead of Lindsay Anderson's if... in being an attack on the corrupting influence of English public schools. I presume you were nervous directing Orson Welles?

Not at all. I'd been told he could be difficult so I made it easy for him to not be difficult. I'd found out what his favourite food and drink was and made sure that his room was stocked with it. He appreciated the gesture. And I *had* found his favourite brandy. He was amazed. He said: "Michael, forget all that nonsense in the contract about me only working from ten to four. I'll work all the hours you want me to work." And he did. And he loved it. We became very good friends. I've still got the letters he wrote to me. He wrote to me all the time.

Did you consult with him on shots?

I had the courtesy to consult with him on the first set-up. He said: "It's your picture, Michael. You set it up. Just call me when you're ready." I called him when the set-up was ready, explained what had been lit, and what I wanted him to do, and he was perfect. Absolutely perfect. And it was quite a complicated set-up. Now, if I hadn't shown him that courtesy, he probably would have started making suggestions, or questioning the set-up.

So essentially, a film director is a behavioural psychiatrist?

Yes! (*laughs*). Orson did complain to me once that I was always filming him from below. He said: "Michael, I don't like to be filmed with the camera low down like that. It makes me look fat." I said: "Orson, I could film you from a helicopter and you'd still look fat!" (*laughs*).

The film got good reviews but isn't often revived, except for the DVD.

A few English critics didn't like it, but in America it was hailed! Hailed! It got a rave review in the New York Times. An absolute rave! ['A Method to Their Iconoclasm:Triumvirate Dissects Mod, Mad Britain' by A. H. Weiler, April 15, 1968: "The

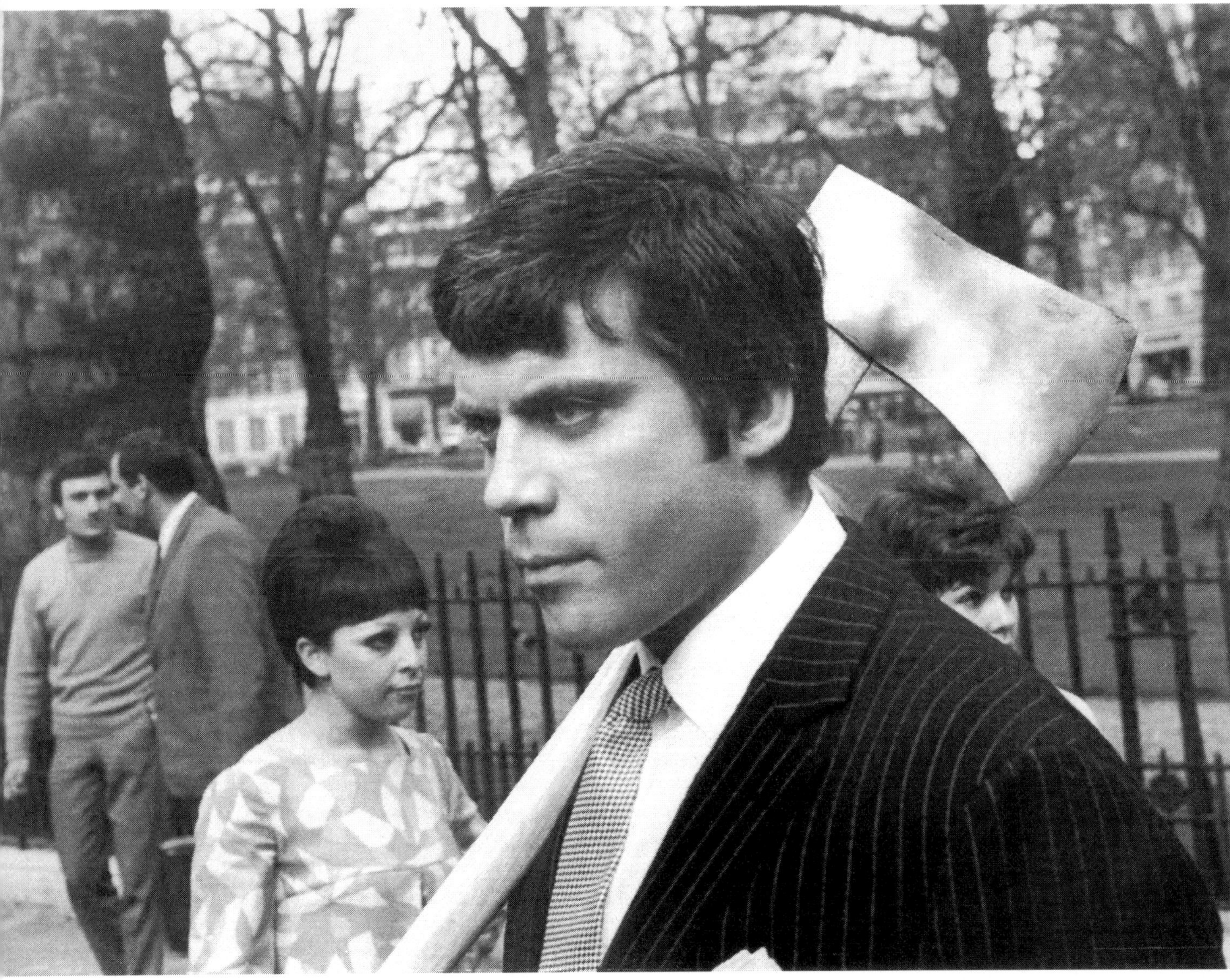

Oliver Reed in *I'll Never Forget What's 'Is Name* (1967). Good film. Terrible title.

ancient idea that you cannot shuck success and recapture youthful ideals underlined in this British comedy-drama... is illustrated in swift, funny, violent, candidly sexy and sometimes poignant strokes that give the picture the towering virtues of honesty and force."]

You followed it with Hannibal Brooks, again starring Oliver Reed. A film made on location in Austria. You were surprised by the help you got from the local authorities and the local people?

It was absolutely extraordinary. I had never done an action film before. For that film, I had an elephant rolling logs onto people, and people rolling down hills, falling out of trains, climbing along cable car wires. We should have had a top American stunt coordinator and a team of thirty stuntmen. I didn't know that's how you did it. So I had one English stuntman who had jumped off the Lutine bell rostrum at Lloyds for me [in *You Must Be Joking!* which also has a few driving stunts]. When I had said: 'Jump!' he jumped. That's all I had. Luckily the villagers in Austria were competitive. And they loved dressing up in Nazi uniforms! They *loved* the uniforms! They announced that: "The villagers of Schlocken will outdo the villagers of Beigle." And they did the stunts. We set them on fire; had them falling over without body protection, no knee-pads, arm-pads, things around the body. They had none of that. They did incredible stunts these people for nothing! Even in those days I should have been paying £2,000 a stunt. I had shots of twenty people all rolling down a hill. And they did it for nothing! For the tuppence they got paid as extras! And for the right to say that they were the best. I liked them for that.

Ken Russell was always at war with the extras union in Great Britain. I asked him why he and he said that 'extras' were the only people on a film who worked for money. The rest worked because they loved it. Because they wanted to be part of something good being made.

He's right. He's absolutely right.

That and the fact that extras sold inaccurate and salacious stories to the press. Didn't Ken Russell visit the set of Hannibal Brooks to persuade Oliver Reed to appear in Women in Love (1969)?

I think it was the day Bobbie Kennedy got shot. A couple of days before, Oliver Reed said to me: "There's a man called Ken Russell coming out to see me. He does television. I don't want to do television, Michael. You've made me a movie star." I said: "Oliver, I've seen what this fellow does. I've never met him but, in my view, you should do it. Because I think Ken Russell is going to become very important and he will help you. Do it." He tried to protest. He adored me, Oliver. He never watched television. Oliver Reed didn't give a shit about the camera-angles of Ken Russell, he was down the pub. There was no way he was going to go back to television. "Oliver," I said: "You should do it. End of story." And he did. I like Ken Russell but what I thought was disgraceful was that he didn't go to Oliver's funeral. Not one person from showbusiness went to his funeral. Was Ken Russell at his funeral? No. There was only me.

It was in Ireland.

So what? It's a thirty-quid flight if you want to go that way. I also helped Oliver to get the job in *Gladiator*. He got the job *entirely* through me. Nobody would employ him. They thought he was useless. He announced his retirement after making my film, *Parting Shots*, because he didn't think he could get any more work. Shortly afterwards, who was the director [of *Gladiator*]?

Ridley Scott.

Ridley. Oliver said to me: "Ridley thinks that because I've just worked with you I should act again. And he wants me to read for him. I'm not going to *read*. I'm a star." I said: "Oliver, I told you to go with Ken Russell and I'm telling you to read for

Ridley Scott. I'm *telling* you. It's a fucking order! Read for Ridley Scott. End of story!" He went and read for Ridley. He got the part. He was happy to be working with David Hemmings again. He told me they spent a lot of time on the set of *Gladiator* talking about *The System*. Then sadly he died. It was a nice way for Oliver to go, on an Oscar winning film. He was a wonderful actor. A wonderful person.

The cinematography on Brooks is fantastic.

It was by a man called Bob Paynter, who was doing documentaries, and I took him on. I had been working with Otto Heller, a brilliant Austrian Jewish cameraman, but he said: "Michael, I can't go over these mountains. I'm too old." I asked the companies who rented lights to tell me who was the best cameraman. Four of them said 'Bob Paynter'. They said: "You've not heard of him, he's only done docu-mentaries, but he's a genius." I hired him. He did six pictures for me. He was then taken up by the man who did *Trading Places*, er...

John Landis.

John Landis. Went to America. Did one of the Michael Jackson videos. He became very successful and, sadly, he became very arrogant. He asked for too much money and got himself [locked] out of the industry. It is true to say that it is not the actors who are the prima donnas on a movie, it is the unit. The actors are easy. Paynter wasn't a world-class cinematographer until he made the movies [for me]. He was a bum going in, and a prima donna coming out. (*laughs*). Geoff Unsworth *was* a world-class cinematographer when I hired him [for *You Must Be Joking!* Unsworth would later do *2001, A Space Odyssey*]. He'd just been nominated for an Oscar for *Becket* (1964). There were only three films shooting in the whole country in January 1964 and we had a stupid B-Picture cameraman, 'Harry', chosen by Charlie Schneer, the producer. Harry went into a little house in St John's Wood, which I was going to use as a location, and said: "This is no good. This is much too small."

I told him: "I've shot in rooms this size many times." "No. It's too small." He want back to Charlie Schneer and said: "Michael Winner is crazy. He doesn't know what he is doing." Charlie Schneer, who was a good fellow, and the only producer at the time who wasn't afraid of the Unit, the Unit ran the film industry in Britain, with overtime bans and all that nonsense, said to me: "Michael, Harry thinks you're crazy."

I said: "Charlie, fire him."

Unsworth wasn't working. He came to see me and I gave him the list of lights we had for the shoot; the most basic lights; the lights they use in shops for photographing babies. We didn't want too many lights. They take forever to set up. I told Geoff: "Here's the list of lights."

He said: "Well, I normally choose my own lights." He looked at the list and said: "I've never used lights like this."

I said: "Geoff, let me tell you something. Harry Boddle, a little schmuck, he was going to make the film using these lights. And if he can make the film using these lights, you, who are a genius, can make the film using these lights."

Geoff looked at list again and he said: "Yes, I can." *That's* what I call a professional. He didn't bring in extra lights, he used what we had. And he lit the film beautifully.

Was the elephant easy to direct?

A nightmare. There were two of them. They are pack animals so you can't have just one. They're dangerous animals. One spent all its time trying to kill Oliver Reed!

How?

Crushing him into the wall. Standing on him. Nudging him over the cliff. Before we started shooting, Oliver told me he was going to sleep with the elephant so he could bond with it. I said:

"Oliver, the elephant is bonded to its trainer. It can only have one master." But Oliver wouldn't listen and he slept with it. Thereafter it kept trying to kill him.

You've made two animal pictures but you've not often worked worked with children?

My very first job was with a child actor. John Howard Davies. David Lean's Oliver Twist. He was making *Tom Brown's Schooldays* (1951). He was fourteen years old. I was fourteen years old and I was trying to get a job in films. He lived near me, and my father knew his father, so I blagged my way into the Daimler which picked him up every morning to take him to Denham Studios. And I arrived at Denham with him. The publicist was amazed. I sold a story about John Howard Davies to the papers and that got me a writing job. My column was syndicated in sixteen newspapers. *[Davies' father would write the screenplay for Play it Cool].*

I know you wrote for Films and Filming in the 1950s. I've got a complete run that I've had bound and which I read all the time. Would you mind if I republished the reviews you wrote?

Please do. I'd love to see them again.

After Hannibal Brooks you made The Games, with Michael Crawford and Ryan O'Neal, a re-creation of the Olympic Games in Rome. I've got the lobby cards but I haven't yet seen the film.

It wasn't a bad film. Again, it got a rave review in The New York Times. But people didn't go to see it because they know they can watch the real Olympic Games on television for free! Ninety-eight of the hundred most watched programmes on television EVER are of the Olympic Games.

But if you'd have held it back for two years it would have been the world's most popular film. You had the star and the writer of Love Story.

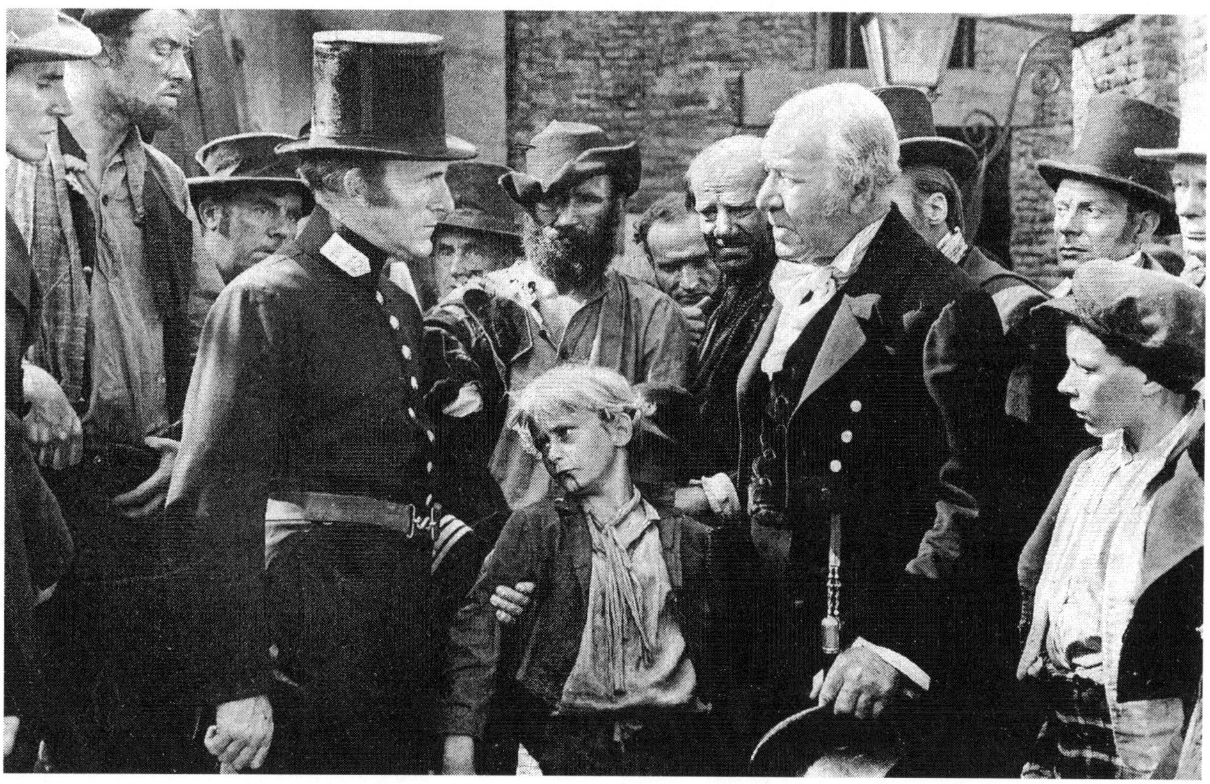

A rather knocked-about John Howard Davies as David Lean's *Oliver Twist.*

True. Paramount screened *The Games* so they could have a look at Ryan O'Neal and decide whether or not to use him in *Love Story*.

And Michael Crawford got his wish to work with Stanley Baker.

Yes, they were friends. For the filming they shared a villa on the Appian Way. It got burgled. Everything got stolen including their passports! Stanley liked to make it known he had 'friends' on the wrong side of the law. So it was particularly hilarious when the wrong side of law tapped him. (*laughs*) He was fuming! Fuming!

I guess that's one of the downsides of shooting in Rome. On the upside though, I read a fantastic quote attributed to you, do tell me if it is true or not. You were in Rome and you gave your location manager a list of the streets you wanted closed, among them the Forum, two miles of roads by the Colosseum, the Trevi Fountain, the St. Angelo Bridge. When the location manager asked for alternatives, you said: "There aren't alternative streets, but there are other location managers." And you got what you wanted.

That's right. I did say that. "If you can't do it, I'll find someone who can." We closed all the streets in Rome by bribing the deputy mayor with $40,000 in a suitcase. Suddenly all the streets were closed. That's how things got done.

That reminds me of the film of yours which I most enjoy, and which I sincerely believe is a masterpiece: Lawman. The premise is superb. The Lawman, Burt Lancaster, rides into town, says he wants these men to stand trial, and if they don't give themselves up by noon he's going to get them. It's a classic scenario. Then

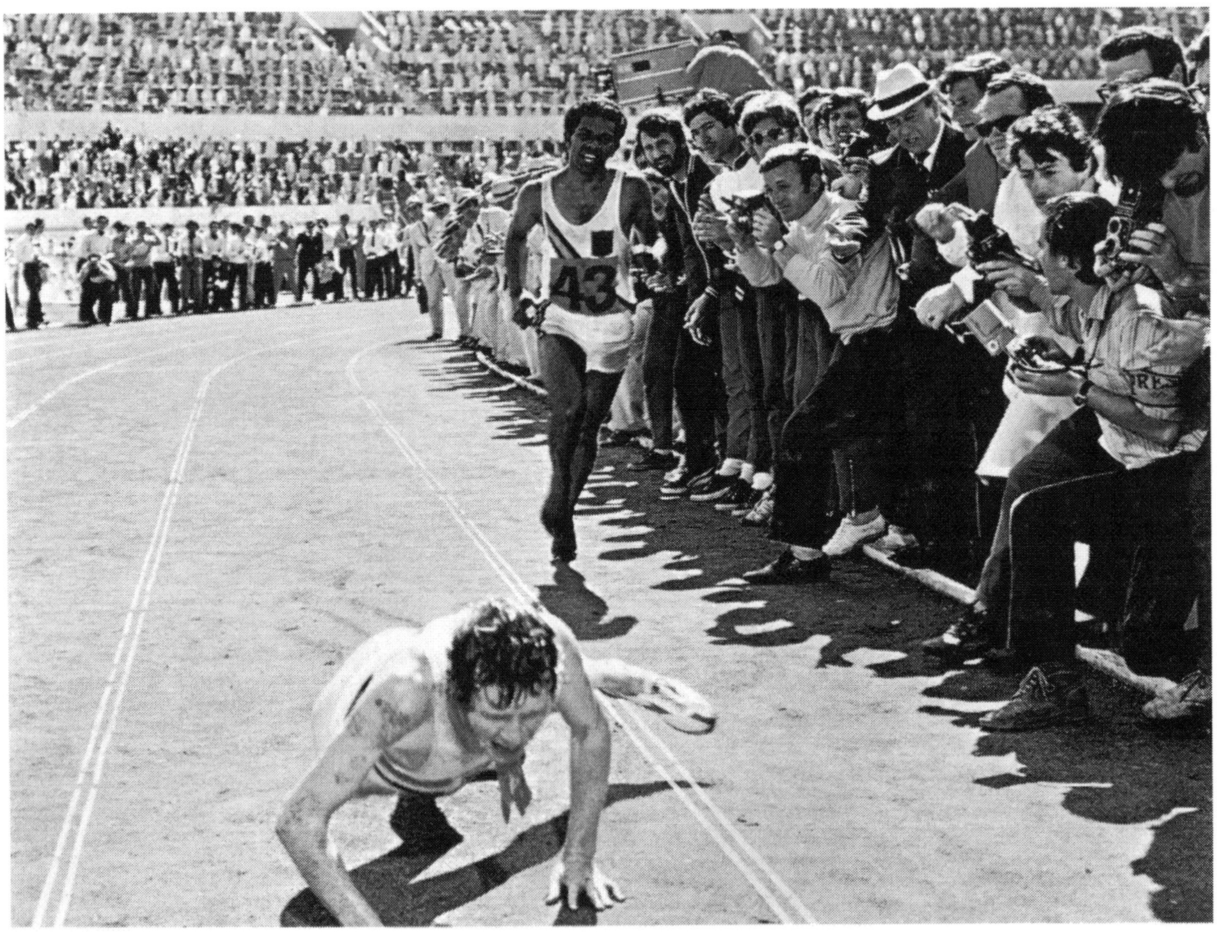

you build in the twists, which take the film deeper. The town is dependent for survival on the purse of a character played by Lee J. Cobb,. The men on the list are Cobb's men. The townsfolk, who are decent people, are against the Lawman. Lee J. Cobb wants his men to stand trial, which is another twist on the premise. He is against violence. Guns no longer rule. There is a stronger weapon, money.

Lee J. Cobb is one of the great actors of all time. In the film, he makes this great speech: "We don't kill him. We buy him. And if we can't buy him we buy the man above him. The shooting days were for younger men."

And that is how America evolved. The whole film gets deeper and deeper and all the characters turn, including the Lawman, who begins to have doubts about what he is doing. And the ending is sensational. Burt Lancaster shooting a man in the back!

When I asked Burt to do the film he went through the script line by line. No actor has ever done that with me. You give them a script and they say "Yes" or "No". Burt went through every fucking line. He was my dearest friend, even though he threatened to kill me three times! When he came to the end of the script, he said: "Why does he shoot the man in the back?" I said: "Because he is a total bastard" (*laughs*). The man drew on him. When you draw on a man in the West all options *end*. That was the Lawman's view. He played by the rules. By his slightly demented rules. He was the Dirty Harry of the West. Gerald Wilson wrote that script. He had it for a long time. It needed about ten changes. He said: "I don't make changes." So I let him sit on it. About six months later, he rang me and said: "What are you doing about my script?"
"I'm waiting for the changes, Gerald."
He rang the next day and said: "I think I can find a way of doing a couple of them." He then did the lot. My God, it was a good script.

It was a bold move, an Englishman setting up a Western from his office in London. Was it difficult raising the money?

United Artists said: "If you can get Burt Lancaster, you can make the movie." That is how movies are made, on the whole. You get Charlie Bronson you can make the movie. That's how *Chato's Land* got made. I went to Paris, where Charlie lived then, and I got him to star in the film. You get Lancaster, you can make the movie. And thank God we got Burt Lancaster. A great actor. I remember, we were shooting the scene where he walks out through the saloon doors. Richard Jordan calls him out and Burt comes through the door, and walks a few steps toward him, and stands on the edge of the boardwalk, and the door swings behind him. He said: "How did it look, Winner?" I said: "Burt, even watching from here, I'm fucking terrified!"

I love the little character touches, the fact he drinks little cups of tea or coffee at the bar.

And plays the flute.

Yes. And the realistic, unsentimental touches, like the coyotes and the vultures tearing the carcass of the horse.

That's how it was. I had all these American professors working on the film because I was terrified of getting the details wrong. And I learned that the Americans know nothing about the West! We had a prop man from John Wayne's company working for us on the set dressing. I said: "What do you use for oil lamps, Charlie?" He said: "Oh, we get them from the supermarket. We buy modern ones and put a bit of dust on them."
"Charlie! You can buy 19th Century oil lamps on the Portobello Road in London for £3 each!" So we bought all the stuff in the Portobello Road and the unit brought it over. After the film, we sold it to John Wayne, for use on another movie. So *Lawman* is far more authentic than American Westerns. *Far more!* It was a risky project and I was determined not to look a fool.

There are some fine directorial touches, very bold tracking shots, great arcs around the gunfighters at the finale. And Jerry Fielding's score is wonderful, the use of the horns in the title track.

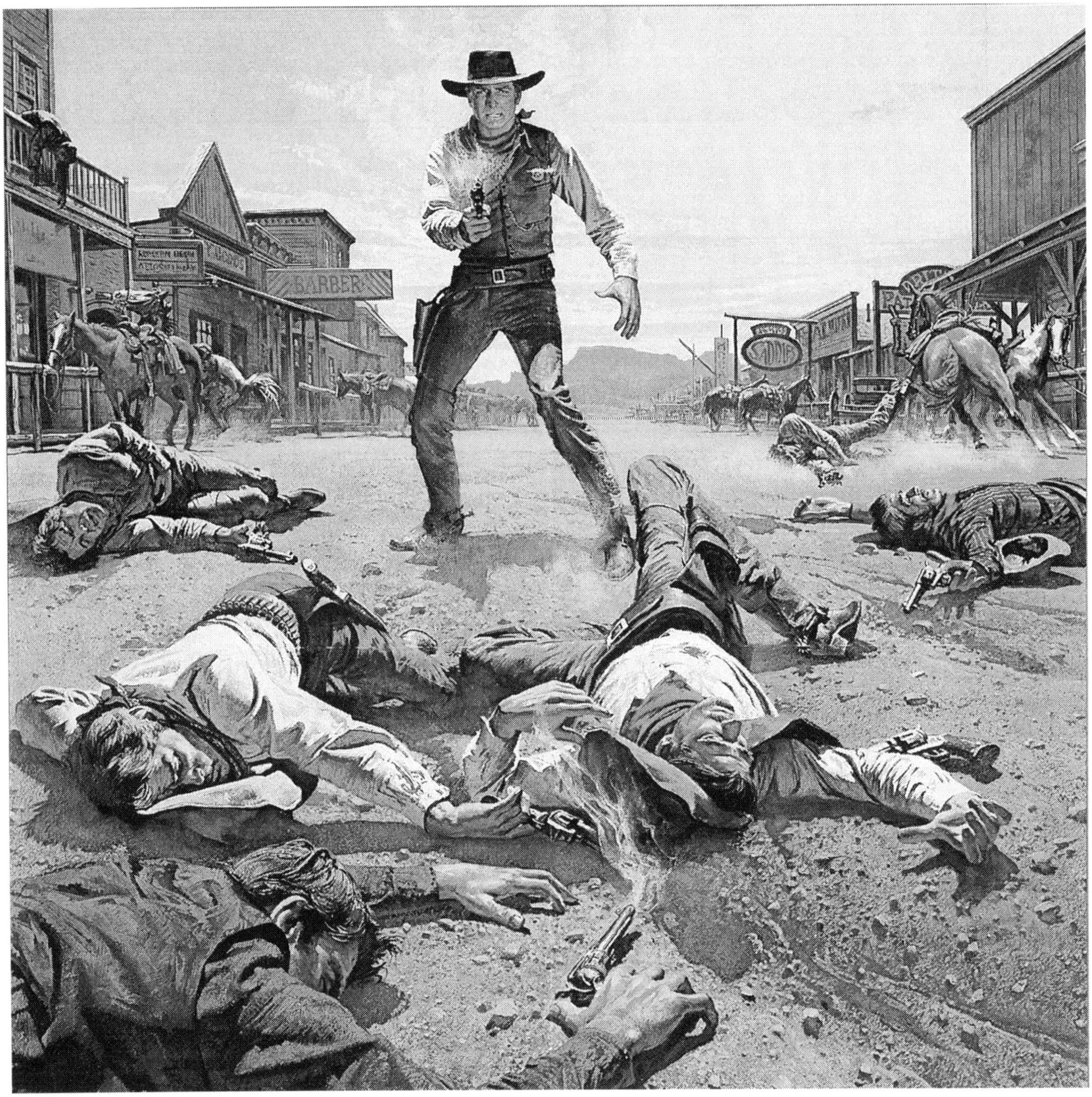

Poster art for Michael Winner's *Lawman* (1970)
The only world-class Western made by an Englishman

He was marvellous. It was Peckinpah who told me to use Jerry Fielding. Jerry did Sam's films and he did Clint's films. Brilliant composer. I would have used him for every film. Sadly he died young. He was one of the blacklisted composers of the McCarthy era and that played very heavily on him. He wrote an English classical score for *The Nightcomers.*

Like Lawman, the main theme is played by the brass, but made to sound a little like English hunting horns.

A genius. He was a wonderful abrasive man who wasn't afraid to give a point of view. I remember him saying: "Michael, you don't know how to dub a movie. When you have people talking you have them talking as loud as the gunshots." Not true, of course!

In Lawman there's a young buck who wants to be a killer, a young man wanting to take on an older man, which is a recurring theme in your work. It's used again in the other film you made with Burt Lancaster, Scorpio. Lancaster is now carrying a bit more weight, but there is still a bit of The Crimson Pirate about him, twirling up the scaffolding at the building site shoot out.

Yes, Burt Lancaster, what a man! The building site was the Viennese subway under construction. There is a scene in that film which I cannot believe I let happen. We held up the traffic in the street at the side of the subway site. All the Viennese traffic was held up. Then we let them go, and filmed Burt and Delon running across the street in front of the traffic. We didn't use stunt drivers! Burt is waving at them as he is running across the road, and he's shouting: "Don't fucking kill me!" I was looking at that scene in real life and I thought: "Fucking unbelievable. They're really doing this!" Burt is old. He's got a bad leg. He's risking his life. The Viennese drivers weren't expecting to see Burt Lancaster running across the road in front of them! Their reactions may not have been so good. You take a lot of risks on movies. The whole thing takes over. And you just do anything to get the shot.

Scorpio, a spy thriller set in Vienna, is again inspired by The Third Man. You paid for the restoration of The Third Man, didn't you?

Yes. They charged me five grand but they spent about £3.80 on it. In *Scorpio* we used the Harry Lime door. The same door where Orson Welles makes his entrance and the cat purrs at his feet. Where he says: "The only life, Harry..." *Fantastic.* We found it by accident. I said: "Fuck me! That's Harry Lime's door!" I was in Vienna only a few weeks ago and I was taken, quite by accident, to where Harry Lime is killed and the little boy runs out and follows them. Opposite the Franz Josef statue. The door is still there. A great door. The Harry Lime door. I'd had a driver look for an hour for the Harry Lime door. [*The phone rings. Winner answers it before the first ring has ended:* "Hello? Spencer I will have to call you back. Where are you?..."]

One of the most remarkable things about Scorpio is that you shot inside the actual C.I.A. complex in Washington.

That was incredible. Incredible! The American production manager asked: "Where do want to shoot the C.I.A. scenes?"
I said: "In the C.I.A. building."
He said: "What if the location manager can't get it?"
I said: "Fire the location manager."
Burt helped us to get it. He knew someone high up. We went down to have a look at the place with Howard Osborne, Head of Internal Security, who turned up in the Nixon tapes! They gave us the building. We took pictures of all the badges and had them printed up in Soho. When we were filming, the Head of Security said: "Michael, where did you get those badges from?" I told him: "Howard, you were there when I photographed them!"
He said: "They look like ours."

I said: "That's the whole bloody point!"

"Three of your agents got in wearing your badges. Will you please not show them so clearly in the film?" But it was too late for that. The film was already under way! And it was written by Gerald Wilson who was barred from America as a Communist! He showed the C.I.A. killing people! Arthur Krim, the head of United Artists, did a lot of work in Washington and didn't want us to film inside the building even though we had permission. He didn't want any trouble in case there was any fall out later. He said: "You can't go, Michael. I disallow you to go there."

I told him I was going to film there.

"Then, you must show them the script."

I said: "They haven't asked for the script. If they want to see the script they can *steal* it."

"No," he said: "If they approve the script you can go." I had no choice. So I sent Howard Osborne a copy of the script although we'd told him we weren't coming. I said: "I've been asked to send you a script." They replied. I think I've lost his fucking letter but I can see it now in front of me. He said: "We've read your script. We thank you very much. We've kept a photocopy of pages 56 and 68." There was nothing on those pages at all! "And as long as your side sorts themselves out we are happy to return to the status quo." So I sent Arthur Krim the letter and he said: "Okay, you can go." Fantastic spirits.

I like the screenplay. They way the hunted turns into the hunter.

Gerald needed a lot of bullying. He was useless without me. He wouldn't rewrite anything unless you bullied him, and he needed a lot of bullying because he was fucking lazy. A lovely man. He realised, when he took his scripts elsewhere, that the producers weren't as hard on him, but nothing got made! What's the point of saying "The script is all right." And nobody makes it! Big deal!

David Sherwin told me that Lindsay Anderson really cracked the whip when they worked on their scripts.

All writers are lazy. You have to lock them in a room and beat them (*laughs*). David Sherwin once worked in my office as a runner. A nice man. Did you see *The Nightcomers*?

Yes. And because I live in Cambridge I had to cycle over to Sawston Hall to have a look at where it was filmed. You'd be heartbroken. The house is an administration centre, I think for a language school. Whole chunks of the grounds are a car park.

Terrible. It was so beautiful that place.

[The house was sold again in 2013]. I liked the way the film was photographed. There are many scenes photographed into the sun, and a lot of scenes shot at the end of the day and in the very early morning when the light is really special.

That was Bob working with winter light. Beautiful.

Three more good things about the film are:

1) It is a plausible prequel to Turn of the Screw, which is no mean feat. 2) It breaks your rule about not working with children, and the kids are fine.

3) Marlon Brando looks so relaxed and comfortable. There's a brightness in his eyes in this film which we do not see again in any film he made after it.

Marlon loved it. He rang me the other day and said: "I've just seen the film again, Michael. You should be very proud of it". He loved making it. His make-up man, Philip Rhodes, who has been with him since they acted together in their twenties in New York, said: "Michael, you have not seen the Marlon Brando that everyone else sees. You caught him on the hop. You kept him laughing." To which I replied: "Philip, the fellow I saw was a delight. He could not be more delightful." He could not have been more professional. Coppola was down there in a cottage, in Cambridge, writing *The Godfather*. We were out in the street shooting, and I said to Marlon: "Is that Francis Coppola on the other side of the barrier."

"Yes."

"Should we ask him through?"

Marlon said: "No. Because you should only have one director on a set." And Marlon was right. That wasn't me being unkind. Brando was a wonderful man. A great, great actor. The best actor in the history of cinema. No question.

Chaplin?

Well, Chaplin didn't have anywhere near the range of Brando.

Brando' is good in your film. I love the looseness in his body language. I'm not sure though about the soft Irish accent. It is skilful but I'm unsure it was right for the character. Whose idea was that?

It was his! It was very good. He didn't want to play it British because he'd played British in *Mutiny on the Bounty*. It was not that incorrect. He wanted to play it Irish. The Irish accent isn't too far from American.

And I suppose adds to the English theme of 'class'; Irish being considered second-class in that environment.

I thought he was incredible. Dr. [Gian Luigi] Rondi, who was in charge of the Venice Film Festival, wanted the film and asked me would Marlon Brando come to Venice?
I said: "Are you going to give him a prize?"
"There is no prize. Everyone who comes is given a plaque or something."
I said: "Well, he is not coming."
Rondi didn't draw breath. He said: "We'll give him the Best Actor prize."
I asked Marlon: "Do you want to go to Venice, Marlon, to get the Best Actor prize? They've never given it before."
He said: "No, thanks." And that was that.

Didn't you lose a bet with Marlon and end up selling condoms in Trafalgar Square?

Yes. That's true. Marlon was in London making *Superman: The Movie* and whenever he is in London we have dinner together. We were on the way to dinner and he asked: "Michael, what is the correct English way to say 'Integral'"?
I said: "Marlon, in England it is in-teg-ral".
He said: "I don't think it is."
"Have a bet. Fifty quid?"
"No, no," said Marlon: "The loser has to sell French ticklers in Piccadilly Circus for an hour." A French tickler is a condom with a bobble on it. I said: "Marlon, don't ponce about, because if you lose you won't do it, and you are going to lose, then our friendship will be severely chipped because, to me, a bet is sacrosanct."
"Michael, I give you my word I will do it."
"Okay, Marlon." We shook hands and we went to dinner. The next day, a Monday, Jay Kanter rings me from the set of *Superman* and I'm told that Marlon is talking about nothing but this bet. He has been hired on the biggest ever contract in the history of movies, eleven million dollars and a percentage for ten days work, which he sued them for seven years over, and the main interest of the day for him is our bet! So I put the phone down and I look up 'integral' in the dictionary. The only pronunciation is 'int-i-gral'. Nowadays in-teg-ral and int-i-gral are both listed but, then, my dictionary was printed in 1971, there was only the one. I rang Marlon to tell him and he says: "Why haven't you rang me before?"
I said: "You've been on the bloody set. I only left you at one in the morning."
"I've sorted out how I'm going to do it," he said. "I'll dress up as a blind beggar. The girls have got me a uniform and a stick."
I told him: "Marlon, *sadly*, you do not have to go because you've won." But the funny thing is, now that I have lost I'm not so keen to do it. About six months later we are talking on the phone I say: "Marlon, I've got to go to Piccadilly Circus because of you."
He said: "You should have gone already. It's ridiculous, Michael. You lost the bet. Pay it."
"I'll go next week, I promise you. I'll send you the photographs." I got a tray made with a sign written on it: 'Purveyors of Sexual Aids to the Gentry, 1st

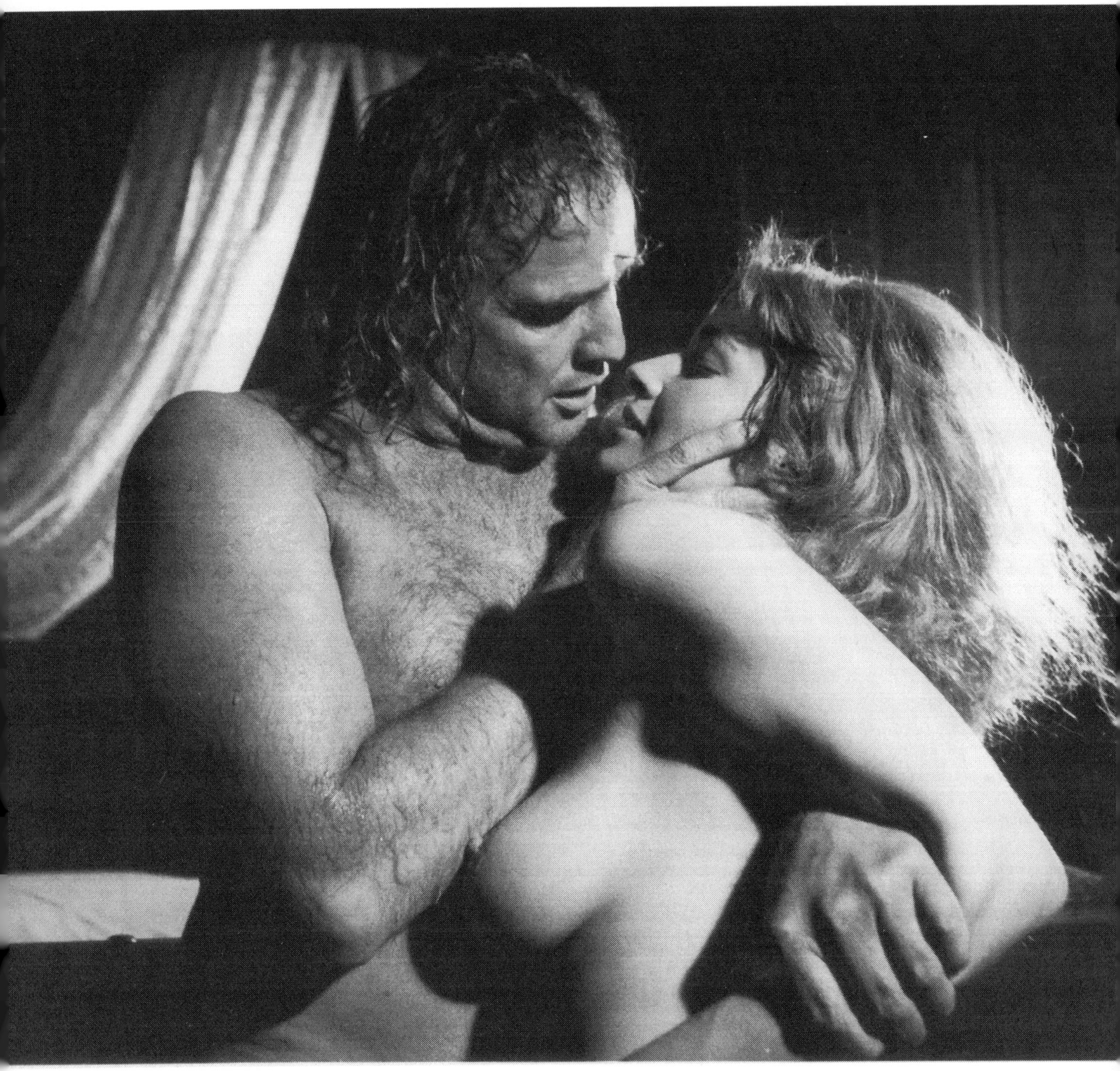

Winner himself took this photograph of Marlon Brando and Stephanie Beacham in *The Nightcomers* (1971)

July, 1977'. We told the police that I would be there for an hour and I would leave if I was arrested but I wouldn't leave voluntarily. They said it would be fine as long as I didn't cause an obstruction. A few days after doing it, Marlon sent me a medallion inscribed: 'Michael, the loser is also a Winner, M.B.' and the date. On the back is a phonetical spelling of 'integral'. I wear it all the time. Every-time he sees me, Marlon says: "You've just put that on for me today." "No, Marlon, I have worn it every day since you gave it to me."
And he said: "Yes, I can see it's scratched. It's well worn." [*Winner shows me the medal*]. He's a lovely man. He's got a sense of fun. A sense of daring. Cheeky. You know what I mean. But everyone goes: 'Oh, he's so depressing. And he's had all these terrible things happen.' And I say: "No". I've walked with all the people who are supposed to be difficult. Bronson. Brando. Mitchum. Burt Lancaster. Faye Dunaway. They were all fine with me. For Faye Dunaway I've got a soft spot. [I was told] The only thing that came out of Faye's caravan on the first two days of shooting *Mommie Dearest* were the wigs, and they came out in pieces because she'd cut them up. Marlon Brando said a great thing. He said: "Michael Winner is the only person who doesn't talk to me like he thinks I want to be talked to." That's a high compliment. I'd talk to him like I talk to you, or me or anybody. I don't ponce about being in terror, you know. Much as I respect him. Give him a bit of fun.

A great actor.

A legend. A fabulous human being. Bless him.

In the year of The Nightcomers*, 1971, Charles Bronson was given a Golden Globe for being the World's Most Popular Actor. In that year he made* Chato's Land*. His first film with you. The following year he was quoted as saying he would only do* The Mechanic *if it was directed by Michael Winner.*

Have you seen *Chato's Land*?

I'm seeing it next week. [I did. I thought it was grim. A humourless film about hate].

That's a great movie. A marvellous film. Get the American version on DVD because it was cut to ribbons in Britain. Again, it has the same writer, Gerald Wilson, and the cast is wonderful: Charles Bronson, Jack Palance, Richard Basehart. Charlie did get me the job on *The Mechanic*. When I had done *Chato's Land*, people asked if I got on with Charlie? I said: "I don't know, but I had dinner with him every night." It was a bit strange because his wife was an ex-girlfriend of mine, way back before he had met her. I didn't tell him that because he would have killed us both. A call came in from Columbia saying 'Charles Bronson will not do *The Mechanic* unless you direct it'. Then the film went to United Artist. We did six movies together, including *The Stone Killer*, a good film which got great notices, and three *Death Wish* movies, of which the first was seriously good. The others were nice meat-and-potatoes work.

The Mechanic *is a very interesting film. Much of it is set on Mulholland Drive, a location brought back into the public eye by David Lynch. Charles Bronson's character, a professional assassin, lives there in a stunning seventies mansion. At home, his uniform is a red bathrobe. He listens to classical music. On his wall is a vision of Hell painted by Hieronymus Bosch.*

Yes. Lindsay Anderson loved the film. He said he didn't understand why the British press didn't like it; why it didn't get the praise it deserved. He said: "It's a marvellous film."

I have heard him enthuse about Charles Bronson. The first fifteen minutes of The Mechanic *are extraordinarily good. Pure cinema. Pure Hitchcock. No dialogue, bits of radio, a few sound effects, and one hell of an explosion!*

It was a clever ending that. The gag at the end. The author had a different end involving a motorcylist who threw a bomb through the fucking window.

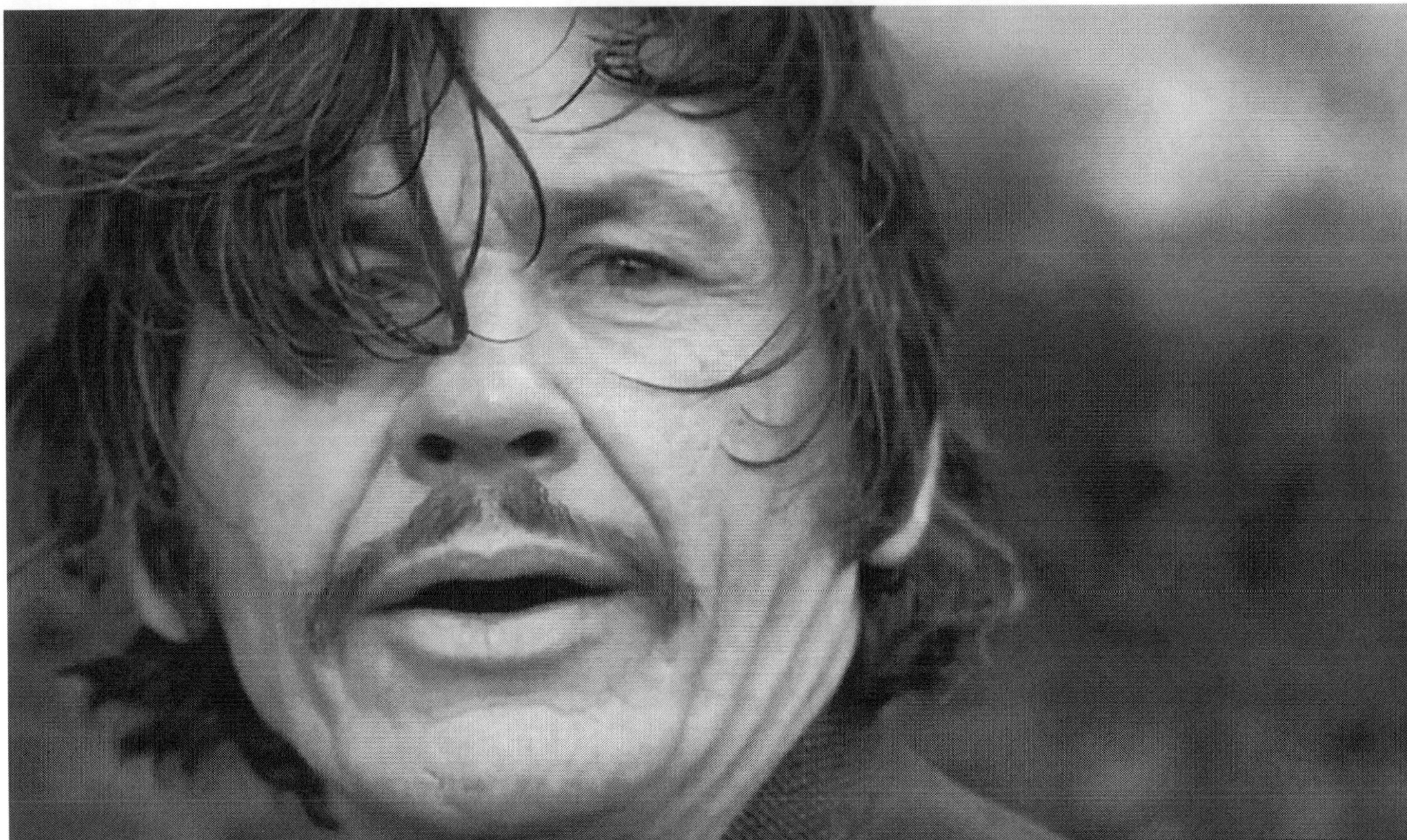

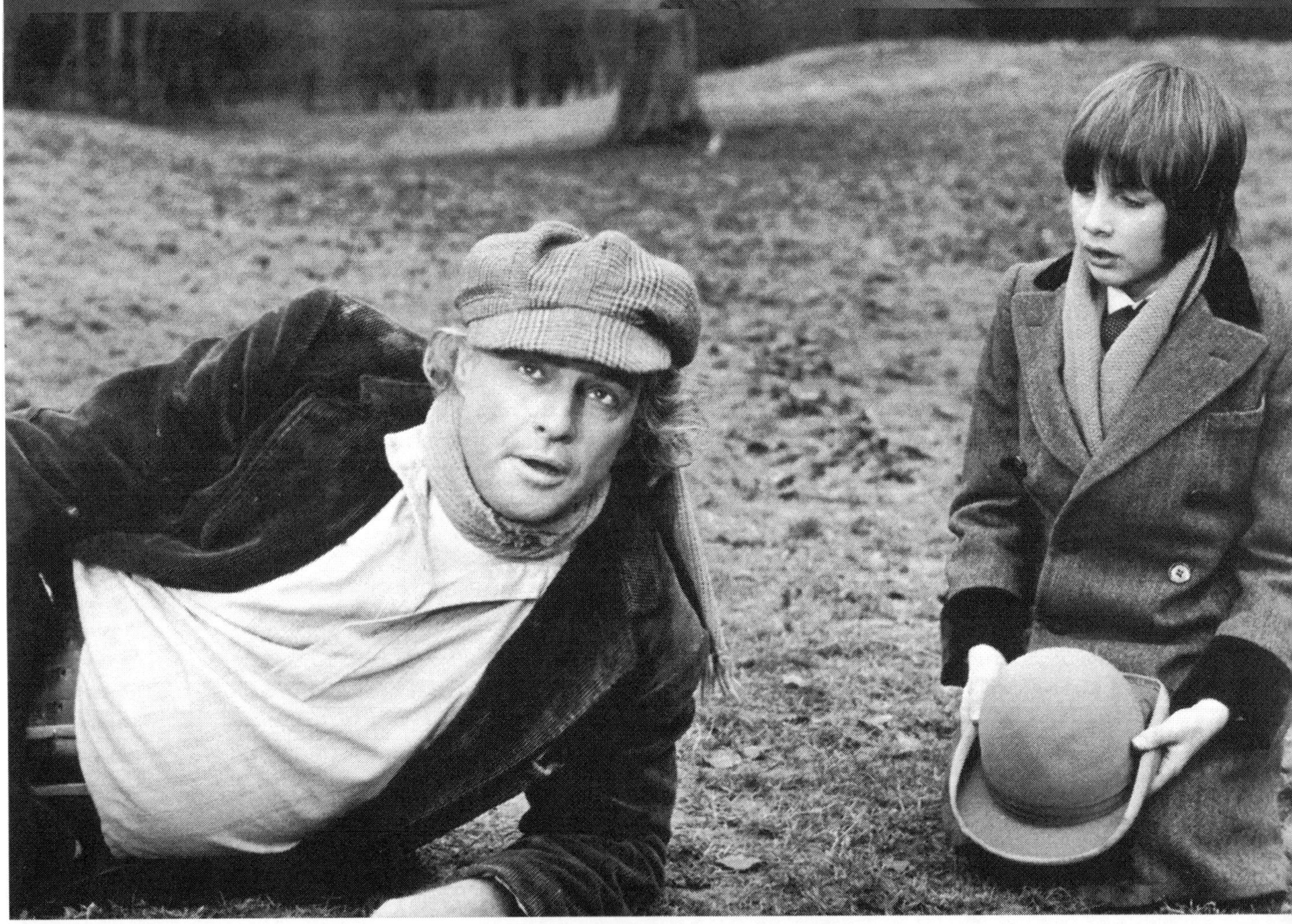

Ridiculous. He had written seventeen endings for the opening sequence and he got very ratty because I rejected them all. He said: "I've written you seventeen endings for that scene and they were all perfectly all right and you keep turning them down. Go fuck yourself!". He went away. Then he came back and said: "I've done one more." I looked at it and I said: "Brilliant. Absolutely brilliant!" And that was the one we used. The script had been around and worked on for about seven years. Originally the characters played by Bronson and Jan-Michael Vincent were two gays, but they took that out.

You'd never get that past Bronson!

Never!!! (*laughs*) Never! I said: "Don't mention that to anyone. If Charlie hears this he'll walk off the set!" He didn't like Jan-Michael Vincent anyway because Vincent was so, sort of 'pretty'. I remember one day when Jan came in and had a cold. Charlie said: "That's a bad cold you've got there, Jan."
Jan said: "That's very sweet of you, Charlie. Thank you for caring about that."
"I don't give a damn about your cold," said Charlie. "I just don't want to catch it!"

I think Jan-Michael Vincent was well-cast.

He was very good. New to the movies. He'd done some very important work on television. His later career is a bit fucked up. He became an alcoholic and addicted to drugs but he was a very nice fellow on *The Mechanic*.

Bruce Weber photographed him during this period and has commented on his generosity as a subject.

He was lovely, but he went mad.

One of the good things about your movies is the delicious unpredictability of the endings. When you watch a Hollywood film you know the ending within the first five minutes. With a Michael Winner film you don't know what's coming up until it hits you. The Mechanic has a startlingly finale. It must be the bleakest end to an action film ever made?

He did a lovely death scene, Charlie. The film originally ended on Catalina and I thought, oh God. I suggested switching it because it would cost less to shoot in Europe, I had never been to Naples and I wanted to go, and it would add a whole new dimension to the film. I knew it would be good for the film. I did the same for the start of *Death Wish* which is set in Hawaii. I had never been to Hawaii so I changed the sequence so I could go to Hawaii *and* because it was very good for the movie. It represented the final idyll.

Before Death Wish, there was The Stone Killer, which has one of my favourite car stunts in it.

Ah, I know the one you mean. You couldn't get away with that now. One of the joys of filmmaking then was seeing how far you could go; sitting back in your chair and watching a real stunt take place right there in front of you; a real person in a real car at real speed on a real street; driving a car into a store-front window, and you walk over to the wreckage and you look inside to see if Charlie Bronson is still alive (*laughs*).

He was a tough man. The real deal.

On the last day of shooting *The Stone Killer*, he said to me: "What are we doing next?" I'd got a script called *Death Wish*. I'd had it for a few years. I said: "I've got a script about a guy whose wife and daughter get mugged and he goes out and shoots the muggers."
"I'd like to do that," he said.
"Make the movie?"
"No. Shoot muggers." (*laughs*)

When the definitive histories of cinema are written, Death Wish will be written up as The Most Talked About Film of 1974. People who have seen it can say that they liked it, and they can say they didn't like it. But no film historian can deny it got the country talking.

The Mechanic, Italian poster

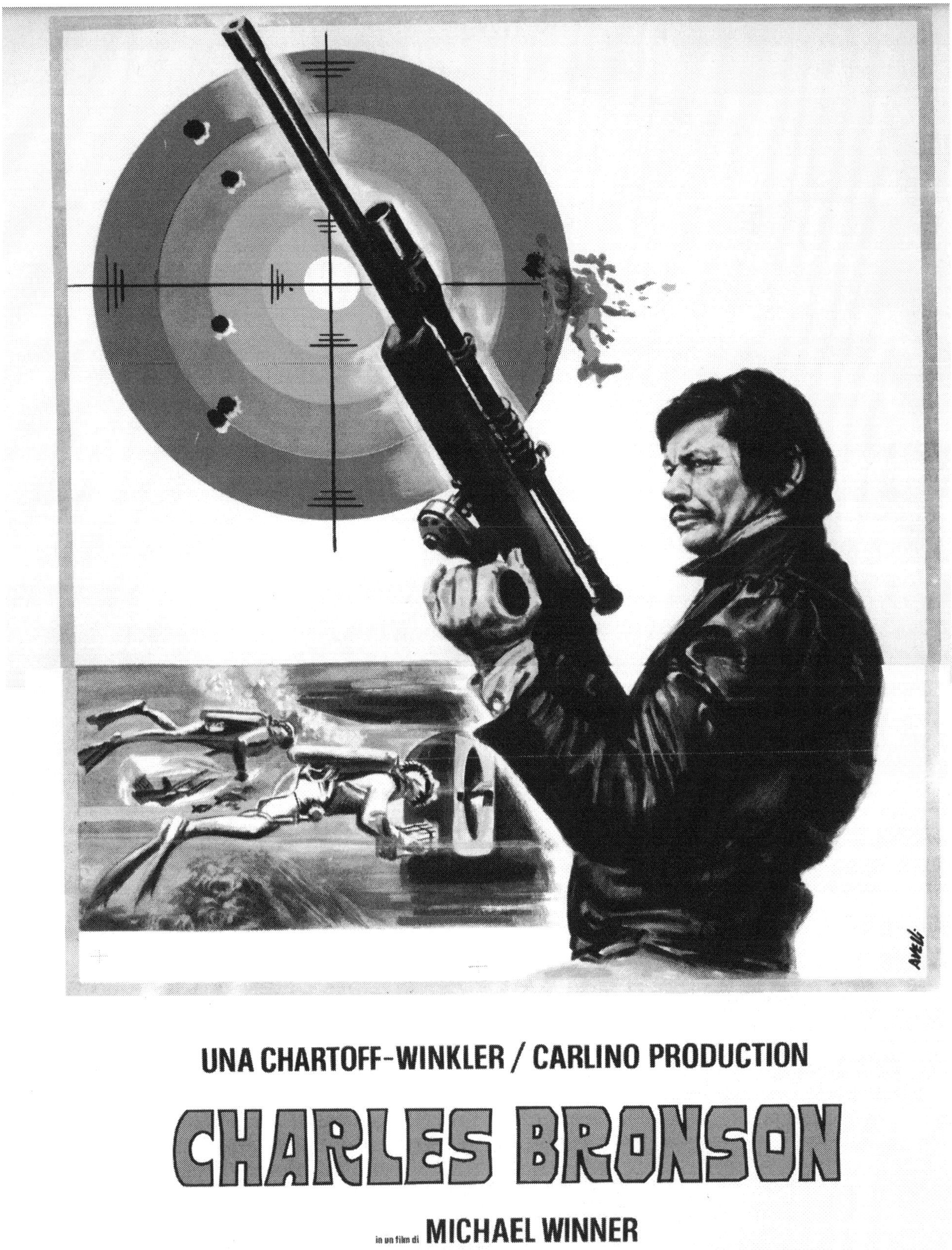

In America they lecture about it in universities. It was a watershed film. Nobody would make a film where the hero shot other citizens. When I was told I couldn't do it, I said, John Wayne does it in The West. "Ah, but that's The West," they said, "That's history." And for three years every studio in America turned it down. The other thing [they had] against making the film was having the word 'Death' in the title. It was totally unacceptable. Films with 'Death' in the title flopped. Dino De Laurentiis told me to change it. He said: "You cannot call it *Death Wish*". I was sitting here, in this house, I have a cinema here and I used to the edit the films here, and I screened the film. Up on the screen came the title *The Sidewalk Vigilante*. They'd changed it! I rang Dino and I told him that *I'd* got the film and *he* hadn't, and that it was coming over to *him* with the title *Death Wish*. End of story.

I bet he gave it a wild title in Italy?

In France it was called *Le Justicier dans la Ville*. The Vigilante in the City. In Germany is was called *Ein Mann sieht rot*. A Man Sees Red. They loved it in Germany [where it became one of the ten biggest earners of all-time]. They loved it everywhere!

Dino was a character wasn't he? He persuaded the Italian government to move the Southern border a few miles North so he could get 'Southern' grants to finance his film studios, Dinocittà!

(*laughs*) I didn't know that! That's marvellous!

Death Wish is a film full of surprises from the opening scene, which you mentioned, the Hawaiian beach, the beautiful red sunsets, and Bronson in his swimming trunks à la Burt Lancaster in From Here to Eternity. Then there is the supporting cast, Jeff Goldblum, Olympia Dukakis...

Christopher Walken. Was in he it? No, he was in the next one.

Christopher Guest, of This is Spinal Tap is in it.

It was Jeff Goldblum's first film. Paramount told me I mustn't have too many black muggers because I'd be thought of as racist. I said: "That is a racist remark. You're saying that blacks like their own muggers. They *don't* like their own muggers! Blacks are mugged by blacks more than anybody else." At that time, more than 95% of muggings in New York were carried out by Hispanics or blacks. And mostly in their own neighbourhoods. I'd never held auditions before in my life, but I held auditions for the muggers. The actors came in, in groups of six, and had to rape a chair (*laughs*). Jeff Goldblum was *fantastic*! And totally unknown. I said to Paramount: "Don't worry fellas, I've got you a Jewish mugger, no one will object if the mugger is a Jew." Goldblum was a nice fellow. I used him again in *The Sentinel* (1977). Vincent Gardenia, who played the police chief, was a great actor.

I've looked through the Academy Award lists of that year and I was surprised Gardenia's name isn't on it. What went wrong there?

Terrible. He should have been nominated. It was a career best performance. I said to Vince at the start of the film: "Vince, in this picture you've got a cold. You are always sneezing and using a spray." Which he loved of course. He died very young too. He was in the second *Death Wish* and he was in *Firepower*.

One of the things I like about Death Wish is that you see black people in positive roles long before the advent of positive discrimination. The officer assigned to Bronson's case is a fine professional black man; the 'hat pin' lady who beats off a mugger, and in doing so revives community spirit, is black, and it's all done without condescension, these are real people, and it done without compromising the realism of the setting. The community looks real. I think you are aided in this by Herbie Hancock's score which almost echoes the music of the streets and which links the film to the blaxploitation genre that was popular at the time, movies like Shaft.

His score was *outstanding!* I was lucky to get him.

On Death Wish 2, you scored another musical scoop by securing the services of Jimmy Page. His first work on leaving Led Zeppelin.

Jimmy Page is my neighbour. He wrote a wonderful score. We used the same music on *Death Wish 3*. I recut it myself for what we call the rough dub, and I said: "Jimmy, I've re-cut your music and put in a few pings and things to smooth over the gaps and it fits the second movie just as well! You can have the credit and you don't have to do anything." He got a fee.

A copy sold on ebay last week for $380.

Which one?

The soundtrack to Death Wish 2.

I've got about a dozen of them upstairs in a cupboard. The old disc. LP. There's a saying that every film is a great success until it's released. You watch your film. You cry. You love it. You *know* it's going to be a success. The film comes out and it's a disaster. *Death Wish* is the only film I made which I didn't think was going to be a success. It was so unlike any Bronson film I had ever done. There is no real action. There are no car chases. It is winter. The deaths are quite quick. The project was originally developed by United Artists who were thrilled when they sold it to Dino because they didn't think it would earn its script money back! I was in Dino's office the day the film opened. At one o'clock the phone rang. It was the manager of the 83rd Street East. He asked for: "Mr. De Laurentiis". I said: "He's not here." He said: "Who am I talking to?" "Michael Winner. The Director of the picture." He said: "Mr. Winner, I can tell you. The theatre is full!" "What do you mean? It's only one o'clock." "It is *full!* We have not seen anything like this since *The Godfather*! They've all come and put their umbrellas and brief cases in the cloakroom and they are all in the cinema." Why should that film be full? A good actor, some good notices, but nothing prepared us for the response. Why was the theatre full?

Its success was repeated here. It broke the all-time box-office record at the Paramount cinema in London. I think part of its appeal is that Bronson isn't playing a superman, he's playing an ordinary Joe. He's half the size of the officer assigned to his case. He runs away after the first acts of violence, then we see his character grow in confidence. I love the scene where he has painted his flat in bold colours and is playing jazz.

I'm glad you noticed that. It's a funny scene. "We can't grieve forever."

It's a very clever film. It could be read as 'a call to arms' and it can be watched as warning against it. You see the dangers of the 'death wish' of Bronson taking the law into his own hands. He gets injured in the last two 'attacks'.

Firepower was going to be made with Charlie Bronson in the Coburn role, but he didn't want to play alongside Sophia Loren. He was too insecure to have a big leading lady. Bless him. We had them both in. We all shook hands at Cannes and Lew Grade announced the film. But I knew Charlie would walk. I'd known him for twenty years and I knew he'd walk and he did. Why? Because he wanted to.

He would have been great, but with O.J. already providing the muscle, Coburn brings something different. It is an interesting film. There is the doppelganger theme you later exploit in Bullseye!, in which you had Roger Moore and Michael Caine playing doubles. In Firepower, James Coburn plays two roles. And, of course, there's Sophia Loren. A real woman.

And let me tell you, the most professional actress. Sophia's a *wonderful* person. Fan-tastic! *Firepower* was originally a *Dirty Harry* sequel for Warners. Three had been written and Clint chose the one he wanted. Warners gave the script to me. They then didn't make it. Carlo Ponti wanted a film for Sophia. I went to see her in Paris. I told her that

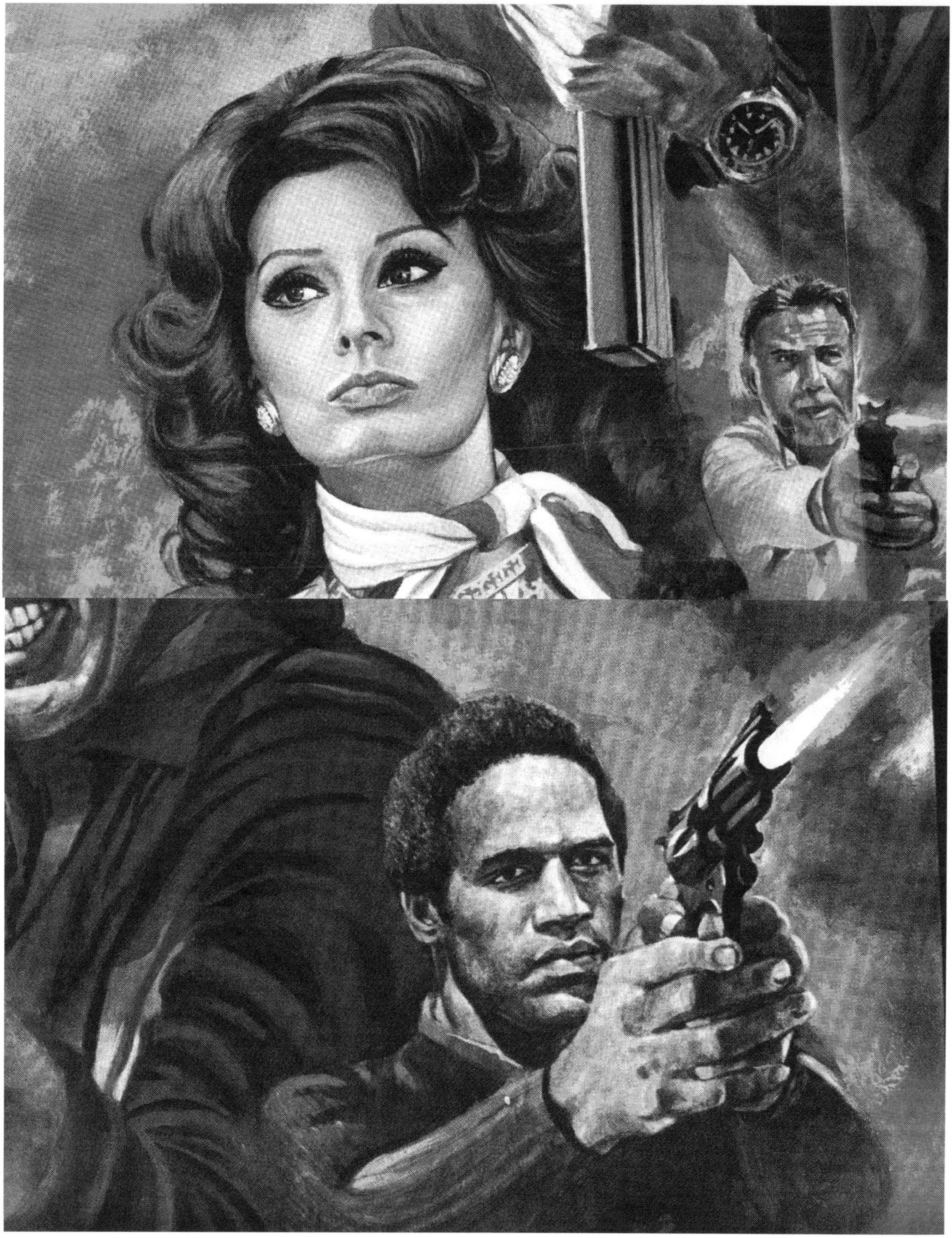

German poster art for *Firepower.* Loren. O.J. and ... is that Eli Wallach?

the part is a jet black Martinique lady with seven lines. She said: "Oh.". Then I said: "But Sophie, in five weeks time, she'll be white and Italian and the star of the picture." We'll work out exactly what we need to do. Which massively changed the film, of course. I had Wilson rewrite it.

Based again on The Third Man, doctored drugs.

Exactly. It was a great fun film to make. We had Eli Wallach, George Grizzard, who was a very big American stage actor.

James Coburn; Jake la Motta.

Who saved my life.

[I'm kicking myself for not taking the bait and asking 'how'?] And O. J. Simpson who is very good in the film.

O.J.'s a very nice fellow. He was perfect in the role. I still like him, even after all the trouble.

I was surprised that his first public appearance after his 'troubles' was standing in front of your house, here, and shaking your hand in front of the world's press.

He's a friend. I always stand by my friends. And he swears he's innocent. He was invited over to speak at the Oxford Union. He rang me up. I said: "Hello, O. J. I haven't heard from you for a while. What have you up to?" (*laughs*).

Firepower has a nice tongue in cheek quality. Sophia Loren goes through literally dozens of costumes. I like the scene where you play on that, when Coburn comes into her room, says he has been shopping, and gives her a designer dress to wear for the next scene, in a casino.

You watch *Hannibal Brooks*, Oliver has a bag this big (*tiny*). And it is full of ropes, stakes, mallets. There is no way all that could fit in his bag! You can get away with almost anything.

I watch Firepower, and I see the glamour, the wit, the action scenes with full-size helicopters and boats, an ingenious plot, real plot twists, believable characters, I see all that is missing from the recent Bond films. I'm surprised you haven't been given the call.

One of my many mistakes is turning down a Bond film. In 1972 I was asked if I would be interested in doing a Bond film, which is close to an offer isn't it? And I said 'No'. What lunacy came over me? I'd still be doing them! I turned down *The Prime of Miss Jean Brodie*, *The French Connection*, and the remake of *King Kong*, which was a hit picture even though it wasn't a great movie.

I enjoyed it. I like the music score for Firepower.

Gato Barbieri. Very famous saxophonist. Amazing.

Bertolucci's man [he scored Last Tango in Paris].

Did you see *The Wicked Lady*?

Only on television and it is always cut. I read in the papers that the censor had banned it to everyone under 18 and was still trying to cut it! You made him back down by naming and shaming him and getting other directors to sign their name to your complaint.

Yes. James Ferman. A failed filmmaker with nothing better to do than to damage other people's films and property. Lindsay Anderson helped me out with that one. [With the campaign to stop the senseless censoring of *The Wicked Lady*]. Schlesinger. Everyone signed the letter. Everyone! The censor had got too big for his boots. It got so bad he would cut things just because he thought he could get away with it. I've got a file this big [*very big*]. It got to the stage where I started to keep transcripts of my conversations with the censors. I thought I had to keep a record because I couldn't believe what I was hearing.

Such as?

Fuses! That was one. On *Firepower*, James Ferman said we had to cut the close-up of a fuse. I said: "James, there have been close-ups of fuses on fire in hundreds of films. Thousands! There were *three* in *The Big Sleep*! and you didn't cut that!

And one in every other Tom and Jerry cartoon.

Exactly.

Wasn't it whips in The Wicked Lady that upset him?

He wasn't upset. He was just trying it on. I like that film. It's a lot of fun. Funnily enough it got rave reviews in England. Very camp. It's got a lot of nudity in it. It was good fun. Just a romp.

But very well lit.

Very well lit by Jack Cardiff.

I love all the work he did from Michael Powell onwards. His colour work certainly helped to put English cinema on the world stage.

Powell lived opposite me. The Director's Guild have put a plaque on the house. For the music, Tony Banks of Genesis wrote a classical score. I thought he did it bloody well.

Of your later work, I did like the TV thing you did about The Diary of Jack The Ripper (1993). It really did scare me. I tuned in thinking I'd give it ten minutes and ended up watching it through and then trying to sleep with the lights on.

Oh, that was good. We've done a couple.

I think A Chorus of Disapproval is the best of the later films. It's a film of a play, but it's more like a film about a theatre group in a very real town than a film of a play.

Alan Ayckbourn helped us find the locations. We drove around everywhere and we got it exactly right. The ending of the film is more realistic and more upbeat. It's an improvement on the play. We had Jeremy Irons, who is excellent in the film, and Anthony Hopkins, who is absolutely outstanding. I was very lucky to get them. I made it just before they both became very big stars.

One big star we've not talked about is Robert Mitchum, perfectly cast as Marlowe in The Big Sleep.

Bob Mitchum is a real gentleman. A real gent. A very intelligent man. When he's not filming he's always got his glasses on and his head in a book. Poetry. Classics. He's like a Midwestern professor. A terrific guy, and what an actor!

The Big Sleep is a big, good-looking film; beautiful cars, great locations. I liked seeing Chandler's name above the title and the fact you returned to his original book and used much of his original dialogue.

It was Chandler's dialogue. Raymond Chandler was educated in England, at Dulwich College. His writing is like poetry. When I took the script to Jimmy Stewart, he read it and said: "I can't do this. I can say these lines. It's so English. So aristocratic." I said: "It's from the book, Jimmy. It's Chandler, line for line."

It was a rare pleasure to see an American source transposed to an English setting, a reversal of what often happens, and it worked well, again, because the locations were perfect. I love the shot that frames the film. The shot through the car window. We are driven to the Colonel's country mansion at the start of the film and we are driven away from it at the end. It sets the mood and the tempo and, of course, the locale.

We got some great locations and a great cast.

Sylvia Miles, whom you worked with on The Sentinel, [a film which had a big influence on the genre re-defining films of Dario Argento and Lucio Fulci] was at the Edinburgh Festival last year. When asked to name her favourite director, she said: "Michael Winner because he always treated me like a lady. Every morning he sent a beautiful car to collect me. He always ensured that I arrived in style."

Sylvia Miles was terrific. I have worked with all the big names. Richard Dreyfuss is in that one. He was looking for an apartment to rent and he came to look at the one we were filming in. I said: "Richard, you're obviously desperate to be in the film. Go over there and talk to Carol and I'll put you in it."

We finished the afternoon talking about English illustrators. Michael Winner had a pre-eminent collection of original artwork including Pooh drawings by E. H. Shepard and watercolours by Arthur Rackham, Lucie Attwell, W. Heath Robinson. In December 2012, he sold the collection at Sotheby's for exactly the cost of the first James Bond film. He died one month later.

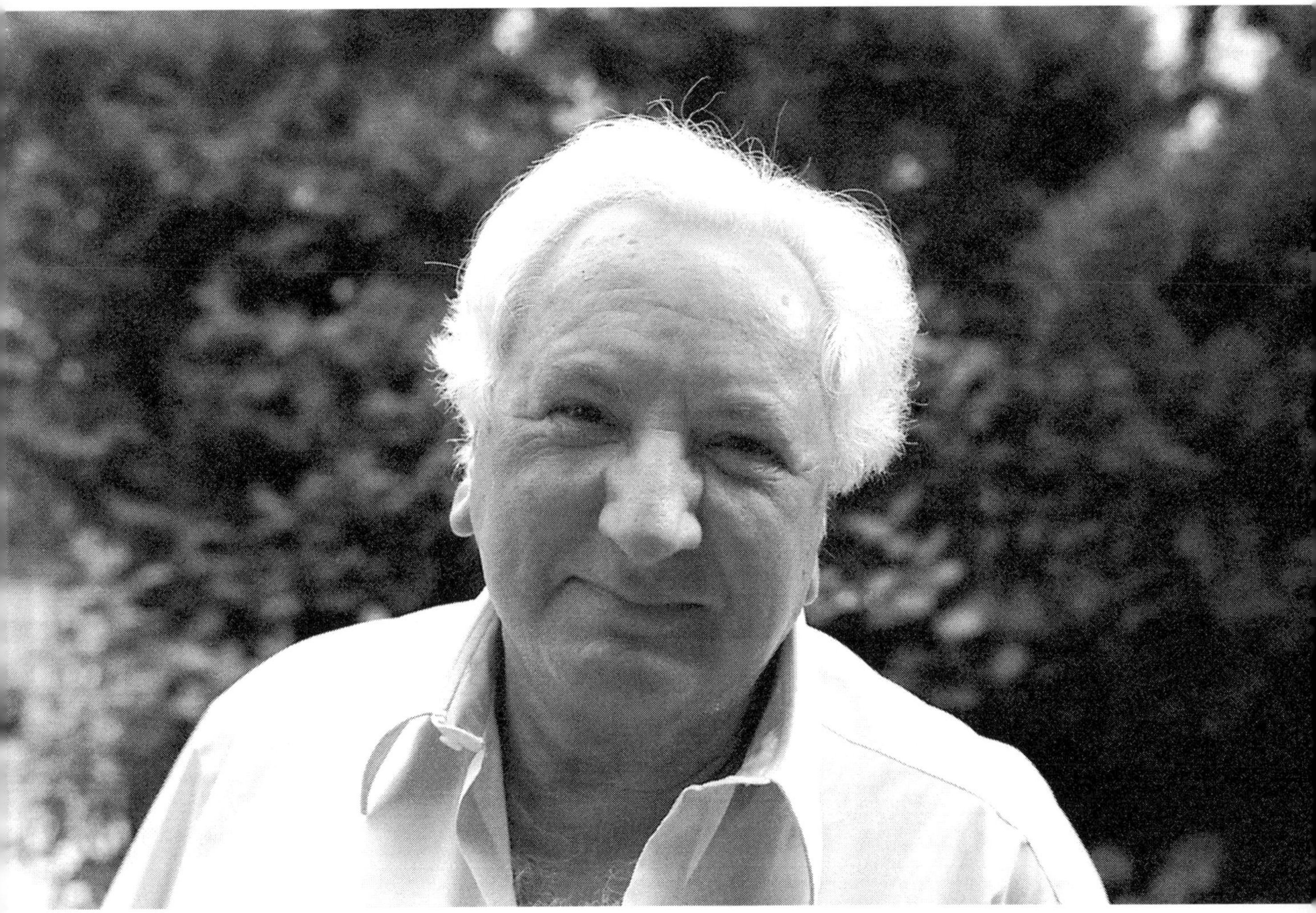

Michael Winner in the garden of his house in Kensington © Sutton

Michael Winner Biting Down On The Censor (who boasts about damaging every print of JAWS)

1.

THE ONE SECOND SHOT OF A FUSE BURNING THAT MR. JAMES FERMAN FELT COULD NOT BE SEEN UNLESS YOU WERE EIGHTEEN YEARS OLD OR OVER!

A transcript of a conversation of March 15th, 1979 concerning the film Firepower between Michael Winner (MW) and James Ferman (JF) concerning a one second shot of a fuse burning prior to a car being blown up. Such shots having been seen for all audiences in films and TV for years throughout the period of film, but not, apparently acceptable to British teen-agers!

JF: There's one problem which came up this afternoon which I think you can probably help us with, which is that we have had a lot of complaints about copyable crimes for teenagers, and we're a bit worried about the close-up of the fuse burning in the petrol tank. Before Coburn sets it alight and the man comes back from pursuing the others.

Could you take away the close-up of the fuse burning?

MW: James, I can't believe what I'm hearing, this I really cannot believe! Everybody knows that you can set light to a petrol tank; it is quite obvious that he sets light to it with a fuse. What is the difference whether it's in close-up or not? We have sixty prints of this picture, are we supposed to throw away sixty prints?

JF: Why do you have to throw them away, just cut it.

MW: So the sound has a great jerk in it and doesn't match?

JF: Jaws went out in this country with 250 prints and five frames were cut out of when Robert Shaw was eaten in to, out of every single print.

MW: What was that an A?

JF: That was an A, yes.

MW: Jaws was an A and this (Firepower) is an AA?

JF: Yeah.

MW: Do you not find that odd?

JF: There are things in this quite different from men fighting beasts -

MW: James, please, I accept the AA without any protest of any kind, but really I'm not going to cut a shot of a fuse burning, what does it get if the fuse burning is in? An X? Are you telling me that if that shot stays in, it's an X?! I'll make an issue of that, publicly.

JF: You will? I see.

Continued

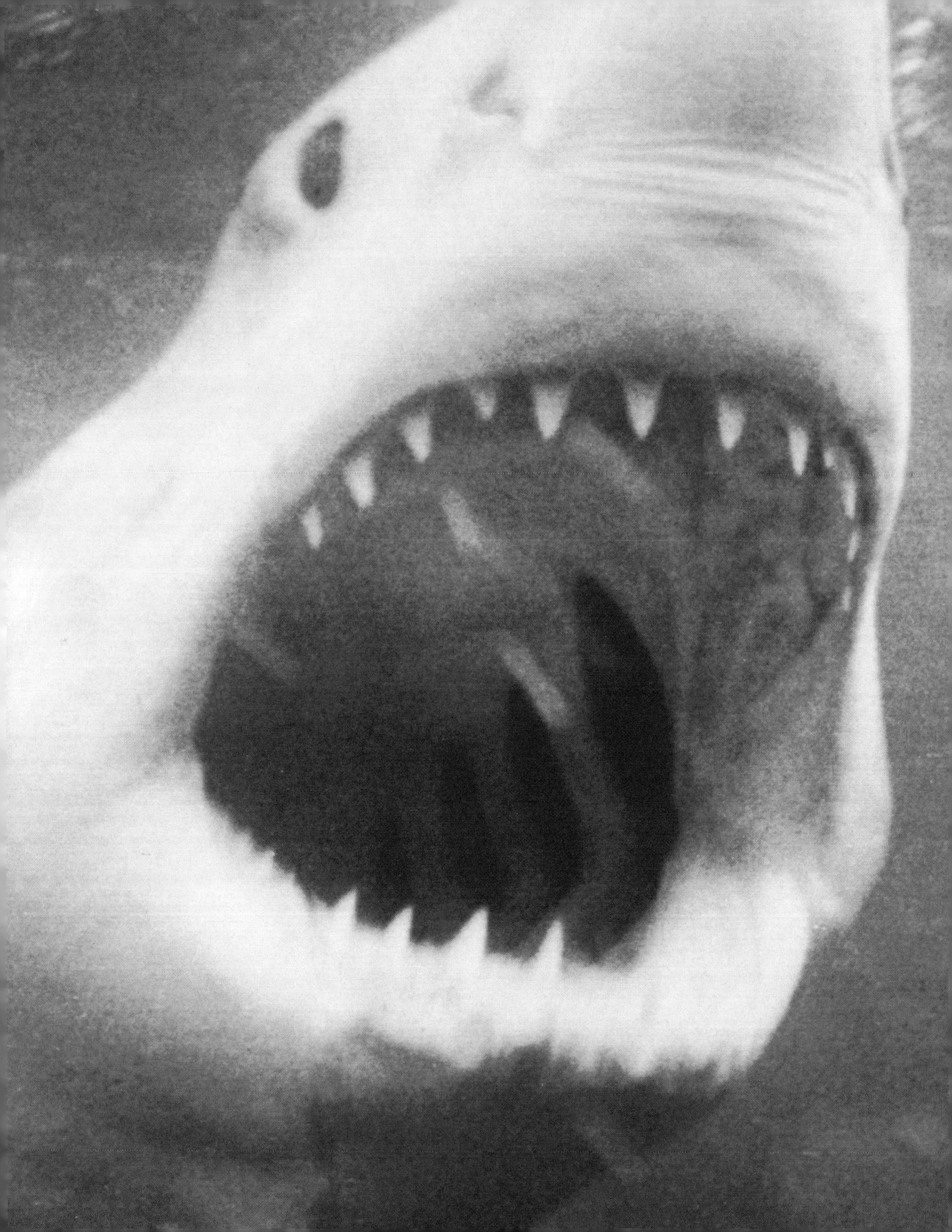

FUSE BURNING 2.

JF: You don't think you're putting ideas in the minds of teen-agers?

MW: No more with an extra shot of a fuse than without, and I think everybody knows when they see firebombs on television and everything else that you can set fire to anything.

JF: Well we talked - that's why we -

MW: I don't think I'm putting things in the minds of teen-agers, definitely not. And certainly not by a close up of the shot. And I don't think with anything else, I mean a teenager can copy anything they see, and this sequence -

we had exactly the same sequence in The Big Sleep, one hundred per cent the same, except it wasn't a burning fuse which is a mechanical device, it was a burning handkerchief, and there were close-ups, three of them, of the burning handkerchief making its way toward the petrol tank of the car - I was not requested to take those out!

JF: I didn't see that.

MW: And there were three of them in The Big Sleep and the sequence lasts longer.

JF: I see, well, I'll...I'll your word on that. I'll tell Alan (the Distributor) he can advertise it AA.

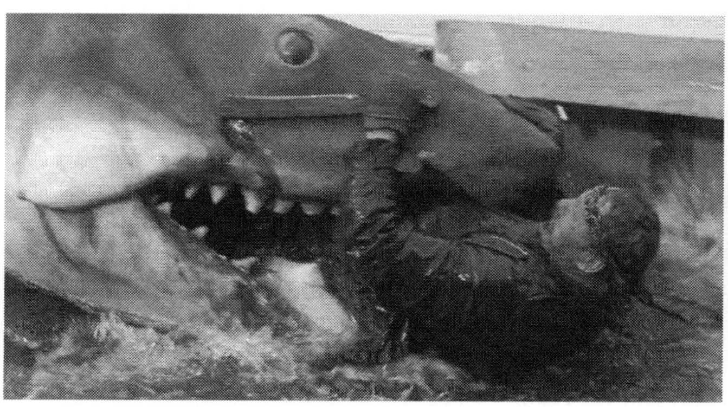

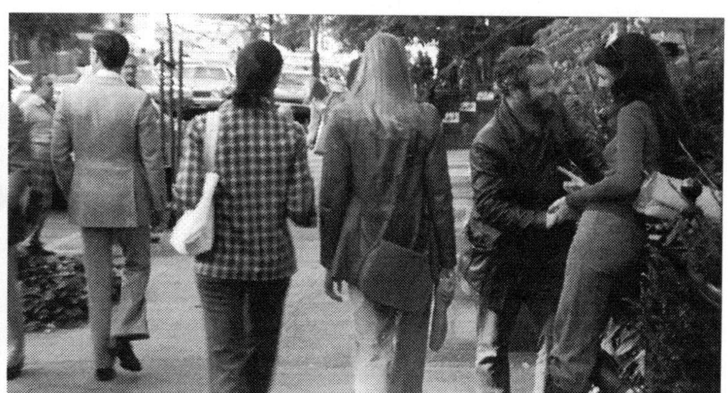

The Sentinel

Michael Winner's Film Reviews

from Films and Filming Magazine (January to July 1956)

Night of the Hunter - With abundant enthusiasm, Charles Laughton ventures into film direction and gives us a weird, haunting picture, about a sex-mad preacher. Unlike most of his fellow-actors who have recently taken a turn behind the camera, Mr. Laughton has something of real worth to offer. He coaxes an enthralling performance from Robert Mitchum, has some of the finest black-and-white photo-graphy I have ever seen and, if that were not a feast, re-introduces Lillian Gish, that great artist of the silent days. Regrettably he seems so busy with new effects that he forgets these are only a means to an end. Laughton's tricks fail at times to live up to their possibilities because he lets his story wander from climax to climax - until it twists round and stabs itself in the back.

The plot is the well-worn one of a man marrying for money, and then killing the missus. In this case the cash is hidden in a child's doll, so Mitchum, as Preacher Powell, has to pursue the offspring until the child reaches the invisible arms of Lillian Gish, as a widow with a big heart and a mania for biblical stories. Miss Gish makes a competent supporting actress, Robert Mitchum a bestially powerful villain, and the two children (Billy Chapin & Sally Jane Bruce) are not too precocious to strain our affections. Miss Shelley Winters, as Ma, is knocked-off about the end of reel two, an accomplishment at which she is becoming thoroughly polished.

Les Clandestines - French call-girls, if we are to believe director Raoul Andre, go about under the names of rare books. This is only one of the not very startling disclosures which are strung together to make this tawdry French thriller about a favourite theme. In this case the man-behind-the-women, turns out to be Alex D'Arcy who has been much better served by Hollywood. The hero, a jail-bird who takes an unconscionably long time to unearth the racket, behaves with a naiveté that would have any self-respecting Frenchman squirming in his cinema seat.

Heidi and Peter - are a couple of children living in a small Swiss village. Some of their insignificant exploits have been chronicled by Director Franz Schnyder to make a film with little appeal to the adult filmgoer. The children, equipped with dubbed American accents, live in a world of pantomime characters and crudely planned incidents devoid of charm or sensitivity. Even the Eastman colour photography is wasted on too many indoor shots instead of concentrating on the scenic beauty of the Swiss mountains. The film will probably appeal immensely to children, its complete lack of subtlety being an advantage for them. Best performance from an all-Swiss cast comes from Theo Lingren as a comic butler. The rest of the characters: crippled rich girls, kindly grandfathers, frustrated nannies, benign schoolmasters, all inhabit a world where adults tread at risk of grave boredom.

Les Grandes Manoeuvres - In order to win a bet, a soldier attempts to seduce a woman; then he falls in love with her. Around this slender situation René Clair has made a slender film. He is too much a master of the cinema for it to be without its good points, but these are regrettably far too few. Clair has wavered between characters and caricatures. The result is that it is hard to feel sympathy for any of his people. *Les Grandes Manoeuvres* - is a precise piece of filming, watched from afar by the audience: but unlike Clair's earlier film work, the comedy and situations are conventional and cold. Partly this is the fault of inadequate subtitles.
Described as a "dramatic comedy", Clair has tried too hard to inject drama into the plot. Gérard

Philipe is conventionally amorous as the philandering officer. Michèle Morgan as his quarry brings a depth to her part of a divorced woman which finds too little support from the other actors. There are some vicious cameos of gossiping provincial women by Lisa Delamare and Jacqueline Maillan. Jean Desailly is excellent as their suffering brother.

The Eastman colour photography flatters the dashing uniforms of the soldiers and the turn-of-the-century French settings, but, if anything, it also helps relegate the story to a fairy-tale level. In the end when M. Philipe, heartbroken and rejected, passes the closed windows of his ex-conquest, every possible variation on an overworked theme has been soundly explored. There remains a pleasant kaleidoscopic picture, which will do Clair no harm but I doubt if it will be remembered among his great contributions to the screen.

Davy Crockett - In his latest non-cartoon film Walt Disney serves a slice of comic-book American history with enough charm and polish to amuse everybody. Accept that *Davy Crockett* has no aspirations other than to chronicle, episodically, the not uninteresting adventures of America's favourite frontiersman, and the film can be easily enjoyed. A cast without stars brings America's past to the screen, headed by fur-capped Fess Parker moving laconically through the title role. All are extremely adequate at personifying such well-known names as Andrew Jackson, Jim Bowie, and George Russell. As can be expected from Disney, the film is pictorially beautiful with picture-book backgrounds of Tennessee, Texas, and old-time Washington. There is some pleasant music, well-integrated animation and brisk direction from Norman Foster. All in all a delightful offering of a tale of considerable novelty to most Englishmen.

Ransom! - Directed by Alex Segal. Starring Glenn Ford. A boy is kidnapped. As a thriller the film is excellent. As a vicious scrutiny of people under pressure it is brilliant.

Papa, Mama, The Maid and I (*Papa, maman, la bonne et moi*): In spite of a rather precious title this bright little comedy turns out to be one of the most unpretentious joys to come out of France for some time. The story itself is a simple chronicle of events in a typical middle-class French family: but Mrs. Dale, French version, is far from cloying. Director J. P. Le Chanois has treated his incidents with a slick, lithe touch, and the film bounces gaily from slapstick to farce, and then to moments of seriousness, all with effervescent ease. Robert Lamoreux is the young man of the family with love-troubles, has an engaging naturalness and a subtle sense of comedy. Fernand Ladoux, as the father, has the most difficult part, requiring at times considerable dramatic ability, and he handles it with ease. Gaby Morlay is similarly excellent as mother, and Nicole Courcel completes the quartet as the maid who has her own idea of her position in the household.

Charley Moon - The old story of a local boy who makes good is dragged out again as a star vehicle for comedian Max Bygraves. The only novelty is that after achieving theatrical fame Mr. Bygraves decides he was better off as a local boy, and wanders back blissfully into a country sunset. Packed into this pleasant, fatuous piece of back-stage hokum is every possible conventional situation and character. There in abundance are affected actresses, Jewish agents, cockney barrow-boys, comic vicars, loud-mouthed sergeant-majors, and tear-jerking children. Mr. Bygraves passes cheerfully through, seemingly unaware of the complete pointlessness of it all. By current British standards, *Charley Moon* is as bright and cheerful as can be expected. Yet close examination of its content reveals how very dreary some of our films have become. Primarily they are dominated by a complete lack of reality or cohesion. Without the strong hand of direction they wander from situation to situation until they finally stop. They are stocked with caricatures instead of *people.*

Lost among the lethargy is the talent of some undoubtedly excellent performers. Dennis Price, as a theatrical ham, is able to over-act consistently and entertainingly throughout his role, and similarly Lou Jacobi, Viv Wise, and Florence Desmond have their moments. Anyone attempting to appear human in the general air of intimate-revue parody is doomed to failure. Thus Mr. Bygraves, too often seeming to mirror Danny Kaye anyway, doesn't stand a chance among the small-part melodramatic scene-stealers, or the inconsequential meanderings of a banal plot.

The Scarlet Hour - With a flourish of subdued trumpets, Paramount introduces two newcomers to star billing in its new Vistavision thriller. They are Carol Ohmart and Tom Tryon who play as neurotic a pair of back-stairs lovers as one could hope to find. Both are competent, and that is really all that can be said of them. The film itself is directed by Michael Curtiz with less skill than he has shown in the past. It is still quite enjoyable, even though the title, which may have had some relevance for the original book, has certainly lost it on celluloid. The plot is a clever one - a glorious mix-up of murder, robbery, romance and secrecy - even though it does fall down rather weakly at the end. The film lacks the personality that made such offerings more than acceptable in the Cagney-Bogart-Lorre-Greenstreet era of mysteries. Today the characters merely fit neatly and uninterestingly into the development of the story, and the shallowness detracts considerably from what could have been a first-rate melodrama.

The Feminine Touch - Having dug endless humour from the medical profession, the British film industry now turns again to dramatise it with this pathetic piece of banal film-making. Gathered for a course for prospective nurses are a bunch of starlets whose effect on this patient was fatal. Directed by Pat Jackson in a series of ill-chosen incidents, the film limps along until it dies quietly under its own anaesthetic. Two compensations filter through. One is Delphi Lawrence as Nurse Pat. Miss Lawrence, with a part as ill-written as the rest, comes through with no little credit. So does veteran Diana Wynyard as the hospital matron. Poor Miss Wynyard appears only three times. Among the candidates for euthanasia are Belinda Lee, George Baker, Adrienne Corri, and Mandy, who keep the lamp burning low.

Twelfth Night - It is difficult enough to make filmic Shakespeare acceptable to English audiences in their native tongue. To distribute a film in which the poetry becomes incomprehensible Russian noises, leaving the original words in crude misspelt subtitles, is a questionable venture. True, this Russian *Twelfth Night* has its curiosity value: but curiosity is satisfied well before the end of 90 minutes. For the rest of the time English audiences must content themselves with some spasmodically worthwhile photography, and suffer the unbearably heavy-handed production of Shakespeare's comedy. Director Y. Fried sets his scene in a sort of Grecian Isle holding a few old ruins which seem to signify a town, and a large castle where lives Olivia with her assorted hangers-on, all of whom would pass Shakespeare unrecognised as they are represented here. The actual story of *Twelfth Night* is not ideally suited to the screen in the first place. It relies on the possibility of mistaking a boy for a woman and vice-versa. Popular as the dilemma may have been in Shakespearean England the treatment it is given in modern-day Russia leaves the love scenes embarrassing and the comedy crude and heavy-handed. All the performances are comparable to third-rate English repertory. This may be a style of acting open to different interpretation in Russia, but over here where subtlety has become the keynote of Shakespearean production, I cannot imagine the film being appreciated or enjoyed.

Smiley - In all their exhaustive foreign travels film-makers have seldom found anything more horrific than the inhabitants of the Australian Bush. Doing no end of disservice to the Australian emigration department, director Anthony Kimmins uncovers an unhappy band of cosmopolitan actors involved in a garish, maudlin story. Against an unattractive background of wooden huts and barbed wire, an even more unattractive tale painfully unwinds itself with the subtlety of a kangaroo on hot bricks. Centre-piece of this band of the doomed is a small boy called Smiley who is saving up to buy a bicycle. With an abundance of childish bonhomie evoked by careful direction, he scrounges around the village in which live the intimate revue characters of Australia. There is the Rev. Ralph Richardson rumbling benignly through his part in an ancient car. With his theological teachings obviously halted at the Old Testament he screams: "Jehovah be with you" at every convenient moment - and quite a few inconvenient ones as well. He ends up punching a young and hulking villain on the nose with miraculously knock-out force. Also around is Chip Rafferty, who has gone a long way since *The Overlanders*, and mostly, I felt in the wrong direction. In this case he is a police sergeant in love with the village school-mistress. John McCallum and a Chinaman called Chow Sing smuggle opium to the Aborigines in chocolate boxes. The whole thing is kept within the Commonwealth by a childish song called *Smiley* sung by zither-playing Shirley Abicair at the start and finish of the picture. It will doubtless all be very much appreciated by young children. Adults, however, are more likely to be Grumpy than Smiley.

John Holmstrom Collection

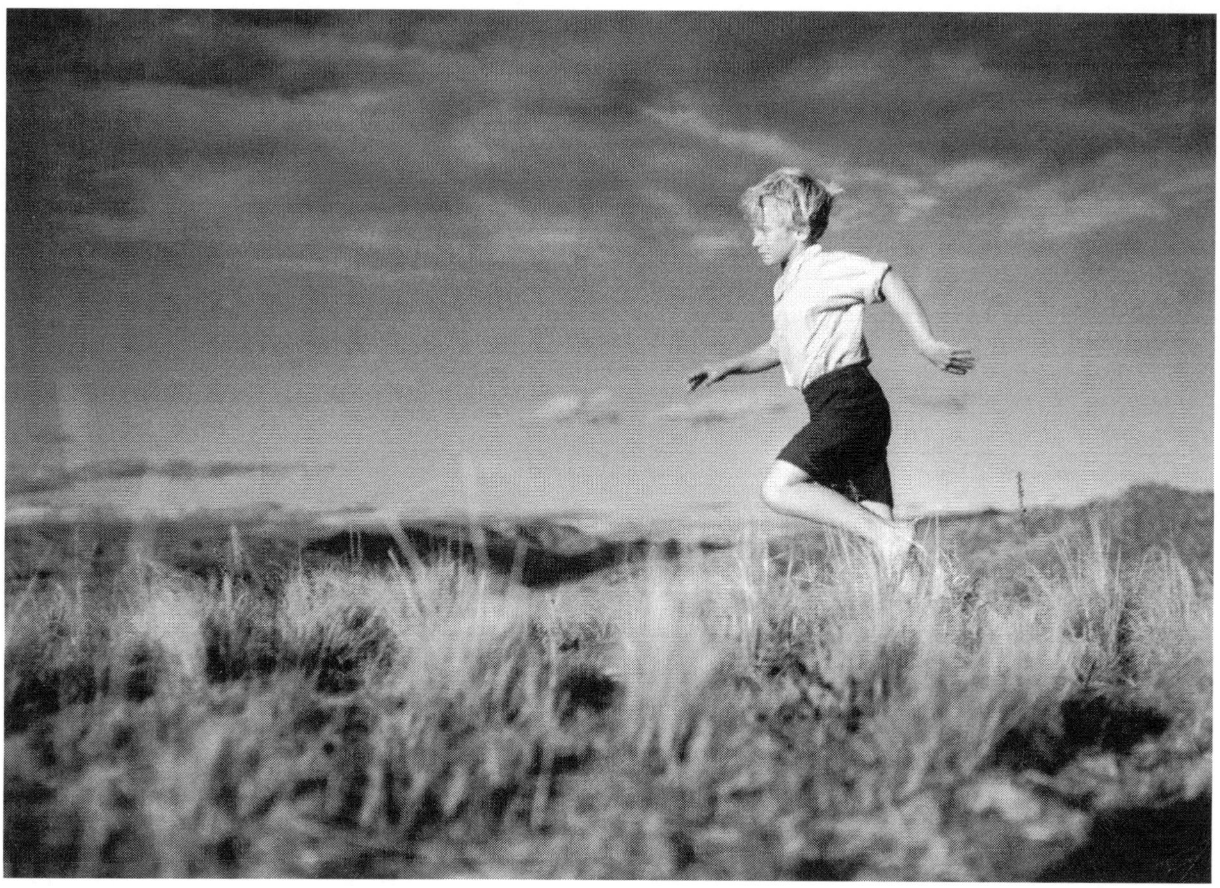

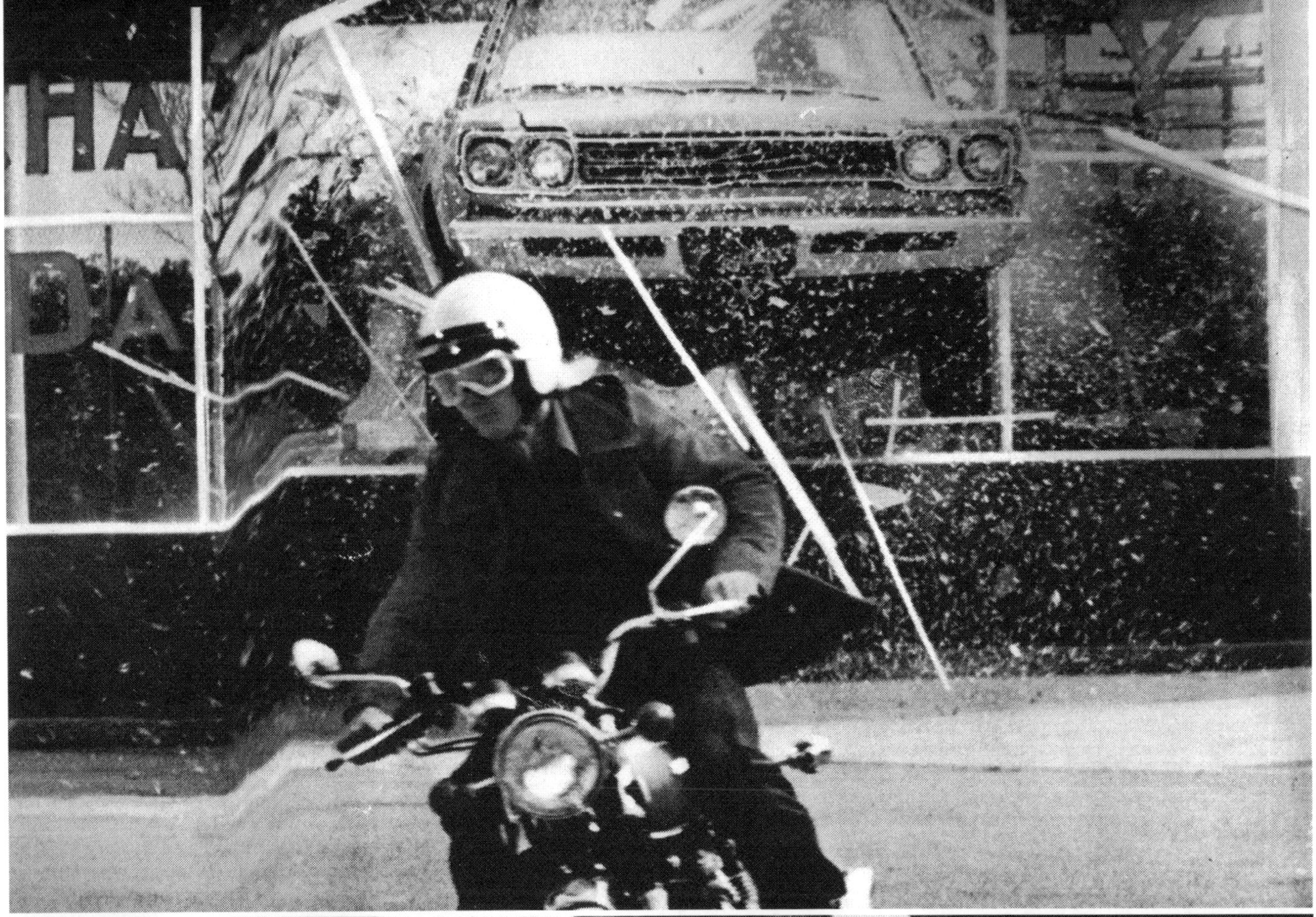

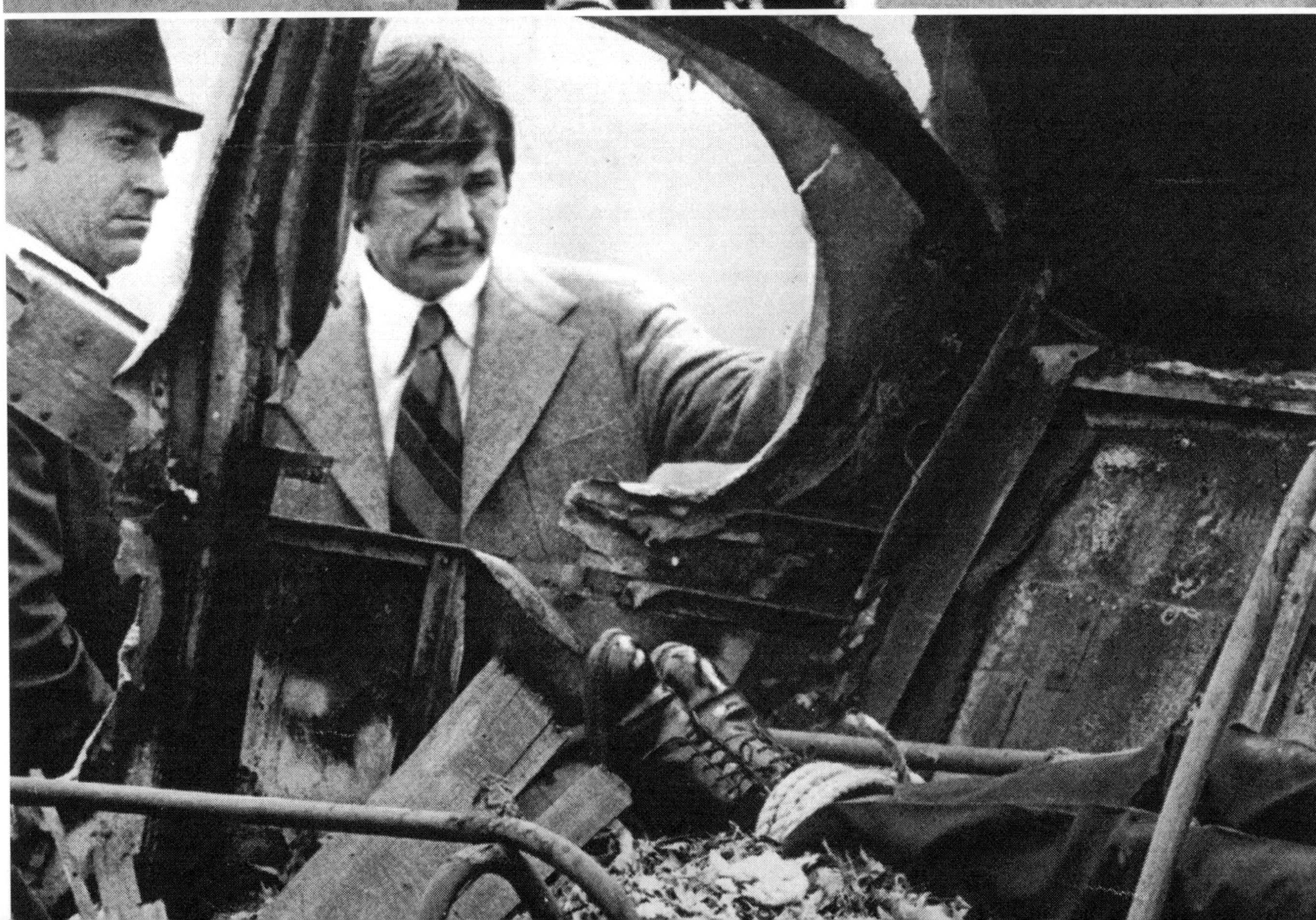

The Stone Killer Cuttings

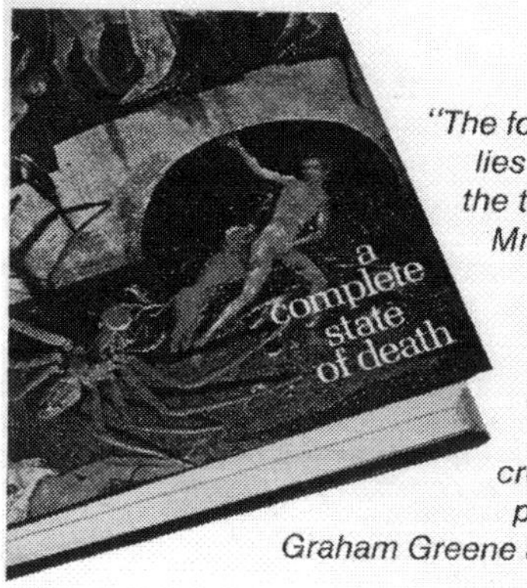

"The force of this brilliant book lies in the characterisation, the terse, electric dialogue. Mr. Gardner is the creator of Boysie Oakes, the bone-headed anti-Bond hero. But he has gone far beyond all that. He has created a real man and puts himself in the class of Graham Greene and Raymond Chandler."
SUNDAY MIRROR

"Derek Torry makes a power-packed debut, backed with a three-star plot...the taut tale should win friends for Torry."
DAILY MIRROR

"In the Greene class for sin-reeking mind-probing."
THE TIMES

"Cracking pace and high suspense."
THE EVENING NEWS

"John Gardner, the creator of Boysie Oakes, has switched to a straight thriller in "A complete state of death," with an equally memorable chief character, Detective Inspector Torry... the start of a new series? If so, it's a promising one."
DAILY TELEGRAPH

"All of it is done with realism, cold calm and colder humour, and works very well indeed."
THE SUNDAY TIMES

"Fast and Exciting."
THE OBSERVER

a complete state of death

To be produced by SCIMITAR FILMS · Screenplay by GERALD WILSON
From the book by JOHN GARDNER · Published by JONATHAN CAPE
A MICHAEL WINNER PRODUCTION FOR UNITED ARTISTS
United Artists

I liked Michael Winner's latest The Stone Killer very much indeed. There are hired assassins, ancient junkies, young creeps, down to a dwarf perched on a seedy hotel's registration desk. In such picturesque details, Winner is obviously recalling his predecessors in the genre, but I think he recalls them honourably. He has at least put a lot of favourite devices into a film that moves with great energy and with an overall economy. With a strange combination of vulgarity and technical elegance, a feeling for when to cut away from an action or a face – whether by accident or design – The Stone Killer keeps turning into exciting cinema, crude, often funny, and sometimes quite brilliantly idiomatic. It may come as close to inspired primitivism as we are likely to get in the movies these days.

Roger Greenspun, The New York Times, August 30th 1973.

This cop plays dirty!

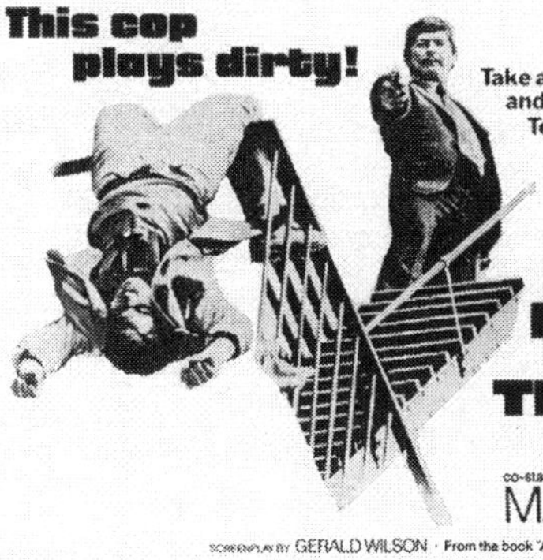

Take away his badge and he'd top the Ten Most Wanted list!

DINO DE LAURENTIIS Presents
CHARLES BRONSON
in a MICHAEL WINNER FILM
THE STONE KILLER X
co-starring
MARTIN BALSAM

SCREENPLAY BY GERALD WILSON · From the book 'A Complete State of Death' by John Gardner
PRODUCED AND DIRECTED BY MICHAEL WINNER From Columbia Pictures

FROM FEB. 21 ODEON LEICESTER SQ.
TELEPHONE: 930 6111
GENERAL RELEASE STARTS MARCH 24

BEATING THE MAJORS AT THEIR OWN GAME

By SUE CLARKE

BRITAIN'S Michael Winner has just returned from America where he has been directing "The Stone Killer" starring Charles Bronson. This is Winner's fifth film in just over two years, and his second financed on what he calls "the new route"—not by a major distributor.

Italian producer Dino de Laurentiis put up £1m. to finance "The Stone Killer" and, according to Winner, is already in profit even before the picture is complete. It has been sold to Columbia for most of the world, but excluded in big markets like Italy, Spain, Germany and Japan.

"Internationally, the American film still sells better than any other," says Winner. "Now continental promoters are turning to make American films in America and are beating the majors at their own game. Men like de Laurentiis and Robert Dorfmann move far quicker, they offer first class up-front deals, they sell territorially, and they don't carry enormous overheads.

"They are much more adaptable and they can work out of a telephone box. Like nomads they are used to pitching their tents in any country, which is what the film industry should do. It's very good for the majors to have this competition."

United Artists financed the preparation for "The Stone Killer" which has a screenplay by Gerald Wilson. But, says Winner, UA wanted to see the grosses on his "The Mechanic" before making a commitment to finance the new production. "The film made $10m. worldwide, but by then it was too late. De Laurentiis had already offered the £1m.

"We did the deal in a phone call. Then I went to Rome for a day because de Laurentiis said he wanted to look into my eyes. I came back with the £1m. to make the film.

"De Laurentiis is a financier, a producer and a distributor. He hasn't got time to sit around on the set—he is much more interested in what you will do next for him. Each time he appears he has a new script.

"He believes in getting a product he can sell and he is realistic about it. I found less corner-cutting on this film than any since the boom time. He has a totally positive attitude, and it's marvellous to work with a man who makes the decisions himself and doesn't have to answer to anyone but himself. He suggested I should edit the

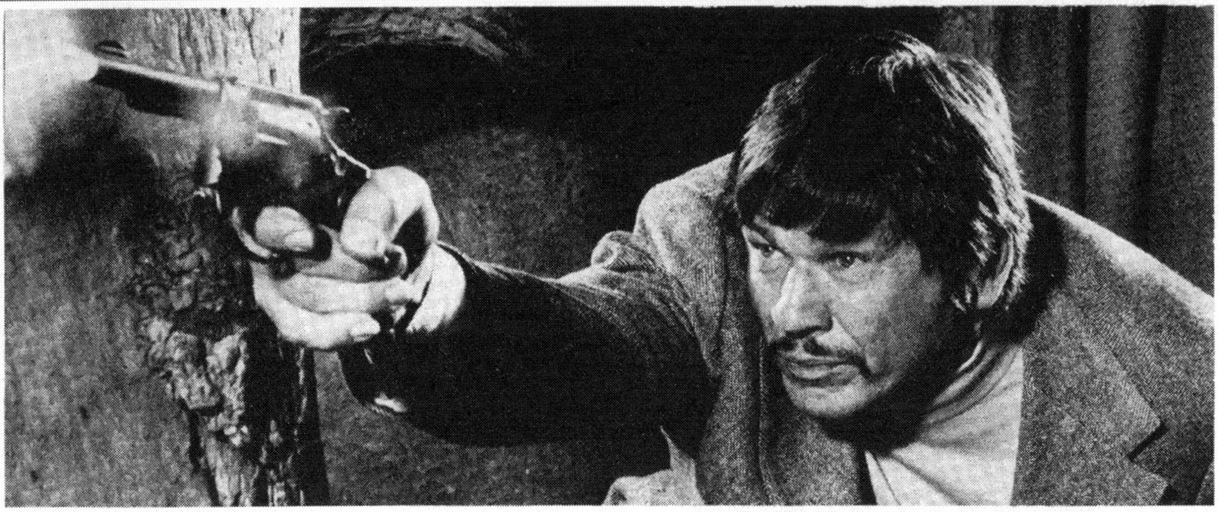

Charles Bronson in an action scene from "The Stone Killer"

picture at his cutting rooms in Rome, but I said I preferred to be in London. That's not a practical answer but he accepted it and I'm editing the film here."

"The Stone Killer" is Winner's third film with Charles Bronson, and Bronson also recently starred in the de Laurentiis production of "The Valachi Papers." Says Winner: "There are only eight or nine bankable stars—Steve McQueen and Dustin Hoffman are working for France's Robert Dorfmann, and Charles Bronson is working for de Laurentiis.

"An actor is sold on his scarcity value which is why prices still rise. Bronson is popular because he has chosen in his career to make films on a commercial basis whereas other stars like McQueen and Newman have tried to add art to their films. There is a very wise saying in Hollywood which is 'If you want art, don't muck about with movies. Buy a Picasso'."

While editing "The Stone Killer," Winner is working on two future projects. One is a whodunnit set in France which Gerald Wilson is scripting; the other is an American army comedy set in Austria which Elliot Baker is writing. "I want to do a subject where not everyone is dead at the end. I'd like to do a film here, but English subjects really don't sell well. It's very regrettable because I would much rather work here. I find Los Angeles an oppressive city to work in, very ugly and very dirty. There is a certain lack of spirit there. It's very ponderous and they take it all very seriously. But they're great workers, and don't care what hours they work or where. They are very highly paid but they earn it.

"Working in America you get fantastic co-operation. In New York they have the Jewish sense of humour and it's very easy to shoot there. You have terrible union problems, you're lumbered with additional staff and high wages, but you can film on Fifth Avenue at 11 am—we screeched our own police cars down the street. That's like stopping Piccadilly. Here you have to have a week's negotiations to get permission to put a generator on a parking meter.

"But it has always been considered rather vulgar to work hard in England. You must remember to show a gentlemanly restraint!"

'If you want art, don't muck about with movies. Buy a Picasso'

Michael Winner

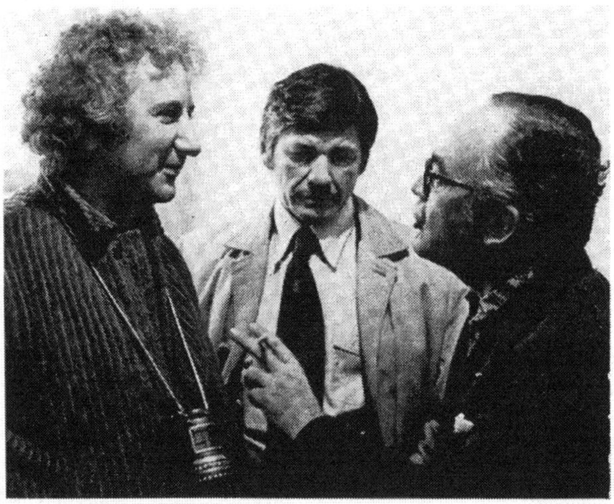

Michael Winner, left, on set with Dino de Laurentiis and Charles Bronson.

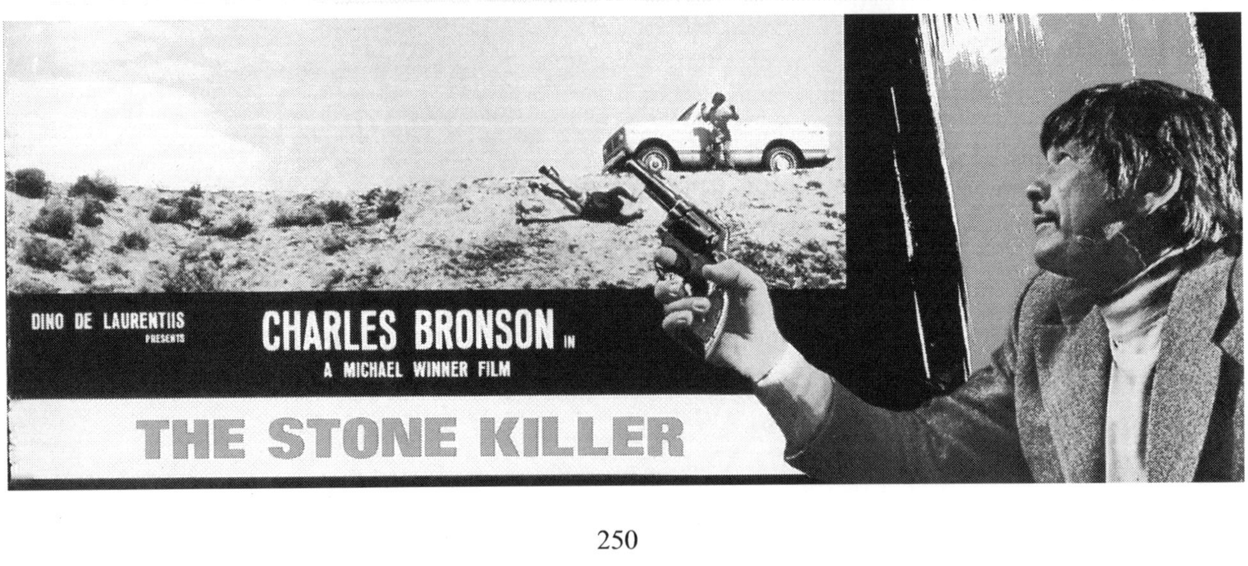

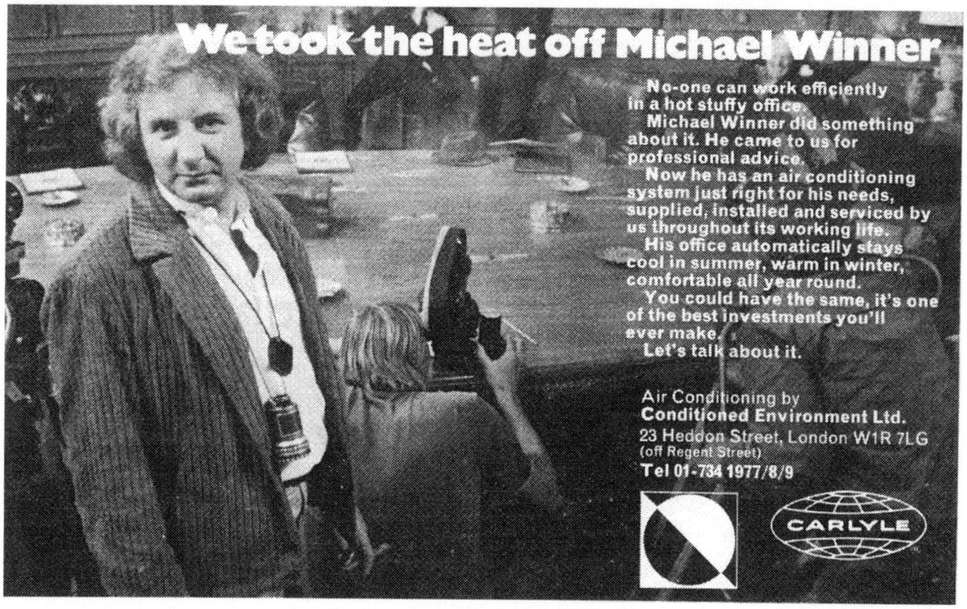

Though famed in his later years for a series of wildly popular "Calm down, dear" insurance commercials, that were referenced in the House of Commons by the Prime Minister, Winner's first print ad was in 1974.

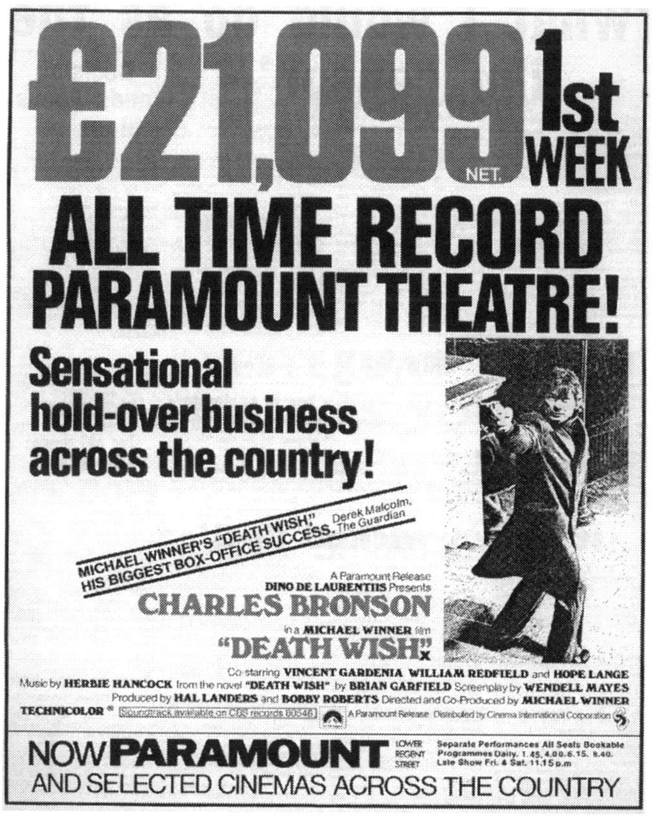

Winner designed his own trade and news publicity. His style was to pack them with rave reviews, except when cash-bells rang.

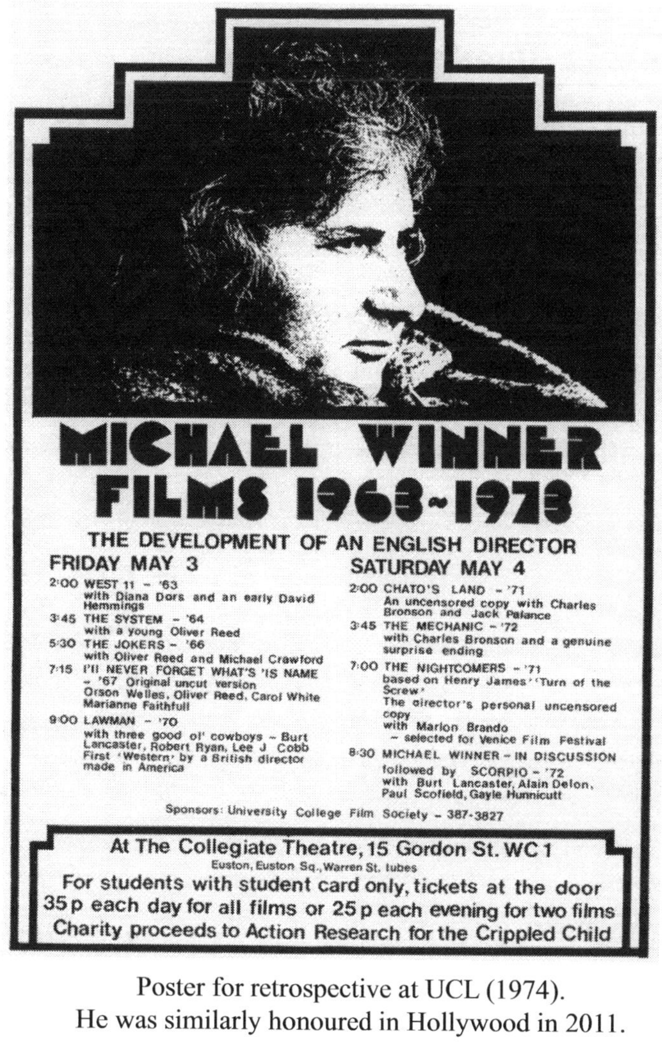

Poster for retrospective at UCL (1974).
He was similarly honoured in Hollywood in 2011.

"Michael said what?"

"That he persuaded Oliver Reed to work with you on Women in Love."

Ken Russell: "But we had already worked together. We knew each other."

"He said Oliver didn't want to go back to making films for television. Though Women in Love wasn't a television film."

Ken Russell: "It doesn't make sense. But if that's what he said, then that's what happened. I've got a lot of respect for Michael."

"He was very specific about the date. The day of Bobby Kennedy was killed, June 6 1968. But I think he's mixing two stories, or maybe Oliver Reed didn't understand that Women in Love was a feature film. It wouldn't make sense that Oliver didn't want to do The Debussy Film, which you started shooting on 1st September 1964. Oliver had done The System for Winner, which had no impact at all in 1964, and you'd just picked up the BAFTA for Elgar (1 February 1964). So perhaps Oliver had cold feet over Dante's Inferno, which you started shooting in 1967? The Jokers had been a hit for Winner, and Oliver would have been making I'll Never Forget What's 'is Name with him. So perhaps that's when Reed grumbled about making a film that would première on television? Sandy Lieberson told me he forced Winner to pay Reed a huge fee for Hannibal Brooks, hundreds of thousands of pounds, which your producers couldn't or wouldn't match for Women in Love. Maybe that's why Oliver was undecided, and that's why you had to go to Austria to persuade him?"

Ken Russell: "Print what Michael Winners says. My only memory of the day was climbing an Alpine mountain with Oliver. We went up and up until he gave up and agreed to do the film. I don't know why he insisted on climbing it."

"You'd made him climb a mountain when you 'found' the Alps in The Lake District when making Dante's Inferno a few months earlier."

Ken Russell: "So I did. We'd already climbed the mountain together."

Michael Winner was disappointed you didn't go to Oliver's funeral.

I wasn't asked. I wanted to go, but funerals are for families. I didn't want to get in the way of the family. I would have gone if they'd asked me to go.

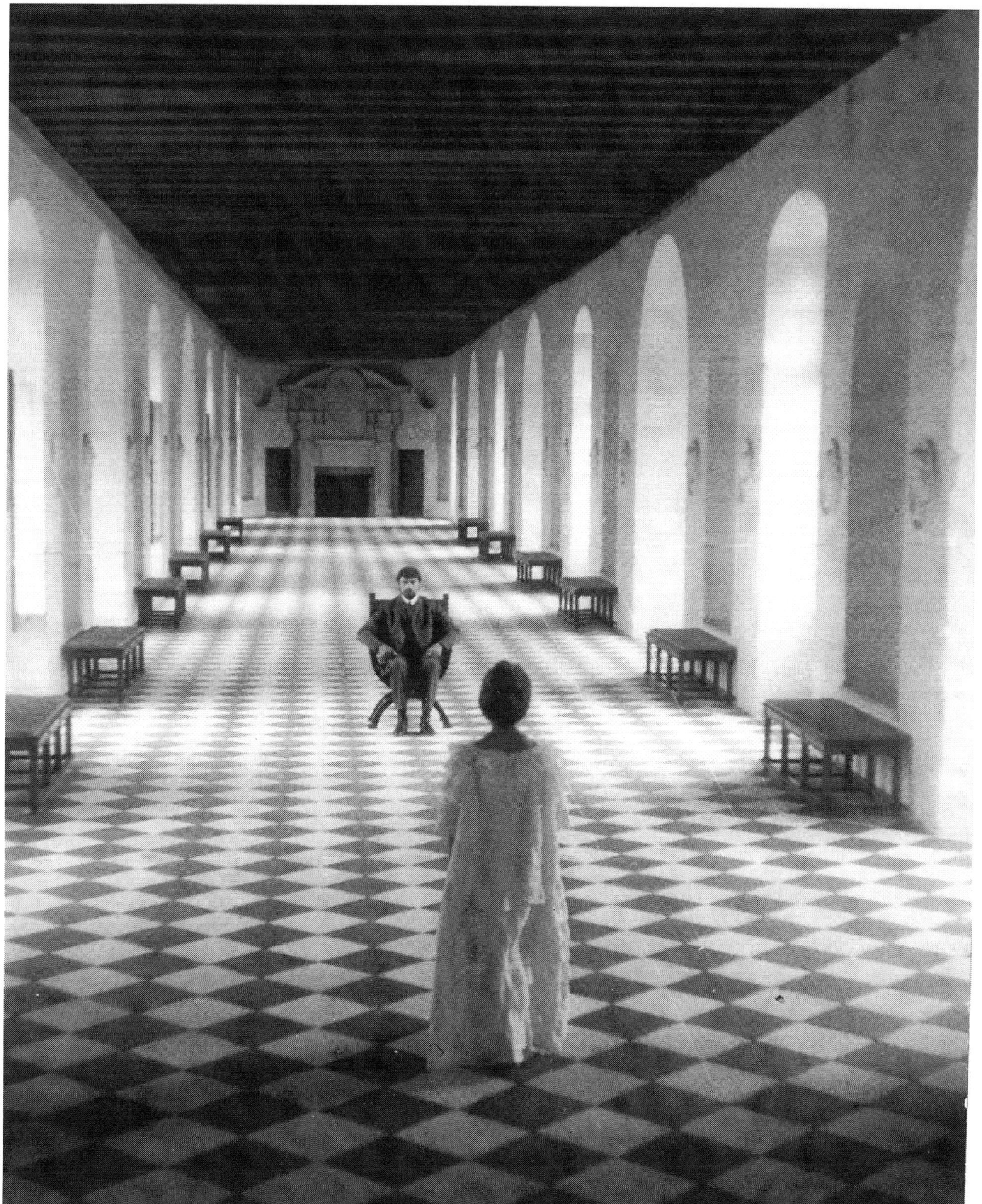

Oliver Reed in Ken Russell's *The Debussy Film* (1965)

Notes

p3. From Anderson's article *British Cinema: The Descending Spiral* (*Sequence* 7, 1949): "Week by week they churn out of the studios for our inspection; and now that their excellence has become almost an economic and political necessity (so that film criticism is regarded by many as a form of national service), the temptation to slash, to sneer rebelliously, is almost irresistible." On David Lean's *The Passionate Friends*: "For a director who has announced that the creation of character is his primary aim, *The Passionate Friends* is indeed a deplorable piece of work. ... none of the leading characters has any inner life, the dialogue abounds in bloodless clichés, and though the handling is full of tricks, it is as lacking in genuine dramatic power as it is in emotion. The stars shine coldly: no minor character is allowed to excite our interest for a moment."

Anderson is probably the only major English filmmaker to dislike Carol Reed's *The Third Man*. Writing in *Sequence 10* (1950): "am less hostile on second viewing, though still reluctant to join in the general acclamations. Difficult to analyse this disapproval. Aesthetically: is the technique too pretentious for the content? Morally: do I disapprove of its "fashionable defeatism" - Reed zithering while Europe disintegrates? Yes."

He made the same point about the imbalance between style and content in a letter he wrote to Sam Goldwyn regarding *Edge of Doom* (1950). Goldwyn was sufficiently impressed by the "very intelligent analysis of my film" to invite Anderson to meet him at Claridge's. Anderson: "He had asked for criticism, I realised, not because he was in the least interested in what people thought of his film, but because he likes to hear it talked about." (*Sequence* 13)

Anderson's most vital article on the failings of English filmmaking is *British Cinema: The Historical Imperative* written in June 1983 and published in Peter Cowie's *International Film Guide* in 1984, eight years before our discussions but I didn't find it until later. Here he writes that the problem with British cinema is The Class System: "a society educated (by a system admirably devised for the administration of Empire) into snobbery and philistinism, deeply divided into mutually contemptuous classes." He particularly despises the "middle-class and middle-brow humanistic appeal" of the British Film Renaissance: "the Oscars won by *Chariots of Fire* and *Gandhi* borne along behind them, like the Ark of the Covenant."

He was unimpressed by the English "Alternative Cinema - Marxist, Trots, semiologists etc., who have substituted a Red Brick puritanism for the old Oxbridge camp, without influencing anything more important than a handful of critics, certain departments of the British Film Institute, and the specialised film programmes on Channel 4. Alternative Cinema has not aimed to transform or take over the British Cinema: it has been content to establish a ghetto of the self-righteous, just as snobbish in its admiration of Wim Wenders and the intellectual criticism of France as were their bourgeois predecessors in their preoccupation with Duvivier or Bergman." What the British lacked: "and I am not speaking just of filmmakers but of critics, "intellectuals" and the whole useless army of institutional, over-subsidised academics. What we lack is a proper understanding of our own traditions, a proper pride in our own achievement. And based on such pride and understanding, the will and the vitality to support our own talent, the imagination to nurture it, the determination to sustain it."

p4. The English Stage Company and Free Cinema both started in 1956: "a year of stimulus and change. Suez, Hungary: the end of sentimental Communism and the birth of a "New Left". (Anderson, June '83). For The ESC at the Royal Court Theatre, Anderson directed the first London performances of *The Long, The Short and The Tall* (1959); *The Waiting of Lester Abbs* (Sully, 1957, with Ian Bannen, Robert Stephens); *Progress to the Park* (Owen, 1959); *The*

Trial of Cob and Leach (Logue, 1959, Mary Ure); *Serjeant Musgrave's Dance*; *The Lily White Boys* (Cookson & Logue, 1960, Finney); *Antigone* (1960, Logue's trans. set in a modern police state: "Anderson's direction, full of gunfire in the wings and sudden changes of tone, kept the nerves warily on the alert, particularly in the brilliantly staged interrogation scene: and Jocelyn Herbert's claustrophobic set and glinting leather costumes increased the impression of power." Peter Carthew, Plays and Players Jan61 p15 1961); *Box and Cox* (Morton, 1961); *The Fire Raisers* (Bullock 1961, with James Booth); *The Diary of a Madman* (1963, with Richard Harris); *In Celebration* (Storey, 1969); *The Contractor* (Storey, 1969); *Home* (Storey, 1970); *The Changing Room* (Storey, 1971 with Warren Clarke); *The Farm* (1973, Storey, with Lewis Collins and Bernard Lee); *Life Class* (Storey, 1974 with Alan Bates).

p4. Laurence Harvey replaced Peter O'Toole for the film. Barry Norman was the BBC film critic.

p5. *O Lucky Man!*'s picaresque structure has an acknowledged antecedent in Voltaire's *Candide*. In France, the film was retitled after Voltaire's maxim that we live in the 'best of all possible worlds'. An unacknowledged and doubtless subconcious influence was Anthony Newley's white-face mime musical, *Stop The World I Want To Get Off* (first performed at the Queen's Theatre on July 20, 1961). Newley rises from tea-boy to tycoon. Anna Quayle played ALL the women in his life. The sets were by Sean Kenny who had designed Anderson's own State of the Nation musical, *The Lily White Boys*.

p5. Anderson's day-to-day account of the making of *O Lucky Man!* is published in *The Diaries*.

p6. Anderson wanted to make a 'life on the road' documentary about Alan Price. Part of that fed into *O Lucky Man!*, and part into a BBC *Omnibus* about Price which Anderson instigated in June 1974. Of the Omnibus: "Not quite what I had originally envisaged ... but some nice things I thought."

p6. *O Lucky Man!* opened at the 686-seat Warner Rendezvous in London in October 1973 and took £7,900 (on tickets priced between £1.65 and 70p) in its first full week (*King Boxer* was playing in the 890-seat Warner West End). It played at the Rendezvous for 21 weeks (replaced by the Palme d'Or winning *Scarecrow*) before transferring for a short run at the Cinecenta 3 (150 seats). *OLM* returned to the West End in October 1974 where it played for 3 weeks at the Warner West End. Curiously, Anderson's Free Cinema colleague, Claude Goretta won two prizes for *L'Invitation* at the Cannes festival where *O Lucky Man!* went unrewarded. To Anderson's disgust, Alan Bridges' *The Hireling* won a share of the Palme d'Or.

p6. McDowell would also play the ballet master in Altman's *The Company* (2003). It was to Altman's apartment we walked on page 34.

p7. Later, Anderson directed McDowell in an off-Broadway revival of *In Celebration* (28.10.84. McDowell: "I honestly think it was one of the best things I ever did - that performance.") and at The Old Vic in *Holiday* (14.1.87 Anderson: "a smooth and agreeable experience, excellently cast").

p7. *Britannia Hospital* was a hit in Paris. It flopped everywhere else, including Australia where, it was championed by Barry Humphries, but marketed as a video nasty: "It's disgusting! It's outrageous! It's offensive!". Its TV première was on UK's Channel 4 on Anderson's birthday - 17th April 1984.

p7. Turning down offers from America was one of Lindsay Anderson's hobbies. Among the films he rejected are *Hurricane* and *Nicholas and Alexandra*.

p8. A U-matic tape of Anderson's edit of the *Wham* film, called *If you Were There*, is in the Anderson archives at Stirling University. George Michael continues to block screenings.

p8. From the NFT talk: "The marvellous thing about Marek Piwowski and his work ... was their instant sense of familiarity, the sympathy of their ironic, poetic humour, their rash and irrepressible feeling... I was making a short film [*The Singing Lesson*] at the Warsaw Documentary Studio. The directors there were not very friendly. "Of course they're not", said my cameraman Zygmunt Samosiuk, "they're all hoping you'll make a balls-up of it". The only one not like that was this shy, friendly and handsome fellow who would come and sit in the cutting room and give me some good advice and moral support. This was Marek Piwowski."

p8. Orson Welles's production of *Rhinoceros* opened at the Royal Court Theatre on 28th April 1960. Every one of its 44 performances sold out. The rhino costume is still on display at the V&A.

p9. Anderson agreed that Hitchcock did his best work in America. In *Sequence* 9 (Autumn '49) he writes: "there are sequences in *Foreign Correspondent* and *Saboteur, Shadow of a Doubt* and *Lifeboat* which outstrip anything in his earlier pictures for the virtuosity and excitement... Hitchcock's progression from *The Pleasure Garden* to *Rope* is aesthetically pleasing; on a graph it would appear a well-proportioned parabola."

p9. Between 1959 and 1970, Ken Russell made 34 short, mid- and feature-length 35mm art films of a standard unmatched in world cinema.

p9. Anderson narrated Kevin Brownlow's feature-length documentaries: *Abel Gance: The Charm of Dynamite* (1968); *Buster Keaton: A Hard Act to Follow* (1987); *Harold Lloyd: The Third Genius* (1989); *D.W. Griffith: Father of Film* (1993).

p10. Anderson and Madonna met on the set of *The Awakenings* (1992), photographed by Ondricek.

p10. *Glory! Glory!* A 206min satirical feature about a TV evangelist, starring Ellen Greene and Richard Thomas. Anderson filmed it in fifteen weeks in Toronto for HBO (May 1988).

p11. The Ken Russell Liverpool Philharmonic film was built around the rehearsals of Mahler's 5th. It was completed, unsatisfactorily, by Don Boyd.

p12. Anderson died from heart failure on 30 August 1994, in France, after swimming in a lake.

p12. John Howlett carried on the theme of teenage rebellion in *Dean* (1977), his book and musical play about James Dean.

p12. Seth Holt's most notable achievement was directing Bette Davis in *The Nanny* (1965). He died almost mysteriously whilst making *The Blood from the Mummy's Tomb* (1971).

p12. Most major filmmakers made commercials, (including Anderson, Donner, Russell, Winner) but they are never discussed, with the singular exception of Ridley Scott, because the commercials rarely add or convey anything of the director's 'style'. Anderson thought his own film style was too "expansive for that very taut medium". Curiously, five commercials made by Joseph Losey in 1960 for Fray Bentos and Horlicks, and available in BFI mediatheques, are recognisably by him. Anderson made 91 commercials between 1963 and 1971 following the success of 17 he made in September 1963 for Mackeson Stout, starring Bernard Miles: "It looks good. It tastes good. And by golly it does you good." Miles and Anderson made a further 13 for Mackeson's the following year, and 7 more in Dec. 1965. Other Anderson ads include a *This Sporting Life* style rugby club (Nottingham) for a Whitebread Tankard (Dec. 1965); four for Kraft crackerbarrel cheese with James Robertson Justice (Nov. 68); and a series for Rowntree's Fruit Pastels (Nov. 1963) with Denis Gilmore, then England's most popular boy on account of his performances as the radio's *Just William.* One of Gilmore's was on youtube the last time I looked: Gilmore's mother is preparing to go shopping and he sings: "Don't forget my Fruit Gums mum!" Naturally, the whipping senior in *if....*, played by Robert Swann, is called 'Rowntree'.

Jeremy Bulloch, who crashes his car and becomes a science experiment in *O Lucky Man!* (and later Boba Fett in the *Star Wars* films) starred in Anderson's June 1971 ad for Ewbank carpet sweepers.

Anderson's 'Fat Chef' Alcan baking foil advert, photographed by Norman Warwick, won the Gold prize at the 1968 USA Commercial Festival.

p12. The Richard Harris films are *Major Dundee*, *The Red Desert*, *The Heroes of Telemark*, *The Bible* and *Hawaii*. The two men didn't see much of each other again. In November 1967, Anderson was Harris' guest at the première of *Camelot*. Early in 1975, they met to discuss making *Passmore* from a script by Storey. In March 1988, Anderson wrote to Harris and offered him a part in *Long Day's Journey Into Night*, which Anderson had been asked to direct in Leicester. Harris declined but said he was open to Lindsay directing him in *Becket* in the West End. Anderson had to decline for he had taken up an offer to direct *Glory! Glory!* ("my last chance, I keep telling myself, to Sell-Out").

Richard Harris's eloquent BFI tribute to Anderson screened on Channel 4 and is on youtube: "Lindsay was an amazing man. Lindsay was a very gentle man. Oxford University. A very intelligent intellectual man, but what he had was a most amazing understanding of violence; which certainly wasn't him at all, because he wasn't a violent man at all. But he had a tremendous understanding of suppressed violence. What I would call 'psychological violence'. I don't mean the violence of *Reservoir Dogs,* but genuine psychological violence, inner passion, volcanic passion, that had a justification when it erupted. It was kind of a social violence of people who are oppressed that Lindsay was always interested in, though he came from a wholly different background to that. The genius of Lindsay, the marvellous thing about Lindsay, was he did all his work as a director without any apparent visual imposition on the actor. He did it all prior. Months beforehand. He almost lived in your ear. You would discuss things with him, over the months, and he'd implant things in your ear. So when you got to do it he had very little to say, because he had done that work prior to shooting. He created the atmosphere that you were not acting anymore. He was the director and you were the actor *prior* to shooting the film but, when you were shooting the film it became a piece of *life*. You *were* Frank Machin (from *This Sporting Life*), and he daren't break the spell, he didn't want to break the spell [so that] Lindsay Anderson [was] talking to Richard Harris. That made it *acting*. One didn't realise how good Anderson really was. Because I thought it was all me. Actors are very egotistical. The folly of youth. Later, as you get older, you recognise that it wasn't all you, Richard. You aren't that great. I've worked now with some of the greatest directors in the world. I've worked with Antonioni; I worked for a long time, but never got to shoot the picture, with Ingmar Bergman. I've worked with John Huston, and I've worked with Marty Ritt. Some of the great directors of the world. And he [Lindsay Anderson] is still the best."

p13. In 1961, Rex Harrison had walked out of the Royal Court's production of Nigel Dennis' *August for the People* after eleven performances, forcing it to close, so he could take up work on *Cleopatra*.

p16. Norland's credits include the 30min *Hetty King Performer* (1970), narrated by Lindsay Anderson.

p20. Philip Harrison's design work includes a Sean Connery trilogy of *Cuba* (1979), *Outland* (1981) and *Never Say Never Again* (1983). He turned down *Alien* three times when it was to be directed by Walter Hill, but gave them the 'industrial trampship' concept which he took back for *Outland*.

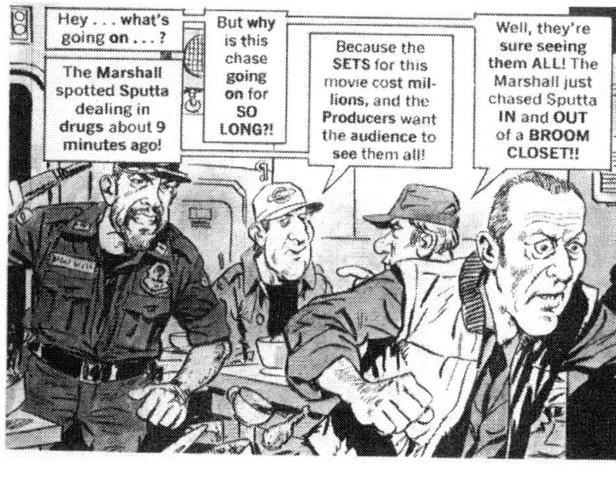

p21. An annual student cash prize in Brickman's name was established in 1978 from financial support from Anderson, Donner, Christie, Schlesinger ...

p43. Anderson's videotaping of *Look Back in Anger* cost $300,000, including his flight by concorde to New York City.

p44. Herbert's theatre work with Anderson: *Serjeant Musgrave's Dance* (1959), *Antigone* (1960), *Cob and Leach* (1960), *Julius Caesar* (1964), *Inadmissible Evidence* (1966) *Home* (1970), *The Changing Room* (1971), *Life Class* (1974), *What the Butler Saw* (1975), *Early Days* (1980), *Hamlet* (1981: "Three towering walls give the acting area the appearance of a crossroads with dark corridors stretching away upstage; and such is the unrelieved austerity of the design that it is a moment of positive luxury when she breaks it with a monochrome projection of Fortinbras's 'little patch of ground' on the back wall." Wardle, Times 21.8.81), *The March on Russia* (1989), *Jubilee* (1990), *Stages* (1992). She designed the world première of Brecht's *Baal* (1963, starring Peter O'Toole and featuring Vivian Pickles). Anderson on Herbert: "The English have so little visual sense that, unless a design is spectacular or crude, they don't actually notice whether it's good or bad but have a purely literary response to a play; it's a missing nerve. I think this applies particularly to Jocelyn since her designs are always totally integrated with the play and are an extension of the poetic heart of the text, executed with extreme sensitivity and intuition... it's almost natural that uncultivated critics wouldn't notice her designs." Workbook p216

p45. Anderson's *Musgrave* press release foreshadowed the 'Which Side Are on You?' theme he would use for the *if....* ad-campaign. "Every now and then there comes a play which by its originality, its boldness and complete lack of compromise, stands out like a landmark - perhaps a signpost. Such plays are seldom universally welcomed, nor are they likely to win immediate commercial success." He printed two reviews side-by-side and asked: 'What Kind of a theatre do you want?'. One was an appalling piece of bilge by Harold Hobson in the *Sunday Times*: 'Another frightful ordeal. It is time someone reminded our advanced dramatists that principle function of the theatre is to give pleasure... It is the duty of the theatre, not to make better men, but to render them harmlessly happy."

p86. Waugh met Chaplin in Hollywood in 1947 on the trip that inspired *The Loved One*.

p87. Meryman was the last to interview Marilyn.

p89. An example of Chaplin's pre-eminence: Peter Daubeny wrote in his memories, *My World of Theatre*, of the Moscow Arts Theatre first visit to London (1958). The Russian actors sent understudies to official receptions, downed tools politely to welcome visitors such as Rex Harrison, but when a visit from Chaplin was arranged: "the whole Moscow Arts Theatre assembled, roaring and stamping like a crowd of football fans... Tarasova said just the fact of meeting him would have made their visit worth while. He was their idol - a legendary figure... For days after, the Company could talk of nothing else but Chaplin's visit. (p162)

p102. *Nothing But The Best* wasn't released on DVD until the summer of 2014.

p104."Heartbreakingly, it became increasingly clear that, whether swinging through some blouse-ripping melodrama like *Marie des Isles*, or smouldering to great effect in early films by Rosi and Vancini, Belinda Lee had, in the end, developed into a skilful, passionate actress." Bob Baker, *Film Dope* No.34

p108. The original play of *The Caretaker* opened at the Arts Theatre Club on 27th April 1960 and was *the* critical and commercial and success in 1960.

p115. Before fame as a comic actor, Dudley Moore scored Anderson's *Serjeant Musgrave Dance* and thereafter became the house composer at the Royal Court Theatre.

p120. In *Luv,* Harrison Ford has a road rage cameo. Wearing a French beret and riding boots, he punches Jack Lemmon on the nose.

p124. A press wit joked that Merchant doesn't speak because her husband, Harold Pinter, objected to the quality of the dialogue.

p125. Donner did sometimes direct new plays, e.g, *The Front Room Boys*, by Alexander Buzo, at the Royal Court (Oct. 1971). His most notable work was directing Vivian Pickles in *Kennedy's Children* (1973).

p125. *Vampira* was the least successful of Donner's major films. It opened at the 1,157-seat Carlton and closed after a mere three weeks and a tiny take of £6,559 (net, less Levy & VAT).

p130. Anderson had peaked McDowell's interest in Dornford Yates by giving him a copy of *Blond Corner.* (Diaries, p344)

p135. Scott was aggrieved by Hollywood's creative accounting, whereby the successes of one film are wiped out by the failures of others, so that profit-share participants are never paid. He raised $1.1m independently to make *The Savage is Loose* (1974), which he directed, produced, acted in and distributed. Similarly, David Prowse was 'locked out' by George Lucas for complaining that *The Return of the Jedi*, which grossed upwards of $500m on a $27m budget, had failed to 'turn a profit'.

p153. Hodges' TV work for *Tempo*, including his films about Pinter, Welles, Tom Jones are on DVD.

p174. *Lady Chatterley* (1993), four-part mini-series, starring Joely Richardson. 15 million tuned in to watch it, but is far from Russell's best work.

p174. Ken Russell making *Isadora Duncan* is an extra on *Ken Russell at the BBC,* a DVD set sold in America and Australia, but rudely prohibited for sale to the British public who financed all the films.

p182. Dorothy Tutin starred in Ken Russell's *Savage Messiah* (1972). He had seen her in the RSC's original production of Whiting's *The Devils* (1961).

p187. The heavily-censored UK release cut of *The Devils* is now available on DVD in the UK and Spain. Warner's have imposed a worldwide ban on the restored version, with the exception of a handful of one-off screenings in London and Belgium.

p189. An aspect of Russell's union problems is told in Falk's clipping from *Cinema TV Today* 3.11.73 p3:

'Keep politics out of movies' say top film men

By Quentin Falk

THE film industry's biggest union is threatened with a major rift if its production policy continues to be dictated by a "politically-motivated minority."

In an open telegram to the General Council of the ACTT, film-makers Ken Russell and Roy Baird state: "We deplore the dictatorial attitude of our union to film production.

"As real film-makers we will not be told by a politically-motivated minority how, where and when we should make our films.

"We employ during the course of our productions hundreds of freelance technicians and craftsmen many more than the small number employed by studios and know that these are totally behind us in endorsing our attitude.

"We have between us commitments to start five location pictures in the coming 12 months any one or all of which could be held by the financing entities involved to be better made as overseas productions.

"We have proven successful over the past six years in forestalling these attempts and have made pictures in the UK.

"Your present attitude would clearly make this utterly impossible in the future."

Blacking

And this week more than 350 members of ACTT, NATKE, ETU, and FFA staged a demonstration outside the headquarters of the ACTT.

Ostensibly they were protesting against the "blacking" (now lifted) of two Euston Film projects "Special Branch" and "The Prison" for Armchair cinema.

Location filming at two condemned buildings, Colet Court in Hammersmith and The Citadel in Clapton had been blacked because the union claimed their members were working in adverse conditions.

But, said Stuart Freeman, spokesman for the protestors: 'This is a blind—the latest in a whole series of attempts over the past 18 months to bring to an end all productions based outside the four major studios—Pinewood, Shepperton, Twickenham, and Elstree."

The union wanted the productions moved into Elstree because Euston Films parent company is EMI.

"The thought that ACTT in accordance with TUC policy has its sights on the nationalisation of the British film industry as a long term measure, and that this is easier in a controlled situation, has no bearing on the immediate subject—the threat to 'black' all 'four wall productions' and the insistence that they must be made in, or based on one of the four studios regardless of the final cost."

Freeman told "CinemaTV Today": "We are not against the studios remaining open but we just defend the right of any film producer to make a film where he wants to, how he wants and when he wants to as long as he works to the existing agreements as laid down by the ACTT and allied unions."

He said that if the "desperately urgent situation" was not acted on now it could mean the loss of livelihood to countless members.

An emergency meeting of the Film branch of the ACTT has been called for 12 November to debate the situation.

Said union General Secretary, Alan Sapper: "We are not against location filming outside or inside." But ACTT condemned productions "wilfully" going outside studio facilities so condemning the viability of the studio and the high craft level of NATKE.

"The policy of ACTT is made by its members and not by me. The buck may stop at me but it does not start with me."

p195. Russell said the 'four thousand years' in a 2009 BBC South interview with Sally Taylor.

p.221. Gilles Vranckx's poster references the British quad for *Savage Messiah*:

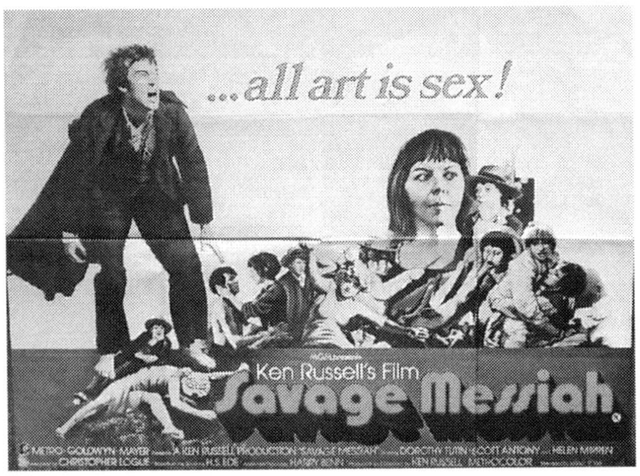

p227. *Saber of London* was directed by Joseph Losey, Richard Lester and others (1955-1957).

p231. *Won Ton Ton* is now on NTSC DVD. Bruce Dern unsuccessfully pitches films about 'a shark which terrorises a New England resort' and 'a girl possessed by the Devil' but has a brief success with dog-to-the-rescue films. Cameos include Jackie Coogan, Dorothy Lamour, Johnny Weissmuller. Fine costumes and set dressing. Weak script. 'Old Hollywood' flops include Schlesinger's *The Day of the Locust* (1975), Peter Bogdanovich's *Nickelodeon* (1976) and Russell's *Valentino* (1977).

p234. Robert Paynter photographed six of Lindsay Anderson's Kelloggs ads, Aug/Sept 1969.

p239. *Scorpio* was one of only two Michael Winner films to top the London box-office (Oct '73). The London council granted it an 'A' certificate in defiance of the State censor who'd slapped an 'X' certificate on it. *Death Wish 2* topped the charts in Feb '82. The original *Death Wish* was kept from the top spot by *The Towering Inferno*. Ken Russell holds the record for the 1970s with five No.1 films.

p254. This famous photograph of a Great White Shark, taken by Valerie Taylor, was included in the *Jaws* press pack and widely used to promote Spielberg's great film, but it's a bit of cheat. It's a more striking image than any in *Jaws*, and had already been used on the lobby cards and poster for *Blue Water, White Death* (1971).

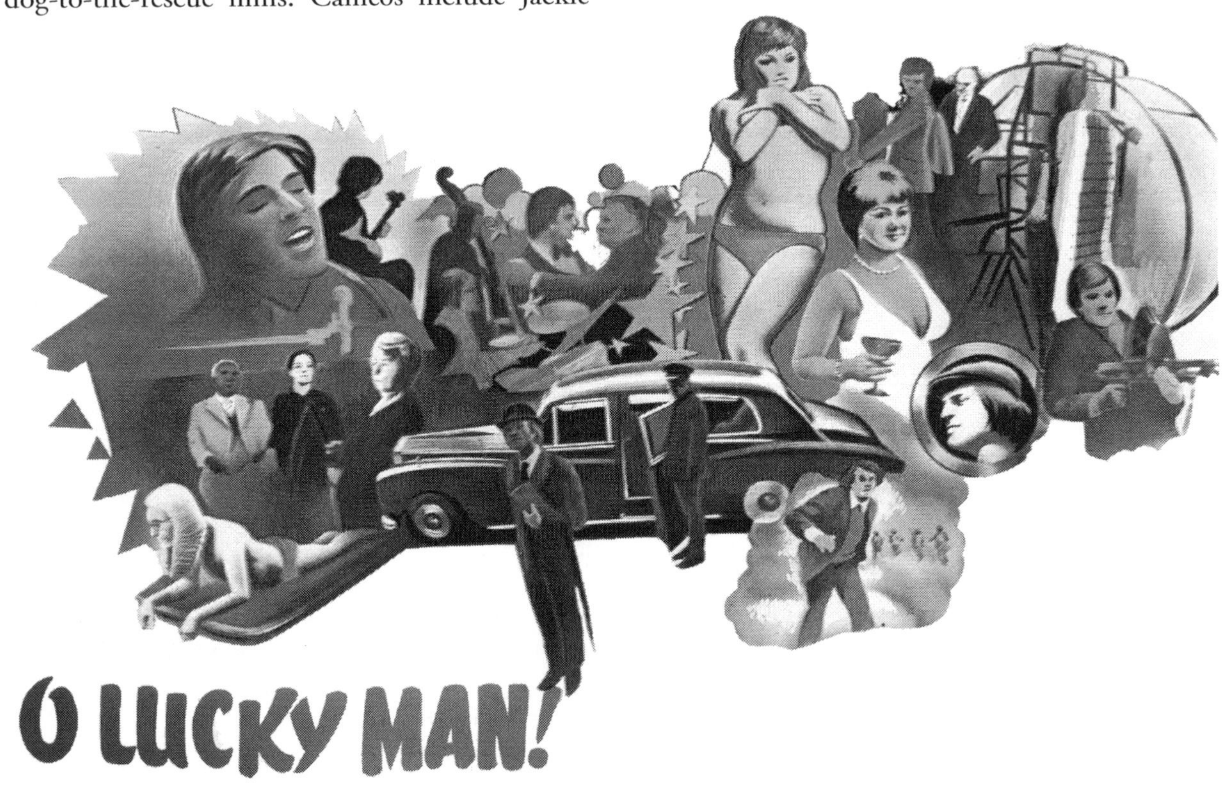

Index

Illustration credits and copyrights

The photographs and advertising prints used in this book are all held in the private collections of the author and his collaborators, and are used in the spirit of promotion and education. This book is a celebration of the work of the artists. All efforts have been made to contact the individual photographers. If any image is incorrectly attributed, please contact the publisher at camerajournal@yahoo.com so this list can be improved. I'd particularly welcome hearing from the set photographers on *if....* and *Tommy*.

AIP 105
American Film Theatre 53
Lindsay Anderson 4, 11, 27, 40, 48, 56, 60, 67
Murray Anderson 12, 18
Artanis Productions 31
Carlino Productions 248
Columbia Pictures 186, 248-250
Frank Connor 2, 67, 69
Constantin Film 127, 249
Roy Export vi, 71, 74, 77, 80, 83-87
Samuel Goldwyn Company 145
Goodtimes 157, 158, 204
Keith Hamshere 147 (bottom)
Jocelyn Herbert 40, 48, 51, 52
John Holmstrom Collection 26-27, 97, 123, 247
David Hurn iii, 160, 163, 178, 181
Anne James 195, 253
Cornel Lucas 100, 102
MGM ii, 103, 105, 112, 152-154, 202
Momentum Pictures 139
Nelson Entertainment 50
Odeon Entertainment 171, 220
Paramount Pictures i, 8, 9, 21, 25, 57, 59, 61-66, 172, 174, 224
Vivian Pickles 175, 177, 188, 193, 196
Rank 103, 105, 106
Ken Russell iii, 160, 163, 181, 182, 185, 189, 191, 194, 196, 201
Paul Sutton 31, 33, 40, 89, 134, 136, 147 (top), 156, 194, 207, 208, 240, 268
Rank 68, 91, 95, 97, 223
Sam Goldwyn 158
Brian Simmons 167
20th Century Fox 123
United Artists 109, 197, 198, 220
Universal Pictures 127, 141, 242, 243
Giles Vranckx 209
Vestron Pictures 206
Warner Brothers ii, 35-38, 46, 48, 58, 149, 192, 199, 200, 201, 205, 234, 260
Michael Winner i, vi, 210, 226, 230, 232, 237, 251

Also By Buffalo Books

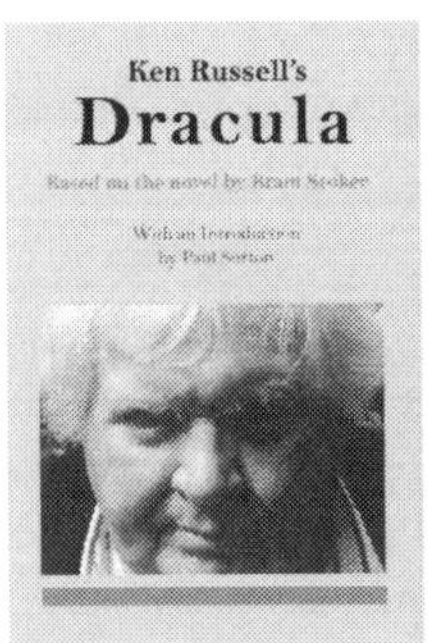

Ken Russell's Dracula

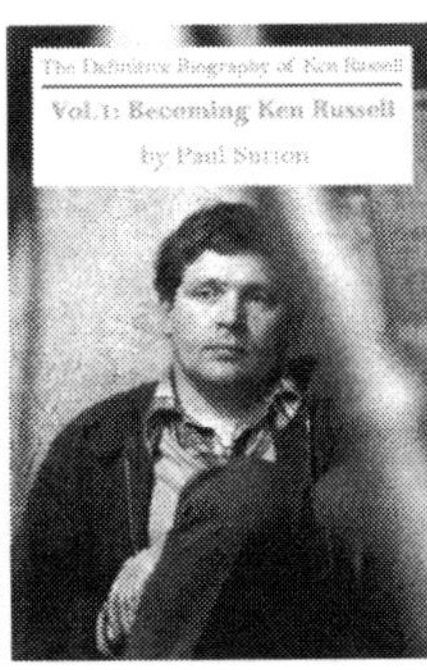

Becoming Ken Russell by Paul Sutton

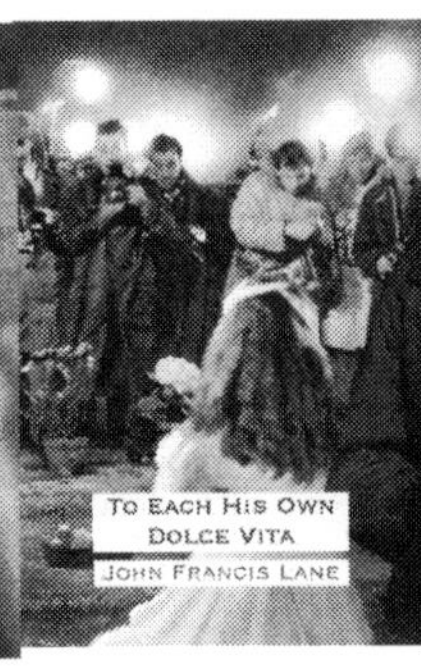

John Francis Lane's To Each His Own Dolce Vita

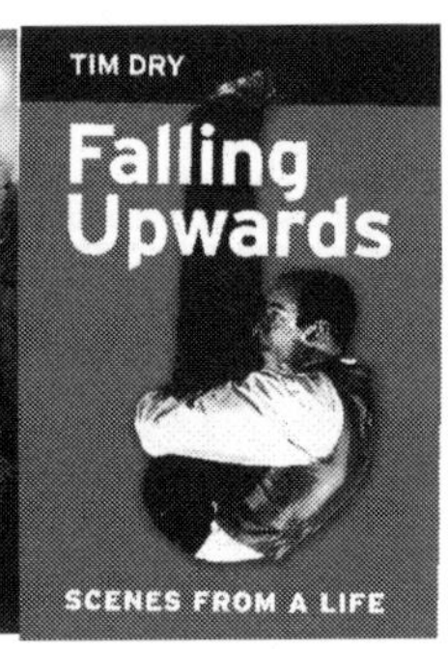

Tim Dry's Falling Upwards

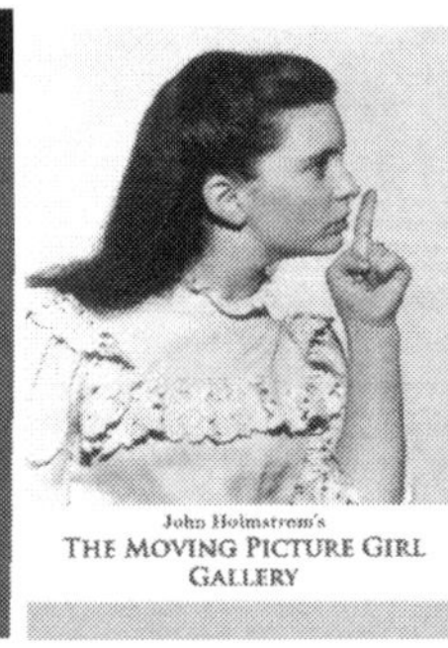

John Holmstrom's The Moving Picture Girl Gallery

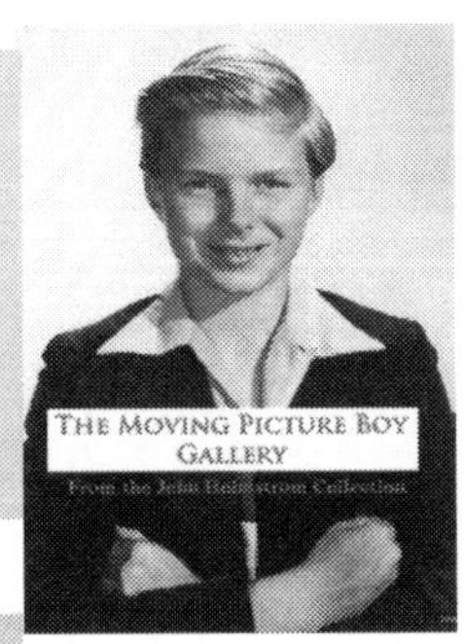

John Holmstrom's The Moving Picture Boy Gallery

6222325R10152

Printed in Great Britain
by Amazon.co.uk, Ltd.,
Marston Gate.